OP
.¹⁹⁵
|.

MUNICH
PROLOGUE TO TRAGEDY

K9.

MUNICH

PROLOGUE TO TRAGEDY

BY

JOHN W. WHEELER-BENNETT

THE VIKING PRESS

NEW YORK

I DEDICATE THIS BOOK
IN GRATITUDE AND AFFECTION
TO
AUBREY AND CONSTANCE MORGAN
AND TO
ISABELLA GREENWAY KING
WHO BETWEEN THEM MADE THE WRITING
OF IT POSSIBLE

Original 1948 edition reissued in 1963 by Duell, Sloan & Pearce, Inc.

VIKING COMPASS EDITION
Issued in 1964 by The Viking Press, Inc.
625 Madison Avenue, New York, N.Y. 10022

This edition published by arrangement with Duell, Sloan & Pearce,
an affiliate of Meredith Press

Printed in U.S.A. by The Murray Printing Company

Third Printing December 1968

CONTENTS

FOREWORD TO THE FIRST EDITION

WRITERS of contemporary history labour under two grave disabilities. They are apt to be too near to the events they attempt to chronicle to be able to establish a proper sense of perspective and they are never in possession of all the relevant material. By the time the archives of Foreign Offices become available to the public the subjects of their revelations have ceased to be " contemporary ", and have passed into the field of what is commonly spoken of as " modern ", history.

In writing this record of the Munich Agreement I have endeavoured to remedy these two disabilities as far as possible. The chief difficulty with which I have had to contend, however, has been to avoid, on the one hand, being too greatly influenced by " hindsight ", and, on the other, appearing to be merely a Cassandra. To find a *via media* between these two extremes is not an easy task.

With regard to original material the contemporary historian has received a windfall in the documentation presented at the Nuremberg Trials. Thanks to the extraordinary capacity of the German official mind for committing to paper and never destroying, the archives of an entire Government machine are in the hands of the Allied Powers, and the selection made public in evidence at Nuremberg provides more comprehensive material than could have been amassed by a single historian in half a century's toil. The gratitude of all workers in the field of international relations is due to the staffs of the Prosecuting Teams of the Four Powers who have rendered this signal service to historical research. As a result of their work we now have, *inter alia*, an almost complete documentary presentation of the German aspects of the Munich Period which would never otherwise have been available. My own particular thanks go to my friends of the British Team, and especially to Colonel H. J. Phillimore and Mr. Patrick Dean, for their many kindnesses.

In addition to this rich field of documentation, I have been given, owing to the great kindness of President Beneš and H.E. Jan Masaryk, to whom I am ever grateful, a very full opportunity of examining the Czechoslovak State Archives for this same period. The records of the British and French Governments for the

Munich Period have still to be published, but I have sought to remedy this deficiency by personal research and enquiry from those protagonists and opponents of the Policy of Appeasement best qualified to speak of that momentous time, and my deepest gratitude is due to them for their kindness and forbearance, and for the unique value of their personal experience. My most sincere thanks are also due to those who have allowed me to make use of their personal records, among whom are the Hon. Harold Nicolson, Mr. Paul Emrys Evans and Colonel Charles Lindbergh, and especially to Sir Robert Bruce Lockhart, whose advice and help have been as unfailing as his friendship.

In the arrangement of this book I have not followed the chronological order of events, nor have I adhered to a strict interpretation of the Munich Period as being between the months of March and October 1938. The Munich Agreement was, as Mr. Churchill said, but the " consequence of five years of futile good intention ", and, in itself, it was but the prologue to the greater tragedy of the Second World War. I have thought it necessary, therefore, to tell, first of all, the story of the Munich Agreement within its restricted time limit ; then to give some account of the five " lost years " which preceded it and of the five months which followed ; and, finally, to record in brief the great events which occurred between Hitler's march into Prague in the spring of 1939 and the outbreak of war six months later.

I would express my warmest gratitude to Professor E. L. Woodward, Montague Burton Professor of International Relations at the University of Oxford, and to Professor L. B. Namier, Professor of Modern History at Manchester University, who, from their great knowledge, have given me much invaluable criticism, wise counsel and friendly encouragement. I am also greatly indebted to those who have read and commented on the MSS., in whole or in part, and particularly to Major-General Sir Neill Malcolm, Mr. and Mrs. Aubrey Niel Morgan and Mr. Isaiah Berlin ; and to my secretary, Mrs. Bagshaw Mann, and to Mrs. P. E. Baker, without whose great help the work would not have been completed, and to Miss Muriel Currey for her technical assistance.

I also wish to acknowledge the generous assistance of H.M. Stationery Office, who have permitted me to reprint as appendices certain documents which had already appeared as Government Publications, and of the Royal Institute of International Affairs in granting similar permission in regard to material reprinted from the *Bulletin of International News* and the annual volumes of *Documents on International Affairs*.

Lastly, I offer the full measure of my thanks and affection to Mrs. Dwight Morrow and Mrs. Isabella Greenway King, to whose most generous kindness and hospitality I owe a great debt of gratitude.

JOHN W. WHEELER-BENNETT

CUERNAVACA, MEXICO ; BLACK ROCK, CONNECTICUT
GARSINGTON MANOR, near OXFORD
February 1945–*January* 1947

POSTSCRIPT

With reference to page 394, note 1, and page 412, note 1, this book had passed its page-proof stage by the date of the publication by the United States Department of State of *Nazi-Soviet Relations 1939–1941*. I have therefore been unable to benefit by the documentary material contained therein. This applies also to the texts of the Secret Additional Protocols to the Soviet-German Pact contained in Appendix N.

J. W. W.-B.

February 1948

FOREWORD TO THE REISSUE

I WELCOME the opportunity of the reprinting of this book to reassert my belief in the views which I held at the time of its first appearance in 1948. Much new material has become available in the meantime: the Nuremberg record, the relevant volumes of the documents of the British Foreign Office and of the German Foreign Ministry, and a host of memoirs. While these contribute invaluably to filling in the details of the narrative of Munich, they do not, I contend, alter in any way my general contention:

" Let us say of the Munich Agreement that it was inescapable; that, faced with the lack of preparedness in Britain's armaments and defences, with the lack of unity at home and in the Commonwealth, with the collapse of French morale, and with the uncertainty of Russia's capacity to fight, Mr. Chamberlain had no alternative to do other than he did; let us pay tribute to his persistence in carrying out a policy which he honestly believed to be right. Let us accept and admit all these things, but in so doing let us not omit the shame and the humiliation which were ours; let us not forget that, in order to save our own skins—that because we were too weak to protect ourselves—we were forced to sacrifice a small power to slavery. It is of no avail to say that we saved Czechoslovakia from that fate which was later suffered by our ally Poland, that, but for Munich, Bohemia and Moravia would have been devastated as were the provinces of Cracow and Lodz and Warsaw. In reality it was the Czechs who saved us; for, had President Beneš elected to fight with Russian support and thus precipitate an Eastern European war, it is impossible to believe that Britain and France could have kept aloof, however reluctantly they might have been dragged into participation."

This, I still believe, represents a true assessment of what happened at Munich.

In the years since this book was first published, historians in many countries have assessed and reassessed the influence which the antecedents and consequences of the Munich Agreement exercised on the final course of world history. The most recent of these "agonizing reappraisals" is, of course, the brilliant, provocative, controversial and, in my view, dangerously misleading work of Mr. A. J. P. Taylor, *The Origins of the Second World War*. Whatever our feelings may be about Mr. Taylor's disturbing thesis, whether we agree or disagree with it, we cannot but be grateful to him for having challenged and provoked us to re-examine the evidence in the case, a process which can only be salutary. Having done this I find myself unrepentantly in disagreement with Mr. Taylor. I cannot accept—on the basis of the facts as stated—the argument that Hitler blundered into war, no matter from however distinguished a source this argument may emanate. I find nothing in the evidence which causes me to depart from the view which I feel proud to have shared with the late Sir Lewis Namier—to whom, incidentally, both Mr. Taylor and I owed so much—that, as early as November 1937, Hitler's plans clearly envisaged the use of war as an instrument of national policy, and that they did not exclude the calculated risk of a general world conflict.

Since this present volume is a reprint, and not a revision, of the original, I cannot add or quote from the new material which has appeared. But I feel that I must draw the attention of the interested reader to two particularly important works recently completed. The first is the revised edition of Mr. Alan Bullock's *Hitler: A Study in Tyranny* which is now available as a Pelican book. Mr. Bullock's original work was rightly hailed as a study of outstanding distinction. In this new edition he has made full use of fresh sources and has rendered his indictment even more enthralling and even more irrefutable. No more valuable book exists on this subject. A very useful contribution has also been made by Mr. E. M. Robertson, whose *Hitler's Pre-war Policy and Military Plans* is to be published by Longmans in 1963. Drawing not only upon the chief published works for this period but also on much contemporary original source material, Mr. Robertson has written a study of great value which presents with damning effect the evidence he has acquired.

It is, I submit, of the very greatest difficulty for the serious student of history to read these two books and avoid reaching the ineluctable conclusion that Hitler was not only guilty of starting the Second World War but had been actively planning his potential aggression against the East, and against the West, for some time. In this story of war guilt, the Munich episode is a vital and fundamental factor, for it was at the conversations of Berchtesgaden and Godesberg that Hitler first made clear to the Western powers his intention, if necessary, of utilizing armed force as a means of treaty revision, regardless of the repercussions which such use might entail. That he would have occupied the Sudetenland on October 1, 1938, there is no denying and he was prepared to run the risk of war in doing so. The same was true of his invasion of Poland a year later, in which he deliberately disregarded the pledges given to that country under the Anglo-French treaties of alliance. That he would have preferred a bilateral war with Czechoslovakia or with Poland only is undeniable, but that he was prepared to hazard the possibility of a general conflict is equally beyond denial.

J. W. W.-B.

December 1962

One great lesson is again taught us, but it is never followed : NEVER *let the Army* and *Navy* DOWN *so low* as to be obliged to go to *great expense* in a hurry. . . . If we are to maintain our position as a *first rate* Power — and of that *no one* can doubt — we must, with our Indian Empire and large colonies, be *prepared for attacks* and *wars somewhere* or *other* CONTINUALLY. And the *true economy* will be to be *always ready.*

QUEEN VICTORIA to LORD BEACONSFIELD, July 28, 1879

This [the Munich Agreement] is the consequence of five years of futile good intention ; five years of eager search for the line of least resistance, five years of uninterrupted retreat of British power, five years of neglect of air defences.

We have been reduced in those five years from a position of security so overwhelming and so unchallengeable that we never cared to think about it. We have been reduced from a position where the very word "war" was considered one which would be used only by persons qualifying for a lunatic asylum.

RT. HON. WINSTON CHURCHILL
in the House of Commons, October 5, 1938

MUNICH
PROLOGUE TO TRAGEDY

SOME REFLECTIONS ON APPEASEMENT

" To avoid war should be the highest ambition of statesman-ship ", wrote Friedrich Gentz to King Frederick William III of Prussia in 1797, and thereby crystallized a verity. " War is a fearful thing," said Mr. Neville Chamberlain on an historic occasion, " and we must be very clear, before we embark upon it, that it is really the great issues that are at stake." The truth of these words is, if anything, more painfully clear in 1947 than in 1938.

It follows, therefore, that to appease, to placate — to agree with an adversary while we are in the way with him — becomes a fundamental purpose of all diplomacy, because it is a necessary condition of our civilized order which it is the purpose of that diplomacy to preserve and develop. At the same time, in any but a strictly pacifist society, the use of force is regarded as legiti-mate, at any rate for self-defence, and a successful foreign policy must, therefore, oscillate between these two apparently opposite poles.

Why, then, has Appeasement acquired the invidious connota-tion which it bears to-day? Some might say, because it has come to be regarded as a unilateral act of policy, as distinct from a mutual agreement, in which each side concedes something to the view-point of the other. Yet this does not seem to be a wholly adequate explanation. Governments may make concessions uni-laterally in pursuit of policy, whatever the principles of that policy may be. But such concessions must never involve the surrender of any fundamental principle upon the preservation of which the claim to loyalty and respect of governments rests. To surrender these is branded as " Appeasement " in the bad sense, and rightly so, for the means, in such cases, openly or covertly, betray the ends which they are called into being to promote. Surrender to blackmail is always damnable because it sets a higher value upon mere self-protection than upon principles, which, in fact, we know to be sacred and inviolable. Such appeasement is justly condemned because it is felt to be an act of treason against

3

all we stand for — the purchase of life at the expense of those ultimate ends of which the pursuit alone makes life worth living. It is in this sense that men of honour are admired, because we consider that in no circumstances will they think it right to sacrifice principle to expediency.

In past centuries men fought with zeal for such ends as the defence and extension of their religious faiths, for the dynastic interests of their monarchs, and for the retention or expansion of their possessions, but, with the gradual development of modern warfare towards totality, there came a growing inclination on the part of civilized peoples to restrict to the barest minimum the issues on which they would have recourse to the arbitrament of arms.

From this tendency evolved the desire for " Peaceful Change " and for the discovery of some method for the settlement of international disputes other than a resort to war with its sacrifice of human life, its destruction of social and economic order, and its inevitable consequences in ruin, disease and death. Parallel with this progression was a similar anxiety to localize and isolate such armed conflicts as did occur, on the principle that the fewer the Powers concerned in a war the less destructive its effects.

This combination of pacific propensities, which was prominent at the Congress of Vienna, resulted in the successful avoidance of a general war in Europe for the next hundred years. There were local wars, indeed, in which relatively few Powers were engaged, but there were many occasions on which issues, of a kind which might in times past have provoked hostilities, were settled by arbitration or diplomatic appeasement, and others in which the solution by pacific means of disputes and differences actually resulted in the promotion of better relations between the Powers concerned than had previously existed. As examples of the first of these categories may be cited the unilateral denunciation in 1870 by Russia of the Black Sea clauses of the Treaty of Paris, and the annexation by Austria-Hungary of the provinces of Bosnia and Herzegovina in 1908 ; while a striking example of the second is the Anglo-French Agreement of 1904, which provided the basis of a firm alliance between the two countries for the next thirty-seven years.[1]

This gravitation toward peace had its defects as well as its virtues. Their general and sincere abhorrence of war afflicted the

---

[1] For an excellent account of this process between 1815 and 1914, see *A History of Peaceful Change in the Modern World*, by C. R. M. F. Cruttwell. (Oxford, 1937.)

Powers with a certain systematic political myopia which obscured the dangers inherent in, for example, the rise of German militarism. The desire to isolate war in this case outran wisdom, for it was clear, from the moment of Bismarck's declaration of the Policy of Blood and Iron in 1862, that Prussia openly regarded war as a definite instrument of policy in the fulfilment of her national ambitions. Thus Denmark was abandoned in 1864 — " I see, my lord, that I can put aside the supposition that Britain will ever go to war on a point of honour ", was the comment of Prince Gortschakov to Lord Napier on receiving the British refusal to participate in intervention against Prussian aggression — while Austria-Hungary and France fought alone and disastrously in 1866 and 1870. There resulted the carefully planned emergence of the German Empire. While guided by the aged Prince Bismarck, who followed the policy of " limited objectives " and always knew when and where to call a halt, this new political manifestation did not prove itself an essential danger to peace, but it became an inevitable agent of destruction under the self-obsessed and irresponsible Wilhelm II.

Under the shadow of the then unparalleled ravages of the First World War, the peace-makers of Paris sought to repair the damage suffered by the machinery for pacific settlement, to strengthen and extend it beyond all previous limits, and to obviate the errors of the past by recognizing the truth that, since peace is indivisible, so must the means of preserving it be indivisible. Under the Covenant of the League of Nations the principle was acknowledged, for the first time, that a wrong done against one State constituted a wrong against all, and it was hoped that by the over-all guarantee of the League against aggression a potential aggressor would be deterred from committing his contemplated crime.

Alas for the imperfections of human nature ; neither the peoples of the world nor their governments were sufficiently in earnest for this plan to become realized in any major degree. The powers of the old Adam of nationalism were too strong for the new international ideal to prevail against them. For a variety of reasons, familiar enough but too numerous to be dealt with here, the system of collective security, as visualized under the Covenant, never materialized in practice, and one by one Japan, Italy, and Germany committed their acts of aggression unchecked and unpunished.

Yet, by a curious contradiction, the will to peace persisted, as strong and stronger than before, among the majority of nations — but it became the will to peace at almost any price. The same mixture of fear and blindness which had afflicted their fathers seventy years before in regard to the rise of German militarism now hampered the peoples and governments of the world in assessing the dangers of its recrudescence in the form of National Socialism. The passionate will to peace — so right, so laudable, so understandable in itself; that same will which had, in Britain, promoted a unilateral reduction of armaments to a point barely compatible with the needs of national defence — now became the progenitor of a profound desire, not to prevent aggression, but to avoid war, and, if war should come, to keep out of it. In following this policy the governments were at one with their peoples, and in Britain, for example, there is no question but that Mr. Anthony Eden voiced the popular opinion of the majority when he declared, as Foreign Secretary, that " nations cannot be expected to incur automatic military obligations save for areas where their vital interests are concerned ".

It is a tragic irony of history that this very will for peace was among the most important contributory factors to the Second World War, for it is clear that early and bloodless victories convinced Hitler that Britain and France would never oppose him by force, or that, if they did so, their opposition would prove negligible. Because of their horror of the concept of war as the *ultima ratio regum*, Britain and France had reduced their armaments and neglected their defences. Because they could not make up their minds as to what their " vital interests " really were, they did not — or would not — realize that they themselves were menaced by the rearmament of Germany, by the reoccupation of the Rhineland, by the unilateral abrogation of the Treaty of Locarno, by the annexation of Austria or by the crippling of Czechoslovakia. In the name of peace and of appeasement they condoned injustice and aggression on the part of Germany because they believed themselves too weak to oppose her and because they hoped against hope that — in accordance with the Führer's promises — each act of depredation would be the last. Not until it was well-nigh too late did Britain and France come fully to realize that German ambitions constituted a direct threat to their own most vital interest of all — their way of life, their tradition of liberty and decency, their " deathless attachment to freedom " ;

when they had so realized, they fought — but for France it was too late.

What, then, is the answer, since all must be agreed that " to avoid war must be the highest ambition of statesmanship " ?

It lies surely, first, in the proposition that disarmament must follow — and not precede — the establishment of an effective system of security; that never again must any peace-loving Power become so weak that, either individually or in alliance with others, it is unable to say " No " to a potential aggressor at the earliest symptom of his aggressive designs; that it should have it within its power to insist that disputes be settled in equity and justice. " The concessions of the weak are the concessions of fear ", declared Edmund Burke in 1775, and this is as profoundly true to-day as it was one hundred and seventy years ago. Appeasement — a necessary and invaluable card in the game of diplomacy — must be played from strength and never from weakness.

The answer lies, secondly, in that, having the necessary force at our disposal, we should arrive at a broader recognition of our " vital interests ", and a realization that the most vital of all, our way of life, to which we have ever pledged " our lives, our fortunes and our sacred honour ", may be threatened by events farther afield than we are at first disposed to perceive.

It was not for Belgium or for Serbia that we fought in 1914; it was not for Czechoslovakia that we might have fought in 1938; it was not for Poland that we fought a year later ; it was in defence of a principle, in the words of Mr. Duff Cooper, " that one Great Power should not be allowed, in disregard of treaty obligations, of the laws of nations and the decrees of morality, to dominate the continent of Europe ". In defence of this principle we have fought many times in the past and must be prepared to fight again in the future, for on the day when we are not prepared to fight for it we shall have forfeited our liberties, our independence, and all the hopes and ideals which we have ever cherished.

Appeasement, then, must ever stop short of this point. But how to realize in time that the point has been reached ? How to prevent Europe from again being plucked like an artichoke, leaf by leaf, until we ourselves remain the tastiest morsel of all — *le fond d'artichaut* ?

To this question the answer was given one hundred and forty years ago :

Expressions like " The fate of this or that part of Europe does not concern us " or " we limit ourselves to the maintenance of order in such-and-such an area " and so on should never again pass the lips of a ruler or statesman. . . . The more vigorously and courageously injustice and force are attacked at their first appearance, the less often will it be necessary to take the field against them in battle. . . . The more sensitive is every part to the injuring of the whole, the less frequent will wars become.[1]

These words, written in the face of Napoleonic aggression, were true after the First World War and are still true to-day. Their purport is clear beyond misunderstanding ; peace is one and indivisible. In an imperfect world, from which the imperfections are not likely to be speedily removed, it must be recognized that, alongside the desire for change and rectification arising from the normal tendencies of evolution and progress, evil, predatory instincts, national passions and hatreds, will continue to exist. Appeasement has its rightful and appropriate place in the solution of problems and disputes by methods of " peaceful change " and pacific settlement, but is inadmissible in dealing with aggression.

Has the world learned its lesson, or are we, in effect, merely taking " an unconscionable time a-dying " ?

[1] *A History of the Balance of Power in Europe* (1805), by Friedrich Gentz, quoted by Golo Mann in *The Secretary of Europe*. (New Haven, 1946.)

PART I

THE DRAMA OF MUNICH

MARCH–OCTOBER 1938

What king, going to war against another king, sitteth not
down first, and consulteth whether he be able with ten thousand
to meet him that cometh against him with twenty thousand?
Or else, while the other is yet a great way off, he sendeth an
ambassage and desireth conditions of peace.

ST. LUKE xiv, 31, 32

CHAPTER ONE

THE LIGHTS ARE DIMMED

(i)

ON the afternoon of November 5, 1937, a group of persons met secretly in Berlin to decide the future policy of Germany. Their purpose was to expand the frontiers of the German Reich, if possible by peaceful means, if need be by war. They were unlike the majority of the governments of Europe, which regarded war as a desperate expedient to be used only as a last resort in defence of those national interests which cannot under any conditions be sacrificed. These persons, following the equally clear doctrines of Frederick the Great, Clausewitz and Bismarck, regarded war as an instrument of policy. Clausewitz had laid down the precept that " war is a mere continuation of Policy by other means ", and, in the mind of at least one of those present at the meeting, the time had come when the use of these means must be envisaged.

A new climacteric had been reached in the history of Germany, and Adolf Hitler had summoned his political and military lieutenants to a frank and full discussion of the future. There were present, in addition to the Führer, Field-Marshal von Blomberg, Minister for War; Colonel-General Baron von Fritsch, Commander-in-Chief of the Army; General-Admiral Raeder, Commander-in-Chief of the Navy; Colonel-General Göring, Commander-in-Chief of the Air Force; and Baron von Neurath, Minister for Foreign Affairs. As they sat round the conference table in the new Reichskanzlei, they listened in amazement to Hitler's exposition of his new " fundamental principles ", which he regarded as so vital that they must be considered, in the event of his death, as his last Will and Testament.[1]

It was nearly five years since the Nazi Revolution of 1933 ; five years which had been devoted to the intensive economic and

---

[1] For the minutes of this meeting at the Reichskanzlei, see Document 386-PS, presented by the prosecution to the International Military Tribunal at Nuremberg.

military rearmament of Germany. Now the time had come to utilize this great machine in the fulfilment of that wider programme for the conquest of *Lebensraum* which had been consciously envisaged ever since the National Socialist Party had come into existence.

Germany's armaments, said the Führer, were at that moment superior in calibre and modernity to those of any other European State, but they would become obsolescent and might even be equalled or improved upon by her potential enemies. Moreover, the economic future of Germany could not be assured by means of *Autarchie* or of an increased share in world commerce and industry. The problem was one of space. It was clear, therefore, said Hitler to his henchmen, that Germany had " nothing to gain from a long period of peace ". The question for Germany's future was " where the greatest possible conquest could be made at the lowest cost ", the objective being not the conquest of people but of " agriculturally useful space ".

The first step in the path of conquest was the immediate consolidation of the Greater German Reich ; an expansion into Central Europe, whence Germany could derive food supplies, raw materials and man-power, to furnish further military excursions to the eastward — to Poland and the rich black lands of the Ukraine. Austria and Czechoslovakia must, therefore, be subjugated as a preliminary to wider conquest.

But how, it was asked, was it possible to carry out so bold a stroke ? What was the " lowest cost " at which such conquest could be made ? Austrian independence was guaranteed by Britain, France and Italy — and incidentally by Germany ; and Czechoslovakia was protected by treaties of alliance with Russia and with France.

" It is true ", replied Hitler, " that we have two hateful enemies to contend with, England and France, to whom a strong German colossus in the centre of Europe would be intolerable, but I personally believe that, in all probability, England, and perhaps France also, have already silently written off both Austria and Czechoslovakia. Britain's difficulties within the Empire and the prospect of her becoming involved in another long and ruinous European conflict will be sufficient to prevent her from going to war with Germany, and without British support an attack by France is hardly probable. There will be no opposition from Italy to the ' removal ' of Czechoslovakia, but the Italian attitude towards Austria will largely depend on whether Mussolini is alive at the time or not.   Russian support for Czechoslovakia may well be counted on, but in this case their intervention must be countered by the speed of our military operations."   The attack on Czechoslovakia would have to be effected with the " speed of lightning " (*blitzartig schnell*).

But, added the Führer, it was not inconceivable that the annexation of Austria and the subjugation of the Czechoslovak Republic might be brought about by peaceful means.   The statesmen of Europe might be bluffed into acquiescence or, more likely still, would purchase Germany's friendship at any price, since he saw every possibility of an Anglo-French-Italian war in the Mediterranean by the summer of 1938.   The German plans must take account of every possible contingency.

There is little doubt that this revelation of policy by Hitler came as a surprise to his hearers, none of whom shared his confidence in success.   Doubts and objections were at once raised. Von Neurath questioned the Führer's optimism on the possibility of a war between the Western Powers and Italy, and the disinterestedness of Britain and France in Central Europe.   For the military, von Blomberg emphasized the strength of the Czechoslovak fortifications, " which would present extreme difficulties to our attack ", and both he and General von Fritsch were dubious as to whether France, even if involved in war with Italy, would not be able to attack Germany in the West.   Von Fritsch indeed believed that France would require only 20 divisions to hold her Alpine frontier against Italy, thereby leaving herself a strong superiority on Germany's western front.   Even Göring, the only other veteran Nazi present, considered that Germany should not embark on this clearly defined programme of conquest until she had liquidated her military liabilities in Spain, where German " volunteers ", fully equipped with arms and material, were making it possible for General Franco to establish a military dictatorship.

But the Führer would brook no opposition.   He accepted Göring's point but swept aside with contempt the objections of the others.   It was possible that the action which they now contemplated would precipitate a general European war, but this prospect must be considered as a risk worth taking.

" The German question ", asserted Hitler, " can be solved only by way of force, and this is never without risk.   The battles of Frederick the Great for Silesia, and Bismarck's wars with

Austria and France, were all tremendous risks. We must place
' force with risk ' at the head of our programme.''

If the doubts of the others were unresolved by this argument,
they were not prepared to incur the Führer's wrath by their
continued objection. When the conference closed at 8.20 that
evening the great decision had been taken ; the fate of Austria
and Czechoslovakia had been settled ; the campaign for *Lebensraum* had been determined.

It is one of Fate's tragic ironies that, at the moment when the
national policy of Germany was about to be directed towards a
programme of expansion, the national policy of Britain should
have developed a trend best calculated to assist the fulfilment of
this programme.

The year 1937 marked as momentous a decision for Britain
as it did for Germany, for it was at this time that the Government
of Mr. Neville Chamberlain, under the direction of the Prime
Minister, resolved to pursue an " all-out " policy of appeasement
toward the totalitarian States of Europe.

The considerations prompting this decision, which will be
treated later in this book,[1] were twofold : first, the deplorably
weak state of Britain's military preparedness ; and, secondly, a
hope (in the case of Germany) that, if only her immediate claims for
the revision of the territorial provisions of the Treaty of Versailles
could be satisfied in Europe, a lasting peace might well result
therefrom.

The British statesmen of the day were not " pro-Nazi ", nor
even " pro-German " ; indeed some of them had shared an
impulse to cry a halt in terms of force to Germany's earlier
violations of the Treaty of Versailles — her announcement, in
March 1935, of the resumption of compulsory military training
and the creation of an air-force, and, a year later, her remilitarization of the Rhineland. But they were accurately interpreting the
general unwillingness to fight which was felt by a majority of the
British people. So long as Hitler confined himself to reclaiming
German territory and incorporating Germans within the Reich,
the British people were not disposed to quarrel with him.[2] Nor
would they listen to the warning voice of Mr. Winston Churchill,

[1] See below, Part II, Chapter Three.

[2] Lord Rothermere, at this moment, was actually advocating the return to Germany
of her former colonial possessions and the formation of " a London-Berlin-Rome
Axis ". (See the *Daily Mail*, May 4 and September 27, 1937 ; also *Warnings and
Predictions*, by Viscount Rothermere (London, 1939), pp. 155-65.)

who vainly endeavoured to awaken England to a true realization of the menace inherent in these seemingly understandable actions of Germany. Even among those who were conscious of danger there were many who believed that, since the opportunity to nip Nazi aggression in the bud had been missed in 1935 and 1936, it was impossible to do so now short of a major military operation, which Britain was in no way qualified to undertake. For Germany had exploited to the full her newly created military machine and had far surpassed the land and air armaments of Britian. If, therefore, Britain was to assert herself again in the councils of Europe, she must play for time until she had rebuilt her defences and re-equipped her armaments. In this camp stood Mr. Anthony Eden, Mr. Duff Cooper and others of the younger Conservative leaders. On the other hand, the Prime Minister himself, Sir John Simon, Sir Samuel Hoare, and Lord Halifax considered appeasement as an end in itself, believing that all that remained was to discover what Germany's demands in Europe amounted to, and to make the best bargain possible to satisfy them by peaceful means.

That these conflicting views were current in London was known to the Führer in Berlin, and his "intuition" deduced therefrom that Britain would not fight for Austria or Czechoslovakia. In order to cloak the magnitude of their ultimate designs, the Nazi leaders spoke with comparative frankness of their more immediate goals in Central Europe, which they represented as the pacific unification of all Germans in one Reich. "I never had a shadow of doubt", wrote Sir Nevile Henderson, the British Ambassador in Berlin, whose opinion carried considerable weight with the British Government, "that his [Hitler's] aims were the incorporation of Austria, the Sudetenland, Memel and Danzig. His claims in these respects were based on the principle of self-determination, and a negotiated settlement in regard to them should not, therefore, have been impossible."[1]

Convinced that only a radical revision of the territorial provisions of the Treaty of Versailles could preserve the peace of Europe, Mr. Chamberlain and his friends were beguiled by the argument advanced by the Nazi leaders in favour of settlement by self-determination — after all, it was only extending to Germans a principle which had been applied under the Treaty to Czechs, Yugoslavs, etc. — and they were impressed by the fact that, in

[1] *Failure of a Mission*, by Sir Nevile Henderson (New York, 1940), p. 99.

January 1935, in a plebiscite conducted by secret ballot and under international police surveillance, the inhabitants of the Saar Basin Territory had voted overwhelmingly for reunion with the German Reich.   The leaders of the Appeasement school were deluded by the German insistence that these territorial changes should be carried out peaceably and in order, and that, once the problems which they presented had been removed, the way would be open, not only to an Anglo-German understanding, but to a general agreement for the preservation of the peace of Europe.

Unheedful of the more cautious views of Mr. Eden, who, having formed a not wholly unfavourable view of Hitler when he first met him in 1934, had soon seen the light and realized the dangers of placing trust in Nazi pledges ; unmoved by the Cassandra-like thunderings which Mr. Winston Churchill continued to pour forth in futile warning, Mr. Chamberlain, in his wisdom, chose this moment, as he later told the House of Commons, to begin the general exploration for the basis " on which we might build up a general scheme of appeasement ".[1]

There is something tragically hideous and pathetic in this belief of Mr. Chamberlain that he could match wits and ex-change troths with Hitler, who, only shortly before, is reported to have confessed that " he was ready to guarantee every frontier and to conclude a non-aggression pact with anyone ", but that " anyone who was so fussy that he had to consult his own con-science about whether he could keep a pact, whatever the pact or whatever the situation, was a fool.   He could conclude any pact and yet be ready to break it next day in cold blood, if that was in the interests of Germany." [2]

Mr. Chamberlain could not know the degree of infamy with which he had to contend, but his own credulity would not have done him credit in an ordinary friendly poker game, and, with the past record of broken Nazi pledges before him, he was culpably credulous in his dealings with Hitler.

The Prime Minister desired to establish a closer touch with the Nazi leaders in order the better to understand what was in their minds.   The Foreign Secretary, Mr. Eden, was not in agreement with this course of action, for he considered that he was already

---

[1] *House of Commons Debates*, February 21, 1938, col. 54.

[2] *Germany's Revolution of Destruction*, by Hermann Rauschning (London, 1939), p. 251.

sufficiently aware of Nazi methods and intentions to mistrust them thoroughly. The establishment of direct contact, however, was persistently urged from Berlin by Sir Nevile Henderson, who was more attuned to the views of Mr. Chamberlain than to those of the Foreign Secretary.

The initiative ultimately came from the Nazis. Someone had told Göring that Lord Halifax, then Lord President of the Council, would prove more *gemütlich* (agreeable) than Mr. Eden and that he even enjoyed a greater degree of Mr. Chamberlain's confidence than did the Foreign Secretary. Forthwith an opportunity presented itself. An International Exhibition of Hunting was to be held in Berlin in the autumn of 1937, under the patronage of Göring as Game Warden of the Reich, and an invitation to visit it was despatched to Lord Halifax as a famous Master of Foxhounds.

Here was that opportunity which Sir Nevile Henderson and Mr. Chamberlain — and even Hitler himself — had sought for the establishment of personal contact between a prominent British statesman and the Nazi leaders, and the private and unofficial nature of the proposed visit was such as " to avoid exciting exaggerated hopes in some quarters and apprehensions in others."[1] The friends of Lord Halifax, of whom Lord Londonderry was one,[2] urged him to go, and he sought Mr. Eden's approval to accept the invitation.

Mr. Eden was not happy about the idea, but he felt that, if a member of the British Government could convince Hitler and Göring that Britain was not disinterested in Central Europe, nothing could be lost and perhaps something gained. He therefore agreed to the projected visit on the natural assumption that Hitler would be in Berlin, or at least that he would travel there to meet so distinguished a visitor. Instructions were accordingly sent to Sir Nevile Henderson, and Mr. Eden departed for Brussels to attend the ill-fated Conference on Far Eastern Affairs (November 3).

The Führer proved agreeable to the idea of a meeting with Lord Halifax, but he showed no inclination to interrupt his

---

[1] Henderson, p. 94.

[2] " I think I may claim ", wrote Lord Londonderry to Ribbentrop on December 8, 1937, " to have been partly responsible for putting the idea into Halifax's head that he should go over to Germany and establish contact with the Chancellor and others in your country " (*Ourselves and Germany*, by the Marquess of Londonderry, K.G. (London, 1938), p. 156).

autumn holiday to receive an unofficial visitor in Berlin. He would be delighted to receive the Lord President — but in Bavaria.

To Mr. Chamberlain this attitude presented no difficulties and he willingly gave his consent, but to Mr. Eden, in Brussels, it was evident that Hitler was pursuing an oriental game concerned with the matter of " face ". The Foreign Secretary considered that, if the Nazi leaders could not take the trouble to see Lord Halifax in the capital of the Reich, it was undignified for a British envoy, however unofficial, to pursue them into their several holiday haunts. Moreover, if the Führer was so little willing to disturb himself that he would not make a journey of a few hours, the value of the meeting became much more doubtful. In all these circumstances, the Foreign Secretary felt the visit to be hardly worth while.

The Prime Minister, more skilled in the ways of business negotiation than in the minutiae of statecraft, swept aside these objections as matters of " diplomatic punctilio ". He set great store upon this forthcoming visit to bring about the first steps in that general process of appeasement which he believed it possible to attain. He was still sincerely convinced that it was possible to " do business with Hitler ", and to this end he disregarded the warnings and objections of his Foreign Secretary and authorized the visit of Lord Halifax to Berchtesgaden.

Thus it came about that on November 10, 1937 — five days after the Führer's secret conclave — the Lord President of the Council arrived in Berlin with the knowledge but not the approval of the Foreign Secretary.

Lord Halifax's first contact with Göring at his castle of Karinhall was on a friendly and amicable basis. Göring frankly told his visitor that every German Government, of whatever political complexion, would consider as an essential part of their policy the incorporation within the Reich of Austria and the Sudetenland, and also the return of Danzig to Germany with a reasonable solution of the Polish Corridor. To this Lord Halifax made no other reply than that the British Government wished all questions affecting Germany and her neighbours to be settled by peaceful means.

" That depends very much on England," Göring answered. " England would be able to contribute very much to the peaceful solution of these questions. Germany does not wish to go to war on these issues, but they must be settled in all circumstances."

The interview with Hitler at Berchtesgaden on November 19, at which Freiherr von Neurath was present, was a more important affair. They made a curious contrast, the cold, detached patrician, and the neurotic hyperbolic dictator; the one a representative of an order which had its roots and traditions in the past, the other concerned less with the past than with the future, of which he considered himself the master. But they were well matched in the art of dialectical fencing. Hitler talked of the difficulties inherent in the transaction of business with democracies, and Lord Halifax replied that, if any agreement between Britain and Germany had to wait until Britain had ceased to be a democracy, he might as well have stayed at home.

There followed a discussion in which the Lord President warily essayed to discover what exactly it was that Hitler wanted, while impressing upon him the fact that Britain could not hold herself disinterested in the fate of Central Europe. The Führer, with equal wariness, was at pains to hide his real intentions.

They touched on a number of subjects, making a *tour d'horizon* of the international situation. The colonial question was considered and the possibilities of reaching an Anglo-German understanding canvassed. When their discussion reached Central Europe, it is to be presumed that Lord Halifax repeated to Hitler what he had already said to Göring; namely, that Britain's anxiety was that any changes which were effected should be achieved by peaceful means and not in a manner which would upset the peace of Europe. There can be no doubt that Hitler gave his visitor no inkling of the fateful decisions which had been taken not three weeks before at the secret conclave of November 5. He doubtless masked his ambition for *Lebensraum* behind a display of moderation and reason. The problem of Austria he regarded as virtually settled. He hoped that that country would soon drop like a ripe plum into his lap — if it did not, he was prepared to do some vigorous tree-shaking, but this fact he would certainly keep to himself; it was not for discussion with foreign visitors. As for Czechoslovakia, Hitler's line had always been that, if the Prague Government would only treat its German minority decently, the Czechs had nothing to fear from Germany, and it was presumably in this vein that he addressed Lord Halifax.

How far Lord Halifax believed Hitler to be sincere in these asseverations of peace, it is difficult to say. The report which he made to Mr. Chamberlain and the Cabinet on his return to

YET ONE MORE CONVERSATION

And why the world is boiling hot,
And whether Peace has wings.

LORD HALIFAX. " But not about Colonies."
HERR HITLER. " Hush ! "

NOVEMBER 24, 1937

Reprinted by the special permission of the Proprietors of " Punch "

London has not yet been published, but it was apparently not of a nature to deter the Prime Minister from the pursuit of his general policy of appeasement, even at the cost of the resignation of his Foreign Secretary. Indeed, he was much pleased with the result.[1] On the other hand, the Lord President himself carried away the impression that Hitler would not be an easy person to deal with and that he would not keep any promise that he made.

To Hitler, on the other hand, who, according to the British Ambassador, had been "impressed by the obvious sincerity, high principles and straightforward honesty" of Lord Halifax,[2] the interview was a further confirmation of the conviction which he had expressed to the conference on November 5, that Britain would not oppose force to the German plans for expansion in Central Europe and that, without the assurance of British support, France would not fight either. The apprehensions of Neurath, Blomberg and Fritsch were groundless, and, if these men persisted in their half-hearted support of his policies, they must be replaced by others more ruthless, more amenable and of greater intestinal fortitude. Nothing must be allowed to obstruct the progress of the German conquest of *Lebensraum*.

And so the fateful year of 1938 dawned with the national policies of Germany and Britain flowing in parallel streams of conquest and appeasement, and, before the autumn leaves had fallen, the streams were to be merged in a meeting of the waters.

(ii)

Four months had passed since the momentous decisions of November 1937; four months during which the protagonists of appeasement in Britain and of conquest in Germany had each strengthened their positions. In Britain, Mr. Eden had at last found it impossible to condone further a policy which could only convey the impression abroad that Britain was prepared to yield to constant pressure. He had resigned on February 20, 1938,

---

[1] " The German visit was from my point of view a great success ", Mr. Chamberlain recorded in his journal on November 27, " because it achieved its object, that of creating an atmosphere in which it is possible to discuss with Germany the practical questions involved in a European settlement. . . . I don't see why we shouldn't say to Germany ' give us satisfactory assurances that you won't use force to deal with the Austrians and the Czechoslovakians, and we will give you similar assurances that we won't use force to prevent the changes you want, if you can get them by peaceful means '." (*The Life of Neville Chamberlain*, by Keith Feiling (London, 1946), pp. 332-3).   [2] Henderson, p. 96.

to be replaced at the Foreign Office by Lord Halifax.[1]

February had also seen great changes in Germany. Hitler had taken advantage of dissensions in the High Command of the *Reichswehr* arising from their disapproval of the marriage of Marshal von Blomberg with a lady with a police record — at which ceremony, incidentally, Hitler and Göring had officiated as witnesses — to dispense with the Marshal and with General von Fritsch,[2] both of whom he regarded as half-hearted and " defeatist " in their adherence to his policies. He had himself assumed the offices of Minister of War and Commander-in-Chief, with General Wilhelm Keitel — popularly known in Berlin as " *Lakaitel* " from his early subservience to Nazi doctrines — as Chief of Staff of all the armed forces of the Reich. He had also replaced the " respectable " Neurath by the evil and malleable Ribbentrop as Foreign Minister.

The first step toward the realization of the programme enunciated by the Führer at the secret conclave of November 5 had already been taken. The unfortunate Austrian Chancellor had met his ordeal at Berchtesgaden on February 12, and now the stage was set for the consummation of the villainy.

In Berlin, in the gigantic structure of the Haus der Flieger, Hermann Göring, newly created a Field-Marshal, was giving an evening party ; one of those fantastic extravagances so dear to his florid soul. A thousand guests — the foreign diplomatic corps, members of the Reich Government, and the hierarchs of the Nazi Party — were gathered in the great hall to be entertained by a performance of his State Opera and Ballet.

The gathering was a brilliant one — in terms of the chromium-plated brilliance of the Third Reich -- but the atmosphere was one of electric tension and impending tragedy. To every foreigner present, and perhaps to some of the German guests also, there was an unseemliness in music and dancing at a moment when a crime of considerable magnitude was in process of being committed — as if the strains of the orchestra had been commanded to drown the last cries of the victim.

---

[1] See below, pp. 268-72.

[2] The details of the *Reichswehr* crisis of February 1938, together with the peculiarly disgusting methods employed to obtain von Fritsch's resignation, were given by Herr Hans Gisevius in evidence before the International Military Tribunal at Nuremberg on April 25, 1946. (See *Proceedings of the International Military Tribunal* (London, 1946–1947), Part 12, pp. 227-33. ; also *Bis zum bitteren Ende*, by H. B. Gisevius (Zurich, 1946), vol. i, pp. 383-459. General von Fritsch met his death in somewhat mysterious circumstances in the Polish campaign of September 1939.

It was the night of March 11, 1938, and Austria was dying.

The day had been one of events happening in rapid succession. Rumours of troop concentration on the Austrian border had circulated in Berlin since morning, but no authentic news was available. Then in the evening had come a dramatic climax. At 7.30 P.M., when Göring's guests were preparing to enjoy his hospitality, the Vienna radio had brought the last despairing message of Kurt von Schuschnigg, delivered in a voice of courage but hoarse and broken with emotion, ending with the invocation : " God protect Austria ". There followed the Austrian National Anthem, in the tempo of a funeral march, and the opening bars of Beethoven's Seventh Symphony ; then a silence as of death, to be broken at length by the excited and breathless voice of Seyss-Inquart urging the Austrian people and army to remain calm and offer no resistance to the events which would follow.

All these things were common knowledge to the assembling guests in the Haus der Flieger — some of them knew much more — and it was evident that every German present was a prey to anxiety. If German troops moved into Austria — and none supposed that they would not — what would Mussolini say ? What would be the reaction of Britain and France, who had guaranteed Austrian independence ? Would the Czechs mobilize ? There was comment on the scanty representation that evening of the army and *Luftwaffe*, on the absence of the Czechoslovak Minister and the presence of his Austrian colleague, who might reasonably be excused for absenting himself.[1]   It was also remarked that at the central table, where were seated the Ambassadors of Great Britain, France, and the United States, the place of the host remained vacant. The Field-Marshal had not yet arrived, though Frau Emmy Göring had preceded him. " Why doth the bridegroom tarry ? " enquired one cynical foreigner of his neighbour.

It was generally known that the British Ambassador had called at the German Foreign Ministry twice during the day [2] and now, when the First Secretary of his Embassy, Mr. Ivone Kirkpatrick,

[1] Sympathy was wasted on this miserable individual. He had already trimmed his sails to the wind. Two days later, on March 13, the day on which Austria was formally annexed to the Reich, he attended the *Heldentag* (the anniversary for the German dead of the First World War) in full uniform, gave the Nazi salute and cried " Heil Hitler " with the rest.

[2] Sir N. Henderson had, in fact, protested officially to Freiherr von Neurath on behalf of His Majesty's Government and his protest had been rejected both orally and in writing. For text of German Note, which Mr. Chamberlain read to Parliament, see *House of Commons Debates*, March 14, 1938, coll. 47-9.

pushed his way to the central table and handed him a communication of obvious urgency, there was a dead silence while the Ambassador read it.[1]

At length, an hour late, Göring appeared, and, lowering his great bulk into the vacant chair, made his apologies.

What had delayed the host of this strange gathering ? Though the Rape of Austria had been designed and planned since the previous November, it had been impossible to make certain in advance of all the *imponderabilia* attendant on such an enterprise. There could be no turning back now ; the die had been cast, and in a few hours German troops would cross the Austrian border, but would the result be a peaceful victory or a general war ? Those very questions, which more than one of Göring's guests was putting to himself, had perplexed the Führer and his lieutenants for many weeks past. What indeed would be the effect on Mussolini ? What the reactions of Britain and France ? Would the Czechs mobilize ? Though determined to go through with his plans, Hitler awaited the answer to these questions in some anxiety, since upon them depended the extent of the operations and their repercussions.

One at least of these problems had temporarily solved itself. France was without a government at this moment, and hence would offer no immediate opposition. But at ten o'clock on the evening of March 11, the time at which Göring's guests had been invited, the other questions still remained unanswered. As to Britain, it was true that on March 3 Sir Nevile Henderson had told the Führer that she had, in fact, washed her hands of Austria, provided that the outcome could be designated as a " reasonable solution reasonably achieved " ; it was true that Mr. Chamberlain in the House of Commons four days later (March 7) had given what might justifiably be interpreted as a " green light " to a peaceful acquisition of Austria ; but the final attitude of the British Cabinet toward the type of *coup* which Hitler was now about to make was still in doubt, and, as a precaution, the Führer's special envoy, Joachim von Ribbentrop, was in London, ready to soothe the ruffled consciences of the British Cabinet.

And what of Italy ? It was not until 10.25 P.M. on the night of March 11 that Prince Philip of Hesse, telephoning from Rome, conveyed to the Führer, then in conference at the Chancellery, the news that, faced with a *fait accompli*, Mussolini had agreed

[1] Henderson, p. 125.

to consider Austria as " immaterial to him " and thereby provoked a paroxysm of hysterical gratitude from Hitler (" Tell him I will never forget him for this, never, never, never ").[1] The conference adjourned. Hitler prepared to visit the country of his birth and Göring departed to his waiting guests.

There remained in doubt Czechoslovakia, and on her attitude depended that of France, for if the Czechs mobilized — and there were rumours both in Berlin and Prague that they were preparing to do so — and an incident occurred, France, who would certainly not fight for Austria, might be compelled to come to the assistance of her Czechoslovak ally.

The German Minister in Prague had received from the Czech Foreign Ministry an official denial of a mobilization rumour which had been current during the day, but it was evident that the Government of Czechoslovakia viewed with considerable alarm the events of the previous few hours in Austria and looked with vivid apprehension towards the future. It was necessary to German policy that they be reassured. Their time had not yet come.

When, therefore, the Czechoslovak Minister in Berlin, Dr. Voytech Mastný, arrived at the Haus der Flieger on that night of March 11, he found himself at once conducted to the private room of the Field-Marshal, who received him with otiose affability. What was happening in Austria, said Göring, was entirely a German family affair. It had no significance whatever for Germany's relations with Czechoslovakia, against whom the Reich harboured no evil intentions. " I give you my word of honour," he said, " that Czechoslovakia has nothing to fear from the Reich." But he asked for reciprocal assurances that the Czechs would not mobilize. Mastný undertook to consult his Government at once, and returned immediately to his Legation.[2] Göring, well satisfied with this reaction, went in to join his guests. But here a shock awaited him. The British Ambassador shook hands with his host " very curtly and coldly ". It was a noticeable affront and might, thought Göring, in nervous anxiety, betoken a stiffening of the British attitude. In a hastily written note, tossed across the wife of the American Ambassador, he invited Sir

[1] See stenographic record of conversation (*International Military Tribunal Document*, 2949–PS) ; also *Proceedings*, I, p. 259. Two days later (March 13) Hitler in Linz reiterated his thanks in the famous telegram : " Mussolini, I shall never forget you for this " (*Dokumente der Deutschen Politik*, Vol. 6, p. 145).

[2] *French Yellow Book* (New York, 1940), pp. 2-3.

Nevile Henderson to a private conference as soon as the ballet had ended.[1] This resulted in a stormy interview, but to Göring's relief there had been no change in the attitude of the British Government. They were still outraged, still protestant, but nothing more. They were not prepared to fight.

Scarcely had host and guest re-entered the great hall than Göring was informed that Mastný had returned, and he hurried out again. The results of the telephone conversation with Prague were highly satisfactory. He had, Mastný said, spoken personally with the Foreign Minister, Dr. Krofta, who had expressed appreciation of the assurance of German good-will and had authorized him to give to the Field-Marshal definite and binding assurances that Czechoslovakia would not mobilize as a result of the occupation of Austria by German armed forces.

Göring was delighted. He could now, he said, share a secret with Mastný. The Führer had absented himself for a few days from Berlin and had vested him, Göring, with full authority for the direction of the Reich. This fact would be made public at noon on the following day, but at the moment it meant that, having previously given assurances to Czechoslovakia in his own name, he could now reiterate them officially in the name of the German Reich and Government ; it was indeed as if the Führer himself were pledging his honour. What more could be required ? Mastný agreed that no higher pledge could be expected and returned to report this additional fact to Prague.

Within the next twenty-four hours (March 12–13) Dr. Mastný had received further and more explicit assurances from the German Foreign Ministry by way of the acting Foreign Minister (Freiherr von Neurath) and the State Secretary (Herr von Mackensen). Not only did the German Reich entertain the friendliest feelings for the Czechoslovak State but the Führer considered himself as still being bound by the German-Czechoslovak Arbitration Convention of October 1925, by which, with certain exceptions, all disputes arising between the two States should be solved by means of pacific settlement. It was hoped and believed that the clarification of the Austrian situation would generally improve relations between Berlin and Prague.[2]

Göring also reaffirmed his pledges, adding for good measure the fact that German troops had received the strictest orders to keep at least 15 kilometres from the Czechoslovak frontier. He

---

[1] Henderson, pp. 125-6.   [2] *French Yellow Book*, pp. 3-4.

again asked for and received a definite statement that no mobilization of Czechoslovak forces would take place.

Well might the Field-Marshal congratulate himself on his work of deception. The attitude of Czechoslovakia had been a definite source of anxiety to the planners of the Rape of Austria and, in their dealings with Italy, they had proposed to use the possibility of Austria becoming " a branch of the Czechoslovak Republic " as one of the excuses for annexation. But the Prague Government had taken the whole thing very quietly and had naïvely accepted the German assurances of good faith. It had been almost too easy, and, on March 12, Göring directed Prince Philip of Hesse to omit from the letter of gratitude which Hitler was sending to Mussolini all reference to the Czechs, since " we can now very agreeably leave Czechoslovakia out of the matter ".[1]

Twenty-four hours later Göring was instructing Ribbentrop in London, by telephone, to inform the British Ministers that " we in no way threaten the Czechoslovak State. On the contrary, Czechoslovakia has now an opportunity to arrive at a friendly and reasonable relationship with us."[2]

Such was the opening movement of the overture to the Drama of Munich — an insidious *Schlummerlied* with which Germany sought to lull Czechoslovakia and her allies into the drugged sleep of false security.

(iii)

Few countries have appeared on paper to be more completely and impregnably protected against aggression than was Czechoslovakia in the spring of 1938. The architects of the Republic, Thomas Masaryk and Edvard Beneš,[3] had wrought well and truly and the world was almost unanimous in admiration of their handiwork. The genius of Masaryk and the vision of Beneš had established a standard of statesmanship rarely equalled in any European country, great or small, and the course of this statesmanship had been directed towards guaranteeing the future safety of Czechoslovakia as completely as possible within the framework of

[1] See stenographic report of the telephone conversation (*International Military Tribunal Document*, 2949–PS).   [2] *Ibid.*

[3] Thomas Garrigue Masaryk, the founder of the Czechoslovak State, was President of the Republic from 1918 to 1935, when he retired, to be succeeded by Edvard Beneš. Beneš had been Foreign Minister of the Republic almost continuously from 1918 to 1935, having played a leading part in the work of the League of Nations, the formation of the Little Entente, and the return of Russia as an active participant in European affairs.

international security. In the first place, she had, as a Member of the League in good standing, that general and over-all guarantee of assistance provided by Article XVI of the Covenant. Both she and Germany were ratified signatories of the Kellogg-Briand Pact of 1928, under which both had renounced war " as an instrument of national policy ", and Hitler had never troubled to denounce this agreement. In addition, Czechoslovakia had the promise of general support from her colleagues of the Little Entente, in the construction of which she had been the chief architect.

More specifically, Czechoslovakia had a treaty of mutual assistance with France, signed in December 1925, pledging each party to come immediately to the support of the other in the event of unprovoked aggrêssion on the part of Germany.[1] A similar treaty concluded with Russia in May 1935 brought the Soviet Union to the aid of the Czechoslovak State immediately the Franco-Czech Pact went into operation. In support of these two latter agreements France had also signed a Pact of Mutual Assistance with Russia in 1935.[2]

With Germany Czechoslovakia had consistently refused to enter into a pact of non-aggression, such as Poland had concluded in 1934, preferring to place her faith in the multiple guarantees of France, Russia and the League of Nations, rather than upon the single plighted word of the Third Reich.[3] She had, however, the arbitration convention signed with Germany in October 1925 as an integral part of the Locarno Agreement, and, in denouncing this general agreement in 1936, Hitler had made a specific exception of the arbitration conventions with Poland and Czechoslovakia. Now, on March 12, 1938, Freiherr von Neurath had explicitly reaffirmed the assurance that Germany considered herself as still bound by this treaty.

[1] There were, in effect, two treaties of mutual assistance between France and Czechoslovakia. The first was signed on January 24, 1924, and ratified on March 4 ; the second, an integral part of the general Locarno Agreement, was initialed on October 16, 1925, and signed on December 5. For the text of this latter Agreement see Appendix A.

[2] For texts of the Agreements of the Soviet Union and France with Czechoslovakia see Appendices B and C.

[3] In his New Year's Message broadcast from London to the Czech people in January 1941, Dr. Beneš said : " Three times between the years 1934 and 1937 Hitler proposed that Czechoslovakia and Germany conclude a bilateral pact of non-aggression. Three times I expressly rejected his proposals, explaining that we would undertake no obligations without the League of Nations and without the Powers with whom Czechoslovakia was bound by treaties. I did not trust Hitler's word, nor did I have any illusions about his signature."

The Czech position was, in fact, the *reductio ad absurdum* of the " pactomania " which afflicted Europe in the years between the wars, and the outcome is a classic example of the failure of the sanctity of treaties when found to be in conflict with other and more overwhelming interests of Great Powers.

The Czechs, however, were among the most realistic of the European nations. They were not, it is true, realistic enough, but, as compared with many of their greater and lesser neighbours, they were considerably more far-sighted and practical in their approach to the German menace. They did not put their faith exclusively in fair words and plighted troths, and they were continually taking stock of their position.

Their defences on the German frontier, for example, were in excellent order. With French assistance, a miniature Maginot Line had been constructed here, providing for a defence in depth behind which the Czech General Staff were confident that their excellently equipped army of forty divisions could hold up any German attack for at least six weeks, by which time, it was supposed, France and Russia would be engaging the aggressor in the West and in the East respectively.

Nor had the Czech Ministry of Defence neglected or ignored the recent signs and portents to the south-east. An *Anschluss* had been considered as a practical possibility since the advent of Hitler to power in 1933, and plans had been made for the development of the national defences on the southern flank as soon as this potentiality should have become an accomplished fact. The Czech calculations had gone awry in that they had expected Schuschnigg's resistance to continue a year longer, but no sooner had the Austrian Federal Chancellor obeyed the fateful summons to Berchtesgaden on February 12, 1938, than every effort was bent upon the strengthening of the defences at this vulnerable spot. These efforts had been still further intensified after the Führer's sinister reminder to the Reichstag, on February 20, that " over ten million Germans live in two of the States adjoining our frontiers ", adding that it was the duty of the German Reich to protect " those fellow Germans beyond our frontiers who are unable to ensure for themselves the right to a general freedom, personal, political and ideological ". No Czech or Slovak doubted that this warning was addressed as directly to Prague as to Vienna.

Nor had the Nazi tactics of the Trojan Horse, so ably practised in Austria, gone unnoticed in Czechoslovakia. It had clearly been the intention of the Reich to create such a situation within the Austrian Republic that the Government of the day must take action against the subversive activities of the Austrian Nazis. A ready-made case had thus been presented for " protection " of this " oppressed " political minority, and casuists in international law might well deem intervention of such a nature as not being " unprovoked aggression " on the part of Germany.

It was well known to the Prague authorities that, should Germany have designs on Czechoslovakia, it would be through the German minority in the Sudetenland that they would strike, using it as a weapon for disruption. Though the Germans in Bohemia and Moravia had never been included within the German Reich, save as a segment of the Holy Roman Empire, there had been, since Hitler's advent to power, a pronounced and increasing tendency on the part of the " activist autonomist group ", the *Sudetendeutsche Partei* (*S.d.P.*), to look towards Nazi Germany as the protector of all Germans and to pose before Berlin as the defenders of an oppressed minority.[1]   This was precisely in line with Hitler's policy of expansion, and the leader of the *S.d.P.*, Konrad Henlein, had been on the pay-roll of the Nazi Party since 1935,[2] a fact suspected by the Czechoslovak Government, though proof was difficult to come by.

In order, therefore, to be forearmed against the Trojan Horse within their borders, the Prague Government had had the prescience, as early as October 1937, to persuade the French Government of the day, that of M. Camille Chautemps, to extend France's commitments in regard to Czechoslovakia to cover the case of internal disorders provoked by Berlin, and in this decision the French General Staff had concurred.[3]

Proud as they were — and justly proud — of the thriving democratic State which they had evolved with such zeal and

[1] It should be remembered that, at the Peace Conference of Paris in 1919, both President Masaryk and Dr. Beneš had wished to improve their frontier with Germany — which had been the former German-Austro-Hungarian frontier — by including a part of the Sudetenland within the new borders of the Reich. The Allied Powers, however, had insisted on the whole area becoming a part of Czechoslovakia (cf. *Guns or Butter*, by R. H. Bruce Lockhart (London, 1939), p. 303). This incident had an interesting sequel some twenty years later (see below, p. 115 footnote).

[2] *International Military Tribunal Document*, 3059–PS. In his interrogation by Czechoslovak officials after his arrest in 1945, Karl Hermann Frank, the Deputy Leader of the *S.d.P.*, testified that the Party had maintained contact with the *N.S.D.A.P.* in Germany since 1933 (*International Military Tribunal Document*, 3061–PS).

[3] *The Grave-Diggers of France*, by Pertinax (New York, 1944), p. 2, footnote.

industry over the past twenty years, the leaders of the Czechoslovak Republic were not unaware of the imperfections which existed in the structure, and had done their best to correct them. It was this very principle of democracy, however, which had defeated the earlier efforts of previous Cabinets to resolve the difficulties arising out of the relationships between the $9\frac{1}{2}$ million Czechs and Slovaks and the 5 million minority nationals ($3\frac{1}{2}$ millions of them Germans) which went to make up the population of the country. For in a democracy reforms can only be enacted by the will of the people, and this will is additionally difficult to ascertain when there are the political prejudices of some dozen or so parliamentary parties to be reconciled and the rival claims of some half-dozen racial groups with which to contend.

But recently released from Austrian tutelage, the Czechs were lacking in the experience necessary in shouldering those burdens of senior partnership in a State of many nationalities, burdens which Britain herself, with her long tradition of administration, still finds onerous and full of difficulty. They were not always as tactful as they might have been in their dealings with their Slovak, German, Ruthenian, Magyar and Polish fellow citizens, nor had they succeeded in carrying out all the promises which had been made to the Peace Conference for the organization of the minorities on a cantonal system analagous to that of Switzerland. With infinite patience, however, the Government of Dr. Milan Hodža had at last completed the intricate negotiations for the formula on which could be promulgated a National Minorities Statute, and it was hoped and believed that this Statute would become law before October 28, the Independence Day of Czechoslovakia.[1]

Thus, having taken every external precaution and being well advanced in the process of solving her own internal problems, Czechoslovakia turned to take stock of her position as the first chords of the *Schlummerlied* floated across the air from Berlin.

The guarantee of the League of Nations, it was reluctantly but realistically acknowledged, was but a broken reed. It had not saved China from Japan ; it had not saved Ethiopia from Italy ; it had not saved Austria from Germany. If any further doubt existed in Prague as to its efficacy, this must have been shattered by Mr. Chamberlain's recent statement in the House

[1] For details of the previous efforts to solve the minority problem of Czechoslovakia, see two admirable studies, *Czechs and Germans*, by Elizabeth Wiskemann (Oxford, 1938), and *Czechoslovakia*, by Edgar P. Young (London, 1938).

of Commons (March 7, 1938), which rang the death-knell of collective security so clearly and resonantly that none could mistake it. " What country in Europe to-day," the British Prime Minister had asked, " if threatened by a large Power, can rely on the League of Nations for protection ? None . . . we must not try to delude small weak nations into thinking that they will be protected by the League against aggression."

There remained for the Czechs the protection afforded them by their system of alliances. Of France they felt certain. To be sure, there were M. Pierre-Étienne Flandin and his friends, who only a few days before (March 7) had demanded that France abandon her commitments in Central Europe and retire behind the mystic safety of the Maginot Line. But the French Chamber had rejected this proposal by a large majority and had reaffirmed the pledges of France to Czechoslovakia. By every reasoning of common sense, by every criterion of political and military security, no agreement was more vitally to the self-interests of both parties than the Franco-Czech Alliance ; for the Bohemian bastion was as essential to the French strategical position as was the aid of France to the Czechs. When, therefore, on March 15, M. Paul-Boncour reaffirmed, on behalf of the Blum Government, the intention of France to stand by her obligation to come " instantly and effectively " to the support of her ally, and when these assurances were reiterated by MM. Daladier and Bonnet a month later, it was no more than the Czechs expected. It was inconceivable that France should abandon her whole system of European alliances, of which Czechoslovakia was the keystone, at the very moment when it might be called into operation.

Similarly with Russia, the Czechoslovak Government was reasonably sure of support, and their expectations were not disappointed. On the very day that Austria was annexed to the Reich (March 13), a deputation of Czech trade unionists was visiting Moscow, and to them President Kalinin took the occasion to reiterate the willingness of the Soviet Government to honour their undertakings to Czechoslovakia. On March 17 M. Litvinov officially repeated these assurances to the Czech Minister in Moscow, and, as an earnest of good faith, proposed on the following day to the British, French and United States Governments that they, with Russia, should confer in order to discuss means of preventing further aggression.[1]

[1] See below, p. 36.

With the attitudes of her two powerful treaty-partners, there-fore, Czechoslovakia had reason to be satisfied. It was unthink-able that France would not come to her assistance in the event of unprovoked German aggression, and, if France came, Russia would come also. But there remained Britain, and Britain was a vitally important factor in Czechoslovak as well as in French calculations.

" If only," as Lord Halifax, in the tragic wisdom of experi-ence, informed the House of Lords on a later occasion,[1] " if only Great Britain would say clearly and unmistakably for all to hear that she would resist any unprovoked aggression against Czecho-slovakia, no such unprovoked aggression would be made."

No truer word was ever spoken ; but this was not Britain's way, nor had it ever been. In 1920 British statesmen had defined the sphere of British interests in Europe as being bound by the Rhine. With Central and Eastern Europe they were not con-cerned and Britain had remained aloof from those aspects of the Locarno Agreement which specifically dealt with Poland and Czechoslovakia. Nor had they abandoned this consistent line of policy even after Hitler had scattered the Locarno Agreement to the four winds in 1936. Mr. Anthony Eden, then Foreign Secretary, had informed his constituents, on November 20 of that year, that " nations cannot be expected to incur automatic obligations save for areas where their vital interests are con-cerned ",[2] and it was still considered at this point that these vital interests did not extend for Britain east of the Rhine. Four months later, in the House of Lords, Lord Halifax was more explicit : " We are unable ", he said, " to define beforehand what might be our attitude to a hypothetical complication in Central or Eastern Europe." [3]

It is true that the mysterious uncertainty with which the British Government enwrapped its foreign policy could be inter-preted in two ways. It kept all parties equally in the dark. A potential aggressor in Central Europe committed his act of aggression with the possibility of British action against him. But of late it had been all too possible to bet comfortably as to which way the British cat would jump — and that the way of least resistance. With the knowledge that the key to French policy

[1] *House of Lords Debates*, October 3, 1938, col. 1303.
[2] Speech at Leamington, November 20, 1936.
[3] *House of Lords Debates*, March 3, 1937, col. 498.

lay, in the final analysis, in London, the Prague Government attempted to elucidate British policy and, if possible, to obtain some gesture from Britain to Germany in favour of Czechoslovakia.

The reactions of the British Prime Minister and Foreign Secretary to the Rape of Austria had been one of genuine dismay. The news of the ultimatum to Schuschnigg had reached Mr. Chamberlain while he was entertaining Ribbentrop and his wife to luncheon at No. 10 Downing Street, on March 11. At the close of the meal, the Prime Minister, Lord Halifax and Sir Alexander Cadogan took Ribbentrop aside and told him how seriously the British Government were disturbed at this new action by Germany, which could not but upset the equilibrium of Europe and delay still further the achievement of that general restoration of confidence which it was the ultimate object of the Policy of Appeasement to attain.

To the Ministers the Nazi envoy said that the removal of the Austrian problem opened up the way for an Anglo-German understanding, and, when Lord Halifax expressed concern regarding Czechoslovakia, Ribbentrop replied that Germany " had no interest and no purpose to do anything in that direction. On the contrary, if we Germans are treated reasonably in that country, we will come to an understanding there also." [1]

Next day Lord Halifax again spoke very firmly to the German envoy, but such was Ribbentrop's conceit — or possibly his anxiety to please — that in his telephone report to Göring he described his interview with the Foreign Secretary as " a great conversation with a man of absolute common sense ". Of Mr. Chamberlain he spoke as giving an " excellent impression of an honourable will for understanding ".

It was against this spell of *Schlummerlied* that the Czechoslovak Minister, M. Jan Masaryk, sought to prevail in an interview which he had that same day (March 12) with this " man of absolute common sense ". In informing Lord Halifax of the double assurance which Mastný had received from Göring on the previous evening, the Minister pleaded the necessity for a positive demonstration by Britain in favour of his country. Why, asked M. Masaryk, should not his Government inform the Foreign Office officially of this double declaration ? " This step would allow you to take official notice of it and then to address a Note

[1] See stenographic report of telephone conversations between Ribbentrop and Göring on March 13, 1938, *International Military Tribunal Document*, 2949-PS.

to Berlin in which the British Government would place on record the assurance given to Czechoslovakia." [1]

Lord Halifax took note of the suggestion and promised to put it before the Prime Minister, with the result that on the following day, in an interview with Göring, Sir Nevile Henderson called attention to the importance attached in London to the German assurances and obtained the consent of the Field-Marshal for a statement to be made by Mr. Chamberlain next day in the House of Commons making public the good intentions of the Third Reich to its Czech neighbours. [2]

Mr. Chamberlain duly reported these facts to the House on March 14 in the course of a debate on Austria, which was the occasion for one of the Prime Minister's rare displays of emotion. In marked contrast with the cold and almost brutal tones in which, only a week before, he had proclaimed the fact that the collective security provisions of the League Covenant were not worth the paper on which they were written, Mr. Chamberlain now flamed in righteous wrath against the annexation of Austria, whose independence Great Britain, France and Italy had been jointly pledged to defend. Not only had Germany flouted this three-Power guarantee, she had actually refused to accept the British protest on the subject, on the ground that the Austrian affair was a purely German family matter, thereby assuming that Britain was not " vitally interested " in Central and Eastern Europe.

It was the cool insolence of the German attitude rather than the depravity of the crime itself which had enraged Mr. Chamberlain, and he energetically denied that the British Government were not within their rights in interesting themselves in the fate of Austria. Were not Britain and Austria both Members of the League of Nations? Were not both, along with Germany, signatories of treaties guaranteeing the independence of Austria? What further proof of interest in Austria was required of Britain?

This somewhat macabre effort — on the part of the Prime Minister to establish the right of Britain to do no more than protest against the violation of pledges which her own inaction was condoning — was concluded with an oracular statement which appeared to give some indication of a change in British policy. His Majesty's Government, said Mr. Chamberlain, were always

[1] *French Yellow Book*, pp. 4-5. [2] *Ibid.* pp. 6-7, 7-8.

interested in Central Europe because what happened there largely affected security elsewhere.[1]

To Jan Masaryk, sitting in the Diplomatic Gallery of the House of Commons, to President Beneš in the Hradschin Palace in Prague, these were words of encouragement and hope. If this could be said by the Prime Minister of Great Britain in regard to Austria, how much more true was it in the case of Czechoslovakia, which was not merely a fellow Member of the League of Nations, but had defensive alliances with France and the Soviet Union and was, in its geographic self, the key to that Central European security in which Mr. Chamberlain had declared Britain to be interested ? In Paris and Moscow, in Warsaw, Belgrade, and Bucharest, in Berlin and Rome, the same question was asked : Did this betoken a new departure in Britain's foreign policy, a new and awakened interest in Central and Eastern Europe ?

Alas for the hopes of those who had prayed that the answer to this question might be " yes " ; the issue was not long in doubt. Under the acid test of realism Mr. Chamberlain's anger subsided ; his protests withered away ; he was once more master of his emotions. On March 19, five days after his speech in the House, there arrived the suggestion of the Soviet Government for a Four-Power Conference to discuss means of preventing further aggression.[2] On March 22 the British Cabinet decided to reject this proposal, and, two days later, Mr. Chamberlain made a second and more important statement on British foreign policy.

This statement of March 24 was a masterpiece of obfuscation. While re-stating the old and obvious, it left the world in complete uncertainty on the essential issues involved in the new situation created by Germany in Central and Eastern Europe. It made crystal-clear what Britain was not prepared to do, but was singularly unclear as to what she might do if faced with certain contingencies.[3]

British interests, said the Prime Minister, fell into three categories :

"We are bound by certain Treaty obligations which would entail upon us the necessity of fighting if the occasion arose, and I hope that no doubts arise that we should be prepared, in such event, to fulfil these obligations."

[1] *House of Commons Debates*, March 14, 1938, coll. 49-50.
[2] See above, p. 32.
[3] *House of Commons Debates*, March 24, 1938, coll. 1403-7.

THE OLD-FASHIONED CUSTOMER

" I wonder if you've got a song I remember about not wanting to fight, but if we do . . . something, something, something . . . we've got the money too? "

MARCH 23, 1938

In this category fell British obligations assumed under the Locarno Agreement — and subsequently reaffirmed after the abrogation of that instrument by Germany in 1936 — to defend France and Belgium against unprovoked aggression, and also British treaty obligations to Portugal, Iraq and Egypt, with whom Britain had formal treaties of alliance.

"Then there are certain vital interests of this country for which, if menaced, we should fight — for the defence of British territories and the communications which are vital to our national existence."

The second category was less specifically described :

"There are other cases, too, in which we might fight if we were clear that either we must fight or else abandon, once and for all, the hope of averting the destruction of those things which we hold most dear — our liberty and the right to live our lives according to the standards which our national traditions and our national character have prescribed for us."

There was also a third category :

"There remains another case in which we might have to use our arms, a case which is of a more general character but which may have no less significance. It is the case arising under the Covenant of the League of Nations which was accurately defined by the former Foreign Secretary : ' In addition, our armaments may be used in bringing help to a victim of aggression in any case where in our judgment it would be proper, under the provisions of the Covenant, so to do '.
"That case might, for example, include Czechoslovakia."

In view of Mr. Chamberlain's remarks on the general guarantee of the Covenant on March 7, and of the subsequent decision of the British Government to do no more than protest against the annexation of Austria, this was but cold comfort to the Czechs. But the Prime Minister had not done ; lest his previous remarks should have raised hopes unduly, he proceeded to demolish them in advance.

It had, he said, been suggested that Great Britain should give forthwith an assurance that she would immediately come with all her power to the support of France in the event of France being called upon, as a result of German aggression, to implement her obligations to Czechoslovakia. It had also been suggested that Britain should at once declare her own readiness to defend

Czechoslovakia against unprovoked aggression and should take the lead in inviting other nations to associate themselves with such a declaration. His Majesty's Government were not prepared to agree to either of these proposals, or to any other which might result in Britain finding herself in a position where the decision to go to war should be automatically removed from the discretion of the Government.

The Prime Minister's only specific reference to the Soviet proposals was to describe them as envisaging " less a consultation with a view to settlement than a concerting of action against an eventuality which has not yet arisen." [1]

Having made it clear that Britain was refusing to give to Czechoslovakia even those frail and ephemeral guarantees of independence which she had so recently found herself unable or unwilling to implement in the case of Austria, Mr. Chamberlain added a passage of some significance. His negative statements had been made with a clarity which left nothing to the imagination, but in turning to the constructive he used phraseology which the guardians of the Oracle of Delphi might well have envied :

"Where peace and war are concerned, legal obligations are not alone concerned and, if war broke out, it would be unlikely to be confined to those who would have assumed such obligations. It would be quite impossible to say where it would end and what governments might be involved. The inexorable pressure of events might well prove more powerful than formal pronouncements, and in that event it would be well within the bounds of probability that other countries besides those which were parties to the original dispute would almost immediately become involved.

"This is especially true in the case of two countries like Great Britain and France with long associations of friendship, with interests closely interwoven, devoted to the same ideals of democratic liberty and determined to uphold them."

In conclusion, Mr. Chamberlain declared that the British Government would continue to lend their influence to the re-

[1] Later, in a debate on a Labour motion of censure on April 4, Mr. Chamberlain described the proposal of the National Council of Labour to unite " the peace-loving countries, and particularly France, the United Kingdom and Russia, to make a common stand against the aggressor " as one which " would be to do what we, at any rate, have always set our faces against, namely, to divide Europe into two opposing camps. So far from making a contribution to peace, I say that it would inevitably plunge us into war " (*House of Commons Debates*, April 4, 1938, coll. 60-61).

vision of relations between nations, whether established by treaty or otherwise, which appeared to demand review, and to exert every effort to " bringing peaceful and orderly solutions " to all disputes arising. He assured the Czechs of Britain's good offices at all times, urged upon them the use of " all the resources of diplomacy " in the cause of peace, and commended the practical steps being taken " to meet the reasonable wishes of the German minority ". " In the meantime ", he added, " there is no need to assume the use of force, or, indeed, to talk about it. Such talk is to be strongly deprecated. Not only can it do no good ; it is bound to do harm. It must interfere with the progress of diplomacy, and it must increase feelings of insecurity and uncertainty."

In making this statement of British intention, Mr. Chamberlain had set himself a peculiarly difficult course to follow. He had made it clear that he would not be deflected from that policy of appeasement which he had enunciated upon entering into office and affirmed on numerous subsequent occasions. In accordance with this policy he had refused a blank cheque to France in the matter of Czechoslovakia, yet had admitted the considerable probability of Britain becoming involved should France be engaged in war as a result of honouring her obligations to the Czechs. In order to square the circle — in order both to have his cake and eat it — it had become vitally necessary for the success of Mr. Chamberlain's policy that France should not become thus engaged.

To bring so complicated a diplomatic ambition to a successful realization would have challenged the agile genius and mental suppleness of a Canning, a Palmerston, or a Disraeli. It was the sort of balancing feat which a skilled diplomatic tight-rope walker might successfully accomplish with everything in his favour. But Mr. Chamberlain was no acrobat ; nor was he supple, agile or diplomatic. His rigidity of mind was one of his salient characteristics. A sincerely honest, not uncourageous, *borné* and obstinate man, he combined considerable personal vanity with a deep and abiding horror of war.

Moreover, he distrusted and disliked the devious ways of diplomacy, preferring the more direct — if no more ethical — conduct of commerce. With the mentality of a business man, he was used to striking a bargain, by which, though the shareholders and investors in some subsidiary company might suffer temporarily, the corporation as a whole would benefit in the long run. He was

J'Y SUIS, J'Y RESTE

Mr. Chamberlain. " I shall wait till it clears a bit before I get down."

MARCH 30, 1938

Reprinted by the special permission of the Proprietors of " Punch "

wedded to the technique and efficacy of the *Kuh-handel*.

This, then, was the key to the Chamberlain policy toward Germany as defined after the return of Lord Halifax from his interview with Hitler at Berchtesgaden in November 1937. Germany desired the realization of certain limited European territorial ambitions. Changes in the map of Europe, the adjustment of national frontiers, were not to be deprecated in themselves but only if they were effected by means so nakedly violent and outrageous that they could not be condoned. The preservation of peace was the essential thing. Now that the Austrians had placidly accepted annexation, war could only come about if Czechoslovakia refused to comply with " the reasonable wishes " of her German minority. No stone must be left unturned, therefore, to persuade the Czechs, by pressure if need be, to make any and every concession to meet these demands, and this must become the key-note of Anglo-French policy.

The effect on Anglo-French relations of Mr. Chamberlain's evasiveness regarding Britain's contingent support of France was disastrous. The Prime Minister's words were so ambiguous as to permit of many interpretations. They allowed the appeasers, such as Georges Bonnet, to proclaim in private conversations that there were really no circumstances in which Britain would follow France, and that France, therefore, must avoid giving a lead, at all costs. The friends of Britain in France, among whom were many opponents of appeasement, did their best to counter M. Bonnet's " whispering campaign " by drawing attention to Mr. Chamberlain's specific references to Britain's arrangements for mutual defence with France, which Mr. Churchill had described as " amounting to a defensive alliance ", but they shared Mr. Churchill's disappointment that, if this were so, it had not been stated in plain words and made effective by a military convention. They were increasingly anxious lest the common desire for appeasement shared by Mr. Chamberlain and M. Bonnet, though it sprang in each case from different motives, should eventually drive France into an intolerable position from which she could only escape with dishonour.[1]

[1] As M. Paul Reynaud, Minister of Justice and leader of the anti-appeasers in the Daladier Cabinet, sadly remarked : " *L'Angleterre déjà se montre trop encline à suivre la mauvaise pente. Si Georges Bonnet l'y encourage elle la dévalera précipitamment. Nous devons, au contraire, arrêter nos amis sur le chemin de danger. Si Paris flirte avec la Gretchen, Londres ne tardera pas à nous montrer qu'elle est toute prête à aller plus loin encore et à lui pincer fesses* " (*De Munich à Vichy*, by Paul Lazareff (New York, 1944), p. 34).

Though determined to obtain French support for bringing pressure upon Prague to accept " the reasonable demands" of Herr Henlein, neither Mr. Chamberlain nor the world at large had any idea of what these demands consisted, but the Prime Minister was fortified in his opinion by telegrams received from both Sir Nevile Henderson in Berlin and Mr. Basil Newton in Prague, urging His Majesty's Government to intervene, together with France, before it was too late, with a view to persuading the Czech Government to readjust their relations with Germany.[1]

There was, however, another factor in Mr. Chamberlain's calculations — the weakness of Britain's armaments and defences. As Chancellor of the Exchequer in the successive MacDonald and Baldwin Governments, he had been fully aware of the meagre sums which had been spent on the armed services and had publicly and consistently pleaded the urgent need for British rearmament.[2] On assuming the Premiership in May 1937 he had announced, as a parallel policy to that of appeasement, his intention of making Britain so strong that she should be everywhere treated with respect.   In pursuit of this exemplary aim, the British Government had immediately announced a gigantic scheme of National and Imperial Defence, involving the expenditure of £1,500,000,000 in five years.   But nearly a year had passed and British rearmament plans were still only in the preparatory stages.   Production had been speeded up in the existing plants but the great new factories had not yet come into operation.   Britain was, in fact, completely unprepared for war, either on the home front or in any of the fighting services, all of which were deplorably short of equipment, arms and trained personnel.

Though this tardiness in rectifying Britain's deficiencies in defence undoubtedly influenced very greatly Mr. Chamberlain's conduct of foreign policy, he repeatedly assured the House of Commons and the nation that the Government were satisfied with the progress of their rearmament programme.   " The almost terrifying power that Britain is building up has a sobering effect

[1] Henderson, p. 130.

[2] In January 1935 Mr. Chamberlain gave the warning that, " if we are to make our contribution to that general sense of security in Europe, we must at all events be sufficiently armed to be able to do so ", and eleven months later, on the eve of the November General Election, he had admitted that " Britain is not strong enough either at sea or on land to make her words good if trouble were to come ".

on the opinion of the world ", he told the House on March 7, a week before the annexation of Austria.[1]

[1] In answer to a question from the Opposition on March 7, as to whether the Air Force Programme was calculated " to provide parity in first-line strength with any European Air Force within striking distance of our shores ", Mr. Chamberlain replied that first-line strength was only a part of Britain's air power and air strength. " We must take account of the aggregate and effectiveness of our resources, and in the various programmes which we have put forward I can tell the House that we are satisfied that we are making the best and most effective use of our resources " (*House of Commons Debates*, March 7, 1938, col. 1560).

The answer came in September 1938 when Britain, on the threshold of war, could muster a total of less than one fully equipped fighter squadron and only a meagre aggregate of anti-aircraft guns for the defence of the country.

It must, however, be remembered that, though deplorably tardy, Britain was on the right track in her aircraft construction — and Germany was on the wrong one. The Spitfires and Hurricanes, though long in coming, proved to be of superior calibre to the aircraft of the *Luftwaffe* in the Battle of Britain.

CHAPTER TWO

LES TROIS COUPS

(i)

NEITHER the world at large nor Mr. Chamberlain was destined to remain long in ignorance of what the Sudeten Activists regarded as their " reasonable demands " upon the Czechoslovak Government. During the weeks that followed, while Britain brought to fruition the latest stage of the policy of appeasement in signing her agreement for Anglo-Italian understanding (April 16), and France indulged in another chaotic welter of Cabinet-making, Adolf Hitler was preparing his next move towards the fulfilment of his desire to destroy the Czechoslovak Republic. Just as Mr. Chamberlain's speech of March 7 had been an encouragement to go forward with the annexation of Austria, so now the Prime Minister's equivocations of March 24 emboldened the Führer to proceed with his further machinations against Prague. Four weeks to the day after Mr. Chamberlain's declaration of policy in the House of Commons, and six weeks after his own triumphal entry into Vienna, Hitler played his next card.

After the completion of the Austrian operation, Hitler had told his Generals that " there was no hurry to solve the Czech question, because Austria had to be digested first ", but that the military plans must nevertheless be pushed forward.[1] Preparations, however, for a " political offensive " against the Czechoslovak Government had been put in hand immediately, and on March 16 Konrad Henlein was informed that he and his party must consider themselves as being under the orders of the German Minister in Prague, from whom they would receive directives on policy, with which they must comply implicitly.[2]

Summoned to Berlin on March 28, Henlein had a personal interview with Hitler and it was at this meeting that the basis of the new move was discussed. The Führer said that the *Sudeten-*

---

[1] See entry in General Jodl's Diary (*International Military Tribunal Document,* 1780–PS).   [2] *International Military Tribunal Document,* 3060–PS.

deutsche Partei must now realize that it was supported by a nation of seventy-five millions who would not tolerate a continued suppression of the Sudeten Germans by the Czechoslovak Government. It was for the Party, therefore, to recognize its responsibilities and play its full role in the great drama of liberation. Its task was to formulate the necessary demands upon the Prague Government to ensure for the Party the privileges which it desired.

On the following day, at a conference in the Foreign Ministry, Ribbentrop went into further details with Henlein as to his immediate future role, but of course gave no hint of the wider aims of the German Government in regard to Czechoslovakia. Henlein was essentially a puppet, not to be entrusted with the great secrets of State.

Although full support had been pledged by the Reich for any demands made by the *Sudetendeutsche Partei*, said Ribbentrop, it was necessary that these demands should be formulated by the Party itself and not dictated from Berlin. They should, however, be of a maximum nature and aim at the granting of full freedom for the Sudeten Germans. In any conferences with the Czech Government the Party must appear as an independent negotiator, in no way relying on the Government of the Reich. Finally, added the Foreign Minister, " do not be satisfied with any compromise agreement with the Czechoslovak Government ".[1]

Henlein gave an admirable performance of an obedient and compliant puppet. On his return to his headquarters at Asch, he at once rejected the proposals of the Czechoslovak Government for a National Minorities Statute and, on April 24, at Karlsbad disclosed the " reasonable demands " of the German Minority.

The eight points of the " Karlsbad Programme " may be summarized as follows : [2]

(1) Full equality of status for Sudeten Germans and Czechs — that is, abandonment of the conception that there was a Czechoslovak State containing a German minority.
(2) A guarantee of this equality by recognition of " the Sudeten group of the German race " as a unified " legal personality ".
(3) Determination of the German area in Czechoslovakia and the legal recognition of its boundaries.

---

[1] *International Military Tribunal Document*, 2788–PS.

[2] *Konrad Henleins Rede in Karlsbad*. Schriften des Deutschen Instituts für Aussenpolitische Forschung (Berlin, 1938).

(4) Full autonomy throughout this German area in every department of public life.

(5) Guarantees for those living outside the areas of their own race.

(6) Removal of " all injustices done to the Sudeten Germans since 1918 and reparation for all damage they have suffered thereby ".

(7) Recognition of the principle of German officials in all German districts.

(8) Full liberty for Germans to proclaim their Germanism and their adhesion to the " ideology of Germans ".

Nor was this all. Lest there should be any doubt as to the meaning of point (8), Henlein proclaimed that the true policy of his Sudeten Germans was " inspired by the principles and ideals of National Socialism ", and he made an additional demand on the Czechoslovak Government, namely, that they should carry out " a complete revision of the Czech foreign policy which up to to-day had led the State into the ranks of the enemies of the German people".

By the mouth of his puppet, Hitler had made clear his imperative requirement for the creation not only of a German but of a National Socialist unit within the Czechoslovak State, and the object of point (4) could only be preparatory to further territorial demands. He had, moreover, indicated that Czechoslovakia must abandon her treaties of alliance with France and with Russia and become entirely dependent upon the German Reich.

From the Führer's point of view it was important that these " reasonable demands " should be put forward ostensibly by the German minority themselves and not directly by Germany. He could then — in the event of their rejection by the Prague Government — appear in his favourite role as " Protector of all Germans ".

The rejection of the Karlsbad Programme by Prague, even as a basis of negotiation, was a foregone conclusion. No government could thus willingly welcome the Trojan Horse within its walls and even offer it hay. But in rejecting it M. Hodža, the Czech Premier, announced (April 25) that he was pressing forward with the Nationality Statute, designed to meet the requirements of all minorities within the State and on which the coalition parties had agreed. It was his hope that this legislation would be hastened through Parliament and placed on the Statute Book by July.

At once the German propaganda machine, directed by the evil genius of Joseph Goebbels, came into operation in support of the Henleinists, and Prague was warned that the time for delay and compromise had passed. What was necessary now in the cause of peace was prompt action by Czechoslovakia.

While the " war of nerves " was in progress, further action of a more forceful character was in preparation. On April 21, that is to say after Hitler's interview with Henlein but before the latter's Karlsbad speech, the Führer conferred with General Keitel as to the means by which the military subjugation of Czecho-slovakia could be brought about. It was not at that moment Hitler's intention to destroy the Czechs without provocation. For political reasons — the susceptibilities of Britain and France — a surprise attack had been ruled out, since it could not be justified before world opinion. The necessary political developments must therefore be provided from within Czechoslovakia, and inde-pendently of the Sudeten agitation. Various means were con-sidered by the Führer and his Chief of Staff and the plan most favoured was the assassination of the German Minister at Prague, which would provide the necessary " pretext " for a " lightning attack ".[1] From his notes of this conversation General Keitel prepared the first draft of the directive for " Operation Green " — the code name for the campaign against Czechoslovakia — which was later to be communicated to the *Wehrmacht*.[2]

In complete ignorance of these cold-blooded calculations in Berlin, the British and French Governments conferred together as to what should be their common policy in view of the Karlsbad Programme. MM. Daladier and Bonnet, the newly inducted Premier and Foreign Minister of France, hurried to London on April 28, bringing with them a Note received from Prague two days earlier, in which the Czechoslovak Government had stated that, while they were ready to go a long way to meet the claims of Sudeten Germans, they could not accept demands calculated to impair the sovereignty and integrity of the State, or to limit their freedom to follow a foreign policy best calculated to preserve its

[1] A similar plan had been considered in connection with the plans for the annexa-tion of Austria : in this case the potential victims under review had been the German Ambassador, Franz von Papen, and his Military Attaché, Colonel von Muff (cf. von Papen's evidence under cross-examination before the International Military Tribunal at Nuremberg on June 18, 1946. The idea was eventually abandoned, but this principle of jeopardizing the lives of German diplomatic representatives abroad gives a new and added unpleasantness to the term " *travailler pour le roi de Prusse*".

[2] *International Military Tribunal Document*, 388–PS, items 2 and 5.

independence. It was added that the Czechoslovak Government reposed complete confidence in the readiness of the French to fulfil their treaty obligations if necessary.

To Mr. Chamberlain and Lord Halifax the French statesmen repeated that they were indeed prepared to carry out their pledges to assist Czechoslovakia in the event of an unprovoked attack on the part of Germany. This attitude, the British replied, was entirely appreciated, but the important thing was that no attack should be provoked by Czechoslovakia, and indeed that there should be no attack at all.

In the course of these conversations, M. Daladier urged upon the British Ministers the desirability of parallel and joint Anglo-French action in Prague and in Berlin. To President Beneš they should advise the widest possible form of concessions to the Sudeten Germans compatible with national security, and to Hitler they should state firmly their intention of assuring the independence of Czechoslovakia should it become menaced. Such action on the part of Britain and France, argued M. Daladier, would not only make clear their attitude to Germany and give confidence to Czechoslovakia, but also sustain the morale of Poland, Yugoslavia and Rumania.

Mr. Chamberlain, however, demurred. He did not believe that Hitler desired the destruction of Czechoslovakia, and feared that such a declaration might precipitate action on the part of Germany which in its turn would lead to war, in which case nothing could save the Czechs from invasion and destruction. The length to which he would go in meeting the French proposals was to agree to a statement by the British Ambassador in Berlin that if, in the course of the negotiations which Britain was earnestly pressing upon Prague, Germany resorted to war, and if France, in discharge of her obligations, were forced to intervene, Britain could not guarantee that she would not do the same.[1]

[1] See extracts from the *procès-verbal* of the Anglo-French Conference of April 28-29, 1938, quoted by M. Daladier in the Constituent Assembly on July 18, 1946 (*Journal Officiel des Débats de l'Assemblée Nationale Constituante*, July 19, 1946, pp. 2678-9) ; also *Défense de la Paix*, by Georges Bonnet (Geneva, 1946), Vol. I, " De Washington au Quai d'Orsay ", pp. 112-19, 351-7.

It should be remembered that both the Beaverbrook and Rothermere press combines were strongly in support of Mr. Chamberlain's policy and were even more disinclined than he to give any conceivable encouragement to the Czechs that they would receive British assistance in the event of German aggression. Indeed the *Daily Mail* of April 30 urged the Government to warn the French that their commitments to Czechoslovakia constituted a challenge to Germany which she might not prove tardy in accepting.

With this M. Daladier had to be content, and it was agreed that the Czechoslovak Government should be urged to go as far as possible to meet the demands of Herr Henlein " within the framework of the Constitution ". It was also hoped that Hitler might be persuaded to bring pressure on Henlein to accept such concessions. At the same time, however, it was made clear to M. Jan Masaryk by Mr. Chamberlain that the Czechoslovak Government were expected to go considerably further in the way of concessions than was at the moment contemplated.

Meanwhile, in pursuance of Mr. Chamberlain's renewed pledges to France of March 24, considerable progress was made in co-ordinating the military effort of Britain and France in the unhappy event that they should find themselves involved in war. Agreements were reached for the unification of command, for frequent staff talks in the three fields of armaments, and for the pooling of purchase of supplies.

The psychological value of these agreements, however, was largely nullified by the effect produced on MM. Daladier and Bonnet of Mr. Chamberlain's unwillingness to give a clear indication of what Britain would do in the event of a German attack upon Czechoslovakia. At this moment M. Daladier, at any rate, was genuinely prepared to honour the obligations of France to her ally. He dared not contemplate a war with Germany, however, without a definite assurance of British support, and instead of this all he could get out of Mr. Chamberlain was a series of conditional and subjunctive clauses. British equivocation at this time weakened the confidence of those in France who would have resisted Germany, and correspondingly strengthened the arguments of those who were seeking for an opportunity of evading France's obligations to Czechoslovakia. The net impression gained in Paris as a result of the conferences of April 28-29 was that in no circumstances would Britain give immediate support to either France or Czechoslovakia in the event of an attack by Germany on the latter, and from that moment the French, consciously or subconsciously, wrote off their own obligations.

From now on, moreover, a distinction must be made in Mr. Chamberlain's conduct of British policy towards France and Germany and his treatment of the Czechs. In his anxiety to prevent France, and, therefore, ultimately Britain, from going to war, he came to view the Czechoslovak Government more and more as an obstacle to the realization of his aims. He knew

nothing of Czechoslovakia — as he subsequently publicly confessed — and his views on the country had been very largely
formed from the despatches of successive British Ministers in
Prague, some of whom had been far from friendly to the Czechs.
In the present contingency the Prime Minister considered that the
sovereignty, the integrity and the independence of Czechoslovakia
were of secondary importance beside the preservation of peace.
If the Sudeten problem could be settled without recourse to war,
the peace of Europe might be preserved indefinitely, and then
all these secondary matters would be of no importance at all.
Mr. Chamberlain was therefore prepared to force the Czechs to
make more and still more sacrifices in the cause of peace, until
he arrived at the position of Shaw's Earl of Warwick, who remarked to the Bishop of Beauvais apropos of the disposal of the
Maid of Orleans : " God grant that her soul may be saved ! But
the practical problem would seem to be how to save her soul
without saving her body." [1]

From the reports received in Berlin it was accurately deduced
that, as a result of the Anglo-French Conference, Britain was still
unwilling to give a " blank cheque " to France in the matter of
Czechoslovakia, and that without this previous assurance the
French themselves were extremely unwilling to honour their
pledges in this regard.[2] Further confirmation of this view was
forthcoming on May 7 when Sir Nevile Henderson informed the
German Foreign Ministry that on that same day an Anglo-French
démarche had been made in Prague, urging the Czechoslovak
Government to go to the utmost limits in settling the Sudeten
problem " within the framework of the Constitution ", and

[1] Bernard Shaw's *St. Joan*, Scene IV.
[2] The French Press of the Right launched its first attack on the treaty commitments of France almost simultaneously with the formation of the Daladier Government on April 10. " *Veux-tu mourir pour la Tchécoslovaquie ?* " demanded *Gringoire* in
a headline, and the campaign reached its height on April 12 when M. Joseph
Barthélemy, an intimate of Laval and subsequently Minister of Justice in the Vichy
Government, contributed an article to *Le Temps*, of which the thesis was that, since
the Franco-Czechoslovak Treaty of Mutual Assistance formed an integral part of the
Locarno Agreement and since Hitler had repudiated this Agreement in 1936, France
was no longer legally bound to give aid and assistance to Czechoslovakia in the event
of German unprovoked aggression. M. Herriot denounced the article as " a stab in
the back of Beneš ", and Bonnet at once assured the Czech Minister that it in no way
represented the views of the Government, but there can be no doubt that the arguments of Barthélemy provided additional ammunition for the appeasers and contributed to the further bewilderment and defeatism of many Frenchmen who were
honestly trying to make up their minds (cf. Bonnet, I, p. 100 ; *The Truth about the
Munich Crisis*, by Viscount Maugham (London, 1944), pp. 71-6).

tendering the good offices of Britain and France in any way which might be helpful in reaching such a solution.

Ribbentrop, on his return to Berlin from Rome, whither he had gone with Hitler to visit Mussolini, told the British Ambassador that this step had been " warmly welcomed " (*herzlich begrüsst*) by the Führer, who regarded the Sudeten problem as a purely internal question for the Czechs to settle with Henlein. As a pendant, however, Ribbentrop added that, in the solution of this " purely internal question ", self-determination in some form or other was essential.[1]

It was at this juncture that Mr. Chamberlain took occasion, at an informal luncheon-party given by Lady Astor for American and Canadian newspaper correspondents resident in London, to give an " off the record " statement of his views on the Czecho-slovak situation. As reported, the substance of his remarks was to the effect that neither France nor Russia, and certainly not Britain, would fight for Czechoslovakia in the event of German aggression, and that the Czechoslovak State could not continue to exist in its present form. Mr. Chamberlain left his hearers with the clear impression that the policy of Great Britain was to bring about a peaceful solution of the Sudeten problem by giving to Hitler the German " fringe " of Czechoslovakia, after which a Four-Power Pact for the preservation of the peace of Europe would be concluded between Great Britain, France, Germany and Italy, to the exclusion of Russia. It may not have been Mr. Chamberlain's intention to give the impression which his remarks, in fact, gave, but no official *démenti* was ever issued when reports of the Prime Minister's remarks appeared in American and Canadian newspapers, and their effect was to create profound despondency and suspicion in Moscow and in Prague and among the friends of Czechoslovakia in Paris.[2]

[1] Henderson, p. 134.

[2] Carefully worded accounts of this event appeared on May 14, from " Augur " in the *New York Times* and from Joseph Driscoll in the *New York Herald-Tribune* and the *Montreal Gazette*. No version was published in England, but it was the subject of acrid discussion in the House of Commons on June 20, 21 and 27, when raised in questions to the Prime Minister by Mr. (now Sir Geoffrey) Mander and Sir Archibald Sinclair. Mr. Chamberlain first dismissed the questions as " restless and mischievous curiosity " ; he then took refuge in the answer that he had given " no authoritative interview " as stated, and finally was driven to a refusal either to confirm or deny the truth of the stories. Lady Astor having first stated that there was " not a word of truth " in the story that the Prime Minister had been her luncheon guest on May 10, subsequently corrected her statement by explaining that Mr. Chamberlain had indeed been at luncheon, but that he had not " given an interview ".

Well pleased with the general progress of events, Adolf Hitler, having allowed the *Schlummerlied* to grow somewhat *piano*, decided upon a step which should make its rendering a little louder. The public reactions abroad to the enunciation of the Karlsbad Programme had been a little too sharp for comfort, despite the unremitting zeal of Government circles in Britain and France to keep official relations on a friendly basis. It would be well to placate public opinion a little for the purpose of deception, particularly in view of the fact that the Führer now meditated a demonstration of force against the Czechs at an appropriate moment.

It was decreed, therefore, in Berlin that Konrad Henlein should go to London. This was not his first visit to Britian. He had been there twice before, the last time in the spring of 1937, when he had talked chiefly with journalists and publicists and had delivered an address of studied moderation at Chatham House (The Royal Institute of International Affairs). He had made a very good impression, this tall, blond, bespectacled young gymnastic instructor, with his athletic build and his somewhat pedagogic method of expression, and he had skilfully concealed his true colours and his Nazi affiliations. He had described himself, in those days, as a loyal citizen of the Czechoslovak Republic, and, while admitting a deep interest in the future of the German Minority of the Sudetenland and a genuine desire to remove what he felt to be certain inequalities and discriminations on the part of the Czechs, there was nothing in his bearing of the declared revolutionary, and many were deceived by his apparent sincerity.

Henlein had gone a long way since then. He was now a leader of an " oppressed minority " and a " little Führer " to boot. During the demonstrations in the Sudetenland in celebration of the annexation of Austria to the Reich, his followers of the *Sudetendeutsche Partei* had pressed about his car to touch even the door-handle or the running-board. Others, more fortunate, caught his raincoat or kissed his hand. Scenes like this had hitherto only occurred in Germany when the Führer passed by.

The growing arrogance of Henlein's bearing in relation to the Czechoslovak Government was reflected both in his own self-confidence and in the increase of support on which he could count from his masters in Berlin. He had rejected out of hand and without examination the proposals which Dr. Hodža had put forward for a National Minority Statute, and when, a month later, the Prague Government refused to accept his own Karlsbad Programme, he had haughtily replied : " I take back nothing " (May 12).

It was not, however, in this guise that Henlein reappeared in London in the second week of May 1938, but rather in an attempt to ape the role of a Garibaldi or a Kossuth ; eager to give the impression of moderation driven desperate by frustration and oppression, yet ever ready to listen to reason. In deference to the strong representations of M. Jan Masaryk he was received by no member of the Government, and it was arranged that, in addition to members of the *entourage* of the Prime Minister and of the editorial staffs of *The Times* and *The Observer*, he should talk with such outspoken opponents of the policy of appeasement as Mr. Winston Churchill, Mr. Eden, Sir Archibald Sinclair and Sir Robert Vansittart, the Chief Diplomatic Adviser to the Government.

To all who would listen to him, Henlein gave assurances that his Karlsbad Programme must not be regarded in the light of an ultimatum but purely as a basis of negotiation. But, whereas it had been hoped that he would benefit from the realistic views expressed without restraint to him by the opponents of appeasement, he was more deeply impressed by those others in London who told him, with even greater realism, of Britain's indifference to the fate of Czechoslovakia and of their conviction that Prague must now choose between " autonomy and separatism ".

It was the views of Mr. Garvin and Mr. Geoffrey Dawson, and not those of Mr. Churchill and Sir Robert Vansittart, that Henlein reported to the Führer in the course of his visit to Berlin on his way back to Asch, and the Führer was well pleased, for he hoped that this betokened a speedy acquiescence with his wishes. He was growing impatient.

(ii)

Early in April the Prague Government had announced that municipal elections would be held in Czechoslovakia on three Sundays in May and June, beginning on May 22, and this decision had governed in great degree the subsequent developments in Berlin and in the councils of the *S.d.P.* The choice of April 24 for the promulgation of the Karlsbad Programme had the object of stampeding the German Minority vote into the Henleinist camp, and it was also decided that the elections should be the occasion of a demonstration which would convince London and Paris, as well as Prague, of the necessity for an immediate settlement of the Sudeten problem.

It had been hinted among Henlein's followers that " *Der Tag* " was at hand. Accordingly the election campaign in the Sudetenland had provoked a number of incidents in which rioting resulted in bloodshed, and on May 13 — at a moment when Henlein was cooing like any sucking-dove in London — the formation of *S.d.P.* Storm Troops was announced for the protection of Party meetings.

An atmosphere of tension had been steadily growing on both sides of the Bohemian frontier and rumours of German troop movements were current. They were, however, to a certain extent discounted by the fact that this was the normal season for spring manœuvres.

The crisis rose to fever-pitch on May 19. On this day troop movements were reported in the German press [1] and Henlein, without warning, declared his inability to pursue negotiations with the Prague Government and departed for Germany. At the same time reliable reports reached both the Czech and the British Intelligence Services that four German motorized divisions under General von Reichenau were concentrated on the Czech frontier, and that full-scale preparations existed for a descent on Bohemia.

The next forty-eight hours saw the greatest exhibition of diplomatic activity and military preparation since August 1914. They also witnessed the last display of unity between Great Britain, France and Russia against German aggression until the latter stages of the Second World War when a liberated France re-entered the battle.

In Prague, on the afternoon of Friday, May 20, the Czech Government, in session in the Hradschin Palace, decided, on the initiative of President Beneš, to order a " partial mobilization ", calling up one class of reservists to the colours, as well as certain technical experts.[2] The operation was executed with smoothness and despatch. That same evening an incident occurred which, it was feared, might touch off the great conflagration. Two *S.d.P.* officials of the District of Cheb carrying propaganda

---

[1] *Leipziger Zeitung*, May 19, 1938.

[2] According to Karl Hermann Frank, who saw the Prime Minister on behalf of the *S.d.P.* on the morning of May 21, Dr. Hodža gave the impression that he had not been entirely in agreement with the President in issuing the mobilization order (*International Military Tribunal Document*, 3061–PS).

material were challenged near the frontier by a Czech policeman. They were motor-cyclists and refused to stop. The policeman fired and both of them were killed.

In Berlin the British Ambassador, under instructions from London, made inquiries as to German intentions. He was assured, both by the State Secretary and by General Keitel, that the tales of troop concentrations were " absolute nonsense " and reported accordingly.[1] But the British Foreign Office was not to be easily put off — it was remembered that Keitel had denied all previous knowledge of the troop movements which had preceded the march into Austria — and Sir Nevile Henderson was instructed to check his facts again. He therefore sent the Military Attaché, Colonel Mason-Macfarlane,[2] and his assistant, Major Strong,[3] on a widespread motor reconnaissance of Saxony and Silesia, where they could find no sign of unusual or significant troop activity (May 21).[4]

Undeterred by the lack of evidence, the British Foreign Office ordered Sir Nevile to make further representations of Britain's anxiety regarding the grave situation which had arisen and to give a warning of what her attitude would be in the event of war — for whether Germany had or had not meditated an attack on the Czechs, the position had now developed as if she had had such an intention. In the course of four interviews with Ribbentrop, the Ambassador repeated Mr. Chamberlain's warning of March 24, that, if France were to fulfil her treaty obligations to Czechoslovakia, the British Government could not undertake that, under pressure of events, they would not themselves become involved.[5] Sir Nevile was supported in these statements by the French Ambassador, and both were received with considerable incivility by Ribbentrop, who angrily denied that Germany had any intention of making an attack on Bohemia. In London, on the evening of the same day (Saturday, May 21), Lord Halifax received the German Ambassador and made it clear to him that a German-Czech war meant a Franco-German war, and therefore perhaps, sooner or later, an Anglo-German war. However, in a Note dated May 22, the British Government informed M. Daladier that their statements to the German Government could in no way

---

[1] These reassurances were repeated to the Czech Government in Prague and to the Czech Minister in Berlin.

[2] Lieutenant-General Sir Frank Mason-Macfarlane, later M.P. for North Paddington, 1944-6.   [3] Major-General K. W. D. Strong, later head of G.2 SHAEF.

[4] Henderson, p. 137.   [5] Henderson, p. 139.

be construed as involving Britain in an obligation to take immediate and joint military action with France in defence of
Czechoslovakia. In the view of the British Government Czechoslovakia could not be saved from destruction even by the combined
military assistance of Britain, France and Russia, and the only
outcome would be a general European war, of which the result
would be — to say the least of it — doubtful.[1]

The response of Czechoslovakia's treaty partners was immediate and gratifying. M. Bonnet announced on May 21,
after receiving the British and Russian Ambassadors, that, if
German troops crossed the Czech frontier, France would at once
come to the support of her ally — assurances which M. François-
Poncet repeated in Berlin — while M. Daladier, in the course of
an interview with the German Ambassador, showed him the
mobilization order lying on his desk, and remarked meaningly :
" It depends upon you, Excellency, whether I sign this document
or not."

The Soviet Government, through M. Litvinov in Moscow and
their representatives in Paris and Prague, also gave proof of their
readiness to stand by their French and Czechoslovak allies in the
event of German aggression, despite the lack of support forthcoming from Rumania and Poland.[2]

To Hitler, sitting in council with his military and political
chiefs at Berchtesgaden, on Sunday, May 22, this display of
unity was nothing short of astonishing. For two days Ribbentrop had received a constant procession of Ambassadors and
Ministers declaring the solidarity of their Governments with
Czechoslovakia. From Prague came reports of a calm and united
nation girt and ready for war ;[3] from Paris and Moscow, the

---

[1] M. Daladier in the Constituent Assembly, July 18, 1946, *Journal Officiel*, July 19,
1946, p. 2679 ; Bonnet, I, pp. 129-30.

[2] The May crisis disclosed one essentially weak spot in the united front which it
was hoped to oppose to German aggression. In response to French inquiries in
Bucharest and Warsaw as to what degree of support for Czechoslovakia might be
expected from these quarters, it became evident that neither Rumania nor Poland
would willingly permit Russian troops to pass through, or Russian aircraft to fly over,
their territory to the assistance of the Czechs. As to action on their own part, the
Rumanian Government refused to move without previous agreement with Poland,
and in Poland Colonel Beck disclosed himself as a willing accomplice of Hitler. Poland,
with the blindness born of an old hatred, desired the break-up of Czechoslovakia in
the belief that her own ambitions would be advanced thereby (*L'Agression allemande
contre la Pologne*, by Léon Noël (Paris, 1946), pp. 205-7 ; Bonnet, I, pp. 130-40).

[3] The municipal elections passed off without incident on May 22, despite the
atmosphere of crisis.

German Embassies reported a determined and unshakable intention to support Prague ; from London came a declaration of " non-neutrality " which gave unmistakable indication against whom Britain would be " non-neutral ". Were these the effete Western Democracies and the treacherous Soviet ally who, the Führer had been assured, would not fight for Czechoslovakia ? Was this a demonstration of faith from that man in London of whom Ribbentrop had brought back such " a really excellent impression " ?

Ribbentrop was summoned from Berlin to Berchtesgaden, but even there the relentless voices pursued him. Late on Sunday a personal message was delivered from Lord Halifax drawing his attention to the danger of precipitating actions leading to a general conflagration which might prove to be the destruction of European civilization.[1]

In face of united opposition abroad it was the unanimous opinion of the Führer's advisers that a political retreat was necessary. This view was voiced with great vehemence by the General Staff, who warned him that the German military machine, while capable of undertaking an unopposed military promenade into Austria, was not yet in a sufficient state of preparedness to conduct a war on two, and possibly three, fronts.

Though it was gall and wormwood to him to do so, Hitler gave the necessary orders, and on the following day (May 23) M. Mastný was again the recipient in Berlin of assurances as to immediate German intentions on his country, but with them was coupled a warning that, unless the policy of Prague towards the Sudeten Minority were radically changed, Germany would be forced to " protect " these Germans. On the same day instructions were issued to Henlein to return to Czechoslovakia and open negotiations with Dr. Hodźa for the peaceful settlement of the Sudeten problem.

So ended a very successful example of collective security. No more satisfactory outcome could have been hoped for. Europe had believed herself to be very near war for two days, but the spectre had been turned away, not by the appeasement of an aggressor but by a determined show of force and willingness to resist on the part of the potential victim and her allies.[2]

[1] Henderson, p. 139.
[2] Just how great this belief was had been illustrated by two events which occurred in Berlin during the crisis. A British resident had some days before booked sleeping

Unfortunately this was not a new flame in the lantern of hope, but the last dying flicker of the burned-out candle, the last upward dart of light before the final darkness.

berths for his family to go to England for the summer holidays, and on the critical Saturday (May 21) the British Naval Attaché, who was also going on leave with his whole family, telephoned the station for berths. When none was available, he asked that an extra sleeping-car be attached to the train. The booking-clerk at once drew the conclusion that, in view of an approaching rupture of relations, the British Embassy were preparing to evacuate the whole colony, and in a few hours it was widely rumoured throughout Europe that the Ambassador had ordered a special train, thus evoking memories of Lord Beaconsfield's *coup de théâtre* at the Berlin Conference. In order to pacify the German Foreign Ministry, Sir Nevile Henderson, while allowing the Naval Attaché to proceed on leave, cancelled the extra carriage and forbade other members of his staff to leave the capital.

The second incident also occurred on the evening of May 21, when the sudden demolition, close by, of a small hotel by dynamite caused Henderson, François-Poncet and Göring to give vent to remarks which betrayed their real anxiety as to the proximity of war (Henderson, pp. 140-41).

CHAPTER THREE

PRELUDE IN PRAGUE

(i)

WHETHER or not the Nazi leaders had actually intended to make a descent in force on Czechoslovakia during the week-end of May 20–22 is of secondary importance beside the fact that Europe at large seriously believed that they had harboured such an intention. As frequently happens, it is not so much the truth that matters as what people believe to be true, and in this case belief was only separated from truth by a narrow margin of time, since Germany was, in fact, contemplating and planning for exactly such an attack at the appropriate moment. The governments of Europe had acted on the belief that, despite vehement and repeated German denials, a further act of aggression was about to be committed by Germany, comparable to that made against Austria two months before.

Moreover, the effects of the crisis in the capitals of Europe were of tremendous importance, increasing the tempo of events in general and, to a major degree, shaping the decisions of future policy.

In Germany, Hitler retired in a black rage and absented himself from all public life for a week. He had been bluffed by the Western Powers, his word had been doubted, and he had been treated to a remarkable and disquieting display of European solidarity in support of Czechoslovakia. He had suffered a major diplomatic defeat and had been placed in an unfavourable light throughout the world at a moment when he particularly wished to give an appearance of sweet reasonableness. His " righteous " wrath was that of a man accused of a crime which he intends to commit but has not yet had the opportunity to carry out. It was upon Beneš and the Czechs that his vindictive mind fastened the cause and responsibility for his humiliation ; for, had the Prague Government not mobilized (even partially), France and Russia would not have supported them and Britain would not have issued that equivocal warning. It was Beneš and the

Czechs who had disseminated these rumours which had caused suspicions to be cast on Germany's *bona fides*. It was Beneš and the Czechs, therefore, who must suffer the penalty of his displeasure and feel the full weight of his revenge.[1]

For a week the Führer brooded in solitude, indulging in alternate bouts of *Weltschmerz* and dreams of revenge. Then on May 28, as he himself subsequently admitted,[2] he took a momentous decision. The Sudeten problem must be settled this year — even if this involved a European war. His General Staff had told him that the Reich was not yet in a sufficient state of military preparedness to face this contingency, and to meet this deficiency Hitler ordered that the strength of the Army and Air Force should be " enormously enlarged ". At the same time, in order to ensure himself against any military interference on the part of France in support of Czechoslovakia, he initiated the immense and formidable fortification on Germany's Western Front which became known as the Siegfried Line.[3]

The original version of the directive for " Operation Green " had been signed by Hitler on May 20. Now he recalled it and, summoning Keitel, ordered a drastic change, so that, when redrafted, it opened with the words : " It is my unalterable decision to smash (*zerschlagen*) Czechoslovakia by military action in the near future. It is the duty of the political leaders to bring about the politically and militarily suitable moment." This directive, when submitted to the *Wehrmacht* commanders two days later (May 30), was supplemented by a general order fixing October 1, 1938, as the dead-line for putting " Operation Green " into effect.[4]

[1] Cf. an undated entry in General Jodl's diary : " The intention of the Führer not to touch the Czech problem as yet is changed because of the Czech strategic troop concentration of May 21, which occurs without any German threat and without the slightest cause for it. Because of Germany's restraint, its consequences lead to a loss of prestige for the Führer, which he is not willing to suffer again " (*International Military Tribunal Document*, 1780–PS).

[2] In his speech before the Congress of the Nazi Party on September 12, 1938, at Nuremberg.

[3] This immense construction project, on which 800,000 labourers of the *Organisation Todt* sweated for three months, cost the Reich some £750 millions — or approximately four billion dollars.

[4] *International Military Tribunal Document*, 388–PS, item 11. This sudden change of plan evidently caused some anxiety in military circles. General Jodl's diary for May 30 reads as follows : " The whole contrast becomes acute once more between the Führer's intuition that we *must* do it this year and the opinion in the Army that we cannot do it as yet, as most certainly the Western Powers will interfere and we are not yet equal to them " (*International Military Tribunal Document*, 1780–PS).

The plan was detailed and comprehensive. It provided for the penetration of the Czech fortifications, " with the utmost daring ", and the destruction of their land and air forces. Surprise was the keynote of the enterprise, and the devastating bombing of cities. But, in so doing, the wider objective of the operation — the contribution which the new conquest would make to Germany's future war potential — was not lost sight of. " In war economy ", ran the directive, " it is essential that, in the field of the armament industry, a maximum deployment of forces is made possible through increased supplies. In the course of operations, therefore, it is of value to contribute to the reinforcement of the total war economic strength by rapidly reconnoitring and re-starting important factories. For this reason the sparing of Czechoslovakian industrial and works installations — in so far as military operations permit — can be of decisive importance to us."

Having cast the die — and to gain time for the necessary measures to be completed — Hitler set himself to break down the barrier of unity which the May crisis had revealed. In this latter project he received surprising support from the least expected quarters.

The annals of history can rarely have afforded so remarkable an example of successful Powers terrified at their own success as that presented by Britain and France after the May crisis. What had been generally believed to be a threat of aggression had been met, and apparently deterred, by an outstanding display of united action on the part of the European Powers concerned. This might reasonably have been accepted as a cause for satisfaction and for the further cementing of those bonds of co-operation which had already proved salutary, at any rate as a warning. The French Government might have been expected to follow up the long-deferred Soviet proposals for consultation between the French, Russian and Czech General Staffs for the possible implementation of their common treaties, and it would not have been extraordinary if the British Government had encouraged them to do so. In any case, in view of the intensified military preparations which Germany had undertaken, and of which there was ample evidence and information to hand, it would have been only common sense for Britain and France to overhaul their own war machines.

In effect, none of these things happened. Instead, Mr. Chamberlain, appalled at the chasm of war which had seemingly opened suddenly at his feet, became more and more determined that never again should he be placed in such an unhappy position, and, instead of taking practical measures to strengthen the powers at the command of those who were opposed to the potential aggressor, he set about weakening still further the position of the victim of aggression.

The tone of Mr. Chamberlain's explanation to the House of Commons on May 23 [1] was almost apologetic to Germany, and the apostles of appeasement in London were openly declaring that the May crisis had been a grave disaster — and particularly the publicity which had attended it. Hitler, it was said, who had hitherto been so reasonable in his attitude, was now presented with an excuse to come down on the side of the extremists and was considering again a solution by force, as in the case of Austria. That Hitler now intended a solution by force was perfectly true, but this he had always intended, if need be, and the events of May had merely increased the tempo of his planning. But British critics of President Beneš were almost as violent in their denunciation as Herr Hitler himself. They feared that the display of support for the Czechs in the May crisis would have the unfortunate effect of encouraging them to believe that their position was secure and, in consequence, to be reluctant to go far enough in satisfying the Sudeten German demands.

It was now also that, among responsible people in London, there began to be repeated what had so long been an insistent refrain of Nazi propaganda, namely, that Czechoslovakia was a ramshackle State — an Austria-Hungary in microcosm — a mere collection of mutually antagonistic races held together by force. This offered an obvious solution to those who, on these grounds, contemplated the placation of Germany, and *The Times* openly urged the Prague Government to grant " self-determination " to the national minorities " even if it should mean their secession from Czechoslovakia ".[2]

The British people were still generally ignorant of, and apathetic to, the dangers of the situation in Central Europe, despite the eloquent efforts of Mr. Churchill to enlighten them. Mr. Chamberlain alternately lulled them into a sense of false security by statements in the House of Commons as to the satisfactory progress of British rearmament, or endeavoured to infuse

[1] *House of Commons Debates*, May 23, 1938, coll. 824-5.
[2] *The Times*, June 3, 1938.

them with his own sincere belief that in war there are no winners.[1] This was an argument he was to employ more vehemently with President Beneš at a later moment in the drama.[2]

Haunted by the prospect that a second Czech crisis would precipitate a situation in which France could not with honour withhold her support from Czechoslovakia, Mr. Chamberlain justifiably bent his every effort towards urging the Prague Government to go to the limit of reasonable concession to the Sudeten Germans and to keeping France in line on their joint policy. War could come only through Czech intransigence, which must at all costs be avoided, and it was therefore under pressure from both London and Paris that the Czech Government agreed, on June 10, to accept Henlein's Karlsbad Programme as a basis for the negotiations which opened four days later.

The official German reaction was reported by Lord Londonderry on his return from Berlin in June, where he had attended a conference of the International Aeronautical Federation. The Marquess, whose visit was " of an entirely private character ", returned with the impression that the German Government entertained an " earnest hope " that the Sudeten problem would be " settled without the new arrangements being brought about with disturbances which could create in the world the impression that the German intentions in these two respects were not of a peaceful or progressive character ".[3]

In Paris, Mr. Chamberlain's efforts were warmly seconded by Georges Bonnet. When M. Bonnet took office as Minister of Foreign Affairs in the Daladier Cabinet in April 1938, the Czech crisis was already looming. Austria had been annexed and the first open mutterings of the next outburst of the *furor teutonicus* had been heard in Berlin. M. Bonnet, after consideration, decided that, whatever the policy of the French Government might be, *his* policy was to abandon the system of French security alliance in face of the Nazi menace, and, in fact, to make any and every surrender in the hope that thereby at least the national independence of France would be preserved. He was prepared to see Germany extended along the Danube — and along the Vistula, if need be — in the pious hope that, in return for French compliance, France would be graciously permitted to continue her

---

[1] Speech at Kettering, July 2, 1938.   [2] See below, p. 155.
[3] Londonderry, p. 156.

existence. The impressions which he had gained from the Anglo-French conversations of April 28-9 had only served to confirm in his own mind the rightness of this policy.[1]

Had M. Bonnet read *Mein Kampf*, of which the *édition intégral* of the French translation had been officially suppressed in 1934 at the request of the German editors ? If so, could he seriously believe that Hitler would allow even a complacent France to exist as a first-class Power ? Had he really convinced himself that those threats to France, so clearly pronounced, could be turned aside by French acceptance of the status of hand-maiden to Germany ?[2]

Whether or not he was acquainted with the political writings of the Führer, Bonnet proceeded to pursue just this policy, and therefore it was an unwelcome shock to him to find himself placed by the events of the May crisis in the position where he was forced to reaffirm the validity of the French pledges to Czechoslovakia. To his intimates he expressed his conviction that the threatened invasion was largely a *ballon d'essai* sent up by the Czechs to test British and French reaction and that " he could never quite forgive the Czechs their stunt of May 21 ".[3] That they should not repeat it he was quite determined, but because there were brave men among his colleagues — Mandel, Reynaud, Campinchi and Champetier de Ribes — between whose views and his own M. Daladier was apt to vacillate, Bonnet could not pursue his course openly.

His tactics were at once both simple and complex. In the Chamber he still gave guarded support to the Czechs against excessive German demands, thinking it inadvisable for the Prague Government to grant minority rights to the Sudeten Germans which would be out of all proportion to their numerical

---

[1] " *Ne faisons pas d'héroïsme, nous n'en sommes pas capables* ", M. Bonnet advised a journalist acquaintance one night as they dined together at Carton's in the Place de la Madeleine, a few days after he had assumed office. " *Les Anglais ne nous suivront pas. C'est très joli de s'instituer le gendarme de l'Europe, mais encore faut-il avoir pour cela autre chose que des pistolets à amorces, des menottes en paille et des prisons en carton. En tout que Ministre des Affaires étrangères, je suis résolu d'aller jusqu'au bout de mon rôle, qui est celui de trouver une solution avant que le Ministre de la Guerre* [M. Daladier, the Premier] *soit obligé d'en prendre une. La France ne peut plus se permettre une saignée comme celle de 1914* " (Lazareff, pp. 32-3).

[2] For example : " The inexorably deadly enemy of the German people is and will be France " (*Mein Kampf*, London, 1939, p. 505) ; also : " We must stop at no sacrifice in our effort to destroy the French striving toward hegemony in Europe " (*ibid.* p. 542).

[3] *The Twilight of France, 1933-40*, by Alexander Werth (London, 1942), p. 176.

importance.[1] Yet he joined with Mr. Chamberlain and Lord
Halifax in bringing pressure to bear upon Prague to accept the
Karlsbad Programme as a basis of negotiation with the Henleinists (June 10). To his British allies, however, he repeatedly
conveyed the impression that France, in the final analysis, could
not fight in accordance with her treaty obligations because of the
weak condition of French armaments, while to his colleagues in
the Cabinet he hinted that the allies of France, especially Russia,
either would not support her in the event of war or, in the
case of Britain, would prefer surrender to resistance, and therefore, since France was the keystone of the arch of European
security, they would prefer that she did not proceed to extreme
measures.

In pursuit of the same policy, Bonnet, in his own office at the
Quai d'Orsay and in the salons and dining-rooms of Paris, would
let drop remarks regarding the inability and unwillingness of France
to resist German aggression ; remarks which he knew would be
retold in Berlin — as well as in London, Moscow and Prague —
through the German Embassy or those more clandestine channels
of Otto Abetz [2] and Fernand de Brinon.[3] Above all, he wished
to confuse the issue and to prevent the Führer's brutality from
being disclosed in all its naked force until after France had
conveniently given way. He had, in effect, accepted the Nazi
programme of the inevitable shift of power in Europe and was
mainly concerned to anaesthetize France into painlessly assuming
her enforced role in the New Order.

That M. Daladier was aware of Bonnet's activities is known ;
that he took no action to correct them and that he tolerated the
continuance of Bonnet in office is the gravest charge against the
French Premier and constitutes, in great part, his personal and
particular contribution to the *débâcle* that was to descend upon

---

[1] *Le Temps* and *Manchester Guardian*, June 4, 1938.

[2] Otto Abetz, Chief Nazi Agent in Paris, was expelled from France in July 1939.
He returned a year later as Ambassador to the Vichy Government and remained in
that capacity until 1944, when he was arrested by French military authorities. In
1949 he was sentenced to twenty years' imprisonment, but was pardoned in 1954.
In May 1958 he was killed in a motor accident.

[3] Count Fernand de Brinon had long been an advocate of a Franco-German
rapprochement, and since the advent of Hitler to power in 1933 had worked for it
with intensified zeal. He was used by both Daladier and Bonnet as " contact man "
with Berlin, and, under the Vichy Government, became " Ambassador " of Pétain to
the German Military Government in Paris. He was arrested by French military
authorities on May 20, 1945, and was sentenced to death on March 6, 1947, on a
charge of high treason. He was executed on April 15.

French policy later in the summer.

For, in the *dramatis personae* of Munich, M. Daladier is the Pathetic Man, " the patriot without strength of will ".[1] It was said of Georges Carpentier that he was an excellent boxer but never a great fighter, and the same is true of Édouard Daladier. His nickname of the " Bull of Auvergne " was apposite only in that he was bovine. He was always a puzzled bull, never a bull who delighted in the battle of the ring. His intellectual integrity caused him to start upon the right road, but his dislike of the disagreeable prevented his removing energetically the obstacles in his path, and allowed him to turn a myopic eye to personalities and events which he knew to be injurious to his Government and to France.

Thus now, when, in July of 1938, he declared that " the solemn undertakings we have given to Czechoslovakia are sacred and cannot be evaded ", he made the statement in all sincerity, yet knowing that his toleration of the ineptitude of General Gamelin as Chief of the General Staff, and of the disingenuousness of Bonnet at the Quai d'Orsay, spelled the very negation of his words as he spoke them.

For the tragedy of Édouard Daladier is that when he became aware of the evils which surrounded him he had not the strength of character to apply the drastic measures necessary to remove them. He preferred to shift the onus of responsibility elsewhere rather than to purge his *entourage*.

Above all, he was, like Mr. Chamberlain, " a man of peace to the depths of his soul ", but his horror of war, unlike Mr. Chamberlain's, which was based on an innate and sincerely Christian devotion to peace, was that of a French soldier who had seen France bled white in 1914–18. M. Daladier's record in that war had been a gallant one — he was not only a fine soldier but a fine officer — but, like so many Frenchmen of his generation, he emerged from the struggle with the conviction that France had fought her last war, and it was this mentality which, in dealing with the brutal energy of the Third Reich, caused France to be defeated before she had begun to fight.[2]

---

[1] Pertinax, p. 85.

[2] As an ex-Service man, M. Daladier had a sincere affection for the *poilus* and shrank from any course of action which would endanger them, whether at home or abroad. " I am anxious not to shed the blood of the little soldiers of France," he said to Louis Lévy on the night of July 7, 1934, when he resigned the premiership rather than employ troops to quell the demonstrations of the French Fascist leagues (*The Truth about France*, by Louis Lévy (Penguin edition, 1941), p. 67).

(ii)

In Czechoslovakia it was undeniably true that the effect of the May crisis was to harden the issue on both sides. The Government had been delighted at the efficiency and speed with which their mobilization orders had been carried out and by the degree of unity which the crisis had evoked throughout the country. The determination of Czechoslovakia to resist aggression was intensified, but the demonstration of support from Paris and Moscow and London seemed to indicate that she would not have to fight alone. It was with new hope, therefore, that the Government embarked on their dual task of solving the German minority problem by means of negotiation with the Nazi puppets in the *Sudetendeutsche Partei*, and of keeping a watchful eye on the manipulators of those puppets in Berlin.

For the *S.d.P.*, also, the situation had hardened. Though under instructions from Berlin to negotiate with Prague, Konrad Henlein felt sufficiently confident of German support to give a significant interview to Mr. Ward Price of the *Daily Mail*. The Czech Government had now, he said, three choices before them : to give to the *S.d.P.* all that it asked for ; to allow a plebiscite for or against secession to Germany ; or to have war. The third course would, he thought, " be simpler still ". Publication of this indiscretion was banned both in Czechoslovakia and Germany, and Henlein, on instructions from Berlin, denied ever having given it, but, under pressure from Mr. Price, he was forced to admit that their conversation had led " to a survey of the theoretically possible development of the Sudeten German problem ".[1]

The official attitude of the *S.d.P.* was declared in a memorandum presented on June 8 to Dr. Hodža in elaboration of the Karlsbad Programme. In it Henlein now demanded that the Czechoslovak State be reorganized into racial areas, that each area should have virtual independence (*i.e.* the establishment of the Sudetenland as a Nazi State within the Republic), and that at the same time each should have an equal voice in the affairs of the central government. It was this memorandum, in addition to the Karlsbad Programme, that the Czech Government, under pressure from London, accepted as a basis of discussion in addi-

[1] The interview was published in the *Daily Mail* of May 26, 1938, and Henlein's " explanation " on June 10, 1938.

tion to their own draft Statute of National Minorities, and the first round-table conference took place on June 23. It is not entirely surprising that the efforts to bridge so yawning a gulf proceeded slowly. The Prague Government, while willing to go a very long way, were fighting to preserve the integrity of the Republic against what was clearly an ill-disguised plan to disrupt it internally. Beneš and Hodža were under continued pressure from London to abandon their purist stand and surrender on the basis of self-determination if need be. Henlein, in accordance with his instructions from Berlin, remained intransigent. His chief representative at the discussions, Ernst Kundt, refused compromise after compromise put forward by Hodža, and dragged the meetings out to an interminable length.[1] In such an atmosphere the conference continued until July 9, when, though the negotiations were not broken off, Henlein was summoned suddenly to the Führer at Berchtesgaden.[2]

Hitler was now ready to quicken the tempo. His military preparations were not yet completed, but it was time to step-up the general situation into an increased atmosphere of crisis. Attacks on Czechoslovakia in the German press and on the radio were resumed.[3] In London and Paris Hitler allowed it to be known that his patience — never his strong point — was becoming exhausted, and that those who had the well-being of Czechoslovakia at heart should give her good advice.

The British Government had watched the dismal course of the negotiations in Prague with rising anxiety and displeasure. Confronted with the rapacity of Germany on the one hand and the unwillingness of Czechoslovakia to commit suicide on the other, they determined on a more drastic course of action.

[1] " Henlein knows why he appointed Herr Ernst Kundt as head of the Sudeten German negotiating committee. He is a master of the tactic of procrastination ", wrote Dr. Sefernik, of the Czech Foreign Ministry, to Eugene Lennhoff on July 15. See Lennhoff, *In Defence of Dr. Beneš and Czechoslovakia* (London, 1938), pp. 120-21.

[2] It was on June 29 that the first orders were given to the *S.D.* (*Sicherheitsdienst*) to be in readiness to act " in case of complications between the German Reich and Czechoslovakia ". A detailed plan of operations was also issued to the *S.D.*, whose instructions were to " follow, whenever possible, on the heels of the entering troops and take over the duties similar to those it had in Germany, to ensure the security of the political life and, as far as possible, the security of all enterprises indispensable for the national as well as the war economy " (*International Military Tribunal Document*, USSR–509).

[3] Speaking in the Olympic Stadium in Berlin, in the presence of the Führer, on June 21, Goebbels stated : " We will not look on much longer while 3½ million Germans [in Czechoslovakia] are maltreated. . . . We saw in Austria that one race cannot be separated into two countries, and we shall soon see it somewhere else."

It was evident that, left to themselves, the Prague Government and the *Sudetendeutsche Partei* would get nowhere in their negotiations, and that, at some moment of his own choosing, Hitler would terminate the discussions in favour of direct action by Germany. The Czechs would undoubtedly resist, and the crisis of May 21 would be repeated *da capo*. If they allowed the situation to drift into war without making every possible effort to avoid the final catastrophe, the British Government felt — and rightly — that they would be held blameworthy. Since direct negotiations had failed, therefore, why should not London and Paris induce Dr. Beneš to accept a settlement at the hands of Anglo-French arbitrators ?

When this proposal was first submitted to the French Government it was rejected by M. Daladier on the ground that direct Anglo-French intervention in the settlement of the Sudeten problem would only serve to assist Germany in ordering Henlein to raise his demands. There then occurred to Mr. Chamberlain " the original and hardy idea " of sending Lord Runciman to Prague.[1]

The inception of the idea was accelerated by events. Early in July Sir Nevile Henderson had telegraphed from Berlin a proposal, which he put forward as his own, that, since there appeared to be no possibility that the *Sudetendeutsche Partei* would accept an agreed settlement on the basis of the maintenance of the national character of the Czechoslovak State, Mussolini should be invited to join with the Governments of Britain, France and Germany in a Four-Power Conference to settle the problem.[2] Shortly thereafter (July 18) there arrived in London the Führer's personal adjutant, Captain Fritz Wiedemann,[3] with an assurance of Hitler's personal good-will toward England and his renewed desire for a peaceful solution of the Sudeten problem. The Führer's patience was being sorely tried by the dilatory processes of the Czechs in

---

[1] *The Observer*, July 31, 1938.   [2] Henderson, p. 144.

[3] Fritz Wiedemann had been Hitler's company commander in the First World War and was attached to the Führer's personal staff in 1936. He was used on a number of confidential missions, several of them to London, where he became associated with Princess Stephanie Hohenlohe-Waldenburg-Schillingfurst (*née* Steffi Richter of Vienna). The Princess accompanied him to the United States on his appointment as Consul-General at San Francisco in 1938, and became an active Nazi propagandist on the West Coast. She was arrested by the U.S. authorities after the declaration of war with Germany in 1941. Wiedemann was sent on a special mission to the Far East in 1942 and was arrested as a war criminal by American military authorities in China in 1945.

redressing the wrongs of their German minority. He would restrain himself for six months, perhaps even for a year, provided no further burden of grievance was added to the sad lot of his fellow Germans, but let but one *Sudetendeutsch* be murdered and he would take immediate action. Once, however, the Sudeten problem had been satisfactorily dispensed with, the way would be clear not only for an Anglo-German understanding but for a Four-Power Pact.

Such a proposal as that of Sir Nevile Henderson's so closely resembled the desired policy which Mr. Chamberlain was alleged himself to have outlined to the American and Canadian correspondents, on May 10 at Lady Astor's,[1] that it could not but have appealed to him. But were there no warning echoes of that " splendid conversation " with Ribbentrop on March 13, when the same formula which Wiedemann now employed had been used in regard to the settlement of the Austrian problem? [2] In any case, it was considered impossible at this juncture to remove the settlement of the Sudeten problem from the field of Czech domestic politics to a conference from which apparently both Czechoslovakia and Russia were to be excluded. They had not got that far yet.[3] But further action must be taken, and immediately, to break the deadlock in Prague. The Anglo-French Agreement of April 28 had recognized the necessity for conciliation and the two Powers had proffered their good offices to the Czech Government. It was now time to insist that these offices be utilized. If the French would not agree, then Britain must act alone. There was no time to be lost, for Lord Halifax was shortly to accompany the King and Queen on a visit of State to the President of the French Republic. Urgent instructions were therefore sent on July 18 to the British Minister in Prague to propose to President Beneš personally the appointment of Lord Runciman as an independent arbitrator. It was this news that Lord Halifax carried across the Channel with him on July 19 and communicated next day to MM. Daladier and Bonnet at a conference which preceded the State dinner given to the King and Queen at the Ministry of Foreign Affairs.[4] It was made clear to the French Ministers that this was a purely British

---

[1] See above, p. 52.   [2] See above, p. 34.
[3] Cf. Henderson, p. 144 : " At that moment, however, it was feared that it would be difficult to exclude other Powers from participating in such a conference ".   [4] Bonnet, I, p. 173.

venture, in which the French Government would not be asked
to participate.

The first reaction of M. Daladier and his colleagues to this
new initiative on the part of Britain was one of almost unanimous
resentment and disapproval. They resented the fact that Britain
had taken this step without prior consultation, or, indeed, notification, and this resentment was allowed to be reflected in certain
organs of the French press well known for their use by successive
Governments as " official leaks ".[1] First, they disapproved of the
idea on the ground that, in intervening directly in the Sudeten
dispute, Britain would be playing Hitler's game by abandoning
her position as a " friendly neutral " and becoming an " interested
party " ; and, secondly, they deprecated the appointment of any
" arbitrator " at all, since this would place the Czechoslovak
Government in an altogether impossible position. In agreeing
to the principle of arbitration the Czechs would have either to
accept the arbiter's award in advance or to accept or refuse it
on presentation. In refusing they would put themselves in the
wrong, while in accepting they would in all probability be placing
themselves at the mercy of Nazi Germany. These same views
were expressed in the strongest manner by the Czechoslovak
Government themselves through their Minister in Paris, M. Stéfan
Osusky. President Beneš was firm in protesting that a purely
domestic question — and Germany, Britain and France had all
publicly stated that they regarded the Sudeten problem as being a
domestic question — could not be the subject of outside arbitration.

In face of this opposition the British proposal was modified.
Lord Runciman should be sent to Prague not as an " arbitrator "
but as a " mediator and adviser ", since the Czechs could not
possibly refuse to accept mediation and advice, and the French
Government were now asked to support the proposal by urging its
acceptance in Prague. The new suggestion was debated at length
in the French Cabinet. Bonnet, Pomaret and de Monzie approved
of it ; Reynaud, Mandel and Campinchi expressed grave doubts
as to its wisdom and sought to safeguard the Franco-Czech
Alliance against sabotage from within. To approve the idea of
the Runciman Mission and to give it support in Prague would, it
seemed to them, endanger the primary basis of France's treaty
with Czechoslovakia. Between these alternatives M. Daladier

---

[1] *E.g.* Pertinax in *L'Écho de Paris* and *L'Europe Nouvelle*, and Geneviève Tabouis
in *L'Œuvre*. In this case cf. Pertinax in *L'Europe Nouvelle*, July 30, 1938.

sought the way of compromise. France would agree " in principle " to the sending of Lord Runciman as a mediator and
adviser, but the attention of Lord Halifax was drawn to the
difficulties which might arise as a result of this departure and the
consequent importance which attached to giving the Czechoslovak Government every guarantee that their national sovereignty would not be impaired and that Lord Runciman should
remain strictly within the terms of " mediator and adviser ".
With this compromise solution the British agreed. Forthwith an
official communiqué was issued to the effect that the two Governments, " marking once more their common determination to
pursue their action of appeasement and conciliation, found that
the complete harmony of views established during the visit of the
French Ministers on April 28-9 had been entirely maintained ".

It was an open secret in Paris that some new development
was brewing in the matter of Czechoslovakia. Amid the festivities
and rejoicings which attended the visit of the King and Queen,
amid the plaudits of the crowds, the displays of military might,
the publicly renewed pledges of Anglo-French amity, there was
an under-current of anxiety. Those who were convinced that the
safety and security of France depended upon the maintenance of
that system of alliances built up so laboriously by Briand and
Poincaré and Barthou sought to reassure themselves that the
abandonment of Czechoslovakia — the keystone of this system —
was not in contemplation. They found small comfort from the
fact that, as the days of the Royal visit drew to a close, the
disciples of appeasement in the Government and in public life
became visibly more smug and satisfied.

The festivities reached their height with the great fête at the
Quai d'Orsay. All Paris was there. The great salons and the
lantern-decked gardens of the Foreign Ministry had never seen
a more brilliant gathering, and in the minds of few present could
there have lurked the thought that within two years these same
halls and gardens would be occupied by the forces of the invader.

Rumour had been rife in Paris all day, and the attention of
many was turned upon two tall figures who stood in long and
earnest conversation beneath the flood-lit emerald trees. What
could the British Foreign Secretary have to say at such great
length to Pierre-Étienne Flandin, the inveterate enemy of the
traditional policy of France in Central Europe ? Among those
who watched were Stéfan Osusky and a friend. " Is everything

going well, *M. le Ministre*?" "Yes, quite satisfactory, quite satisfactory, really *quite* satisfactory," replied Osusky with agitated emphasis. "Any new developments expected?" "No, no; nothing new, everything *quite* satisfactory." At this moment Flandin concluded his conversation and passed through the open windows into the salon. He was smiling broadly. The friend turned to speak again to the Czech Minister, but he had gone.[1]

On the same day, July 22, Mr. Chamberlain in London had had a very long talk with the German Ambassador, Herr von Dirksen; a talk so long that attention to its length was drawn in *The Times* of the following day. The Ambassador, it was believed, had indicated the seriousness of the Sudeten situation, saying that, if the Prague Government did not accept the expanded terms of the Karlsbad Programme, it would be impossible for Henlein to restrain his followers. Bloodshed would follow and Germany would be forced to intervene. He urged a solution on the lines of a Four-Power Conference already adumbrated by Henderson. Mr. Chamberlain talked of a German guarantee of non-aggression.[2]

Such was the position when Lord Halifax returned to London. Discussions continued throughout the week-end and the decision was finally taken to evade the issue of a Four-Power Conference by despatching Lord Runciman to Prague with the terms of reference agreed upon in Paris.[3] Mr. Newton, who had already reported to President Beneš the substance of von Dirksen's conversation with the Prime Minister, was now instructed (July 25) to inform him of the subsequent British action which would be announced in both Houses of Parliament on the following day.[4]

The description of the circumstances which surrounded the despatch of Lord Runciman and his Mission to Prague which Mr. Chamberlain gave to the House of Commons, on the eve of the adjournment of Parliament for the summer vacation, was as remarkable an example of prevarication as that Chamber can ever have heard. The British Government, said the Prime Minister, "*in response to a request from the Government of Czecho-slovakia*", had agreed to propose that a person with the necessary qualifications should investigate the Sudeten problem on the

---

[1] Werth, p. 189.   [2] *The Times*, July 23, 1938.
[3] At this time a proposal was made that the French should send an envoy of their own in a position analogous to that of Lord Runciman, but this was rejected by M. Daladier (Bonnet, I, p. 181).
[4] *House of Commons Debates*, July 26, coll. 2955-60.

spot, and should endeavour, if necessary, to suggest means for bringing the negotiations then in progress between the *Sudeten-deutsche Partei* and the Czech Government to a successful conclusion. The choice of the Government had fallen on Lord Runciman, who would function " not in any sense as an arbitrator but as an investigator and mediator ". He would " of course, be independent of His Majesty's Government — in fact he would be independent of all governments. He would act only in his personal capacity."

Mr. Chamberlain continued : " With regard to the *rumour that we are hustling the Czech Government, there is no truth in it.* Indeed the very opposite is the truth. Our anxiety has been rather that the Czech Government should not be too hasty in dealing with a situation of such delicacy." The Prime Minister concluded with the expression of his belief that " throughout the Continent there is a relaxation of that sense of tension which six months ago was present ".

There were three outstanding statements in Mr. Chamberlain's announcement which constituted grave divergences from the facts. First, there had been no request from Prague for the offices of any individual, whether in the role of arbitrator, mediator or investigator ; [1] and secondly, the British Government, though doubtless with the best of intentions, had not ceased to " hustle the Czechs " since the initial Anglo-French *démarche* of May 7. The crisis of May 21 had placed Mr. Chamberlain in a stronger position *vis-à-vis* Prague, since he could, and did, now say that, as Britain had stood by Czechoslovakia in one crisis, Czechoslovakia must reciprocate by making terms with the Sudeten Germans before another developed. [2] In the third place, the *détente* in the European situation, to which Mr. Chamberlain so optimistically referred, was purely fictional in character, since at the very hour that he spoke the Foreign Office and War Office were possessed of accurate reports on the feverish preparation afoot in Germany for the mobilization of her military reserves, her sources of man-power in labour, and her civil strength. When

[1] Even so impartial a chronicler as the editor of the annual volume of *Documents on International Affairs*, published by the Royal Institute of International Affairs, describes this statement as " presumably a diplomatic fiction intended to avoid the appearance of foreign interference in Czechoslovak internal affairs " (*Documents on International Affairs*, 1938 (London and New York), vol. ii, p. 148).

[2] " The dramatic week-end of May 21 has left the ball at Chamberlain's feet," commented Ferdinand Kuhn in the *New York Times* of August 3 ; " it is still possible for him to lose the game for the Czechoslovak Republic."

a State with Germany's past record is thus energetically engaged, the tension in Europe can scarcely be described as being in a state of relaxation.

The conception of mediation between the Prague Government and the *Sudetendeutsche Partei* was not in itself a bad one, since it was justifiable to use all legitimate means of preventing war. Criticism may, however, justly be made of the method by which the Czechoslovak Government were forced willy-nilly to accept it, and also of the composition of the Runciman Mission itself. No member of the Mission had background or experience of either Central European politics or minority problems. Nor was the personality of Lord Runciman, with its nineteenth-century liberalism and its general lack of imagination, the ideal one for the leader of so delicate an expedition.

Moreover, the attempt of the Prime Minister to disclaim responsibility for Lord Runciman's Mission deceived no one, more especially since a senior member of the Foreign Office, Mr. Frank Ashton-Gwatkin, was attached to the staff of the Mission. There was not a responsible man in Europe who did not believe that the Runciman Mission carried the full weight and authority of the British Government, and in many quarters there was general belief that the French Government were equally in support of this new venture.

The situation at the close of July could not but have afforded satisfaction to Adolf Hitler. His military preparations and his plans for deception were proceeding quite admirably. He had, it is true, failed in his original objective of lifting the Sudeten problem out of the sphere of Czech domestic politics into that of Four-Power discussions, to the exclusion of Russia and Czechoslovakia, but, by a judicious amalgam of blackmail and cajolery, he had succeeded — perhaps more fruitfully — in bringing Britain and France into the open as publicly intervening in the dispute. Both countries were inevitably and vitally concerned for the success of the Runciman Mission and would urge upon the Czechoslovak Government the granting of those liberal concessions which Germany, through the *Sudetendeutsche Partei*, had demanded. The Führer was careful, however, in his relations with London and Paris to exacerbate any ill-feeling which might have been caused on this issue by laying the full burden of responsibility on Britain,[1]

---

[1] When officially informed of the British Government's intention to send Lord Runciman to Prague, Ribbentrop replied that the Government of the Reich must

but, for all that, the Western Powers had been manœuvred, in the eyes of the world, into the position of accomplices in the Führer's plans. They were doing Hitler's work for him and there was no shadow of doubt in Berlin as to the nature of Lord Runciman's instructions.[1] Meanwhile the military preparations for placing Germany *en état de guerre* were proceeding apace, though the Führer was adhering more and more to the opinion that in the final issue the Western Powers would not fight for Czechoslovakia.

(iii)

" If the nation is justified in packing up for its holidays with a free heart it is not only because of Lord Runciman's devoted pilgrimage of peace to a cockpit of discords but on broader and more guarded grounds. The pilgrimage is the original and hardy idea of the Prime Minister himself." With this note of gay optimism Mr. Garvin waved his readers off on their summer vacations, confident in the ultimate triumph of what he believed to be right.[2] Neither his optimism as to the future nor his approbation of the Runciman Mission was unanimously endorsed.

On a sultry August day two groups waited under the glass roof of the Wilson Station at Prague for the arrival of the Paris express. One of these groups comprised the " welcoming committee " of the Czechoslovak Government, together with Dr. Smutny, the President's *chef de Cabinet*, the Lord Mayor of Prague and the British Minister, Mr. Basil Newton ; the second was composed of representatives of the Czechoslovak and foreign press. At the last moment a deputation of the *Sudetendeutsche Partei* arrived in a great hurry and waited aloof from the others, eyed with suspicion by both. The train drew slowly into the station ; a mountain of luggage was disgorged ; a number of gentlemen and one lady descended from a *wagon-lit* with the consciously superior air of Britons on foreign soil ; and, finally, a stooping, bald-headed man with a clean-shaven, beak-nosed face

reserve their attitude towards the Mission " and regard it as one of purely British concern ".

[1] On August 3 the official organ of the German Foreign Ministry, the *Deutsche Diplomatische-politische Korrespondenz*, defined the task of the Runciman Mission as being " to expose Czech subterfuges, and to establish the facts and conditions in their true character, in order, perhaps, to draw appropriate conclusions ".

[2] *The Observer*, July 31, 1938.

WHAT'S CZECHOSLOVAKIA TO ME, ANYWAY?

JULY 18, 1938

By courtesy of Mr. David Low and the " Evening Standard"

emerged, carrying a brief-case. The Runciman Mission had arrived.[1]

Lord Runciman shook hands warmly with the two groups of " greeters ", and, passing the representatives of the press with scarcely a nod of salutation, walked quickly to the waiting automobile. " The hangman with his little bag came creeping through the gloom ", quoted one journalist to another as they left the station.[2]

Installed at the Hotel Alcron, Lord Runciman received the press, and somewhat shocked them by going out of his way to thank the representatives of the *Sudetendeutsche Partei* for welcoming him at the station. He hoped, he said, to be " the friend of all and the enemy of none ", and expressed the hope that, when the troubles which he had come to investigate had been explored, " we shall get to the bottom of some of them, especially if we set to work in a spirit of good-will and the exercise of patience ".[3]

The Mission began its labours on August 4 with the usual ceremonial calls. It then set about digesting the mass of documentary evidence in the case, and from this stage proceeded to negotiation by means of personal interviews. All concerned worked hard and unsparingly with that tense devotion to detail and duty which is characteristic of British Civil Servants.

To many observers in Prague that summer — of whom I was one — it seemed, however, that the Mission was functioning in a vacuum of unreality. Lord Runciman had come to mediate between the Government of Czechoslovakia and the *S.d.P.* of Konrad Henlein. But Henlein could not negotiate. He was not a

[1] Lord Runciman's Mission, in addition to himself, consisted of Mr. Frank Ashton-Gwatkin, head of the Economic Section of the Foreign Office ; Mr. Robert Stopford, formerly Secretary of the Simon Commission on Indian Constitutional Reforms and of the " Standstill Committee " on Germany's foreign debts ; and a Member of Parliament, Mr. Geoffrey Peto, who had been Lord Runciman's Parliamentary Private Secretary in the House of Commons from 1931 to 1935. They were assisted by Mr. Ian Henderson, the British Consul at Reichenberg in the Sudetenland, and also by a young Englishman, Mr. David Stephens, a Treasury clerk who had made a considerable study of German minorities in Central Europe in the course of extensive bicycling tours carried on during his holidays.

[2] *Ballad of Reading Gaol*, by Oscar Wilde, Part III. Mr. Gedye's quotation is slightly at fault ; the correct text is : " The hangman, with his little bag, went shuffling through the gloom ".

[3] *Betrayal in Central Europe*, by G. E. R. Gedye (New York, 1939), pp. 383, 423. William Shirer, who was also among the waiting journalists at the Wilson Station, expressed himself succinctly : " Runciman's whole Mission smells ", he recorded in his diary that evening (*Berlin Diary* (New York, 1941), p. 121).

free agent. He was operating, not very skilfully but very patently, under orders from Berlin. He could not even give answers to the questions which members of the Mission put to him without an interval for " consideration and consultation ", which meant that he had to refer to his masters before replying. His lieutenants, Kundt, Frank and Sebekovsky, were more skilful masters of procrastination, but it was evident from the first that the *S.d.P.* had said its last word in the Karlsbad Programme and the Memorandum of June 8, and would retract nothing from the position therein defined. Behind them stood the German Reich, rapidly girding its loins for battle, equally intractable and determined that the issue should be settled in accordance with its wishes.

On the other hand was the Czechoslovak Government, sensible of the fact that the minority situation within the Republic was imperfect and that previous delays to remedy it must now be paid for by reasonable reforms, but equally determined to fight rather than surrender to the demands of the *S.d.P.*, which would entail the establishment of a Nazi *imperium in imperio*. Once this was effected, the autonomous Sudetenland would either secede to the Reich or remain as a destructive factor within the Czech State. In either case Czechoslovakia would have lost her national defences and her " Little Maginot Line " and would lie naked and exposed to German caprice. Moreover, it must be remembered that the demands of the *S.d.P.* included the abandonment of the alliances of Czechoslovakia with France and with Russia. No State could thus voluntarily invite self-destruction, and, since it was clearly the emasculation of the Czechoslovak State at which Hitler and Henlein were aiming, no concession by the Prague Government, short of complete surrender, could prove acceptable to them. The gulf between the two parties was therefore unbridgeable and the Runciman Mission was doomed to failure before it began its work. Its activities only served to pejorate still further a situation already critical ; to render more facile the circumstances which Hitler required for his final coup.

Among the foreign observers in Prague there was a steadily increasing anxiety, a sense of suspicion and of imminent and impending tragedy. Again and again reference was made to the newspaper reports of the fateful luncheon at Lady Astor's and of the refusal of Mr. Chamberlain to " confirm or deny " them in the

House of Commons. Did this really represent British policy? That was the question incessantly asked of the British by the Czechs, and the French and Americans also. It was debated among the British themselves. To a man the Americans believed it was indeed the intention of the British to " sell the Czechs down the river ", and the British, while denying it, became uncomfortably aware of the uncertainty of their denials.

But this uncertainty was not reflected in Czech official circles. Whether one talked with President Beneš, or with the Premier, Dr. Hodža, or with Dr. Krofta, the Foreign Minister, or with General Syrový, Inspector-General of the Army ; in the Hradschin or in the Czernin Palace or in the offices of the General Staff, the impression was the same : a definite willingness to make all reasonable concessions, a grim determination to fight rather than accept voluntary dismemberment.

Though the President regarded as polite blackmail the manner in which he had been asked to receive Lord Runciman and his Mission, he also entertained the hope that this new departure on the part of the British from their traditional policy of refusing to be directly concerned in Central Europe betokened a more definite participation in Danubian affairs. If this were so, the incursion of Lord Runciman might have its compensations, and Dr. Beneš retained his belief that Britain and France would not abandon the fundamental position which they had taken up in London on April 28 — namely, that Czechoslovakia should give all possible satisfaction to the demands of her German citizens " within the framework of the Constitution ".

There was not, however, the same undivided opinion in Czechoslovakia as to the value and desirability of the Russian guarantees, though these were constantly reaffirmed throughout the summer. Within the Army and in certain of the political parties, notably the Agrarians, there was a suspicion of the warmth and sincerity of these Russian promises ; a fear, not that Russia would abandon Czechoslovakia but that, having once encompassed her in a bear-hug, she would never let her go. Many of the older general officers of the Czech army had fought against the Bolsheviks in 1918 and had no love for them. One of these was General Jan Syrový, Inspector-General of the Army, who had lost an eye during the great anabasis of the Czech Legions across Siberia. " We shall fight the Germans," he said to me, " either alone, or with you and the French, but we don't want the Russians in here. We should never get them out." And Dr. Hodža, himself a leader of the Agrarian Party, though less outspoken, was also apprehensive of what the ultimate results of Russian intervention on behalf of Czechoslovakia would be.

There were those, also, who recalled that, in the past, there had been voices in Russia which had warmly espoused the cause of the Sudeten Germans and had even denied that Czechoslovakia existed as a nation.[1] It was difficult for those with long memories to adjust themselves to the rapid reversals of policy of which the Soviet Union is capable, and they feared that the friendship of to-day might wither on the morrow.

By the middle of August the Runciman Mission had achieved exactly nothing. Lord Runciman had called briefly on President Beneš and had not seen Henlein. He had, however, spent two successive week-ends at the castles of members of the Kinsky family, Count Zdenko and Count Ulrich, who guarded the borders of their estates with Henleinist Storm Troopers and who brought him into contact both with leaders of the *Sudetendeutsche Partei* and with members of the former Austrian aristocracy, who were equally antagonistic to the Prague Government. Members of the Mission had conferred with representatives of both the disputant parties and had expressed surprise when informed that the *Sudetendeutsche Partei* was not the only German party in the Sudetenland but that there were four others, which also constituted a not entirely negligible political factor in that area and in no way shared the views of their more " activist " compatriots.[2]

---

[1] At the Third Congress of the Comintern at Moscow in June 1923, M. Manuilsky, the Ukrainian leader who, twenty-three years later, was to represent his country at the General Assembly of the United Nations, had declared : " *Il n'y a pas de nation tchécoslovaque : la Tchécoslovaquie a 13 million ½ habitants, dont* 44% (6,000,000) *sont Tchèques. Elle s'est annexé des régions d'industries textile, minière et verrière dont la population exclusivement allemande est de 3,700,000 habitants.*"

The Congress had thereupon adopted the following resolution :

(1) *Le Congrès constate qu'il n'y a pas une nation tchécoslovaque : l'État tchécoslovaque, outre la nationalité tchèque, comprend des Slovaques, des Allemands, des Hongrois, des Ukrainiens et des Polonais.*

(2) *Le Congrès estime nécessaire que le parti communiste de Tchécoslovaquie, en ce qui concerne ces minorités nationales, proclame et mette en pratique le droit des peuples à disposer d'eux-mêmes, jusque et y compris celui de se séparer.*

(See *La Question nationale et coloniale* — the official report of the committee on this subject to the Third Congress of the Third International — (Paris, 1924), pp. 211 and 432.)

[2] These four parties were the German Social Democratic Party — the most influential — the German Agrarian Party, the German Christian Socialist Party and the German Small-traders Party. The information does not appear to have made

HIGH STAKES

DAREDEVIL RUNCIMAN (*to Messrs. Hodža, Henlein and Hitler*). " Mind if I take a hand, boys? "

AUGUST 10, 1938

In mid-August, however, two things occurred which marked the beginning of that steady process of deterioration which continued, without halt or intermission, till the climax six weeks later. On August 15, in view of the fact that the National Minorities Statute had completely failed to meet the demands of Hitler, the Czechoslovak Government produced " Plan No. 2 ", which the *Sudetendeutsche Partei* summarily rejected two days later. On the same day orders were issued in Germany for large-scale military manœuvres with troop concentrations in Saxony and Silesia.[1]

The effect upon London of this concatenation of events was one of alarm and despondency. Mr. Chamberlain's tight-rope act was making greater demands in agility and equilibrium than the Prime Minister could readily supply. It was now clear that Germany meant business in every sense of the word, that the tempo of events in Czechoslovakia would be geared to the period of the Congress of the Nazi Party, which was to open at Nuremberg on September 5, and that the high point of danger in that period would be the Führer's speech on the night of September 12. Less than a month, therefore, remained in which to find a solution to the Sudeten problem, a solution which would at the same time satisfy Czechoslovakia and also prevent Germany from going to war, thereby precipitating a general European conflict.

As a result of this discovery there followed a curious compromise in British policy. An elucidation of Mr. Chamberlain's obscurantism of March 24 was now becoming imperative. That vague contingency which " might include Czechoslovakia " was looming up before him and it was perilously possible that he might have to put his name to that " blank cheque " to France which he had originally refused. Yet the Prime Minister did not wish to alarm the country, which was still peacefully enjoying its summer holidays, reassured by his optimistic statement in the House of Commons on July 26.[2] Whatever warnings were conveyed to

much impression, since throughout his Report Lord Runciman refers to the *Sudetendeutsche Partei* as the sole representative of the Sudeten German Minority, making no mention even of the Social Democrats.

[1] *International Military Tribunal Document*, 388–PS, item 16.

[2] In France also the holiday season was not disturbed by any undue perturbation. "Nothing much is likely to happen while Runciman is in Prague : ' *qu'ils se débrouillent* ' was the general attitude " (Werth, p. 191), and on August 17 M. Léon Blum was writing in the *Populaire* : " French opinion remains calm, serious and perfectly self-assured. The Government shows neither nervousness, emotion nor precipitation. In my view this is right in all respects."

Germany, therefore, must not be repeated in public. At the same time it was absolutely necessary that the Czechs should make every concession, possible or impossible, to prevent the final cataclysm.

Accordingly Lord Runciman was encouraged, and Mr. Newton was instructed, to press forward along these lines in Prague, while Mr. Chamberlain and Lord Halifax made a direct appeal to the Führer. In a personal message conveyed by the British Ambassador through the Reichskanzlei, and not through the German Foreign Ministry, the Prime Minister and the Foreign Secretary drew Hitler's attention to the inevitable apprehension which the abnormal German military preparations had caused abroad. Such preparations could not fail to be interpreted as a threat of force to Czechoslovakia, where they might provoke the taking of counter-measures and would certainly jeopardize the chances of Lord Runciman's success in his efforts at mediation.

To this approach the Führer did not deign to reply directly. Its sole effect was to provoke a protest from Ribbentrop at its having been sent through the Chancellery and not through him. The German Foreign Minister refused to discuss any internal measures which the Reich Government might see fit to take, and expressed the opinion that " the British efforts in Prague had only served to strengthen Czech intransigence ".[1]

In face of this attitude the British Inner Cabinet, composed of Mr. Chamberlain, Lord Halifax, Sir Samuel Hoare and Sir John Simon, took decisions on August 24 which involved three important steps. It was agreed to utilize the occasion of a speech by Sir John Simon at Lanark on August 27 to restate publicly the Prime Minister's unspecific warning of March 24,[2] and that this should be followed up by a much stronger message to be delivered by Sir Nevile Henderson to the Nazi leaders at Nuremberg on the eve of the Conference, to the effect that, if Germany committed an act of aggression against Czechoslovakia and France went to the aid of her ally, Britain would inevitably be drawn into the war in support of France.[3] It was also agreed to ask the French

---

[1] Mr. Chamberlain's statement in the House of Commons, September 28, 1938, and Henderson, pp. 146-7.

[2] See above, p. 39. For the text of Sir John Simon's speech, see *The Times*, August 29, 1938.

[3] Sir Nevile Henderson was recalled to London on August 28 to receive his instructions. He returned to Berlin on August 31. Mr. Newton, the British Minister at Prague, was also recalled to London at this period, for consultation.

Government to repeat once more their intention to stand by their treaty obligation to the Czechs. At the same time the British Ambassador was instructed secretly to begin negotiations for the establishment of a " personal contact " between the Prime Minister and the Führer.[1]

Meanwhile in Paris the attitude of the French Government had been one of " wait and see ". They had contented themselves with informing the British that the only settlement acceptable to France would be one within the existing frontiers of Czechoslovakia and compatible with her full and continued sovereignty over all her territory. In face of the German mobilization the Government had shown neither nervousness, emotion nor precipitation. Indeed, they did nothing at all. Since Britain had assumed the initiative in the Anglo-French relations with Czechoslovakia it was for her to continue to exercise it, and, taking their line from M. Bonnet, the Government refused to pursue any action unless assured in advance of British support. It is true they had been told by the Soviet Ambassador that, on August 22, Moscow had informed the German Government that Russia would honour her pledges to Czechoslovakia, but these pledges only became operative after France had honoured her own ; it was decided to await the statement of British policy which they were informed was imminent.

The promised statement was, in effect, Sir John Simon's repetition at Lanark on August 27 of Mr. Chamberlain's declaration of March 24 that, if war broke out, " it would be quite impossible to say where it would end and what Governments would become involved ". " That declaration holds good to-day," said Sir John. " There is nothing to add or to vary in its contents." This, the French thought, was fairly satisfactory, though not quite tough enough, and they might not have taken any definite action even then had it not been for a sudden appearance, two days later, of the Führer himself, on the bridge between Kehl and Strasburg, accompanied by the Chief of Staff of the *Wehrmacht*, General Keitel, the Commander-in-Chief of the Army, General von Brauchitsch, and six other high-ranking general officers.

This event did shock the French Government out of their apparent lethargy ; and orders were hastily issued for the manning of the Maginot Line — an operation which was not, however, completed till September 5 — and M. Bonnet reaffirmed, in

[1] Henderson, p. 147.

answer to British " needling ", at a speech at Pointe de Grave on September 4, that " in all cases France will remain faithful to the pacts and treaties which she has concluded ". But having done this the Government sat back and awaited further developments from Britain and from the Nuremberg Congress.

In the meantime the situation in Czechoslovakia had gone from bad to worse. Under the stimulus of urgent messages from London, and of the rejection of " Plan No. 2 " by the *S.d.P.*, Lord Runciman summoned Henlein to meet him for the first time at Schloss Rotenhaus, the home of Prince Max Egon von Hohenlöhe-Langenburg, on August 18. The interview was unsatisfactory in that Henlein had already informed Lord Runciman, through Ernst Kundt, that he considered further negotiations impracticable since the Prague Government would not accept the Karlsbad Programme *in toto*. In the discussion which followed, Henlein showed himself manifestly unwilling to talk openly on any point diverging from his " set piece " without further " discussion or consultation ".[1]

After further conferences between Mr. Ashton-Gwatkin and Dr. Hodža in Prague, and with Henlein again at Marienbad, there emerged the blue-print of a further offer by the Czech Government, " Plan No. 3 ", with which Mr. Ashton-Gwatkin flew to London on August 24. He was back two days later. The details embodying further concessions were worked out with President Beneš, and on August 28 Lord Runciman, who was this time spending the week-end with Prince Clery in Bohemia, presented " Plan No. 3 " to Henlein, with the advice that he seek the direct opinion of the Führer in person.

Such a departure may have been considered unusual for a " private individual " whose mission was to mediate between two groups of Czechoslovak citizens, but these were unusual circumstances, and on the whole Lord Runciman's action was understandable. It was now completely apparent to all that Henlein and his followers were merely the puppets of Berlin, and, though it may be argued that, on discovering this fact, Lord Runciman

[1] According to Karl Hermann Frank, however, members of Lord Runciman's Mission expressed to Prince Hohenlohe views which indicated a partiality for the demands of the *S.d.P.* The Prince passed on this information to the Party Executive, who, in turn, informed the German Minister. " These reports ", said Frank, " represented one of the most valuable political services rendered to the German Reich. They provided Hitler with invaluable information, indispensable for the carrying-out of his international policy ; he arrived at the conferences with the British with a strong card in his hand " (*International Military Tribunal Document*, 3061–PS).

should have thrown up his assignment and come home, it was equally inconceivable that he would do so. Henlein would have referred the Prague proposals to Berlin in any case and in bidding him do so Lord Runciman was but recognizing the existing and inevitable situation.

But the effect of this direct approach was most unfavourable. Hitler interpreted it as a sign of weakness and decided to utilize it as the first stage of the " pretext " envisaged in " Operation Green ". The time for direct action had come and the occasion of his speech to the Party Congress was most suitable. Delaying tactics must be employed therefore until September 12, but in the meantime the situation in the Sudetenland must be allowed to deteriorate.

After two separate flights to Berchtesgaden, therefore, Henlein returned on September 2 with the rejection of " Plan No. 3 ", but also with Hitler's new and secret instructions. He had decided to take the settlement of the Sudeten German problem into his own hands, the Führer had told Henlein, since the British, in sending Lord Runciman to Prague, had turned it into an international affair. The *Sudetendeutsche Partei* must, therefore, continue the negotiations with the Government in order to give the impression that the final crisis was not imminent. At the appointed time Hitler would give his further instructions, but, in the meantime, not even the negotiating committee of the *Sudetendeutsche Partei* must suspect that the continued conversations with the President, the Prime Minister and Lord Runciman were not *bona fide*.[1]

In conformity with these orders Henlein announced on his return that, although " Plan No. 3 " was unacceptable, he and his representatives were still prepared to continue the search for a formula of settlement, although, he added, " the eight points of the Karlsbad Programme are a minimum ". Despite this further evidence of intransigence, Lord Runciman declared that he had " not lost all hope " and proceeded to urge upon President Beneš the necessity of making further and still greater concessions to the views of the *Sudetendeutsche Partei*.

It was now that Dr. Beneš put forward his last and greatest effort to reach a compromise. He realized — none better — that, in making concession after concession piecemeal to the demands of Henlein and of the Reich, he had weakened his position by giving

---

[1] Henlein did, in fact, inform Frank of his conversation with Hitler.

the impression that the bottom of the barrel had not yet been reached. However, he calculated, as against this, that in going to the limit in deference to the urging of Britain and France he would place his country in an unassailable moral position, a position which those who had urged these concessions upon him could not fail to respect and support. He realized that, to the majority of Englishmen, Czechoslovakia represented no vital interest, but he had seen Mr. Chamberlain's policy pass from a cold disdain of collective security to an active participation in the internal affairs of Czechoslovakia, and he believed that such an interest could not be wholly bad. He had recognized the added difficulties which France had now to face in coming to the military assistance of the Czechs by reason of the new German fortifications ; but had not France repeatedly reaffirmed her pledges to Czechoslovakia, despite these new difficulties ? And was not the continued existence of an independent Czechoslovakia essential to the security of France ? He was aware of the dissension within his own country regarding Russian assistance, but, in any event, the Russian guarantees did exist and Moscow had very recently reaffirmed them in Prague and Paris and in Berlin.

The sacrifices which Dr. Beneš was being called upon to make were growing greater and heavier, the stakes with which he was playing were getting higher and more risky. If Mr. Chamberlain and M. Daladier had to consider the public opinion of their countries, Dr. Beneš could not afford to ignore that of his own. He would be criticized abroad — he was indeed already being criticized — for not having made the final concession earlier, but Czechoslovakia was a democracy — just as Britain and France were democracies — and her leader could not outrun the mandate of the people. For this reason the President had himself handled the latter phases of the negotiations with the *Sudetendeutsche Partei* and the conversations with Lord Runciman. He had taken the responsibility on his own shoulders, and it was on his authority that the terms of the Second and Third Plans had not been made public, lest the degree of concession which they contained should provoke an outcry of protest from the Czech population.

Nor, indeed, was Dr. Beneš blind to the fact that imperfections did exist in the structure of the Czechoslovak State, and that it fell short of that cantonal organization on the Swiss model which President Masaryk and he had in 1919 told the Peace Conference of Paris it was their ambition to attain. Left to himself Beneš would have made more rapid progress towards the attainment of this ideal, and, since his election to the Presidency in 1935, he had used all his influence and authority to persuade successive Governments to make further progress. But Czechoslovakia had both the benefits and the drawbacks of a democratic form of government. Her political parties were rigid and bureaucratic in nature, and it was exceedingly difficult to obtain their common approval for any agreed formula. Moreover, in almost every case, the leadership of the parties was in the hands of men who had grown old and weary on the battlefield of the pre-war Austrian Parliament or in the early struggles of the Republic; men who lacked that vision and political sagacity which were so necessary in these critical days and which the President himself possessed to so remarkable a degree. The party leaders, unimaginative and inelastic, could not or would not follow the enlightened lead of Dr. Beneš, and it was for this reason that the inter-party negotiation which had preceded agreement on the National Minorities Statute had lasted for almost a year. The President, on his own authority, had now gone considerably further than the Statute in his subsequent negotiations, feeling that he must make every possible concession, in the same spirit in which Serbia, in July 1914, had accepted all but the most humiliating terms of the Austro-Hungarian ultimatum. Would not the Czechs now have nearly the whole world on their side, as opinion had everywhere then rallied to the Serbs?

It was with this end in mind that President Beneš prepared to make the ultimate sacrifice in the vain search for a formula which should both satisfy the Henleinists and yet remain " within the framework of the Constitution ". He was under no illusions as to the prospects of success; he knew that the concessions which he was about to make would spell defeat and not victory to the Sudeten leaders, who had never desired or expected an agreement by negotiation; he realized that what he was about to do might precipitate the final catastrophe, since the present proposals would certainly be rejected and he could do no more than offer all. Nevertheless for this gambit he determined upon a stratagem of audacity and surprise.

Summoned to the Hradschin Palace on September 4, the *Sudetendeutsche Partei* leaders, Kundt and Sebekovsky, were received by President Beneš with bland calmness. Without preliminaries he pushed a blank sheet of paper towards them, saying: " Please write your party's full demands for the German minority. I promise you in advance to grant them immediately."

Kundt was thunderstruck. He stared incredulously at the President. Sebekovsky sat in angry, suspicious silence.

" Go on ; I mean it. Write ! " said the President.

The Sudeten leaders, still fearing a trap, were reluctant to commit themselves in holograph. They shifted uncomfortably in their chairs. This was something very different from what they had expected from their interview. They had been prepared for intransigence and a lecture from the little doctor on loyalty to the State, but this was most unexpected. The President was surrendering but he was conducting the affair as if he, not they, were the victor.

" Very well ; if you won't write it down, I will," said the President. " You tell me what to say," and drawing the blank sheet of paper to him, he unscrewed his fountain pen and sat waiting. So at the dictation of the leaders of the Sudeten German Party, the President of the Czechoslovak Republic wrote down what came ultimately to be "Plan No. 4", and he signed the copy which he gave to Kundt and Sebekovsky.[1]

With the exception of refusing to accept the demand that Czechoslovakia should reorientate her foreign policy, the Fourth Plan did indeed embody almost all the Eight Points of the Karlsbad Programme, including that which would establish for one section of the population a totalitarian system within a democratic Czechoslovak Republic ; and in handing it to Lord Runciman, President Beneš made it abundantly clear in an accompanying Note that these last concessions had been made by him and his Government under the direct pressure of the British and French diplomatic representatives. He expressed the view that it was very unlikely — " because of the well-known plans of the Berlin Government and the aims of Henlein and his Party " — that even this proposal would be accepted by the Germans.[2]

Lord Runciman could not deny these facts. In his view the Fourth Plan not only embodied almost all the Karlsbad Eight

[1] Cf. G. E. R. Gedye's interview with President Beneš published in the *Daily Herald*, October 8, 1945, and confirmed to me by President Beneš in July 1946.

[2] The full text of the Fourth Plan was not published in 1938, though a summary appeared in the *Prager Presse* of September 10, 1938. In 1942, however, the Czechoslovak Government-in-Exile communicated the text to the Royal Institute of International Affairs, who included it in *Documents on International Affairs*, 1938 (Oxford, 1943), vol. ii, pp. 178-84.

Points, but " with a little clarification and extension could have been made to cover them in their entirety ". But, as the President had so truly written, " even this plan is very unlikely to be accepted by the Germans ". The unconditional concession by the Czechoslovak Government of their most extreme demands created consternation in the Sudeten camp, where it completely dislocated the carefully prepared schedule for a campaign of terror and agitation which would, by September 12, have created the degree of tension desired for Hitler's speech at Nuremberg.

" My God, they have given us everything ! " was the horrified exclamation of Karl Frank, the Deputy Leader of the *Sudetendeutsche Partei*, when the Fourth Plan had been rapidly read in party conclave on September 5. The details were telephoned to Henlein at Asch, who found them so little to his liking that, without waiting for the text, he departed next morning to attend the Nuremberg Congress as Hitler's guest. Frank, too, flew to Germany and found in Berlin as widespread consternation at the Czech surrender as he had left at home. The order went forth for the revolt of all Germans in Czechoslovakia at the first excuse. Promptly there occurred an incident at Morawska-Ostrava on the morning of September 7, where, in the course of a street demonstration, a *S.d.P.* Deputy was alleged to have been struck by the riding-whip of a Czech mounted policeman. This was sufficient excuse for the general rupture of the negotiations with the Czech Government. The Party had no longer time for talking ; action was now in order and they flung themselves whole-heartedly into the work of fomenting civil disturbance in the Sudetenland.[1] Henlein, returning to Asch for a flying visit on September 7, brought with him the Führer's final instructions and returned at once to Germany to organize the Sudeten German Legion, of which, ten days later, he was appointed the Commander.

And so the negotiations, which had opened on June 23, closed with the *Sudetendeutsche Partei* flying in dismay from the fruits of their own victory — that victory in which they had been so warmly assisted by Lord Runciman and the Governments of Britain and France. They had left the field to President Beneš, who had given them their victory in the certainty that they would reject it, and whose reward had been to read in *The Times*

---

[1] It is of interest to note that as early as August 26 instructions had been issued to members of the *Sudetendeutsche Partei* " to forgo no longer the right of self-defence " but to resist attacks by " Marxist terrorists ".

of September 7 a proposal for further sacrifices by Czechoslovakia
on a scale which the *Sudetendeutsche Partei* themselves had never yet
put forward — namely, the cession of territory to Germany; and
they had left behind them the Runciman Mission regarding in
some dismay the results of its handiwork.

There was little more for the Mission to do, and for nearly a
week they rested from their labours and awaited their leader's
decision to return to London. On Saturday, September 10, came
Göring's venomous diatribe from Nuremberg and President
Beneš's calm, dignified broadcast to the nation describing the
principles and purpose of the Government's last offer. Lord
Runciman also made a public appearance that week-end, when
he spoke a few words from the steps of Count Czernin's Schloss
Petersburg to a demonstration of five thousand of Henlein's
followers, including several hundred Storm Troopers in uniform.

But it was for September 12 that all Czechoslovakia, and all
the world, was waiting. On that day Hitler was to speak to his
assembled legions at Nuremberg and it was fully believed in
Prague, as elsewhere, that the speech might well determine the
issue of peace or war. The listening Czechs carried their gas-
masks with them, for who could tell whether, within an hour of
the beginning of the speech, the first German bomber would not
be overhead ? [1]

The speech did not bring war, however ; it dripped venom ;
it abounded in the grossest insults to President Beneš and his
countrymen — who can forget the naked hatred in Hitler's voice
as he articulated the words " *Ich spreche von der Tchechoslovakei* " ?
But it did not bring war and it did not even demand a plebiscite.
To the *Sudetendeutsche Partei*, however, it brought the signal for
revolt, and revolt they did in earnest, so that for two days there
was hand-to-hand fighting in the Sudetenland. By September 15
the rising had been quelled, and Lord Runciman and his Mission,
having made — in Mr. Ashton-Gwatkin's odyssey to Asch and
Eger on the night of September 13-14 — a last and fruitless
effort to persuade Henlein to reopen negotiations, returned to
England unwept in Prague.[2]

[1] Gedye, p. 429.
[2] Konrad Henlein fled to Germany on September 16 and returned in October
after the Munich Agreement had been signed, as Reich Commissar for the Sudeten
Territory, a position which he continued to occupy for the next seven years. He was
arrested by the Czech Resistance Movement in May 1945 and later committed
suicide.

CHAPTER FOUR

THE DRAMA OF MUNICH

(i)

CURTAIN-RAISER AT NUREMBERG

THE approach of the Nazi Party Congress at Nuremberg darkened the international horizon like a fast-moving tornado. Beneath its threat feverish efforts were made in London and in Paris to stem disaster ; to deflect the path of the Nazi phenomenon in this direction or that ; above all, to guide it away from Britain and France.

Would Hitler order an attack on Prague if the Czechs had not surrendered by the time he addressed the Congress (September 12) ? If so, would Britain and France and Russia stand together ? Could the Czechs be dragooned into giving the Sudeten Germans a blank cheque in the formulation of their future ? Could Germany be deterred by a determined display of force from a final recourse to the arbitrament of war ? These were the questions which assaulted the minds, and even penetrated the dreams, of those who held the reins in London and Paris and Moscow and in the capitals of the smaller countries. And a further question began to drum in the ears of certain national leaders with an ever-increasing beat as event piled upon event : What is there in it for me ?

When the Congress opened on September 5, the ostensible position of the various parties had been made clear. The *Sudeten-deutsche Partei* stood pat upon the Karlsbad Programme ; the Czechoslovak Government, in offering the Fourth Plan, had gone to the limit of concession in meeting this Programme ; Germany, with a considerable part of the *Wehrmacht* already on manœuvres, preserved a sphinx-like official silence as to her intentions, though her press and radio left the world in no doubt as to what these intentions might be ; Britain, with the Fleet about to take up its positions for annual exercises, had assured Germany that she would inevitably be drawn into war should France discharge her treaty obligations to the Czechs, and had urged France to reaffirm these obligations ; France, having manned the Maginot Line, had made such a reaffirmation, albeit in a somewhat lukewarm manner ; the Soviet Union had repeated its assurances in Berlin, London, Paris, and Prague, and had invited Britain and France to join in political discussions and staff talks and in a joint *démarche* to the League of Nations. At a glance it might have been thought that the united front toward Germany, which had been established on May 21, was still in virile being. This, however, was far from true. The façade remained but the structure behind it had crumbled.

The first sign of open appeasement in the ranks of the British press came not from the combines of Lord Beaverbrook and Lord Rothermere, nor from the network of the Lords Camrose and Kemsley, nor even from Printing House Square ; it appeared in a quarter where it might least have been expected, the Left. In the *New Statesman* there appeared, on August 27, an editorial comment to the effect that " the strategical value of the Bohemian frontier should not be made the occasion of a world war ". The fact that such a view should be expressed in a paper whose Liberal-Labour sympathies were supposed to lie with the Czechs could not be ignored in Berlin and Prague, where it encouraged the Nazis and *Sudetendeutsche Partei*, and was equally a source of no little depression to Czech Liberals and Social Democrats.

But this encouragement and this despondency were to be increased very shortly. On September 6 and 7 two newspapers of standing, importance, and influence delivered themselves of similar opinions. " Can Prague still persist in counting 3,200,000 Germans among its loyal subjects ? If so, all will be well. But if not, then the two races which cannot agree to live together within the framework of the centralized Czech State must be separated. In any case, a peaceful solution *must* be found." So wrote Émile Roche, the close collaborator of Caillaux, of Flandin, and of Bonnet, in *La République* on September 6 : and, on the following morning, *The Times* put the thing a little more suavely :

" It might be worth while for the Czechoslovak Government to consider whether they should exclude altogether the project, which has found favour in some quarters, of making Czecho-slovakia a more homogeneous state by the cession of that fringe of alien population who are contiguous to the nation with which they are united by race."

Under pressure from the French Embassy and the Czech

Legation the Foreign Office at once issued a *démenti* to the effect that the editorial views of *The Times* did not represent the policy of His Majesty's Government. But the damage was done. The similarity of the suggestion advocated by *The Times* to the views which Mr. Chamberlain had refused to deny he had expressed at Lady Astor's luncheon was unmistakable. Here were the particular paper in Paris which was known to be the mouthpiece of the French Foreign Minister, and the particular paper in London which every foreigner believed to be inspired by the British Government of the day, both in agreement that the Sudetenland should be ceded to Germany— a view which had so far been advanced by none of the interested parties, not by Hitler, nor Henlein, nor Lord Runciman, and which had been associated in the public mind only with the British Prime Minister. And was it not known that the editor of *The Times*, Mr. Geoffrey Dawson, was a personal friend of Lord Halifax ?

What did it profit that Sir Nevile Henderson should continue to pour out his stream of warnings at Nuremberg to Göring, to Ribbentrop, to Goebbels, to Neurath — to everyone except Hitler [1]— when these recipients of his admonitions could read, in what was widely believed to be a Government-inspired journal, proposals exceeding any that they themselves had so far advanced ? What were the renewed pledges of French loyalty worth when it was known in Berlin that those organs of the press, which admittedly owed their inspiration to the bureau of the Foreign Minister, were openly advocating the abandonment of Czechoslovakia ? Where, indeed, lay the danger of the Soviet threat when it was an open secret that the Russian proposals had been pointedly ignored in London and in Paris ?

The effect on the international barometer was instantaneous. There is no question but that the editorials in *The Times* and *La République* destroyed what slim sliver of hope may have ever existed for the success of the Fourth Plan submitted by the Czechoslovak Government to the leaders of the *Sudetendeutsche Partei* on September 5. The encouragement which these two articles gave

[1] The idea of a warning to Hitler by the Ambassador, which had originally been in the minds of the British Government, had been abandoned on the earnest insistence of Sir Nevile Henderson that, in the first place, the Führer would refuse to receive him, and secondly that, if such a communication were made to Hitler through Ribbentrop, it would inevitably become public and the effect would be so to enrage the Führer as to make an immediate attack on Czechoslovakia unavoidable (Henderson, p. 150.)

to Hitler and to Henlein is equally beyond doubt. How could it
be otherwise ? The sweeping concessions which President Beneš
had made in the Fourth Plan had caused the greatest consternation. The *S.d.P.* no longer had a leg to stand on ; they had
won too soon and too much to justify their continued agitation
against the Prague Government. Here, however, was miracu-
lously presented a pointed invitation to go further and to demand
outright secession.

This public — if unofficial — indication in London and Paris
of a willingness to put further pressure on Prague was as clear an
affirmation as Hitler required of his confident belief that France
would not fight for the Czechs, and, if France did not fight,
neither would Russia nor Britain. Accordingly, on September 9
he gave the order for " Operation Green " to begin on September
30 and authorized the Sudeten revolt of September 13-15, while
treating with a cynical contempt the warnings conveyed by M.
Bonnet and General Gamelin to the German Ambassador in
Paris on September 8 and by Sir Nevile Henderson to Ribbentrop
on the following day. He was confident now that the united
front of May 21 had been shattered once and for all, and that
under the necessary pressure Britain and France would deliver
up the Czechs in due course. " Operation Green " could still be
put into effect, but the final act of war might not be necessary.

Yet, though the Führer's reasoning was ultimately proved to
be correct, it need not have been. All was not lost at that moment.
The Foreign Office *démenti* had been perfectly correct. The
thoughtless irresponsibility of *The Times* did not voice at that
moment the views of His Majesty's Government. The Foreign
Office was opposed to the surrender of Czechoslovakia and Mr.
Chamberlain himself had travelled a long way from his original
stand in March. When, on September 11, he declared that
" Germany cannot with impunity carry out a rapid and successful
military campaign against Czechoslovakia without fear of intervention by France and by Great Britain ", he was perfectly
sincere. He had consulted with the Leaders of the Opposition,
and with Mr. Churchill and Mr. Eden, before making this statement, and had found that they were squarely behind him in
supporting France in the event of German aggression.[1]

[1] Mr. Chamberlain's statement was made to British journalists, but its content
was given simultaneously to representatives of the foreign press by an official of the
Foreign Office. On receiving news of this statement M. Bonnet ordered one of his

And yet, despite the sincerity of Mr. Chamberlain's statements, the British Government still refused to give to France that firm indication of support which might have given French policy just that extra modicum of steel which it required. On September 10, the day preceding Mr. Chamberlain's declaration, M. Bonnet had put to the British Ambassador this question : " If Germany should attack Czechoslovakia, and France, in the discharge of her treaty obligations, should then mobilize and say to Britain : ' We are going to march, come and march with us ', what would be the reply of the British Government ? " Sir Eric Phipps had referred this enquiry to London and after two days received from Lord Halifax the reply that M. Bonnet's question, " though plain in form, cannot be dissociated from the circumstances in which it might be posed, which are necessarily at this stage completely hypothetical ". On the excuse that His Majesty's Government could not commit the Dominions " in advance of the circumstances of which they would desire themselves to judge ", Lord Halifax could only reply to M. Bonnet's question that, while the British Government " would never allow the security of France to be threatened, they are unable to make precise statements of the character of their future action, or the time at which it would be taken, in circumstances that they cannot at present foresee ".[1]

In view of this renewed refusal on the part of Britain to face realities, it is not entirely surprising to find the elements of resistance in the French Government wilting in their determination. Everything seemed to be fated to confirm the worst of Bonnet's doubts regarding Britain. Were not he and Flandin and Caillaux correct in their estimate of Britain's willingness to help France? And, if they were right about Britain, why should they not also be right about Russia?

And there were other factors which provided M. Bonnet with a " confederate season " for his defeatist campaign. Despite General Gamelin's confidence in the " over-all " efficiency of the French war potential, it soon became evident that in at least one of the armed services France lagged sadly behind Germany. The Chief of the Air Staff, General Joseph Vuillemin, had returned

officials to telephone all diplomatic correspondents of the French press instructing them to minimize the importance of the Prime Minister's declaration (Lévy, p. 86). M. Lévy, as diplomatic correspondent of the *Populaire*, was one of those who received this instruction.

[1] A copy of Lord Halifax's letter is printed in English as an appendix to M. Bonnet's Memoirs (Bonnet, I, pp. 359-61).

from the Reich in July with a terrifying report of German preparedness in the air, the main aspects of which had subsequently
been confirmed by the French Intelligence. Now there also
arrived from Germany Colonel Charles Lindbergh, who had made
a competent study of the position.

At the request of M. Daladier, the American Ambassador,
Mr. William C. Bullitt, invited Colonel Lindbergh and M. Guy
La Chambre, the Under-Secretary for Air, to dine at his house at
Chantilly on the night of September 9. M. La Chambre gave the
gloomiest possible picture of French aviation. The position, he
said, was desperate ; Germany had so long a lead that France
could not catch up with her for years, if at all. The Reich was
producing between 500 and 800 war planes a month, according to
French information, whereas France was only turning out 45 to
50 planes a month and Britain about 70 per month.[1] What were
Colonel Lindbergh's views ?

Lindbergh assured him that he could give no opinion as to the
number of planes in production in Germany or in any other
European country, but he confirmed M. La Chambre's view as
to German air superiority in general, for he had been forced to
the conclusion that the German air fleet was stronger than those
of all the other European countries combined.[2] Profoundly
depressed, M. La Chambre reported on his conversation to the
Premier and to Bonnet.[3]

All this was grist to Bonnet's mill, and he made the best use of
it in the worst way. To the British Ambassador, Sir Eric Phipps,
he deprecated General Gamelin's optimism as to the outcome of a
war with Germany, stressing only the views of Vuillemin and
Lindbergh on the greatly expanded strength of the *Luftwaffe*.
In the Cabinet and outside he consistently maintained that no
firm stand could be expected from Britain, and that, even if Russia
should fight, she was of no use at all ; an army, he said, which
had so recently as 1937 " decapitated " its General Staff in the
great military purge, could scarcely prove an effective ally. He
recapitulated the views of Lindbergh and Vuillemin on the

---

[1] In August 1938, when the metallurgical workers took their paid holidays, the
aircraft output fell to 13. In September France had a total air force of 700 planes,
of which most were obsolete and none was modern. She had no reserve planes and
not a single up-to-date bomber. Cf. evidence of M. Guy La Chambre before the
Riom Tribunal on March 6, 1942. (See *The Riom Trial*, by Lieut.-Col. Pierre Tissier
(London, 1942), pp. 61-4.)

[2] I have consulted Colonel Charles Lindbergh's record of this conversation.

[3] *Ci-devant*, by Anatole de Monzie (Paris, 1941), p. 37.

German Air Force and added to them the highly unfavourable report of the Japanese Military Attaché on the Soviet Air Force. He deliberately misrepresented the assurances given him recently by M. Litvinov,[1] and, though he maintained the *convenances* with regard to the Czechs, he made no secret of his real views to the friends of Germany. Indeed all Paris knew these and marvelled at his retention in office.

Herein, then, lies the core of the tragedy. When France might have stood firm Britain discouraged her; later, when, in desperation at the failure of the way of compromise, Britain looked to France for a lead, she was met with defeatism, apathy, and infirmity.

Such was the position when, on the evening of September 12, Hitler mounted the rostrum to address his cheering legions at Nuremberg. The world waited upon his words. The issue of war and peace, it was felt, hung on the thread of his rhetoric. Would he continue on the violent brutal note which Göring and Goebbels had sounded two days earlier? Would he declare his patience to be at an end and send his bombers southward to enforce his demands?

But Hitler was not yet ready to move. The date for " Operation Green " was still September 30. His speech had a place in the prepared schedule of that operation but it was not the signal to march. It was, however, a masterpiece of political warfare.

Hitler abused the Czechs, and especially President Beneš, with a coarse brutality which made the stomach turn. His insults were punctuated by the barbaric shouts of " *Sieg Heil !* " uttered in terrifying staccato and vibrating through the air in waves of hate. He disclosed for the first time his fury at the crisis of May 21 and the military preparations which he had set afoot a week later. He enlarged on the rapid completion of these preparations, of the great fortification which now stretched along

---

[1] On September 11 M. Bonnet, at Geneva, conferred with M. Litvinov and with M. Comnen, the Rumanian Foreign Minister. On this occasion M. Litvinov repeated his assurances that Russia would support France in accordance with the Pact of 1935 and informed him that Rumania had agreed to permit Russian troops to pass through her territory to the assistance of Czechoslovakia as soon as the League of Nations had pronounced Czechoslovakia to be a victim of aggression. He therefore advocated to M. Bonnet the urgent necessity of a joint *démarche* to the League. M. Bonnet again refused this suggestion and, in reporting the results of his conversations to the French Cabinet on the following day, said that the Russians and Rumanians had " wrapped themselves in League procedure " and had shown little eagerness for action.

Germany's western frontier, cutting off France from her ally. He stressed, to the crescendo of frenzied applause, the invincibility of the Reich. But he did not declare war. He told the Sudeten Germans that if they could not obtain justice and assistance for themselves, they would get both from the Reich, but he added that it was the business of the Prague Government to discuss matters with the representatives of the *Sudetendeutsche Partei*. Nor did he clearly define his intentions, restricting himself to a demand for a rapid settlement of the Sudeten problem by means of self-determination. And then he ceased to speak and the air was again filled with the thunder of " *Sieg Heil!* " and the braying of trumpets.

The speech had exactly the results which its author could have desired ; it confused the issue and produced a number of conflicting reactions. In the Sudetenland it was the signal for revolt, but Lord Runciman still made further efforts towards mediation. In London Mr. Chamberlain felt that the general effect had been " to leave the situation unchanged with a slight diminution of tension ".[1] In Paris chaos and confusion reigned supreme.

September 13 was a fateful day for France, for she stood at the cross-roads, and none knew it better than the Premier, Édouard Daladier. He had long sought to reconcile the warring elements within his Cabinet, to compromise between activism and defeatism which in the long run meant between patriotism and betrayal ; he had juggled — and with no mean skill — with those conflicting personalities about him, but it seemed that to-day he could no longer evade the issue, that a decision must be taken.

The choice before France was clear. If she failed to react to Hitler's speech, his next demand would be for outright annexation of the Sudetenland. Yet opposition in support of the Czechs might — and, on the face of it, would — mean war, and could France fight ? On the previous day M. Daladier had been assured by General Gamelin, in the presence of General Georges and General Billotte, that in the event of war " the democratic nations would dictate the peace ". Such was the very phrase, and the Chief of Staff had backed it up in a letter setting forth the reasons for his confidence.[2] But would the democratic nations stand together ? And was Russia to be counted on ?

[1] Mr. Chamberlain's speech of September 28 (*House of Commons Debates*, September 28, 1938, coll. 5-26).
[2] *Servir*, by General Gamelin (Paris, 1946), II, pp. 344-6 ; Pertinax, p. 3.

All day the Cabinet met in continuous session. The debates were fierce and acrimonious ; the fate not only of Czechoslovakia but of France was in the balance. The chief advocates of resistance numbered six (MM. Reynaud, Mandel, Champetier de Ribes, Campinchi, Zay, and Queuille), and with all the strength at their command they pleaded and demanded that France should now assert herself, not only in the interests of the Czechs, but in her own, and oppose further demands by Germany. They stressed the fact that, while France was perhaps not fully prepared for war, Germany had not yet completed her rearmament ; that Britain and Russia would support her ; that the forces of the Little Entente, and even Turkey, might be counted on ; and that it was always possible that a determined stand taken now would avoid war, both immediately and hereafter. But, if Czechoslovakia was abandoned, the whole structure of French security was menaced.

Though the principal disciples of appeasement in the Cabinet were but four (MM. Bonnet, de Monzie, Pomaret, and Chautemps) they were powerfully supported from without, and their outside supporters were better organized than those of the resisters.[1] They frankly believed that Hitler would not be intimidated by a united front and that it was not worth risking a war for Czechoslovakia. They repeated once more their well-worn arguments : Britain was unwilling, Russia unprepared to fight. Vuillemin had reported that the German Air Force was " gigantic " ; Lindbergh had confirmed the great superiority of Germany in the air. In the event of war France would be held up on the West Wall[2] and Russia would never get her troops through Rumania. The Czechs would be overwhelmed before assistance could reach them. London, Paris, and Prague would be bombed and laid in ruins. It was futile, it was madness, to resist German demands. In any case the situation had gone too far to be corrected by palliatives. If Hitler was to have been " warned " by France it should have been done before the Nuremberg speech. He had committed himself too far now to withdraw. He would certainly fight.[3]

---

[1] That very morning Stéphane Lauzanne, in the *Matin,* had advocated a plebiscite in the Sudetenland, and on September 16 Flandin, in the columns of the *Evening Standard,* assured the British public that France " will refuse to fight a war to save peace ".

[2] For German military opinion on this point see below, p. 161, footnote.

[3] Werth, pp. 219-21 ; Pertinax, pp. 398-9.

As if to reinforce these arguments there arrived from Prague, late in the afternoon (September 13), the news that the *Sudetendeutsche Partei* had presented an ultimatum to the Czech Government demanding the withdrawal of martial law in the Sudetenland, and, on receiving a refusal, had finally broken off all negotiations.

Faced with this dilemma, Daladier characteristically hesitated. He attempted to assess the position impartially, to weigh the pros and cons— and if possible to discover some way of evading a decision. In his mind the pledged word of France stood against the horrific prospect of the slaughter which would inevitably result from a decision to honour that pledged word. The losses to France would be enormous, both materially and in the lives of her sons. The military preparedness of France, despite that brave parade which had passed in gallant grandeur before the King of England so recently, was not complete. Could French arms sustain the assault of German might ? France was weary and divided internally, she was weighed down with the inertia born of victory. Germany was virile, alive, strong with the rejuvenation born of defeat. Could France, even with Britain and Russia, prevail against these ruthless robots ?

And there were other questions which beset the Premier. Was it really true that the security of France depended upon the frontiers of Czechoslovakia ? Might there not be something in Flandin's thesis of retiring behind the mystic impregnability of the Maginot Line ? If Czechoslovakia fell into German hands, would the Reich necessarily and automatically become masters of Central Europe ? Dared he order mobilization ?[1]

Himself inclined to resistance, M. Daladier sought the easier way of surrender, but he salved his conscience by a decision to surrender, not directly to Hitler, but to Mr. Chamberlain. By this means he shifted the onus of responsibility from his own shoulders and removed the conduct of affairs from the hands of Bonnet. With pitiable lack of courage he determined to place the whole burden of negotiations upon Britain.

Sir Eric Phipps was attending a performance at the Opéra-

[1] It is said that on this day (September 13) M. Flandin, when leaving the office of the Prime Minister in the Ministry of War, encountered M. Caillaux, who had just had an interview with President Lebrun at the Elysée. Said Caillaux : " *Je vais dire à Daladier que le ministre qui signerait l'ordre de mobilisation serait passible du poteau de Vincennes, et c'est une expression que je peux employer parce que je m'y connais* " (*Le Chemin de Munich*, by Paul Lombard (Paris, 1938), p. 230).

Comique that evening of September 13. He had seen M. Daladier twice in the course of the day and had reported to London the division which existed in the Cabinet and the state of irresolution in which he had found the Premier. In his opinion the French would not fight in any circumstances. Now an urgent message was brought to him in the theatre asking him to come again, and immediately, to the rue St. Dominique. There in the Ministry of War he was closeted with M. Daladier for a long time. The news of the Ambassador's summons had spread like wildfire and as he descended the stairs he found a little knot of correspondents in the hall. To their earnest and anxious enquiries he replied with one enigmatic remark : " *Il faut que cette chamaillerie cesse.*" [1]

This obscure sentence might well have meant that an end was to be brought to the bickering by the adoption of a determined stand on the part of Britain and France, and it was so interpreted by some of those who heard it, but in effect the exact opposite was the case. For the word to London which Sir Eric took away with him to his Embassy was that France was divided in her counsels, that there was a majority in the Cabinet for abandoning Czechoslovakia and that Mr. Chamberlain was invited, nay, implored, to make the best bargain with the Führer that was obtainable, a request which M. Daladier reaffirmed personally to the Prime Minister by telephone later in the evening.

Mr. Chamberlain's immediate reaction to this new development was to set in operation his plan for a personal interview alone with Hitler,[2] and he so informed M. Daladier, who may or may not have envisaged such a result of his action.[3]

And so the " curtain-raiser " of Nuremberg was finished and the curtain rose on the Drama of Munich.

(ii)

ACT I : BERCHTESGADEN

Mr. Chamberlain's decision to fly to Berchtesgaden was one which required courage, vigour, and audacity, and he was

---

[1] Werth, p. 221. [2] Henderson, p. 151.

[3] M. Daladier, in a statement on September 14, said that he had taken " the initiative to establish a personal and direct contact with Mr. Chamberlain with the object of examining with him the possibility of adopting an exceptional procedure which would allow for the examination with Germany of the most effective measures to assure a friendly solution of the differences which separate the Sudeten Germans and the Prague Government, and in consequence to maintain the peace of Europe ".

entirely justified in taking it. Up to that time it had been recognized that if France, as the ally of Czechoslovakia, had decided to make a stand in giving aid to the Czechs, Britain would sooner or later have been forced to come to her support. " We should be drawn in," the Prime Minister told a visitor on September 10, " because we could not stand aside if the security of France were imperilled. Hitler must know that : our Ambassador has made it plain to all his chief Ministers." [1]

But France had now abdicated the position of leadership. Enquiries made in Paris on September 13, by the British Ambassador, as to what attitude the French Government intended to adopt as a result of the Sudeten ultimatum and the consequent rupture of the negotiations at Prague had disclosed a hopeless confusion and disunity which had reached its climax in M. Daladier's midnight appeal. Since the burden of averting war had been thrown, full weight, upon Mr. Chamberlain's shoulders, he was justified in employing exceptional methods to meet an exceptional emergency.

He was justified also in refusing M. Daladier's proposal to accompany him. Mr. Chamberlain rightly judged that the presence of M. Daladier, representing a disunited Cabinet, would be more of an incubus than an asset. It was now no longer a question of keeping France from going to war for Czechoslovakia, which had been his earlier objective, but of preventing her from " running out " altogether.

And there were other considerations. Hitler's demands for a settlement of the Sudeten problem by self-determination had received warm support from the Japanese Government, who in an authorized statement had re-echoed the Führer's accusation that Czechoslovakia was a pawn in the hand of the Comintern for the bolshevization of Europe.[2] It was thus possible that, in the event of war, the Anti-Comintern Pact of 1936 might provide a serious factor in hampering Russian aid to Czechoslovakia by a Japanese attack on the Soviet Union, and, though this prospect did not appear to agitate Moscow, it undoubtedly played a part in Mr. Chamberlain's calculations.

Now, as throughout the whole Czech crisis, the Prime Minister was disposed to discount the Russian pledges of support to Czechoslovakia. It was his belief that Russia, who, it was said, would

[1] *Munich, Before and After*, by W. W. Hadley (London, 1944), p. 66.
[2] *Contemporary Japan*, December 1938, pp. 581-2.

like nothing better than to see the capitalist States at each other's throats, would either not fight at all once she had, by her incitement of the Czechs, precipitated a war, or, if she did fight, would, by reason of the bad state of her armaments and the difficulties of logistics, be able to offer little of value in the way of assistance.

With regard to the first of these arguments it can only be said that, on the face of all the available evidence, the record of the Soviet Union throughout the crisis of 1938 was one of impeccable conduct and there is no clear reason to believe that she would not have honoured her promises to Czechoslovakia ; certainly the German General Staff were of this opinion. How valuable her assistance would have been, on the other hand, it is difficult to say. Since both Poland and Rumania had categorically refused to permit the passage of Soviet troops through their territories, the only contribution which Russia could have made would have been in the air, yet Russian and Czech aircraft had not been standardized. Even with the best will in the world, therefore, Russia could have brought but meagre assistance at the outset. Nevertheless it was vitally important to have even this meagre assistance thrown into the proper balance of the scale rather than to have it neutral or hostile, as in the case of Poland in 1939.

It is certainly true that no action which Mr. Chamberlain had taken previously in his career had won such unanimous applause as his decision to fly to Berchtesgaden. On September 14 it seemed that, despite Lord Halifax's reference to " hypothetical circumstances ", the threat of war was very near. The weather was perfect, the full glory of an English September, but Londoners went about their business under the weight of impending tragedy. There was no panic ; there was even a calm resignation to the horror of war if need be, but the air was charged with tension, and, as night drew on, London retired to a restless, fitful slumber.

Then came the sudden announcement on the B.B.C. of the Prime Minister's intention, and at once the blanket of depression was lifted. Many did not know of the decision till they read it in their newspapers next day, and smiles greeted the morning sun on September 15. The first reaction was one of surprise ; the second of admiration. The courage of a man of nearly seventy setting out on his first flight [1] to beard the dragon in his den took

---

[1] Mr. Chamberlain had, as a matter of fact, taken a brief demonstration flight over the Birmingham airport, but this can scarcely be considered as an aerial experience.

hold upon the imagination of Englishmen and appealed to their sense of sportsmanship. " Good luck to the old boy ; I didn't know 'e 'ad it in 'im," was a costermonger's comment, and a stockbroker expressed the same approval in his own terms : " Quite right. He's gone to see the head of the firm." Those with longer memories and a liking for historical traditions re-called the energy and drive of the Prime Minister's father : " It's Joe over again — it's what Joe would have done," they said.

Mr. Chamberlain's initiative inspired the Poet Laureate to a paean of praise,[1] and was approved of by even the severest critics of his foreign policy. " It is an effort to stave off war which has seemed to be growing dreadfully near," said the *Daily Herald*, " and, as such, it must win the sympathy of opinion everywhere, irrespective of party." [2]

To many Englishmen — ignorant of the diplomatic background of Mr. Chamberlain's expedition — it seemed that the Prime Minister had taken a step which would render impossible a repetition of the lack of clarity in Britain's policy in 1914. How often had it been said that the failure of Mr. Asquith and Sir Edward Grey to make clear to Germany that Britain would fight in support of France or in defence of Belgium had materially contributed to the outbreak of the First World War ? There were few in England who doubted that, while making every effort to preserve peace, Mr. Chamberlain would tell Hitler clearly and firmly that an attack by Germany on Czechoslovakia would be met by the united opposition of Britain, France, and Russia.

It was not, however, with this intention that Mr. Chamberlain took to the air on September 15, with the unanimous approval — in which were mingled relief and high hopes — of a united British public, an approval so unanimous that it amazed even the Prime Minister himself. His object, as he himself described it later, was to " find out in personal conversation whether there was any hope of saving the peace ", but in his own mind he knew what that involved. Convinced that the flight of Henlein to Germany on the previous day could betoken nothing else than immediate action by Germany, the Prime Minister was confident of what his line of action with Hitler should be. If France could not, or would not, fight in support of her ally, Britain, having no direct

---

[1] See Mr. John Masefield's poem " Neville Chamberlain " in *The Times* of September 16, 1938.

[2] *Daily Herald*, September 15, 1938.

obligation to Czechoslovakia, was concerned only with averting the catastrophe of war. This would involve a further surrender on the part of the Czechs, but it was France, not Britain, who had betrayed them.

Mr. Chamberlain had chosen as his companions in adventure Sir Horace Wilson, Chief Industrial Adviser to the British Government, and Mr. William Strang, head of the Central Department of the Foreign Office.[1] It was a matter of some remark that the Prime Minister should be accompanied by the Chief Industrial and not the Chief Diplomatic Adviser to the British Government on a journey which involved so delicate an act of diplomacy as the vivisection of another country, but Sir Robert Vansittart had been among the opponents of the Chamberlain policy of appeasement and at the end of 1937 had been " promoted " from the position of Permanent Under-Secretary of State for Foreign Affairs, in which capacity he was the head of the Foreign Office, to the newly created sinecure of Chief Diplomatic Adviser to the Government, in which post he was neatly side-tracked. He was succeeded as Permanent Under-Secretary by Sir Alexander Cadogan.

Sir Horace Wilson, on the other hand, had early attracted the attention of Mr. Chamberlain as an adept at settling industrial disputes — he was said to have a great capacity for " seeing the other fellow's point of view " — and was an ardent supporter of the Appeasement policy. He was trained in the field of industry and commerce, having no diplomatic experience, and was in every way, therefore, in greater *rapport* with the Prime Minister's mental approach to the problem than could Sir Robert Vansittart have been.[2]

---

[1] They were joined at Munich by the British Ambassador, and Mr. Ivone Kirkpatrick, First Secretary of the British Embassy in Berlin.

[2] Even after the failure of the policy of Appeasement, Sir Horace Wilson remained in high favour at No. 10 Downing Street until the advent of Mr. Winston Churchill as Prime Minister in May 1940. Sir Robert Vansittart was created a Privy Councillor on Mr. Churchill's assumption of office, and a peer on his retirement in 1941.

Mr. Harold Nicolson has very fairly compared this adventure of Mr. Chamberlain and Sir H. Wilson to " the bright faithfulness of two curates entering a pub for the first time ; they did not observe the difference between a social gathering and a rough-house ; nor did they realize that the tough guys assembled did not either speak or understand their language. They imagined that they were as decent and as honourable as themselves " (*Why Britain is at War* (Penguin Special, 1939), p. 106).

It is not without interest that, in order to distract the attention of the Prime Minister from the unusual experience and possible effects of his first journey by air, Sir Horace Wilson regaled him during the flight with a selection from the laudatory letters and telegrams which had arrived at No. 10 Downing Street before their departure. Mr. Chamberlain was thus wafted to Berchtesgaden in a cloud of commendation.

In Mr. Strang [1] the Prime Minister had an adviser thoroughly reliable and widely experienced, who had accompanied Sir John Simon on his visit to Berlin in 1935 and Mr. Eden on his European odyssey of the same year. He alone of the three had seen Hitler before ; none of the three spoke German.

At last the weary seven-hour journey by plane and train and motor-car was finished, and at four o'clock, after the briefest interval for refreshment, Mr. Chamberlain's car drew up to the steps of the Berghof. Hitler, concealing his heart-felt satisfaction at the event,[2] made no gesture to go to meet his guest, but with General Keitel and a few members of his entourage awaited him on the top step. Together they turned and went into the house.

And so began the first of those three historic meetings between Mr. Chamberlain and the Führer ; between an elderly and respectable politician of sixty-nine, and a ruthless political adventurer of forty-nine ; between a man of sincere beliefs who was prepared to make almost any sacrifice in order to preserve peace, and a cold, cynical, contemptuous creature who regarded war as merely another weapon in the German armoury for the achievement of his ambitions. Democracy faced Dictatorship across a tea-table in Bavaria ; the representative of a Power grown weak and lethargic from the fruits of victory encountered the master of a people which had arisen lean, virile and vengeful from the ashes of defeat.[3]

The discussion, which began with banal exchanges and lasted three hours, was held *à deux* save for the presence of Hitler's personal interpreter, Dr. Schmidt. That Mr. Chamberlain should be unsupported by any of his advisers and should even be without his own interpreter — Mr. Kirkpatrick, a brilliant linguist, was available for this purpose — had been the novel idea of Sir Nevile

[1] Mr. (now Sir) William Strang was later special envoy to Moscow for the abortive negotiations for an Anglo-Franco-Soviet Pact in the summer of 1939, and was subsequently British Representative on the European Advisory Commission, 1944–5. After the surrender of Germany he became Political Adviser to the Commander-in-Chief of the British Forces of Occupation.

[2] It is recorded that, on receiving the first intimation of Mr. Chamberlain's willingness to come to Berchtesgaden, Hitler could scarcely believe his luck. " *Ich bin vom Himmel gefallen* (I fell from heaven) ", he said with a chuckle, when later recounting the story to a foreign diplomat (*Diplomatic Prelude :* 1938–1939, by L. B. Namier (London, 1948), p. 35). This reaction is certainly more in character than the " official " one which Hitler later gave personally to Mr. Chamberlain, namely, that his first thought had been : " I can't let a man of his age come all this way ; I must go to London " (Feiling, p. 363).

[3] Cf. *Cymbeline*, Act III, scene 6 : " Plenty and peace breed cowards : hardness of hardiness is mother ". Mr. Chamberlain was not a coward but he had an abiding horror of war — there is a difference.

Henderson, who wished to exclude Ribbentrop from the discussion. The result, however, was not felicitous, for Mr. Chamberlain was never furnished with Dr. Schmidt's record of the proceedings [1] and had therefore to reconstruct from memory his own version of the conversation.[2]

Mr. Chamberlain had left London with the object of exploring the Führer's mind and, if possible, arriving at the basis of some compromise which should at the same time preserve the peace of Europe and involve the Czechs in as small sacrifices as possible. But he speedily found that the position was much more acute and much more grave than he had imagined. " In courteous but perfectly definite terms " Hitler told him that he had made up his mind that the Sudeten Germans must have the right of self-determination and of " returning ", if they so wished, to the Reich.[3] If they could not achieve this by themselves, he would assist them to do so, and, rather than delay further, he was prepared to incur the risk of a world war.

At one point in the monologue — for Mr. Chamberlain did most of the listening — the Führer complained of " British threats " and the Prime Minister replied that Hitler must distinguish between a " threat " and a " warning ". There might, he said, have been just cause for complaint if Hitler had been told that in no circumstances would Britain go to war with Germany, when, in fact, there were conditions in which such a contingency might arise.

Mr. Chamberlain was convinced, however — and correctly — that the Führer was not bluffing and that an immediate invasion of Czechoslovakia was in active preparation. But Hitler's attitude had aroused in the Prime Minister all the inherent dislike of the Briton for being " pushed around ". He had naturally assumed that the fact that Hitler had agreed to their meeting presupposed a disposition to discuss a basis of a possible compromise — a kind of respectable *Kuh-handel*; else why should they meet at all? This, however, was evidently not the case, and Mr. Chamberlain considered that he had been treated cavalierly by a man twenty

---

[1] Henderson, pp. 153-4.

[2] It was this version that the Prime Minister gave to the House of Commons on September 28, 1938 (*House of Commons Debates*, September 28, 1938, coll. 5-26). See also his personal account written immediately on his return (Feiling, pp. 366-8).

[3] It is doubtful if Mr. Chamberlain, who was not well acquainted with German history, was aware of the lie inherent in the Führer's use of the word " return ", which was usually employed in connection with territory detached from Germany after the First World War.

years his junior, in that he had apparently been brought on a fool's errand. With asperity and courage, therefore, he asked why he had been allowed to travel all this way when he was evidently wasting his time. To this Hitler replied that, if he could receive " there and then " the assurance that the British Government would accept the principle of self-determination, he would be prepared to discuss ways and means of carrying it out ; but if no such assurance were forthcoming there was no purpose in continuing their conversations.

The Prime Minister could not, of course, give such an assurance " off his own bat ", but he played for time. He would consult his colleagues in the Cabinet as expeditiously as possible, provided Germany would refrain in the meantime from active hostilities. This Hitler agreed to do, provided his hand was not forced by Czechoslovakia. He also agreed to a further meeting.

With that sum total of success Mr. Chamberlain headed back to London next day (September 16) and in the evening presided over a full Cabinet, at which he gave a detailed account of Hitler's plans for solving the Sudeten problem.[1] Lord Runciman, who, in answer to a summons from London, had returned that same day from Prague, also attended the Cabinet meeting and presented the outline of his own recommendations for the solution of the same problem.

Taken together these two reports may be said to comprise the basis of British foreign policy until the conclusion of the Munich Agreement, and their interrelationship is not without interest.

Though communicated in essence to the Cabinet on September 16, and presented officially to the Prime Minister and to President Beneš on September 21, the report of the Runciman Mission was not made public until September 28, when Mr. Chamberlain had already been to Berchtesgaden and to Godesberg.[2] Despite the fact that the report is dated September 21, certain portions of it give the impression of having been written at a later period. Indeed the document falls very naturally into two sections : the first, in which Lord Runciman retailed his early efforts at media-

[1] Tribute must be paid to the physical endurance of Mr. Chamberlain during this period. After fourteen hours' travelling and three hours' conference with Hitler, he had an audience with the King and met his colleagues in Cabinet before dinner on the evening of the 16th, when, after a brief adjournment, the meeting was resumed until a late hour.

[2] For text of the Runciman Report, see below, Appendix D.

tion and their failure, and the second in which he made his recommendations. It is the second part that gives the appearance of having been written under the influence of " hindsight ".

After expressing his opinion that the turning of the Sudeten Germans to Germany for help and their eventual desire to join the Reich was " a natural development in the circumstances ", Lord Runciman delivered himself of the opinion that the frontier districts between Czechoslovakia and Germany, where the Sudeten population was in an important majority, " should at once be transferred from Czechoslovakia to Germany, without even the formality of a plebiscite ".

Now, when Lord Runciman and his colleagues left Prague on September 16, no one had even suggested the transfer of Czech territory to Germany without a plebiscite. The *Sudetendeutsche Partei* had never made such a demand, and Hitler himself on September 12 had confined his demands to " self-determination ". Indeed only in *The Times* editorial of September 7 had this suggestion ever been mooted, and the Foreign Office had officially denied that these views represented in any way the policy of His Majesty's Government. It would seem, therefore, that either Lord Runciman, when in Prague, formed opinions as to the solution of the Sudeten problem which far outstripped anything that either Hitler or Henlein had then proposed, and that these opinions had immense influence upon the Cabinet, or that in the writing of his report he was influenced by what had been told him of the Führer's demands upon the Prime Minister.

With regard to those portions of Czechoslovak territory where the German majority was not so predominant, Lord Runciman proposed that a basis of local autonomy should be found for them within the frontiers of the Republic on the lines of the Fourth Plan. He had four other recommendations :

(1) That those parties and persons in Czechoslovakia who have been deliberately encouraging a policy antagonistic to Czechoslovakia's neighbours should be forbidden by the Czechoslovak Government to continue their agitation : and that, if necessary, legal measures should be taken to bring such agitations to an end.

(2) That Czechoslovakia should so remodel her foreign relations as to give assurances to her neighbours that she will in no circumstances attack them or enter into any aggressive action against them arising from obligations to other States.

(3) That the principal Powers, acting in the interest of the

peace of Europe, should give to Czechoslovakia guarantees
of assistance in case of unprovoked aggression against her.

(4) That a commercial treaty on preferential terms should be
negotiated between Germany and Czechoslovakia if this
seems advantageous to the economic interests of the two
countries.

Of these recommendations, the first was so designed as to
muzzle all criticism of Germany in Czechoslovakia while granting
full and free rights of expression to the German minorities within
the Czechoslovak State, as agreed to in the Fourth Plan.

The second and third points, however, again raise the question
of the time factor in the writing of the report. Though the reorientation of Czechoslovak foreign policy had been a part of the
Karlsbad Programme, it had not been included in the eight points
and no one, not even Lord Runciman, had urged President Beneš
to consider it. It was not, in fact, until after Mr. Chamberlain's
conversation with the Führer that this became a matter of practical
consideration, and from it arose the corollary of a Four-Power
Guarantee to Czechoslovakia to replace her French and Russian
alliances. This point also had never been discussed in Prague.

After a discussion of the reports of the Prime Minister and
Lord Runciman the Cabinet adjourned on the night of September
16, pending the arrival of MM. Daladier and Bonnet, who had
been invited for Sunday. But the Inner Cabinet met throughout
the week-end in constant session. It is to be believed that in
these discussions there was a sharp division of opinion: one
school holding that the transfer to Germany of a minority of
Czechs within the German minority was indefensible, and another,
to which Sir John Simon, Sir Samuel Hoare and the Prime
Minister himself subscribed, which held firmly that Britain should
not enter into commitments beyond the Rhine.

With the arrival of the French Ministers on the 18th there
ensued conferences which were, in Mr. Chamberlain's words,
" guided by a desire to find a solution which would not bring
about a European war, and, therefore, a solution which would not
automatically compel France to take action in accordance with
her obligations ".[1] In other words, the object of the conference

[1] See Mr. Chamberlain's speech in the House of Commons, September 28, 1938.
M. Daladier, in the Chamber on October 4, was even franker : " *Nous nous trouvions
devant l'alternative suivante : Ou bien dire ' non ' aux revendications des Allemands des Sudètes
et par là pousser le gouvernement tchèque à l'intransigeance et le gouvernement allemand à
l'agression, provoquer un conflit armé qui aurait eu pour conséquence rapide la destruction de la*

was to force the Czechs to accept the principle of self-determination. In effect, however, the position of Great Britain was made considerably clearer to the French than it had ever been before. Lord Halifax had written on September 12 that Britain " would never allow the security of France to be threatened ", but Mr. Chamberlain now interpreted this view as meaning that France could not expect British intervention unless and until her own territory were attacked. Even then there would inevitably be a time-lag occasioned by the necessary consultation with the Dominions and other constitutional procedure. If and when Britain did enter the war, she could supply in the first six months only 150 aircraft and two non-mechanized divisions.[1] In these circumstances the French were advised to pursue a policy of the greatest caution.

In the discussions which followed, there was a notable change in M. Daladier's behaviour. In April he had been vigorous and forceful, refusing to contemplate any eventuality in which France would not defend her ally against aggression. Now he seemed heavy and lethargic, altogether under the influence of Bonnet. It would seem that he was shocked at the results of his own action in appealing to Mr. Chamberlain to seek a direct approach to Hitler. The situation with which he was now faced defeated him. He sat glum and silent, acquiescing in Bonnet's sardonic acceptance of the transfer to Germany of the territory of France's ally, and only venturing himself to insist, against a certain amount of British opposition, that, in return for the sacrifices which were to be demanded of Czechoslovakia, Britain and France should bind themselves to guarantee the new frontiers of that State. He won his point, but only at a price. Mr. Chamberlain and his colleagues insisted, in their turn, that such a guarantee should be general (*i.e.* that Germany should be included) and that it should replace the present system of Czech treaties of mutual assistance, and with this M. Daladier was forced to content himself.

But of what value and what efficacy could such a guarantee be to either France or her ally when at the same moment the whole strategic frontier of Czechoslovakia was handed over to the Reich ? " *Nous nous sommes penchés sur les cartes* ", M. Daladier subsequently related, and such an examination could only have

Tchécoslovaquie. Ou bien essayer un compromis. . . . Nous avons choisi la paix " (*Le Temps*, October 5, 1938).
    [1] *Carnets secrets de Jean Zay* (Paris, 1942), p. 2 ; Bonnet, I, p. 272.

disclosed that a defenceless and indefensible frontier between Czechoslovakia and Germany would result from the acceptance of the German demands by the Prague Government. Why, then, did M. Daladier attach so much importance to the association of Britain with such a guarantee ? Was it not because he wished to salve his conscience for the betrayal of an ally and to bring back something from the conference which would placate the Resistance Group in his Cabinet ?

The course which the conference would take was one which the Czechs themselves had foreseen only too well. To be forearmed, and to make his country's position perfectly clear, M. Jan Masaryk had, during the afternoon of the 18th, presented a Note to the conference recalling the fact that Czechoslovakia's life was at stake and warning the Ministers that she would not accept responsibility for decisions reached in her absence, even by her friends and allies.[1]

It was all to no purpose. Late that night the " Anglo-French Plan " was born. The conference agreed to recommend to the Governments of Britain and France that they should urge upon Prague the immediate acceptance of the " direct transfer to the

[1] According to M. Daladier's account of these conversations before the Constituent Assembly on July 18, 1946, he had received from Prague on September 17 " une proposition officieuse " to the effect that Czechoslovakia would be prepared to cede certain mountain salients, with a population of some 800,000 to 900,000 inhabitants, to Germany, and had reported this fact to the British Government (*Journal Officiel*, July 19, 1946, p. 2680).

No such proposition was ever made officially by the Czechoslovak Government, but the statement had its origin in two separate incidents. In their anxiety to gain some further concession from Prague, MM. Daladier and Bonnet had instructed the French Minister to urge on President Beneš the need for accepting some frontier rectification. The President refused, but, in the course of his conversations with M. de Lacroix, he recounted the occasion of the offer which President Masaryk and he had made to the Peace Conference in 1919 (see above, p. 30, footnote). " But what was possible in 1919 is not possible now, in the present circumstances ", added Dr. Beneš to M. de Lacroix. In reporting on his interview to Paris, M. de Lacroix retailed the story in his turn and this was seized upon by the Premier and Foreign Minister as a veiled offer of concession.

Simultaneously there arrived in Paris a Social Democratic member of the Czechoslovak Government, who, on behalf of the Czech Social Democratic Party, asked the support of M. Léon Blum and the French Socialist Party. This unofficial envoy also repeated the story of the offer at the Peace Conference to Blum, but only as a fellow Socialist and member of the Second International. M. Blum, who himself was anxious to avoid war at any cost, at once sought an appointment with the Premier and again told him the story.

In view of this double event M. Daladier sought to justify his agreement in the Anglo-French Plan by the thought that Czechoslovakia had herself meditated a minor rectification of her frontier with Germany twenty years before.

Reich of all territories with over 50 per cent Sudeten inhabitants ".
In return for this concession an Anglo-French guarantee was
offered for the new Czech frontier.

The proposals of the conference were submitted to the two
Cabinets on the following day, and met with some opposition
both in London and Paris,[1] but, whereas Mr. Chamberlain was
able to carry his colleagues into eventual agreement, M. Daladier
was forced to make concessions. The Resistance group, MM.
Reynaud, Mandel and Champetier de Ribes, exacted from the
Premier and from M. Bonnet a solemn undertaking not to bring
any pressure to bear on the Czech Government, who must be
free to decide for themselves.[2]

A fig for M. Bonnet's promises : he went straight from the
Cabinet meeting to his office in the Quai d'Orsay, where he
received the Czech Minister, M. Osusky, and communicated to
him the terms of the Anglo-French Plan. For an hour Osusky
protested and pleaded for French support in resisting what were
virtually the demands of Germany. His pleas were met with a
terse and sardonic " *Acceptez* ", and Osusky left the room white
with anger and despair, saying to the journalists as he passed
through them : " Here you see the condemned man. He has
been sentenced without being heard."

The Berchtesgaden visit is, in many respects, of greater
historical importance than the Munich Conference itself ; it set
in motion a procession of events to which Munich was the tragic
climax and the inevitable sequel. For, once direct appeasement
had been begun on the basis of personal contact, it was almost
impossible to stop the process without the certainty of war.
From then on the issue depended on a time-table, a schedule of
evacuations and frontier delimitations, on neither of which, once
the main principle of surrender had been accepted, would it
have been possible to have obtained full public support for war.

---

[1] Mr. Herbert Morrison, Dr. Hugh Dalton, and Sir Walter Citrine, representatives
of the National Council of Labour, were received on September 19 by the Prime
Minister, who informed them of the situation. The Council thereupon issued a manifesto declaring that they had " heard with dismay of the reported proposals for the
dismemberment of Czechoslovakia under the brutal threat of force by Nazi Germany
and without prior consultation with the Czech Government ", and denounced it as
" a shameful betrayal of a peaceful and democratic people ". When, however, British
Labour sought the support and solidarity of the French Socialists and the C.G.T.,
they were shocked to find no approval of their action but only shamefaced acquiescence
in the decision of the Government.

[2] Werth, p. 227 ; Lombard, p. 236 ; Zay, pp. 5-7.

Before Mr. Chamberlain went to Berchtesgaden he had believed that Germany had not really intended to go as far as to risk war in order to attain her ambitions, but his meeting with the Führer convinced him that this risk would not only be taken, but taken immediately if Hitler's demands were not granted. " I have no doubt whatever," Mr. Chamberlain later told the Commons, " that my visit alone prevented an invasion, for which everything was ready". This, of course, was not entirely true, since the earliest date for the X-Day of " Operation Green " was September 30, and at no time did Hitler deviate from this time-table.¹ But Mr. Chamberlain had carried away an accurate impression of the Führer's inflexible determination to march into the Sudetenland, and it was clear to him that, if peace were to be preserved, Hitler's demands on Czechoslovakia must be granted ; and once this principle had been accepted, it seemed virtually impossible to go to war later over ways and means. The historic moment of decision, therefore, was at Berchtesgaden, and, though the subsequent tide of events might ebb and flow, the ultimate outcome was inevitable.

For France the decision which Mr. Chamberlain took at Berchtesgaden, and which MM. Daladier and Bonnet ratified in London, was even more vital. By her agreement to abandon Czechoslovakia France destroyed her own military security, but she also abdicated her right to be considered a Great Power and began that fatal descent which ended in the Avernus of Vichy, and on which Munich was but a milestone.²

The Berchtesgaden meeting was also important for Hitler. Though he had been persistently certain that Britain, and therefore France, would not fight for the Sudetenland — he was so sure that he had only moved five extra divisions to supplement the normal defence force on the Western Frontier ³ — and was

---

¹ Hitler's undertaking not to attack the Czechs before receiving Mr. Chamberlain's reply was no concession at all, since there was a fortnight to go before the appointed day.

² It is notable that during the fateful four weeks between September 4 and Munich, neither M. Daladier nor M. Bonnet made a single public speech.

³ *International Military Tribunal Document*, R-150. In German General Staff circles there had been changes of opinion as to the probability of French intervention. A directive issued by Hitler to the *Wehrmacht* on June 18 stated categorically that " there is no danger of a preventive war by foreign States against Germany " ; the Führer continued : " However, I will decide to take action against Czechoslovakia only if I am firmly convinced, as in the case of the occupation of the demilitarized zone and the entry into Austria, that France will not march and therefore that England will not intervene " (*International Military Tribunal Document*, 288–PS, item 14).

quite undeterred by Mr. Chamberlain's debating point on the differentiation between " threats " and " warnings ", he received impressions during his conversations with the Prime Minister which gave additional confirmation to his convictions. These impressions the Führer passed on to his uncertain Southern ally — and to good effect. It was not until after the Berchtesgaden meeting had convinced the Italian Government of the weakness of the Western democracies that Mussolini began his series of speeches in the leading cities of Italy (September 18–26) in which he consistently intimated that, in the event of war, Italy would support her Axis partner.

The Führer, moreover, was materially aided by the fact that, by allowing the German proposals to be submitted to Prague as the " Anglo-French Plan ", the British and French Governments had automatically made themselves to some degree the accomplices of Hitler in the eyes of the world. Had the German ultimatum been transmitted — as was later the case after Godesberg — as a purely German document, it would still have been open to both Governments to give such advice, or apply such pressure, to the Czechs as they might see fit in order to ensure its acceptance, and their hands would have been a good deal cleaner. As it was, Britain and France allowed themselves to appear before world public opinion as Hitler's willing bailiffs.

(iii)

First Entr'acte : Prague

In telegrams from London and Paris, M. Jan Masaryk and M. Stefan Osusky had to some extent prepared President Beneš and the Prague Government for the decisions of the London conference, which had indeed been to some degree anticipated ever since the news of Mr. Chamberlain's flight to Berchtesgaden. It was not, however, until noon on September 19 that the " Anglo-French Plan " was officially presented by Mr. Basil Newton and M. de

Two months later, however, the opinion was expressed, in a German Air Force directive dated August 25, that " the basic assumption is that France will declare war during ' Operation Green ' ", but " only if *active military assistance from Great Britain* is definitely assured " (*International Military Tribunal Document*, 375–PS). Both documents assumed that Russian intervention was probable. Later still, on September 8, in conversation with Jodl, General Stülpnagel wondered whether the Führer was as confident as he had been in June that the Western Powers would not intervene and if he had not secretly decided to go ahead with " Operation Green " even in face of such intervention (*International Military Tribunal Document*, 1780–PS).

Lacroix.[1] In it the Czech Government were told that the territory
in question might be handed over either directly or as a result of
a plebiscite. This territory would probably have to include areas
where the Germans numbered more than 50 per cent of the inhabitants. The British and French Governments hoped to be
able to arrange adjustments of the frontiers, where advisable and
possible, by some international body " including a Czech representative ", and the same body would also be charged with the
question of the possible exchange of populations, " on the basis
of the right to opt within a specified time limit ". There followed
the declaration of the British and French willingness " to join in
an international guarantee of the new boundaries of the Czechoslovak State against unprovoked aggression ", but one of the
principal conditions of such a guarantee would be " the safeguarding of the independence of Czechoslovakia by the substitution of a general guarantee against unprovoked aggression in place
of the existing treaties which involve reciprocal obligations of a
military character ". A reply was requested " at the earliest
possible moment ", as Mr. Chamberlain wished to renew his
conversations with Hitler by Wednesday (September 21), " or
earlier if possible ".

Since his experiences of Lord Runciman, President Beneš had
lost confidence and hope in Britain, but the Note of September 19
brought him the defection of France also, and, in addition,
demanded his renunciation of Russia. Not only was Czechoslovakia to be stripped of her strategic frontier but her subsequent
security was to be left to nebulous sureties of a " general guarantee " ; the world had seen the value of such guarantees in the
case of Austria.

No Chief of State could be placed in a more hideous predicament, but none was better equipped in cool courage and grim
determination than Edvard Beneš. He faced the matter squarely
and examined each appalling detail. Alone with his conscience
and in constant discussion with his Cabinet, he probed the situation in every aspect, seeking desperately for some glimmer of
hope. To accept was impossible. To surrender the strategic
frontier and also to create a Czech minority of some 800,000 souls
in Germany was unthinkable. Yet to reject the demands would
be to precipitate a European war, and this responsibility, in the
eyes of Britain and France, would rest upon his shoulders.

[1] For text of the Anglo-French Plan, see Appendix E.

Not even at this hour was the President prepared to abandon all faith in France. Admittedly it was not the France he had known in the past, the France of Poincaré, of Briand, and of Barthou, men who had forged with him the Franco-Czech Alliance, the Locarno Agreement, and the Little Entente; it was true that the reins of government were to-day in other hands, those of Daladier, a weakling, and of Bonnet, a defeatist, but they were not all France, and in the Cabinet were friends of Czecho-slovakia — Reynaud and Mandel — who could not be a party to this sacrifice. If only he could talk with them and know their minds; but telegrams in cipher took time and the telephone to Paris crossed not only French but also German territory, and was certainly tapped in both countries. He must take his decision alone, as he had so often to do in those dark days, this lonely little democrat who sat in the palace of kings.

For a day and a half the President sat in endless session with his Cabinet and his military advisers. No voice was raised for accepting the Anglo-French Plan, but General Syrový and General Krejcy warned him that the risk involved in resisting a German attack would be very great unless French assistance were assured. Finally a way of compromise was found. They would not accept the demands of Germany, which Britain and France had presented to them, but their rejection should not be an unqualified negative. They would propose the reference of the whole dispute to arbitration under the provisions of the German-Czech Treaty of 1925, which Hitler and Neurath had assured them in March was still considered as valid and effective.[1] Such a procedure would bring a reasonable solution in harmony with the dignity of all the interested parties.

This decision was hastily embodied in a Note, and to it was added a special plea to France, to whom Czechoslovakia had " always been bound by esteem and devoted friendship as well as by an alliance to which no Government and no Czechoslovak individual would ever be a traitor ". To the two Powers " a supreme appeal " was addressed, begging them to reconsider their point of view, for " in these crucial moments it is not merely the fate of Czechoslovakia which is at stake, but that of other nations as well, and notably that of France ".[2]

How futile were these efforts of the Prague Government to avoid their fate. On receiving the Note from Dr. Krofta at 5 P.M.

---

[1] See above, p. 26.   [2] For text, see Appendix F.

on September 20, Mr. Newton said at once that, if Czechoslovakia persisted in her rejection of the Anglo-French proposals, Britain would certainly declare herself disinterested in the fate of the Czechs. M. de Lacroix associated himself with this attitude on behalf of France. With a heavy heart Dr. Krofta returned to the Cabinet meeting and reported to the President.[1] The last spark of hope had died and the Ministers in despair awaited the official reaction to their Note. Their suspense was not long.

The Cabinet adjourned at eight o'clock in the evening, and at once the Premier, Dr. Hodža, received M. de Lacroix and sought an explanation of the French attitude. Mr. Newton's remarks had been more or less expected, but the fact that the French Minister had made no protest against the statement of his British colleague but had actually agreed with him was a terrible shock. Hodža now put the question bluntly to the Minister : could Czechoslovakia count on French help or could she not ? M. de Lacroix, a good friend of Czechoslovakia, was deeply moved. He wept. It was some time before he could reply, but when he did speak it was to say that, although he had received no definite instructions, he was convinced that French support would not be forthcoming. If this were so, said Hodža, the President must be immediately informed ; but again the French Minister pleaded that he had no official instructions. Then, said the Premier, he must ask for them in the most explicit terms, for it was vital that the Czech Government and Army should know what the attitude of France was to be. M. de Lacroix agreed to ask.[2] On telephoning to Paris he was asked by M. Bonnet to communicate so important a matter by cipher telegram.[3]

The telegram which M. de Lacroix then sent was curiously at variance with the request which he had been asked to make by Dr. Hodža.[4] According to the French Minister, the Czecho-

[1] *Munich, Before and After*, by Hubert Ripka (London, 1939), p. 78.

[2] This account is taken from Dr. Hodža's own version of the incident as published by Professor Hubert Beuve-Méry in *L'Europe Nouvelle*, October 29, 1938, and confirmed by Dr. Hodža in a conversation with me in New York in 1941.

[3] Ripka, p. 42.

[4] The text of M. de Lacroix's telegram was as follows :

" 20 septembre 1938
" (télégramme réservé No. 2219-220)

" *Le président du Conseil vient de me convoquer. D'accord m'a-t-il dit, avec le président de la République, il m'a déclaré que si je venais cette nuit même déclarer à M. Benès qu'en cas de guerre entre l'Allemagne et la Tchécoslovaquie à propos des Allemands des Sudètes, la France, à*

slovak President and Premier, with the support of the Chiefs of
the Army, would, despite the Note of refusal already despatched
to London, accept the Anglo-French Plan if they received written
confirmation that the French Government would not support
them if they rejected it, but they needed such a confirmation in
order to accept. Dr. Hodža was reported as urging this course
of action on the French Government as the only means of preserving peace.

What is the explanation of this misrepresentation? Had
M. de Lacroix misunderstood what Dr. Hodža had said to him?
Or had he, in his agitation, placed a different emphasis on the
proposals which had been made to him, thereby giving them an
interpretation more exactly in accord with the views of M.
Bonnet? Or does this incident accord with other evidence that
Dr. Hodža, himself a Slovak and a member of the Agrarian Party
(who were strongly opposed to any action which might bring
Russia into a war as the sole ally of Czechoslovakia), was intrigu-
ing behind the President's back in order to bring about a situation
in which Czechoslovak resistance would be rendered impossible?
Whatever the explanation, there can be no doubt that the French
Foreign Minister, when he received the telegram late on the night
of September 20, was delighted with the contents, which he at once
telephoned to M. Daladier and later used for his own purposes.[1]

The receipt in London and Paris on the evening of September
20 of the Czech Note of refusal was the signal for an outburst of
petulance and anger. Had the Czechs no conception of the
gravity of the situation? How could they talk of arbitration
when Hitler was prepared to seize them by the throat at any
moment? It was intolerable that they should endanger the continuation of the negotiations between Mr. Chamberlain and the
Führer, and then precipitate a European war which in any case
could only end in their own destruction.

The Inner Cabinet met in London and sat till 10.30 P.M.
There were telephone conversations with Paris, with M. Daladier

cause de ses engagements avec l'Angleterre, ne marcherait pas, le président du Conseil convoquerait
immédiatement le Cabinet dont tous les membres étaient dès à présent d'accord avec le président de
la République et avec lui-même pour s'incliner.

"Les dirigeants tchécoslovaques ont besoin de cette couverture pour accepter la proposition
franco-anglaise. Ils sont sûrs de l'armée, dont les chefs ont déclarés qu'un conflit seul à seul avec
l'Allemagne serait un suicide. M. Hodža déclare que la démarche qu'il suggère est le seul moyen
de sauver la paix. Il désire que tout soit fini avant minuit si possible ou, en tout cas, dans le
courant de la nuit. Le président du Conseil fera la même communication au ministre d'Angleterre."

[1] See below, p. 125.

and M. Bonnet, who had not dared to acquaint their Cabinet colleagues with the terms of the Czech Note. At length it was agreed, with the approval of President Lebrun and in view of M. de Lacroix's telegram, that the utmost pressure must be exerted on the Czech Government to bring them to their senses, and instructions were accordingly sent to the Legations in Prague.[1]

It was after midnight when President Beneš went to bed for the first time in three days, but his slumbers were not destined to be of long duration. Scarcely an hour had passed before Mr. Newton and M. de Lacroix were urgently demanding immediate audience, and it was a quarter past two (September 21) when they confronted the President and Dr. Krofta with the British and French replies.

The message of the two envoys was tantamount to a peremptory ultimatum. The Czech proposal to refer the Sudeten problem to arbitration was dismissed as in no way meeting the critical situation, and President Beneš was bidden to " withdraw that reply and urgently consider an alternative that takes account of realities ". The realities were clearly and forcefully set out. Britain and France were determined, if possible, to prevent a European war, and incidentally an invasion of Czechoslovakia. If the Czech Government, by their refusal to accept the Anglo-French Plan immediately and unconditionally, prevented the two Powers from accomplishing their peaceful aims, Czechoslovakia would stand before the world as solely responsible for the war that would ensue, and in which she would fight alone in so far as Britain and France were concerned ; for, in face of such culpable obstinacy, both Powers would wash their hands of the whole business.

Mr. Newton left with President Beneš a copy of the instructions which he had received from Lord Halifax,[2] but M. de Lacroix made only a verbal statement, which culminated in the unequivocal phrase : " *La France ne s'y associera pas* ".

This then was the final confirmation of the statements which the two Ministers had made personally on the previous evening when the Czech Note had been handed to them. This was the answer to the further reply which M. de Lacroix had made to

[1] In making public the essential documents on the Munich crisis, neither the British nor the French Government saw fit to include the text of the Czech reply to the Anglo-French Plan.

[2] These instructions were communicated to Parliament on October 5, 1938, by Lord Stanhope and Mr. R. A. Butler, Under-Secretary of State for Foreign Affairs.

Paris at the request of Dr. Hodža. This was the *coup de grâce* to
the last hopes which the President had cherished for the ultimate
support of France. Beneš showed no sign of emotion at this
critical juncture. It was as if he had risen above the present
difficulties and was already looking towards the future when the
injustices of to-day should be redressed. He was concerned now
with the record of his country at the bar of history.

The President accepted Mr. Newton's paper and with his
own hand recorded M. de Lacroix's statement, but he wished to
have the betrayal of France in writing — the President knew his
Georges Bonnet very well — and he demanded a written confirmation of what the French Minister had said verbally. In so
doing M. Beneš had one last flicker of optimism. It was, he
thought, impossible that such a document as he had requested
could be given without the approval of the French Cabinet ;
he therefore hoped that those amongst Bonnet's colleagues who
were friends of Czechoslovakia would be aroused to opposition
on this vital issue and that the policy of the Foreign Minister
might just possibly be reversed.

But alas for the hopes of Dr. Beneš : he knew his Bonnet very
well but not well enough. Though he obtained his first objective,
he failed in his second and wider aim. M. Bonnet was simply
too slippery for him.

The Foreign Minister of France was in conference with his
disciple and sycophant, M. Jean Mistler, President of the Foreign
Affairs Committee of the Chamber, when M. de Lacroix telephoned from Prague.[1] To the request for a written statement he
at first refused to commit himself, and then suggested that the
Minister himself prepare a paper in accordance with his instructions. M. de Lacroix was adamant. He had suffered much in
the last few days in shame and humiliation at his country's policy
and now he insisted on nailing down the responsibility for that
policy where it belonged. He demanded that M. Bonnet dictate
to him at once over the telephone the political statement which
Dr. Beneš had requested.

After consultation with Mistler it suddenly occurred to Bonnet
that even this event might be turned to his own advantage. He
thereupon dictated a Note which, though it lacked the frank
brutality of the earlier " *la France ne s'y associera pas* ", conveyed
unmistakably, though none the less exactly, the same message.

[1] Pertinax, p. 400 ; de Monzie, p. 33.

M. Bonnet had thus defeated the wider objective of President Beneš. He had taken the initiative himself in confirming the sense of the verbal message of French abandonment and had at the same time provided himself with a weapon with which to oppose and confuse the friends of Czechoslovakia among his Cabinet colleagues.

When later in the day the Cabinet met, and the Premier reported the terms of the Czech Note and the subsequent Anglo-French ultimatum delivered that morning, there was the fiercest opposition from Reynaud, Mandel, and Champetier de Ribes, who declared that not only had Bonnet broken his pledge to them that no pressure would be brought to bear on the Czechs to accept the Anglo-French Plan,[1] but that French and Czech security had been betrayed and destroyed without reference to the Cabinet.

At this point M. Bonnet produced the telegram from M. de Lacroix of the previous day requesting, on the part of the Czech Government, a definite statement of French intentions,[2] and also gave his own version of the telephone conversation with the Minister earlier that morning. From this evidence, he told his colleagues, it was clear that Beneš and Hodža did not wish to fight and that they sought from France a face-saving formula which would enable them to recede with grace from their previous attitude of intransigency. By offering them a *non possumus* in regard to her treaty obligations, France was in reality playing the game of the Czech leaders in helping them to keep face before their own people. Beneš and Hodža, argued M. Bonnet, were resigned to losing the Sudetenland, but, so long as the majority of Czechs continued to believe that France would support Czechoslovakia against German aggression, the leaders were powerless to act in accordance with their better judgement. The true course of friendship, therefore, was for France to strengthen the hands of the Czechoslovak Government by destroying the confidence of the Czechoslovak people in France.[3]

This casuistry had its effect. Confused and frustrated, distrusting Bonnet profoundly yet unable to refute his arguments,

---

[1] See above, p. 116.   [2] See above, p. 122.

[3] The arguments of M. Bonnet were not confined to the audience of his colleagues. They appeared with embellishments in *La République*. When informed by the Czechoslovak Minister in Paris of these newspaper stories, both President Beneš and the Czechoslovak Government protested vehemently against any such allegation. After the signature of the Munich Agreement the Government of General Syrový also issued an official denial that any such approach had been made from Prague to Paris.

the Reynaud group temporized. They had intended to resign forthwith and to publish their reasons for so doing. They now contented themselves with placing their resignations in the hands of M. Daladier and leaving it to him to make them effective at his own time.[1] M. Bonnet had triumphed after all.[2]

While he was being thus slandered and betrayed in Paris, Dr. Beneš was facing his own ordeal in Prague. Dawn was breaking over the baroque beauty of the Old Town and over the starker grace of the New City as the French and British envoys left the Hradschin Palace (September 21), and from six o'clock onwards the President was in continuous consultation. He conferred with his Ministers, with the Presidents of the Senate and the Chamber, with the party leaders, and with the heads of the Army. He was almost unrecognizable now from the ravages of fatigue and disaster, but his iron will and strong peasant body continued to carry him through to the end.

The position which he described was clear in every terrible aspect. Either Czechoslovakia must surrender to the demands of the Western Powers or those Powers would become her enemies, among whom must also now be numbered Poland and

[1] Ripka, pp. 86-93; Pertinax, pp. 399-400; de Monzie, pp. 34-5; Werth, pp. 229-30; Zay, pp. 8-9, 15-17; *Chronique de septembre*, by Pierre Nizan (Paris, 1939), pp. 90-92.

[2] In justice to the Diplomatic Service of France it must be said that there did exist among its members brave men who were opposed to the policy of their Minister. Within the Quai d'Orsay itself, these numbered the Secretary-General, M. Alexis Léger; the senior Ministerial Director, M. René Massigli, and the Director of the Press Department, M. Pierre Comert. All suffered at the hands of M. Bonnet for their opposition, but when the *débâcle* occurred in 1940, though all were opposed to the Vichy régime, only one rallied to the cause of General de Gaulle. M. Léger retired to Washington, where he found employment in the Library of Congress; M. Comert went to London and published a newspaper, *La France*, which was almost equally hostile to Pétain and to de Gaulle. It remained for M. Massigli alone to join the forces of the General, with whom he served first as Commissioner for Foreign Affairs in the French National Committee at Algiers, and subsequently as Ambassador in London.

The political evolution of the French Embassy in London is also not without interest. During the crisis year of 1938, the Ambassador, M. Charles Corbin, could not have been a stronger opponent of his country's policy of surrender, and in this attitude he was supported by his Counsellor and First Secretary, MM. Roger Cambon and Roland de Margerie. When, however, the disaster of 1940 struck France, this admirable team failed to respond to the greatness of the hour. The Ambassador and the Counsellor resigned, and retiring, the one to Argentina and the other to Sussex, took no part in the struggle for the liberation of France. On the other hand, M. de Margerie, who had inveighed so strongly against the policy of Munich, accepted the post of Consul-General at Shanghai at the hands of the Vichy Government. He was, however, but a half-hearted Pétainist, and was reinstated in the French diplomatic service after the establishment of the Fourth Republic.

Hungary, since both these countries, at the instigation of Germany, were demanding the equality of treatment for their minorities with that conceded to the Sudeten Germans.[1]

There remained Russia. In the course of the day there came the report of M. Litvinov's speech at Geneva before the Assembly of the League of Nations, in which he again reaffirmed the Soviet pledges to France and Czechoslovakia,[2] and this was followed later by a personal message from the Foreign Commissar, delivered by the Soviet Minister, M. Alexandrovsky, to the effect that, in the event of war, Russia would stand by Czechoslovakia whatever the Western Powers might do.

On receiving this offer the President at once asked the Soviet Minister what steps his country was prepared to take to ensure Russian support. To this M. Alexandrovsky replied, after consultation with Moscow, that Czechoslovakia must first submit her case to the League of Nations, who would proclaim Germany an aggressor. When this had been done, Soviet assistance would be immediately forthcoming. But, argued Dr. Beneš, by the time the rather cumbrous machinery of Geneva had been set in motion, Germany would have attacked and Czechoslovakia would have to withstand the full force of the onslaught alone, since France and Britain were " disinterested " and Russia would not move until after the League's pronouncement. Again M. Alexandrovsky consulted Moscow and again he returned to the Hradschin Palace. Now he brought a further pledge. The Soviet Government would come to the support of Czechoslovakia, he now reported, as soon as Moscow was informed that the League had been seized of the case and would not wait for a decision to be reached at Geneva.

[1] Representations to this effect were made by the Polish and Hungarian Ministers in Prague on September 21 and 22.

[2] M. Litvinov stated that he had officially informed the French Government, in answer to an enquiry received a few days before, that " our War Department is ready immediately to participate in a conference with representatives of the French and Czech War Departments, in order to discuss the measures appropriate to the moment ". He had also suggested that, independently of this consultation, the question should be raised at the League of Nations, in order to mobilize public opinion and to ascertain " the position of certain other states, whose passive aid might be extremely valuable " (*Against Aggression*, collected speeches of Maxim Litvinov (New York, 1939), p. 129). This last reference was doubtless directed to Rumania, the only channel for Russian assistance to Czechoslovakia, since Poland was now openly ranged on the side of Germany. When sounded by President Beneš on the matter of facilitating the passage of Soviet troops and aircraft through and over Rumania, King Carol had begged that the request should not be pressed.

But this offer served only to bring into the open the latent fear and suspicion of Russia which were harboured in certain Czech circles. Dr. Hodža and the Ministers of the ·Interior and of Defence, all members of the Agrarian Party, were opposed to resistance with Russia as a sole ally, and the Bureau of the Agrarian Party was strongly of the same opinion.[1]

All day the conferences continued, but to Dr. Beneš they could have but one end. " We have been basely betrayed," he repeated again and again, but he knew that they must capitulate. The end came at five o'clock in the afternoon when the Czechoslovak acceptance of the Anglo-French Plan was handed to the British and French Ministers.[2]

In resigning themselves to their fate, the Czechoslovak Government placed on record their assumption that Britain and France would regard the principle of the guarantee of Czech frontiers as an integral part of Czech acceptance, and that they would therefore not permit a German invasion of Czechoslovak territory, which would remain Czechoslovak up to the moment of its transfer after the delimitation of the new frontiers by the International Commission in agreement with the Czechoslovak Government. Even in the midst of disaster Dr. Beneš had an eye to the future.[3]

Czechoslovakia, who had faced with courage the threats of her enemies, bowed her head at the desertion of her friends. Against her better judgement, and yielding only to the most ruthless pressure, she sacrificed herself in the cause of peace.

" We had no other choice, because we were left alone." [4]

(iv)

ACT II : GODESBERG

" European peace is what I am aiming at and I hope this journey may be the way to get it," said Mr. Chamberlain to the

[1] According to some authorities certain members of the Agrarian Party threatened to open the frontier to Hitler if the Government decided to accept assistance from the Red Army. (See *La Tragédie tchécoslovaque*, by Paul Buk (Paris, 1939), p. 55.)

[2] *Czechoslovak Archives.*

[3] The British Minister was at once instructed to inform President Beneš that His Majesty's Government were " profoundly conscious of the immense sacrifices to which the Czechoslovak Government had agreed, and the great public spirit they had shown ".

[4] Czechoslovak Government Statement of September 21, 1938. Dr. Hodža's Cabinet resigned on September 22 and was succeeded, after wild popular demonstrations in favour of resistance, by a Government of National Concentration under General Syrový, who pledged himself to defend to the last the honour and integrity of the Czechoslovak State.

assembled newspaper men at Heston airport as he departed for his second conference with the Führer,[1] and he had good reasons to be satisfied with the results of his efforts during the past week. In every respect he had carried out the undertaking given to Hitler at Berchtesgaden ; the British Government had accepted the principle of self-determination as a solution for the Sudeten problem ; the French Government had given their approval, and together they had bludgeoned the Government of Czechoslovakia into acquiescence. Moreover, Czechoslovakia had not given, either by word or deed, the slightest provocation to Germany, though throughout the week the German press and radio had not ceased to vilify and insult the Czechoslovak people, their President and their Government.

The Prime Minister could justifiably anticipate the opening of the second stage in that plan for peace which he had agreed upon with the Führer, namely, the discussion of the ways and means of implementing the principle already accepted by all parties. It was this confidence which prompted Mr. Chamberlain to take with him on this second journey — in addition to Sir Horace Wilson and Mr. Strang — Sir William Malkin, the head of the drafting and legal department of the Foreign Office.[2]

Mr. Chamberlain's confidence in his success received further confirmation on his arrival at Cologne. He was received with every mark of deference. An S.S. guard of honour awaited his inspection and a band greeted him with " God Save the King ". The streets through which he drove to the Petersburg Hotel at Godesberg were decorated with the swastika and the Union Jack and the good people of Cologne and Godesberg demonstrated their unconcealed pleasure at seeing one whom they recognized as the harbinger of peace.

Before his meeting with Hitler in the late afternoon of September 22, Mr. Chamberlain conferred with the British Ambassador, who presumably told him of a conversation he had had with Göring during the previous week. " If England makes war on Germany," the Field-Marshal had said, " no one knows what the ultimate end will be. But one thing is quite certain. Before the war is over there will be very few Czechs left alive and little of

---

[1] *The Times*, September 23, 1938.
[2] Sir William Malkin was killed in an air disaster in the Atlantic as he was returning from the San Francisco Conference, August 1945.

London left standing," [1] and he had gone on to disclose how well Germany was informed of the unprepared state of Britain's air defences. As a final remark, he threw in that the German Air Force was numerically superior to that of Britain, France, Belgium and Czechoslovakia combined, and of this statement Sir Nevile Henderson had no reason to doubt the accuracy.[2]

Such a report would, however, have had little effect on Mr. Chamberlain, since he was confident that all danger of war was now virtually over and that what would emerge from the forthcoming discussion that afternoon would be a concrete plan for peace. It was in this happy frame of mind that he was ferried across the Rhine to the Hotel Dreesen,[3] where the Führer had established his quarters.[4]

Mr. Chamberlain opened the proceedings with an account of his achievements since their first meeting at Berchtesgaden, and informed Hitler of the details of the Anglo-French Plan which the Czechs had accepted. He went on to outline the steps which in his opinion should be taken to effect the peaceful transfer of the Sudeten territory in the shortest possible time.

This, however, was not at all in accordance with the Führer's programme. He had indeed proceeded along quite contrary lines. What he had anticipated was a message from Mr. Chamberlain that, though Britain and France could not associate themselves with the German demands on Czechoslovakia, they

[1] That Göring knew of what he spoke has been subsequently confirmed in detail. " Operation Green " provided not only for the destruction of Prague by aerial bombardment but also for the use of poison gas against the civil population of Czechoslovakia (*International Military Tribunal Document*, 388–PS).

[2] Henderson, p. 156.

[3] The owner of this hotel, Herr Dreesen, had been an early member of the Nazi Party and had achieved a certain intimacy with Hitler during the days of the struggle for power. He had, in fact, provided free board and lodging on a number of occasions and the Führer was wont to retire to this hotel when in need of rest and contemplation. It was there that he took the final decision to carry out the Blood Purge of June 30, 1934, and it was from there that he left by air with Goebbels for Munich in order to direct personally the arrest and execution of Ernst Röhm, Edmund Heines and other S.A. leaders.

[4] On the occasion of the second meeting with Mr. Chamberlain, Hitler was accompanied by Goebbels, Himmler, Ribbentrop; von Weiszäcker, the State Secretary of the Foreign Ministry; von Dirksen, Ambassador in London; General Keitel; Dr. Gaus, head of the Legal Department of the Foreign Ministry; von Domberg, Chief of Protocol; and the inevitable Schmidt as interpreter. The conversations were not *tête-à-tête* on this occasion, for Sir Nevile Henderson had learned his lesson at Berchtesgaden. The Prime Minister was supported by Sir Horace Wilson, and sometimes by the Ambassador, while Mr. Ivone Kirkpatrick acted as interpreter and took notes of the proceedings. Ribbentrop was present at some of the discussions. (See Henderson, p. 154.)

would nevertheless not regard an occupation by Germany of the Sudeten areas as a *casus foederis* ; or there was the alternative of an unwilling declaration by France of support for the Czechs, but only in the event of British assistance being assured, and this, the Führer felt, despite Mr. Chamberlain's differentiation between " threats " and " warnings ", was improbable.

The position which Hitler had assumed was simple beyond belief. He intended to send his troops into the Sudeten areas by October 1, 1938. That was all there was to it. As he had phrased it in his directive of May 30 : " It is my unalterable will to smash Czechoslovakia by military action in the near future ",[1] and the moment was now approaching when the future should become the present. At the appointed time " Operation Green " would go into effect, whether France and Britain objected or not. His agreement with Mr. Chamberlain at Berchtesgaden had seemed entirely fatuous, and the task which the British Prime Minister had undertaken to perform appeared to be one of those Herculean labours which are assigned on account of their impossibility. In his shrewd and careful planning Hitler had never foreseen that Mr. Chamberlain would return from London with so wholesale a compliance with the German demands.[2]

So assured was he of the contrary that he had simply ignored this possibility altogether, and had proceeded, in accordance with the schedule of " Operation Green ", to deploy seven divisions along the Czechoslovak frontier and to place the Sudeten German Free Corps under the German High Command ; to foment the Slovaks to begin their agitation for autonomy ;[3] and to mobilize the Poles and Hungarians to take such action as would satisfy their demands on Czechoslovakia in the event of a peaceful settlement, and would force the Czechs to fight on all fronts in case of war.[4]

[1] See above, p. 61.

[2] He so confessed later to Mr. Chamberlain, who repeated the fact to the House of Commons on September 28, adding, with a certain *naïveté*, that he did not think for one moment that Hitler was deliberately deceiving him.

[3] *International Military Tribunal Document*, 2858–PS.

[4] The British Government had been made aware of these claims by the Hungarian Minister and the Polish Ambassador in London on September 19 and 20. The Government had, however, only " taken note " of these representations, on the ground that they were concentrating all their efforts on the Sudeten problem. (See Mr. Chamberlain's statement to the House of Commons, September 28, 1938.)

To the hesitant objections of the Hungarians, who feared the consequences to themselves of such depredations, the Führer had remarked trenchantly that " only those could eat at the feast who had participated in the preparation of the dish " (*International Military Tribunal Documents*, 2796–PS and 2797–PS).

Hitler himself had been faithful to his part of the Berchtesgaden bargain after his own peculiar fashion, and had taken no
military action against the Czechs until Mr. Chamberlain's
return — though he had not curbed the tide of abuse which
flowed out incessantly over the German radio. But this good
faith was but part of a greater infamy. He had made no attack
upon Czechoslovakia because the scheduled moment for this had
not yet come, but he was not averse to using this fact to delude
Mr. Chamberlain as to his *Bundnisfähigkeit*. And meanwhile the
time-table of " Operation Green " moved relentlessly and dia-
bolically forward.[1]

Everything had gone smoothly until this sudden surprise move
by Mr. Chamberlain, who had made a similar manœuvre to that
which had called forth Karl Hermann Frank's horrified exclamation on reading the Czech Government's " Plan No. 4 " : " My
God, they have given us everything ! "[2]

And so, when Mr. Chamberlain had finished his opening
remarks and looked confidently down the green baize-covered
board-room table for the Führer's reactions, there was a moment
of incredulous silence. Then, to crystallize the matter, Hitler
asked directly : " Do I undertand that the British, French, and
Czechoslovak Governments have agreed to the transfer of the
Sudetenland from Czechoslovakia to Germany ? " " Yes,"
replied the Prime Minister. There was another pause, a longer
one this time, and then the Führer replied incisively : " I am
extremely sorry, but that's no longer of any use (*Es tut mir
fürchtbar leid, aber das geht mir nicht mehr*)".[3]

He went on to explain that the dilatory processes which the
Prime Minister had proposed presented too many opportunities
for evasion by the Czechs. The Sudeten areas in the north, west
and south, where the German population constituted more than

---

[1] It would appear, however, that Hitler had had some advance indication of the
acceptance of the Anglo-French Plan, which he had not yet entirely believed, before
his meeting with Mr. Chamberlain on September 22. General Jodl records that at
11.30 A.M. on the previous day (September 21) he received a telephone message from
Hitler's Adjutant : " The Führer has received news five minutes ago that Prague is
said to have accepted unconditionally ". At 12.45 a second message arrived authorizing continued preparations for " Operation Green ", but adding the warning that
everything must be in readiness for a peaceful occupation (*International Military Tribunal
Document*, 1780–PS). The premature announcement of the Czech acceptance of the
Anglo-French Plan was made by the Agence Havas. The report came ostensibly from
London but it is alleged to have been issued personally by M. Bonnet in Paris (*Suicide
of a Democracy*, by Heinz Pol (London, 1940), p. 82).

[2] See above, p. 92.   [3] Henderson, p. 158.

50 per cent of the population, must be evacuated by all Czech troops and officials and occupied by German troops ; a plebiscite would be held in November, and, in accordance with its results, a new frontier would be drawn by either a German-Czech or an International Commission. In addition, certain other areas, in which the German minority was less than 50 per cent but still substantial, would also be subject to a plebiscite, but for the moment these areas might continue to be occupied by Czech officials. Both German and Czech troops were to be withdrawn from the disputed areas during the plebiscite, the details and the organization of which were to be in the hands of a joint German-Czech Commission. Moreover, the Führer refused to participate in any international guarantee of the new Czech frontier or to negotiate a non-aggression treaty with Czechoslovakia until such time as the claims of the Polish and Hungarian minorities had been satisfactorily settled.

Mr. Chamberlain was, to use his own phrase, " profoundly shocked " at this new development, which in his view constituted a breach of the agreement reached at Berchtesgaden. He recapitulated the terms of that agreement and the record of his own efforts to fulfil it. He could not be expected now to be fobbed off with the rejoinder that the success of these efforts was no longer adequate.

A debate of some acrimony followed, Hitler reiterating the failure of the Anglo-French Plan to meet the new contingencies, Mr. Chamberlain refusing to accept the new German proposals. During this time the Prime Minister was treated to a typical example both of the Führer's theatre-craft and of his temperamental nature. In the course of the discussion they were frequently disturbed by couriers who handed urgent despatches to Hitler. These the Führer would scan swiftly, and then, his face contorted with rage, would shout : " Two more Germans killed by the Czechs ; I will be avenged for every one of them. The Czechs must be annihilated." At length, after three hours, and many repetitions of this scene, Mr. Chamberlain withdrew, "full of foreboding ", but not before he had exacted from Hitler an extension of his assurance that he would not move his troops into Czechoslovakia while the negotiations continued, a concession which it was easy for the Führer to make since the zero hour for " Operation Green " had not yet arrived.

As the Prime Minister prepared to leave the Hotel Dreesen,

Hitler, still fulminating, followed him out on to the terrace. Suddenly he stopped speaking, and one of those curious lightning changes of temperament occurred. " Oh, Mr. Prime Minister," he said in a soft and almost tender voice, " I am so sorry : I had looked forward to showing you this beautiful view of the Rhine . . . but now it is hidden by the mist." [1]

That night the deadlock seemed to be complete and all Mr. Chamberlain's high hopes of peace appeared to be in ashes.[2] There were gloomy consultations with London and with Paris, which bore fruit next day in a message to Prague from the British and French Governments that they could no longer advise Czechoslovakia not to mobilize.[3]

But on the morrow (September 23) Mr. Chamberlain, having slept on the matter, decided to make one more effort. He had not been satisfied that in conversations carried on through an interpreter he had been completely understood by the Führer, and forthwith, " soon after breakfast ", he sat down to write him a letter in which he sought the basis of a compromise.[4] He admitted the German claim to the predominantly German areas of the Sudetenland and was certain that the Czechs would accept the Führer's proposal for the " adjustment " of the frontier beyond this predominantly German area. But he felt sure that the occupation by German troops of areas which would become part of the Reich at once " in principle ", and very shortly thereafter by formal delimitation, would be regarded by public opinion in Britain and France as " an unnecessary display of force ", and the Führer must realize that it was impossible for him (Mr. Chamberlain) to put forward any plan " unless I have reason to suppose that it will be considered by public opinion in my country, in France, and indeed in the world generally, as carrying out the principles already agreed upon in an orderly fashion and

---

[1] Mr. Chamberlain thus described the scene during his visit to Paris, with Lord Halifax, in November 1938 (*Tragedy in France*, by André Maurois (London, 1940), pp. 12-13).

[2] The authorities are at variance as to whether a second meeting for the following day was actually arranged on the evening of September 22. Mr. Chamberlain told the House of Commons that " we had arranged to resume our conversation at half-past eleven the next morning ", but Sir Nevile Henderson records that " the first interview at Godesberg thus ended without any reference to a subsequent meeting " (Henderson, p. 160).

[3] Ripka, pp. 128-30 ; Buk, pp. 79-81 ; also *Czechoslovak Archives*. The Czech mobilization was actually ordered at 10.20 P.M. on September 23 and was completed within twenty-four hours.

[4] *British White Paper*, Cmd. 5847, No. 3.

free from the threat of force ". Moreover, the Czech Government " would have no option but to resist such an occupation " and this would mean " the destruction of the basis upon which a week ago you and I agreed to work together ". He therefore proposed, as an alternative suggestion, that, " if the Czech Government agreed ", the policing of certain areas, pending their formal transfer to the Reich, should be carried out either by the Sudeten Germans themselves or by existing forces, possibly acting under neutral supervision.

All morning long the British delegation awaited an answer. The Prime Minister and the Ambassador impatiently paced the terrace of the Petersburg Hotel with its lovely view of river and mountain. Lunch-time came and went and still there was no reaction from the opposite bank. It was not until late in the afternoon that the Führer's answer was received.

The truth was, as was seen from the text of the reply, that Mr. Chamberlain's letter had thrown Hitler into one of those paroxysms of rage which justified the nickname of " *Teppichfresser* " (carpet-eater) by which he was familiarly known in the Party.[1] The Führer's reply was a furious tirade which, though it contained much abusive and explanatory material, constituted no sort of modification of his previous demands, either along the lines suggested by the Prime Minister or any other.[2]

In contrast with this vulgar outburst, Mr. Chamberlain's reply was courteous and brief.[3] He had exhausted all his efforts and also the usefulness of his presence in Germany. By the hand of Sir Horace Wilson and Sir Nevile Henderson he requested a Memorandum of the German proposals for transmission to Prague, and intimated his intention to return to England.

Again there was an interminable delay. It is to be believed that the Prime Minister's refusal to renew personal contact had caused some alarm among the more moderate members of the Führer's *entourage*, though it is probable that Hitler himself remained unimpressed. However, by evening he had quieted down and an invitation to a further conversation at 10.30 P.M. was extended and accepted.

It was at this meeting that Mr. Chamberlain received the Memorandum for which he had asked, and for the first time he was confronted with a time-limit. The Czechs were required to begin the evacuation of the predominantly German areas at

---

[1] Shirer, p. 137.   [2] *British White Paper*, Cmd. 5847, No. 4.   [3] *Ibid.* No. 5.

8 A.M. on September 26 and to complete the operation by September 28.[1]

" But this," said the Prime Minister, as he read the paper, " is nothing less than an ultimatum."

" Nothing of the sort," replied Hitler. " It is not a *diktat* at all : look, the document is headed by the word ' Memorandum '." [2]

It was then that Mr. Chamberlain's anger, humiliation and disappointment became too much for him to restrain. He had suffered much disillusionment in the last thirty-six hours and this cynical casuistry was more than he could stand. In his own words, he spoke " very frankly ".

" I dwelt with all the emphasis at my command [he later told the House of Commons] on the risks which were incurred by insisting on such terms, and on the terrible consequences of a war if war ensued. I declared that the language and the manner of the document, which I described as an ultimatum rather than a memorandum, would profoundly shock public opinion in neutral countries, and I bitterly reproached the Chancellor for his failure to respond in any way to the efforts which I had made to secure peace." [3]

These words are revealing of Mr. Chamberlain at this moment. His charges against the Führer are disclosed as based on an innate horror of war, a dread of what the reaction of public opinion might be, and a deep resentment of the blow to his personal vanity : for he had pledged his reputation on the preservation of peace.

That he was eloquent is clear, and the effect on the Führer of this elderly and irate business man's outburst was unexpected. He agreed to extend the time limit to October 1 — the ultimate date for putting " Operation Green " into execution — at which time German troops would enter Czechoslovakia, and with his own hand made certain marginal alterations, which, although minor in character, did to some extent mitigate the severity of the demands — if it is possible to allay the severity of a death sentence. It was this amended version of the Memorandum that the Prime Minister consented to transmit to the Czechoslovak Government, though he made it clear that he could neither accept it personally nor recommend it to Prague.[4]

---

[1] *House of Commons Debates*, September 28, 1938, col. 21.   [2] Henderson, p. 161.
[3] *House of Commoms Debates*, September 28, 1938, col. 21.
[4] For text see Appendix G. The Memorandum was entrusted to the British Military Attaché, Colonel Mason Macfarlane, who, travelling by plane and motor-

So concluded the formal conference, but the two chief protagonists lingered a little together. The Führer was in one of his guileful moods. " You are the only man to whom I have ever made a concession," he said, thus applying balm to Mr. Chamberlain's wounded vanity, and he went on to assure the Prime Minister that the annexation of the Sudetenland represented the last of his territorial ambitions in Europe. With the incorporation of these areas in the Reich he would have brought the last sizable German minority back into the Fatherland. He had no design upon the new Czechoslovak State, and he wanted no peoples in his German Reich other than Germans. He was prepared to guarantee the new Czech frontier as soon as the Polish and Hungarian claims had been settled. His great desire, reiterated Hitler, was to be on friendly terms with England, and, once this Sudeten question could be got out of the way peacefully, he would gladly resume the personal contact which the meetings at Berchtesgaden and Godesberg had established. He had no doubt that the little difficulties which existed between them in the matter of the German colonies could be settled " without a mobilization ".

Hitler's motive in making the concessions in the time-limit of the Memorandum, and later in lavishing these blandishments on Mr. Chamberlain, may be ascribed both to duplicity and caution. The extension of the time-limit was in reality no concession at all, since, as we now know, the ultimate effective date for " Operation Green " had always been October 1, and the actual date selected for the Operation to begin was September 30. But it left the impression with Mr. Chamberlain that he, and he alone, had wrung an indulgence from Hitler.

But the motive went deeper than that. Though Hitler had determined as early as November 1937 that the independence of Austria and Czechoslovakia must be destroyed, he had not at that time decided upon military action as the medium in the case of Czechoslovakia. That was a decision which had only been taken on May 28, 1938, and incorporated in a general directive to the *Wehrmacht* two days later. Hitler had then determined that Czechoslovakia should suffer conquest at the hands of the German military machine. But this did not necessarily mean war. It

---

car, and even partly on foot, placed it in the hands of the British Minister in Prague on the night of September 24. It was then communicated by Mr. Newton to the Czechoslovak Government.

meant that the Sudetenland would be occupied by German troops before it was annexed to the Reich — that is to say, while it was still Czech territory. If the Czechs accepted, the military might of Germany would have achieved one more bloodless victory ; if, on the other hand, the Czechs resisted, their resistance would be crushed by the united forces of Germany, Hungary and Poland. This might mean war with France, and ultimately with Russia and Britain, and, though the Führer's intuition told him that such would not be the case, he was prepared, in any event, to take the risk of a general war. The General Staff, however, were not enthusiastic about embarking on such a venture. Though they were confident of the outcome in the case of Britain and France, they had a healthy respect for the Czech fortifications. Moreover, they were traditionally opposed to a " two-front war " and were, therefore, the more apprehensive of a conflict which might indeed engage them on three fronts, since they did not rule out the possibility of Russian intervention. In view of these considerations, there is no doubt that, while ready to implement " Operation Green " on the Führer's command, they urged him to gain his ends peacefully if possible.

Hitler, while contemptuous of their lack of political insight, saw the force of their argument. Though he was prepared to go to war to attain the achievement of his ambitions, even he had no desire to make war simply for the fun of it. Hitler was ever mindful of his basic principle — to achieve the greatest conquest at the lowest cost ; he was also keenly conscious of the fact that the threat of force is often as productive of results as the use of force itself, particularly when force is there to back the threat when necessary.

The Führer had been genuinely impressed by Mr. Chamberlain's ability to comply with demands that were seemingly incapable of fulfilment and to obtain the assent of the French and Czechs also. The Prime Minister must, therefore, be sent home with the conviction of Germany's unalterable determination to occupy the Sudetenland as well as to annex it, even at the risk of war, but he must also carry with him the belief of the Führer's personal good-will and admiration of his abilities. As a result of this dual impression Mr. Chamberlain might feel impelled to exercise once again that great capacity for concession which he had already demonstrated.

It was for this reason that Hitler spoke softly to the Prime

Minister at the conclusion of the Godesberg conference. He had nothing to lose thereby, and perhaps something to gain, but in the meantime the preparations for the destruction of Czechoslovakia proceeded with relentless precision.

(v)

Second Entr'acte: London, Paris, Prague and Berlin

What must have been the thoughts of Mr. Chamberlain as he flew back to London on that Saturday morning (September 24)? He had set out two days before with such high hopes, and these hopes had been shattered on the intransigence of Hitler's vengeful ambition. Yet was the Führer so adamant after all? Had he not made concessions in the face of Mr. Chamberlain's righteous anger? Had he not given assurances that what he really desired was peace and friendship with Britain? In that case must not the Czechs be made to endure even the greatest sacrifices demanded in the Godesberg Memorandum? After all, when the principle of transfer had been accepted, it would be childish to quarrel irreparably on the minutiae of procedure. The Czechs could not be allowed to plunge the world into war over a matter of detail. " Is the position hopeless, sir ? " someone had asked him the previous night as he returned late and weary to the Hotel Petersburg. " I would not like to say that," he had answered. " It is up to the Czechs now."[1]

Whatever his thoughts may have been when the Cabinet met that evening, the Prime Minister endeavoured to do exactly that which he had assured Hitler it was impossible for him to contemplate, namely, to persuade his colleagues to accept the new German demands, in the light of the Führer's subsequent promise, and to put pressure on the Czechs to do likewise. " I know Hitler will keep his word and prove better than his word," he declared.

Differences of opinion had long existed in the Cabinet on the subject of foreign policy. The group of which Mr. Duff Cooper, the First Lord of the Admiralty, was the acknowledged leader, had been anxious and uneasy at the continued willingness of the Prime Minister to yield ground in the face of every pressure. They had, with great reluctance, accepted the " Anglo-French

[1] *The Times*, September 24, 1938.

Plan " on the ground that peace must be preserved at nearly any price. Now, however, confronted with new and harsher demands, they could not support Mr. Chamberlain's desire for acquiescence with the terms of the Godesberg Memorandum.

" If I were a party to persuading or even suggesting to the Czechoslovak Government that they should accept that ultimatum," Mr. Duff Cooper later declared, " I should never hold my head up again," and many of his colleagues supported him, assuring the Prime Minister that it would be impossible to get his policy through the House of Commons.

The Cabinet adjourned without having reached a decision. It met again next morning at 10.30, and now there was a new development of great importance. In the watches of the night Lord Halifax had reached a grave decision — he could no longer accept the Prime Minister's view. It is believed that he now urged Mr. Chamberlain to reject the Godesberg terms and to give assurances to France that Britain would support her if she were called upon to honour her obligations to Czechoslovakia.

The Prime Minister still hesitated. He was unwilling to take a step which might bring war within measurable distance. He was unwilling even to contemplate the possibility of war, and rejected proposals for preliminary measures of mobilization and defence. The discussion was long and anxious. At one moment, despairing of action, Mr. Duff Cooper offered to resign but was asked by the Prime Minister to reconsider so drastic a decision.

Finally, in face of the majority opinion of his colleagues, Mr. Chamberlain agreed both to the rejection of the Godesberg terms and to the giving of assurances to France.

In so doing the Government had the unanimous support of the majority of the British press and public. Even Mr. Garvin, no friend of the Czechs, declared that " the Nazi Power last week threw off the mask before the British Prime Minister and demanded in effect his total capitulation on their own soil. They counted that their armed advantage had made them already masters of the earth. Not yet." [1] The *Daily Telegraph* on the 26th published the text of the Godesberg Memorandum, describing it as an attempt to exact " an abject and humiliating capitulation ", and was joined in its protests by both *The Times* and the *Manchester Guardian*.

There did not lack those, however, who, in public life and in

[1] *The Observer*, September 25, 1938.

the press, attempted to minimize the differences between the terms of the Anglo-French Plan and those of the Godesberg Memorandum, and to demonstrate that what Hitler now required was, in fact, little more than the Czechs had themselves already conceded.[1] But these were in the minority. The bulk of the British public were deeply shocked at the rapacity of the German demands and were united in applauding their rejection by the British Government. With reluctant determination, the British man-in-the-street again faced the prospect of war and did not flinch from it.

Similarly in Paris the atmosphere had hardened in favour of resistance. M. Daladier had regained his courage and — for the moment — his command of the situation. Though shocked and aghast at the pass to which France had been brought by his abdication of her rights in favour of Mr. Chamberlain, M. Daladier now exhibited more of his bull-like characteristics than he had shown for some time. He had shaken off his lethargy and, with the support of General Gamelin, who, to do him justice, had consistently argued that French diplomacy had been completely out of proportion to her military strength, the Premier did not hesitate to order a " partial mobilization " on September 24.

In the Cabinet also he was a new man, dominating the meetings and refusing to be browbeaten or side-tracked by his slippery Foreign Minister. Thus, despite the energetic efforts of M. Bonnet inside the Government and of MM. Flandin and Caillaux outside, the French Cabinet unanimously rejected the terms of the Godesberg Memorandum on the morning of September 25, shortly before the departure of the Premier and M. Bonnet for London.

In Prague the Government of General Syrový, after a long Cabinet meeting with the President, declared the Godesberg terms to be " absolutely and unconditionally unacceptable ", and their Note of rejection, penned by the gallant son of a great father, was delivered by its author, Jan Masaryk, to Lord Halifax on Sunday afternoon. Few State documents have displayed more simple, poignant dignity.[2] M. Masaryk wrote from the deep suffering of his heart, with the fate of his father's life-work trembling in the balance.

---

[1] For a comparison of the terms of the Anglo-French Plan, Godesberg Memorandum and the Munich Agreement, see Appendix J.

[2] *British White Paper*, Cmd. 5847, No. 7.

His country, wrote the Czechoslovak Minister, had accepted "the so-called Anglo-French Plan for ceding parts of Czechoslovakia . . . under extreme duress ", on the understanding that it was to be the end of the demands to be made of it " and because it followed from the Anglo-French pressure that these two Powers would accept responsibility for our reduced frontiers and would guarantee us their support in the event of our being feloniously attacked ". Now had come a further set of demands, at the contents of which the Czechoslovak Government were amazed.

" It is a *de facto* ultimatum of the sort usually presented to a vanquished nation and not a proposition to a sovereign State which has shown the greatest possible readiness to make sacrifices for the appeasement of Europe. . . . The proposals go far beyond what we agreed to in the so-called Anglo-French Plan. They deprive us of every safeguard for our national existence. We are to yield up large proportions of our carefully prepared defences, and to admit the German armies deep into our country before we have been able to organize it on the new basis or make any preparation for its defence. Our national and economic independence would automatically disappear with the acceptance of Herr Hitler's plan. The whole process of moving the population is to be reduced to panic flight on the part of those who will not accept the German Nazi régime. They have to leave their homes without even the right to take their personal belongings, or, even in the case of peasants, their cow."

M. Masaryk concluded with the brave and simple words :

" Against these new and cruel demands my Government feel bound to make their utmost resistance, and we shall do so, God helping. The nation of St. Wenceslas, John Hus, and Thomas Masaryk will not be a nation of slaves." [1]

Thus, when the British and French Ministers met in Downing Street on Sunday afternoon (September 25), the deadlock seemed complete. The Governments of Britain, France and Czechoslovakia had rejected the terms of the Godesberg Memorandum and war appeared to be round the corner. The prospects of international solidarity behind Czechoslovakia, on the other hand, were not altogether unfavourable. To offset the open hostility of Poland and Hungary and the half-hearted support of Rumania, there was the clear warning which had been given to the Polish

---

[1] No truer prophecy was ever made ; for, although condemned to six years of Nazi servitude (March 1939–May 1945), the Czech nation never became slaves.

Ambassador in Moscow on September 23 that the Soviet Government would denounce the Russo-Polish Non-Aggression Treaty if Poland joined in an attack on Czechoslovakia. On the same day, moreover, M. Litvinov had stated categorically at Geneva, before the Sixth Committee of the League Assembly, that Soviet commitments to Czechoslovakia still held good even though Prague had accepted the Anglo-French Plan, which involved the " eventual denunciation of the Soviet-Czechoslovak Pact ".[1]

At their first meeting, on September 25, Mr. Chamberlain gave to the French Ministers a detailed account of his experiences at Godesberg, withholding nothing of the rapacity of the new German demands. All were agreed that the Czechoslovak Government could not be pressed to accept them. But what would be the result of their refusal ?

" If Germany then invades Czechoslovakia what will you do? " asked Mr. Chamberlain of M. Daladier.

" In that case France will come to the assistance of the Czechs ", was the reply.

But with what will you fight ? the British Ministers asked. Can you put the requisite number of troops into the field? Are your mechanized forces equal to those of the Germans ? Is your air-force capable of opposing the *Luftwaffe* ? How will you meet the rain of bombs which will fall on Paris and your railways, stations and air-fields ? Do not forget that the Czechs will be overwhelmed in a few days at most, and that then you will have to face Germany alone.

Under this inquisition M. Daladier writhed distractedly, for he knew that the answer to all these questions was a qualified negative, and he knew also that not until France did stand alone against Germany would Britain consider coming to her aid.

" Do you then suggest that France should remain aloof if Germany attacks Czechoslavakia ? " he demanded of Mr. Chamberlain, and the Prime Minister replied: " It is not for the British Government to express an opinion as to what France should do ; that is a matter for the Government of France." [2]

They separated that night without a word having been uttered concerning British assistance to France, and the only decision taken was to call General Gamelin to London for further discussions next day.

[1] *League of Nations Official Journal*, Special Supplement No. 189 (Geneva, 1938), pp. 31-5.   [2] Bonnet, I, pp. 268-9.

When the French Chief of Staff arrived from Paris (September 26) he brought with him a breath of optimism. The General had been angered at the news that the report which he had given to M. Daladier on September 12 on the military situation [1] had been transmitted to London by M. Bonnet in an emasculated form. He now repeated the substance of it, which was that, in the event of war, despite their discrepancies in armaments, " the democratic nations would dictate the peace ". When M. Bonnet attempted to rebut this with reference to the Vuillemin Report on the weakness of French aviation, General Gamelin snapped back: " It is the whole and not the part that counts," and hoped that he had convinced his audience.[2]

Encouraged by the persistent optimism of his Chief of Staff, M. Daladier's spirit revived. He again repeated the decision of France to support the Czechs in the event of German aggression. Mr. Chamberlain then made his announcement. He appreciated fully the position of France, he said, and he was prepared to take measures to support her. He would make a final appeal to Hitler to accept a solution by negotiation rather than resort to force, and he would couple with it the warning that " if, in pursuit of her treaty obligations, France became actively engaged in hostilities against Germany, the United Kingdom would feel obliged to support her ".

This declaration of policy, although it fell short of the automatic commitment which the French would have preferred, was a considerable advance on the statement of Lord Halifax to M. Bonnet of September 12.[3]   Indeed, in recognizing the treaty obligations of France as a potential *casus foederis*, Mr. Chamberlain had gone much farther than the existing undertakings which Britain had assumed toward the French at Locarno and had renewed in 1936. At any rate, on paper the British statement of September 26 constituted a departure from the traditional policy that Britain's commitments should not extend beyond the Rhine and a marked progress towards the granting of that " blank

---

[1] See above, p. 101 ; also Gamelin, II, pp. 351-2.

[2] Pertinax, p. 3.   Subsequent events in 1940 proved General Gamelin to be substantially wrong in his calculations, but he was confident enough of them two years before.   Shortly after the Anglo-French conference of September 25-26, he protested in writing to Mr. Hore-Belisha, the Secretary of State for War, against a memorandum from London transmitted to him by the British Military Attaché in Paris, which indicated that M. Bonnet's views had carried more weight than his among certain of the British Ministers attending the conference.

[3] See above, p. 98.

cheque" which Mr. Chamberlain had so firmly refused to countenance on March 24.[1] As such it was a revolutionary development
of considerable importance.

The conference concluded with an agreement for united action
in the event of unprovoked German aggression, and for the further
pursuit of any peaceful solution of the dispute between Germany
and Czechoslovakia on the basis of the Anglo-French Plan.

It is, however, surprising that, in view of the resolute attitude
of Russia and the appeal, which arrived during the discussion of
the 26th, of President Roosevelt to all parties in the dispute to
recall and abide by their obligations under the Pact of Paris of
1928,[2] the British and French Ministers should have given no
consideration either to finding a basis for common action with
the Soviet Government in the event of war, or of attempting to
enlist the services and assistance of the United States Government
in the work of mediation. The vital necessity of joint action with
Russia on the outbreak of hostilities appears to have been totally
ignored in the conversations, despite the fact that during them
General Gamelin received a repeated assurance from Marshal
Voroshilov, *via* the Soviet Military Attaché in Paris, that Russia
anticipated that Poland would join with Germany in any attack
upon Czechoslovakia and that he (Voroshilov) was therefore
preparing for active military operations in Poland. The General
informed the British and French authorities of this report, but,
we know, M. Bonnet consistently minimized both the good faith
and the value of Russian intervention, despite the official and
public declarations of Moscow of her readiness to consult.[3]

Incredulous, as always, of the good faith of Britain, M. Bonnet
remained sceptical of the undertaking given by Mr. Chamberlain.
On his return to Paris the Foreign Minister sought to determine
the degree of British support on which France could rely in the
event of war. Would Britain mobilize immediately? Would she
introduce conscription at once, and would she undertake to bear
half the cost of the war?

By a curious coincidence these same views were shared by
Pierre-Étienne Flandin, who in a letter to *Le Temps* stated that it

---

[1] See above, pp. 38-9.
[2] See *U.S. Department of State Press Releases* (Washington, D.C., 1938), vol. xix,
No. 470.
[3] Gamelin, II, pp. 348, 352. It should be noted that M. Bonnet, in his memoirs,
makes no mention of the report received by General Gamelin of the conversations
between his Chief of Staff and the Soviet Military Attaché in Paris.

was evident that " the French Government could not order a general mobilization unless the same measure is taken in the British Empire; it being understood, of course, that mobilization would involve the introduction of conscription in the British Empire, where it does not at present exist. Our British friends should, in all loyalty, be informed — and I have no doubt that MM. Daladier and Bonnet have done this — that the French Army would be unable alone, or even with the help of a small British contingent, to bear the strain of land operations on three fronts." [1]

M. Bonnet carried his scepticism into the Cabinet meeting of September 27, where he clashed on the subject with M. Daladier.[2] The French Premier was disposed to believe that Mr. Chamberlain had meant what he said, but there was doubt in his mind as to just how great the measure of British support could be. M. Daladier remembered the two divisions and the 150 planes of which the British had talked a few days earlier, and he awaited anxiously the replies to M. Bonnet's enquiries. Late that night they were delivered by Sir Eric Phipps and, alas for M. Daladier's hopes, they were as elusory and Laodicean as Bonnet had prognosticated.

In reply to the question, would they mobilize immediately? the British Government replied by pointing to the action which they had already taken in ordering the Fleet to battle stations and in calling up the reserves. With regard to the issues of conscription and the equal division of war costs the British returned an evasive answer.[3] Again an opportunity had been missed of giving to the French an earnest of good faith.

The truth is that, though Mr. Chamberlain had in all sincerity pledged Britain's support to France, he was determined that this pledge should only be implemented after every effort and every sacrifice for peace had been exhausted. War was not yet a

[1] This letter appeared on September 26 in the afternoon edition of *Le Temps*, which is dated September 27, 1938. On the following day (September 27), M. Flandin actually posted up in the streets of Paris a proclamation inviting French citizens to refuse to comply with any military measures. The proclamation was immediately confiscated but M. Flandin remained at large.

[2] The Foreign Minister was giving his colleagues an erroneous account of a conversation which had taken place the previous day between Mr. Chamberlain and M. Daladier, at which he, Bonnet, had not been present. He concluded his remarks with the statement that France could not count on British help. At this point Daladier interrupted him with the question : " What do you know about it, since you were not there ? " (Lévy, p. 87). [3] Bonnet, I, pp. 272, 279, 367-8.

certainty and he strove desperately to prevent it from becoming so, even to the extent of discouraging the French — and the French were not averse to being discouraged.

Adolf Hitler was to speak in the Sportspalast in Berlin on the night of September 26, and, just as two weeks before at Nuremberg, all diplomatic activity was geared to this event. Mr. Chamberlain hoped that the suggestion of a settlement by conference would appeal to the Führer. He had conceived the idea of a Four-Power meeting some long time back and it was with reluctance that he had not seized the opportunity in July when it had been suggested by Sir Nevile Henderson.[1] At that time it had been felt difficult to exclude " other Powers " from such a conference and for that reason the proposal had been abandoned. Now, however, the situation was different. Russia, clearly the " other Power " referred to, had been, in July, a treaty partner with Czechoslovakia and an integral part of her system of security. But, in accepting the " Anglo-French Plan ", the Czechs had agreed to denounce their French and Russian Alliances of Mutual Assistance, which were to be replaced by an international guarantee. Yet in the original concept of this guarantee it had evidently been intended to invite the Soviet Union to participate. " France and Russia will begin by extending to Czechoslovakia their guarantee against unprovoked aggression in place of their former treaties of mutual assistance ", Lord Halifax had told the French Ambassador, " and Britain will give the same assurance in her turn ".[2] This had been on September 22, but in the meantime Mr. Chamberlain had returned from Godesberg with the very definite impression that the Führer would not be prepared to join in any guarantee arrangement which included Russia. It seems probable, therefore, that on Mr. Chamberlain's return the idea of Russian participation was discarded and that, when he then spoke to M. Daladier of a Four-Power conference, the Prime Minister was already thinking in terms of Italy, and not Russia, as the fourth Power.

Even before the arrival of the French Ministers the idea of a meeting of the Powers had been in Mr. Chamberlain's mind, and, when he and Lord Halifax received M. Jan Masaryk on Sunday afternoon (September 25), the Prime Minister had suggested that Czechoslovakia should consent to negotiate, " through an inter-

---

[1] See above, p. 70.
[2] Telegram from M. Corbin to M. Bonnet, September 22, 1938 (Bonnet, I, p. 260).

national conference in which Germany, Czechoslovakia and other Powers could participate ", to seek means of implementing the Anglo-French Plan. No indication was given, however, to M. Masaryk as to any restriction which might be placed on the number of " interested Powers " to be included. After consultation with Prague, the Czechoslovak Minister replied by letter to Lord Halifax (September 26) that his Government would be ready to assist in any effort to " find a different method of settling the Sudeten German question from that expounded in Herr Hitler's proposals, keeping in mind the possible reverting to the so-called Anglo-French Plan ", which nevertheless had " many unworkable features ".[1]

The suggestion was then discussed with MM. Daladier and Bonnet. As in the case of the despatch of Lord Runciman's Mission, the French Ministers, while distrustful of the method proposed, eventually agreed to it in principle, provided that France was not associated with the proposal or bore any direct responsibility. Accordingly the industrial *fidus Achates*, Sir Horace Wilson, was despatched to Berlin on the 26th with a letter which he was to deliver to the Führer before his Sportspalast speech at 8 P.M. In his letter Mr. Chamberlain, after recapitulating a number of arguments already used unsuccessfully with Hitler, proposed, in view of the fact that the Prague Government had rejected the terms of the Godesberg Memorandum — a course in which she had the sympathy of Britain and France — that direct negotiations for the transfer of the predominantly German territories of the Sudetenland should take place in a conference between representatives of the German and Czechoslovak Governments, at which, if desired by both parties, " I am willing to arrange for the representation of the British Government ".[2]

What this proposal was expected to achieve, save as a forlorn hope, it is difficult to say. The Führer had been quite explicit, both in speech and in writing, that the Godesberg Memorandum represented his last word on the subject and could be either taken or left. Doubtless Mr. Chamberlain was banking on the fact that he was " the only man to whom Hitler had ever made a concession " and hoped to repeat the performance. If he hoped to exercise a moderating force on the Führer's speech he was greatly disappointed.

Hitler was already in a bad humour when he received the

[1] *British White Paper*, Cmd. 5847, No. 10.   [2] *Ibid.* No. 9.

British Ambassador and Sir Horace Wilson at the Reichskanzlei on Monday afternoon, and the purport of their message did not improve his temper. He could scarcely be persuaded to listen to the end of the Prime Minister's letter, interrupting the reading of it with such shouts as " *Es hat keinen Sinn, weiter zu verhandeln* " (" It's no use talking any more ").[1] He was clearly working himself up into a rage as a preliminary to his speech, and a few hours later the world listened aghast to the naked animal passion of his fury.[2]

With the snarl of a wild beast he declared openly that, if " that Beneš " had not yielded up all the Sudetenlands by October 1, Germany would occupy them by that date with himself as the first soldier of the Reich.[3] His attack on President Beneš was vile and venomous, an amazing onslaught by one Chief of State upon another. The responsibility for war was placed in the hands of the President : " Now let M. Beneš make his choice."

Yet, in the throes of his anger, Hitler was shrewd enough to make a bid to Mr. Chamberlain. He praised the Prime Minister's efforts for peace ; he repeated " that, when the claims of other minorities have been satisfied, we will guarantee the integrity of the Czech State " ; he reiterated that " after the Sudeten German question is regulated we have no further territorial claims to make in Europe ". Germany wanted no Czech within the Reich, neither had she claims against France or Poland. In a sweeping god-like gesture he guaranteed the inviolability of all Germany's territorial neighbours. " This is no mean phrase. It is our holy will."

It was a shrewd and brutal speech and it had two very interesting and diverse effects in London. Scarcely had the last howl died away on the radio of Britain when the Foreign Office released a communiqué to the effect that, " if a German attack is made upon Czechoslovakia, the immediate result must be that

---

[1] Henderson, p. 163.

[2] For German text see *Völkischer Beobachter*, September 27, 1938 ; for English translation see *Hitler's Speeches, 1922-1939*, translated and edited by Norman H. Baynes (Oxford, 1942), vol. ii, pp. 1487-99.

[3] According to Ciano, Hitler had that afternoon informed the Italian Ambassador, Signor Attolico, that troops would move into Czechoslovakia at 2 P.M. on Wednesday, September 28. (See speech by Count Ciano, before the Fascist Chamber, November 30, 1938, *Giornale d' Italia*, December 1 and 2.) It will be remembered, however, that the X-Day for " Operation Green " was September 30, and on both September 26 and 27 Jodl records in his diary that " in no case will X-Day be before the 30th " (*International Military Tribunal Document*, 1780-PS).

France will be bound to come to her assistance and Great Britain and Russia will certainly stand by France ".[1]   This statement, issued by those who believed that surrender to force had gone far enough, was, apparently, an attempt to commit France irrevocably to subsequent action, and contains the only reference to co-operation with Russia in any British document of the period.   It was based on the statements which had been made by MM. Litvinov and Maisky on September 23, at Geneva, to Lord de la Warr and Mr. R. A. Butler, and which left the impression that Russia was prepared to intervene with France and Britain in defence of the Czechs, and to attend a three-Power conference or a meeting of the League Council in London in order to discuss the situation. The statement was a brave but fruitless gesture, for it was immediately sabotaged in Paris by M. Bonnet, who, on being questioned by journalists, replied that he had no confirmation of it, adding that it was manifestly the work of Sir Robert Vansittart, who was no longer of any importance in the conduct of British foreign policy, and had been endorsed " by an obscure underling ".[2] M. Bonnet was certainly not going to be caught on any such limed twig as that.   As for M. Daladier, he made no reference to the communiqué until after the Munich Agreement was safely signed.

Mr. Chamberlain's own public reaction to the Sportspalast speech was issued shortly after midnight on Monday the 26th, when he had already received a report by telephone from Sir Horace Wilson on his first interview with the Führer.   He appreciated the German Chancellor's reference to the efforts which he had made to save the peace, declared the Prime Minister, and he would not abandon those efforts.   Since Hitler had no faith in the promises of the Czechoslovak Government, the British Government regarded themselves as morally responsible for seeing that these promises were carried out, " fairly and fully " and with " reasonable promptitude ", provided the German Government would agree to the settlement of the terms of transfer by discussion and not by force.   " I trust that the Chancellor will not reject this proposal." [3]

---

[1] *House of Commons Debates*, March 1, 1939, col. 1230.

[2] Werth, p. 243 ; also *Après Munich : veux-tu vivre ou mourir ?* by Pierre Dominique (Paris, 1938), pp. 12-13.   The communiqué, which had never been shown to Sir Robert Vansittart, was to have been broadcast in German by the B.B.C. that same evening, but for " technical reasons " this did not take place.

[3] *The Times*, September 27, 1938.

The views of the Chancellor were revealed to Sir Horace Wilson and the British Ambassador when they had their second interview with him on the following morning (September 27). The answer which Sir Horace could carry back to London, said the Führer, was that the Czechs had two alternatives open to them : either to accept the terms of the Godesberg Memorandum or to reject them. They had apparently chosen the latter. " I will smash the Czechs " (" *Ich werde die Tschechen zerschlagen* "), Hitler repeated several times with evident pleasurable anticipation. He, Hitler, had said his last word.

In that case, said Sir Horace, he was charged by the Prime Minister to warn Herr Hitler in all solemn sincerity that " if, in pursuit of her Treaty obligations, France became actively engaged in hostilities against Germany, the United Kingdom would feel obliged to support her ".

" I can only take note of that position," replied Hitler ; " it means that if France elects to attack Germany, England will feel obliged to attack her also."

In vain Sir Horace protested that it meant nothing of the sort ; that the decision of peace or war rested solely with Hitler ; that even now it might be possible to get the Czechs to see reason. The Führer would have none of it. " If France and England strike ", he screamed, " let them do so. It's a matter of complete indifference to me. To-day is Tuesday ; by next Monday we shall all be at war." [1]

Rising to his feet, and speaking this time at " dictation speed ", Wilson repeated the Prime Minister's warning — and, as he left the room, the Führer's storm of fury burst.

Sir Horace Wilson returned to London that afternoon, and the news which he brought to the Prime Minister and the Inner Cabinet was so disquieting that a decision was at once taken to declare a State of Emergency by Order in Council, to mobilize the Fleet, and to call up the Auxiliary Air Force. The Prime Minister also sent the following telegram to President Beneš:

" I feel it my duty to inform you and the Czechoslovak Government that His Majesty's Government have received from Berlin

[1] Henderson, pp. 164-5. It is not entirely clear why Hitler specified Monday as the day on which Britain and Germany would be at war. September 30, the day on which " Operation Green " was due to begin, was a Friday, and Monday would therefore be October 3. It is probable that, though the action of France would presumably be automatic, the Führer believed that constitutional processes would delay a British declaration of war until Parliament met on the Monday.

information which makes it clear that the German Army will receive orders to cross the Czechoslovak frontier immediately if, by to-morrow (September 28) at 2 P.M., the Czechoslovak Government have not accepted the German conditions.[1] This means that Bohemia would be overrun by the German Army and nothing which another Power or Powers could do would be able to save your country and your people from such a fate. This remains true whatever the result of a world war might be. His Majesty's Government cannot assume the responsibility of advising you what you should do, but it believes that this information should be brought to your notice without delay." [2]

And thus President Beneš, who had already been made responsible by Hitler for the outbreak of war, was also held similarly responsible by Mr. Chamberlain.

How terrible a dilemma confronted Edvard Beneš as he sat alone in his office in the Hradschin Palace that September afternoon. He weighed the choice before him. If he accepted the Godesberg terms he drove a dagger into the heart of his own country, condemning her to a living death as the defenceless victim of Nazi caprice, to be devoured and dismembered at the Führer's whim, and at the same time destroying one of the great bastions of European security. If he rejected the terms and resisted the advance of the German armies, he would deliver up the peaceful citizens, the fair lands and the ancient cities of Bohemia and Moravia to fire and sword and devastation from the air. By so doing he would also precipitate a far wider conflict, which might end God knew where. The full tragedy of the quandary

---

[1] A confusion appears to have arisen in London as to the import of Göring's statement to Sir N. Henderson on September 27. According to M. Bonnet (*French Yellow Book*, No. 15), Göring said that, " if the Czechoslovak Government had not accepted the terms of the Godesberg Memorandum on the next day, September 28, by 2 P.M., measures of mobilization would be immediately taken and followed by action ". This appears to have been interpreted in London as an indication that German troops would actually cross the Czech frontier on the 28th, whereas the X-Day of " Operation Green " was always September 30, at the earliest, and was never changed. (See above, p. 61.)

[2] *Czechoslovak Archives*. This conviction on the part of the British Government that Czech resistance to a German attack would be ineffective — a conviction, be it noted, which was not shared by the German General Staff — was based on adverse reports from the Military Attachés at Prague and Berlin. Their views influenced British policy not only towards Czechoslovakia but also towards France ; for, at the same time that Mr. Chamberlain sent his warning to Dr. Beneš, the British Ambassador in Paris presented a Note to M. Bonnet which urged the French Government to take no military action — and particularly no action of an offensive nature — without preliminary consultation with the British, in order to avoid, if humanly possible, the unleashing of a world war in which Czechoslovakia could certainly not be saved from destruction (Bonnet, I, p. 280).

had been set out in cold sharp detail. The British Government could not assume the responsibility of advising him, they simply posed the problem starkly. They did not even give him contingent assurances of support in the event of his electing to resist.

Twenty-four years before, in August 1914, a ruler of another small people was confronted with a similar quandary. King Albert of the Belgians also depended on the good faith of France and Britain and had turned to them for help in the face of German menaces. What, one wonders, would have been the result if, at the eleventh hour, King Albert had received from Mr. Asquith and Sir Edward Grey a telegram similar to that which now lay before President Beneš ; if Poincaré and Viviani had threatened to withdraw their guarantee from Belgium ? The issues, though not similar in all aspects, are sufficiently parallel to warrant comparison.[1]

To Beneš, as he weighed his choice, there passed in review all that had happened since the final stages of this grim drama had opened in the summer. He was not given to reverie ; he was normally a man of action, but just now he looked back across the past few weeks with their burden of tragedy and disillusionment and surrender. The unctuous " impartiality " of Lord Runciman ; the cynical desertion of Bonnet ; the petulant bewilderment of Mr. Chamberlain ; the evident embarrassment of Mr. Newton and M. de Lacroix at the instructions with which they had to comply ; the vitriolic abuse of the Führer and his jackals, which hurt less than the cold abandonment by Czechoslovakia's friends — all these memories came to him. And there were others, happier thoughts which shone out in the night of despair : the magnificent solidarity of his fellow Czechoslovaks in the face of danger, and the most recent manifestation of this national unity which had come only that day in the form of a manifesto of support from the former Austrian aristocracy, who had never before recognized the republican régime ; the proffered support of Russia, of which new proof had also arrived that day in the

---

[1] It is true that, in the case of Belgium, Britain held from the first the position of a guarantor of the Treaty of London, whereas she had no other obligation to Czechoslovakia than the mutual engagement of membership in the League of Nations. But at the time Mr. Chamberlain sent this telegram he had already specifically informed both the French and German Governments of Britain's intention to support France in the discharge of her undertakings to Czechoslovakia, and, by the Anglo-French Plan, which Prague had accepted under pressure, Britain had agreed to join in a guarantee of Czechoslovakia's frontiers. Britain had therefore assumed, to a great extent, the responsibilities of a guarantor.

form of a member of the Soviet General Staff anxious to confer with the Czechoslovak Air Force; and perhaps, above all, the acts of individual loyalty such as that of General Faucher, the head of the French Military Mission, who, resigning his commission in protest against the policy of his country, had offered his services to Czechoslovakia.

The President walked to the window and looked out over the leafy slope to the river, the swiftly flowing Vltava. In the courtyard beneath, the guard was changing, the Legionaries wearing their traditional Russian, French and Italian uniforms, symbolic of the armies with which they had fought for liberty and freedom in 1914–18 when Czechoslovakia was still an unborn State. The shadows were lengthening; soon the lights would begin to come out in the darkness. Would it be the last night that they would shine peacefully over Prague? Was it possible that this time to-morrow the city might be laid in ruins from German bombing?

The President turned back into the room. He must decide. The answer for Berlin must be sent to London that nrght.[1]

Perhaps fortunately for Dr. Beneš, the responsibility of choice was removed from his hands. Already the swift passage of historic events had left Prague in a back-water, and, before he could reply to the Prime Minister's telegram, his Foreign Minister, Dr. Krofta, was bringing a second and most urgent message which he had received from the British Legation.

This new document did exactly what Mr. Chamberlain's previous telegram had said was impossible : it contained advice from the British Government.[2] It also represented Mr. Chamberlain's final effort to reach a compromise between the national honour of the Czechs and the predatory instincts of the Germans, between the Anglo-French Plan and the Godesberg Memorandum. Faced with the Führer's intransigence, Mr. Chamberlain had accepted, in principle and in a restricted sense, the military occupation of Czech territory, and also a mitigated version of the Führer's time-table, which the British Government would under-

[1] Mr. Chamberlain had expressly stated that he desired that any reply which the Czech Government might make to the Godesberg Memorandum should be transmitted through him as intermediary (*Czechoslovak Archives*).

[2] The inconsistency between the two telegrams was so apparent to Mr. Newton — as he explained to Dr. Krofta — that, before delivering the second, he had asked London whether it was not already out of date, to which he had received the reply that he must urgently present the proposals to the Czechoslovak Government (Ripka, p. 195).

take to see was carried out.[1] The first areas in the Sudeten Zones were to be handed over on October 1, on which date German troops would occupy Cheb and Asch, outside the Czech fortifications. Provision was made for an Anglo-German-Czech Delimitation Commission, which should have under its command certain international observers, a unit of the British Legion,[2] and, ultimately, four battalions of British troops. Another tripartite body was to be responsible for the withdrawal of Czech troops and State police. The fixing of " the broad outlines for the protection of the minorities in the ceded areas, and for the right of option and removal of property ", and for the determination of the new frontiers " with the greatest expedition " (i.e. by October 31), was also to be in the hands of this body. German troops would carry out a progressive occupation, from October 3 to 10, of territory in which it was agreed " that settlement was complete ". The question of the withdrawal of troops and the replacement of Czechoslovakia's present system of alliances by an international guarantee would be subjects for subsequent negotiation between Germany, Great Britain, France and Czechoslovakia.

The most surprising aspect in the document was the statement that " the only alternative to this plan would be an invasion and a dismemberment of the country by force, and that Czechoslovakia, though a conflict might arise which would lead to incalculable loss of life, could not be reconstituted in her frontiers, *whatever the result of the conflict may be* ".

In effect Czechoslovakia was being warned by Britain and France (for the French Government had associated themselves with these new last-hour proposals) that if she resisted aggression, except on the terms of her rather dubious allies, she would be condemned to dismemberment, even if she and her allies won the war; the inference being that it was clearly not worth while fighting at all. There was even a latent threat that the rejection by Czechoslovakia of these new proposals would constitute " provoked aggression " on her part against Germany, in which

---

[1] *Czechoslovak Archives.*

[2] The British Legion had offered its services in any capacity required in connection with the settlement of the Sudeten problem, and had been requested by the British Government to supply a force of 1000 volunteers for police duty in plebiscite areas. The President of the Legion, Major-General Sir Frederick Maurice, had been received by Hitler on September 25, and had discussed the matter with him. The force was never used and was disbanded on October 17, 1938.

case France, and subsequently Britain, would be released from any obligation towards her.

There can be few parallel cases in history in which a small State has been subjected to such simultaneous pressure from two groups of Great Powers, of which one group had recently agreed to protect her in the event of " unprovoked aggression ".

But Mr. Chamberlain was unaware of any lack of ethics in this latest approach. To him the preservation of peace in Europe was the major task, for which no sacrifice, whether his own or another's, was too great. He still hoped that these new concessions to Hitler might bring counter-concessions in return, and that the deadly, seemingly unavertable, approach of war might still be avoided.[1] The despatch of the new proposals to Berlin and to Prague[2] was his final act on September 27 before he made his broadcast to the British nation at 8.30 P.M., and he may well have thought he had made his last bid to save his country from destruction.[3]

It is a tragic irony that there were no two sadder men in London that evening than Jan Masaryk and Neville Chamberlain. Throughout the crisis, the Czechoslovak Minister had maintained an amazing and courageous dignity and restraint under the most difficult circumstances. He had even preserved to some degree his gallant gaiety of spirit. Despite the fact that it was his country — the country that Thomas Masaryk and Edvard Beneš had fashioned so bravely out of the ruins of 1918, and cherished so zealously thereafter — which was being discussed and parcelled out, he had been forced to stand by in the rôle of an observer, to listen to the brutal threats of his enemies and half-hearted promises of his friends. But he had not been a passive spectator. No man could have done more for his country than had he behind the scenes, and the fact that the Czech cause had so

---

[1] Mr. Chamberlain had yet to learn the truth of the remark which Lincoln Steffens made to President Wilson in the course of the Paris Peace Conference apropos of the Fiume compromise : " Mr. President, you cannot commit rape a little ".

[2] The proposals were delivered in Prague at 9.30 P.M. and in Berlin at 11 P.M. (Ripka, p. 195 ; Henderson, p. 166).

[3] The Czechoslovak Government accepted the British proposals, together with the " time-table ", on September 28, but in so doing they pointed out that the proposals departed in several respects from the " Anglo-French Plan " and that in others they were impossible of fulfilment within the time specified. In particular, it was stated that the Czechoslovak Government could not evacuate their territory, demobilize their troops and abandon their fortifications before the delimitation of the new frontier and the international guarantee were in operation (*Czechoslovak Archives*).

many sympathizers in Britain was due in no small measure to the affection with which they regarded Jan Masaryk and their respect for his integrity.

And now the tragic game was almost played out. Tomorrow the war might begin — for M. Masaryk had no doubt but that his people would fight, even if alone. Sick at heart and very lonely despite his many friends, he waited silently at his Legation to hear the Prime Minister's broadcast.

Across the Park, at No. 10 Downing Street, Mr. Chamberlain sat before the microphone. His world was in ashes and he was deathly tired. The peace of Europe, to preserve which he had laboured so earnestly, was hanging by a hair to-night and his sense of duty had impelled him to speak to the British public. The address which he made is the most complete revelation of his whole attitude towards the crisis. It is all there : the overwhelming horror of war and the consequent determination to spare no effort to protect his country from that horror, despite the personal sacrifice and public stricture which might be involved ; the greater sympathy for the German case than for that of the Czechs, but, at the same time, the bewildered puzzlement at the Führer's implacable hatred and the tenacious obstinacy of the Czechs, which together threatened to bring about a war over the details of a matter that had already been settled in principle ; the continued and incomprehensible belief in Hitler's promises ; and the evident lack of perception of the deeper issues at stake.

Starting from his horror of war — " so horrible, fantastic, incredible . . . because of a quarrel in a far-away country between people of whom we know nothing . . . impossible that a quarrel that has already been settled in principle should be the subject of a war " — he reviewed briefly, for he would make his detailed statement in Parliament on the morrow, his negotiations with Hitler at Berchtesgaden and Godesberg. He had vividly realized how the Führer felt that " he must champion other Germans, and his indignation that grievances have not been met before this ". After Berchtesgaden Hitler had got " the substance of what he wanted ", and the Prime Minister found his attitude at Godesberg " unreasonable ". If it arose from a doubt of the intention of the Czechoslovak Government to carry out their promises Britain had offered to guarantee their words :

" And I am sure the value of our promise will not be underrated anywhere. . . . I shall not give up the hope of a peaceful solution [said the Prime Minister in a voice of infinite weariness], nor abandon my efforts for peace as long as any chance for peace remains. I would not hesitate to pay even a third visit to Germany if I thought it would do any good. But at this moment I see nothing further that I can usefully do in the way of mediation."

He warned the British people to keep calm and to take part in the work of defence, though the precautionary measures taken did not necessarily mean that war was imminent. And then, in his final passage, his whole soul was revealed :

" However much we may sympathize with a small nation confronted by a big and powerful neighbour, we cannot in all circumstances undertake to involve the whole British Empire in a war simply on her account. If we have to fight it must be on larger issues than that. I am myself a man of peace to the very depths of my soul. Armed conflict between nations is a nightmare to me ; but, if I were convinced that any nation had made up its mind to dominate the world by fear of force, I should feel that it must be resisted. Under such a domination life for people who believe in liberty would not be worth living ; but war is a fearful thing, and we must be very clear, before we embark on it, that it is really the great issues that are at stake, and that the call to risk everything in their defence, when all the consequences are weighed, is irresistible." [1]

Despite the faint hope held out to them by the Prime Minister, the majority of his listeners went to bed in the belief that Britain and Germany would be at war within the next twenty-four hours. The broadcast was the climacteric of three days of steadily increasing tension and anxiety, and, in retrospect of the Second World War, it is difficult for those who have survived the blitzes and V-bombings to understand or to recapture the sense of fear and apprehension which oppressed Britain in these days. Our imagination had been whetted by the works of those uninhibited writers of " next war " fiction, who had assured us that within a week of the outbreak of hostilities London would be rendered uninhabitable by bombings and by gas.[2] The actuality, when it came two years later, was hideous enough, but not so horrific as those nightmares of the unknown which rode us during the September nights of 1938.

The A.R.P. had been mobilized on the Sunday (September 25), even before the end of the Anglo-French Conference, and deep cellars and basements had been commandeered for shelters.

[1] *The Times*, September 27, 1938.   [2] See below, p. 269.

On the following day came the evacuation of school children to the country and the clearing of hospitals for casualties, of which, it was said, fifty thousand were expected during the first few days. In these days, too, began the somewhat futile process of " fitting " the population for gas-masks, which were only to be distributed " in emergency " and, in any case, were virtually non-existent,[1] and there spread through the city the word that old sheets were being solicited to eke out the deficiency in London's supply of coffins. The population of London were adjured by King and Premier to " keep calm and dig ", and as a result there appeared in parks and squares and public places that system of pitiful little " slit-trenches " which were supposed to give shelter from aerial bombardment. On the Horse Guards Parade and on West-minster Bridge single anti-aircraft guns were mounted, with a meagre supply of ammunition, and a lonely Spitfire — one of the very few existing at that time — patrolled the skies above the city.

Yet, though many a Londoner went about with a sensation of sick apprehension at the pit of his stomach, there was no panic, no undue rush to leave for safer quarters, nothing comparable to the fear-crazed exodus from Paris, where a third of the population fled the city. The man-in-the-street, frightened but stoical, went about his business with a prayer in his heart and an occasional eye cocked skywards. There was a quiet, fatalistic accept-ance of the probability of war and a widespread popular sympathy with the justice of the Czech cause.

There were even those who urged a stronger policy upon the Government, a policy which they believed to be more in conson-ance with the national dignity and honour of Britain, and it was the ardour of such as these — a group of Conservative back-benchers, active and vociferous in criticism of their party — that Sir Thomas Inskip, the Minister for Co-ordination of Defence, essayed to dampen on this same evening of September 27 by emphasizing the unpreparedness of Britain and France for war and the disasters which might result from their becoming involved in hostilities.[2]

[1] M. Bonnet records that in the course of the Anglo-French discussions of Sep-tember 25-26 he received from the Minister of the Interior in Paris a message to the effect that there were no gas-masks available for distribution to the people of Paris and requesting that a million might be supplied from Britain. On enquiry M. Bonnet was informed that the British supplies were sufficient for the population of London only. There were not even enough for other cities (Bonnet, I, p. 270).

[2] Summoned urgently to London by Ambassador Joseph P. Kennedy, Colonel Lindbergh had arrived from France on September 21 and had given to Mr. Kennedy,

To Mr. Chamberlain also it must have seemed that war was almost inevitable, that the issue which he had so consistently and earnestly sought to avoid was now inescapable. After his hectic activities of the past ten days he was reduced to the Micawber-like policy of waiting for something to turn up. Amazingly, he was not disappointed.

At ten o'clock that night there was delivered to the Prime Minister from the German Embassy an "immediate and important" personal letter from the German Chancellor. It was a reply to that which Mr. Chamberlain had sent to the Führer by Sir Horace Wilson and had evidently been written after he had recovered from the outburst of rage in which Sir Horace had left him that afternoon.

Attempting to justify his attitude towards the Czechs, Hitler repeated his definite assurances that, once the Sudeten Germans were incorporated in the Reich, he would cease to be interested in Czechoslovakia, and would do nothing to infringe her independence. He did not contemplate a total occupation of the country. His troops would not go beyond the designated line and would be withdrawn before the plebiscite. As for the Czech population in the occupied areas, "nothing whatever will occur which will preserve for those Czechs a similar fate which has befallen the Sudeten Germans consequent on Czech measures". The procrastination of the Prague Government and the distortion of German intentions, which they had consistently made, were designed solely "to mobilize those forces in other countries, in particular in England and France, from which they hope to receive unreserved support for their aims and thus to achieve the possibility of a general war-like conflagration". He therefore urged the Prime Minister to continue to use his good offices, which he, Hitler, sincerely appreciated, "to spoil such manœuvres and bring the Government in Prague to reason at the very last hour".[1]

What were the motives for this letter, which had been written well before Hitler had received Mr. Chamberlain's last proposal for a compromise backed by a British guarantee of execution?

both orally and in writing, his views on the vast preponderance of Germany's air forces over those of all the European Powers combined, including Russia. These views were already shared by M. Guy La Chambre, with whom Colonel Lindbergh had dined on September 9 (see above, p. 99), and they were now communicated by Mr. Kennedy to the Prime Minister, for the information of his colleagues.

[1] *British White Paper*, Cmd. 5847, No. 10.

Why had the Führer's rage at noon cooled by sundown to those honeyed words of sweet reasonableness ?

There are some who ascribe the change to anxiety and caution, and Sir Nevile Henderson found the letter " indicative of a certain nervousness ". It is true that the opposition within the German High Command to a general European war had increased considerably since the apparent intention of Britain, France and Russia to fight had been made evident. Generals von Rundstedt and von Reichenau were even dubious of the success of the campaign against the Czechs in the event of outside intervention.[1]

There were signs that the German people themselves, while suitably inflamed against the Czechs, had no stomach for a wider

[1] During a staff conference at the Berghof on August 10, 1938, of which Jodl made a record that night in his diary, a number of Generals attempted to draw the Führer's attention to the defects of Germany's military preparations, with " rather unfortunate results ". Especially outspoken was General Wietersheim, who endorsed the opinion of another officer (not present) that " the Western Fortifications can only be held for three weeks ". In a rage Hitler shouted that, if this were true, " the whole Army was good for nothing ", the Western Fortifications would be held " not only for three weeks but for three years ". He then read them a " curtain lecture " on the defeatism and despondency prevalent in General Staff circles. " The vigour of the soul is lacking," he cried, " because in the end you do not believe in the genius of the Führer " (*International Military Tribunal Document*, 1780–PS).

It is alleged that on September 26 a deputation of the German General Staff, consisting of Generals Hanneken, Ritter von Leeb and Colonel Bodenschatz, had called on the Führer, who had refused to see them. They came again the next day and were again refused audience. This time, however, they left at the Reichskanzlei a memorandum representing their emphatic opposition to any declaration of war. A summary of the memorandum was published by Professor Bernard Lavergne in *L'Année politique française et étrangère* (Paris, November 1938). If the story is true, this memorandum would have been received by Hitler before he wrote his letter to the Prime Minister.

More direct measures of opposition on the part of the German Army were disclosed by General Franz Halder, Chief of the General Staff, during his interrogation by the Allied Military Intelligence Officers after his arrest in July 1945. According to his story, a group of general officers, headed by himself and including Generals von Witzleben, Beck, Otto von Stülpnagel, Graf Brockdorf, Commander of the Potsdam Garrison, and Graf Helldorf, Police President of Berlin — all of whom were later associated with the abortive *Putsch* of July 20, 1944 — had planned to arrest and depose Hitler in order to prevent war. Their plans were frustrated by the announcement of the Munich Conference.

This story appeared and reappeared throughout the evidence for the defence at the Nuremberg Trials and was particularly stressed by both Schacht and Gisevius. There is contemporary corroboration that such a plot was, at any rate, talked about in September 1938 ; Mr. Vernon Bartlett, on his return from Berchtesgaden (whither he had accompanied Mr. Chamberlain as a newspaper correspondent), informed Mr. Harold Nicolson (who noted it in his diary on September 20) that while there he had been approached by a former acquaintance on the German General Staff, who said that Mr. Chamberlain's decision to meet the Führer had forestalled a plot by the Army to arrest Göring and Himmler, and even Hitler himself, if he persisted in his policy of war.

conflict. That very afternoon a motorized armoured division passing through Berlin in the light September rain had been greeted in silence by the crowds in the streets, and two such well-qualified observers as the British Ambassador and William L. Shirer were convinced that this negative demonstration, which Hitler himself had witnessed from the windows of the Reichskanzlei, had deeply impressed him.[1]

Moreover, the Führer's ally to the south, Benito Mussolini, who, in a series of speeches begun on September 18, had been pouring forth a torrent of abuse of the Czechs, support for Hitler and praise for Mr. Chamberlain, was becoming perceptibly less enthusiastic at the prospect of a war waged in alliance with Germany against an Anglo-Franco-Russian combination. On September 20, at Gorizia, he had cried exultantly : " If there is drama, we shall face it ",[2] but a week later, at Verona, he was begging Britain and France to forsake the Czechs, who, " left to rely on their own strength, would be the first to recognize that it was not worth their while entering on a conflict concerning the outcome of which there could be no doubt ".[3]

Hitler had also received that day a second appeal from President Roosevelt that the dispute between Germany and Czechoslovakia be referred to a " conference of all the nations directly interested ", and inferring that, in the event of a recourse to war, Germany alone would be held responsible by the world.[4]

It is possible that this concatenation of factors may have influenced the Führer towards moderation and have caused him to write his conciliatory letter to Mr. Chamberlain, but it is much more likely that he was actuated by motives far deeper and more subtle.

The letter was phrased in as shrewd a wording as can be conceived to appeal to a man of Mr. Chamberlain's psychology. It was moderate and flattering, and calculated to pique the Prime Minister on his two weak spots — the obstinacy of the Czechs and the " war-mongers " in Britain. It was an appeal from one man of the world to another in an attempt to come to a reasonable agreement by brushing aside unnecessary details and obstacles. It implied that, if only this problem could be handled by the Führer and Mr. Chamberlain and their friends, the whole thing could be settled amicably and satisfactorily. It was really only these wretched Czechs who continued to frustrate Mr. Chamberlain's admirable efforts for peace.

And there is another aspect. From the earliest days of his political thought — as evidenced in *Mein Kampf* [1]— Hitler's attitude to Britain had been one of spiritual ambivalence.

There is a Freudian "love-hate complex" for England throughout his writings and his policies. Hitler admired and hated England for exactly the same reason, namely, that she had beaten Germany in war, and that she occupied a position in the world similar to that to which he wished to raise Germany. There was a curious sincerity in his protestations that he desired an Anglo-German understanding — which there never was in Ribbentrop's — and he regretted, or perhaps he even failed to understand, that Britain, because of unspecified pledges to a decadent France, should be dragged by the heels into a war between Germany and Czechoslovakia, in which she could have no possible interest.

It seemed to Hitler — as it had to Kaiser Wilhelm II before him — that the proper disposition of *Weltmacht* was that Germany should be dominant on the continent of Europe, and Britain outside it, and he repeated this again and again. Thus he did not wish to enter into active hostilities with Britain in 1938, any more than he did in 1939 ; and the same motif is to be found in his policy of 1940, when after the collapse of France he proposed a peace along these very lines. [2]

It is believed that these were the factors which influenced Hitler at this juncture, far more than the opposition of his Generals, whom he despised as " objective, defeatist cosmopolites " and whom he was frankly ignoring on the basis of his own intuition, or the lack of enthusiasm for war among the German people, who could always be whipped up by propaganda and dragooned by the power of the State. His outburst of rage in the presence of Sir Horace Wilson was an example of his antagonism for Britain, but his later letter was a manifestation of

[1] Mr. Chamberlain, it should be stated, had not at this moment read *Mein Kampf*, of which only an abridged edition existed in English. It was not until after his return from Munich that he requested the Foreign Office to prepare and translate suitable extracts for his perusal.

[2] Speech before the Reichstag, July 19, 1940. For text see *My New Order*, Hitler's speeches from 1922 to 1941, edited by Count Raoul de Roussy de Sales (New York, 1941), pp. 768-81.

his liking and admiration, combined with the subtle thought that Mr. Chamberlain might always be caught by the butter — and, as the March Hare remarked, " it was the best butter."

But whatever the Führer's motives may have been, there is no doubt that his letter came as an Angel of Light to the unhappy Mr. Chamberlain. War, then, was not inevitable ; the door had not been slammed, and he quickly got his foot inside.

There was but one solution now : a reversion to his original idea of a four-Power Conference, with a Czech representative also present, which he had proposed to Jan Masaryk on Saturday (September 25). Mussolini's assistance must be invoked as an impartial but interested party and the French must be brought into line.

The Prime Minister telephoned to Paris. M. Daladier and M. Bonnet were now delighted with the idea — M. Bonnet especially so.[1] The idea of a Four-Power Conference had been discussed in the Chamber of Deputies that afternoon, where M. Louis-Oscar Frossard had warmly advocated it. As a result of these conversations both Mr. Chamberlain and M. Bonnet sent messages to the Duce urging him to support the proposal,[2] and the Prime Minister at once telegraphed a reply to Hitler.

He was ready, he said, to come to Berlin at once to discuss arrangements for the transfer of the Sudeten Territory with the Führer and a representative of the Czechoslovak Government, and with those of France and Italy, if Hitler so desired. " I feel convinced we could reach agreement in a week ", he wrote, and added : " I cannot believe that you will take responsibility of starting a world war which may end civilization for the sake of a few days' delay in settling this long-standing problem ".[3]

But Mr. Chamberlain had reckoned without Georges Bonnet, and Georges Bonnet was wedded to the twin thought that there should be no war and that Hitler should get what he wanted. The French Foreign Minister had already that day denied all

---

[1] In the golden days which followed Munich, M. Bonnet's admirers sought to claim for him the honour of initiating the idea of a Four-Power Conference on the night of September 27-28. (See Thouvin in *L'Intransigeant*, October 8, 1938 ; also *Le Quai d'Orsay*, by Paul Lombard ; *Histoire secrète de la négotiation de Munich*, by A. Fabre-Luce.) The overwhelming mass of evidence, however, shows that, though he afterwards became very active indeed, M. Bonnet took no action until after Mr. Chamberlain had received Hitler's letter. The original initiative lay, therefore, with the Prime Minister.

[2] For text of Mr. Chamberlain's message to Mussolini see *British White Paper*, Cmd. 5848, No. 2.   [3] *British White Paper*, Cmd. 5848, No. 1.

knowledge of the British Foreign Office communiqué of September 26 pledging France, Britain and Russia to support Czechoslovakia,[1] and he had authorized the Agence Havas to deny categorically the statement that a general mobilization had been ordered in Germany for 2 P.M. on September 28.[2] He was doing his best to keep France anaesthetized. Now while Mr. Chamberlain was sending messages to the Führer and the Duce, M. Bonnet telegraphed his own explicit instructions to the French Ambassador in Berlin.[3]

The instructions were of such a nature that when M. François-Poncet received them at an early hour on the morning of September 28 he could not at first believe his eyes, and in any case he had some difficulty in gaining access to the Führer. Ironically enough it was only through the intervention of Sir Nevile Henderson and Göring that he was received by Hitler at all.[4] However, he finally gained audience at 11.15 A.M. and the Führer, when he had read his message, talked with him for an hour " in altogether a different tone", as M. François-Poncet afterwards said, "from that which he had used previously with my British colleague ". The interview was interrupted at 11.40 for a hurried conversation between Hitler and the Italian Ambassador, who had arrived with an appeal from Mussolini for a stay of twenty-four hours in the German mobilization. When he returned, Hitler said to Poncet : " I cannot say no to your suggestion. I will give you a written answer this afternoon." [5]

Well might the Führer acquiesce in the suggestion which M. François-Poncet had brought him, for it was no less than a wholesale surrender on the part of France. M. Bonnet's pro-

---

[1] See above, pp. 149-50.

[2] In his circular despatch of October 2, informing the French Diplomatic Corps of the results of Munich, M. Bonnet admitted his full knowledge of this mobilization order (*French Yellow Book*, p. 13).

[3] At the same time M. Daladier, as Minister of War, instructed General Gamelin to advise (*conseiller*) the Czech General Staff to evacuate immediately the territories of the Sudetenland (*L'Histoire d'un jour. Munich, 29 septembre, 1938*, by Louis Thomas (Paris, 1939), p. 212).   [4] Henderson, pp. 167-8.

[5] *Souvenirs d'une Ambassade à Berlin*, by André François-Poncet (Paris, 1946), pp. 327-9; Bonnet, I, pp. 284-6; Pertinax, pp. 401-2; Henderson, pp. 166-7; Werth, pp. 254-6. M. François-Poncet's visit to Hitler was thus officially described in a Havas communiqué from Berlin on September 29 : " M. François-Poncet was received by the Führer [on September 28]. The conversation lasted about an hour. It is said that the French Ambassador submitted to him some new suggestions from the French Government with a view to a peaceful settlement of the German-Czech conflict. According to well-informed sources it is said that the proposals provide for the occupation of the Sudeten country by German troops."

posals were ostensibly intended to be presented as a last-minute effort to placate Hitler in the event of his rejection of the British proposals, which had been already received by President Beneš and were at that moment still reposing in Sir Nevile Henderson's brief-case. The Führer, therefore, received the French offer before he had read the British, and it was considerably more generous.[1]

Where Mr. Chamberlain had offered one zone, M. Bonnet offered three, all of which were to be occupied on October 1, though it was stipulated that the Czechs must retain their fortifications. There was, however, an air about the Note which seemed to indicate that even this did not represent the last word in French amenability and that, provided that Hitler did not go to war, further pressure might be brought upon Prague to accept further demands if they were forthcoming. It was the climax of the betrayal of Czechoslovakia, seeming to justify the bitter comment of an English author, written years before, that " France, among a multitude of virtues, has one vice, unpardonable to Northern men : she turns from a fallen friend ".[2]

When Sir Nevile Henderson arrived with Mr. Chamberlain's letter at 12.15, Hitler greeted him with the news that " at the request of my great friend and ally, Mussolini ", the German general mobilization had been postponed for twenty-four hours. But he would not agree to send a reply to the letter until he had further consulted the Duce. However, the Führer was once again interrupted by the indefatigable Signor Attolico, this time in order to bring Mussolini's enthusiastic endorsement of the proposal for a Four-Power Conference. After this it was all plain sailing, and by lunch-time the invitations to Munich had been despatched.[3]

In reality, however, the whole thing had been settled well before Mr. Chamberlain's letter was even placed in the hands of the Führer, and the principal factors in assuring a " peaceful settlement " had not been the faint-heartedness of Mussolini ; nor the opposition of the German General Staff ; nor the last-minute qualms of Göring ;[4] nor the appeals of President Roose-

---

[1] The governing phrase of M. François-Poncet's instructions was that he should make to Hitler personally " *une proposition qui, reprenant les modalités d'application de cette dernière suggestion britannique, comporterait une occupation immédiate d'un territoire plus important* " (Bonnet, I, p. 283).

[2] H. Seton Merriman, *Barlasch of the Guard* (1904).   [3] Henderson, p. 169.

[4] Göring was apparently quite unprepared for the final *démarche* of the British and French Governments, and, on the morning of September 28, considered war as almost

velt; nor even the mobilization of the British Fleet : [1] the principal factors were the Laodicean policy of Britain and the ignoble conduct of France.

Hitler had neither " climbed down " nor " lost face ". He had had everything he wanted handed to him on a silver salver. In postponing mobilization for twenty-four hours, he had given away nothing, since the threat of it remained suspended like a Damoclean sword during the ensuing discussions, and in any case the striking force was already on the Czech frontier. He would get his military occupation of the Sudetenland none the less. The Czechs would be crushed and " that Beneš " would be humbled. And the Führer's intelligence told him, moreover, that once the war tension in Britain and France had been relaxed it would be a very difficult task to persuade the peoples of those countries again to screw their courage to the sticking-place and resign themselves once more to the prospect of war.

But of these events the world at large was, of course, ignorant as yet. September 28, " Black Wednesday ", dawned bright and clear over Paris and over London. Men and women woke with an eerie feeling that this was " the last day ",[2] and that by to-morrow night Paris and London might be in flaming ruins. In each capital there were some who remembered that, if this were so, Prague might have disappeared even earlier. In Paris they were fighting for seats on trains, and the roads out of the city were choked with traffic ; in London they were digging trenches.

The morning newspapers brought confirmation of the measures to which Mr. Chamberlain had referred in his broadcast of the night before. A State of Emergency had been proclaimed ; the Auxiliary Air Force Reserve had been called up ; the Fleet had

---

inevitable. " A great war can hardly be avoided any longer," he said. " It may last seven years and we will win it " (*International Military Tribunal Document*, 1780–PS. Jodl's diary entry for September 28).

[1] How powerful a factor the mobilization of the British Fleet constituted in the Führer's calculations it is difficult to judge, but it should be remembered that on February 20 he had told the Reichstag that " German economy has been so organized that as a whole it can at any time exist wholly independent of other nations and stand on its own feet. *The thoughts of a blockade can clearly be dismissed as an ineffective weapon.*" (See Baynes, vol. I, pp. 930 *et seq.*)

[2] I recall that while shaving that morning the hymnal injunction to " live this day as if thy last " came into my head and remained with me much of the day.

been mobilized.[1]   This last measure gave particular satisfaction in London, ever partial to the Navy.   " That'll make old 'Itler look out ", was a frequent remark, though there were those who reminded themselves — and, inevitably, others — that the mobilization of the Fleet had not stopped Germany from going to war in 1914.

It was known that the Prime Minister would meet Parliament that afternoon to report on his negotiations with Hitler and the subsequent situation.   It was impossible not to recall a parallel event on August 4, 1914, when Sir Edward Grey had addressed the House on a terribly similar occasion.   Would Mr. Chamberlain close his speech with an ultimatum to Germany?   The gloom deepened as the day drew on.   About lunch-time came a rumour that the German mobilization, ordered for two o'clock that afternoon, had been postponed, but people did not know whether to believe it or not; it brought, nevertheless, a lift of optimism.

It seemed as if all England walked in spirit with the Prime Minister from Downing Street to the Palace of Westminster that afternoon.   The House of Commons was filled to overflowing. Members sat on the steps between the benches.   The Press Gallery was packed.   Behind the grille of the Ladies' Gallery Mrs. Chamberlain was seen to be in her place.   The seats set apart for distinguished strangers had rarely been so full.   Lord Halifax sat with the Archbishops of Canterbury and York in the crowded Peers' Gallery and, in the Diplomatic seats, the representatives of all the " interested Powers " — von Dirksen, Corbin, Maisky and Jan Masaryk — were herded in intimate proximity.

Despite the tenseness the House of Commons adhered strictly to its established ritual.   There were Prayers at 2.45, followed by Questions, at which time the relevant Minister dealt with such vital matters as War Insurance Risks and Unemployment. Apart from the general uneasiness there was no sign of excitement.   Everything was done decently and in order.   When the Prime Minister entered the Chamber, there was subdued applause, for the moment was too poignant for lively demonstration, and

---

[1] Full credit for the mobilization of the Fleet must be given to the First Lord of the Admiralty, Mr. Duff Cooper, who, wearied of waiting and delay, gave the actual order on his own authority at 8 P.M. on September 27, and reported the fact at the Cabinet meeting which was held at 9.30 P.M., after the Prime Minister's broadcast. Mr. Chamberlain endorsed the order and agreed that full publicity should be given to it on the following day.

he was applauded again by his supporters when he rose to speak.[1]

Mr. Chamberlain gave to the House a detailed report of the events in the pitiful story of the Czech crisis, from the decision in July to send Lord Runciman and his Mission — how long ago that seemed — to the happenings of the previous night, and supplemented his account with a White Paper, issued that morning, which contained some of the documents in the case.[2] Neither the speech nor the White Paper gave a complete picture, even from the British standpoint ; there were some remarkable omissions in both.[3] But the Prime Minister told his story in deep earnestness and sincerity, and the House listened silent and enthralled.

It was 4.15 P.M. and Mr. Chamberlain had been speaking for some eighty minutes when the now historic scene took place. To Lord Halifax in the Peers' Gallery there came an urgent message and he hurried out. In a few moments Lord Dunglass, one of the Prime Minister's Parliamentary Private Secretaries, was seen to bend over the back of the Treasury front bench and to hand two sheets of paper to the Chancellor of the Exchequer, who was sitting next to Mr. Chamberlain. Sir John Simon tried to attract the attention of the Prime Minister, but Mr. Chamberlain's attention was riveted on what he was saying. He had reached that point in his narrative at which Signor Mussolini had intervened with the Führer at his, Mr. Chamberlain's, request, and had secured the postponement of the German mobilization. " Whatever views hon. members may have had about Signor Mussolini in the past," he was saying, " I believe that everyone will welcome his gesture of being willing to work with us for peace in Europe."

At this point Sir John Simon, after two unsuccessful efforts, succeeded in distracting the Prime Minister from his text. Mr. Chamberlain paused to read the paper handed to him, then he

[1] It had originally been intended that the Prime Minister's speech should be broadcast, and a microphone had been installed on the table of the House of Commons for the first time in history. At the last moment, however, it was agreed among the leaders of the Government and the Opposition that this departure from tradition would create a precedent which might entail difficulties in the future. Thus, though the apparatus still remained on the table, it was not used.

[2] *Correspondence respecting Czechoslovakia*, September 1938, Cmd. 5847.

[3] For example, in neither the speech nor the White Paper was there any reference made to the Reply of the Czech Government to the Anglo-French Plan ; nor to the Anglo-French Ultimatum of September 21 ; nor to the most recent British proposals to Hitler ; nor of Mr. Chamberlain's telegrams to President Beneš of September 27, one of which contained the statement that, even if war ensued and the Allies were victorious, Czechoslovakia could not expect to be reconstituted within her existing frontiers.

whispered to Sir John : " Shall I tell them now ? " and the Chancellor nodded assent. When the Prime Minister again faced the House he was smiling :

"That is not all [he said]. I have something further to say to the House yet. I have now been informed by Herr Hitler that he invites me to meet him at Munich to-morrow morning. He has also invited Signor Mussolini and M. Daladier. Signor Mussolini has accepted and I have no doubt M. Daladier will accept. I need not say what my answer will be. (Interruption.) We are all patriots and there can be no hon. member of this House who did not feel his heart leap that the crisis has been once more postponed to give us once more an opportunity to try what reason and good-will and discussion will do to settle a problem which is already within sight of settlement. Mr. Speaker, I cannot say any more. I am sure that the House will be ready to release me now to go and see what I can make of this last effort. Perhaps they may think it will be well, in view of this new development, that the Debate shall stand adjourned for a few days, when perhaps we may meet in happier circumstances." [1]

" Thank God for the Prime Minister ! " cried an unidentified member, and with that cry touched off a demonstration of mass-hysteria which the Mother of Parliaments had never before witnessed. So great was the relief — so great, hon. members suddenly realized, had been their fear — that tears mingled with the cheering, as the whole House stood throwing its Order Papers in the air.

Not quite the whole House ; there were two that day who did not join in the ovation to Mr. Chamberlain. Mr. Anthony Eden walked out of the Chamber pale with shame and anger. With equal courage, Mr. Harold Nicolson, despite the threats of those surrounding him, remained seated.

To Jan Masaryk the scene appeared fantastic, amazing, and he could scarcely believe his ears as to what he had just heard the Prime Minister announce. Was it possible that at this eleventh hour Britain and France had completely abandoned Czechoslovakia ? that the Four Powers were about to settle the fate of his country without her voice even being heard ? For a moment he stood alone in the Diplomatic Gallery, looking down at the weeping, cheering throng beneath. Then he left the House of Commons, not to enter it again for four years.

From Mr. Chamberlain and Lord Halifax Jan Masaryk sought explanation in the latter's room at the Foreign Office. He was

[1] *House of Commons Debates*, September 28, 1938, col. 26.

told that Hitler had only consented to a conference on condition that Czechoslovakia and Russia were excluded. Public opinion in Britain and France, it was said later, would not support their national leaders if they now refused to go to Munich because the Czechs and the Russians were not to be represented.

Jan Masaryk stood silently mastering his emotions. Then he faced the two gaunt Englishmen across the table : " If you have sacrificed my nation to preserve the peace of the world, I will be the first to applaud you," he said. " But if not, gentlemen, God help your souls."

(vi)

ACT III : MUNICH

" When I was a little boy," Mr. Chamberlain remarked to the assembled press and Cabinet in a moment of gay reminiscence, at Heston next morning (September 29), " I used to repeat, ' If at first you don't succeed, try, try, try again '. That is what I am doing. When I come back I hope I may be able to say, as Hotspur says in *Henry IV*, ' out of this nettle, danger, we pluck this flower, safety ' ",[1] and with that he flew off to Munich.[2] It was noticeable that he maintained this high pitch of optimism throughout the proceedings, and, by their conclusion, had become positively exalted.

The Prime Minister was riding on air now in every sense of the word. His own sense of relief was very great. The spectre of war had been terribly near to him — to all of us — in the last twenty-four hours, and now that it had been turned aside Mr. Chamberlain was determined that no power on earth or in Heaven should allow it to return. He was going to Munich to reach an agreement come what might, and in the fulfilment of this purpose he was not going to allow himself to be frustrated by the Czechs or even by the French, if M. Daladier proved obstructive.[3]

---

[1] *Henry IV*, Part I, Act I, Scene 3.

[2] Mr. Chamberlain was accompanied on this occasion by Sir Horace Wilson, Sir William Malkin, Mr. Strang and by Mr. Ashton-Gwatkin, who had been a member of the Runciman Mission.

[3] It was this determination to reach a pacific settlement at all costs which prompted the quip soon current in London that what Mr. Chamberlain had really said to Hitler at Munich was : " Don't be vague, ask for Prague ". The Prime Minister had, in fact, sent word to President Beneš that " it is absolutely necessary that the conversations at Munich should reach speedy and definite results. . . . This can be reached only if the Czechoslovak Government is resolved to give a wide discretion to Mr. Chamberlain and not to hinder his decision by making absolute conditions " (*Czechoslovak Archives*).

It was perhaps for this reason that he made no attempt to arrange a prior meeting with M. Daladier, either *en route* or at Munich, at which they might have arranged some plan of campaign or at least prepared a united front. But, whereas the two Dictators had met at the old Austrian frontier and travelled to Munich together, the two representatives of Democracy did not meet until the opening of the conversations.

M. Daladier was equally at fault, but he was at least ashamed of the whole affair and of his own weakness. Before leaving Paris he had had his usual conference with General Gamelin, at which the Chief of Staff had stated, specifically and in writing, the extent to which territorial concessions in the Sudetenland might be accepted without endangering the over-all strategical position of French security. There must, he said, be no question of Czechoslovakia being reduced to such a position of weakness that she had to be eliminated as an asset to Britain and France from the strategical concept in the event of war. For this purpose the Czech system of defence fortifications and the main railway trunk lines must remain unimpaired and under Czech control. Above all, the Germans must not be allowed to cut off the Moravian corridor.[1]

But, alas ! the General did not accompany his chief to Munich — that was to be strictly a civilian affair, although General Keitel accompanied Hitler — and it was left to Alexis Léger to shoulder the burden of keeping M. Daladier up to the mark. He did his best. No man could have done more. But it was useless ; however much M. Léger might twist his tail, " the Bull of the Auvergne " would not fight. He would snort a bit and even stamp his feet, but there was no full-throated bellow, no lowering of the horns, no final charge.

The two Caesars and their aides were in great fettle ; Hitler with the swagger of a conqueror, Mussolini " cocky as a rooster ", Göring obesely gloating. This was their day and they knew it, and, while they preserved a certain decent modicum of reserve in the presence of their French and British colleagues, among themselves they did not hide their contempt for these champions of Western Democracy.[2]

---

[1] Gamelin, II, p. 358 ; Pertinax, p. 5.

[2] " It is terrible. I always have to deal with nonentities," said Hitler to Ribbentrop, as they watched Mr. Chamberlain and M. Daladier drive away after signing the Pact ; and, later, when drawing up the plans for the attack on Poland, the Führer remarked, " I have seen these miserable men at Munich."

In reality the Munich Conference was but a ceremony. Its very existence meant that in all essentials Hitler had won his demands. There was no attempt to return to the Anglo-French Plan, which had been accepted by the Governments of Britain, France and Czechoslovakia, and discussion turned on reaching a compromise between the terms of the Godesberg Memorandum, which had been rejected by these same three Governments, and the recent proposals which had been put forward by Britain and France on September 27–28. A new proposal, representing a synthesis of these two plans, had been tactfully prepared in advance by Mussolini and it was this draft, edited by Sir Horace Wilson, which formed the basis of the conversations.

During the early part of the discussions, which began before luncheon, M. Daladier, mindful of Gamelin's warnings, did put up some argument and showed a combative spirit. But " at no stage of the conversations did they become heated ",[1] and, when Göring took the Premier of France in hand, his objections soon subsided. " M. Daladier is the very kind of man I like," the Field-Marshal said after it was all over, adding " *und er ist so elastisch* ". By dinner-time general agreement had been reached, subject to the discussion of details.

At half-past two on the morning of September 30, 1938, the Munich Agreement was signed by the representatives of the Four Powers, amid the flashlights of press photographers and the whirring of movie cameras. The only untoward event which marred the ceremony was the sudden discovery that the ink-well was empty.[2]

As a last-minute concession the Czechoslovak Government had been permitted to send two representatives to Munich, but only to give information to the British and French delegations. Accordingly Dr. Voytech Mastný, to whom Göring had given in March such glib assurances as to Germany's good intentions toward Czechoslovakia, and Dr. Hubert Masarik, of the Foreign Office, duly arrived in Munich and were kept in suspense through-

---

[1] Henderson, p. 171.

[2] Though dated September 29, 1938, the Munich Agreement was not actually signed until the small hours of September 30. Exactly eight years later, September 30, 1946, two of those present at the ceremony, Göring and Ribbentrop, heard themselves pronounced guilty of all charges brought against them at Nuremberg and on the following day were sentenced to death by the International Military Tribunal.

Of the actual signatories of the Munich Agreement Mr. Chamberlain died on November 9, 1940 ; Mussolini was executed by Italian patriots on April 28, 1945, and Hitler committed suicide on April 30, 1945. Only M. Daladier survives.

out the day. At seven o'clock they were joined by Mr. Ashton-Gwatkin, who, with evident embarrassment, informed them that a general agreement had already been reached and that it was much harsher than the terms of the Anglo-French Plan. He said no more. After a further three hours' interval the unfortunate Czechs were taken to Sir Horace Wilson, who outlined the terms of the agreement and gave them a map on which the territories to be ceded and evacuated were marked. The Czechs tried to protest, to draw attention to particular towns and areas the retention of which was vital to them. Sir Horace refused to listen and left them alone with Mr. Ashton-Gwatkin.

Dr. Mastný and his colleague again repeated their arguments, but to no avail. The only answer which they received was that the British favoured the proposals. "And", said Mr. Ashton-Gwatkin as he rose to go, "if you do not accept you will have to settle your affairs with the Germans absolutely alone. Perhaps the French will tell you this more gently, but you can believe me that they share our views. They are disinterested."

Again they were left alone. Finally, after the Agreement had been signed at 2.30 A.M., they were summoned to the Conference room. The Germans and Italians had withdrawn and there were Mr. Chamberlain and his advisers, together with M. Daladier and M. Léger. Daladier, slumped in his chair, remained silent throughout the interview; it was Mr. Chamberlain who did the talking. He made them a long speech and then handed them the text of the Agreement. M. Léger than informed them, "with superficial casualness, but harshly enough ", that no comment or reply was expected from them, as the Agreement was regarded as accepted, but that the Prague Government must be ready to send a representative to Berlin, at the latest by five o'clock that afternoon, to take part in the first session of the International Commission.[1]

Mr. Chamberlain yawned unrestrainedly throughout the interview. He was very tired, but as he said later, "*pleasantly* tired".

The unfortunate emissaries set out at six o'clock by air for Prague, escorted by Mr. Ashton-Gwatkin and bearing with them the text of the Agreement.[2] Simultaneously M. Daladier was

---

[1] This account is based on Dr. Masarik's report to the Czechoslovak Foreign Office (*Czechoslovak Archives*).

[2] The text and protocol of the Munich Agreement had, in fact, been already communicated to the Czechoslovak Government by the German Minister a little after 5 A.M. on the 30th, that is to say, a little more than 3½ hours after its signature (*Czechoslovak Archives*).

telegraphing his " deep emotion " to President Beneš, and the assurances that " it was not by my choice that no representative of Czechoslovakia was present ". Nevertheless he instructed the French Minister " to make sure of the President's agreement ".[1]

Dr. Beneš met with his political and military advisers throughout the morning, and also conferred with the party leaders. Pressure was applied both to him and to Dr. Krofta by the British and French Ministers, leaving no scintilla of doubt as to what the fate of Czechoslovakia would be if she failed to accept her fate.

The President thought of Russia, who had once more pledged her aid should Czechoslovakia elect to resist. Beneš had now to choose between submission to the demands of Germany, Britain and France or fighting a war with the sole support of Russia. If he chose the former course he knew the sacrifice which would be imposed upon his country, but if he chose the latter he realized that he, and he alone, would stand before history as having precipitated a second World War, which could only entail the devastation and destruction of his country and which might mean the victory of Germany over the combined forces of Russia and Czechoslovakia, and even over those of Britain and France, if, after an inevitable delay, they reluctantly elected to participate.

Moreover, to fight with Russian support alone was to court civil war in Czechoslovakia itself, and the President knew it. The Agrarians, the strongest political group in the Czechoslovak Cabinet, had made no secret of their opposition to any such proposal.

Dr. Beneš debated his decision, pacing up and down the terrace of the Hradschin Palace, weighing all the factors as impartially as possible. Finally he decided upon submission and peace — even though this would mean his own exile abroad.

Indeed, there was no other choice before the leaders of Czechoslovakia. Threatened, traduced, betrayed, they were now compelled to submit utterly, and at 12.30 P.M. the decision was announced. Czechoslovakia had surrendered.

Under the provisions of the Munich Agreement,[2] the Sudeten German territory was ceded to Germany, and, for the purposes of evacuation, was divided into four zones, occupation of which by German troops would begin on October 1, and continue progressively until October 7. The execution of the evacuation by the Czechoslovak Government, without destruction of, or damage

---

[1] *French Yellow Book*, p. 12.   [2] For text, see Appendix I.

to, existing installations, was guaranteed by Britain, France and Italy, and the conditions of the evacuation were to be laid down by an International Commission in Berlin consisting of the Secretary of State in the German Foreign Office, the British, French and Italian Ambassadors, and a representative of Czechoslovakia.

The Commission was also charged with ascertaining the remaining territory of predominantly German character which was to be occupied by German troops by October 10 ; with determining the territories in which plebiscites were to be held and in fixing the conditions for these plebiscites ; and with the final delimitation of the frontier. The right of option into and out of the transferred territories was permitted and had to be exercised within six months, and a joint German-Czech Commission was to be entrusted with working out the details and facilitating the transfer of the population.

The International Commission was also empowered to recommend to the Four Powers, " in certain exceptional cases, minor modifications in the strictly ethnographical determination of the zones which are to be transferred without plebiscite ".

The Czechoslovak Government was required to release, within one month, all Sudeten Germans serving prison terms for political offences,[1] and also to discharge from the military and police forces all Sudeten Germans who should desire their release.

Britain and France agreed to guarantee the new frontiers of Czechoslovakia, and Germany and Italy would join this guarantee as soon as the question of the Polish and Hungarian minorities in Czechoslovakia had been settled. It was also agreed that, if these minorities questions had not been satisfactorily settled within three months, the four Heads of Governments would meet again to consider them.

Such were the terms of the Munich Agreement. What had been gained ? In the first place, Mr. Chamberlain had won his debating point that settlement should precede action, the fundamental upon which he had insisted at Berchtesgaden and at Godesberg. The principle of peace by negotiation had been upheld.

But what had it produced ? On paper there were two important concessions from the terms of the Godesberg Memo-

---

[1] No similar reciprocal agreement was included for the release from German prisons of the numerous Czech citizens who had been arrested and held as hostages on Hitler's orders (*International Military Tribunal Documents*, 2854–PS and 2855–PS).

randum : first, a Czechoslovak representative would sit on the International Commission at Berlin, having equal voting power with those of the Four Powers ; and, secondly, the ruling that " in exceptional cases " the Commission might depart from the strict ethnical rule that all the predominantly German population areas of Czechoslovakia belonged automatically to Germany. By this means M. Daladier, at any rate, had hoped to safeguard Czechoslovakia's national defences and economic existence. There was also a further concession in the right of option and the transfer of populations.

In making these concessions, however, Hitler had given away very little, and he had only given way on these points in the secret knowledge that he would get it all back later. But, naturally, of this neither Mr. Chamberlain nor M. Daladier was aware, and it cannot therefore be held against them.

In effect, however, Hitler had gained everything. He had said that his troops would enter the Sudetenland by October 1, and they would do so — the only difference being that now they would not have to fight their way in, and would complete the occupation in ten days without resistance. He had inflicted a defeat of the first magnitude on France and on Britain without firing a shot. They had been forced to participate in the dismemberment of a small State for which the only historical parallels were the partitions of Poland in the eighteenth century.

In addition, Hitler had paved the way for his next step, already premeditated : the total destruction of the Czechoslovak State. He had shattered the French system of security, driven Russia out of the European alignment, and isolated Poland. Such were the fruits of Munich.[1]

" The Pact of Munich is signed," wrote Jodl in his diary, with mingled relief and satisfaction, " Czechoslovakia as a Power is out. . . . The genius of the Führer and his determination not to shun even a World War have again won victory without the use of force." [2]

Apart from the Führer himself, perhaps the only individual who had the slightest inkling of these catastrophic consequences

---

[1] As Mr. Churchill later summed up the position in the House of Commons : " At Berchtesgaden . . . £1 was demanded at the pistol's point. When it was given [at Godesberg], £2 were demanded at the pistol's point. Finally [at Munich] the Dictator consented to take £1 : 17 : 6 and the rest in promises of good-will for the future " (*House of Commons Debates*, October 5, 1938, col. 361).

[2] *International Military Tribunal Document*, 1780–PS.

was Édouard Daladier. Certainly there was no sadder man in Munich that day. He was sunk in the depths of despair, so weary and defeated that, when asked by correspondents in the Regents Palast Hotel whether he was satisfied with the Agreement, he could not utter a sound and stumbled out of the door in silence.[1]

For France, that day at Munich had been disastrous. She had sacrificed her whole Continental position and had abandoned her main prop in Eastern Europe, her most faithful ally. On the flight back to Paris, M. Daladier was assailed by fears for his own safety when the truth became known. As the plane circled above Le Bourget, the Premier could see a dense throng of people on the airfield. Were they waiting to lynch him, he wondered? Would he be torn in pieces by this dark, waiting mob? The plane landed, the crowd surged forwards, and, as M. Daladier stepped out, he heard that they were cheering. " The fools," he thought, " they are *cheering* me. For what? " Then a figure, with arms outstretched and coat flying open, embraced him, and he found himself in the arms of Georges Bonnet.

M. Bonnet did not go to Munich. It was not necessary. From Paris his unseen presence had made itself felt. He knew that M. Daladier would seek some amelioration of the Godesberg terms. He felt that a good impression would be created if some minor concessions were made. Through his own channels he counselled moderation to Berlin on the understanding that all that was conceded would be regained in the end. Still he had had a *mauvais quart d'heure* when, on the previous day, it seemed that M. Daladier was really putting up a fight. He had taken immediate steps. He had telephoned. He had had others telephone. His cronies, Pierre-Étienne Flandin and Joseph Caillaux, had stood ready with articles which would blast M. Daladier in the press if he resisted successfully. His fears, however, had been groundless.[2]

Now it was all over, and with an embrace he welcomed back his chief to a cheering and bedecked Paris. With soft words he drove from the Premier's mind all those doubts and fears and pangs of conscience which had beset him. M. Daladier accepted his triumph with a mixture of cynicism and contempt, and sank back into that fatal malaise which had brought him to Munich and was to bring him to Riom.[3]

---

[1] Shirer, p. 145.   [2] Pertinax, p. 402.
[3] M. Daladier's triumphal entry into Paris had been carefully organized by Bonnet, who had seen to it that the exact route of his drive from Le Bourget to the Ministry of

How very different were the reactions of Mr. Chamberlain as he flew home from Munich. The events of the last twenty-four hours, though at the time they had seemed to be " one prolonged nightmare ",[1] now proved to be a source of unalloyed satisfaction to him. It had been a near thing, but they had pulled it off. Peace had been preserved and the Czech affair settled as conveniently as could have been expected. Hitler had been really very reasonable on the whole, and they seemed to understand one another. And those crowds who had cheered him every time he had appeared in the streets of Munich. No one could say that the Germans were not a peace-loving people. Why, they abhorred the idea of war as much as he did and were as relieved and thankful for its passing. Ah well, there was a new era opening for everyone now.

For the Four-Power Agreement on the Sudetenland was not the only document which the Prime Minister was bringing home in his brief-case. Mindful of the Führer's oft-repeated promise that once the Sudeten problem had been settled the way would be clear for an Anglo-German understanding, Mr. Chamberlain, in the first flush of his post-Munich enthusiasm, had presented to Hitler that morning a declaration whereby, in view of the fact that the question of Anglo-German relations was " of the first importance for the two countries and for Europe ", he and the Führer were resolved that " the method of consultation shall be the method adopted to deal with any other questions that may concern our two countries, and we are determined to continue

---

War in the rue St.-Dominique was broadcast in advance by the Paris radio. The people had had time, therefore, to gather in the streets and, in some cases, to decorate their houses. In his efforts to convince M. Daladier that Munich had not been a defeat but a victory, it is said that Bonnet had endeavoured to have all the church bells rung in welcome but that this proposal had been rejected with some heat by Cardinal Verdier, Archbishop of Paris, who had long been a friend of Czechoslovakia — and so continued till his death in April 1940 — despite the reproaches of the defeatists in Paris, and even the reproof of the Papal Secretary of State, Cardinal Pacelli (now Pope Pius XII), at the International Eucharistic Congress at Budapest in May 1938 (De Monzie, p. 210).

There was also a movement, set on foot by Bonnet, to have one of the Paris streets re-named " Rue du 30 Septembre ", but this piece of folly was also prevented, largely on account of the opposition of the Municipal Council of Paris.

The welcome accorded to M. Daladier by his colleagues recalls the Memorandum addressed to M. Caillaux by his Cabinet on the occasion of his return from Berlin in 1911 after a similar, though lesser, appeasement : " We have the honour of having supported you in serving, together with the peace of the world, the dignity and grandeur of France " (*Mes Mémoires*, by Joseph Caillaux (Paris, 1943), vol. ii, p. 218).

[1] Feiling, p. 376.

our efforts to remove possible sources of difference and thus to contribute to assure the peace of Europe ".[1]

Hitler, though possibly surprised and undoubtedly pleased at this new proof of Britain's confidence in him, had found no difficulty in signing the declaration, to the Prime Minister's immense satisfaction. " I've got it ! " he cried exultantly to his colleagues on his return to the hotel, patting his breast pocket with pride, and it was this paper which he flourished so triumphantly at the assembled Cabinet and pressmen on his arrival at Heston and of which he broadcast the terms before leaving the airfield.

There may have existed some doubt in his mind as to the lasting efficacy of all he had accomplished. It is recorded that, as he drove away with Lord Halifax through the cheering crowds, he remarked : " All this will be over in three months " ; [2] but his faith would appear to have reasserted itself later and there can be no doubt as to his subsequent elation.

And how, indeed, should he not be elated on that great day when he was being hailed as a Messenger of God by his fellow countrymen but lately delivered from the spectre of war? When, as *The Times* declared, " no conqueror returning from a victory on the battlefield had come adorned with nobler laurels " ? [3] How, with his curious psychological make-up, could he have failed to believe in his own triumph with the congratulations of his Sovereign and his colleagues ringing in his ears and the densely packed crowds in Downing Street crying " Good old Neville ! " under his windows ?

Mr. Chamberlain that day achieved a state of elation for which both Britain and he himself were to pay dearly in the future, but it would have taken a greater man than he not to have been momentarily deceived by the transitory glory of the hour. And all England was responsible in some measure for his deception.

The windows on the first floor of No. 10 stood open and Mr. Chamberlain showed himself to the crowd. The cheering redoubled and broke into " For he's a jolly good fellow ". The Prime Minister looked on smiling, then he said : " My good friends : this is the second time in our history that there has

---

[1] For text see Appendix K.   [2] Feiling, p. 382.
[3] *The Times*, October 1, 1938. The British press was almost unanimous in acclaiming Mr. Chamberlain. For a study of the editorials of October 1–2, 1938, see Hadley, *op. cit.* pp. 93–110.

come back from Germany to Downing Street peace with honour.
I believe it is peace for our time." [1]

But Mr. Chamberlain did not lose all sense of judgement. To
his credit be it said that he refused to consider the suggestion of
a National Fund of Thanksgiving in his honour.[2] When the
Conservative Central Office urged him to go to the country
in a General Election and thus exploit his present overwhelming
popularity, he rejected this idea also, on the advice of one of
his nearest colleagues — Lord Halifax.

When, however, he was advised to take the action he had intended to take had war come, and reconstitute his Cabinet as a
truly National Government by bringing into it the leaders of the
Labour and Liberal Parties, together with such outstanding Conservative figures as Mr. Churchill, Mr. Eden and Lord Cranborne,
thereby strengthening its character, he would not be so guided.
At no time was it easy for Mr. Chamberlain to become reconciled
with his political opponents; magnanimity was not his *forte*. Moreover, there was now no need, he felt, for precipitate action of this
kind. He had signed an accord with the Führer to settle all matters
arising between Britain and Germany by the method of consultation, and it would be alien to the spirit of that accord if he now took
into his Cabinet men who were presumably inimical to Hitler and
who had been publicly branded as " war-mongers " in Germany.
That would be tantamount to indicating that he doubted the
good faith of the Führer's signature on the Anglo-German
Declaration, and nothing was then further from his thoughts
than this.[3]

The truth is that Mr. Chamberlain had developed as blind a
confidence in his political intuition as ever the Führer subsequently achieved, and his faith in his own influence with Hitler
was as great. " You see," he is said to have replied to one of his

[1] The parallel was perhaps an unhappy one, since Lord Beaconsfield was defeated
in the General Election of 1880. Mr. Chamberlain also survived his unlucky
prophecy by nearly two years (until May 1940). There exists, however, another and
more significant parallel. When M. Caillaux, as Premier, returned from Germany
in 1911, after his visit of appeasement, Mr. Asquith telegraphed the following
instruction to the British Ambassador in Paris : " Tell M. Caillaux that he comes
back from Berlin like Lord Beaconsfield bearing on his flag ' Peace with Honour '."
(Caillaux, vol. ii, p. 238.)

[2] *The Times*, October 1 and 3, 1938.

[3] Mr. Chamberlain's only effort in this direction was an offer made on October 25
to Lord Samuel, the Liberal Leader, to join the Government as Lord Privy Seal.
The offer was refused (*Memoirs of the Rt. Hon. Viscount Samuel* (London, 1945), pp.
278-9).

Cabinet colleagues who had pointed out to him that Hitler had made promises in the past and broken them, " you see, my dear fellow, this time it is different ; this time he has made the promises to me."

(vii)

Epilogue : London, Paris, Berlin and Prague

When Parliament reassembled on Monday, October 3, the gilt had already begun to wear off the gingerbread. The country had slept off its debauch of emotion over the week-end and had awakened with something of a bad taste in its mouth. The threat of personal danger had receded sufficiently for many in Britain to remember the Czechs and to recognize that that very deliverance from war which they had celebrated on Friday with such rejoicing had been purchased with the sacrifice of Czechoslovakia. By Monday morning many realized that there was room for guilt and humiliation and even shame along with that sense of relief which was still their predominant feeling.

Profiting by these quickening throes of conscience, the friends of Czechoslovakia in England, notably Professor Seton-Watson and Mr. H. Wickham Steed, sought to mobilize opinion by enlightening Members of Parliament on some of the aspects of the pre-Munich story which had been omitted or glossed over by the Prime Minister in his statement of September 28.[1] And with this additional ammunition the Debate promised to be lively. What Mr. Chamberlain had done was undoubtedly approved by the vast majority of his fellow countrymen, but there was increasing criticism of the means which had been employed to do it, and the necessity for its having to be done at all. Though very few then appreciated fully the futility and danger inherent in the Munich Agreement, the conditions of the peace so narrowly won were deplored everywhere.

Within the ranks of his own Government Mr. Chamberlain had been faced with severe censure and revolt. At one moment

---

[1] Professor Seton-Watson circulated to all Members of Parliament a memorandum summarizing the text of the Czechoslovak Reply to the Anglo-French Plan and of the joint *démarche* made by the British and French Ministers at Prague on September 21, neither of which was referred to by Mr. Chamberlain nor published in the White Paper. In the course of the Debate, Sir Samuel Hoare described Professor Seton-Watson's version of what had happened at Prague, in this latter case, as " substantially, I might say totally, inaccurate ". Subsequent disclosures, however, have shown Dr. Seton-Watson to have been substantiated on all counts.

during the week-end it had looked as though a number of the younger element would secede, but, under pressure from their elders, the " Young Turks " subsided and it was only Mr. Duff Cooper, the First Lord of the Admiralty, who resigned.

In the House of Commons debate, which opened on October 3 and continued for four days, much of the criticism of the Prime Minister was deprived of its force by the fact that many of his critics — with certain outstanding exceptions — by their past actions, whether positive or negative, had been confederate or contributory to the policy which had reached its tragic climacteric at Munich. The Labour and Liberal Opposition had consistently opposed even those insufficient attempts at rearmament which the MacDonald-Baldwin-Chamberlain administrations had made since 1934 ; they were, therefore, in part responsible for the parlous condition into which the state of British defences had fallen by 1938. There were those among Mr. Chamberlain's own followers who had disowned his policy of appeasement, even, in the case of Mr. Eden, to the point of resigning from his Cabinet in protest, but they had not joined Mr. Churchill in issuing a clarion call to arouse Britain to a consciousness of her own peril.

After the resignation of Mr. Eden the dissident Tories were divided into two groups ; the followers of Mr. Churchill consisting of Mr. Brendan Bracken, Mr. Robert Boothby and Mr. Duncan Sandys, and the followers of Mr. Eden comprising some twenty members, including Lord Cranborne, Sir Sydney Herbert and Mr. Harold Macmillan. Both groups were in sympathy with each other and neither was under any illusion as to the real nature of the Nazi régime ; some had held all along that nothing but a firm and determined policy could prevent the Dictators from practising aggression, others had only arrived at this conclusion by progressive stages. Many of them had felt in the early days of the Third Reich that at least an effort should be made to reach a peaceful agreement with Germany. All, however, were united at the time of the Debate in their disapproval of the policy which had made the Munich Agreement necessary and they denounced it as disastrous and deplorable. But, by the terms of the Resolution before the House, Members were required to approve not only the Munich Agreement itself but also the policy which led up to it. Such a requirement placed the dissident Tories in a quandary. Though they considered

Mr. Chamberlain's policy in regard to Italy and Germany to have been calamitous, they felt that once he had gone to Munich he had no option but to sign the Agreement. They could not, therefore, vote against the Resolution, nor could they support it. It seemed to them that the only honest course was to abstain from voting at all, and this was the course followed by both the Churchill and the Eden groups.

The Opposition, moreover, ignored in their attacks two important factors: that the Prime Minister had been first deserted by the French, and that, throughout the crisis, His Majesty's Governments in the British Commonwealth had been overwhelmingly opposed to the pursuit by the United Kingdom of a policy toward Germany which would involve them in war. There had been no more fervent supporters of Mr. Chamberlain's thesis of appeasement than those who directed national affairs in Ottawa, Canberra and Pretoria, and they continued to support him until the events of the following March awoke all of them to a sense of terrible reality.

But the fundamental and salient weakness of the Opposition was that, in the majority of cases, they evaded the issue of peace and war. Just as, on September 28, no one of them had interrupted Mr. Chamberlain's speech to protest against the acceptance of the Berchtesgaden terms, so now, with one exception — Mr. Duff Cooper — no Member of the House was sufficiently certain of himself to stand up in his place and say that the terms of the Munich Agreement should have been rejected at the price of war, because no Member of the House was sufficiently assured that the people of Britain would have endorsed such a rejection. They said, which was not true, that there would have been no war, because Hitler was bluffing ; they said, which was possible, that a different attitude on the part of the Prime Minister would not only have averted war with Germany, but also the mutilation of Czechoslovakia and the humbling of Britain and France ; but they would not say that at Munich or at Godesberg Mr. Chamberlain, in face of what certainly was not bluff, should have taken a determined stand, saying : "Very well, we shall fight." Whether Britain should or should not have accepted Hitler's challenge at that moment is another question, but it was clear from the debate that very few of the Prime Minister's critics, had they been responsible for the direction of affairs, would have picked up the gage.

Many Members of Parliament, of all parties, shared the sentiments expressed by Mr. Victor Raikes : " There should be full appreciation of the fact that our leader will go down to history as the greatest European statesman of this or any other time ".[1] A heartfelt sense of thankfulness for the avoidance of war was the underlying and predominant feature of the debate, and it is significant that nearly all speakers, opponents as well as supporters, paid tribute to the unremitting efforts of Mr. Chamberlain in this regard.

It was upon the fundamental issue of war and peace that the Prime Minister and his team — Sir John Simon, Sir Samuel Hoare and Sir Thomas Inskip — based their case. " I feel convinced that by my action I did avoid war," said Mr. Chamberlain. " I feel equally sure that I was right in doing so " ; it was on this note of challenge that he asked for his vote of confidence — without consideration of non-essentials. " How many of those among us are there ", asked Sir John Simon, " who, if we could undo what was then done, would reject the settlement to which the Prime Minister put his hand on Friday, and instead — because it was the only alternative — would fling the world into the cauldron of immediate war ? "

The Opposition were on safer ground when they criticized the Government for their treatment of the Czechs, who, in Mr. Herbert Morrison's phrase, had been " lost and betrayed ", and of whom Mr. Eden gave so glowing an encomium. Against these shafts the Government had no other protection than to join in the chorus of praise and eulogy for the gallantry, sacrifice and self-control of the victims of Munich. As Shelley wrote of Lord Eldon, they " wept well ".[2] " It is the Czechs who kept the peace of Europe," declared Mr. Chamberlain ; " it is their sacrifice which has averted war " ; and in the House of Lords, Lord Halifax echoed, in a tribute to President Beneš, that " without his help it would have been impossible to avoid a European war ". They were very sorry for the Czechs, the Government said ; they would do all in their power to implement the guarantee of the new frontiers which they had undertaken — and which Sir Thomas Inskip declared that they already regarded as " a moral obligation " ; as a solatium, they proposed to grant immediately an advance of ten million pounds sterling in answer to a request

[1] *House of Commons Debates*, October 3, 1938, col. 97.
[2] Cf. " The Masque of Anarchy "

received for a loan of thirty millions.[1] The Government speakers pointed out, however, that even as a result of Munich the Czechs were infinitely better off than they would have been had they been invaded.

It was reserved for members of the Prime Minister's own Party to place before the House the wider aspect of the Czech crisis and the Munich Agreement. In a speech of high oratory and great courage, Mr. Duff Cooper gave the reasons for his resignation, among them being his inability to persuade his colleagues to view the situation other than in the parochial terms of Czecho-slovakia. It had been said that the people of Great Britain and the Commonwealth were not prepared to fight for Czechoslovakia, and this, he admitted, was perfectly true. But it was not for Czechoslovakia that they would have been fighting.

" It was not for Serbia that we fought in 1914. It was not even for Belgium, although it occasionally suited some people to say so. We were fighting then, as we should have been fighting last week, in order that one Great Power should not be allowed, in disregard of treaty obligations, of the laws of nations and the decrees of morality, to dominate by brutal force the continent of Europe. . . . For that principle we must ever be prepared to fight, for on the day when we are not prepared to fight for it we forfeit our Empire, our liberties and our independence." [2]

He went on to question the wisdom of the Prime Minister's confidence in Hitler's good-will and enumerated the broken promises with which the path of the Nazi régime had been paved in the past.

These same doubts were echoed by Mr. Richard Law, son of a former Conservative Prime Minister, who wished he could see any very strong grounds for Mr. Chamberlain's statement that he had brought back " Peace with Honour ".

"We have now obtained [said Mr. Law], by peaceful means, what we have fought four wars to prevent from happening, namely, the domination of Europe by a single Power. I see those

[1] Mr. Chamberlain's statement (*House of Commons Debates*, October 3, 1938, col. 46). This financial transaction caused very bitter feeling between the protagonists and opponents of Munich. According to one source, an opponent remarked in the Smoking Room of the House of Commons : " The world is changing. Values have improved. Two thousand years ago a man could reckon on receiving thirty pieces of silver if he went in for betrayal. Now a nation has to pay out thirty million pieces of gold if it goes in for betrayal." The speaker was at once knocked down by a fellow member and went home in a cab with a bloody nose (*Guilty Men*, by Cato (London, 1940), p. 62).   [2] *House of Commons Debates*, October 3, 1938, col. 32.

ideas which most of us, I think, value in England, ideas of decency and fairness and liberty, at a discount in the markets of the world." [1]

But it was Mr. Winston Churchill who, in unforgettable eloquence, proclaimed unerringly the cause and the consequence of the humiliation of Munich.

" It is [he said] the most grievous consequence which we have yet experienced of what we have done and of what we have left undone in the last five years — five years of futile good intention, five years of eager search for the line of least resistance, five years of uninterrupted retreat of British power, five years of neglect of our air defences. . . . We are in the presence of a disaster of the first magnitude which has befallen Great Britain and France. Do not let us blind ourselves to that. It must now be accepted that all the countries of Central and Eastern Europe will make the best terms they can with the triumphant Nazi Power. The system of alliances in Central Europe upon which France has relied for her safety has been swept away, and I can see no means by which it can be reconstituted. The road down the Danube Valley to the Black Sea, the resources of corn and oil, the road which leads as far as Turkey, has been opened." [2]

The Prime Minister, however, was undeterred by the strictures of his critics, or by the unrelieved gloom of their forebodings. He was conscience-proof against the darts of the first, and profoundly convinced that the second were rooted in fallacy.

It is perhaps remarkable that, in a debate on a policy based on " peace for our time ", the only issue on which there was complete unanimity of opinion was the vital necessity for the rapid completion of Britain's rearmament. Mr. Churchill, Mr. Attlee and Mr. Duff Cooper urged it for the Opposition. Mr. Chamberlain and his chief lieutenants pledged it on behalf of the Government. There was an alarming frankness in the bland confessions of Sir John Simon and Sir Samuel Hoare, and of the Prime Minister himself, that certain gaps and deficiencies had disclosed themselves in Britain's defences, but that these would be filled up and made good. What, one wondered, had become of that " almost terrifying power that Britain is building up " of which the Prime Minister had spoken with awe in the previous March, and which, he had told the House, was having " a sobering effect on the opinion of the world " ? [3]

---

[1] *House of Commons Debates*, October 3, 1938, col. 114.
[2] *Ibid.*, October 5, 1938, coll. 366, 367-8.   [3] See above, pp. 43-4.

Now he gave a solemn assurance that there would be no relaxation, as a result of the Munich Agreement, of the Government's programme of rearmament, but it was apparent, even as he said the words, that he did not appreciate the urgent necessity, not only of completing this programme as rapidly as possible but also of awakening Britain to the gravity of the situation in Europe. He did not do so, because he did not himself perceive that the situation was grave.[1] Thus, while he paid lip-service to rearmament, it was patent that his greater enthusiasm and zeal were centred on the development of that new era of which, he was confident, the foundations had been laid at Munich.

"Ever since I assumed my present office [he told the House] my main purpose has been to work for the pacification of Europe, for the removal of those suspicions and those anxieties which have so long poisoned the air. The path which leads to appeasement is long and bristles with obstacles. The question of Czechoslovakia is the latest and perhaps the most dangerous. Now that we have got past it, I feel that it may be possible to make further progress along the road to sanity."[2]

In the minds of not a few of those who listened to the Prime Minister there occurred the thought that so far, in order to "get past" these obstacles on the road to sanity in a peaceful manner, it had been necessary to condone the illegal rearmament of Germany, to acquiesce in the reoccupation of the Rhineland, to do no more than protest against the annexation of Austria, and, finally, to approve the dismemberment of Czechoslovakia. Moreover, after each of these depredations Hitler had declared that his ambitions were satisfied. But that Mr. Chamberlain harboured no further suspicion or anxiety regarding Germany was very clear, for he continued, apropos of the declaration which he had signed with the Führer :

"[It] is something more than a pious expression of opinion. In our relations with other countries everything depends upon there being sincerity and good-will on both sides. I believe that there is sincerity and good-will on both sides in this declaration. That is why its significance goes far beyond its actual words."[3]

[1] Once only in the course of the debate did Mr. Chamberlain strike a note of warning, and then only of the mildest resonance. "It is possible," he said, "that we may want great efforts from the nation in the months that are to come, and if that be so, the smaller our differences the better " (*House of Commons Debates*, October 6, 1938, col. 548).   [2] *House of Commons Debates*, October 3, 1938, col. 48.

[3] In almost similar words Addington had defended the Peace of Amiens before the House of Commons during the debate on ratification in 1802 : " This is no

Such sublime faith as this was unlikely to be shaken by force of criticism or the gloom of counter-prophecy, and, in the final words with which the Prime Minister closed the debate, he charted his course for months to come :

" Our policy of appeasement does not mean that we are going to seek new friends at the expense of old ones, or, indeed, at the expense of any other nations at all . . . [Our objective] is to obtain the collaboration of all nations, not excluding the totalitarian States, in building up a lasting peace for Europe."

He asked for a decisive majority in support of this policy and was accorded it by 366 votes to 144.[1]

In contrast with the debate in the House of Commons, the discussion of the Munich Agreement in the French Chamber of Deputies on October 4 was lacking in dignity, length and interest. In view of the fact that, despite repeated requests that Parliament be recalled, the whole Czech crisis had occurred without reference to, or consultation with, the Chamber, it is perhaps extraordinary that the whole debate lasted barely six hours. The statement of M. Daladier, though given with great assurance, was in no way as detailed as that of Mr. Chamberlain and was unsupported by any documentary evidence.[2] No mention was made of the historic Cabinet meeting of September 13, or of the French ultimatum to Prague on September 21, and the story of Berchtesgaden, of Godesberg and of the two Anglo-French meetings in London was left vague and obscure. Indeed, as M. Louis Marin, almost the last veteran of the great days of Poincaré and Barthou, subsequently remarked in the discussion, without the record of the House of Commons debates, the British White Paper and the Czech documents, France would be in absolute ignorance of what had happened.[3] Yet M. Daladier claimed for the negotiations that " perhaps for the first time in the history of the world everything was done and said in public ".

In defence, or explanation, of his own attitude after Godesberg, M. Daladier said :

ordinary peace, but a genuine reconciliation between the two first nations of the world ". Later in the debate he added : " I am well persuaded that, whatever happens, it is the wisest course for us to husband our resources at present that we may be the better prepared, if that should be our lot, to exert ourselves with energy and effect ".

[1] A vote taken immediately before on the motion to adjourn gave the Government a majority of 369 to 150.

[2] For text of M. Daladier's speech see *Le Temps*, October 5, 1938.

[3] Werth, p. 270.

" In those days of anguish there were two currents of opinion in France. Both could be found inside every political party, one might even say in the heart and conscience of every Frenchman : one was the hope in future negotiations, the other the faith in intransigent firmness. As the head of the Government I recognized from the outset that both these movements of opinion represented the infallible instinct of the French people. I felt that the truth lay in the synthesis of these two currents of opinion and not in their juxtaposition. What the French people desired was that the irreparable should be avoided. The irreparable was German aggression. If this happened, we, for our part, would have asked you to fulfil France's obligations."

The Premier's account of the events of the night of September 27–28 differed from that of Mr. Chamberlain. The initiative of bringing in Mussolini, thereby ensuring a Four-Power discussion, was claimed for himself and M. Bonnet. No details of the final proposals submitted to Hitler by the French Ambassador were forthcoming ; they were described merely as being of " a precise nature and capable of immediate and practical application " (" *des propositions précises et d'application immédiate et pratique* ").

" I accepted the invitation to Munich. It was not a question of discussing procedure or of submitting counter-proposals. It was a question of saving peace which many believed to be definitely lost. I said " yes " and I regret nothing. No doubt, I would have preferred that all the nations directly concerned be represented. But there was no time to lose. The least delay might have been fatal."

Here is a complete confession of panic. There was no attempt to explain or to regret the abandonment by France of an ally of twenty-seven years' standing. Instead the Czechs were told that, " thanks to the good-will of all, Munich is an unquestionable improvement on Godesberg ", and that, while Czechoslovakia had certainly been reduced in territory, she could " continue her life as a free country, and we shall do our best to help her ".

It was evident that M. Daladier's hopes for the future peace of Europe were not as rosy as Mr. Chamberlain's. He was more deeply concerned with the fate of France, and he was desperately anxious that the apparent unity of purpose which had been achieved, at least superficially, during the past few days should not be dissipated. " This country is in need of a moral transformation," he warned the Deputies, with truthful candour. " My dear friends, do not let us allow this unity to be shattered through idle quarrels and unimportant polemics."

In the debate which followed, the Government were charged with unpardonable weakness and lack of preparedness by M. Péri, for the Communists, and M. de Kérillis, from the Right. Neither M. Bonnet nor M. Flandin spoke. Indeed, the latter was feeling a little uncomfortable. In a burst of enthusiasm he had sent a telegram of congratulation to Hitler, Chamberlain and Mussolini, and, through the carelessness of a postal official, the Führer's reply, in which he assured M. Flandin that he had watched his activity for the past years " with great interest and sympathy ", had come into the hands of the Foreign Affairs Committee of the Chamber, where it was destined to cause its recipient some embarrassment.[1]

At the conclusion of the discussion M. Daladier received a vote of confidence of 543 to 75.

The debate disclosed the overwhelming desire for peace which possessed France at this time to the exclusion of all other considerations. This desire varied in degree and motive, from the doctrinal pacifism of the Left to the opportunist neo-pacifism of the Right, but the combination produced a powerful anti-war trend in public opinion. As M. Daladier had said, for each individual the Munich Agreement was a *cas de conscience*, an inner conflict between his national honour and his love of peace. But the energetic defeatist elements in the Government had seen to it that, in the endeavour of the French public to weigh the pros and cons of the situation, the scales were consistently weighted on the one side. The fact that it was not only the existence of Czechoslovakia but the security of France which was at stake was never presented to them. The result was exactly that which these elements desired that it should be. With only false balances with which to reach a conclusion, the people of France decided that national honour was not a sufficient incentive for fighting a long and bloody war in defence of a small and unhappy ally.

Yet while Mr. Chamberlain and M. Daladier were receiving their plaudits and their votes of confidence in London and in Paris, the very concessions which they claimed to have exacted from Hitler were being swept away in Berlin.

---

[1] The sending of this telegram and the wording of Hitler's reply figured among the charges which M. Flandin was called upon to face during his trial before the High Court of Justice at Versailles (July 25-8, 1946). Owing largely to the intervention of Mr. Winston Churchill and Mr. Randolph Churchill, the Court took a lenient view of M. Flandin's conduct and merely inflicted on him the loss of civic rights for a period of five years.

It had been said persistently by the defenders of the Munich Agreement that, however harsh its terms may have been, they were very much better than those of Godesberg, and M. Daladier had derived particular conscience-balm from those two concessions which he had succeeded in gaining ; namely, the representation on a footing of equality of a Czech member on the International Commission, and the right of the Commission to depart in certain cases from the strict ethnical rule in order to safeguard Czechoslovakia's national defence and economic existence.[1]

When, however, the International Commission met in Berlin on October 1, the three Ambassadors and M. Mastný found that they were dealing, in reality, not with the amiable Staatssekretär von Weizsäcker, but with the steely adamant of General Keitel and General von Brauchitsch. It was the German General Staff, relieved and delighted at having achieved another " bloodless victory ", who called the tune, and the German Foreign Ministry — and ultimately the Commission itself — who danced to it. Plans were already in course of preparation for the ultimate destruction of what remained of Czechoslovakia, and the General Staff was determined that the " temporary " settlement now under discussion should result in the complete military and economic impotence of the victim.

The Commission met for the first time on October 1, on which day German troops began their occupation of the First Zone. Its pressing duty was to delimit the Fifth Zone of the " remaining territory of preponderantly German character ", which was to be occupied by German troops on October 10, and it was in this connection that the concession regarding the departure from the ethnic rule was supposed to apply.

The Czech member produced the figure of the 1930 census as a basis of decision, but this was immediately rejected by the German Secretary of State, who claimed that, since the whole principle of the cession of the Sudetenland to Germany was on the basis of the situation of 1918 — a completely new contention, never advanced before — the statistics used must be those of the last census held under the Austro-Hungarian Empire, that of 1910. The principle of this census had been very largely political, as the Vienna officials of the day had been anxious to prove a preponderant number of Germans in the Empire. For this purpose nationality had been recorded, not by mother-tongue, but in

[1] See above, pp. 176-77.

accordance with the language most used in daily life ; because the Czechs who lived in the Sudetenland used German in their day-to-day transactions they could therefore be registered as Germans.

Dr. Mastný protested that, if this basis were adopted, it would constitute a violation of the Munich Agreement and would, in effect, result in terms even harsher than those of the Godesberg Memorandum. He received a certain qualified support from the Italian Ambassador, but none from the British or French. Weizsäcker, under pressure from Keitel and von Brauchitsch, carried the dispute to Ribbentrop and ultimately to Hitler, who replied with an ultimatum demanding immediate occupation of the language-line of 1910.

With faint hope Mastný turned to M. François-Poncet. Surely France, despite all her recent cruelties, would not, in her own interests, allow the last of the Czech fortifications to fall into German hands and permit the economic destruction of Czechoslovakia. It was now that Georges Bonnet completed the role which he had played *in absentia* at Munich. When M. François-Poncet asked for guidance on the issue of the language-line in the Fifth Zone, he received it in no uncertain terms. Speaking by telephone from his room in the Palais Bourbon,[1] so that his officials at the Quai d'Orsay should not be aware of the content of his instructions, M. Bonnet ordered the French Ambassador to support the German claim and to vote for the 1910 census figures as a basis of settlement.[2]

In desperation Dr. Mastný sought the doubtful sympathy of Sir Nevile Henderson, but here he found neither comfort nor understanding. The British Ambassador was in no two minds as to what his action should be, and, without referring the matter to London, he too accepted the dictate of the German General Staff.[3]

Thus, on October 5 — the day on which M. Daladier received his vote of confidence in the Chamber and one day before Mr. Chamberlain received his in the House of Commons — a decision

---

[1] The Chamber of Deputies.   [2] Pertinax, p. 4.

[3] Sir Nevile Henderson gives his reasons for supporting the German claim without reference to London, as follows : " I hoped thereby, firstly, to avoid plebiscites ; and, secondly, to pin the Germans down to a line of their own choosing, which they would find it difficult afterwards to modify again to their renewed advantage ; and, thirdly, because the German contention was actually, in my opinion, the better founded of the two theses " (Henderson, p. 175).

was taken in defiance of every principle which was believed to be inherent in the Munich Agreement and which left the Czecho-slovak State no more than a truncated and subjugated body. By four votes to one the International Commission, under threat and pressure from Hitler and the German Army, accepted the German claim, and it was not surprising that, a week later (October 12), they arrived at the unanimous opinion that, in view of this decision, " plebiscites may be dispensed with ".[1]

Within a week of signature, therefore, the Munich Agreement, with the concurrence of all the signatory Powers, was stripped of even those few limitations which had been laid on Nazi demands. No vestige of success remained to Mr. Chamberlain and M. Daladier — save that this victory for German arms had been a bloodless one.[2]

By the amended terms of the Munich Agreement Czecho-slovakia was deprived of the last of her defensive line of fortifica-tions. She ceded to Germany nearly 11,000 square miles of territory with a population of 2,800,000 Sudeten Germans — and 800,000 Czechs. Nor was this all. Having taken so formidable a stand upon the strict application of the ethnic rule, the German General Staff did not hesitate to abandon it when convenient in order to effect their main purpose of achieving the military and economic impotence of Czechoslovakia. For this reason the frontier, when finally drawn, left a quarter of a million Sudeten Germans within the border of the new Czechoslovak State.

[1] Communiqué of the International Commission. Text in *Prager Presse*, October 14, 1938. The final delimitation of the frontier became a matter for direct negotiation between Germany and Czechoslovakia as the result of an agreement " concluded privately " between the two Governments. The results of these negotiations, which were described as a " realistic working arrangement ", were the subject of a Protocol signed in Berlin on November 20. (For text see *British Blue Book*, Miscellaneous, No. 11, 1938, Cmd. 5908.)

For map of final settlement of November 20, see opposite. Maps to illustrate the German demands at Godesberg and the subsequent agreement at Munich will be found in Appendix G, and Appendix I.

[2] Speaking at Leeds on January 20, 1940, Lord Halifax frankly admitted : " The Munich settlement gave Germany all she immediately wanted. In applying the Agreement, every contentious point was decided in Germany's favour " (*Speeches on Foreign Policy*, by Viscount Halifax (Oxford, 1940), p. 347). It is somewhat surprising to find that in the " Special Note " summarizing Lord Halifax's speech, in the *Bulletin of International News* of the Royal Institute of International Affairs (vol. xvii, p. 82), that usually admirable and impartial publication entirely omits the important admission contained in the second sentence of the passage quoted above.

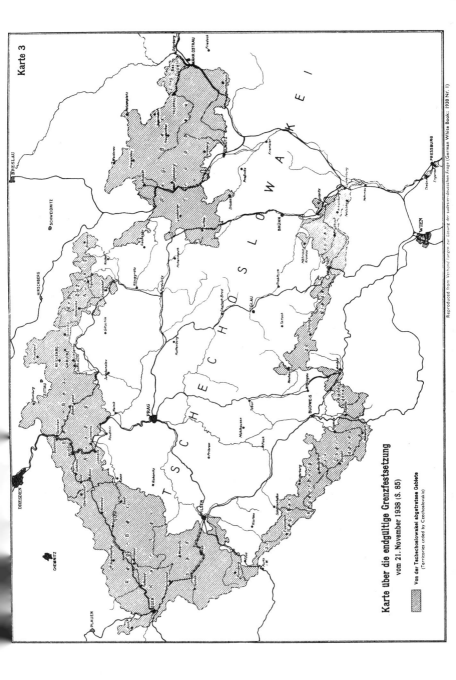

Karte 3

Karte über die endgültige Grenzfestsetzung
vom 21. November 1938 (S. 85)

Von der Tschechoslowakei abgetretene Gebiete
(Territories ceded by Czechoslovakia)

In addition to these sacrifices in territory and population, Czechoslovakia suffered staggering economic losses. These losses corresponded to that part of the plan for " Operation Green " in which had been scheduled the " war potentials " which Germany intended to obtain from a subjugated Czecho-slovakia. The new frontier had been so drawn as to dislocate completely the whole system of railway communication — on the maintenance of which General Gamelin had laid such emphasis with M. Daladier — and to deprive her of 66 per cent of her coal and 80 per cent of her lignite. Her industrial losses, according to German statistics, amounted to 70 per cent of her iron and steel, 80 per cent of her textiles, 75 per cent of her railway carriage works, 80 per cent of her cement, 90 per cent of her porcelain, 86 per cent of her glass, 86 per cent of her chemicals, 90 per cent of her news-type, 40 per cent of her timber, and 70 per cent of her electric power supplies.[1]

Such was the peace from which, M. Daladier had assured the Chamber of Deputies, all provisions had been eliminated " which might have figured in an armistice imposed by a victor on his defeated foe ". Such was the settlement which Mr. Chamberlain had acclaimed as " Peace with Honour ". The German Führer, to whose sincerity and good-will Mr. Chamberlain was even then paying tribute in the House of Commons, was apparently not willing to give the Prime Minister even these grounds of justifica-tion. At this very moment he was, in concert with his High Command, drawing up plans for seizing the remainder of the Czechoslovak State, with the result that, on October 21, a secret directive to the *Wehrmacht* was issued over the signatures of Hitler and Keitel, which gave the alert for this operation :

" The future tasks of the armed forces and the preparations for the wars resulting from these tasks will be laid down in a later directive. Until this directive comes into force, the armed forces must be prepared at all times for the following : (1) period for the liquidation of the remainder of Czechoslovakia ; (2) period for the occupation of Memelland." [2]

In Prague, meanwhile, the shadow of death was fast gathering round the democratic State which had been founded by Thomas Masaryk and Edvard Beneš. German troops crossed the frontier on October 1, and on the following day (Sunday) this prayer was

---

[1] Ripka, p. 492.   [2] *International Military Tribunal Document*, C-136.

ordered to be read in all Catholic churches by the Cardinal-Primate of Bohemia :

"The land of St. Wenceslas has just been invaded by foreign armies and the thousand-year-old frontier has been violated. This sacrifice has been imposed on the nation of St. Wenceslas by our ally, France, and our friend, Britain. The Primate of the Ancient Kingdom of Bohemia is praying to God Almighty that the peace efforts prompting this terrible sacrifice will be crowned with success, and, should they not, he is praying to the Almighty to forgive all those who impose this injustice upon the people of Czechoslovakia."

In Protestant churches the same prayer was offered, substituting the name of "John Huss " for that of " St. Wenceslas ".

President Beneš himself resigned on October 5, under pressure from Berlin, and left the country, only to return when it had been liberated from Nazi thraldom.   In departing he charged his countrymen to " remain united, brave and faithful ", and from his exile he laboured unceasingly for their liberation.[1]

General Jan Syrový, already Premier, succeeded as Chief of State *ad interim*, and it was clear from his first public pronouncement that under his guidance the new Czechoslovak State, having lost all faith in the support of the Western democracies — no one in Prague ever considered the Anglo-French guarantee as a serious commitment — was ready to embark on a " policy of collaboration " with Germany.

[1] On October 1 Göring summoned M. Mastný in Berlin and bluntly told him that Germany could no longer tolerate Dr. Beneš as head of the Czechoslovak State. Unless the President resigned, Germany would treat Czechoslovakia with absolute ruthlessness in the application of the Munich Agreement.   Dr. Beneš, therefore, resigned on October 5 and left Prague on the following day for his country estate in Southern Bohemia.

Certain of the more zealous of the President's enemies urged General Syrový to put him on trial on a charge of having attempted to ruin the Czechoslovak State. This proposal was rejected, but Dr. Beneš's life was no longer safe in his own country. He retired to England on October 22, and later toured the United States.   M. Jan Masaryk, who resigned as Minister to the Court of St. James in December 1938, did likewise.   In their American addresses both men pleaded the cause of their country and warned their hearers against the Nazi menace, but, with remarkable magnanimity and restraint, neither uttered a word of reproach against Britain or France.

On the outbreak of war Dr. Beneš formed the Czechoslovak National Committee in London, which was recognized by Britain as a Provisional Government on July 18, 1941, with himself as President and M. Masaryk as Foreign Minister.

The story of the struggle for their recognition is eloquently told by Sir Robert Bruce Lockhart, who was appointed British Representative to the National Committee in 1939, in his *Comes the Reckoning* (London, 1947).

President Beneš re-entered Prague with the Provisional Government on May 16, 1945.   M. Masaryk returned on July 6.

" The Government [said General Syrový] is anxious to carry out loyally the decisions taken by the four Great Powers at Munich, while doing its utmost to preserve and safeguard the vital interests of our new State. The principle, in accordance with which the Government will direct its foreign policy, may be expressed very simply : friendly relations towards all, and especially towards our neighbours. The establishment of such relations is clearly dictated as a result of our realization that if we want to live safely and content we must collaborate with our neighbours."

The first translation of this policy into concrete terms was the announcement from Prague on October 21 that the Government had informed the Soviet Minister that, in view of the new situation, Czechoslovakia was " no longer interested in the Russian alliance ".

There was another significant indication, of which I was a witness. Much sympathy had been aroused in Britain by the sorry plight of the refugees who had fled from the Sudetenland before the advance of the German occupying forces. With vivid memories of what had happened in Germany and in Austria to those who, by reason of race, nationality or political creed, had found themselves in opposition to the principles of the Third Reich, thousands of Czechs, as well as Jews and those Sudeten Germans who had been members of the Social Democratic and Communist Parties, had fled from their homes and were living behind the new Czech frontier in circumstances of great privation.

In response to a letter to *The Times*, signed by Major-General Sir Neill Malcolm, at that time League of Nations High Commissioner for Refugees, Viscount Duncannon and myself,[1] the Lord Mayor of London, Sir Harry Twyford, opened a Mansion House Fund for the relief of these unfortunate people, to which many men and women in Britain, moved to make a definite act of thanksgiving for their deliverance from war, contributed generously and gladly.[2]

The Lord Mayor wished to superintend personally the setting-up of a committee for the distribution of these funds, and, accompanied by Sir Neill Malcolm and myself, he flew to Prague on October 10.[3] On arrival we found that the situation was even

---

[1] *The Times*, October 4, 1938.

[2] The total amount subscribed to the Lord Mayor's Fund for the Relief of Czechoslovak Refugees was £318,000.

[3] Our journey was not without adventure. We flew in a Belgian aircraft from London to Brussels, where we changed into a Swedish plane for Prague. No sooner had our original plane taken off to continue its journey to Cologne than it exploded,

worse than we had anticipated. The German Government had demanded that all those who were registered residents of the recently occupied areas on October 1 and who had since fled were to be returned forthwith, and the Czech Government had complied with this demand. As a result those refugees who had already arrived were being rounded up by the Czech police preparatory to forcible return and those arriving by road and train were turned back immediately.

For many of those who had loyally supported the Czech Government against the agitation and intrigues of Konrad Henlein, return to their homes was tantamount to a death warrant. Already the Sudeten Legion and the Henleinist Storm Troops were going from house to house with lists, arresting their former political enemies and working off old scores on the spot.[1]

With Sir Neill Malcolm and General Faucher, formerly head of the French Military Mission and a close friend of General Syrový, I went to plead with the Chief of State that in the case of at least some of these political refugees a respite of a fortnight should be granted in order that emergency refugee organizations abroad might take charge of them and visas be procured for their departure.

General Syrový had changed greatly since I had seen him in August. Then he had been calm, friendly and completely confident that, rather than surrender, Czechoslovakia would fight — if need be alone. Now, having had to eat his words, he was a very different man. His single eye glared at us balefully and the black patch over the empty socket seemed more sinister than before. His falsetto voice trembled with emotion as he rejected our plea. " Not fifteen days, not fifteen minutes," he said. " The Germans have asked for them and back they go." Then, rising to his feet and bringing the interview to an end, he said, more quietly but in tones full of meaning : " In this affair, messieurs, we have been willing to fight on the side of the angels, now we shall hunt with the wolves."[2]

all passengers and crew being killed. On our return journey we were informed by the Belgian Security Police that the explosion had been caused by a time-bomb secreted in the plane.

[1] In a public speech on October 7, Konrad Henlein announced that, as newly appointed Reichskommissar for the Sudetenland, he would imprison all political opponents " until they turn black ". He threatened that " all those who fled and have been subsequently returned will be treated in the same way ".

[2] To return to Prague after Munich was, for an Englishman, a most humiliating experience, and the fact that one's profound feeling of relief that war had been avoided

Such is the story of the Munich Agreement, the great humiliation of the Western democracies ; a settlement of which it may be written, as Sheridan said of the Peace of Amiens, that " every man ought to be glad but no man can be proud " — the great exception being Mr. Chamberlain. The best that could have been said for it was that, though irretrievable in itself, it had at least gained — at a terrible price — a breathing-space in which Britain and France might prepare, materially and spiritually, for the forthcoming and inevitable conflict. Had this been true, the Czechs would not have been sacrificed in vain. In fact, however, Munich only stands as a milestone between the years which the locusts had eaten and the months which they were about to devour.

was tempered with a deep sense of shame only added to the discomfiture. The Czechs were not in general openly hostile but they were, which was worse, contemptuous. They did not hesitate to say that they had been betrayed, and who could blame them?

The refusal of General Syrový to grant a stay of repatriation for the refugees discounted to a very great extent the efforts of the Lord Mayor. " He is just bringing us conscience money," many people said bitterly. " He should use it to buy a magnificent wreath in the British Colours to be placed on the nameless graves of the victims of the Nazis " (Gedye, p. 478).

In point of fact a number of prominent refugees, such as Dr. Wenzel Jaksch, leader of the Sudetan Social Democrats, did escape to London and Paris.

PART II

FIVE YEARS

(1933-1938)

It is always a temptation to a rich and lazy nation
  To puff and look important and to say :—
" Though we know we should defeat you, we have not the time
    to meet you,
  We will therefore pay you cash to go away."

    .   .   .   .

It is wrong to put temptation in the path of any nation,
  For fear they should succumb and go astray ;
So when you are requested to pay up or be molested,
  You will find it better policy to say :—

  " We never pay *any*-one Dane-geld,
    No matter how trifling the cost ;
  For the end of that game is oppression and shame,
    And the nation that plays it is lost ! "

RUDYARD KIPLING, *Dane-geld*

CHAPTER ONE

EUROPE ASLEEP

(i)

WHEN Adolf Hitler came to power in Germany on January 30, 1933, the continent of Europe was in the latter years of a period of which the watchwords — at least outwardly — had been " Peace, Retrenchment and Reform ". This period, which had been inaugurated with the acceptance of the Dawes Plan for Reparation Payments in 1924, had reached its peak a year later in the Locarno Agreements of 1925, and its anti-climax in the Kellogg-Briand Pact for the Renunciation of War in 1928. The chief objective of policy among the European Powers had been to bring Germany back to the fold of the body politic of Europe, while seeking to violate as little as possible the provisions and safeguards of the Treaty of Versailles. This procedure became known as " Peaceful Change ".

The European Powers, great and small, had, moreover, endeavoured to protect themselves against future aggression — whether from Germany or from any other source — by a system of bilateral and multilateral pledges, so that by the close of 1932 Europe was enmeshed by a web of alliances, pacts and treaties of mutual assistance, in addition to the general guarantees and instruments of the League of Nations. On paper the Continent was well insured against all forms of international violence, but in reality all that this " Pactomania " had produced was a flimsy structure, destined to collapse at the first test of its strength.

Under the freezing winds of the Great Depression, the fortunes of " Peaceful Change " had withered and declined. The forces of nationalism, apparently dormant during the comparative peace and plenty of the 'twenties, revived with renewed vigour under the influence of economic disaster and were in full flower on both sides of the Franco-German border by the close of 1932. The *Annus Terribilis* of 1931 marks the first turning-point from peace to war, but it must be remembered that great progress had been made towards reaching an agreement between Germany and the Allied Powers before the inauguration of the Third Reich.

Within Britain and France there had matured strong forces of opinion which called for a revision of the Treaty of Versailles, by common consent, in Germany's favour. German economy, it was said, must be relieved from the crippling burden of reparation payments if Germany was not to relapse into economic chaos. Similarly, if the Allied Powers could not themselves agree upon a measure of disarmament, compatible with the general reduction envisaged at Versailles and to which the disarmament of Germany was specifically stated to be a preliminary measure, then Germany must be allowed to increase her military establishment beyond the restrictions imposed by the peace treaty to a level at which the Allied Powers could agree to reduce their own armaments, thus establishing an equality of status.

Above all, it was pointed out, unless concessions were made by the Allied Powers to the German Government of the day in the matter of treaty revision in order to strengthen their position so that they could, by their own success, check and harness the great wave of national awakening which was sweeping over Germany, the rising tide of National Socialism would carry Hitler to the supreme power in the German Reich.

The failure of Stresemann's Policy of Fulfilment to bring forth what the German people regarded as satisfactory results, and the alluring prospects promised under Hitler's Policy of Repudiation, were driving Germans of all ages, but more especially the youth of Germany, into the ranks of the National Socialist Party, which by the close of 1931 had achieved the position of the largest single party in the country, with a registered membership of over a million.[1]

Unable to ignore these warnings of approaching disaster, the Allied Powers made shift to meet the situation by diplomatic methods: Concessions which, had they been made earlier to Heinrich Brüning, might have achieved their object, were made wholesale to the Government of the egregious Franz von Papen, which had virtually repudiated the reparation payments and withdrawn from the Disarmament Conference. In consequence the Lausanne Agreement of July 1932 abrogated the reparation

[1] In the elections of 1930 the Nazi Party had increased their representation in the Reichstag from 12 to 108 seats, showing a total poll of six and a half millions as against 800,000 two years before.

clauses of the Treaty of Versailles — save for a final token pay-
ment of 3 milliard marks, which everyone tacitly agreed should
never be made — and von Papen was able to announce to the
German people that the " War Guilt " Clause (Article 231) had
been erased from the Treaty of Versailles with the lapsing of
Part VIII (Reparation), of which it formed the first article.[1]
Although this was a unilateral statement and found no echo either
in the Lausanne Agreement or in the other European capitals, it
remained unchallenged by any of the Allied Governments.[2]

Similarly the Agreement of December 11, 1932, granted to the
Government of General von Schleicher in the matter of rearmament that status for Germany of " equality of rights within a
system which would provide security for all nations " which
had been consistently refused to Brüning, and procured, thereby,
the return of Germany to the Disarmament Conference.[3]

Thus, when Hitler came to power, the way to treaty revision
by peaceful means had already been cleared of its two most
outstanding obstacles, and, had he elected to follow this same
path, his achievement might have been more successful and more
durable.

It was evident from the first, however, that the new régime in
Germany had no pacific intentions. Though the Government
declaration in the Reichstag on March 21, 1933, called for
" a long-term consolidation of peace by the really great national
Powers, in order to restore the mutual confidence of the peoples ",
a monument was almost immediately thereafter erected in West
Prussia, looking towards the Corridor and bearing the inscription :
" Never forget, Germans, of what blind hate has robbed you.
Bide the hour which will expiate the shame of this bleeding
frontier." This, it was felt, interpreted more accurately both the
spirit and the policy of the new Germany.

As the spring drew on to summer, there was no neighbour of
the Reich who was not in a ferment of anxiety, and the world
at large was nauseated by the brutalities of the Brown Terror
which convulsed Germany. At the Disarmament Conference the

---

[1] Article 231 of the Treaty of Versailles read as follows : " The Allied and
Associated Governments affirm and Germany accepts the responsibility of Germany
and her Allies for causing all the loss and damage to which the Allied and Associated
Governments and their nationals have been subjected as a consequence of the war
imposed upon them by the aggression of Germany and her Allies ".

[2] *The Wreck of Reparations*, by J. W. Wheeler-Bennett (London, 1932), ch. viii.

[3] *Disarmament Deadlock*, by J. W. Wheeler-Bennett (London, 1934), pp. 82-5.

German delegates maintained an attitude of complete obduracy and intransigent non-co-operation, and on May 12, in a speech at Münster, Vice-Chancellor von Papen announced that " on January 30, 1933, Germany struck out the word ' pacifism ' from her vocabulary ".

The effect on public opinion in Britain and France of this terrifying phenomenon in Central Europe was one of bewilderment and confusion. Whereas the " anti-Germans " remained consistently hostile, the former Germanophiles became hopelessly divided between those who secretly admired the Nazi régime or feared it to the point of appeasement, and those who, while sincerely detesting the cruelties of National Socialism, retained a belief in the fundamental decency of the German people, and waited hopefully for " the other Germany " to rise up and expel the Nazi forces of evil. Some placed their faith in the Army, some in the Churches, some in the Radical and Communist elements of the Left.

As the revolution in Germany increased in fury and bestiality there followed a further shifting of political thought outside the Reich. Those who had always suspected Germany of malevolent intentions, ever since the signing of the Peace Treaty in 1919, now joined hands with those who had become " anti-German " since the Revolution, and made common cause in demanding that Germany should be restrained by force from her aggressive policies ; the original " anti-Germans ", because of their inherent phobia, and the " anti-Nazis ", because of their belief that only by the military destruction of National Socialism could " the other Germany " be liberated from the thraldom under which its own strange lack of preparedness and comprehension of danger had placed it. These incongruous allies were united against the forces of appeasement, which, prompted by a strange amalgam of reluctance, misplaced confidence, and lack of understanding, struggled to maintain the peace of Europe by the method of giving in to the Nazis and even of condoning certain of their criminal actions.

Thus, as early as the summer of 1933, there were those in London and in Paris and in Warsaw who were advocating a preventive war on Germany for the preservation of peace.

In effect, however, the chief contributory factor to the bewilderment and division of counsel which afflicted all schools of thought in Britain and France from 1933 to 1939 was a fundamental ignorance of the German character and a complete inability to comprehend the lengths of evil, dishonesty and deception to which the Nazi mentality could extend. It seemed incredible to many in Britain and in France that the German people, who had but recently emerged from the depths of defeat, should again permit themselves to be led into the ways of aggression by a wanton adventurer. The capacity of the Germans for sheep-like conformity to leadership was not appreciated, nor the fact realized that this new political phenomenon combined all the guile of the old pre-war duplicity of Prussian diplomacy with a new and ruthless deceit of unplumbed depths.

For this reason, therefore, while there was an immediate reaction in Britain and in France against any further concession to Germany in the matter of treaty revision — and especially regarding the revision of the territorial provisions of the Peace Treaties — there was a general tendency among Governmental circles in both countries toward wishful thinking and to the hope that, when the first blast of Hitler's exuberance had been exhausted, the situation would settle down to a more normal condition which would lend itself to settlement by negotiation.

These illusions were fostered by the Führer's speech on May 17, 1933, before the Reichstag, which could scarcely have been equalled by Stresemann or Brüning. " No fresh European war ", Hitler declared, " was capable of putting something better in the place of the unsatisfactory conditions which to-day exist. . . . The outbreak of such a madness without end would lead to the collapse of the existing social order in Europe." He then repeated the basis of Germany's claim to equality, but added : " Germany is at any time ready to assume further international security obligations if all nations are prepared to do so and Germany benefits thereby. Germany is also ready without further ado to dissolve her entire military forces and destroy the weapons left to her if other nations will do the same. If, however, they are not willing to carry out the disarmament stipulations of the Treaty of Versailles, then Germany must at least maintain her claim to equality."

The effect of the speech was a diplomatic and tactical victory for Hitler, who had suddenly extricated himself from the position of being responsible for the breakdown of the Disarmament Conference and had placed the onus for such a collapse — if such there should be — at the door of the Allied Powers. Nor was the Führer content with words. Two days after the speech, his representative at Geneva had withdrawn all previous objections raised by Germany and had accepted as a basis for discussion the Draft Treaty submitted by the British Government (May 19).

To the optimists in Europe the new development betokened a justification for their wishful thinking. Hitler had succeeded in his first diplomatic campaign and had established a balance on the credit side. He had given proof of his *Bundnisfähigkeit* (" pact-worthiness ") and had dispelled many of the reservations which the leaders in France and Britain had entertained in regard to entering into written agreements with him. It was now held that nothing could be lost in concluding a pact with Hitler, and indeed that the more agreements to which he could be persuaded to put his name the more difficult it would be for him to practise the aggression which all had feared. Forthwith, in a naïve attempt to contain the Führer by paper obligations, there was signed the Four-Power Pact between Britain, France, Germany and Italy (June 8, 1933), which was intended to provide not only the formula of success for the Disarmament Conference but also the foundation for a new Concert of Europe.

(ii)

Alas for the hopes thus engendered ; the advancing summer brought no hope of fulfilment. Nazi propaganda in Austria clearly aimed at the overthrow of the Federal Government and the union of that country within the Reich, and in this campaign the German Legation in Vienna made no secret of its connection with the Austrian Nazi Party.

Moreover, it soon became apparent, despite the Führer's pious asseverations, that Germany had made up her mind to rearm. The spirit of martial glory had descended upon her and the way seemed open for military expansion. Germany would not be baulked of it. Already the longing for military display, the swagger of a uniform, the glamour of a band, had been re-awakened in the German people. The drab respectability of the Weimar Period had been swept away and replaced by the tawdry brilliance of the Third Reich. Newer and smarter uniforms were making their appearance every day ; social distinctions between the S.S. and the S.A., between staff and battalion, between Guard and Line, were manifesting themselves. Already many men, for whom life seemed to hold no other future than the unattractive humdrum existence of clerk or salesman, were back in uniform as commanders of labour camps, as instructors in " war sports camps ", as experts in the secret areas where S.S. were being trained by N.C.O.s from the *Reichswehr*. Thoughts of promotion were filling their minds and they were looking eagerly forward to the day when the officer corps of the *Reichswehr* should be doubled, in the hope that there would be a commission for them. Others were waiting to take their places in the labour corps.

After fifteen years the labour and effort which General von Seeckt had expended on the reorganization of the German Army were finding their reward. Not only was the *Reichswehr* the most efficient military force in the world, but it was no longer a disgraceful profession in Germany ; no longer was there the difficulty, as there had been in the early years, of getting the right type of young man as an officer. A commission was an eagerly sought and highly prized privilege now. The Nazi revolution had restored to the Army its old prestige and honour, and, borrowing a leaf from the book of Mr. Florenz Ziegfeld, was " glorifying the German soldier " [1] ; the stigma of 1918 had been removed. " The German people know ", had said the Chancellor, " that no new war will take place which will gain for our country more honour than was in the last war. Germany is not in need of rehabilitation on the battlefield, for there she would never have lost her prestige." [2]

But, though Hitler added that the Nazi revolution which had redeemed Germany was not " the expression of a desire to win new laurels on the battlefield ", this sentiment was not altogether shared by the rank and file of the S.A. and S.S. Many of these young men had been blooded for the first time during the Brown Terror and their atavistic and combative instincts had been aroused. They had been hailed as the saviours of Germany from the degradation of Marxism and the Weimar system, and had been nurtured on the injustices which Germany had suffered under the Peace Treaty. They were young, they were ambitious, above all they were unemployed, and all the efforts of the Government had failed to absorb them into the economic life of the country ; what better glory, then, than to avenge Germany's external

---

[1] Mr. Florenz Ziegfeld, the great American theatrical producer, proclaimed to the United States, when he first produced the famous " Ziegfeld Follies ", that he was " glorifying the American girl ".

[2] See the Chancellor's speech at Nuremberg, September 3, 1933.

wrongs as they had purged her of internal pollution ? " When
we've dealt with these Marxist swine," said one of them to me,
" we'll have a slap at those —— Poles."

And the effect of all this was not lost upon France, where now
the word " disarmament " was beginning to reassume that
identical sense which it had acquired during the Peace Conference.
It was impossible to ignore the fact that with the S.A., S.S.,
Stahlhelm and Prussian Police, Germany had more than two
million men in uniform, in addition to the very efficient *Reichswehr*,
and, though it is by no means true that the uniform makes the
man, it is truer in Germany than in any other country. It was
also known beyond doubt that large numbers of the S.A. and
S.S., armed with rifle, bayonet and steel helmet, co-operated
closely with the *Reichswehr*, and that they were organized in seven
areas parallel to the seven military districts — and this despite the
Chancellor's statement that " there is only one body in Germany
which bears arms — and that is the Army ".

In Paris the facts were known and appreciated that German
boys of between eleven and sixteen were being given morning
exercises in the technique of throwing hand grenades, and that
in the curricula of German universities and technical institutions
courses in " Poison and Combat Gas ", " Military Utilization of
Electrical Means of Transmission " and " The Maintenance and
Perfecting of the Military Aptitude of the Individual and of the
People " were making their appearance.

More disturbing still was the large increase in German im-
portations of nickel, leather, manganese and other features more
usually connected with the manufacture of munitions.[1] The

[1]   GERMAN IMPORTS OF NICKEL, TUNGSTEN, CHROMIUM, ETC.,
                        AND SCRAP IRON

Germany	1932		1933	
	Quantity, Kilos	Value, Rm.	Quantity, Kilos	Value, Rm.
(a) Nickel, crude : coins, waste and scrap	1,571,000	4,161,000	3,143,700	7,726,000
(b) Nickel : bars, sheets, castings, forgings	56,800	254,000	109,600	450,000
(c) Chromium, cadmium, tungsten and other base metals suitable for metal wares, crude and waste	476,700	1,188,000	896,300	934,000
(d) Scrap and old iron, etc. .	43,507,300	1,205,000	262,190,400	7,545,000

military preparedness of German industry was a topic of continual speculation and discussion in France. Germany, like other countries, had learned a hard lesson in the Great War and had not altogether forgotten it. By reason of treaty restrictions she had abandoned the maintenance of large peace-time effectives, and the equipment of her field army and of her national army no longer depended on warehoused stocks of material but upon industrial transformation for war production, and it was known that adequate plans for the organization of such a transformation existed.

To France it seemed as if her patience were being tried unduly highly, and to this M. Paul-Boncour made significant reference on September 3, at the unveiling of M. Briand's memorial at Trébenden. " How easy it is to observe the contrast between a peaceful manifestation such as this and the agitations which surge to the very boundaries of our territories ", he declared, and added that, if French patience with Germany were due to a feeling of weakness, that would be grave ; but France knew herself strong enough to resist violence, and the recent visit of the Premier to the frontier defences was the best reply to proceedings of which the least he could say was that " they deeply trouble the atmosphere of peace so necessary to European restoration ".

In Great Britain the repercussions of the European situation were of a different nature, and produced among thinking people two divergent schools of thought, both of which were more long-sighted than the views expressed in Europe, and treated the question of disarmament in relation to the whole vast problem of Treaty revision. The one school held that, unless some specific guarantee were given, Europe would most certainly drift back to war which, as in 1914, would gradually engulf the whole world. It was maintained that, even though minor rectifications of the Peace Treaties were made, Germany would not be content, but would demand and would prepare to take more by force, unless it were made absolutely clear by Great Britain that she meant to oppose such unilateral revision, if need be also by force. It was thought, therefore, that, unless such additional guarantees of security were given, either France or Poland might precipitate war before Germany had had time to rearm, or that Germany, if given time, might re-establish a hegemony over Europe which would threaten the rest of the world as it had in 1914.

The view of the second school was far more isolationist in character. It urged that Great Britain should resolutely refuse to form part of any special system of European security, and that the main object of her policy should be to co-operate with the Dominions and the United States in trying to form a non-European or Oceanic *bloc*, actively interested in the prevention of war and prepared to carry out its obligations under the Covenant, " as these are generally understood to-day ". Apart from these commitments Britain should be entirely unpledged to any special or automatic economic or military action.

This school of thought — and in this particular aspect it was surprising to find the Round Table Group and the Beaverbrook Press in a startling degree of agreement — considered further that the provisions of the Locarno Treaty must in any case be reviewed, and that any special obligation which Great Britain might undertake on her own account in Europe as a modification of the Locarno system should be undertaken in the interests of her own security and should be limited to a renewal of the guarantee to Belgium and a declaration never to permit the return of Alsace-Lorraine to Germany. In no case, however, should Great Britain form part of a balance of power in Europe involving her inevitable liability to belligerency whenever a European war broke out.

There was no indication as to whether either of these views was held by the British Government, which still maintained a masterly silence on all subjects connected with foreign affairs, save that on September 16, 1933, at Cupar, in Fifeshire, the Foreign Secretary, Sir John Simon, vouchsafed a gleam from the dark lantern, and disclosed the fact that he was shortly going to Geneva " to find out if there was even now some way in which we can secure an agreed Disarmament Convention ".

A blow was dealt the isolationists of Britain, however, by Mr. Stanley Baldwin, then Lord President of the Council, on October 6, when he described their views as " both crude and childish ", and gave a categorical reaffirmation of Britain's pledges to France and Belgium. " What Great Britain has signed she will adhere to ", he declared, but he added that the Treaty of Locarno was " the most difficult " of the agreements entered into since the war.[1]

It remained, however, for M. Daladier, Premier of France, to voice the question which all Europe was asking. What did

[1] Speech at Birmingham. See *The Times*, October 7, 1933.

Germany want ? he demanded at the Radical Party Congress at Vichy (October 10). Publicly the German Government proclaimed their desire for peace, and, by diplomatic channels, their wish to draw closer to France. Yet why was German youth trained for fighting ? Why this refusal to take the first step towards disarmament ? Why this demand for the right to construct material which would have to be destroyed soon afterwards if the Disarmament Convention were signed ?

Events were now moving with great rapidity towards a climax. Though all now knew that a crisis was inevitable, few had any conception of what its magnitude and its gravity would be.

When the representatives of Britain, France, Italy and the United States met in Geneva on October 9 for the meetings of the Bureau and the General Commission of the Disarmament Conference, they had already agreed among themselves that, at the present juncture and in view of the evidence then forthcoming from the Reich, Germany could not be granted immediately that equality of status in armaments which she had demanded. A " probationary period " of five years was regarded as desirable and it was this proposal which was put before the German representatives on the night of October 11.

Hitler at once took energetic action. He summoned his Cabinet on October 13, haled the aged President von Hindenburg to Berlin from the seclusion of his East Prussian retreat,[1] issued a statement that the Four Powers' proposals were " incompatible with the principle of international politics " and, on the following day (October 14), announced the formal withdrawal of Germany not only from the Disarmament Conference but also from membership in the League of Nations.

(iii)

October 14, 1933, was a momentous date in world history. On that day the second or Locarno period in the years between the wars came to an end and the world entered upon an uneasy progress towards a new conflict ; a period which finally terminated on September 1, 1939.

More important, however, is that this date marks the first trial of strength between Hitler and the former Allied Powers,

[1] President von Hindenburg's estate at Neudeck in East Prussia was already currently referred to in Germany as " the smallest concentration camp ".

a contest in which, to his intense surprise, he won an easy victory. To those who were in Berlin on that evening it was clearly apparent that the gravest anxiety and apprehension permeated every stratum of German official life, both political and military, and to this the Führer himself was no exception.

There was no more disturbed man in the Reich than Adolf Hitler in the days immediately succeeding October 14. He had taken his decision to withdraw from Geneva in full anticipation of some military action on the part of France and her allies, and every hour he expected news of a French occupation of the Ruhr, of Czech troops in the brown coal country of Saxony, or of a Polish invasion of East Prussia. Gradually, in the silence which reigned in Paris, in Prague and Warsaw, Hitler discovered that he had achieved a major diplomatic victory, which was to bring him a genuine expression of public support in the German elections of November 12. With the success of his first act of defiance the Führer had taken the measure of his opponents and forthwith conducted his policy accordingly.

CHAPTER TWO

HOW GERMANY NEITHER
SLUMBERED NOR SLEPT

(i)

WHEN, in December 1924, Adolf Hitler emerged from his detention in the Bavarian fortress of Landsberg, he brought with him the MSS. of the first part of *Mein Kampf*, in which he had obligingly set down for all to read the blue-print of his political intentions. The book was a phenomenal failure.[1] When the first volume appeared in 1925, at the exorbitant price of Rm. 12, even the Führer's intimates found it heavy reading, and two years later, when volume two was published, the reading public of the world still remained unappreciative of the vital and stark gospel of ruthlessness which lay enmeshed within its author's turgid prose.

Unrecognized at home and unknown abroad, the warnings of *Mein Kampf* passed unheeded by the political leaders in Britain and France — and in Germany.[2] This was unfortunate, since

[1] Max Amann, the first business manager of the *Völkischer Beobachter*, alleged that twenty-three thousand copies of the first volume of *Mein Kampf* were sold in the first year, but there is no supporting evidence for the statement. Contemporary issues of comic papers, such as *Simplicissimus*, depicted Hitler in cartoons as hawking his book from door to door.

[2] The degree to which *Mein Kampf* was ignored in political circles was very great. Brüning had never read it until after his fall from office, and had von Papen done so he would scarcely have made a coalition with a man who had written that " no really great achievement has even been effected by coalitions, but has been due to the triumph of one individual man. . . . The national state therefore will only be created by the adamantine will-power of a single movement, *after* that movement has won through, having defeated all others ".

In France, when Hitler came to power in 1933, only M. Louis Barthou had read *Mein Kampf*, and, in Russia, M. Litvinov claimed that he had read the book immediately on its appearance. Sir Nevile Henderson first read it in 1937, *en route* from Argentina to take up his post in Berlin.

A somewhat bowdlerized translation appeared in English in 1933, but a complete translation was not made until 1938 (in America) and 1939 (in England). A French edition was published in Paris in 1934 but almost immediately withdrawn at the request of Hitler's literary agent.

this largely unoriginal work [1] gave the key to that technique of strategy which Adolf Hitler was to practise with such amazing success both in internal politics and in international affairs.

Basically the cardinal principle of Hitler's political strategy was " Divide and Conquer ", but to this was added the military concept of " Limited Objectives ", that is to say the attainment of complete command of one unit or situation before passing on to another. To attain this end all means were justified and the greatest duplicity was advocated. Taking his cue from Nietzsche's superman, who " would rather lie than tell the truth because lying requires more spirit and will ",[2] Hitler developed the thesis that " in view of the primitive simplicity " of the average mind " it is more readily captured by a big lie than a small one. . . . Consequently, even from the most impudent lie something will always stick." [3]

By an apt application of these two precepts, Hitler rapidly re-established his former hold on the Nazi Party, which had languished during his imprisonment. His next step was towards the achievement of power in the Reich. Here the thesis of the " Great Lie " was ably developed. The technique adopted was that of " professed peaceful intentions as a cloak for aggressive designs ", and on this basis was operated the principle of " Divide and Conquer ".

When the National Socialist Party entered the arena of " constitutional politics " with 12 deputies in the Reichstag of 1928, it was confronted with a solid mass of opposition from the Nationalist Conservatives on the Right to the Communists on the Left. Yet in two years it had increased its parliamentary representation to 107 and its vote to six and a half millions (1930) ; in four years (1932) it was the largest single party in the Reichstag, with 230 seats, and Hitler was contending with Hindenburg for the Presidency of the Reich ; and in five years (1933) the Führer was summoned to assume the Chancellorship.

This phenomenal record of achievement, though greatly aided by economic and political conditions at home and abroad, was chiefly effected by the method of promising all things to all

---

[1] Many of the ideas and precepts in *Mein Kampf* were derived from the writings of Gobineau, Houston Stewart Chamberlain, Ludendorff, Haushofer, Rosenberg, the American military writer, Homer Lea, and the *Protocols of the Elders of Zion*.

[2] *The Will to Power*, the Complete Works of Friedrich Nietzsche (Edinburgh and London, 1910), vol. xv, p. 367.

[3] *Mein Kampf*, p. 252.

men, thereby splitting the united front of opposition, and of ruthlessly suppressing those who could not be thus beguiled.

Hitler promised rearmament to the Army, and frightened the Nationalists and the German People's Party with the bogy of Communism. He promised Socialism to the masses and restoration of privilege to the Conservatives ; he promised legal government to the President and to the Centre Party, and a " night of long knives " to the S.A. He threatened and bludgeoned the Social Democrats into submission and he suppressed the Communists. By the autumn of 1933 he stood forth before the German people as the Leader of a " Constitutional Revolution ", with a strong foreign policy which should liberate them from the shackles and injustices of the Treaty of Versailles.

After the withdrawal of Germany from Geneva in 1933, Hitler was faced with a situation in international affairs almost parallel to that within the Reich in 1928. From the West, where France and Belgium looked anxiously across the Rhine, southwards to the apprehensive republics of Austria and Czechoslovakia, to the East where Poland stood on guard, all Germany's neighbours stood allied in fear and distrust, and behind them Britain, Italy and Russia were in no happier state of mind.

Hitler met this situation with exactly the same technique as that which he had employed within the Reich itself. He took the measure of the opposition and began to probe for the weak spots in the united front. He was not yet ready for war. He had made his gesture of October 14 because he needed it for home consumption. The risks had been great but the results justified the taking of them. The German people had accepted this gesture and were now more united behind him. But neither they nor he desired war at this moment. Germany must be rearmed before the ultimate trial of strength was undertaken. In order to achieve this, both Germany and the world must be reassured as to Germany's peaceful intentions. With this end in view Hitler invoked the technique of the *Schlummerlied*. He lulled the Western Powers into a sense of false security with promises and pledges and pacts ; then, quickly achieving his immediate objective by a bold and well-planned stroke, he resumed the lullaby almost before the Powers had been fully awakened to his achievement.

It was in accordance with this policy that Hitler launched a " Peace Offensive " in November 1933, reminiscent of similar activities in the latter years of the First World War.

The first step was taken on November 15, three days after the elections, when the Chancellor summoned the Polish Ambassador to a conference, at the end of which it was announced that full agreement had been established and that both countries would take up direct negotiations on all German-Polish problems " in order to consolidate peace in Europe. They renounce the use of force in adjusting their mutual relations ".[1] Nothing could be more gratifying, and, flushed with success, Hitler next approached Czechoslovakia with a similar proposal for a joint declaration renouncing the use of force. But the Czech diplomacy was more wary than the Polish ; the German proposals, though renewed on three separate occasions, met with no success in Prague, where the indefatigable Dr. Beneš continued to keep watch and ward over the heritage of the Little Entente.

Somewhat abashed, Hitler turned his attentions to France. Franco-German relations were anything but friendly, and the fact that in the course of one Sunday afternoon's drive outside Berlin the French Ambassador's car had been stopped and searched by Nazi patrols five times had done little to improve them. An attempt, however, must be made to demonstrate the peaceful intentions of Germany towards France, and to this end the Chancellor received the Comte de Brinon, of the *Matin*, on November 16, and gave him an interview in which he surveyed the points at issue between France and Germany, asserting that he was only pursuing the policy of Stresemann and Brüning, and that Germany had abandoned all claims to Alsace-Lorraine. His predecessors had not had the whole German people behind them as he had, for now the whole nation had approved his policy and knew what he wanted. " I am deeply convinced that once the question of the Saar is settled there will be nothing, absolutely nothing, to divide France and Germany."

There was no dispute in Europe sufficiently important to justify a war, said the Führer. A bad treaty was responsible for the difference between Poland and Germany, but this dispute was not worth a war. He was not quite mad — " a war would not settle anything ; it would only make matters worse — it would mark the end of our races, which are the *élite* of humanity, and in time Asia and Bolshevism would rule Europe. . . . I have a great deal of work to do at home. I have restored the German's

[1] The German-Polish *rapprochement* was made formal by the joint declaration of January 26, 1934, which provided for a ten-year pact of non-aggression.

sense of honour ; I want to restore his joy of life. . . . I shall need years to restore Germany's prosperity. Do you really think I want to upset my work with a new war ? "

Hitler summed up his attitude in the words : " Not a single German for a new war ; every German for the defence of the Fatherland ". If France wished to make of Germany's helplessness the keystone of her security, no agreement could be reached between them, " but if France is prepared to look for security in a free agreement with Germany, I am willing to listen, to understand and to act. The equality demanded by Germany is absolute moral equality. As for practical equality, it can be achieved by stages, and we are prepared to discuss the details."

In conclusion, he said that in leaving Geneva he had done the right thing, for in doing so he had helped to clear up the situation. " We shall not return to Geneva," he said. " The League of Nations is an international Parliament in which the conflicting groups of Powers can only quarrel. The differences, instead of being settled, only grow worse. But I shall be only too glad to enter into negotiations with anyone who wants to talk to me."

Toward England the method was more indirect. The Ministry of Propaganda made great use of those Englishmen who had been carried away by the more emotional and sentimental aspects of the Nazi régime and were prepared to undertake " conversation work " in their own country. In addition, the frequent visits to London of " Putzi " Hanfstängel won many converts in Mayfair. Not a few Englishmen, who had at first been convinced that the " new presbyter was but old priest writ large ", and that the Nazi régime in Germany was but a recrudescence of prewar Prussianism, began now, under the force of the German " peace offensive ", to waver in their opinion and to wonder whether, after all, there was not something fine and genuine and hardy about the Nazi movement, which only wished to be let alone, to purge Germany from the decadence of the post-war years. It is said that the chairman of a well-known peace organization was at this time only with difficulty dissuaded from sending a congratulatory telegram to the Chancellor on the spirit of his peace policy.

It will at once be seen that it was profoundly difficult to counter the German " peace offensive ". . If Germany's neighbours rejected her advances, they laid themselves open to the charge of sabotaging the peace of Europe by refusing to enter into *bona fide* negotiations for a settlement. If, on the other hand, they accepted the German proposals, they placed themselves in a position of disadvantage in the event of Germany's bad faith, which they more than suspected. Never was it truer that Europe feared — in this case — the Germans even when they brought gifts, but on the whole it was felt better at least to discuss the gifts, even though it meant looking them in the mouth rather more than is usually considered courteous.

Thus it was that Hitler engaged in desultory negotiations with the Western Powers and Italy for the solution of Germany's claims for armament equality and her possible return to Geneva. These conversations, doomed from the start to failure, dragged on for six months or so, but he was able to turn them to his own advantage.

All was not well within the Third Reich, nor within the Nazi Party. The S.A., those brown-shirted paladins of the Revolution, were proving a serious embarrassment. Two and a half million strong, armed with rifles and revolvers, they constituted an *imperium in imperio*, a Praetorian Guard disgruntled at the non-fulfilment of their hopes in regard to socialism and war, who threatened to imperil the relations of the Führer with the Army.

Faced with these contumacious followers on the one hand, and a Europe unconvinced of his pacific intentions on the other, Hitler determined to sacrifice the one to the other. The disarmament negotiations presented him with a golden opportunity of disembarrassing himself of the Brown Army, which had become a threat and an incubus ; he therefore offered Mr. Eden in February 1934 the complete disarmament of the S.A. and a material reduction in their numbers, and he repeated the offer two months later.

When these negotiations failed, Hitler seized an opening to consolidate his position with the Army. In exchange for a pledge from the Army chiefs to acknowledge him as Reichsführer and Commander-in-Chief on the death of President von Hindenburg, he agreed to liquidate the S.A., and therefrom resulted the massacre of June 30, 1934.[1]

The clandestine rearmament of Germany was by this time virtually a *secret de polichinelle*. It was a matter of open comment within the Reich, and jokes about perambulators ordered in

---

[1] *Hindenburg, the Wooden Titan*, by J. W. Wheeler-Bennett (London, 1936), pp. 453-6.

parts and, when assembled, turning out to be machine-guns, were generally current. The publication of a greatly swollen military budget in March 1934 precipitated the collapse of the Disarmament Conference in the following June,[1] but still the world hesitated and German military preparations proceeded unchecked.

On March 15, 1935, Hitler, now Führer and Chancellor of the Reich in succession to Hindenburg, made his second act of defiance in the unilateral revision of the Treaty of Versailles. By proclamation he decreed the re-establishment of compulsory military service in Germany and announced the creation of the *Luftwaffe*.

The response of the Powers was a spirited display of finger-shaking at the Stresa Conference in April and the conclusion of pacts of mutual assistance with Russia by France and Czechoslovakia in May. An attempt to negotiate an " Eastern Locarno " Agreement proved abortive, as neither Germany nor Poland would consent to participate in a general agreement with Russia. The Führer kept his hands free of general commitments, but he made his usual protestations of peaceful intentions. In a speech to the Reichstag on May 21, 1935, Hitler produced a peace plan which embraced proposals for collective security, limitation of armaments, and the control of the " poisoning of public opinion by irresponsible elements, by word of mouth or by writing ". He also offered to accept a 35 per cent rate of British naval strength and declared that " Germany neither intends nor wishes to interfere in the internal affairs of Austria, to annex Austria or to conclude an *Anschluss* ".

" Even from the most impudent lie something will stick ", Hitler had written, and he was right. Out of this maze of mendacious promises he obtained the one thing that he wanted. On British initiative there was signed on June 18, 1935, an Anglo-German Naval Agreement which accorded to Germany, with certain reservations, particularly in the matter of submarines, a permanent naval strength in relation to the total aggregate strength of the members of the British Commonwealth of Nations in the proportion of 35 : 100.

Hitler's policy of " Divide and Conquer " was working successfully. The structure of opposition was beginning to crumble. Recognizing France as the primary and hereditary enemy of Germany — he had proclaimed as much in *Mein Kampf* — Hitler had deliberately proceeded to undermine her position and to

[1] Wheeler-Bennett, *Disarmament Deadlock*, pp. 220-38.

render null and void the elaborate system of alliances and agreements with which successive French governments had sought to substantiate the security of France. The first breach had been effected with the Pact of Non-Aggression with Poland, which had caused a rift in Franco-Polish relations. Now the conclusion of the Naval Agreement with Britain caused a distinct coldness between London and Paris, for the French Government had not been consulted in advance and regarded this action as a breach of the Stresa Front and a tacit recognition by Britain of Germany's right to rearm.

Profiting by the situation, Hitler concentrated the full force of his propaganda machine upon France, and, by means of Nazi agents and dissident Frenchmen, contrived to disseminate the seeds of civil and moral dissension within the body politic of the French Republic, seeking to render it a helpless and divided force.

With Italy the Führer had an even easier task. Mussolini's early hostility to National Socialism, both as an imitation of his own Fascism and as rendering Germany once again a power factor in Central Europe, had given way before his own imperial ambitions in Ethiopia. These Hitler fostered and aided by refusing to be bound by the system of economic sanctions imposed upon Italy by the League of Nations in September 1935, thereby placing the Duce under an obligation.

Against Russia the antagonism of the Third Reich was always open in propaganda, but the policy adopted in diplomacy was more subtle. Hitler sought to use Poland as a cat's-paw to pull the Russian chestnuts out of the fire for Germany. Gradually but surely the Führer had been developing his plans for a wider *Lebensraum* for Greater Germany. These plans were directed ultimately against Russia but primarily against Poland, and it was Hitler's diabolical artifice to employ one potential victim of aggression in the destruction of another.

Thus, when he signed the Pact of Non-Aggression with Poland in January 1934, the Führer, and also Göring, impressed upon the Poles the evil which the pre-Hitler Germany of Stresemann and Brüning had consistently worked with Russia against Poland, who had, they said, been the intended victim of the Rapallo Policy,[1] given the means and the opportunity. This, said the

[1] In April 1922, in the course of the Genoa Conference, the German and Soviet Governments signed at Rapallo a Treaty of Friendship and a secret agreement

Nazi leaders to Marshal Pilsudski and Colonel Beck, was all changed now; the Third Reich entertained only the friendliest feelings toward Poland and was ready and willing to give her all support and protection against the menace of Soviet aggression.

In short, beginning with 1935, it became one of the chief objectives of Nazi foreign policy to exacerbate Soviet-Polish relations and to dazzle Poland with promises of gigantic territorial aggrandizement. In all their conversations with the Polish leaders the Nazi chiefs were studiously modest in their own prospective demands upon Russian territory. These, they said, were confined to the annexation of the Baltic States and the transformation of the Baltic Sea into a German lake. Germany had not the slightest design upon the Ukraine, not even upon a part of it, and looked upon this fertile land as the perquisite of Poland, to whose Western Ukrainian Provinces, taken from Russia in 1921 by the Treaty of Riga, it should be united.[1] With these honeyed words the Nazi leaders pushed Poland forward against the Soviet Union, while at the same time preparing for the destruction of the Polish State.

All was now ready for the next coup; the stroke only waited upon the occasion. It was not long in coming. On February 27, 1936, the Franco-Soviet Pact, which had been signed in the previous May but ever since had hung fire in the Senate and the Chamber, was finally ratified by France. Hitler's reply was dramatic and forceful, but in full accordance with his general use of the technique of the *Schlummerlied*. While all the world waited for his reaction, the Führer received M. Bertrand de Jouvenel of the *Matin* and gave to him an interview in which he expressed the warmest and most conciliatory sentiments towards France.[2] Then having administered his soporific, he summoned the Reichstag on March 7 and denounced the Locarno Agreement on the ground that it had been violated in spirit by the Franco-Soviet Treaty, which " it is an undisputed fact . . . is directed against Germany ". He then announced that, as he spoke, the demilitarized areas of the Rhineland were being occupied by German troops. Concurrently, in keeping with his policy of " action and deception ", he offered a twenty-five years' non-

providing for mutual assistance in the re-equipping of the Russian and German armies. The Rapallo Policy remained the basis of German-Soviet relations until the advent to power of Hitler and the National Socialist Party in 1933.

[1] *Polish White Book*, p. 26.
[2] *Le Matin*, February 28, 1936; François-Poncet, p. 250.

aggression pact to France and Belgium, with Britain and Italy as guarantors. In language which was by now becoming familiar, the Führer argued once again that Germany was a peace-loving nation which had never had a square deal. "There is no better proof of Germany's love for peace", he declared, "than the fact that the German people, in spite of its great numbers, has secured for itself such a modest share in the world's area and the world's goods."

This step was the boldest which Hitler had hitherto taken and yet it was not so daring as it appeared. Hitler was not unaware of the situation prevailing in Britain and in France, and he had good reason to believe that he would meet with little real opposition. France was actually divided both socially and politically, and there was clear evidence of this in the debates on the ratification of the Franco-Soviet Pact.[1] French visitors to Berlin in the winter of 1935-6 said openly that France would not fight against the remilitarization of the Rhineland, and both Britain and France had for some time favoured a negotiated solution of the position in the Rhineland and had said as much to the Führer.

In these conversations, however, emphasis had been laid on the point that concessions in the Rhineland would constitute a "revision", and not an "abrogation", of the Locarno Agreement, and Hitler had repeatedly declared his intention of observing this treaty.[2]

When, therefore, his Generals, who could not conceive that France would allow so great a threat to her security to materialize without protest, opposed the Führer's plan on the grounds that it would certainly mean war and that Germany's armaments were not yet ready to meet the Western Powers on terms of equality, Hitler scornfully overrode their opposition. He contemptuously conceded their condition that they would only consent to undertake the operation on the understanding that the occupying troops should immediately be withdrawn from the demilitarized zone in the event of any armed opposition from France. Hitler dared the Western Powers to do their damnedest, and their damnedest was very little indeed. At a meeting of the Council of the League on March 19, at which representatives of Italy, who had formally been declared an aggressor, and Germany, who had formally resigned her membership, were permitted to attend as "interested parties", Germany was found guilty of infraction of both the Treaty of Versailles and the Locarno Agreement, but

---

[1] See below, p. 251. [2] François-Poncet, pp. 245-6.

that was all. No penalty was inflicted or even discussed. Instead, the British Government asked for elucidation on various parts of the latest German peace plan and the French Government made counter-proposals which Hitler characterized as " a sky-scraper of pacts and visions ".

Confident from the first that nothing would happen, and encouraged by the complete justification of his confidence, the Führer now turned to a more definite form of political and military aggression.

(ii)

The months between the spring of 1936 and the winter of 1937 constitute the final phase of that " Preparation for War " period in Nazi history. During the years 1933-8 Hitler neither desired nor courted war ; but he prepared with intensifying energy for that time when his ultimate policy of expansion, his campaign for *Lebensraum*, could only be carried out at the risk of a general European conflict. So long as only the intangibles of the Treaty of Versailles were concerned, or those provisions which concerned purely German territory, the political intuition of the Führer told him that no real opposition would be encountered from Britain, France or Italy, nor, consequently, from Poland or Russia, since neither would fight alone or together.

But when, in November 1936, Hitler had announced the resumption of full German sovereignty over the Kiel Canal and those German rivers which had been placed under an international régime by Part XII of the Treaty of Versailles, he had freed the Reich proper from the last of her shackles. Reparation (Part VIII) had disappeared before his advent to power ; Disarmament (Part V) had been abrogated in 1935 ; the demilitarized zone of the Rhineland (Part III, section III) had been reclaimed for German militarism in 1936. The German Reich, as defined by the treaty, was now clear of all restrictions and enjoyed, by unilateral treaty revision, the full exercise of its sovereignty.

Hitler's ambitions, however, extended further than this. He sought to restore to the Reich those territories reft from Germany in Europe and in Africa, to add other German peoples to that Reich, and to achieve for the whole a living-space in other parts of Europe. This concept of a *Deutschtum* stretching from Jutland to the Brenner and from the Strasburger Kirche to the Riga Dom had been clearly indicated in *Mein Kampf* as but a stepping-stone to greater things. The expansion for *Lebensraum* was there indicated as developing towards east and south-east Europe, to those territories which had been colonized by Germans in the Middle Ages. " We begin again where we left off six centuries ago ", Hitler had written, and in his mind was a vision of the rich black fertility of the Ukraine and the Caucasus.[1]

This dream of territorial expansion had been ever present with the Führer, both before and after his accession to power. He had talked of it to his Party comrades before the Revolution and to his chosen confidants in the years which followed. It had inspired writers and journalists in post-war Germany even before 1933. All the old ambitions of the Pan-German League again took fire. The teachings of Adolf Lehr and Ernst Hasse were merged with those of Rosenberg and Haushofer into one flaming gospel of *Lebensraum*. But, as the time approached for the dream to become translated into reality, Hitler himself became more and more reticent, not because he was weakening, but because he wished to throw dust in the eyes of the Western Powers and to delude them with his protestations of peace until the last possible moment, thereby giving himself as long as possible to outstrip them in the race for rearmament which would inevitably follow their discovery that they had been duped.

Thus Hitler used the months of 1936 and 1937 to great profit. His programme of rearmament was bringing forth formidable results and the economic and financial organization of the Reich, under the joint genius of Hermann Göring and Hjalmar Schacht, was placing Germany upon a self-sufficient footing for war. But, while these matters were in progress, Hitler developed a two-edged political offensive against Russia and against France.

By the autumn of 1936 secret negotiations which the Führer had set on foot in the early summer bore fruit in the form of the Rome-Berlin Axis (October 25) and of the Anti-Comintern Pact with Japan (November 23) by the provisions of which the contracting Powers undertook to co-operate against the activities of the Third International and to take severe measures " against those who, at home *or abroad*, are engaged, directly or indirectly, in the service of the Communist International or promote its subversive activities ".[2]

[1] *Mein Kampf*, p. 699.
[2] The Anti-Comintern Pact was subsequently adhered to by Italy, Spain, Manchukuo and Hungary.

In concentrating his attack on the Comintern and not specifically upon the Soviet Union, Hitler displayed an acute sense of political warfare. In France and in Britain there was in Conservative circles an inherent and growing distrust of Communist activities, and this fear was to some extent shared by many members of the Socialist and Labour Parties in both countries, who were separated from Moscow by the deep and abiding chasm of ideology which divides the Second International from the Third. Thus, by attacking " Communism " rather than " Russia ", Hitler divided his antagonists on a doctrinal basis, causing them to neglect the possibility of co-operation with the Soviet Union for fear of the Trojan Horse of the Comintern.

In a similar manner Hitler utilized to his own advantage the civil war which broke out in Spain in July 1936. The Soviet Union, together with the Leftist elements in Britain and France, espoused the cause of the constitutional Government of Spain, which was promptly branded as " Communist " by the propaganda of Germany and Italy, who afforded material aid in men, weapons and equipment to General Franco.

The whole conflict was therefore immediately placed on an ideological level of Fascism versus Communism, and Hitler lost no opportunity in the next three years of gleaning every possible advantage from the situation thus created. Britain and France were bitterly divided internally on the Spanish policy of their Governments. The sessions of the Non-Intervention Committee were rendered sterile by the deadlock which ensued between the German and Italian representatives on the one hand and the Soviet representative on the other. Meanwhile German military experts utilized Spain as a proving ground for many weapons and devices, which were further perfected and developed as a result of their practical application. The ultimate victory of General Franco contributed still further to the political isolation of France, since she had an unfriendly, instead of a friendly, neutral to the south-west in the event of war, and must, therefore, detach more troops to guard that frontier than would otherwise have been necessary.

By the close of 1937 Germany's preparedness for war was complete. The preference for guns rather than for butter had brought forth results. Her rearmament had reached its apogee and could hold that peak level for a certain time. Her economy was geared to a strict régime of rationing and output on a war level. She had reached a point at which, in the estimation of her Führer, she had "nothing further to gain from a prolonged period of peace ".

The time had come to begin the realization of that dream conceived twelve years before in the fortress of Landsberg, and in this spirit Hitler summoned his political and military lieutenants to that secret conclave of November 5, 1937,[1] at which time he declared to them the new policy for Germany; a policy which must be carried through even at the risk of a second World War; a policy which envisaged the annexation of Austria, the subjugation of Czechoslovakia, the destruction of Poland, the conquest of *Lebensraum* in Russia and — ultimately — a Germany paramount in the arbitrament of the world's destiny. It was *Weltmacht oder Niedergang*, and, by October 1938, it looked as if the Führer were to achieve *Weltmacht* without opposition.

[1] See above, p. 11.

CHAPTER THREE

HOW BRITAIN AND FRANCE
SLEPT FITFULLY

(i)

IN January 1933 neither Britain nor France was equipped materially or spiritually to confront a world climacteric, such as the advent of Adolf Hitler to power in Germany, with that determination for sacrifice and action which the situation demanded. The Great Depression of 1930–31 had rocked the economic structure of both countries upon its foundations, and, in the process, had brought little to improve Anglo-French relations. Both countries were governed by political combinations which had been created as a result of emergency, and had as little in common as most coalitions. In Britain the conduct of foreign affairs was guided by the combined genius of Mr. Ramsay MacDonald and Sir John Simon, and in Paris the inspired statesmanship of Briand had given place to the bewildered leadership of Édouard Daladier, a pacifist *malgré lui*.

The approach of both Powers to the German question was through the problem of disarmament, but it was very different in each case. The British objective was to secure the maximum degree of reduction in armaments compatible with the preservation of the European balance of power, whereas the aim of France was to disarm as little as possible and to maintain her hegemony in Central and South-Eastern Europe. But, whereas Britain displayed a pertinacious determination in pursuing her line of policy, even to the point of unilateral disarmament, French policy — save for a brief moment under Louis Barthou — displayed neither the steely adamant of Poincaré nor the pliant guile of Briand. Behind a crumbling façade of bluster the dry rot of moral decay had entered into the body politic of France.

The story of Britain and France, between the first mutterings of Teuton violence in January 1933 and the successive thunderclaps of 1938 and 1939, is one of miscalculation and underestimation of Germany, and a lack of understanding and co-ordination between themselves. It marks a low point in the statesmanship and leadership of both countries.

(ii)

In Britain it has become axiomatic to associate the policy of appeasement almost exclusively with the names of Mr. Neville Chamberlain and Lord Halifax. It should, however, be remembered that Mr. Chamberlain only became Prime Minister in May 1937 and Lord Halifax did not take charge of the Foreign Office until February 1938. For the greater part of the period between 1933 and 1938 the Prime Minister of Great Britain was either Mr. Ramsay MacDonald or Mr. Stanley Baldwin, while the direction of the Foreign Office was successively exercised by Sir John Simon, Sir Samuel Hoare and Mr. Anthony Eden. Since the policy of appeasement toward Germany began to develop with the establishment of the Third Reich, the responsibility and the credit for its development must, therefore, be shared by the predecessors of Mr. Chamberlain and Lord Halifax.

Since the inauguration of the League of Nations in 1920 Britain had taken very seriously the obligations incurred under the Covenant, more particularly those involving the reduction of armaments, and this tendency had been further encouraged with the increase of economic burdens. In an honest but fatal endeavour to achieve universal disarmament, successive Governments had reduced the armaments of Britain to a point at which many believed them to be no longer compatible with the demands of national defence, in the vain hope that others would be moved to emulate such an example of unilateral rectitude. The appropriations for the armed services had fallen from £116 millions sterling in 1926-7 to £110 millions sterling in 1930-31, and, when the estimates for 1931-2 showed a further decrease of only £66,200, the attitude of the Labour Government was one of apology that they had not been able to make the reduction greater.[1] Under the insistent pressure of necessity occasioned by the economic crisis of 1931, the National Government of Mr. MacDonald and Mr. Baldwin reduced the armaments expenditure

---

[1] A note of warning had, however, been sounded by the Socialist Secretary for War, Mr. Tom Shaw, who stated frankly in Parliament : " It is impossible for me in the circumstances to recommend any further unilateral disarmament, because the figures are against it ; experience is against it ; and, in my opinion, the prospects of the future are against it " (*House of Commons Debates*, March 10, 1931, col. 1020).

for the year 1932-3 to £102·7 millions, and the Labour Party, now in opposition, expressed the view that the reduction fell far short of what was expected. At this moment it was believed by all parties that the risk of financial disaster was far greater than the menace from any rival Power.

Moreover, in the distribution of the appropriations among the three services it was evident that Britain had not become really air-minded and that the British Fleet was still regarded as the greatest single factor in national defence. The attitude of the British Government towards air power was still dominated by the rather hopeless statement of Mr. Baldwin in November 1932 that it was as well for the man-in-the-street to realize " that no power on earth can protect him from being bombed : the bombers will always get through " — a statement which, though it did not have the effect of improving British air strength, materially influenced the attitude of the British public towards war, causing them to regard it with increasing horror.

But the British attitude toward Germany was not only affected by a very natural disinclination to fight, though this in itself was considerable. There had grown up in England a " guilt complex " in regard to Germany, born partly of a national and traditional tendency to resuscitate a defeated enemy ; partly as a result of the masterly propaganda campaign directed from Berlin to " mobilize sympathy " for Germany and to defeat the Treaty of Versailles as a dictated peace ; partly from a disapproval of the attitude of France.

The policies of Stresemann and of Brüning had commanded considerable support in Britain and had produced a corresponding criticism of France in that her opposition to them had prevented the achievement of a greater degree of treaty revision. It had been believed by many that, had concessions been made to the Weimar régime in respect of reparation and armaments, the National Socialist Party would have been deprived of much of its most persuasive propaganda material and would either have withered away or become so weakened as to make it a controllable force in German politics.

Thus, when the Weimar régime perished on January 30, 1933, those former friends of Germany in Britain found themselves perplexed and irreparably divided. There grew up among them two schools of thought, between which there could be no compromise : the one which held that the establishment of the Nazi Power had changed everything and that the forces of aggression inherent in totalitarianism must be opposed by every possible means, not excluding war ; the other, which argued that if the Treaty of Versailles had been unjust before 1933 it was equally unjust afterwards, and that, if the more forceful demands of Hitler for treaty revision were met forthwith, Germany might still not be lost as a constructive force in the general policy of Europe.

Others, moreover, believed that the interests of Britain were more closely allied with those of Germany than of France, and welcomed the emergence of a strong government in the Reich as an added bulwark against the spread of Communism toward Western Europe.

There remained one other important factor. Human imagination, and particularly British imagination, could not conceive of the depths of infamy and turpitude to which this new phenomenon in Germany could descend. It was not realized that Europe had become confronted by a Power which recognized no law save that of force, no code save that of deceit, no canon of principles save that " Necessity knows no Law " and that " Might is Right ".

Such, then, were the constituent elements of the British attitude towards Nazi Germany at the establishment of the Third Reich : weakness in armament, infirmity of purpose, and a lack of realization of the immensity of the danger ahead. Other factors were added with the course of time, but basically these three remained unchanged.

(iii)

The reaction of France to the apparition of National Socialism in control of Germany was somewhat different from that of Britain. Both externally and militarily she was in a stronger position than Britain to meet the crisis. France possessed a network of alliances which, at any rate on paper, assured her, in the event of unprovoked aggression on the part of Germany, of the immediate assistance of Britain, Italy, Belgium, Poland and Czechoslovakia, and, although no military alliance existed with Yugoslavia and Rumania, there was no doubt as to where their sympathies lay. To the south, the leaders of the recently proclaimed Spanish Republic were men who, during the First World War, had been ardently pro-Ally, and, further eastward, a pact of non-aggression, signed with the Soviet Union in 1932, had dispelled the nightmare of Germany and Russia combining against France.

Nor had France permitted her armaments to decline to the same degree as had Britain; indeed, in the six years since 1926, she had doubled her military expenditure, which in 1933 stood at more than 17 milliard francs (approximately £130 millions sterling). The French Army was still rated the most efficient fighting machine in Europe and the French Air Force was the largest in the world, having an effective, though obsolescent, strength of 2,375 planes.

But a new element was emerging, an element strange and contradictory. In 1930 the construction had begun of the great system of fortifications on the eastern frontier of France, known as the Maginot Line, and, as its wonders and strength became apparent, an insidious mysticism developed in French military and political thought. Designed by its creator, M. André Maginot, as a more practical guarantee of French security than pacts of non-aggression and treaties of alliance, the Maginot Line grew to be a strange factor of appeasement. It represented the feeling of French self-sufficiency, the abandoning of the interests of France in Europe, the weakening of collective security and the adoption of a purely defensive policy toward Germany. The illusion evolved that France was so secure behind her magical defences that she could afford to allow Germany to increase her own armament strength and even to replace France in the hegemony of Central and South-Eastern Europe. For many Frenchmen the Maginot Line came to possess that mystic quality of security with which many in Britain had invested " the silver sea, which serves it in the office of a wall ".

Economically, however, France was in a worse position than Britain in 1933. Whereas Britain, the United States, and even Germany had begun to recover from the worst effects of the Great Depression by that time, France was just descending into the lowest trough. Those to suffer worst were the middle class, the *rentiers* and the holders of Government securities, who were torn between their yearning to enter the ranks of the wealthy and their fears of being thrust into the legions of the proletariat. Ever since 1919 successive French Governments had re-echoed the glib promise of Clemenceau's Finance Minister, Louis Lucien Klotz, that " the Bosche will pay ".[1] But now it was revealed to

---

[1] It will be remembered that, in speaking of M. Klotz, M. Clemenceau is said to have complained that " it was his bad luck to have as Finance Minister the only Jew who couldn't count ".

them that not only would Germany not foot all the bills, but that their very economic existence was menaced, their *rentes*, their property, their farms, shops and factories endangered. Terrified, they watched the slow but steady drift of popular opinion from Socialism to the extreme Left, and it was with relief and sympathy that they listened to Hitler's denunciation of Communism. If this new Germany were to prove a rampart against the Red menace, they thought, it might not be so bad after all.[1]

On the Right, too, there were surprises. The French Conservatives, so traditionally alert to every sign of the German menace, greeted the Nazi Revolution with surprising calm — an attitude which contrasted strangely with the apprehension with which they had regarded a less provocative régime across the Rhine — and there were many in England who wondered whether this astonishing absence of nerves reflected a fatalistic indifference or a failure to comprehend the gravity of the situation. " I expected it ever since I read Léon Blum's statement that the Nazis were doomed," was André Tardieu's cynical — and sole — comment on receiving the news of Hitler's appointment as Chancellor. " Whenever Blum makes a prediction — just count on the opposite to happen. You'll never fail to guess right."

Among the leaders of the Right, one man — the septuagenarian Louis Barthou, last veteran of French diplomatic grandeur, who claimed that he alone among French Cabinet Ministers had read *Mein Kampf* in the unexpurgated original German — saw clearly the danger to France. " If we take that fatal step," he said, with reference to potential concessions to Hitler, " we shall be faced with new and higher demands in a short time. One day we shall have to make a stand. It is better to make it now while we still have the trump cards in our hands." He remained of this opinion until his assassination, which may not have been unconnected with his views.[2]

Like the Petite Bourgeoisie, the Right welcomed the outspoken

---

[1] It was this reaction of the *rentiers* which materially contributed to the split in the ranks of the Socialist Party in July 1933. The Right Wing of the Party seceded from the leadership of M. Blum, and, under the title of " Neo-Socialists ", affiliated themselves with the Radicals. Their leaders were Adrien Marquet, the Mayor of Bordeaux, and Marcel Déat, both of whom later achieved notoriety in the Vichy régime of Marshal Pétain.

[2] Shortly after the appointment of Adolf Hitler as Chancellor, I was shown in Berlin a list of prominent anti-Nazis abroad who, it was said, had been marked for death. The list included King Alexander of Yugoslavia, Chancellor Dollfuss, M. Louis Barthou and M. Duca, the Rumanian Prime Minister. All these persons were assassinated within two years of the Nazi Revolution.

attacks of Hitler upon Communism which dulled the instinctive fears aroused by the equally manifest Pan-German tendencies of the Nazi Party. There was general agreement not to take seriously the blue-print of *Mein Kampf*, with its clear warning that France must be first isolated and then annihilated. French conservatism was beginning to waver between class interest and national security, and, with the birth of this uncertainty, Hitler had achieved his first victory over France in political warfare.

To Édouard Daladier, the Radical leader who, with infinite difficulty and little stability, had formed a Government two days after Hitler's appointment as Chancellor, the Nazi Revolution presented new opportunities of success. If he could reach an understanding with this new and regenerated Germany, he might at one stroke free France from the age-long threat of invasion and, in alliance with the parties of the Right, create a sufficiently strong Government to relieve her from the menace of Communism also.

M. Daladier saw himself as the saviour of France both within and without. He hated Communism and he hated war. He had fought with courage in 1914–18 and he dreaded a repetition of the horror and bloodshed of those terrible years. He feared that a successful war could only deliver France into the hands of the extreme Left ; that in the final analysis France was faced with a choice between an understanding with Germany and a gradual domination by Russia. Of these alternatives he had no difficulty in making his choice. Ignoring alike the warnings from Marshal Pilsudski regarding the progress of German rearmament and the offer of Polish assistance in checking it,[1] M. Daladier despatched to Hitler an unofficial envoy, the Comte Fernand de Brinon, an individual introduced to him by his Minister of Finance, Georges Bonnet, who had long used him as a confidential agent.

In his *Campaign of 1812 in Russia*, General von Clausewitz had written : "A great European country of civilization cannot be conquered without the help of internal disunity ". Doubt and divided counsels were already, in 1933, providing the premonitory symptoms of this disunity in France.

(iv)

It was, however, the initiative of Mr. Ramsay MacDonald which set on foot the first movement of appeasement toward

_____
[1] See below, p. 283.

Germany. Some months before the advent of Hitler to power, Mussolini had adumbrated the idea of a pact between Britain, France, Germany and Italy for collaboration in preserving the political and economic stability of Europe.[1] Mr. MacDonald now considered this a favourable moment at which to follow up these adumbrations. In the course of a brief visit with Sir John Simon to Paris on March 9, 1933, the Prime Minister discussed the matter *in thesi* with M. Daladier and found him not unsympathetic.[2] The British Ministers then passed on to Geneva, where Mr. Mac-Donald presented the British Draft Convention to the Disarmament Conference, somewhat like an unwanted child deposited on the doorstep of a foundling asylum, and departed abruptly for Rome.

This visit of the British Prime Minister and Foreign Secretary to Italy, which was unkindly described as " the journey of two harlequins to the home of pantomime ", was seized upon by Mussolini as an opportunity to present a draft of a Four-Power Pact (March 18), and this Mr. MacDonald brought back with him to Paris.

As originally conceived, the Four-Power Pact claimed to present " an effective policy of co-operation among France, Britain, Germany and Italy in order to maintain peace ". It paid lip-service to the Covenant, recognized the claim of Germany to equality in armaments, and provided for further treaty revision. It ignored the Soviet Union, and also the French Treaties of Alliance in Central and South-Eastern Europe, and sought to establish a Western European oligarchy with Germany as a charter member.

Despite the efforts of all parties to keep the terms of the Italian proposals secret, it was inevitable that they should become common knowledge. The effect was disastrous. Suspicion and disunity were general in every quarter. Poland made haste to forestall the apparent desertion of France by reinsuring herself with Germany.[3] With equal despatch the Soviet Union proceeded to take measures which should ensure her own security and also nullify the Pact itself if possible.[4] In Prague and Belgrade and Bucharest the greatest anxiety was evinced at this apparent intention of France

---

[1] Mussolini had publicly advocated a Four-Power Pact for the first time in a speech at Turin on October 23, 1932, during the celebrations of the tenth anniversary of the March on Rome.

[2] It was immediately after these conversations that Daladier despatched de Brinon to Berlin.   [3] See below, p. 284.   [4] See below, pp. 275-76.

to abdicate her leadership in Central and South-Eastern Europe. And in France itself the disclosure of the terms precipitated a violent quarrel between M. Herriot and the Premier, which resulted in French counter-proposals of a very different character.[1]

As a result of these repercussions the Pact, when finally signed in June 1933, was a comparatively innocuous and already still-born document.[2] But it had provided Adolf Hitler with an indication of the readiness of Britain and France to accommodate him, and it had sown a harvest of misgiving across the continent of Europe.

But M. Daladier did not despair of arriving at a complete and permanent reconciliation with Germany. His aversion to war was genuine and very deep, and he was, moreover, a dreamer of dreams. As summer drew on to autumn and the portents of Germany's aggressive policies became less and less veiled, the French Premier, undeterred by warnings at home or storm signals abroad, conceived the idea of a meeting with Hitler somewhere on the banks of the Rhine, at which the Führer and he, two former front-line soldiers, should jointly dedicate a memorial to the settlement of the age-old Franco-German feud and the beginning of a new era of Franco-German amity. This web of moonbeams was rudely shattered by the departure of Germany from Geneva in October 1933, but that he should even have regarded the idea as possible is significant of M. Daladier's capacity for self-delusion.

(v)

Hitler's act of defiance in leaving the Disarmament Conference and the League of Nations[3] disclosed the extent to which disunity of opinion had developed among and within the other Powers. From the Conference itself came only an expression of regret and scarcely even of anger,[4] while in Britain and France there was no singleness of thought.

The immediate reaction in Britain to the events of October 14 was one of anxiety as to whether they would entail war, and, if so, whether Britain could keep out of it. There was a keen sense of popular resentment against Germany for having precipitated the crisis, and certain extremist factions publicly advocated the use

---

[1] For an account of the negotiations for the Four-Power Pact, see Wheeler-Bennett, *Disarmament Deadlock*, ch. vii, " Roman Interlude ".

[2] The Pact never came into force, as both Britain and Germany failed to ratify it.

[3] See above, pp. 213-14.　　　　[4] *British White Paper*, Cmd. 4437.

of sanctions against the Reich, ranging from economic boycott to thoroughpaced intervention and preventive war. As against this there were many who believed in Germany's case for equality, and who, while deprecating her precipitate action, still felt that her claims should be met in all justice.

From then onwards, rival schools of thought in Britain battled for the soul and attention of the thinking public. The struggle was between those who saw in Hitler's Third Reich a challenge and a menace to Western civilization and those who still experienced a sense of guilt at the inequalities created by the Treaty of Versailles and who urged patience and a new deal. Both were deeply sincere in their beliefs, but the chasm which divided them was clearly unbridgeable, and it was in recognition of this lack of public unity that the Government formed their policy.

It was now evident that, unless checked by force, Germany had every intention of rearming, and the British Government, in full cognizance that they would not have the support of the electorate in taking forceful action, endeavoured to achieve with France a common policy for the legalization and regulation of German armaments.

In France, on the other hand, while public opinion was almost wholly apathetic, it was the official circles which were divided. The French General Staff would willingly have indulged in a preventive war had they been sure of the willingness of the French Army to fight and of adequate support from Italy, Britain and the United States ; when, however, it was discovered that their sole supporter was M. Paul-Boncour, the Foreign Minister, their enthusiasm subsided and they accepted the fatalistic ruling of their War Minister, M. Daladier, who, though grieved at this interruption of his dreams, was certainly not one to fight.

And so no penalty was exacted from Germany for her open defiance of the Allied Powers. Britain and France, while regretting the necessity, set about humouring Hitler on the ground that the more agreements the Führer was persuaded to sign, the more difficult it would be for him to break any of them — a line of reasoning which displayed both faulty logic and an ignorance of the Führer's capacity for treaty-breaking.

Both Britain and France lent an ear to the new crescendo of the *Schlummerlied* which came gustily across the Rhine in the form of Hitler's peace offensive of November 1933.[1] M. Daladier actually

[1] See above, pp. 217-19.

contributed to this performance by permitting the egregious de Brinon to make a further visit to Berlin, whence he indited to the *Matin* an extravagant picture of a peace-loving Hitler, eager above all things to avoid a European war and to reach an understanding with France.[1]

The effect in Central and South-Eastern Europe of this Anglo-French policy was catastrophic. In every capital of the Little Entente, in the Balkan States and in Budapest and Vienna, the leaders of the Government watched anxiously for the lead which they anticipated from Britain and from France ; they wondered, each for a different reason, whether it was conceivably possible that the Western Powers could permit this German challenge to go unanswered, and, when they found that it was indeed so, each began to take his line accordingly. In Czechoslovakia the Agrarian Party urged an understanding with Hitler, and similar tendencies marked the activities of the followers of Codreanu in Rumania and of Stoyadinovitch in Yugoslavia. In Hungary General Gömbös declared secretly for a *rapprochement* with Germany, and in Austria the National Socialists redoubled their efforts to destroy the Federal Chancellor Dollfuss.

By January 1934 the shifting of French political currents had swept M. Daladier from power, but not from the Ministry of War in the rue St.-Dominique, where he continued to serve in the successive Cabinets of MM. Albert Sarraut and Camille Chautemps. The British Government, meanwhile, had elaborated new proposals which envisaged the immediate recognition of German equality in armament. These were submitted to the French Government on January 28, and would certainly have been acceptable to MM. Chautemps, Sarraut, Daladier and Bonnet, had not an internal eruption caused their temporary eclipse.[2]

[1] M. Daladier's action was taken to counter the activities of M. Georges Mandel, who exposed the secret rearming of Germany in a speech to his constituents which he repeated to the Chamber on November 9. In the same week the *Petit Parisien* published a series of articles disclosing the extent of German rearmament and also of the Nazi propaganda methods in France and other countries. In the interests of Franco-German amity, M. Daladier rushed the Comte de Brinon to Berlin and at his request *Le Matin*, the organ of the French Steel Trust, published the famous interview on November 17.

[2] See Wheeler-Bennett, *Disarmament Deadlock*, pp. 202-13. An interesting by-product of the British proposals was the interest displayed in them throughout Great Britain, where they became the topic of heated criticism and defence alike on public platform and around dinner-tables. At one of the latter, when it was advanced in support of the proposals that Britain now had clean hands, the rejoinder was at once forthcoming : " So had Pontius Pilate ".

In December 1933 the Stavisky scandals had laid bare the state of corruption in France. Public attention was drawn to the fact that not only could a common swindler successfully evade the law and avoid imprisonment but that he could actually acquire accomplices in high places. Taking advantage of this weakness in a democratic State and encouraged by the success of Hitler's successive *coups de main* in internal and external affairs, the Fascist Leagues in France determined upon direct action. On February 6, 1934, they attempted to overthrow the French Republic by an *assaut dans les rues* and marched upon the Chamber of Deputies. The Chautemps Cabinet fell in panic. Daladier, called back to restore order, could not avoid giving the order to fire on the mob. Sixteen were killed, and Daladier at once resigned next day. " I could not shed the blood of the little soldiers of France ", he said, and rather than do so he allowed the Government of the French Republic to accept defeat at the hands of a street mob.[1]

Interesting as this is as an indication of M. Daladier's character and his affection for the *petits poilus*, the events of February 6–7 were of the deepest significance for France. From that date the nation was split in two, and as the years passed the chasm became deeper and wider. The road to Munich, to Bordeaux and to Vichy begins in the Place de la Concorde, and France began to travel along it in February 1934, for from then on there was an increasing number of persons in France who viewed the parties of the Left as a greater menace to the " good life " than Adolf Hitler, and upon every hand in Paris for the next six years one heard repeated the names of those who would one day take over dictatorial power in France — the names were always the same though sometimes the individual emphasis would change : Pétain, Laval, Marquet and Weygand.[2]

Whatever may have been the shortcomings of the Doumergue Cabinet, which succeeded to power on February 9 and remained in office for nearly a year, the Premier, by entrusting the Quai d'Orsay to M. Louis Barthou, ensured a complete reversal of French foreign policy. For the next ten months Europe was treated to a display of diplomatic virility emanating from

[1] Two of the Fascist Leagues, the *Camelots du Roi* and the *Ligue d'Action Française*, were dissolved by Presidential Decree in February 1936 after the murderous assault on M. Blum. Similar action was taken against the *Croix de Feu*, the *Jeunesse Patriote*, the *Parti Franciste*, and the *Solidarité Française* on June 18 in the same year.

[2] All four of these persons were members of the Government formed at Bordeaux on June 16, 1940, to negotiate the surrender of France.

Paris which recalled the robust policies of Clemenceau and Poincaré.

Louis Barthou, long remembered in French politics as the maker and breaker of Cabinets and the wrecker of international conferences, was the last of the traditional French foreign ministers who believed that France must be the first Continental Power in Europe. Like Clemenceau he was haunted by the fear that partnership with Great Britain would mean that France would be the horse and Britain the rider. At no time was this relationship acceptable to him — more especially when there came from London proposals for the regulation and legalization of German armaments — and he therefore treated with some degree of suspicion the covert enquiries which the British Government made on March 19 as to what French expectations from Britain in the realm of security might be. Barthou still held confidently to the thesis — already regarded as *vieux jeu* in London — that, if France would only have faith in her own strength and remain true to the network of alliances which bound her to Central, Eastern and South-Eastern Europe, she could meet the German menace with a calm assurance that it would either crumble or be destroyed. He did not believe in yielding to German demands, holding that concessions bred further concessions and that to break the sequence was as well-nigh impossible as to wrest oneself from the talons of a blackmailer.

Old-fashioned he might be, but M. Barthou was certainly vigorous. He threw himself with zealous energy into the task of repairing the breaches in France's diplomatic relations caused by the pallid policies of his predecessors. In April he visited Prague and Warsaw. President Masaryk and Dr. Beneš received him royally and were duly reassured, on the word of France, as to the Franco-Czechoslovak alliance. But in Warsaw M. Barthou met with failure. Marshal Pilsudski received him coldly and refused to budge from his reinsurance agreement with Hitler. Now it was Poland who rode on her high horse. "I could not make him change his mind", said Barthou sadly, as he left the Bellevue Palace.

Undeterred, however, he went to Geneva in May, where he said a warm "Yes" to his hitherto inveterate enemies the Bolsheviks in the matter of their entry into the League of Nations, and an equally forceful "No" to his hitherto supposedly warm friends the British, in regard to Sir John Simon's proposals to concede equality of armament to Hitler, even after the publication of the German military budget had disclosed the degree of rearmament which already existed.   Indeed M. Barthou's clash with the British Foreign Secretary in the General Commission of the Disarmament Conference on May 31, 1934, will not easily be forgotten by those who witnessed it, and the discomfiture of Sir John was so apparent that he returned immediately to London, leaving the remainder of the work of the session to be handled by Mr. Eden.

When the Disarmament Conference finally collapsed under the combination of German aggression and French intransigence, M. Barthou hurried off to complete his round of calls on the *cortège habituel* of France.   In June he visited Bucharest, where the jubilant Rumanians made him an honorary citizen, and Belgrade, where King Alexander received him as a sovereign.   In each capital Barthou gave assurances of French assistance in the event of German aggression, and urged co-operation with France and Russia in the creation of an " Eastern Locarno " Agreement, which should include Germany also.   His plans in this direction were entirely frustrated by the common refusal of both Germany and Poland to sit at the same table with the Soviet Union, but when he returned to Paris at the end of June the seemingly indefatigable M. Barthou could tell reporters : " I think I have checked him [Hitler] in Eastern Europe.   But it will require hard work to keep him in check."

That Hitler did not underestimate the danger which M. Barthou's vigour and strength represented to German designs in Central and South-Eastern Europe may be judged from the fact that the French Minister's train was unsuccessfully bombed on June 19 by the Nazis on its journey across Austria.   But Hitler had not long to wait.   On October 9, at Marseilles, King Alexander of Yugoslavia and Louis Barthou were assassinated by Croatian terrorists, with arms allegedly supplied from Germany.   Two of the leading opponents of Nazi expansion had been eliminated at one stroke and the conduct of French foreign policy passed into the hands of Pierre Laval and Georges Bonnet.

The last spark of French resistance to Germany expired with the death of Louis Barthou.   To the man who had said " a promise from Nazi Germany is not enough " succeeded, in the Quai d'Orsay, the man who declared : " I shall not hesitate to conclude an agreement with Berlin, if it is possible ", and before the year closed Joachim von Ribbentrop was being entertained in Paris by Pierre Laval.

(vi)

Whether it is true, as was widely believed in London at the time, that the British Government heaved a collective sigh of relief at the disappearance of M. Barthou from control of French foreign affairs it is impossible to say, but it is certainly true that Pierre Laval was more attuned than was his predecessor to the general line of British policy.

The Government, however, were labouring under grave difficulties at home. The need for rearmament was being borne in upon them, but they were aware that Britain was still as yet predominantly pacifist. Mr. Churchill might cry, " Wake up, England ! " and the National Union of Conservative and Unionist Associations might " record their grave anxiety in regard to the inadequacy of the provision made for imperial defence ", but the country as a whole was still absorbing such pacifist pabulum as Mr. Beverley Nichols's *Cry Havoc* and was wholly unawakened to the danger on the Rhine.

Within a week of the withdrawal of Germany from Geneva the leader of the Labour Party, Mr. George Lansbury, declared that he would " close every recruiting station, disband the Army, dismantle the Navy, and dismiss the Air Force. I would abolish the whole dreadful equipment of war and say to the world ' Do your worst '." [1]

The whole country respected Mr. Lansbury as a sincere pacifist, and this statement might have passed as an expression of his own personal views, but in the same month the electors of East Fulham rejected a Conservative candidate, who stood openly for " a bigger Navy, a bigger Army and a bigger Air Force ", in favour of a Socialist who satirically remarked that apparently his opponent's only solution for the country's difficulties was to prepare for war. A Conservative majority of 14,521 became a Socialist majority of 4,840.

Faced with this situation at home and considering the views of many of its members, it is not surprising that the first steps taken by the National Government toward rearmament should be feeble and tottering nor that they should meet with vehement opposition. In July 1934, after the collapse of the Disarmament

[1] *The Star*, October 23, 1933.

Conference and the bloody examples of Nazi ruthlessness offered by the Purge of June 30 and the assassination of Dollfuss ; after the publication of the German military budget in March had proclaimed the open rearmament of Germany in all fields but more especially in the air — the British Government almost diffidently introduced a measure to increase the Royal Air Force by forty-one squadrons (July 19).

At once the Labour Party tabled a motion of censure, regretting that " His Majesty's Government should enter upon a policy of rearmament neither necessitated by any new commitment nor calculated to add to the security of the nation, but certain to jeopardize the prospect of international disarmament and to encourage a revival of dangerous and wasteful competition in preparation for war ".[1]

In his speech supporting the motion, Mr. Attlee, then parliamentary leader of the Labour Party, attacked the Government both for their responsibility for the failure of the Disarmament Conference and for embarking upon a programme of unilateral rearmament. The collective strength of the League of Nations was, in his opinion, sufficient to protect the country.[2]   Three months later, at the annual Labour Party Conference at Southport, Mr. Attlee announced : " We have absolutely abandoned any idea of nationalist loyalty ".[3]

Later in the year Mr. Churchill called the attention of the House to the existence in Germany of " an illegal air force rapidly approaching equality with our own ".[4]   This Mr. Baldwin vehemently denied, though he admitted that an air force did exist in Germany. He assured the House that there was neither " menace " nor " emergency ", and " that Germany's air strength was not fifty per cent of our strength to-day ". He added that " His Majesty's Government are determined in no condition to accept any position of inferiority with regard to what air force may be raised in Germany in the future ".[5]

That Mr. Baldwin was woefully mistaken in his estimates he was frankly to admit at a later date, but this incident is significant of the whole psychology of the Government approach in those fatal years. It was known and admitted that an illegal air force

[1] *House of Commons Debates*, July 30, 1934, col. 2325.
[2] *Ibid.* coll. 2340-51.
[3] Southport Conference, October 1934.
[4] *House of Commons Debates*, November 28, 1934, coll. 866-9.
[5] *Ibid.* col. 883.

existed in Germany, but in their wisdom the Government decided not to alarm the electorate on this score. At the same time they deluded themselves by completely underestimating the rapidity with which Germany could build aircraft and tanks. With the construction of warships and the time required therefor they were familiar, but they were apparently unable to compute the increase of those formidable new weapons capable of being made in immense quantities by mass production.

Yet the very fact that illegal rearmament was in progress in Germany should surely have sent Mr. Baldwin to the country in a campaign, similar to that which Mr. Churchill was waging single-handed, with the object of arousing the British people to an awareness of danger on the Rhine, which he himself had admitted to be Britain's frontier in Europe. Instead he applied the soothing syrup of statistics to the first awakening cries of the British public and lulled them back into the fitful slumber of their false security.

(vii)

Thus matters stood at the opening of 1935. In Great Britain, with a General Election looming before the National Government and the country enthusiastically in favour of collective security but equally averse to rearmament, the conduct of foreign policy was divided between the frank and open appeasement of Sir John Simon and the distressed idealism of Mr. Eden. In France, Pierre Laval, who, since the beginning of his tenancy of the Quai d'Orsay in October 1934, had followed a policy of reaching agreements with both Germany and Italy at any price, was beginning to gather his fruits.

In January 1935 Laval displayed such ostentatious indifference toward the Saar plebiscite that even the most resolute opponents of Hitler lost courage to vote against the return of the territory to Germany. The result of the referendum provided Hitler not only with a success but a triumph. In the same month the French Foreign Minister concluded his agreement with Mussolini, in which he was alleged to have granted the Duce a free hand, in so far as France was concerned, in regard to the projected Italian aggression against Abyssinia.

It may be imagined, then, with what satisfaction M. Laval responded to the British suggestion that new proposals should be submitted to Hitler for the restitution of the balance of power in Europe. On February 3 the two Governments agreed upon a basis of negotiation which comprised three separate agreements, a Western Air Pact, an Eastern European Pact of Non-Aggression and Mutual Assistance, and an agreement to respect the independence of Austria. These proposals had been put forward by the British in a vain attempt to reach some kind of arrangement somehow. Somewhat to their surprise, Hitler agreed to discuss them (February 14), and invited a British Minister to come to Berlin on March 7.

At the same time (March 4) the British Government issued a White Paper on Imperial Defence which set forth their record in regard to the " risks of peace " which they had incurred as a result of their policy of " unilateral disarmament ". It was confessed that " disarming ourselves in advance, by ourselves, by way of an example, has not increased our bargaining power in the disarmament discussions at Geneva ", and the Government now felt that it " could no longer close its eyes to the fact that adequate defences are still required for security ".[1]

It might have been thought that the Service Estimates which accompanied this *apologia pro vita sua* would betoken an opening of a real programme of rearmament, but so confident were the Government that this would prove an unpopular act in an election year that the Estimates put forward showed only an increase of £10 millions over the 1934-5 figures, and of these only the Air Estimates carried any provision for an actual increase in size. But even these meagre proposals were attacked by the Labour Opposition, who presented the confusing paradox of demanding that Britain should carry out her collective obligations, while voting against any measures which would bring her armaments strength up to the sufficient potential to enable her to do so.

At the same time, the Government Estimates were attacked by Mr. Churchill on the score of inadequacy. He warned the House that the Lord President (Mr. Baldwin), far from having spoken the truth in the previous November, when he had stated that Germany's real strength in the air was not 50 per cent of our strength in Europe to-day, had been grievously in error. Germany had now a front-line strength of at least 600 planes and a productive capacity of 125 per month.[2]

[1] *British White Paper*, Cmd. 4827.
[2] *House of Commons Debates*, March 19, 1935, coll. 1053 and 1058.

The answer came not from the Lord President of the Council but from the Führer. Hitler had professed indignation at the publication of the British White Paper on Defence. He had at once " caught a cold " and in consequence was forced to postpone the visit of the British Ministers arranged for March 7. Then he hurled his new bombshell of defiance in the shape of a unilateral repudiation of Part V of the Treaty of Versailles, the reintroduction of conscription, and the announcement of the official existence of the *Luftwaffe* (March 15).

Hitler had calculated that neither Britain nor France would do more than protest on paper, and he was exactly right. The Notes duly arrived expressing the pain and sorrow of the writers at this infraction by Germany of the Treaty of Versailles. But public opinion, either in Britain or in France, was not deeply stirred. To the British, certainly, the matter of German rearmament had been written off for some time as a foregone conclusion, and there were many who experienced a curious sense of relief that one of the so-called injustices of the Treaty of Versailles had been redressed, albeit illegally. In neither country would there have been any degree of support for punitive measures against Germany, even had the Governments concerned contemplated taking them — which they certainly did not. In the French Chamber only a handful of deputies applauded M. Franklin-Bouillon's slashing attack on Laval and Flandin for their " abdication in the face of German rearmament ", and in the House of Commons Sir John Simon announced that, far from cancelling the projected visit of himself and Mr. Eden to Berlin, it was the intention of the Government to press forward with it — " To refuse to do so, to cancel your engagement . . . why, Sir, it leads you nowhere ".

And go to Berlin he did, with disastrous results for Anglo-French relations; for, while in April Britain, France and Italy were going through the motions of censure toward Germany at the Stresa Conference; while the Council of the League was uttering its hollow words of protest at Geneva; while in May M. Laval was — tongue in cheek, to be sure — concluding his Pact of Mutual Assistance in Moscow,[1] Sir John Simon remained silent on the fact that in the course of his discussions with the Führer in March, while he may have deprecated the German action of March 16, he had so far condoned it as to propose that

[1] See below, p. 278.

" German representatives should come to London for a preliminary discussion with a view to a naval agreement in the future ".[1] From these discussions emerged the Anglo-German Naval Agreement of June 18, 1935.[2]

The decision of the British Government to save what they could for themselves from the *débâcle* of the military clauses of the Treaty of Versailles is understandable, but that they should have done so without first consulting the French Government was not only unethical but stupid. Moreover, it was clear either that the British historical sense was at fault or that there was a definite intention to humiliate France, since the date selected for signing the agreement was the hundred and twentieth anniversary of the defeat of France at the hands of the British and Prussians at Waterloo.

What appeared to the French to be an underhand transaction on the part of Perfidious Albion was long remembered and unforgiven. It was remembered in turn by Pierre Laval, Pierre-Étienne Flandin and Georges Bonnet. It was to bear fruit a year later in a further and deeper misunderstanding between the two countries, and Adolf Hitler himself could not have devised a better and more effective instrument to create ill-feeling between Great Britain and France.

(viii)

It was in the summer of 1935 that a curious political phenomenon made its appearance in Britain in the shape of the Peace Ballot, which was organized with the blessing of the Labour and Liberal Parties and also of many members of the League of Nations Union.

The results of this mass interrogation, published on June 27, disclosed that 11½ million people took part in it, and that the overwhelming majority were for disarmament. The usual confusion was, however, apparent between disarmament and collective security. Whereas nearly 10½ millions voted in favour of an all-round reduction of armaments, and more than 9½ millions were for a total abolition of military aircraft by international agreement, 10 millions favoured the application of economic and

---

[1] Mr. Ramsay MacDonald's statement in Parliament (*House of Commons Debates*, May 2, 1935, col. 574).
[2] See above, pp. 221-22.

non-military sanctions to an aggressor nation and nearly 6·8 millions were even prepared for military sanctions if necessary.[1]

The Peace Ballot made no mention of rearmament in the event of no agreement being reached for an international reduction, and it was widely disputed whether those who voted for the application of military sanctions really understood that they were, in fact, voting for war. But there was no disputing the fact that the results of the ballot constituted a serious political lobby in Britain, perhaps the first since the agitation on the Corn Laws. It was a demonstration in favour of disarmament and of an undiminished belief in the efficacy of the League of Nations despite the defection of Germany. As such it had to be taken seriously by the Government.

A moment of testing was soon forthcoming. Mussolini's expansionist plans had now matured and in October he invaded Abyssinia, with the approval of Adolf Hitler and the tacit consent of Pierre Laval. Forthwith the League of Nations proclaimed Italy an aggressor State, accepted her resignation from membership, and ordained that economic sanctions should be imposed upon her.

In all this movement of condemnation Sir Samuel Hoare, the British Foreign Secretary, played a leading rôle, with the full support of the British Government behind him. Collective security, which had for so long been the nostrum of the Labour Party, had now been adopted as a panacea by the National

---

[1] The questions in the Peace Ballot were as follows :

(i) Should Great Britain remain a Member of the League of Nations ?
   Answers : YES. 11,166,818.   No.   357,930.

(ii) Are you in favour of an all-round reduction of armaments by international agreement ?
   Answers : YES. 10,542,738.   No.   868,431.

(iii) Are you in favour of the all-round abolition of national military and naval aircraft by international agreement ?
   Answers : YES. 9,600,274.   No. 1,699,989.

(iv) Should the manufacture and sale of armaments for private profit be prohibited by international agreement ?
   Answers : YES. 10,489,145.   No.   780,350.

(v) Do you consider that, if a nation insists on attacking another, the other nations should combine to compel it to stop by—
   (a) economic and non-military sanctions ?
   (b) if necessary, military sanctions ?
   Answers :
   (a)   YES. 10,096,626.   No.   639,195.
   (b)   YES.   6,833,803.   No. 2,366,184.

(In the above figures abstentions, doubtful and other non-effective votes are omitted.)

Government, which went virtuously to the polls in November with collective security and the application of sanctions figuring prominently in their programme. Rearmament was not emphasized. The Conservatives were convinced that any mention of an increase of armaments would result in the country returning the Labour Party with a majority.

The House of Commons which emerged from the election of November 1935 was predominantly Conservative, but in forming his Cabinet Mr. Baldwin maintained the fiction of a Nationalist Government by retaining the services of the representatives of miniscular " splinter parties ", such as Sir John Simon and Mr. Ramsay MacDonald. The Government had been returned with an overwhelming majority and a clear mandate to pursue a policy, though no one in the course of the campaign had stood up and told his constituents in plain language that sanctions might mean war, and few of the electorate had any conception that this was, in fact, the case.

The first action of the Government was to fly in the face of this mandate by evolving with France the Hoare-Laval Plan, which would have conceded to Italy control over a considerable portion of Abyssinia. The effect was immediate and pyrotechnic. Considered *in vacuo* there was much to be said for the Hoare-Laval compromise, both as a solution of the Abyssinian problem and in order to keep Italy on the right side in regard to Germany. But to have sprung it suddenly upon an electorate, which had but six weeks before pronounced clearly and specifically against such a policy, was little short of political lunacy. The country seethed with resentment, and the Government, threatened with a revolt within its own ranks, withdrew its approval of the plan and hurriedly jettisoned Sir Samuel Hoare, along with the principle of Cabinet responsibility.

Sir Samuel Hoare, whose brief career at the Foreign Office had begun with the Anglo-German Naval Agreement and ended with the Hoare-Laval Plan, was succeeded by Mr. Anthony Eden, and Britain settled down again with a confidence that her *preux chevalier* would worthily perform the charge which had been laid upon him.

In France also public opinion was suddenly and unexpectedly stirred to its depths by the Hoare-Laval Plan. Laval himself received a bare majority of twenty in the Chamber, and, when he decided to attempt to carry on the government until the general elections in the following year, he found himself confronted by an irate Édouard Herriot.

That guardian of the public conscience of France could no longer condone the machinations of Pierre Laval. A leakage of imformation had enabled Pertinax and Mme. Tabouis to publish the terms of the compromise before Mussolini had had time to accept them, with the result that in Britain and in France public opinion rose in protest. Thereupon M. Herriot announced the withdrawal of his support from the Premier, and Laval fell — but unfortunately to rise again, unlike Lucifer, whom he otherwise closely resembled.

But despite its outburst of righteous indignation at the frank *realpolitik* of the Hoare-Laval Plan, the British public was still not prepared to apply sanctions to Germany over the revision of the Treaty of Versailles, and if this was true of Britain it was still more true of France. Hitler was not unaware of this fact, and he laid his plans accordingly.

The new Government of Albert Sarraut and Pierre-Étienne Flandin decided to submit for ratification the Franco-Soviet Pact which Laval had signed in Moscow in May 1935 and had subsequently persistently side-tracked. At once a political hurricane was unleashed and the tragedy which had hampered Franco-Russian relations before the First World War was now re-enacted, but with the rôles reversed. In 1906 the parties of the Left had denounced the close friendship of France with a reactionary and imperialist Russia as a threat to the Republic; thirty years later their arguments were repeated *mutatis mutandis* by the parties of the Right, who feared that an alliance with Soviet Russia would encourage and strengthen the influence of the French Communists.[1]

Throughout the debates on ratification there was little apparent awareness of either the immediate or the ultimate menace which was brewing across the Rhine. The discussions were redolent only of that bitter class struggle which was now cleaving France in twain, draining her energies, dissipating her strength, and blinding her judgement to the ever-growing danger from Germany.

Nor were Anglo-French relations as cordial at the opening of 1936 as could have been wished or, indeed, as the situation in

---

[1] " We will accept the Franco-Soviet Pact when there are no longer seventy-two Russian deputies on the benches of the French Chamber " was the view expressed by Henri de Kérillis during the debate.

Europe demanded. The episode of the Anglo-German Naval Agreement still rankled in Paris, and in London there was little liking among Conservative circles for the French pact with the Soviet Union. Moreover, the fiasco of the Hoare-Laval Plan had somewhat cooled the zeal for combined action with France, and, on the other hand, it was felt that the French were not pulling their weight in the matter of sanctions against Italy.

This unfortunate concatenation of misunderstandings continued in face of the persistent rumours of Hitler's intention to remilitarize the Rhineland and was responsible for a lack of co-ordination in Franco-British policy.[1] For example, when on February 12 Mr. Eden was asked in the House of Commons to give " an assurance that the provisions of the Treaty of Locarno, requiring that this country should immediately come to the help of France or Germany in the event of a flagrant breach . . . of Article 42 or 43 of the Treaty of Versailles concerning the de-militarized zone ", would be carried out so long as the Treaty had " not been abrogated by general consent of the parties ", he stated categorically that the Government intended to stand faithfully by its obligations as specified in the Treaty of Locarno.[2] Yet when, in mid-February, the British Ambassador in Paris, Sir George Clerk, reported that he had sought to elicit from M. Flandin what France would do in the event of a German attempt to occupy the Rhineland, the reply which he received from the Foreign Office, of which Mr. Eden was at that time in charge, was to the effect that in future it would be preferable for His Majesty's Ambassador not to discuss " hypothetical questions " with the French Government. Three weeks later, on March 7, Hitler marched.[3]

Nevertheless, when the time of testing came, Mr. Eden was well in advance of the leaders of France, of public opinion in Britain, and of the majority of his Conservative colleagues in the House of Commons. His parliamentary statements showed a real appreciation of the situation. He admitted that, since Germany had committed a breach of the Treaty of Locarno, France was

---

[1] Mr. Eden had raised the subject tentatively with the French and German envoys during the funeral obsequies of King George V in December 1935. He had found the first vague and uncertain, and the second full of glib assurance. At the same time, however, General Gamelin informed General Sosankowski, the Second Inspector-General of the Polish Army, that, in the event of a military coup by Germany in the Rhineland, France would mobilize immediately.

[2] *House of Commons Debates*, February 12, 1936, col. 918.

[3] *Water under the Bridge*, by Sir Nevile Henderson (London, 1945), p. 185.

entitled to take action, and that, if she did so, Britain would honour her obligations. The French Government, however, made no more than a demonstration of wishing to be held back, despite the fact that they had also the assurance of Polish support.[1]

In neither Britain nor in France, however, was there any indication of any public support for any measure which would, or might, involve a war with Germany.

In Britain the old " guilt-complex " again became apparent; it was said that really Hitler had a " pretty good right " to occupy German territory if he wanted to, and there was a general inclination to take the Führer's peace offer of March 7 [2] at its face value. Under the title of " A Chance to Rebuild ", *The Times* optimistically suggested that Hitler's action might be turned to good account as the opportunity for broadening and strengthening the collective system in connection with Germany's offer to re-enter the League and to negotiate a general European settlement. " The old structure of European peace, one-sided and unbalanced, is nearly in ruins. It is the moment not to despair but to rebuild." [3]

Similarly in France, the deciding factor which dissuaded MM. Sarraut and Flandin from taking military action was the flat statement of General Gamelin that such action would necessitate an order for general mobilization, and this order, with France in her present state of disunity and a General Election imminent, they dared not give.

For these reasons, though Britain and France still retained a combined armament superiority over Germany, it came about that this latest act of Nazi defiance was allowed to pass unchallenged save for verbal protests. The British and French Governments duly expressed their disapproval, and the Council of the League of Nations adopted a resolution merely registering the fact that Germany was a law-breaker. Both Britain and France, however, were soon involved in a discussion of the Führer's new peace plan, which had been the jam round the pill of Nazi ruthlessness.

Thus the *Schlummerlied* began again and Adolf Hitler was permitted to win the first battle of the Second World War without firing a shot. He, and only he, appreciated the issues at stake : that within eighteen months Germany would have over-topped Britain and France in armaments and that this was therefore the

---

[1] See below, p. 287.   [2] See above, pp. 223-24.   [3] *The Times*, March 9, 1936.

last occasion on which they could speak from strength ; that the crumbling of the structure of Locarno would result in the falling away of Belgium to neutrality and the consequent jeopardizing of the Allied left flank in the event of war ; that all the treaty commitments linking France with her European allies, Poland and Czechoslovakia, had become, at one blow, far more difficult to carry out, since France would now have to batter her way into Germany through a system of fortifications set up against the Maginot Line.

These consequences, so crystal clear to Adolf Hitler, were apparently or deliberately ignored by Frenchmen, who were now desperately divided on the social and ideological issue of the Popular Front, and by Englishmen, who remained unmoved by the eloquent warnings of Mr. Churchill or even by the admission of Mr. Baldwin that his calculations as to German air strength had been startlingly inaccurate.

The failure of Britain's leaders to grasp the true situation and to warn the country was grave enough, but the British public cannot escape their share of responsibility. They gave the stamp of approval to the policy which, in time, brought them so near to disaster.

(ix)

The year 1936 marked the beginning of British rearmament and its chief protagonists were Mr. Neville Chamberlain, Mr. Anthony Eden and Mr. Duff Cooper. Convinced that realities must be faced and that disarmament must follow and not precede the establishment of a sense of security, Mr. Chamberlain had, as early as September 1935 in a speech at Kelso, warned the country of the dangerously low level to which the national defences had fallen, with the result that on the Continent the knowledge of Britain's weakness had " shaken the confidence of our friends in our ability to carry out our obligations, and encouraged others, who are not so friendly to us, to think that we can be treated with indifference, if not with contempt ".[1]

A month later, at the Conservative Party Conference at Bournemouth, the Chancellor of the Exchequer had advocated ex-

[1] *The Times,* September 23, 1935. Mr. Chamberlain had, indeed, been aware of the situation as early as 1934, when he had advocated the first serious expansion of the Air Force. " Either we must play our part in pacification, or we must resign ourselves to the staggering prospect of spending £85 million on rearmament ", he wrote in his diary on March 25 of that year (Feiling, p. 252).

pansion of the Navy and the Air Force (in contrast to Mr. Baldwin, who was still harping on the need for disarmament)[1] and was bitterly attacked by *The Economist*, which pronounced his speech to be " a regrettable departure from British tradition " and one which " certainly will not help to promote national agreement on foreign policy if collective security is to be used as an excuse for unilateral rearmament ".[2]

By the spring of 1936 the British public were catching up with the views of Mr. Chamberlain, Mr. Eden, and Mr. Duff Cooper, though they still lagged well behind those of Mr. Churchill. Rearmament for defence and for purposes of collective security was admitted as legitimate and permissible, but Mr. Churchill was still regarded as an irresponsible war-monger prancing in the jungle of his imagination and beating on the tom-tom of his own verbosity. Public opinion, generally, was not prepared to regard the Nazi movement as a revolutionary crusade for the domination of Europe even after Hitler's Rhineland coup. The Führer's propaganda was so effective that the reaction of the average Briton to Germany's wholesale shattering of the Treaty of Versailles and of the Locarno Agreement was one of numb acquiescence. Nor did the Government, if indeed they saw the picture any more clearly, attempt to break down the barrier of illusion. Thus the vital effort of national unity, by which alone Britain could be saved, was lacking and the progress of both Government and electorate toward rearmament was faltering and half-hearted.

Nevertheless the advocates of rearmament had their way with their Cabinet colleagues ; the White Paper on Defence, of March 3, 1936, made definite provisions for an increase in the armaments of the country, and it was carefully stated that the scheme was subject to alteration according to any change in the international situation.[3] Thus when the Service Estimates were presented to Parliament on March 11, they called for an expenditure of £158,211,000, which by the end of the year had mounted to £188,163,000. This showed an increase of £50 millions over the estimates of 1935–6, and was nearly double the figure for 1931. The Navy received an allotment of £70 millions, which was supplemented in May by a further £10 millions, and at once embarked upon a three-year building programme which, by the

---

[1] *The Times*, October 4, 1935. [2] *The Economist*, October 12, 1935.
[3] *British White Paper*, Cmd. 5107.

outbreak of the Second World War, had restored the Fleet to a pitch of high efficiency.

The Air Estimates were nearly doubled, and it was announced that the building programme had once more been " revised to keep abreast of changing circumstances ". Even the Army, which was admitted to be smaller than in 1914, received a grant for four additional battalions " to mitigate the present difficulties of policing duties ".

As an earnest of general intent and good-will, the Prime Minister announced the appointment of Sir Thomas Inskip as Minister for the Co-ordination of Defence, a position of which the terms of reference combined licence to elicit the requirements of all the fighting forces with complete lack of authority to do anything about them.

The Labour Party opposed these defence measures with a fervour as fanatical as it was sincere, and undiminished by the fact that they were now swimming against the tide of public opinion, which had become reconciled to rearmament for defence. The Opposition voted against the measures, not, as it carefully pointed out, because it wanted Britain to continue to neglect her armaments, but because the rearmament programme was part of the Government's foreign policy and the beliefs of the Labour Party were predicated on the theory that " security cannot be achieved by competitive armaments ".

Mr. Churchill assailed the Estimates as a Peace Budget, but the leaders of the Labour Party attacked them, both within the House and outside, as a War Budget. Mr. Attlee complained bitterly on this score in a broadcast address on April 22, 1936, and a day later Mr. Arthur Greenwood bewailed the fact that " we are faced now with rising charges year by year for rearmament against an undefined enemy and to an undefined amount ".[1] Sir Stafford Cripps went even further and declared that "every possible effort should be made to stop recruiting for the armed forces ".[2]

These statements, it should be remembered, were made in the face of repeated examples of ruthless disregard by National Socialism for treaty obligations and of frequent indications of the growing strength of German armaments. The Estimates were passed by virtue of the Government's majority, but the picture given abroad was one of a country uncertain of itself, reluctant and half-hearted.

---

[1] *House of Commons Debates*, April 23, 1936, col. 424.   [2] *Forward*, October 3, 1936.

While the British sleeper evinced this first dim impulse of awakening, across the Channel the French sleeper was sinking further and further into the depths of nightmare. The May elections of 1936 had given the combined forces of the Left, the Socialists, the Communists and the Radicals, a vote of 5½ millions, as against 4·3 million votes cast for the parties of the Right and Centre. The Popular Front was born, and its leader, M. Léon Blum, conceiving himself in the rôle of a " French Roosevelt ", set about giving France a " New Deal ". Like many reformers, he was not content " to make haste slowly ", and the comprehensive programme of social legislation which he introduced resulted in the great " sit-down " strikes of June and the dislocation of the industrial productive system of the country consequent on the Matignon Agreement.

At a moment when France should have been concentrating on the reconditioning of her Air Force in face of the modern equipment of the *Luftwaffe*, her plane production fell to almost nothing and remained at this near-zero for the next two years. As a result the French Air Force in September 1938 was an outmoded and dubious asset, and, moreover, the failure in French production had its repercussions on British rearmament, which had been planned with the expectation that the French Air Force could be counted on to supplement production figures.

Nor was this the only effect of the Popular Front upon the international situation. M. Blum's reforms brought into the open for the first time the bitter and unyielding conflict which was destined to destroy France. The politico-ideological battle, long fought in secret, was now joined in the open field, and, when the Right made their counter-attack in the late summer and early autumn, there arose the slogan, " Rather Hitler than Blum ", which carried such comforting assurance to Berlin. The never-flagging forces of Nazi propaganda fanned every flame which could consume the soul of French resistance to German ambitions, and the fuel was all too plentifully at hand. It is one of the injustices of history that Léon Blum, *un homme du bon volonté par excellence*, should have contributed — albeit involuntarily — to the downfall of France.[1]

But the fault of France did not lie only in the field of produc-

---

[1] M. Blum made a brilliant defence of his policy at his trial before the Riom Tribunal in 1942, in the course of which he disclosed much of the opposition which hampered the fulfilment of his programme for economic and industrial reorganization.

tion. Such rearmament programme as existed was necessarily closely interrelated with the war plans of the Supreme War Council and of the General Staff, and these bodies were still unable to make up their minds which weapon they wanted and in what quantities. Their hesitation and vacillation were described by General Mittelhauser before the Riom Tribunal : " From 1936 onwards the Supreme War Council discussed the importance of the use of tanks and airplanes, but without arriving at any agreement. In 1938 the Germans already had two armoured divisions completely organized and prepared to take the field, while we had not been able to organize even one division by the beginning of the war." [1] In vain had Colonel de Gaulle pleaded for a mechanized army designed for assault. He was ignored in Paris and the only person to benefit by his advice was General Guderian of the German Army, who at that time (1934) was planning the mechanized columns which were to sweep through France six years later.[2] No military authority in France would listen to this apostle of the Army of the Future, and, as late as the summer of 1939, Marshal Pétain, in a preface to a book [3] which elaborately disproved both the possibility and probability of France being again invaded, decried the tank as a weapon of assault but admitted its potential value as a defensive weapon supported by natural and man-made obstacles. The fact remains that, whether for offensive or defensive uses, France at the outbreak of war possessed but two divisions of tanks to Germany's ten.

(x)

The month of July 1936 witnessed the death of collective security as conceived in the spirit of the League of Nations and

[1] Evidence given before the Riom Tribunal on March 18, 1942, quoted by Pierre Cot in *Le Procès de la République* (New York, 1944), vol. ii, pp. 63-4.

[2] In 1936 the name of Charles de Gaulle was better known in Berlin than in Paris. The publication of his book, *Vers l'armée de métier*, in 1934, though practically ignored in France, had caused a profound impression in German military circles, where, in an atmosphere of greater mental emancipation, experiments were being made with all types of military formations. A comparison of the composition of the " Armoured Division " put forward by de Gaulle in 1934 with that of the *Panzerdivision* which Guderian actually created in 1935, indicates the great influence which the one exercised on the other, a fact to which the German military reviews of the time did not hesitate to bear testimony. It was not until the tribute which Paul Reynaud paid to de Gaulle in *La France militaire* (Paris, 1937) that France became in any way " de Gaulle-conscious ".

[3] *Une Invasion, est-elle encore possible ?*, by General Chauvineau, with a preface by Marshal Pétain. (Paris, 1939.)

the beginning of a three-year period in which aggression was openly practised by certain Great Powers and tacitly condoned by the remainder. For the record of history, therefore, it is important to remember that the policy of appeasement by Britain and France of German aggression against other States — as distinct from condoning treaty infractions on the part of Germany — began not under the Governments of Mr. Chamberlain and M. Daladier, but under those of Mr. Stanley Baldwin and M. Léon Blum.

On July 4 — the hundred and sixtieth anniversary of American Independence — the Assembly of the League of Nations admitted the fiasco of sanctions, and, in the presence of the luckless Haile Selassie, withdrew the measures imposed upon Italy, thereby assuring her conquest of Abyssinia.[1] A fortnight later, July 17, the smouldering fires of discord within the Spanish Republic flamed out into open civil war.

The international aspects of the Spanish Civil War produced the most fantastic diplomatic paradox of modern times. In the first place, it was not officially speaking " a war ", nor was it in any sense purely " civil ". Its unofficial nature rendered inapplicable the neutrality legislation recently enacted in the United States, since this only referred to war between nations, and yet both armies in Spain were augmented by contingents from many nations.

For the Spanish War represented the first clash upon the field of battle between the forces of Democracy and the forces of Fascism, and was recognized as such by hundreds of young men in Britain, France and the United States of America who joined with political refugees from Germany and Italy in forming the International Brigades of the Spanish Republican Army. Opposed to them were the legions of " volunteers " with which Hitler and Mussolini sustained the wavering fortunes of General Franco. The third great dictatorship, that of Joseph Stalin, placed itself squarely behind the established constitutional

[1] Mr. Eden had made a desperate effort to save the system of sanctions in March 1936 by announcing that Britain was prepared to impose an oil embargo on Italy if the other nations would do the same. The United States would give no clear answer and the occupation of the Rhineland disposed of any inclination which M. Flandin may have had to risk hostilities with Italy. By June it was patent that not only the defeat of Abyssinia but of the League of Nations was imminent, and Mr. Eden, in a speech of considerable courage, told the House of Commons on June 12 that, as Britain had taken a leading part in imposing sanctions, she must take the initiative in lifting them ; this he proceeded to do at Geneva in the following month with the approval of M. Blum.

Government and thereby contributed no little to the paradoxical complexities of the whole episode, for the struggle in this respect became not a conflict between Fascism and Democracy but between Fascism and Communism — in other words, an international civil war between totalitarian Powers.[1]

The immediate reaction of Britain and France to the Spanish War was to maintain a strict neutrality and to localize the conflict if humanly possible. In pursuit of this laudable objective they established early in August, on the initiative of M. Blum,[2] the European Non-Intervention Committee, to which — after much urging, procrastination and recrimination — Russia, Germany, Italy, Portugal and twenty-one other countries ultimately adhered. The programme of the Committee called for an arms embargo on both sides, but from the earliest days of its existence it was patent that only two members, Britain and France, were faithfully observing this policy.

Men, arms and equipment continued to arrive in Spain from Germany, Italy and Russia. The Axis Powers openly declared for Franco in October and officially recognized his government on November 18 ; while, on October 15, Stalin telegraphed to the Spanish Communists that " the workers of the U.S.S.R. would merely fulfil their duty in rendering the revolutionary masses of Spain every possible assistance ". British and French cargo ships, trading on their lawful occasions into Spanish ports, were attacked and sunk by aircraft and submarines supplied to Franco by Germany and Italy, and their Governments did no more than

---

[1] Cf. Virginio Gayda, on November 20, 1936 : " It must be said very clearly that Italy is not prepared to see on Spanish soil a new centre of the Red Revolution " ; and Joseph Goebbels, on September 9, 1937 : " It is here [in Spain] that the decision must be taken between Bolshevism and authority ".

[2] According to M. Louis Lévy, an intimate of M. Blum, the French Premier endeavoured, in the course of a visit to London in July, to persuade the British Government to intervene on the side of the Republicans on the ground that they were the legitimate and constitutional Government of Spain, and, above all, friendly to Britain and France. He apparently met with but lukewarm support, and, on his return to Paris, encountered fierce opposition within his own Cabinet, led by MM. Chautemps and Yvon Delbos, from the Presidents of the Chamber and the Senate, MM. Herriot and Jeanneney, and from the President of the Republic, M. Lebrun, who is reported to have threatened to resign. M. Blum himself contemplated resignation, but was, according to M. Lévy, persuaded not to do so by a representative of the Spanish Government on the ground that the withdrawal of the Government under a Socialist Prime Minister would be the worst solution from the Spanish Republican point of view. In face of these arguments M. Blum assumed the responsibility of sponsoring the policy of Non-Intervention, with which the British Government immediately concurred (*The Truth about France*, pp. 113-15).

protest. The German warship *Deutschland*, bombed by a Republican plane while on patrol, was " revenged " by a savage bombardment of the open port of Almeria by her sister ship, the *Leipzig*. No war could have been prosecuted with greater military or ideological ferocity.

Yet amid this belligerent atmosphere the Non-Intervention Committee dragged out its unhappy existence for three years. It laboured diligently but in a vacuum of unreality, and its efforts were doomed to failure almost from the beginning, for it was impossible to deny that intervention on a grand scale was indeed an established fact. There were even some successes for the Non-Intervention Policy, such as the Nyon Agreement of September 17, 1937, which put a stop to the wanton piracy then rampant in the Western Mediterranean ; but in the main the Committee itself had an almost unmitigated record of failure. Russia, on the one hand, and the Axis Powers on the other, kept announcing that each would enforce the embargo when the other did, and neither proceeded to do so. Nor were the efforts of Mr. Eden to reach a direct agreement with Italy for the withdrawal of the Black Shirt Volunteers any more successful. Mussolini signed a " gentleman's agreement " on January 2, 1937, but without appreciating the meaning of the term, and in the end it was Mr. Eden and not the Black Shirts who withdrew.

But the tragedy of the Non-Intervention Committee's failure was not only that it added to the general lack of regard and respect for international authority, but that it contributed to the lack of unity in Britain, and, more particularly, in France, where the complexities of the internal situation obscured the national vision in respect of the greater external dangers.

In Britain, in Conservative and Catholic circles, there was a certain amount of support for Franco but no enthusiasm for intervention. The Labour and Liberal Parties, with some reluctance, endorsed the policy of non-intervention at the outset,[1] but, as it became clear that no one, save Britain and France, was adhering to this policy, the Labour Party began to demand that assistance should be sent to the Republican Government, because, as Dr. Hugh Dalton expressed it, " General Franco must not be allowed to win ". In July 1937 the National Council of Labour recommended that the Spanish Government should be allowed to

[1] The Trades Union Congress approved, by an overwhelming majority, the Government's policy of non-intervention on September 10, 1936.

buy arms and ammunition in Britain, and a few months later Mr. Noel-Baker was calling upon the Government to bring pressure upon M. Blum to open the French frontier and to lift the embargo on the sale of arms to Madrid.[1]

Their anxiety to assist the Spanish Government did not, however, prevent the Labour Party from continuing to criticize and oppose the Government's policy of rearmament. This policy, they insisted, should be correlated with the moribund system of collective security under the League of Nations and not with the purposes of national defence, which was identified as a policy of isolation. Nor would the Opposition measure up to the potential ultimate issue of intervention in Spain, which, like that of sanctions, would almost inevitably have been war. When confronted with this issue by Mr. Eden in the House of Commons, the Opposition leaders would not face it, and again and again sought refuge in evasion on the ethical grounds that Fascism must not be allowed to triumph, a contention which no one in England was prepared to deny but which no one was prepared to fight for.

In France the inner conflict was far more bitter. M. Blum was assailed from the Left, where the Communist leader, Maurice Thorez, urged armed intervention on behalf of Madrid, and from the Right, where Henri de Kérillis, later to become a leading opponent of appeasement, advocated the recognition of Franco's Junta at Salamanca as the legitimate Government of Spain.

A frenzied opposition manifested itself throughout the Right of French public opinion, an opposition which extended from platonic sympathy with Franco to the smuggling of firearms and oil across the Spanish frontier, the support of diplomatic manœuvres on behalf of Franco's agents in Paris, and the open menace of civil war in France if the Government in any way took action to benefit the Republican cause.

A section of the Right played directly into the hands of the totalitarian Powers by denouncing the Government, in the press and in Parliament, for the alleged sending of planes and war materials to the Republican forces, thereby furnishing Germany and Italy with an excuse for their own intervention.[2] Others

---

[1] *House of Commons Debates*, October 28, 1937, col. 290.

[2] Of these M. Brosselette wrote in *L'Europe Nouvelle* : " Rarely, indeed, has irresponsibility been pushed to this point. The peak, which seemed to have been attained during the Ethiopian affair, has been surpassed. This time it is not against Ethiopia that a foreign Power is being aided ; it is against France herself that Germany and Italy are being excited " (*L'Europe Nouvelle*, August 8, 1936).

repeated, consciously or unconsciously, the line of propaganda purveyed by Goebbels, and became more and more closely identified with the political ideology of National Socialism. For the first time it became clear that there existed in France elements which relied upon help from without in their opposition to Léon Blum.[1]

From this welter of disunity and divided counsels in Britain and in France Adolf Hitler derived no little satisfaction. He was becoming increasingly certain that the moral and physical infirmity displayed by the Western Powers ensured that they would offer no grave opposition to the fulfilment of his ambitions, or that, if opposition were forthcoming, it would be of such a nature as to be easily dispensed with.

It was the misfortune of Britain and France that by their policy of non-intervention they gained both the contempt of their opponents and the mistrust of their friends. In Eastern and South-Eastern Europe the smaller nations viewed with the utmost concern the success of the Axis Powers in the prosecution of their policies of ruthless and cynical disregard for international agreements, and many sought reinsurance of their independence in Berlin. Czechoslovakia alone remained loyal to the spirit of her French Alliance, and, in tragic confidence, looked for a reciprocal attitude from France. In Western Europe, the Netherlands and the Scandinavian countries declared that they could no longer undertake to be bound by the decisions of the League in matters concerning collective security, while Belgium sought refuge in the old formula of the neutrality which had not prevented her from being the cockpit of the First World War and was to prove powerless to save her from participation in the Second.[2]

---

[1] The hatred of the extreme Right for M. Blum had already been demonstrated on February 13, 1936, when a murderous assault was made upon him by members of the *Camelots du Roi* demonstrating in the streets of Paris on the occasion of the funeral of Jacques Bainville, the celebrated historian of the Right. The bitterness of the press campaign later unleashed may be judged from the fact that M. Roger Salengro, Minister of Interior in the Blum Government, committed suicide on November 17, 1936, as a result of a persistent series of attacks upon his character and his honour published in *Gringoire*. He was alleged to have been a deserter from the Army in the First World War, and, despite the evidence produced by General Gamelin that there was no shadow of truth in the charge, but rather that Salengro had been sentenced by a German Court for refusing " to work against France ", the attacks continued in the press, ultimately driving the Minister to take his life. Eight years later (December 29, 1944) Henri Béraud, the leading contributor to *Gringoire*, was condemned to death in Paris on a charge of actions " calculated to harm France or her allies ".

[2] Alarmed at the collapse of the Disarmament Conference, the Rhineland reoccupation, and the Franco-Soviet Alliance, all of which appeared to betoken the

By the summer of 1937 the old order of the League of Nations had virtually disappeared and Europe looked with vivid apprehension to what New Order should succeed it. Was its form to be dictated from Berlin and Rome, or shaped in London and in Paris?

(xi)

On May 28, 1937, Mr. Stanley Baldwin and Mr. Ramsay MacDonald, who between them had governed England as successive Prime Ministers for the last thirteen years, both retired from the National Government and were succeeded respectively by Mr. Neville Chamberlain as Prime Minister and Lord Halifax as Lord President of the Council. A new team and a new policy had emerged in Britain.

Mr. Baldwin had been bored with foreign affairs and had left their conduct almost entirely to Mr. Eden. Mr. Chamberlain found them a new and fascinating interest, and, although he retained Mr. Eden as Foreign Secretary, he took a far greater part in the evolution of policy than his predecessor.

The new Prime Minister had his own views on what the future policy of Britain should be, and, in formulating them, he was guided by two essential and vital factors, which he developed in a series of speeches both in Parliament and in the country. These factors were, first, " the re-establishment of our defence forces ", and, secondly, " the removal of the causes which are delaying the return of confidence in Europe ".

Mr. Chamberlain on entering office found Britain in a deplorably bad condition in regard to her armed services.[1] The

growing strength of Germany, the Belgian Government denounced the Franco-Belgian Military Alliance of 1920 and confined their commitments to those involved in the Four-Power Agreement of March 19, 1936, which replaced the Locarno Agreement. Later, on October 16, King Leopold III announced that the international position of Belgium was now almost equivalent to that which she occupied in 1914. Finally, on April 26, 1937, Britain and France reaffirmed their guarantee to Belgium, while releasing her from any reciprocal obligation save that of resisting a violation of her neutrality. This was followed on October 13, 1937, by a declaration by the German Government that Germany also would defend Belgium against aggression.

[1] This was particularly true of the air arm, where the programme laid down in previous years had fallen below schedule. An air programme cannot be continually expanded except at very great expense, and every time that Hitler had made a move several hundred planes had been added to the British production programme. The original organization of factories had been planned to produce about a thousand aircraft by 1938, and, in face of the later additions, unless enormous sums were voted for factory expansion, the programme could not be maintained on schedule.

British Government had at last awakened to the paucity of the national defences, and the White Paper which Mr. Chamberlain himself, as Chancellor of the Exchequer, had presented to Parliament on February 16 [1] took cognizance of this situation and made certain provision for its reparation. To bridge the gap between existing and essential armament it was proposed to spend £1,500,000,000 over a period of five years ; a fifth of this sum was to be borrowed in the form of a Defence Loan.[2]

This was a great step forward, but it was inevitable that a lag should occur between the demand for increased armaments and the full realization of the extra productive capacity which that demand had created. The " shadow factories ", for which provision had been made in the Defence Bill of 1936, were still little more than on paper in 1937, and the whole rearmament programme would only come to its full fruition in 1939 and 1940. For the next two years Britain would be in that precarious stage in rearmament which Germany had so cleverly camouflaged by clandestine activity.

Yet throughout these crucial years of 1937 and 1938, when the leaders of the fighting services were giving it as their considered professional opinion that Britain must either increase her armaments with the utmost celerity or seek to appease her potential enemies abroad, there continued a constant conflict between the Service Ministers and the Treasury as to the degree of expenditure necessary for national rearmament. The full realization of the gravity of the situation seemed to be wanting ; there was a refusal to admit the inexorable argument of fact.

Mr. Chamberlain himself was determined first to concentrate all his efforts upon avoiding war, at least until such time as Britain was sufficiently strong to avoid a knock-out blow. With regard to this ambition there were few in Britain who could quarrel with

---

[1] *British White Paper*, Cmd. 5374.

[2] The attitude of the Labour Party to these new proposals was interesting. At its annual conference in October 1936 the Party had modified their attitude towards rearmament, but a strong minority had opposed this decision. When the new Defence Estimates were put forward in 1937 the Party continued to vote against them, and on March 14, 1937, Sir Stafford Cripps, in a speech at Eastleigh, exhorted workers engaged in armaments industries to make use of " the most glorious opportunity that the workers have ever had. . . . Refuse to make munitions, refuse to make armaments." (See Sir Bernard Partridge's cartoon in *Punch*, March 24, 1937.) By a vote of 45 to 39 a Labour Party meeting in July decided not to vote in future against Service Estimates, but merely to abstain. The Party Executive, however, was opposed to this change of tactics, and amongst those voting against it were Mr. Attlee, Mr. Herbert Morrison and Mr. Arthur Greenwood.

COUNSEL AGAINST THE DEFENCE

Sir Stafford Cripps, K.C. (Ex-Law Officer of the Crown, at Eastleigh, March 14). " To-day you have the most glorious opportunity that the workers have ever had . . . Refuse to make munitions, refuse to make armaments.

MARCH 24, 1937

the Prime Minister. For the first time since 1918 the whole country was aroused to the necessity of rearmament, though it remained divided on the use to which these armaments should be put. There were still some stalwart paladins of the League of Nations who believed that Britain should place less dependence upon the sword of her own armaments and more upon the somewhat doubtful buckler of the Geneva brand of collective security. The British Government, they argued, should not allow themselves to be intimidated by the Dictators but should place their trust in the League and pursue a vigorous League policy.

This gallant if impracticable thesis was forcefully sustained by the Labour Party in the House of Commons and by Lord Cecil and Lord Davis in the Upper House, but it had little relation to reality. There had been no more doughty warrior for the League than Mr. Anthony Eden, but he spoke for many when he frankly told the Council that, while the League could be legitimately proud of its achievements, certain weaknesses existed in its structure, caused by the defection of some of its important members, which made it unable to fulfil all the hopes that had been built upon it, and that, regrettable and deplorable though this might be, it was no good shutting one's eyes to unpleasant facts.[1]

The unpleasant facts were these. Britain should perhaps have been more zealous in support of the League in the past, but she had not been ; she should have been more aware of the danger from Germany in 1935 and 1936, but she had not been ; she should have begun rearming in 1934, but she had not done so. In consequence the authority of the League had fallen into desuetude ; Germany had got a head start in rearmament and Britain's defences were in a parlous condition. Collective security, as defined at Geneva, was dead, but it still remained a responsibility for Britain, as Mr. Eden had stated as early as November 1936, to use her armaments " in bringing help to a victim of aggression in any case where, in our judgement, it would be proper under the provisions of the Covenant to do so . . . for nations cannot be expected to incur automatic military obligations save for areas where their vital interests are concerned ".[2]

In other words, Britain should build up her armaments with all possible speed and avoid armed conflict with Germany on all but her vital interests. A war postponed might mean a war

[1] Speech at the 100th session of the League Council, January 27, 1938.
[2] Speech at Leamington, November 30, 1936.

avoided, but Britain's vital interests must be safeguarded at all costs.

Between the views of Mr. Chamberlain and Mr. Eden there existed no greater difference than the interpretation of what Britain's vital interests were. Both were men of peace, loathing the idea of war, of which Mr. Eden had had first-hand experience ; both sought desperately to find the formula which should preserve Britain and Europe from a contest which would rock not only the foundations of their own way of life but of Western civilization itself. What divided them, however, was the degree of sacrifice which could legitimately be made by Britain in the cause of peace without bringing her to the position where her word and her bond were doubted in the councils of Europe.

Mr. Chamberlain honestly believed that some sort of agreement could be worked out with Germany and with Italy for the peaceful solution of Europe's problems. Himself essentially a business man, he could not conceive how any problem could possibly be settled by a recourse to arms, nor could his mentality envisage that any other national leader in Europe, whether democratic or totalitarian, could think otherwise. He was confident, therefore, that if certain compromises, certain business deals, could be arrived at, so that the Dictators in Berlin and Rome would not have to go to war to save their popularity at home, Europe might have peace and the lion lie down with the lamb.

There was a *naïveté* in this approach which, in looking back across the years, is startling. It must, however, be remembered that in 1937 Mr. Chamberlain's attitude to peace and war was very representative of the national reaction of Britain. The British public had been brought to the point of recognizing the necessity for increased armaments by the sheer pressure of events, but in that process they had lost no modicum of their deep-seated horror of war.

Indeed, the very circumstances which had revealed to Britain her own vulnerability had, if anything, increased this horror. Mr. Churchill had warned the country in vain of the approaching danger, but his jeremiads had gone unheeded until the war in Spain, with its pictures of terrified refugees looking fearfully skywards, had aroused the emotion of the fear of death from the air in the hearts and minds of the British public. Lord Trenchard's warning in the House of Lords of thousands of planes dropping in a few hours more bombs than were dropped during the entire period of the First World War ;[1] the gloomy picture drawn by the author of *War over England*[2] of the horrors of London during an air raid ; the widely publicized theories of the Italian General Douhet,[3] describing a *Blitzkrieg* of the air which would paralyse a country at the outbreak of war — struck a chill into the hearts of Londoners, who recalled Mr. Baldwin's disheartening statement that " the bomber will always get through ".

The fear of this new type of warfare, in which there would be no distinction between the civilian and the soldier, impelled the British public to subscribe freely to Defence Loans which would provide them with protection, but it also tended to make them endorse almost any policy which would prevent the necessity of this protection being called into effect.

There is no doubt that this widespread hatred of the thought of war, which he himself so keenly shared, materially affected Mr. Chamberlain in the formulation and execution of his policy, and also contributed to its failure. He made considerable and realistic efforts to build up Britain's armaments, but he was so deeply, so desperately, anxious to avoid war that he could not conceive of its being inevitable. He was so confident, so hopeful, of the success of his policy of appeasement that his very confidence and hope blinded him to the greater realities of the situation. And Britain shared his difficulty. Like a boxer who " cannot work himself into the proper psychological and physical condition for a fight that he seriously believes — and hopes — will never come off ", the British people could not think themselves into the necessary state of mind for real preparedness because they hoped so dearly that they would never be called upon to fight.[4]

Such was the background of Mr. Chamberlain's approach to the German problem and the spirit in which he sent Lord Halifax to Berlin and Berchtesgaden in November 1937.[5] His immediate object was to gain a clearer idea of the problems which, in the view of the German Government, had to be solved if Europe was to arrive at a condition of affairs " in which nations might look at one another with a desire to co-operate instead of regarding each other with suspicion and resentment ". His ultimate aim, as he

[1] *House of Lords Debates*, November 18, 1936, col. 214.

[2] *War over England*, by Air Commodore Lionel Charlton (London, 1936).

[3] *The Command of the Air*, by General Giulio Douhet (London, 1927).

[4] *Why England Slept*, by John Kennedy (New York, 1940), p. 157.

[5] See above, pp. 17-19.

told the House of Commons, was to achieve " a general settlement, to arrive at a position where reasonable grievances may be removed, where suspicions may be laid aside and when confidence may again be restored. That obviously postulates that all those who take part in such an effort must make their contribution towards a common end." [1]

Alas for Mr. Chamberlain's hopes and confidence. He could not know that, ten days before his envoy had arrived in Germany, the secret Nazi conclave of November 5, 1937, had decided upon a programme of territorial expansion which, far from making " a contribution towards a common end ", was to be carried out even at the risk of provoking a world war. [2]

Mr. Chamberlain persisted in his policy of appeasement in defiance of current warnings and in disregard of the opposition of his Foreign Secretary ; by the close of the year, the divergences of opinion which existed between the Prime Minister and Mr. Eden had developed into what was virtually an impasse, which sooner or later must end in the dissolution of association.

Early in January 1938, President Roosevelt had revived an idea, which he had long cherished, of appealing to the Governments of the world, in view of the unmitigated horror which must inevitably attend the outbreak of any modern war, to reach an agreement which would cover the essential principles of international conduct; the most effective methods of achieving a general limitation and reduction of armaments; the means of promoting economic security and welfare among all nations through equality of treatment and opportunity; and measures for assuring the maximum respect for humanitarian considerations in the event of war. If other States were willing, the United States was prepared to take the initiative in proposing that certain Governments should join in drawing up tentative proposals for subsequent submission to all nations as a basis for universal agreement. [3]

It is doubtful whether this grandiose and idealistic scheme would ever have achieved the ultimate purposes which Mr. Roosevelt had in mind — which included the conclusion of peace

[1] *House of Commons Debates*, December 21, 1937, coll. 1804-5.
[2] See above, p. 11.
[3] *The Time for Decision*, by Sumner Welles (New York, 1944), pp. 64-6. The President had in mind, if his proposals were accepted, the creation of a working committee of ten nations, representing all regions of the world, which should work out concrete proposals upon which a definite argument might be based.

between Japan and China ; it might, however, have attained his immediate goal of arousing the interest of public opinion on a world scale to an awareness of the proximity of the danger of war, and might also have had a tonic effect of encouragement on the small countries which had become increasingly aware of the lack of leadership among the Great Powers and the consequent abandonment of all interest in their affairs.

It would also have been of the utmost value that the President of the United States, by such a public *démarche*, should show his concern for European affairs ; in any case it would have provided a further opportunity to buy time for preparation in the event of war, and it would have placed Germany and Italy and Japan firmly " on the spot ", since they would have had either to accept or refuse the President's proposals.

It was precisely this which Mr. Chamberlain did not desire to happen, and, when confidentially sounded on the President's proposals on January 12, 1938, he did not scruple to reject them — on the ground that Germany and Italy would utilize the opportunity to delay settlement of the specific points which must be settled between themselves and Britain and France " if appeasement were to be achieved " — without even consulting Mr. Eden, who was, at the moment, on holiday in the South of France.

Now it had always been the policy of the Foreign Secretary to march in the closest step with the United States, and the President's proposals would have commended themselves very warmly to him, though he, like others, might have entertained doubts as to their ultimate success. When, therefore, he heard of Mr. Roosevelt's initiative and of the Prime Minister's reply, he returned at once to London, and not only sent a private message to the President but so worked upon the Prime Minister that a second and very different answer was sent to Washington before the end of the month ; but by that time the situation in Europe had so deteriorated that Mr. Roosevelt reluctantly decided to postpone his projected appeal.[1]

When, therefore, the Prime Minister proposed in February to enter upon a further process of appeasement with Italy in the form of a " gentleman's agreement " in the Mediterranean — which was to be concluded without any *quid pro quo* elsewhere in Europe and even without the intention that Italy's former undertakings, hitherto unheeded, to withdraw her " volunteers "

---

[1] Welles, pp. 66-8 ; Feiling, p. 336.

from Spain should be carried out — Mr. Eden could contend with the situation no longer. In deference to his own beliefs and his fundamental view of what constituted Britain's "vital interests", he resigned on February 20, and with him went the Under-Secretary of State, Lord Cranborne. Both made it clear in their statements to the House of Commons that they were leaving the Ministry not, as Mr. Chamberlain sought to represent, on a specific point of policy in regard to Italy, but because they could no longer find themselves in sympathy with "the outlook and approach" of the Prime Minister and the majority of their colleagues, nor could they any longer condone a policy which could only allow the impression to gain currency abroad that Britain was prepared to yield to constant pressure.[1]

They were succeeded at the Foreign Office by Lord Halifax and Mr. R. A. Butler, and for the next year the policies of Britain and Germany, though directed towards opposite goals, were to run strangely parallel, the one playing into the hands of the other with hideous effect. The disillusionment of Britain was more rapid than that of her Prime Minister, but both were finally to awaken to the sound of Hitler's mechanized columns rolling into Prague.

[1] *House of Commons Debates*, February 21, 1938, coll. 45-52.

CHAPTER FOUR

HOW RUSSIA SLEPT WITH
ONE EYE OPEN

Of all the States concerned, Russia was more immediately conscious of the danger to herself and to Europe which was presented by the National Socialist Revolution in Germany. The Soviet Union was, therefore, less susceptible to the spell of the Nazi *Schlummerlied* than was any of her neighbours. The advent of Hitler to power meant, in a sense, far more to the Soviet Union than to any other Power in Europe, and the dislocation of her foreign policy was also greater. To Britain and France the rupture of the Locarno policy of Stresemann and Brüning was a disillusionment and a shock, but for the Soviet Union the termination of the Rapallo policy of Brockdorff-Rantzau and Maltzan and Seeckt entailed a complete reorientation of all aspects of foreign policy.

Perhaps it was because of the extreme Russian sensibility to the problem of security, perhaps because of the acute ideological antithesis which existed between National Socialism and Marxism, that the Government of the Soviet Union was more vividly aware of the menace of the Third Reich than were the majority of the Western Powers. But, whatever the cause, Soviet leadership and Soviet diplomacy were quick to recognize both the dangers and the advantages which might accrue from this new manifestation. Russia was concerned for her own safety from the militant Moloch which was gradually emerging in Central Europe, but she was also alive to the fact that the effect of this apparition might redound to her own benefit, since it would inevitably force the Western Powers to woo Russia from her isolation back to active membership in the family of Europe.

The calculation of Moscow proved exactly right. The appearance of the Nazis, after the elections of September 1930, as the second largest party in the Reichstag, was sufficient of a shock to be descried as a danger signal in the European capitals and caused many, who had hitherto held aloof from alignment with Russia, to look upon her with a decidedly more friendly eye.

Poland and the Eastern European States regarded with growing apprehension the increase of Nazi strength in Germany and became more and more inclined to secure their Eastern frontiers by a *rapprochement* with Russia, thereby freeing their hands to deal with the new phenomenon in Central Europe. In this policy they were supported by France, who shared their anxiety, and, as the guarantor of the security of some of them, was not averse to finding a new partner with whom to share the burden of this responsibility.

The result of this new development was a further crop of treaties of neutrality and non-aggression concluded by Russia, in 1931 and 1932, with France, Finland, Poland, Estonia and Latvia,[1] complementing the provisions of the Protocol of Moscow with which M. Litvinov had supplemented the Kellogg-Briand Pact in February 1929.[2] Rumania still stood aloof, hampered to a certain extent by internal dynastic troubles. But the increasingly earnest tone of the representations made by the Polish Minister at Bucharest began to have their effect, and the French Government had at the outset made the final conclusion of a Franco-Soviet Pact conditional upon the signature of similar treaties by both Poland and Rumania. A Soviet-Rumanian Treaty, however, remained the missing link in the chain. Negotiations were conducted intermittently and agreement was reached upon the general lines of a pact, but the question of Bessarabia still constituted an obstacle in the way of final agreement.[3]

[1] These treaties were concluded on the following dates : with France on November 29, 1932 ; with Finland on January 21, 1932 ; with Poland on November 23, 1932 ; with Estonia on May 4, 1932 ; with Latvia on February 5, 1932.

[2] *Disarmament and Security since Locarno*, by J. W. Wheeler-Bennett (London, 1932), pp. 249-55.

[3] Rumania had been allowed to occupy the Russian province of Bessarabia in 1919 and her possession had been recognized by Britain, France, Italy and Japan in the Agreement of October 28, 1920. Russia, however, had never accepted the position and continued to regard Bessarabia as a lost province of which she had been illegally dispossessed.

Rumania now required a specific reference to Bessarabia which would signify Soviet recognition of her sovereignty and of the Dniester as their common frontier, and would include the province in the non-aggression undertaking. The Soviet Government, on the other hand, would not concede this point as it would amount to a tacit acquiescence in the Rumanian " occupation ". M. Litvinov was, however, prepared to include a provision that any attempt to solve by force any existing territorial or other disputes would be a violation of the pact, but to this the Rumanian Government would not agree.

Direct negotiations having failed, M. Herriot obtained from the Soviet Government, on the occasion of the signature of the Franco-Soviet Treaty on November 29, 1932, a reaffirmation of " its pacific intentions towards Rumania ", and of its willing-

But the new situation in Germany outran the steps taken to counteract it, and, with the advent of Hitler and the Nazis to power in January 1933, there was a further manifestation of desire on the part of Europe to reach a fundamental understanding with the Soviet Union which would ensure at least the neutrality of that Power in the event of an infraction of peace.

The Soviet Union had expected a more spirited reaction on the part of Britain and France to the advent of Hitler, and it is not impossible that she would have supported any co-ordinated effort to suppress the National Socialist régime in its natal state. It was with considerable anxiety and suspicion, therefore, that Litvinov learned of the preliminary negotiations for a Four-Power Pact which would not only admit Germany to the European Club but would put her on the election committee. Russia did not belong to this select assembly and was thoroughly distrustful of it, and M. Litvinov proceeded to take his own measures both to checkmate Germany in the East and to " euchre " the attempt of the Four Powers to establish an oligarchy from which Russia was excluded.

In response to the general demand in Eastern Europe for additional security against National Socialism, M. Litvinov returned to the old gospel which he had preached since 1928. He had then endeavoured to bring some sense of reality into the provisions of the Kellogg-Briand Pact by inserting in it a clear definition of aggression and potential penalties for those so branded. Now, with the support of the agile-minded Nicholas Politis of Greece, he persuaded the Security Committee of the Disarmament Conference to adopt a comprehensive resolution on these lines and, in the course of the London Economic Conference (June–July 1933), secured its adoption in the form of a Convention by all Russia's treaty partners in Eastern Europe and the Middle East, with the exception of Lithuania and Finland.[1]

ness to leave the possibility of signature open to Rumania for a period of four months. At the same time the Soviet Government declared their fidelity to a " policy of non-recourse to violence for the solution of litigious questions, as also their obligations under the Pact of Paris of August 27, 1928 ". The Rumanian Government, however, insisted on their conditions, and the negotiations were allowed to drop.

[1] The States signing the Convention of July 3, 1933, were the U.S.S.R., Afghanistan, Estonia, Latvia, Persia, Poland, Rumania and Turkey. A separate Convention was signed between the U.S.S.R. and Lithuania on July 5, thus bringing one of the defaulters into line, and in the meantime, on July 4, the Little Entente, together with Turkey, had also signed a Convention identical with the other two but containing an additional article extending the right of adherence to other countries. Finland adhered to this instrument on July 23.

The effect of this forceful campaign against aggression constituted a considerable diplomatic success for the Soviet Union. The Kremlin had viewed with alarm the conclusion of the Four-Power Pact and the gradual development of the German-Polish *rapprochement*, and M. Litvinov's offensive had now succeeded in offsetting these to Russia's advantage.

The Four-Power Pact had attempted, unsuccessfully, to create an oligarchy of European Powers to which Germany, but not Russia, would be admitted, and the Soviet answer to this development had been to create for herself a position in Eastern Europe without peer or rival. By exploiting the alarm and despondency engendered among the smaller States by the growing danger of Nazism, and the apparent lack of intention of the Western Powers to check it, M. Litvinov had crystallized this apprehension into a form which, while it could not be described as a threat to Germany, was nevertheless a means of mutual protection. In so doing, he had placed his country among the leading diplomatic Powers of the world, and the world could no longer ignore the fact.

The results were immediate. During the summer there developed a Russo-Polish *rapprochement* of surprising warmth — so great, in fact, that both sides realized that it could not endure — and both Italy and France paid court to Moscow. Mussolini took advantage of M. Litvinov's visit to Rome to sign with him (September 2) a Non-Aggression Pact similar to that already negotiated with France, and, in the course of a second visit by the Soviet Foreign Commissar in December — by which time Germany had left Geneva — the Duce made every effort to disabuse him of the idea that the Four-Power Pact was in any way directed against the Soviet Union, and urged the necessity of Russia's participation in the League of Nations.

The reaction of France was even more positive. For France the danger of a rearmed Germany represented a reason for restoring the *entente* with the Great Power in Eastern Europe, and French policy, urged on by the French General Staff, began to incline more and more to the forging of a tangible link in the chain of Franco-Soviet friendship. A military alliance, similar to that of 1895 with Imperial Russia, was openly advocated and the more clamorously when, in June of 1934, the Disarmament Conference reached an ignominious demise. And so began the period of the Russian " return to Europe ", a courted and fêted prodigal, over whom there was more joy in Geneva than over many of the more zealous devotees of the Covenant.

But it was not all easy going.   There were many obstacles to be overcome before Russia entered the portals of the League as a fully-fledged member.   Not the least of these was the restoration of diplomatic relations between the Soviet Union and the States of the Little Entente.   From February to June 1934 the indefatigable Dr. Beneš laboured without ceasing to bring his allies into line.   He succeeded in the case of Rumania, but failed to persuade Yugoslavia to follow suit : the Belgrade Government, however, agreed to support the candidacy of Russia at Geneva.

There were certain reservations in Moscow as to the advisability of joining the League, and it was first desired that a military alliance with France should be a necessary prerequisite.   To this the French demurred on account of the provisions of the Locarno Agreement under which France had incurred certain reciprocal obligations together with Britain, Italy and Germany.   Accordingly in May 1934, Louis Barthou and Maxim Litvinov agreed upon a tentative alternative for an " Eastern Locarno " Pact which should extend the provisions of the existing treaties concluded in 1925 between Germany, Poland, Czechoslovakia and France to include Russia, the Baltic States and Finland.   The combined efforts of Britain and France failed to induce Germany or Poland [1] to agree to such a proposal, and in face of these difficulties, and of the rapidly deteriorating situation in Europe generally, the Soviet Union agreed to enter the League without further preliminaries.   She was accordingly elected to membership and to a permanent seat on the Council on September 15, 1934.[2]

With considerable enthusiasm, born of a growing sense of danger, the Soviet Union threw itself into the work of building up a system of European security against potential Nazi aggression — a policy which the Nazis themselves at once described as one of " encirclement " of Germany.

The announcement by Germany on March 16, 1935, of the unilateral repudiation of the military clauses of the Treaty of Versailles, the consequent reintroduction of compulsory military service, and the creation of an air force, was the signal for open

[1] Poland did, however, on May 5, 1934, renew for a period of eleven years the Treaty of Non-Aggression signed with the U.S.S.R. on July 25, 1932.

[2] Soviet membership of the League terminated on December 14, 1939, when, as a result of her attack on Finland, the Council, by resolution, decided that " by its own actions, the Soviet Union has expelled itself from the League of Nations ".

panic in the capitals of Europe. Though the Stresa Conference (April 14, 1935) gave the appearance of a united front in the face of this new example of Nazi ruthlessness, nothing could in fact be further from the truth. Italy, already meditating a descent upon Ethiopia, was not disposed to take any part in sanctions against Germany, and scarcely was the ink dry on the Stresa Declaration than Britain was condoning the rearmament of Germany by opening negotiations for an Anglo-German Naval Agreement, which was finally signed on June 18.[1]

The effect on France was to revive once more the flagging interest in Franco-Soviet relations. These had flourished under the trenchant realism of Louis Barthou but had languished when, on Barthou's assassination in October 1934, the reins of power had passed into the soiled hands of Pierre Laval. Now it was as if the ghost of Barthou rose and pointed the way, and Laval was stirred to sign a Franco-Soviet Treaty of Mutual Assistance in Paris on May 2, 1935, and subsequently to make a visit to Moscow (May 13–15).[2] This was what Russia had originally proposed just a year before at Geneva, but, to safeguard the French commitments under Locarno and to assuage the fears of certain strata of the French political world, who feared the effect on Germany — and on France — of an out-and-out Treaty of Alliance with Russia, an important Protocol was appended to the Franco-Soviet Treaty. By this, Germany was invited to join as a contracting party, either at the time of signature or subsequently, thereby transforming the treaty into a tripartite agreement of non-aggression and mutual assistance. The Protocol also made provision for the ultimate conclusion of a multilateral " Eastern Locarno " agreement as previously proposed by Barthou and Litvinov, which would include France's Central and Eastern European protégés and Russia's Western neighbours.

The uncertainty of this illusory palladium did not, however, satisfy the needs of Dr. Beneš, who perceived more clearly than any other European statesman the inherent menace of a Nazi Germany. Anxious to reinsure the frontiers of Czechoslovakia against future aggression, Beneš concluded, on May 16, 1935, his own treaty with Moscow, identical with that signed two weeks previously between France and Russia, which, in effect, was

[1] See above, pp. 221-22 and 247-48.
[2] With a certain Puckish humour the Soviet authorities took the occasion of M. Laval's visit to the Bolshoi Theatre to give the first programme of the revolutionary ballet *Paris en Flammes*.

designed to bring Russia to the assistance of Czechoslovakia, in the event of German aggression, immediately France implemented those obligations incurred under the Franco-Czech Treaty signed in October 1925 at Locarno.

It was the ratification of the Franco-Soviet Treaty by France on February 27, 1936, which Hitler seized upon as his excuse to make his fresh act of defiance in reoccupying the demilitarized zone of the Rhineland and denouncing the Locarno Agreement; and that the Western Powers meekly acquiesced in the double infraction of treaty obligations came as a shock to the Soviet Union.

A process of disillusionment had begun in Russia with the conclusion of the Anglo-German Naval Agreement in the previous June. It began to be believed in Moscow that the protestation of Britain against the potential aggression of Germany could be stilled if such were to be to her advantage, and that a tacit condoning of German depredation in Europe might always be possible if Britain did not consider herself directly threatened and if such depredation could be effected by peaceful means.

This impression in the Kremlin was strengthened after the failure of Britain and France to apply sanctions to Germany in March 1936. It was impossible, thought the Russians, to consider as serious the weighty admonition of the League Council when all that could or would impress Germany was a strong and determined display of force, and this impression was soon to be enhanced by the refusal of Britain and France to do more than protest against the intervention of Germany and Italy in the Spanish Civil War. Soviet diplomacy would have endorsed whole-heartedly the dictum of Jules Cambon : " You can't seduce Germany, you have to rape her ".

The Soviet contempt for the Western diplomacy and for the institutions of Geneva was soon to be coupled with a growing suspicion that in London, in Paris and in Warsaw there existed political elements who would willingly deflect the menace of German aggression from themselves by directing it against Soviet Russia, and the day might well come when Germany and Poland might march eastwards together with the tacit support, or at least the benevolent neutrality, of Britain and France.

The increasing campaign of Hitler against Bolshevism and the formation of the Anti-Comintern Front ; the open defection of Italy from the anti-aggression camp and the equivocation of

Colonel Beck ; the cries of " Rather Hitler than Blum " which began to re-echo in Paris ; and the obscurity which characterized the pronouncements of Mr. Chamberlain in the House of Commons — all combined to convince the Kremlin that, in the final analysis, Russia constituted a common enemy of all, bourgeois capitalist States and dictatorships alike, and that, in their profound hostility and suspicion of the Soviet " way of life ", the Western Powers would connive at a Fascist-Marxist war in the hope that, in the course of such a conflict, both sides would be exhausted to the point of extinction, or at least to that of impotence.

An added source of concern was the discovery of treason within the structure of the Soviet Union itself, and this Stalin eradicated with a ruthlessness which appalled the Western Powers and caused them to wonder what, if anything, there was to choose between the rival brands of authoritarian government. It was also pointed out in London and in Paris that a State which had recently been forced to decimate its General Staff and liquidate a considerable number of its leading citizens on a charge of high treason was scarcely in a position to prove an effective ally in war. There can be no doubt that the Treason Trials in Moscow during 1936–8 materially influenced the decisions of the British and French Governments in regard to their policy toward Russia.

In the meantime, the Soviet Government lost no opportunity of making crystal clear their attitude in regard to Germany. The two States clashed head-on over the issue of the foreign intervention in the Spanish Civil War, and the Kremlin was impartially caustic, both as regards the reprehensibility of German and Italian policy and the supineness of Britain and France in allowing this policy to go unchecked. Indeed, throughout the year 1937, M. Litvinov, a grotesque caricature of an angry angel painted by Rubens, constituted himself, whether at Geneva or the Far Eastern Conference at Brussels, the denouncer-in-chief of Fascist aggression on the one hand and of the timidity of the Western Powers and the League of Nations on the other.

The result of these tactics was to render hostility toward Moscow in London and Paris almost as acute as in Berlin and Rome, and the pressing issue of resistance to German aggression became obscured in the floating vapours of suspicion. Britain and France suspected the U.S.S.R. of wishing to precipitate a general European conflict to the greater glory and advancement of the

Dictatorship of the Proletariat. The Soviet Union, for its part, believed the Western Powers guilty of a desire to embroil Germany and Russia for the advantage and preservation of bourgeois-capitalism. Only Germany and Russia knew that between them was a gulf of ideology which, despite all appearances to the contrary, could never be bridged or filled, a fundamental conflict of thought and reason which could only cease with the utter defeat of one of them. And so began the strange procession of events which, despite the fantastic contradictions of the Pacts of Munich and of Moscow, was to lead to Stalingrad, to Potsdam — and whither ?

CHAPTER FIVE

HOW POLAND WALKED IN HER SLEEP

THE traditional policy of Poland — a policy which, so far, has resulted in four Partitions — is that of a canary who has persistently but unsuccessfully endeavoured to swallow two cats. Geographically placed between two powerful and acquisitive neighbours, with neither of whom she had a defensible frontier, Poland has for centuries been torn between her hatred of Berlin and her hatred of Moscow. As a corollary, she has proved a cardinal factor in the seemingly contradictory series of *rapprochements* and alienations which has distinguished the relations between Prussia and Russia for the past two hundred years ; since, in general, it is true to say that when separated by a buffer State the two great Eastern European Powers have been friendly, whereas—save for the nineteenth century—the reverse has been the case where there has been a contiguity of frontiers.

With the bitter lessons of history to guide her, it might reasonably have been expected that Poland, when resurrected by the Peace Conference of Paris in 1919, might have evolved a modicum of worldly wisdom, but it was very soon evident that this was not the case. Within three years of her reappearance as a sovereign State, after an eclipse of a hundred and twenty-five years, Poland had become involved in armed conflict with three of her immediate neighbours and had gone far to alienate permanently the affections of the fourth.[1]

Scorning alike the experience of the past, the decisions of the Peace Conference, and the authority of the League of Nations, Poland contrived to annex the province and city of Vilna from Lithuania (1920) and a considerable portion of the Western Ukraine and White Russia from the Soviet State (1921). She had also sponsored the " irredentist " movement of the freebooter Korfanty in Upper Silesia (1921), while the dispute with Czechoslovakia over the possession of Teschen provided a lasting source of enmity between the two countries. " *La Pologne c'est le rhumatisme*

---

[1] " *Les Polonais sont devenus les Napoléonais* " was the *mot* of Paris.

de l'Europe ", was the exasperated comment of Aristide Briand on one occasion.

For a State whose very independence was an inevitable magnet to Germany and to Russia, and who had been awarded large tracts of former German territory which a regenerated Reich would inevitably seek to regain, Poland had not pursued a course of outstanding intelligence. She placed her reliance on the traditional friendship of France — had not Marshal Foch ordained that Poland must be *grande et forte, très forte* ? — and in the treaties of alliance and mutual assistance which this policy had brought forth,[1] but in other respects Poland had taken little thought to protect herself against the enmities which her chauvinistic policies had engendered.

But however much the policy of Poland may have been lacking in wisdom between 1919 and 1933, it must be admitted that she was not only the first to sound the tocsin of alarm on the advent of Adolf Hitler to power, but also to propose effective, if drastic, methods for nipping this new menace in the bud. It seemed clear beyond peradventure to the aged Marshal Pilsudski, who had spent much of his life in and out of German and Russian prisons and had an acute appreciation of both countries, that Poland, who now stood in possession of the Corridor and in control of the Free City of Danzig, would be marked for early attention on Germany's programme for treaty revision, and he lost no time in summoning assistance from his French ally.

In March 1933 Pilsudski warned M. Daladier that German rearmament was progressing far more quickly and in much greater degree than was generally supposed. It had already passed beyond the stage of plans and blue-prints and was in actual being. The Marshal, it is said, proposed that direct action should be taken to crush the Hitler régime by means of a " preventive war " by France, Britain and Poland, and even offered to provide the necessary " incident " in Westerplatte. Daladier at first demurred and then refused so radical a solution of the problem. A month later Pilsudski again repeated his offer and supported his contention by an *aide-mémoire*.

This time Daladier did not deign any kind of reply at all. Instead, to Pilsudski in the Bellevue Palace at Warsaw there came rumours and reports of a Four-Power Pact. Once convinced

[1] A Franco-Polish Treaty of Alliance was signed on February 19, 1921, and this was further supplemented by a Treaty of Mutual Guarantee on October 16, 1925.

that, far from taking direct action to destroy the menace of National Socialism, France and Britain were actually negotiating secretly with Germany and Italy for an understanding at the expense of Poland, the Marshal did not hesitate to take his own measures. He flung himself into the vanguard of the race for appeasement and won by a short head, at the same time nullifying the immediate efforts of his competitors.

Ignoring in his turn the French assurance that the contemplated Pact would in no way affect the Franco-Polish Alliance, Pilsudski summoned his Ambassador from Berlin and charged him to sound out the possibilities of a German-Polish Agreement. The result was the famous interview of May 2 between Hitler and M. Wysocki, which bore fruit seven months later in the Non-Aggression Pact of January 26, 1934.

In recognition of the apparent disinclination of France to consider seriously the treaty obligations which she had entered into with Poland for their mutual protection, Pilsudski during the summer of 1933 sought to improve his relations with Russia, with whom he had already negotiated a pact of neutrality and non-aggression in 1932. He accepted the Litvinov Convention for the Definition of Aggression,[1] and initiated an exchange of visits by Polish and Soviet Chiefs of the Air Staffs. He also welcomed a cultural *rapprochement* which involved, in addition to a visit to Warsaw by Radek, the presentation by a high official of the Soviet Commissariat of Education of a file of the prison records referring to the Marshal's period of exile in Siberia from 1890 to 1905, in exchange for the gift to the Lenin Institute in Moscow of all the papers which Lenin had left at Cracow at the time of his hurried departure in 1914 at the outbreak of the First World War.

To crown all, the Soviet and Polish Governments agreed to raise their respective legations in Warsaw and Moscow to the rank of embassies, and in February 1934 the Marshal despatched his Foreign Minister and political protégé, Colonel Joseph Beck, to Moscow to return the visit which Chicherin had paid to Warsaw in 1926.

So far the Marshal had contrived, not unsuccessfully, to re-insure himself with Berlin and with Moscow. But the day was shortly to arrive when he could no longer maintain this difficult feat of equilibrium.

[1] See above, p. 275.

When, in June 1934, the Disarmament Conference disintegrated from sheer inanition, the control of French foreign affairs was in the vigorous hands of M. Louis Barthou, who alone among the statesmen of France appreciated to the full the menace of Hitlerism and the inevitable failure of any attempt to contain it by threats or arguments. Jettisoning simultaneously the pacific policies of Aristide Briand and the pusillanimities of Édouard Daladier, Barthou strove to meet *Realpolitik* with *Realpolitik*, and embarked upon a course which was frankly designed to oppose any potential German aggression in Eastern Europe. In collaboration with M. Litvinov he endeavoured to construct an " Eastern Locarno " Pact which should include both Poland and Germany.[1]

This time, however, it was Pilsudski who baulked at taking action which might antagonize Germany. Eighteen months before he had called for a " preventive war " to destroy German military power before it should attain sufficient size and strength. France had refused. In the meantime German armaments had increased and France and Britain had done nothing to improve their own position in this respect. The position was therefore more serious than in March 1933.

Pilsudski suspected Barthou of wishing to maintain Poland in the position of a junior ally, instead of recognizing her as the " Sixth Great Power in Europe " ; he suspected France of wishing to subordinate Polish interests to her own ; he suspected the part which Dr. Beneš was playing as *entrepreneur* between Paris, Moscow and the capitals of the Little Entente. Above all, he suspected Russia of having designs of her own upon Poland, and believed that an anti-German structure, of which Poland was an advanced block-house, could only result in driving Hitler to return to the Rapallo policy and to tempt Russia out of the new combination at the expense of Poland. He therefore refused to be a party to this new alignment.

Here was an interplay of suspicion and chagrin similar to that which played so tragic a rôle in Anglo-French relations. Daladier's refusal of Pilsudski's offer in 1933 and his failure to inform the Poles of the Four-Power Pact negotiations had resulted in the Hitler-Wysocki interview and the German-Polish Treaty. This, in its turn, had been largely responsible for Barthou's proposal for an Eastern Locarno, and these proposals were sub-

[1] See above, pp. 242, 277.

sequently wrecked by Pilsudski's suspicion of what lay behind them.

And in all these complexities the only party to reap benefit was Adolf Hitler. In the midst of these mutual recriminations and suspicions he flourished " like a green bay tree ".

But, having refused to enter a general alignment in company with France and Russia, Poland found herself cast back on the uncomfortable friendship of Germany. Here the predicament was equally great, and it was at this moment (May 1935) that Marshal Pilsudski died, leaving the fortunes of his country in the less competent hands of Colonel Beck.

The first advances had been made from Berlin before the old Marshal's death, however. In January 1935 both Hitler and Göring had taken occasion to emphasize to the Polish Ambassador, M. Lipski, the community of interest which existed between Germany and Poland in resisting their common danger from Soviet aggression.[1] Subsequently, at the ceremonies which attended Pilsudski's funeral — that memorable occasion at which Marshal Pétain first met Göring — these overtures were renewed in a somewhat more concrete form, and when Beck made an official visit to Berlin in July it was openly suggested to him that Poland's retrocession of Danzig and the Corridor to Germany might be amply compensated for at the expense of Russia, whose Ukrainian territory might round off the present Polish frontier to the south-east.

Beck recoiled from the advances of Hitler and Göring, as had Pilsudski from those of Barthou and Litvinov. Forthwith he evolved that strange policy — impossible of achievement — of which the keynote was " Not a millimetre nearer to Berlin than to Moscow ". No more fatal line could have been adopted, since it was inevitable that such conduct would arouse the suspicion and ultimately the hostility of both Germany and Russia. Poland seemed fated to become the victim of her own geographical position and her own problem of existence.

With all his major Polish-German problems unsettled and having refused point-blank to adhere to the Franco-Soviet Pact of May 1935, to which an additional protocol had been attached in the hope of transforming it from a bilateral into a multilateral agreement, Colonel Beck elected in July to pick a quarrel with Czechoslovakia on the subject of Teschen and the treatment of the

[1] *Polish White Book*, pp. 23-5.

Polish minority. This dispute reached so grave a point that, on November 5, the Czechs proclaimed a state of siege in Teschen and withdrew the *exequaturs* of certain Polish consular officials. The Polish Government retaliated by a similar cancellation in regard to Czech consuls in Cracow and Poznan, and Beck himself sought, by devious means and indirect pressure, to encompass the defeat of Beneš in the Czechoslovak presidential elections. His efforts failed, however, and President Beneš was elected on December 18, 1935, by 342 votes out of 440. But Beck's activities were not forgotten.

Nevertheless, Poland made a further gesture of solidarity with France on the occasion of the Rhineland reoccupation. Early in 1936 the French Ambassador in Berlin, M. François-Poncet, returned from a visit to Paris and informed his Polish colleague, M. Lipski, in the name of his Government, that France would undoubtedly mobilize in the event of a military coup by Germany in the Rhineland. This was in accordance with the information given by General Gamelin to General Sosnkowski in London in December 1935,[1] and, in view of this double assurance, the Polish Government at once offered a *casus foederis* to France on March 9, 1936; a fact which became known in Berlin.

When, however, it was found that France had little or no intention of taking effective action, the Polish Government had to extricate themselves from a somewhat delicate situation. This was done by means of an official statement in the *Gazeta Polska* of March 19, which condemned the " regional principles " of Locarno and declared that, as peace was indivisible and war in Europe could not be localized, the matter of organizing peace must also be indivisible.

As a result of this incident, Poland found herself being wooed, later in the year, by both France and Germany.

General Gamelin visited Warsaw in August 1936 and sought to renew the old ties of comradeship between the French and Polish General Staffs. Gone, however, were the days of 1921 when the Polish Army could be described by M. Poincaré as " the French Army on the Vistula "; to Gamelin's approaches the reply of Colonel Beck and Marshal Smigly-Rydz was that of the Swiss mercenaries — " *Pas de l'argent, pas des Suisses* ". As a result, the Marshal later flew to Paris and signed (September 6)

[1] See above, p. 252 (footnote 1).

the Rambouillet Agreement for a military loan to Poland of 2000 million francs.[1]

Meanwhile Hitler continued his proposals for a common front against Russia, and declared publicly on January 20, 1937, that any nation soliciting Russian help would seal its own death warrant.[2]

Now, however, the tragedy of Poland began to assume new proportions. In November 1937 Hitler took the final decision to achieve *Lebensraum*, if necessary at the risk of a general European war.[3] His ultimate objectives were Poland and Russia, but for the final attainment of his ambitions he had first to annex Austria and subjugate Czechoslovakia. These operations, however, were merely preliminary to the isolation of Poland.

Colonel Beck was hopelessly deceived by Hitler's stratagems. Desperately holding on his difficult course between Berlin and Moscow, he contributed his full share to the situation which so materially assisted the fulfilment of the Führer's schemes. When M. Yvon Delbos, the French Foreign Minister, visited Warsaw in December 1937, Beck told him that the *Anschluss* was inevitable and could not be opposed. This both disheartened the French in the consideration of any plans they might have been contemplating to implement their guarantee to Austria and increased their suspicion of Beck's policy, which was written off as pro-German.

After the *Anschluss* had become an accomplished fact in March 1938, Polish policy veered backward and forward in the tempest of European politics. Steadfastly refusing to yield to the German demands in the matter of Danzig and the Corridor, Beck still rejected the idea of a joint front against Russia.

In the months which followed, however, when it became apparent that Britain and France were bent upon compelling Czechoslovakia to cede the Sudetenland to Germany, Beck could not resist the urge to seize the opportunity of settling his account

---

[1] The circumstances of the Rambouillet Loan Agreement were unusual throughout. The original amount was for 2 milliard francs, but, because the franc was devaluated three weeks after the Agreement had been signed, the sum was proportionately increased. One half of the loan was to be given by France in kind, in supplies of armaments and machinery for armament factories in Poland ; the other half was to be paid in cash. The financial part of the Agreement was carried out, but the deliveries in kind were first delayed by the frequent strikes and dislocation in French industry, and subsequently cancelled because in 1937 and 1938 the French military authorities opposed the transfer of military equipment to Poland on account of France's own shortage and also because of the new orientation of Polish foreign policy.   [2] *Polish White Book*, p. 36.   [3] See above, p. 11.

with Beneš once and for all. Still ignorant of the fact that Poland was marked for the next victim of Nazi aggression, Beck yielded to the bait of Teschen, which Hitler extended as the price of Polish co-operation in the destruction of Czechoslovakia, and refused steadfastly to permit the transit of Soviet troops through Polish territory. When the final climax came at Munich, Poland shared with Hungary the odium of the jackal. It is to be recorded to Beck's discredit that when, after the Munich Agreement had been signed, the British and French Ambassadors in Warsaw sought to mitigate the Polish demands upon the unfortunate Czechs, he refused to receive them.[1] Blinded by his desire to join in the humiliation of President Beneš, Colonel Beck little thought that within a year he too would have passed into exile.

Such is the story of a period (1933–8) which Mr. Churchill stigmatized as " five years of futile good intention and an eager search for the line of least resistance ". It is the back-drop against which the Drama of Munich was played, and, at the same time, it provides the reason why that drama was of tragic rather than heroic proportions.

The course of the events which immediately followed between March and October 1938 has already been chronicled in this book ; there remains to be seen what lessons were learned from this humiliating experience and how they were applied.

[1] The Poles, said a Frenchman at this time, " are like the ghouls who, in former centuries, crawled about the battlefield to kill and rob the dead and wounded ".

PART III

FIVE MONTHS

(NOVEMBER 1938-MARCH 1939)

O ye who lead, take heed !
Blindness we may forgive, but baseness we will smite.
WILLIAM VAUGHN MOODY (1869–1910)
An Ode in Time of Hesitation

CHAPTER ONE

THE "GOLDEN AGE" OF APPEASEMENT

(i)

" I T is indispensable that the Western democracies should draw a lesson from the dramatic events of last week," wrote M. François-Poncet from Berlin, in prophetic warning, on October 4, 1938. " It is necessary that, while continuing to affirm their will to peace and neglecting no means of reaching an understanding with the totalitarian States, they should nevertheless eliminate all causes of internal weakness, that they should fill up as quickly as possible any gaps in their armaments, and that they should give to the outside world tangible proof of industry, cohesion and strength. This is the price we must be prepared to pay if Europe is not to undergo again, after a respite of uncertain duration, crises similar to the last one just settled at the Munich Conference after threatening for several days to degenerate into general pandemonium." [1]

Here was charted the course of sanity for Britain and for France ; the only course which would bring their troubled barques of state, if not to peace, at least to safety. Had Mr. Chamberlain returned to London, not with garlands but in sackcloth, and urged Britain to embark upon a policy of " blood, sweat, toil and tears ", our national record would have been cleaner and we should have been the better prepared, both morally and materially, for the ultimate conflict. Had the British people been made aware that what Mr. Chamberlain had, in effect, brought back from Munich was not peace but a breathing-space before war, the lamentable state of unpreparedness in 1939 and 1940 might have been repaired, and Lord Gort might not have had to write with that magnificent humility and restraint which characterized his Dunkirk despatch : " Improvised arrangements, made at short notice, can only lead to the shortage of essential equipment, the production of inferior articles and the unskilful handling of weapons and vehicles on the battle-field ".[2]

[1] *French Yellow Book*, p. 18.
[2] Para. 6 of Field-Marshal Viscount Gort's Second Despatch, July 28, 1940. (See Supplement, of October 17, to the *London Gazette* of October 10, 1941.)

But the leaders of France cannot plead even the excuse of self-delusion which had so grievously afflicted Mr. Chamberlain. M. Daladier had not been deceived at Munich. He knew that he had put his hand to a second Peace of Frankfurt, that he had bought for France, with the life of a most loyal ally, nothing more than a precarious respite. He had every right to maintain that the Munich Settlement was preferable to a war, but he had no conceivable right to allow the people of France to remain deluded. It was his imperative duty to cry a warning through the length and breadth of France, a warning that her peril was now even greater than before.

Above all, there was but one way only to justify the staggering sacrifices which had been demanded of Czechoslovakia — the strict fulfilment of the guarantee which Great Britain and France had undertaken to the new truncated State, a guarantee which the British Government, as they announced on October 4, felt themselves under a moral obligation to consider as now being in force.[1]

But Mr. Chamberlain and M. Daladier did none of these things.

In Britain there was a conscious effort to applaud the policy of the Prime Minister and to repose faith in his faith and confidence in his wisdom. Though the Labour and Liberal Parties raised their voices in denunciation and anxious warning, they were too weak to carry conviction, and the Conservative Party, together with the majority of British opinion, were almost solidly behind the Prime Minister.

Those Conservative back-benchers who had had the temerity to criticize their leader's policy on his return from Munich learned to their sorrow the truth of Voltaire's dictum : " *Il est dangereux d'avoir raison dans les choses où des hommes accrédités ont tort* ". In their constituencies they were submitted to bitter attacks by their local associations, though in no case was a motion of censure carried against them.[2]

As for the Conservative leaders who had passed into opposition, they had to stand fire from two quarters. On October 9 the Führer, breaking silence for the first time since the Munich

[1] See Statement of Sir Thomas Inskip (*House of Commons Debates*, October 4, 1938, col. 303).
[2] Those who suffered most heavily in this respect were Mr. Paul Emrys-Evans, Mr. J. P. L. Thomas, the late Captain Ronald Cartland, Sir Derrick Gunston, and Lord Cranborne. Mr. Harold Nicolson, although not a Conservative, felt the weight of the Government's displeasure and was strongly criticized by his constituents.

Conference, delivered a speech at Saarbrücken which might normally have been calculated to arouse the resentment and anger of any British Prime Minister. After complimenting in somewhat patronizing tones " the two other statesmen who strove at the last moment to find a way to secure peace ", Hitler warned his Germans that " it only needs that in England, instead of Chamberlain, Mr. Duff Cooper or Mr. Eden or Mr. Churchill should come to power, and then we know quite well that it would be the aim of these men immediately to begin a new World War ".[1]

It was the same technique which Hitler had employed with Mr. Chamberlain in his celebrated letter of September 27, 1938, when he had appealed to the Prime Minister to circumvent the " war-mongers " of Britain,[2] and it had exactly the same effect. Far from seeming to resent a calumniation, by the head of a foreign State, of distinguished fellow citizens who had been his colleagues, Mr. Chamberlain took occasion to indicate his sympathy for Hitler's point of view. On November 1, in the House of Commons, he contended that criticism of Munich was equivalent to a bird fouling its own nest, and reaffirmed his confidence in the Führer's good faith regarding both the Munich Agreement and the Anglo-German Declaration.[3]

Similarly when Dr. Walter Funk, the German Minister of Economics, on his return to Berlin from an extensive tour of South-Eastern Europe made immediately after Munich, announced that he had " great economic construction plans " for the Balkan countries — plans which would make them economic satellites of Germany — Mr. Chamberlain hastened to accept as natural this creation of German commercial hegemony in Central and South-Eastern Europe. For geographic reasons, he assured the House of Commons, Germany must be considered as occupying " a dominating position " in that region. Appeasement could scarcely go further.

This willingness to see Hitler dominant in Central and Eastern Europe was not, however, merely a by-product of the general trend of British diplomacy. It was of far greater significance than that, and represented one of the prime factors in the

[1] Baynes, vol. ii, p. 1358.

[2] See above, p. 160.

[3] *House of Commons Debates*, November 1, 1938, coll. 74, 88. Encouraged by this display of support, Hitler repeated his attacks on the British " war-mongers " at Weimar on November 6, and at Munich on November 9. (See Baynes, vol. ii, pp. 1546-7, 1555-9.)

whole political situation. Behind the general desire for peace and for an " accommodation " with Hitler, there lay, if not in the mind of Mr. Chamberlain himself, at any rate in the minds of some of his advisers, the secret hope that, if German expansion could be directed toward the East, it would in time come into collision with the rival totalitarian imperialism of Soviet Russia. In the conflict which would ensue both the forces of National Socialism and of Communism would be exhausted, and, since it was believed by those who held these opinions that Bolshevik Russia was of greater danger to Britain than Nazi Germany, the prospect of Hitler defeating Stalin, and greatly weakening himself in the process, was not unwelcome.

These views, which were held even more strongly in Paris than in London, were known in Berlin — where they entirely coincided with the Führer's plans for the first stages of his programme for *Lebensraum* — and in Moscow — where they convinced Stalin of the impossibility of attempting to continue co-operation with the Western democracies.

England was more divided over the Munich Agreement than by any other political issue in Europe since the Radical legislation of Mr. Asquith and Mr. Lloyd George in 1909–11 engendered such bitterness in the country. The division was not exclusively on party lines, for, though the greater part of the " anti-Munich " forces were to be found among the Socialists and Liberals, and the Conservatives constituted the main support for the Government, there were sizable minorities in both camps. In the country as a whole, families were divided and friendships sundered. Social life became actually endangered, since no hostess could guarantee that any dinner-party would not break up in passionate recrimination. In West End clubs and East End public-houses ; in railway trains and in suburban parlours ; wherever men and women met together, the subject was debated with heat and acrimony. The sense of humiliation was strong, if wrathfully suppressed, and gradually, as the autumn drew on to winter, there came a change in the defensive line of argument used by the supporters of Mr. Chamberlain. At first, they had said : " He has brought us peace and laid the foundations of a new system in Europe " ; then they had argued : " Well, anyway we couldn't have fought. The Germans are too strong for us. We'd have been wiped out " ; now, as they watched the grim passage of events in Europe, they said confidently : " At any rate he gave us time to get our defences

in order ". To this their opponents replied : " What are you
doing with it ? "

When Parliament reassembled in November, the mood of
many members had changed from that emotional sense of relief
which had prevailed in October. There was a marked tendency
to avoid extolling the Agreement of Munich as a great achievement of statecraft, and also an increasing inclination on the part of
many supporters of the Government to take the view that the less
said about the past the better it would be for all. Yet none
would join in calling upon England to awake from her lethargy
and work for her salvation. It remained for Mr. Churchill, that
Knight of the Dolorous Blast, and his faithful esquire, Mr.
Brendan Bracken, to contend with the enshrouding darkness in
urging Britain to assume the Armour of Light.

Meanwhile Mr. Chamberlain and his intimate advisers, Sir
John Simon, Sir Samuel Hoare, Sir Thomas Inskip, and the Lord
Chancellor, Lord Maugham, pursued the path of appeasement
with unruffled complacency, perverse intransigence, and complete
disregard of every warning of disaster. On November 2, the day
on which the German and Italian Governments, in flagrant
disregard of the stated terms of the Munich Agreement, had
settled, to their own satisfaction, the claims of Hungary upon the
helpless Czechoslovak Government [1] by the Vienna Award, the
Prime Minister announced that " the time was ripe to take a
further step forward in the policy of appeasement " and to bring
into force the Anglo-Italian Agreement concluded in the previous
April, at the price of Mr. Eden's resignation. The House of
Commons supported him by 345 votes to 138.[2]

It was into this atmosphere of " cloud-cuckoo land " that a
bombshell exploded a week later. In Paris on November 7, a
seventeen-year-old Polish Jew, Herschel Grynszpan, apparently
grief-crazed by the sufferings inflicted on his parents in Germany,
shot and fatally wounded Baron vom Rath, a young Third
Secretary of the German Embassy, who died three days later.
His death was the signal for a fifteen-hours' pogrom throughout
the Reich, during which nearly every synagogue in Germany was

[1] Annexed to the Munich Agreement was a Four-Power Declaration that if,
within three months, the problems of the Polish and Hungarian minorities in
Czechoslovakia had not been settled between the respective Governments, the
heads of the Governments of the Four Powers would meet again to discuss the
matter. (See above, p. 176.)

[2] *House of Commons Debates*, November 2, 1938, col. 332.

burned, and Jewish shops systematically sacked and destroyed. Thousands of Jews were dragged from their homes at dead of night, and, having been first forced to witness the demolition of their property, were removed to the horrors of concentration camps.

The synchronization of the attacks and the fact that the outrages were committed by S.A. men and members of the Hitler Jugend in uniform, while the police took no steps to protect the victims or their property, indicated that the outburst of savagery, which occurred during the celebrations of the fifteenth anniversary of the Bürgerbrau *Putsch* of 1923, was planned and organized in advance.[1] There was even a suggestion that Grynszpan was in similar character with van der Lubbe, the Nazi cat's-paw who was arrested and executed in connection with the Reichstag fire in 1933. Two days later (November 12), physical atrocities were succeeded by legal penalties. A fine of a milliard marks (about £80 millions) was imposed on the German Jewish community for the murder of vom Rath ; in addition, the Jews were forced to repair, at their own expense, all the damage they had suffered, which in Berlin alone was estimated at 13 million marks, while, as from January 1, 1939, Jews were pronounced to be excluded from the economic life of the Reich.

A shudder of horror passed through the civilized world. The President of the United States at once recalled the American Ambassador from Berlin. In Britain the reaction was immediate and sincere. The opponents of appeasement pointed to the events in Germany as a justification of their scepticism as to " Peace for our Time ", and the apologists for Munich were in the forefront of those who lifted up their hands and voices in reprobation.

Thus Lord Londonderry, at that time an inveterate friend of Germany, made haste to denounce as " detestable " the acts which Hitler had ordered or allowed to be committed, and Lord Baldwin, who only a month before, during the Munich debate in the House of Lords, had warmly applauded Mr. Chamberlain's policy, was so deeply moved and horrified that he broadcast (December 8) a public appeal for funds to aid those Jews who, as a result of German bestiality, had been " despoiled of their goods,

---

[1] This was subsequently proved to be true on the admission of Julius Streicher in his memorandum on the Jewish question, dated April 14, 1939 (*International Military Tribunal Document*, 406–PS).

and driven from their homes ".[1] The German press retorted by
venting upon him some of the insults which they had recently
lavished on President Beneš. Whereupon Mr. Chamberlain, who
had allowed similar vilification of Messrs. Churchill, Eden and
Duff Cooper to pass unheeded, was at last moved to deprecate
the attacks of Germany upon a British public figure. As a result,
German journalists in London were ordered by their Embassy to
boycott the dinner of the Foreign Press Association on December
13, at which the Prime Minister was the guest of honour and
they, in part, the hosts.

It was at this time that Mr. Chamberlain found himself confronted with a situation within his own Government similar to
that immediately after his return from Munich which culminated
in the resignation of Mr. Duff Cooper.[2] Three Junior Ministers,
after considerable searchings of heart, conveyed to the Prime
Minister the disquiet which they felt with regard to the composition of the Cabinet. They named certain Ministers whom they
considered as incompetent in their present offices and intimated
that unless changes were made they themselves would be forced
to resign.[3] The Prime Minister was clearly impressed by their
arguments, for shortly afterwards certain important governmental
changes were made, and of the three Ministers who had complained, two remained in office.[4]

But in the main Mr. Chamberlain remained undeterred and
unwavering. " Europe is settling down to a more peaceful state ",
he assured an audience at Guildhall on November 9 — one day
before the Jewish pogroms — and at the dinner to the Foreign
Press he denounced criticisms of Munich as " no service to
democracy or to the chances of further international co-operation ". He persisted in the belief that " the wish of our two
peoples remains still as it was recorded in the Munich Declaration — namely, that never again should we go to war with one
another, but that we should deal with any difference between us
by the method of consultation ". The Declaration rather than
the Munich Agreement itself had now become his touchstone.

---

[1] The response was immediate and generous. In a few weeks over £300,000
had been subscribed, together with a further £600,000 to the Fund for Jewish
Refugees raised by the Council for German Jewry.   [2] See above, pp. 182-83.

[3] *The Second World War*, by Alfred Duff Cooper (London, 1939), p. 98.

[4] On January 28, 1939, Sir Thomas Inskip was appointed Secretary of State for
the Dominions, to be succeeded as Minister for Co-ordination of Defence by Admiral
of the Fleet Lord Chatfield.

" When I signed it I meant what was in that document," he assured the House of Commons in November, " and I am convinced that Herr Hitler meant it too when he signed it."

The belief that he, and he alone, could deal with Hitler still prevailed with the Prime Minister, who had discovered some strange affinity of spirit between himself and the Führer. " It is not that Mr. Chamberlain believes that Adolf Hitler is, like himself, a member of the Birmingham Corporation," said someone at this time, " but he does believe that he is a member of the Manchester Corporation."

But for the moment the Chamberlain legend was still strong over England. The year 1938 closed with the odds of 32–1 being laid at Lloyd's against Britain becoming involved in war before December 1939, and the remarkable spectacle of the Lord High Chancellor of England demanding in a public speech, with reference to the " war-mongers ", that those who would " make war against another country without having counted the cost ought to be impeached " and either shot or hanged. Lord Maugham continued, with unconscious irony, that " there has never been a Prime Minister in the history of England who has in nine months achieved such agreements as those Mr. Chamberlain has made with Eire, Czechoslovakia, Italy and with Hitler at Munich ".[1]

(ii)

Whereas the " Golden Age of Appeasement " found Britain divided and uneasy, it disclosed France to be in a state of political disunity and moral collapse. In Britain the division of opinion was not essentially along party lines ; in France it followed a doctrinal cleavage of the most unbridgeable nature. With the exception of the extreme Left, France was pacifist with varying

Speech by the Lord Chancellor, Viscount Maugham, at the Constitutional Club, December 14, 1938. (For text see *The Times*, December 15, 1938.) Though these views were expressed with a violence rarely equalled by holders of Lord Maugham's august office, they were indicative of the depth of feeling which the Munich Agreement and the Policy of Appeasement had engendered in England. They were equalled in fervour by the other side. When an opponent of appeasement quoted to a friend Walpole's historic words : " They may ring the bells now, they will be wringing their hands soon," he received the grim rejoinder : " And we shall be wringing their necks."

Lord Maugham's views on the Munich Agreement did not change with the passage of time and events. In the course of the Second World War he published a spirited defence of Mr. Chamberlain's policy (*The Truth about the Munich Crisis*, London, 1944).

degrees of sincerity and interest.   In the debate on Munich the only party to vote against the Government was the Communist Party, and to France this represented the deep chasm of her future.   The Communists represented *bellicisme* ; the Communists represented the Soviet Union ; Stalin wanted war in order to undermine the social fabric of France.   Such was the line of argument.[1]

In the main, therefore, the rift in French opinion was not for or against the abandonment of France's position in Europe, not for or against the security of France against Germany, but for or against the security of the " good life " of France against Communism.   From Fascist and reactionary elements of the Right, from the Clericals and the Radicals, from the upper and the petty bourgeoisie, from all those elements who had long cried " Rather Hitler than Blum ", the cry now went up, " Rather Hitler than Stalin ".   Many among the Right actually feared a victory over Germany as much as a defeat of France at her hands, and the fundamental reason of the opposition of the Right to war in 1938 — and, indeed, later — was expressed by M. Thierry Moulnier : " Not only was defeat and devastation of France possible, but a German defeat would mean the crumbling of the authoritative systems which constitute the main rampart to the Communist revolution, and perhaps the immediate bolshevization of Europe. In other words, a French victory would really have been a defeat for France."[2]   The same view was more tersely expressed by Léon Bailly, who, when writing of the Four-Power Concert which had emerged from Munich, declared : " The primary advantage of this assemblage is that Russia is evicted from it.   Too much could not be done to remove her from Europe, to send her back to Asia, to her internal struggles."[3]

The surrender which M. Daladier made at Munich was not only the abandonment of Czechoslovakia, the Maginot Line of France in Central Europe, it was not only the abandonment of

[1] The attitude of the French Communist Party at this time stands out in marked contrast to the defeatist and even treasonable policy which it pursued after the Soviet-German Pact of 1939.   So detrimental to the safety of the State and the general war effort did the activities of the French Communists become that on September 26, 1939, M. Daladier dissolved the Party by decree.   The Communists, however, went far to redeem their record by the gallantry of their efforts in the Resistance Movement in France from 1941 to 1945.   But this second change of front only provided further proof of the complete subservience of the Party to Moscow.

[2] *Combat*, November 1938, quoted in *L'Europe Nouvelle*, July 29, 1939, p. 817.

[3] *Le Jour*, October 3, 1938.

what Georges Duhamel called " the Descartes Line ", the outer rampart of French culture in Europe ; [1] it was a surrender to those elements which were prepared in due course to barter away the soul of France for an illusory mess of pottage, and it allowed France to become the prey of rampant rival ideologies.

The vote which M. Daladier obtained on October 5 was not a strict vote of confidence on the Munich Agreement ; it was a motion on adjournment, which implied agreement. The new majority which was thus obtained ranged from the extreme Right to the Radicals — a majority of 618 to 75 — and M. Daladier immediately asked, and was accorded, plenary powers to deal with the internal and external problems of France.

If M. Daladier had hoped thus to out-manœuvre the Right he was speedily undeceived. Scarcely had the powers been granted to him than their price was made perfectly clear, first by M. Caillaux, then by a group of Right Wing deputies, and finally by Big Business. They demanded the appointment of an Ambassador to Rome — a post which had been vacant for a year, owing to the unwillingness of successive French Governments to accord recognition of Italy's conquest of Abyssinia by accrediting a representative to the Court of the King of Italy as Emperor of Ethiopia ; they demanded the recognition as soon as possible of General Franco's régime in Spain ; they demanded the abolition of the forty-hour week, the dismissal of the Finance Minister, M. Marchandeau, who was believed to be inclined towards planned economy and exchange control, and, finally, the dissolution of the Communist Party. As an earnest of what M. Daladier might expect if he failed to accept their ultimatum, they staged a minor " flight from the franc ", and a certain amount of capital left the country.

The effect was immediate and complete. M. François-Poncet was translated from Berlin to Rome. At the Radical-Socialist Congress at Marseilles (October 27) the Premier bitterly assailed the Communists and a resolution of the Congress pronounced the Popular Front to be officially dead. M. Marchandeau and M. Reynaud changed places in the Cabinet. M. Daladier had surrendered to his new allies as completely as he had surrendered to Hitler.

In the meantime, M. Bonnet had embarked on his own account upon a policy of wholesale appeasement of Germany and the

---

[1] *The White War of 1938*, by Georges Duhamel (London, 1939), p. 43.

abandonment of France's remaining allies in Eastern Europe, the Soviet Union, Poland, and Rumania. The Foreign Minister's first act after the Munich Conference was to purge his *entourage* at the Quai d'Orsay of those elements who opposed or criticized his policies. Thus M. René Massigli, the Political Director of the Foreign Office, suddenly found himself appointed Ambassador to Ankara, while M. Pierre Comert, head of the Press Division, was *limogé* to the position of assistant director of the American Division. He was succeeded in the Press Department by M. Bressy, " an ' appeasement ' enthusiast, with little experience, and a profound distrust, of the Press ".[1]

Nazi propaganda became rampant in Paris, and, cheek by jowl with it, appeared a flood of works defending the policy of Munich. Books appeared, published *à compte d'auteur*, describing Hitler as " the creator of a new European Order " and as the leader of the crusade against Bolshevism. Attacks were printed on Dr. Beneš and the Czechs accusing them of having deliberately imperilled the peace of the world, both directly, by attempting to plunge Europe into war, and indirectly, by having constituted an out-post in Prague for Bolshevik intrigue and propaganda. At the same time those journalists who had opposed the policy of appeasement and who continued to do so — for example, Pertinax, Mme. Tabouis, Émile Buré, Élie Bois, and even Henri de Kérillis — were denounced in the *Munichois* press as being in the pay of Moscow.[2]

It was at this period, too, that a figure who had long been an avowed admirer of Hitler now made an open appearance as a Nazi propagandist operating a private news agency — it was Paul Ferdonnet, later to become notorious during the Second World War as the radio " Traitor of Stuttgart ".[3]

Meanwhile Georges Bonnet, with the approval of the Premier but without the knowledge of his Cabinet colleagues, was pre-paring a diplomatic coup which should crown his own efforts for appeasement. Both M. Daladier and M. Bonnet had been somewhat perturbed by the way in which Mr. Chamberlain, without previous consultation or notification, had concluded at Munich a joint declaration with Germany, to the exclusion of

---

[1] Werth, p. 305.

[2] Lazareff, p. 85.

[3] Ferdonnet was arrested after the liberation of France and shot as a traitor on August 5, 1945.

France. To the French leaders, ever suspicious of British diplomacy since 1935, this behaviour savoured somewhat of the Anglo-German Naval Agreement of that year, which had also been concluded without the French being previously consulted.[1]

M. Bonnet now proceeded to lay plans for an agreement with Germany, analogous to, but more far-reaching than, that which Mr. Chamberlain had signed with Hitler. In addition to the provisions for solution by consultation and non-resort to war, M. Bonnet sought to gain the approval of Germany for a mutual declaration perpetuating the *status quo* of the Franco-German frontier. Such a promise, thought he, would enable him to present a tangible asset of the policy of appeasement to the people of France. If Germany agreed to the perpetual renunciation of Alsace and Lorraine, what further major points of disagreement were there between the two countries ? If both States agreed to resolve by way of consultation any disputes which might from time to time threaten the " good-neighbourliness " of their relations, was there really any need for the continued military alliances in Eastern Europe ? Would not the way now be open for the " Withdrawal behind the Maginot Line " and the " Retreat on the Empire " which Pierre-Étienne Flandin had been advocating for so long ?

Moreover, Bonnet was conscious of the fact that, though M. Daladier had now virtually sold out to the Right, he was neither happy nor secure in his new environment. M. Bonnet's earnest desire had always been to become Premier of France. He saw the chances of this possibility steadily improving and he counted upon his agreement with Germany to improve them still further.

The negotiations were opened on October 19, when M. François-Poncet was granted a farewell audience by the Führer prior to his departure to Rome. Hitler, as might be expected, was not inimical to an agreement which might prolong the weakness and deception of a State whom he regarded as a prime enemy of Germany. He moved, however, with shrewdness and caution, and, wrote the Ambassador to Bonnet, he " did not at once ask that France should renounce her pact with Soviet Russia ".[2] Conversations continued between François-Poncet

---

[1] Bonnet, I, p. 292.

[2] *French Yellow Book*, p. 23. Hitler could not have been unaware of the violent campaign then being waged in the French press and even in the Chamber of Deputies against the Soviet Alliance. He had no reason to urge France to abandon the treaty, since she was already on the way to doing it herself.

and Ribbentrop, and before the Ambassador actually left Berlin he was able to report that the drafts were in preparation (October 24).[1]

The murder of vom Rath on November 7 and the consequent pogroms in Germany provoked only the slightest ripple in the even course of the negotiations. There was little public expression of deprecation in France at the horrors which Herschel Grynszpan's rash action had induced ; there was no demonstration of sympathy for the dispossessed Jews any more than there had been for the Czechoslovak refugees from the Sudetenland. Actual anti-Semitism in France itself was at a height almost unparalleled since the Dreyfus Affair, and newspaper attacks against the two Jewish members of the Cabinet, Georges Mandel and Jean Zay, were of frequent occurrence.[2]

In these circumstances Bonnet had little difficulty in persuading the majority of the press to " play down " the Jewish pogroms in the Reich, but he failed in his attempt to utilize the incident to establish a still more totalitarian hold upon public expression of opinion in France. Bonnet prepared and submitted to the Minister of Justice two draft decrees ; the first would permit the Government, on the initiative of the Foreign Minister alone and without waiting for a protest from abroad, to take action against any paper which had published anything considered offensive against the head of a foreign State. The second draft decree was conceived with an eye to the forthcoming proceedings against Grynszpan, and provided that any trial likely to have " international repercussions " should be heard *in camera*.

M. Marchandeau refused to sign these two decrees, which were calculated to protect the Dictators from attack, but Bonnet retaliated by placing so many obstacles in the way of bringing Grynszpan to trial that, ten months later, at the beginning of the Second World War, his case was still unheard.[3]

Nor did Bonnet allow himself to be deterred, any more than Mr. Chamberlain had been deterred, from the path of appeasement by the fact that, by the Vienna Award of November 2,

---

[1] *French Yellow Book*, p. 29.

[2] Both M. Mandel and M. Zay were murdered by the Vichy Militia in 1944.

[3] Grynszpan was never brought to trial before a French court. He was still in prison when the Germans invaded France and his surrender by the French authorities was among the first demanded by the Gestapo under the notorious Article 19 of the Armistice Agreement of June 22, 1940, by the terms of which German political refugees in France were to be handed over " on demand " (Lazareff, p. 93).

Germany and Italy had broken the Agreement of Munich. In fact he accepted without demur the view which Hitler expressed to M. François-Poncet that, by avoiding a Four-Power discussion on the subject of the Hungarian and Polish claims on Czechoslovakia, he had relieved Britain and France from a considerable embarrassment which might have involved " a definite danger ".[1]

It was at a Cabinet meeting on November 23, the day that Mr. Chamberlain and Lord Halifax arrived in Paris for a conference, that Bonnet fully informed his colleagues of his negotiations with Hitler and Ribbentrop. Germany was now prepared to enter into a formal declaration, he reported, and her Foreign Minister would come personally to Paris in order to sign it. The Cabinet was astounded. Both the President and the Premier felt that public opinion should have been prepared in advance and that the arrival of Ribbentrop in Paris at this moment might create an unfavourable impression, not only in France but in those States with whom France still had treaties of alliance.[2] MM. Zay and Campinchi feared hostile demonstrations and public disorder, and M. de Monzie proposed that, in that case, the ceremony should take place at Strasbourg. Reynaud declared that both the Declaration and the visit should be postponed, " for, though the Agreement may be to our advantage, the trip is surely to theirs ".

Bonnet, however, was adamant. Ribbentrop should come, and he should come to Paris. Germany, he said, had consented to this new accord " merely to be agreeable to France " ; she saw little benefit to be derived from it for herself. After much discussion it was finally agreed that the ceremony should take place in Paris between November 28 and December 3.[3]

But things were not to go quite as easily as that. When the news of the Declaration and of the impending visit of Ribbentrop was made public, the Communist Party, in an ill-advised gesture, persuaded the *Confédération Générale du Travail* to join in calling a general strike for November 30. It may have been that the Party were inspired by a genuine desire to arouse the working classes to the awareness of the dangers of the Munich policy, but

---

[1] *French Yellow Book*, p. 25.

[2] This was more especially true since Ribbentrop had stated, only a week before, at Düsseldorf, that " slowly but surely, the old world is crumbling. No threat can hinder the rise of Germany " (November 17).

[3] de Monzie, pp. 56-7 ; Zay, pp. 36-8 ; Lazareff, pp. 94-5.

they had not the courage to say so in their discussions with the *Confédération Générale du Travail* and the strike appeared to be called on purely professional lines. It was unsupported by the public, who desired nothing more than peace and quiet, and was easily broken by the energetic measures taken by Daladier. But it marked the final rupture of the Popular Front and a major factor in the growing national disunity of France.

And so, on December 6, for the third time since Bismarck had proclaimed the German Empire at Versailles, a German Foreign Minister came to Paris;[1] two days later, in the Salle de l'Horloge at the Quai d'Orsay, the room in which the Covenant of the League of Nations had been adopted and the Kellogg-Briand Pact had been signed, Georges Bonnet and Joachim von Ribbentrop placed their signatures to a Franco-German Declaration of Friendship.[2]

The Declaration was accompanied by two statements which differed considerably in tone. Whereas M. Bonnet expressed the pious hope that the accord to which they had put their hands would do good to the cause of peace in Europe in general, Ribbentrop said nothing at all about world peace but dwelt merely on Franco-German relations.[3] His visit passed off without major incident, owing to the fact that every precaution was taken to avoid any untoward annoyance. Heavily guarded, he was driven about Paris, where the streets were empty of even an interested public. The two Jewish Cabinet Ministers were omitted from those invited to M. Bonnet's reception at the Quai d'Orsay, lest their presence should embarrass the guest of honour ; but Mme. Campinchi, the wife of the Minister of the Navy, refused the invitation on the ground of a previous engagement at the Czechoslovak Legation,

---

[1] The two previous occasions were the journeys of Count Brockdorff-Rantzau to receive (and reject) the terms of peace between the Allied and Associated Powers and Germany in May 1919, and of Dr. Stresemann to sign the Kellogg-Briand Pact in August 1928.   [2] For text see below, Appendix L.

[3] Otto Abetz also came to Paris in the train of Ribbentrop, bringing with him the story of how " terrified " the Führer had been at the time of Munich ; how he had seized on the intervention of the Duce to back-down and avoid war. This line of propaganda was effective both with the *bellicistes* and the *Munichois*. It confirmed the first in their erroneous impression that Hitler was " bluffing " and that Germany was not really strong enough to fight a war, and it further convinced the second that the determined statesmanship of Chamberlain and Daladier had scared Hitler into making an Agreement far less acceptable than he had intended ; in fact, that Munich was a diplomatic victory for Britain and France ! This was one of the more subtle moves of Joseph Goebbels, for, as has been shown, the Führer held unwaveringly to his intentions in the matter of Czechoslovakia despite the timidity of many of those around him.

and M. Jeanneney and M. Herriot, the Presidents of the Senate and the Chamber, also absented themselves.

On the face of it the Franco-German Declaration contained nothing which jeopardized the commitments of France under her treaties of alliance in Eastern Europe. The gist of its contents had been communicated to the Soviet and Polish Ambassadors, and whereas the first had received the news " without comment ", the second had " shown himself very favourably disposed towards the project ".[1] But did M. Bonnet pledge himself to Ribbentrop in a private conversation ? Both have repeatedly given the lie to each other. Which speaks the truth ? [2]

According to his own record, M. Bonnet certainly said nothing in the conversations on December 6 before third persons which altered France's official position *vis-à-vis* her allies, and he even allowed M. Léger to remind Ribbentrop that, since the Vienna Award of November 2 had finally settled the last of the Czecho-slovak minority questions, the time had now come for Germany and Italy to join in the guarantee of Czechoslovakia's frontiers. Yet Ribbentrop's notes of the conversation disclose Bonnet, by his remark that conditions had changed fundamentally since Munich, as accepting the German Minister's view that the French military alliances with Czechoslovakia and Poland were remains of the Versailles Treaty, which Germany — having regained her strength — could no longer endure. Furthermore, according to Ribbentrop, Bonnet did not contradict the state-ment that Czechoslovakia must now be regarded as within the German sphere of influence, but indicated, on the contrary, that France regarded the Four-Power guarantee to Czecho-slovakia as something " to which no special importance was to be attached ".

Apart from this recorded conversation, however, there were two meetings between Ribbentrop and Bonnet — one at the Hôtel Crillon and the other during a visit to the Louvre Museum, where Bonnet had offered to serve as a guide — at which they

---

[1] *French Yellow Book*, pp. 29, 34-5.

[2] M. Bonnet's record of his official conversation with Ribbentrop is contained in a circular despatch to the French Embassies dated December 14, 1938 (*French Yellow Book*, No. 32).

Ribbentrop's record was published in Berlin in 1939 : " *Auszug aus der Aufzeichnung über die Unterredungen zwischen dem Reichsminister des Äussern von Ribbentrop und dem französischen Aussenminister Bonnet am 6.12.1938 in Anwesenheit des Botschafters Grafen Welczeck und des Generalsekretärs am Quai d'Orsay Léger sowie des Gesandten Schmidt* ".

were entirely unattended and of which no record was apparently
kept by either party.[1]

Whatever the truth of these accusations and rebuttals may be,
the fact remains that on his return to Germany Ribbentrop spoke
earnestly to M. Coulondre, the new French Ambassador, on the
necessity of " creating zones of influence in the East and South-
East ".[2] For his part, M. Bonnet, who had already rebuffed King
Carol of Rumania during his visit to Paris in November, now
made a very characteristic appearance before the Foreign Affairs
Committee of the Chamber on December 14. Under question--
ing from Henri de Kérillis on the subject of France's Eastern
alliances, Bonnet first replied that " if Poland, Russia, and
Rumania defend themselves we shall of course come to their aid "
— the implication being that they would not resist and that France
would certainly not encourage them to do so — and then, by
devious means, he persuaded the Committee to adopt a resolution
requesting the abrogation of the Soviet and Polish alliances.[3]

" You celebrated Czechoslovakia's misfortunes too soon, my
friend," said Paul Reynaud to the Polish Ambassador, as they
dined together two nights after the conclusion of the Ribbentrop
visit. " It won't be long before the Germans are after you."
M. Lukasiewicz was incredulous. " They would never dare," he
said. " We're stronger and more intelligent than the Czechs ;
and, anyway, they are leaving the Czechs alone now."

" By March," Reynaud answered, " they will have swallowed
Czechoslovakia ; and in August they'll attack Poland."

" You almost sound as if you wished it," said the Ambassador.

" No," replied Reynaud sadly, " but I refuse to close my eyes
to realities." [4]

[1] As the crisis developed toward war in the spring and summer of 1939, the two
Foreign Ministers became increasingly vehement in their mutual accusations of
mendacity on the subject of what had and what had not been agreed during the
famous Paris visit. The final salvos were fired in an exchange of letters in July 1939
(*French Yellow Book*, pp. 197, 212-15). M. Bonnet, however, in the second volume of
his memoirs, which is due to appear in 1948, will have the opportunity of the last word.

[2] *French Yellow Book*, p. 42.   [3] Werth, pp. 329-30 ; Pertinax, p. 404.

[4] Lazareff, p. 97. Among a collection of Polish State Papers published by the
Germans after the capture of Warsaw in 1939 there appears a despatch from M.
Jules Lukasiewicz, Polish Ambassador in Paris, dated December 17, 1938, in which
he says frankly that Bonnet, when acquainting him with the general purport of the
conversations with Ribbentrop, " voluntarily stressed the fact that he confessed to
the German Minister that he regretted both the alliance with us [Poland] and with
the U.S.S.R.", and that he had given to Ribbentrop " a French promise not to oppose
German economic expansion in the Danube basin ". The Ambassador gives it as
his own opinion that if " France should see herself forced to comply with her obliga-

M. Bonnet's willingness to accord a free hand to the Reich in Central and Eastern Europe, and indeed to accommodate German ambitions in any way, was not due entirely to mere supine cowardice nor to a dislike and distrust of the Russians. Bonnet, in his curious way, was devious rather than pusillanimous; more disingenuous than cowardly. He needed assistance from either Britain or Germany in the rapidly deteriorating condition of Franco-Italian relations, which had culminated in a scene in the Fascist Chamber on November 30 when the assembled deputies had shouted their demands for " Tunis ! Corsica ! Nice ! " into the stonily smiling face of the French Ambassador. Since it had been the announcement of the projected visit of Mr. Chamberlain and Lord Halifax to Rome in January which had touched off this remarkable demonstration of Italian aggression, it is not perhaps surprising that Bonnet should have turned to Germany rather than to Britain.[1] In return for a free hand in Central and Eastern Europe, he hoped that Germany might intervene directly with her Italian ally in the interests of France.

Bonnet had mentioned the unfortunate episode in the Fascist Chamber to Ribbentrop during the latter's visit and had received the rather chilling reply that " Mediterranean matters lay outside the scope of German interests ", and that the only practicable means of improving Franco-Italian relations was through a continued *rapprochement* between France and Germany.[2]

It was now, however, that M. Bonnet's contortions occasioned him considerable embarrassment. Despite his efforts, direct and indirect, to keep his desire to appease Italy discreetly in the background and to play down the question of France's obligations to her Eastern European allies, the ghost of French honour persisted in walking. The Italian demands on France had evoked a demonstration of French solidarity which was unexpected. France's Empire was inviolate, no foot of it must be yielded, no compromise must be envisaged. M. Daladier's triumphal tour through the " demanded territories " of Tunis, Corsica, and Nice

tions to us as a result of the alliance, greater efforts would be made to break away from them than to fulfil them " (*Third German White Book* (New York, 1940), Fifth Document, pp. 25-8).

[1] The attitude of His Majesty's Government towards the Franco-Italian dispute was indicated by the Prime Minister on December 12 : " There is no treaty or pact with France which contains any specific requirement that Great Britain should render military assistance to her should Italy embark on war-like operations against France or her possessions " (*House of Commons Debates*, December 12, 1938, coll. 1580-81).

[2] *French Yellow Book*, pp. 39-40.

in January 1939 was as popular an act as that statesman had ever performed, and his enhanced prestige on his return to Paris was an indication to Bonnet that if he seriously entertained ambitions for the Presidency of the Council of Ministers he must trim his sails accordingly.   Daladier had appeared as the champion of the French Empire, the friend of Britain, the protector of the bourgeoisie against Communism, and the guardian of the honour of France.   M. Bonnet, therefore, took his cue accordingly.

The Foreign Affairs debate in the Chamber on January 26 and 27 was the occasion for an expression of grave anxiety and acrid comments from numerous critics of the Goverment's conduct of the foreign policy of France.   It was now that Bonnet surpassed himself.   His speech was in the patriotic tradition of the highest order.   For France a " policy of withdrawal " would be both unthinkable and disastrous.   " Not an inch of French territories will be ceded ", not a jot or tittle of France's interests abandoned — (" Bonnet has been bought by the French Government ", was the grim jest circulating in the Chamber before the end of the Foreign Minister's speech) — France turned especially to " the great Anglo-Saxon communities who have given us their word to be at our side.   There is Great Britain, whose friendship towards us is precious, and there is the United States, whose President has addressed to us words which have touched our hearts."

In regard to Italy, Bonnet assured the Chamber that " between 1936 and 1938 the Italian Government had not at any moment called in question the Agreement of January 1935 ",[1] but he did not confess that even as he spoke he had received news of the official abrogation of this Agreement.

Finally, he declared that never had the relations between France and her Soviet and Polish allies been marked by such " close and constant contact ".   With both countries " France has maintained her traditional friendship.   The engagements entered into by France with Soviet Russia and Poland remain in force."   The Government secured a vote of confidence by 360 votes to 234.

It was not only in regard to the Franco-Italian Agreement that Bonnet had misled his hearers ; the whole speech was a tissue of lies from beginning to end, and, according to the German

---

[1] This agreement was signed as a result of Laval's visit to Rome.   (See above, p. 245.)

Ambassador, Count Welczeck, Bonnet admitted as much to him a few days later, saying that " often in foreign political debates in the Chamber things were said which obviously were meant for internal consumption and were not meant to go beyond the frontiers ".[1]   Even before this conversation M. Coulondre had informed Ribbentrop, apropos of Bonnet's speech, that there was no danger of French policy proving a source of suspicion to Germany in Eastern Europe.[2]

In the case of Italy M. Bonnet had been still more fantastically mendacious.   Having assured the Chamber of Deputies that the honour and interests and territories of France were safe in his hands, Georges Bonnet, in the tradition of Louis XV, without a word to his Cabinet colleagues or his advisers in the Quai d'Orsay, despatched early in February two secret emissaries to Rome and Berlin over the heads of his Ambassadors.   To Mussolini he sent Paul Baudouin, President of the Banque de l'Indo-Chine, an intimate of Laval and subsequently the Foreign Minister of France to negotiate the Armistice of 1940,[3] with offers of a share in the Suez Canal directorate, of special privileges for Italians in Tunis, and of what amounted to the surrender to Italy of Djibuti and the railway to Addis Ababa.   To Ribbentrop went Count Fernand de Brinon in an effort to enlist German pressure upon Italy to accept the proposals.[4]

Ribbentrop had also been informed of the Baudouin proposals by Ciano.   The German Foreign Minister did not desire that a *détente* should occur in Franco-Italian relations.   If France and Italy composed their differences, France would be relieved of an embarrassment and would be the more free to deal with Germany, and Italy would have lost the *raison d'être* for an alliance

[1] *Der deutsche Botschafter in Paris an das Auswärtige Amt*, Berlin, February 13, 1939.

[2] M. Coulondre's account of his own words is that " France had no intention of giving up either her friendships or her interests in any part of the continent. . . . Nothing, however, in her attitude could give rise to suspicion on the part of the Reich " (*French Yellow Book*, p. 59).   Ribbentrop's version of the Ambassador's remarks, however, was to the effect that France " will undertake no policy in Eastern Europe that would disturb Germany " (*Aufzeichnungen über die Unterredung des Reichsministers des Auswärtigen mit dem französchischen Botschafter am* 7.2.1939.   Berlin, 1940.)

[3] M. Baudouin, who had evaded immediate capture after the liberation of France, was arrested by frontier guards at Hendaye on April 1, 1946, in an attempt to escape into Spain, and was handed over to the French authorities.   He was sentenced on March 3, 1947, to five years' imprisonment with hard labour, confiscation of property, and national degradation.

[4] Baudouin was received by Ciano on February 2 ; de Brinon saw Ribbentrop during the same week (February 4 and 5).

with the Reich.   Without hesitation, therefore, Ribbentrop decided to torpedo the Baudouin Mission, and through his own channels he revealed it to the press and the " grapevine ".[1]

Alas for M. Bonnet's discreet machinations, he had been outwitted by Ribbentrop.   Gossip in Paris, which he had so often used to his own advantage, proved a fickle jade and turned against him.   The story went the rounds with zest and embellishment.   An official *démenti* was at once issued and M. Coulondre, on his own authority, hastened to repeat his Minister's denials to Ribbentrop.   With a cold brutality the German Foreign Minister assured the Ambassador that he had the best reasons for knowing that, not for the first time, M. Bonnet was lying.[2]

Thus was France served at a moment when her last chance of rebuilding her national resistance to the inevitable invader was passing swiftly and unseized.   The sands of life of the Third Republic were running out in the glass, and, though France was to survive, it was only to be by bitter expiation.

(iii)

In the course of the Munich debates in the House of Commons and in the Chamber of Deputies in October 1938, the only points upon which the proponents of appeasement were on the defensive, the only points on which they displayed a sense of contrition, were the unfortunate fate of the Czechs and the disquieting lack of national preparedness in Britain and France.   The Four-Power Guarantee of the rump of the Czechoslovak State and the pledge to repair the deficiencies in their armament and defences had been the conscience balm which the British and French

---

[1] *Ciano Diaries* (New York, 1946), pp. 17, 20-21, 23, 47.

[2] See Pertinax, pp. 234-5 ; also, *J'accuse*, by André Simone (London, 1941), p. 216. This incident is not recorded in the *French Yellow Book*, the contents of which were carefully edited and selected by Bonnet and by M. Charles Rochat, whom Bonnet had appointed Political Director in succession to M. Massigli.   So humiliated was M. Coulondre by his interview with Ribbentrop that he came directly to Paris on February 10 to protest to the President and to M. Daladier against the outrageous conduct of the Foreign Minister.   He wished to resign on the spot and was only dissuaded with difficulty from so doing.

Despite this set-back, however, Daladier and Bonnet continued to negotiate with Ciano on the basis of the original Baudouin proposals until the middle of May 1939, but from April 25 onwards the discussions were conducted between Ciano and the French Ambassador, and were no longer entrusted to secret agents (*Ciano Diaries*, pp. 49, 72, 80).

Governments had extended to those in their countries who demanded some relief from their sense of guilt and humiliation.

It is true that both Mr. Chamberlain and M. Daladier had been moderately guarded in their references to the guarantee to the Czechs, but other batsmen in the British team scored heavily on it. Sir Samuel Hoare had assured the House that the guarantee " will be more effective than either the Franco-Czech Treaty or the Soviet-Czech Treaty . . . and may make the new Republic as safe as Switzerland has been for many generations ".[1] Sir Thomas Inskip went still further and solemnly declared that " His Majesty's Government feel under a moral obligation to Czechoslovakia to treat the guarantee as being now in force. In the event, therefore, of an act of unprovoked aggression against Czechoslovakia, His Majesty's Government would certainly feel bound to take all steps in their power to see that the integrity of Czechoslovakia is preserved." [2]

No undertaking could have been more clearly given or understood, and there were many hon. members who went home on the adjournment of Parliament deriving comfort and consolation both from this clear-cut obligation towards the hapless Czechs and from the concomitant statement of Lord Halifax that " if only Great Britain would say clearly and unmistakably for all the world to hear that she would resist any unprovoked aggression on Czechoslovakia, no such aggression would be made ".[3]

But, when Parliament reassembled on November 1, it was evident that much of the Government's fervour for the guarantee had already wilted. All was not well in Central Europe, and the problems arising from the claims and demands of Hungary and Poland upon the prostrate Czechoslovak State were developing in such a manner that for some time it had appeared that there could only be two alternative outcomes : either the Four Powers would agree to enforce the claims of Warsaw and Budapest or they would disagree among themselves, and Britain and France, having already committed themselves in advance to the guarantee, would be called upon to come to the assistance of Czechoslovakia in the event of unprovoked aggression by Poland or Hungary— or Germany.

In fact, however, Britain and France were delivered from their

---

[1] *House of Commons Debates*, October 3, 1938, col. 156.
[2] See above, p. 185. [3] *House of Lords Debates*, October 3, 1938, col. 1303.

dilemma by the simple fact that there was no Four-Power discussion at all.   Ribbentrop and Ciano met at the Belvedere
Palace in Vienna on November 2 and arbitrarily settled the
Hungarian claims without reference to Mr. Chamberlain or
M. Daladier.[1]   France and Britain were firmly and ruthlessly
ignored, and, despite the fact that the Vienna Award constituted
a clear and flagrant breach of the Munich Agreement, no word
of protest was raised from Downing Street or the Quai d'Orsay.
Indeed both the British and French Governments were profoundly
grateful to Hitler for having thus, in his own words to the French
Ambassador, " avoided a definite danger ".[2]

When Mr. Chamberlain addressed the House of Commons on
November 1, it was evident to all that Britain and France were
being excluded from the determination of the Hungarian-Czecho-
slovak frontier and that it was only a matter of a very short time
before the world would be confronted with a *fait accompli*.   In
these circumstances the Prime Minister continued to do a balancing
feat between not going back on commitments already made and
not defining those commitments with any degree of clarity.[3]   Thus,
though he declared that Sir Thomas Inskip's declaration still
remained the policy of His Majesty's Government, he added
that he could not enlighten the House as to " what the terms of
the guarantee will be and who will be partakers in that guarantee ".

This was tantamount to saying that what Sir Thomas Inskip
had pledged the word of His Majesty's Government to as " a
moral obligation " was a guarantee of which the terms and extent
were as yet unspecified and indeed unknown.   But Mr. Chamberlain had not done.   If he could not give the House any information
as to what the terms of the guarantee included, he could at least
tell them what they did not include, and this, apparently, was
specifically frontiers.   " We never guaranteed the frontiers as they
existed," he informed Mr. Wedgwood Benn.   " What we did was
to guarantee against unprovoked aggression — quite a different
thing. . . . Our guarantee was against unprovoked aggression
and not the crystallization of frontiers."

It was clear, therefore, that the Hungarian claims did not
constitute an act of unprovoked aggression any more than the
Vienna Award constituted a breach of the Munich Agreement,
and that the pledge given by Sir Thomas Inskip in the name

[1] See below, p. 338.   [2] See above, p. 306.
[3] *House of Commons Debates*, November 1, 1938, coll. 80-82.

of His Majesty's Government was not worth the paper on which it was recorded in Hansard.[1]

As for the French participation in the guarantee, we have seen how M. Bonnet had treated this matter in his conversations with Ribbentrop,[2] and how he had accepted, without scruple, Hitler's jeering remark to François-Poncet on the error which Britain and France had made in guaranteeing Czechoslovakia's frontiers before they had even been clearly defined,[3] a statement which at least showed that the Führer's interpretation of the terms of the guarantee differed from that of Mr. Chamberlain.

Neither Britain nor France was anxious to pursue the subject further and it was not until December 22 that the German State Secretary, Baron von Weizsäcker, in response to a prod by the French Ambassador, asked with apparent *naïveté* whether the whole matter of a Four-Power Guarantee could not be forgotten. " Since Germany's predominance in that area is a fact, would not the guarantee of the Reich be sufficient ? " In any case, Germany was in no hurry to settle the matter ; and they would talk about it again after the visit to Berlin of the Czechoslovak Foreign Minister in January.[4]

The unfortunate Foreign Minister did, indeed, proceed to Berlin, on January 21, 1939, and had astonishing interviews with Hitler and with Ribbentrop.

It was useless, M. Chvalkovsky was told, to cherish any hopes of assistance from Britain or France in the matter of the guarantee. So long as Mr. Chamberlain was in power, Britain would not risk a war and France was neither minded nor able to resist the policies of Germany and Italy. The Czechoslovak State must realize, therefore, that it was completely at the mercy of the German Reich, which had now secured assurances of " active military support " from Hungary and Poland. Germany, therefore, was the only Power who could, in practice, guarantee the independence of Czechoslovakia, and she was prepared to do so on certain conditions.

[1] Mr. Chamberlain's reservations did not go unnoticed by the German Ambassador in London, who reported to Berlin two days later : " It is noteworthy that Mr. Chamberlain refrained from entering into any details concerning the character of the final guarantee, and that he spoke only of a British ' offer ', without designating this guarantee as a goal of British foreign policy. Furthermore it is interesting, in view of the conditions prevailing at the time, that he referred solely to the case of unprovoked aggression, but did not speak of a guarantee of the frontiers in the sense of a guarantee of the sovereign territory of the State " (*Second German White Book*, No. 256, p. 277).   [2] See above, p. 308.   [3] *French Yellow Book*, p. 25.   [4] *Ibid.* p. 46.

The price demanded from Chvalkovsky for the German guarantee was of a nature so exorbitant that it amounted to an ultimatum. Czechoslovakia must leave the League immediately, and must assimilate her foreign policy to that of Germany by adhering to the Anti-Comintern Pact ; it was not sufficient to state that Czechoslovakia was no longer interested in any treaty, as had been done in the case of the pact with the Soviet Union.[1] Complete neutrality must be guaranteed by Prague. A preferential treaty must be negotiated with Germany, whose consent must be obtained before any new industry could be established, and Czechoslovakia must surrender a part of her gold reserve to Germany. The Army was to be drastically reduced, and all officials of the Republic inimical to the German Reich dismissed. Finally, Germans in Czechoslovakia should be allowed to wear Nazi insignia and to display the Swastika banner, and the Czechoslovak Government must enact anti-Semitic laws on the Nuremberg pattern.[2]

Only after the Czechoslovak State had been thus reduced to mere grovelling impotence would Germany give effective guarantee to her frontiers, and Chvalkovsky was bidden to hold his tongue concerning the terms after his return to Prague. What had passed in Berlin was to be between himself and Ribbentrop, for the Government of the Reich was not yet ready to drop the mask in their relations with London and Paris.[3]

Meanwhile Mr. Chamberlain and Lord Halifax, in their conversations with Mussolini in Rome (January 11–14), had ascertained that the Duce was not unwilling to join in a guarantee of the Czechoslovak State, provided he were satisfied with its complete neutrality, and also that it possessed a constitution favourable to his views and that the frontier had been actually and finally delimited.[4] Italy had, therefore, also repudiated her undertakings at Munich and was now considering participation in the guarantee on terms quite different from those originally agreed upon ; terms which, like those elaborated in greater detail by Germany, involved the complete abandonment by Czechoslovakia of all semblance of independence and sovereignty.

[1] See above, p. 197.
[2] Report of M. Chvalkovsky to the Czechoslovak Cabinet on January 23, 1939 : *Czechoslovak Archives* ; and Minutes of the interview with Hitler : *International Military Tribunal Document*, PS–2795. See also PS–2796 and PS–2906.
[3] *French Yellow Book*, pp. 55-6.
[4] *House of Commons Debates*, January 31, 1939, coll. 39-40.

With what seemed unpardonable tardiness — assuming that they were giving any serious consideration to the situation at all — the British Government took no action until the meeting of the Council of the League, more than a fortnight later, where Lord Halifax informed M. Bonnet that the British Cabinet had decided to make a *démarche* in Berlin " to sound the Government of the Reich on its intentions " respecting the Czechoslovak guarantee, and suggested that the French take parallel action (February 4).[1] A further delay of four days occurred before the joint *démarche* was made,[2] and even so it remained unanswered until March 2, when the reply was wholly in the negative and the strongest exception was taken in no uncertain terms to this unwarranted and undesirable interference by Britain and France in a sphere of influence which was clearly recognized as being that of Germany.[3]

Before this reply had been received, however, both Paris and London had been informed by the French Minister in Prague (February 18) of the conditions demanded of M. Chvalkovsky in Berlin ; [4] yet neither this amazing information nor the crushing snub from Berlin prevented Mr. Chamberlain from saying on March 10 that all signs pointed to a tranquil political future and easing of the economic situation in Europe, or M. Flandin from declaring that " the prophets who worked so hard, and are still working, to alarm public opinion in France now see their sinister predictions given the lie one by one ".

It is beyond doubt that this matter of Britain's participation in the international guarantee to Czechoslovakia, together with the surrender of the Czech gold in the Bank of England,[5] is among the most discreditable episodes in the whole sordid and tragic story of Munich. The Munich Agreement itself may be excused on the ground of expediency, and Mr. Chamberlain had a strong argument in Britain's lack of preparedness and in the fact that she had no specific obligation to Czechoslovakia — though he persistently ignored the mutual obligations which existed between them as fellow Members of the League of Nations. But this was not true after Munich. Britain had assumed a position *vis-à-vis* Czechoslovakia exactly analogous to that of France. She may have been unwise to do it, but she had done so.

---

[1] *French Yellow Book*, p. 35. [2] *Ibid.* pp. 59-60.
[3] *Ibid.* pp. 61-5. [4] *Ibid.* p. 60.
[5] See below, p. 358 (footnote 2).

Her word had been passed, and Mr. Chamberlain in his broadcast to the British people on what seemed to be the eve of war (September 27) had said : " I am sure the value of our promise will not be underrated anywhere ".

This guarantee had been given by Britain and France and accepted by Czechoslovakia as part of the Anglo-French Plan of September 19. The Czechs had agreed to the Plan on the specific condition that the guarantee formed an immediate and integral part of it. Yet the guarantee did not save Czechoslovakia from the infringements and breaches of the Munich Agreement which evolved from the sessions of the International Commission in Berlin.

The guarantee had been a salient feature in the defence of the Munich Agreement in the House of Commons and the Chamber of Deputies. His Majesty's Government had declared that they regarded it as being already in force and also as " a moral obligation ". Yet this did not save the Czechoslovak State from the arbitrary decisions of the Vienna Award, taken without the " by-your-leave or thank-you " of Britain and France and in flagrant defiance of the Munich Agreement.

Now, in March, the British and French Governments accepted, apparently without offence, an insolent statement from the Government of the German Reich that their interference was undesirable in Eastern Europe.

The truth of the matter was that Mr. Chamberlain had never liked the idea of the guarantee in the first place. When the matter was first discussed after his return from Berchtesgaden, he shared the views of Sir John Simon and Sir Samuel Hoare that Britain's commitments should not be extended east of the Rhine. It was M. Daladier at the Anglo-French Conference of September 18 who had forced the guarantee on the British in order to be able to bring back to Paris some sop to Reynaud's Resistance group in the Cabinet. It is doubtful whether at any time the French Premier's interest in the idea of a guarantee went beyond the scope of domestic politics. He expected greater opposition to his policy of appeasement and he wished to be forearmed against it. Now, however, he had become the " Man of the Right ", a " *pas-prisonnier, mais* " (in Rostand's phrase) of the Pacifist-Patriots. The guarantee was no longer important to him politically, and indeed was an obstacle to the good relations which Bonnet had established with Germany. Thus Mr. Chamberlain and M. Daladier were at one in their anxiety to free themselves from an incubus.

And so a guarantee to defend a defenceless and undefendable frontier, which had originally been offered in order to bribe a small State to commit suicide, was now jettisoned in order to lay the ghost of that small State, which, though dismembered, still survived.

With the decline of Mr. Chamberlain's interest in the guarantee may also be seen that faint and gradual, that involuntary and reluctant, awakening from " the great dream of peace ". The Prime Minister was just beginning to realize that he had been indulging in wishful thinking — a state of mind which he was not to abandon fully until the very verge of war had been reached. By the New Year (1939) Mr. Chamberlain was beginning to feel twinges of disappointment at the attitude of Germany, and disappointment developed into the first pangs of disillusionment as the months wore on and virtually no dividends were apparent from the heavy investment made in appeasement.

The Prime Minister was torn within himself. He had genuinely believed in, he had been honestly convinced of, the rightness of his policy and the good chances of his success. He had dwelt to the point of exaggeration on the achievements of the Munich Settlement and in his self-delusion he had resented and rejected all criticism. He had pledged himself absolutely to appeasement, banking all on the willingness of the Dictators to fulfil and co-operate. He dared not fail. His vanity and his obstinacy and his dread of the international consequences of failure made him willingly blind to many of the signs and portents about him, and, when he half-perceived them, he could not bring himself to warn England of her danger.

" The outlook in international affairs is tranquil ", said Mr. Chamberlain on March 10, 1939, with all the information at his disposal.

(iv)

The aspect of the Munich Crisis which had most disturbed the British public was that which touched themselves most closely, namely, the revelations of the deficiencies and defects in Britain's defences. They had been lulled into a sense of false security by

Mr. Chamberlain's assurances in the past — " the almost terrifying power that Britain is building up has a sobering effect on
the opinion of the world " (March 7, 1938) — and they were
appalled at the bland confessions of the Prime Minister, Sir John
Simon, Sir Thomas Inskip, and Sir Samuel Hoare, in the course
of the Munich debate, that " certain gaps and deficiencies had
disclosed themselves in Britain's defences ", a fact which many
had seen for themselves during those anxious September days.[1]
If the Munich debate had disclosed anything it was the unanimous
demand that British rearmament should be pushed forward with
all celerity and force, and to this Mr. Chamberlain had pledged
himself.

But little confidence was aroused by the statement of the
Minister for the Co-ordination of Defence (Sir Thomas Inskip),
on October 26, that " now we are in the middle of the third year
of rearmament, there is almost everything — I think I may say
everything—a stream which might fairly be called a flood of
the armaments and equipment which we need to complete our
defences." [2] This was a little too much, even for the credulous,
to believe. If British armaments were in such a healthy state on
October 26, why had Britain been found in such a parlous condition a month before ? Only a miracle could have wrought so
great a change in four weeks and it was generally believed that
the days of that sort of miracle had passed.

In fulfilling his rearmament pledges Mr. Chamberlain was
faced by two dilemmas. A gigantic drive for national defence
would undoubtedly be interpreted by the Führer as a want of
confidence in the good faith of Germany and the spirit of the
Anglo-German Declaration. On the other hand, a full mobilization of Britain's resources in man-power and labour would
undoubtedly meet with strenuous opposition from the Socialist
Party, who had been consistently antagonistic to any measure
savouring of conscription. The ink was scarcely dry on the
Munich Agreement and the indignation of the Socialist Party was
still hot in their throats, when Mr. Arthur Greenwood let it be
known that they were not in a mood to tolerate any Derby Scheme,

---

[1] Not long after the September crisis a senior Civil Servant in the Air Raids
Precautions Department said at a semi-public lecture : " We have no illusions
about the state of unpreparedness of the country to receive a sudden air attack.
We are not prepared. We have hardly begun to prepare. We do not know how
all the failures that occurred during the crisis can be avoided next time."

[2] Speech at Stubbington. For text, see *The Times*, October 27, 1938.

or any attempt to establish conscription by backstairs methods,[1] and, during the months which followed, although Mr. Attlee and his colleagues stressed their willingness to co-operate in any scheme for voluntary National Service, they remained obstinately opposed to industrial and military conscription.

Moreover, neither Capital nor Labour was ready or willing to accept those whole-hearted sacrifices without which the goal of national effort could not be maintained. It is true that this unwillingness was due in part to conflicting vested interests of the two parties, but in very great measure the Government of the day was responsible for the lack of psychological preparedness in the nation. No attempt had been made to rouse Britain to an awareness of her danger, but rather had there been every effort to save her from alarm and despondency.

When Mr. Chamberlain met Parliament on November 1, he had, therefore, to walk warily. He announced the creation of a new Ministry of Civil Defence, with Sir John Anderson at its head, charged with special jurisdiction over A.R.P. and also with " determining arrangements for national voluntary service ", but he made no mention of national conscription, either for military service or for labour in factories. He emphasized the progress of the rearmament programme as a whole, but, far from endorsing the light-hearted optimism of the Minister for the Co-ordination of Defence regarding the output for the third year, he exhorted the House to remember that it was indeed the third year of a plan only intended to be completed in five years.

Mr. Chamberlain gave no indication that he and his colleagues had any intention of attempting to accelerate the completion of this programme in a shorter period ; indeed, he said, " I doubt whether it would have been possible, if we had endeavoured to do so, to squeeze a five-year programme into three years ".[2]

---

[1] Lord Derby in October 1915 introduced the method of voluntary recruitment which became known as the " Derby Scheme ". It proved, by its failure to produce the necessary man-power for the armed services, to be the forerunner of the Conscription Act of March 1916. Sir John Simon, at that time a fervent opponent of compulsory military service, resigned his position as Home Secretary in the Coalition Government of Mr. Asquith over this decision.

[2] The Prime Minister did appoint a committee of six people outside the House of Commons " to receive representations as to any delays, defects or difficulties in supply or production under the rearmament programme ". The purpose of this committee, however, was to enquire into the deficiencies in the *existing* programme and not to accelerate the pace of the schedule.

Above all, the Prime Minister rejected the proposal of the Liberal Party to set up a Ministry of Supply, because " the disadvantages would outweigh the advantages " and because " we are not now contemplating the equipment of an army on a Continental scale ". He turned the arguments of the Labour Opposition against their Liberal allies by the admission that "such a Ministry would have to have compulsory powers if it is to function effectively " ; he was satisfied, however, that in order to obtain the supply of labour which was required " it was not necessary to introduce compulsion ".[1]

It may be imagined what effect this most guarded statement had in France. When Mr. Chamberlain and Lord Halifax visited Paris on November 23, they had not only to contend with the hostile element in the crowds, who shouted " *Vive Eden !* " and " *A bas Munich !* " but also with a hostile French Cabinet who demanded of them assurances regarding the strengthening of a British Expeditionary Force in case of emergency, in order to mitigate to some degree the loss of the 40 divisions which Czechoslovakia would have been able to put into the field. This demand presented grave difficulties for Mr. Chamberlain. The maximum strength of any potential British Expeditionary Force had hitherto been fixed at from two to three divisions, and the present armament programme made no allowance for any increase in this number. Nor could the Army be increased without the introduction of conscription, and conscription could not be introduced without causing national alarm at home and distrust and suspicion in Germany. The vicious circle was complete.

The British, however, riposted with a request to France to strengthen and increase her Air Force, whose weakness had been alleged as one of the chief reasons for her policy of surrender before Munich. A large Air Force had been the subject of rival press campaigns both by the French Government and by M. Frossard, formerly Public Works Minister in the Daladier Cabinet, who had recently resigned after a difference of opinion with the Premier. M. Frossard was genuinely anxious to improve the national defences of France, but the Government press were more earnestly concerned with using the clamour to justify the surrender of Czechoslovakia. Both parties demanded " 5000 aeroplanes " ;

[1] *House of Commons Debates*, November 1, 1938, col. 86. It is, however, true that the British Government placed substantial orders for planes in the United States which enabled the American aircraft industry to " tool up " for increased production.

by the outbreak of war, France had actually an air fleet of 494 modern fighter craft and no heavy bombers.[1] This was the ultimate answer to the enquiries of Mr. Chamberlain and Lord Halifax in November 1938.

When the British Defence Estimates were submitted to Parliament in February 1939 [2] they did indeed show a notable increase on those for the previous year — an increase of £135 millions. The Chancellor of the Exchequer, Sir John Simon, estimated that the requirements of the three Services for the fiscal year 1939–40 would total £523 millions as compared with £388 millions in 1938–9. With the addition of expenditure on Civil Defence the total vote asked from Parliament was £580 millions, a sum which exceeded that for 1938–9 (including supplementary estimates) by £175 millions. The available revenue and the unexhausted borrowing powers of the Government were not sufficient to meet this expenditure, and the Chancellor sought, and was granted, an increase of the limit of Defence borrowing from £400 millions to £800 millions.

The personnel of all three Services had been increased during 1938, the Chancellor informed the House, and he further reported that, in the case of the Royal Air Force, the number of first-line aircraft would reach 1750, " the number for which the programme due for completion at that date provided ". The Secretary of State for Air (Sir Kingsley Wood) had promised, on November 10, 1938, that the Air Force programme would be increased and accelerated, and Sir John Simon now gave an added assurance that this would continue.

The realization of the Productions Estimates for the Air Force exceeded expectations.[3] Together with the arrangements for Civil Defence,[4] they were destined to have the most encouraging

---

[1] Figures quoted in *Deuxième Bureau Report* dated August 23, 1939, cited in defence evidence by M. Guy la Chambre during the Riom Trial of 1942. (See *Le Procès de Riom*, by J. le Coquet (Paris, 1945), p. 99; also Tissier, p. 63).

[2] *White Paper*, Cmd. 5944.

[3] According to figures released by Sir Stafford Cripps, as Minister of Aircraft Production, in 1944, 2827 planes were produced in 1938 as compared with 7940 in 1939 (*Daily Telegraph*, June 21, 1944).

[4] The achievement of Sir John Anderson in the matter of A.R.P. was outstanding. " Anderson shelters " provided protection for 10 million persons. The system of evacuating school children from London was perfected to a nicety, and arrangements were also made for finding nearly 200,000 beds in existing hospitals and institutions within twenty-four hours of a state of emergency being declared. For the inspiration and organization which these projects demanded, great credit is due to Mr. Walter Elliot, the then Minister of Health.

results of any aspects of the defence and rearmament programme. For, though the financial requirements of the armed services were voted by the House with little opposition, and though the Secretary of State for War stated (March 7) that in the event of war Britain would send a Field Force of 19 divisions, plus two cavalry divisions, to France,[1] and though the Prime Minister, in an excess of enthusiasm, was moved to say (February 22) that " our arms are so great that, without taking into account the Dominions contributions—

> Come the three corners of the world in arms,
> And we shall shock them ",[2]

the fact remains that these were but illusory dreams.

Mr. Hore-Belisha confessed in Paris in June that if war came immediately he would be able to send at once to France " not more than six divisions ",[3] and when war did come three months later he was only able to send four.[4]

As to Mr. Chamberlain's proud boast, the answer came in tragic passages from Lord Gort's despatch, of which the accuracy, sincerity, and honesty are undoubted : " I had on several occasions called the attention of the War Office to the shortage of almost every nature of ammunition. . . . There was a shortage of guns in some of the anti-tank regiments of the Royal Artillery, while armour-piercing shells for field-guns had not, by May 10 (the date of the German attack), been provided. . . . It was clear from the outset that the ascendancy in equipment which the enemy possessed played a great part in the operations. . . . He was able to employ at least five [out of ten] armoured divisions against the British rearward defences. On the other hand, the British armoured forces in the theatre of war amounted to seven divisional cavalry regiments equipped with light tanks, one regiment of armoured cars of an obsolete pattern, and two battalions of infantry tanks, the latter, except for twenty-three Mark II tanks, being armed with one machine gun only."[5]

---

[1] *House of Commons Debates*, March 8, 1939, col. 2173.

[2] Speech at Blackburn (*The Times*, February 23, 1939).

[3] In conversation with André Maurois (*Tragedy in France*, p. 19).

[4] The I and II Corps, which landed in France in September 1939, consisted of two divisions each ; it was not until the end of January 1940 that Lord Gort was able to report that his two corps, each consisting of three divisions, stood at 222,200 men. (See para. 15 of Lord Gort's despatch of April 25, 1940.)

[5] See paras. 10 and 60 of Lord Gort's despatch of July 25, 1940.

(v)

Wherein lay the cause of this display of political myopia in British leadership ? It certainly was not in the reports received from Germany, whence the British and French Embassies continued to pour out a threnody of warning. Sir Nevile Henderson had returned to England after Munich — so he said later —"thoroughly disheartened " and " with the utmost misgivings as to Hitler's good faith and the honesty of his ultimate intentions towards the Czechs ".[1] M. François-Poncet had written, as early as October 4, that " they [the Germans] are scanning the horizon in search of new demands to formulate, new battles to fight out, new prizes to conquer ".[2]

At no moment between October 1938 and March 1939 was there any indication from Hitler that he regarded the Munich Agreement as valid and binding upon anyone except the Czechs, and, though the depths of his intrigues and villainy could not be plumbed at that time, the outward and visible signs of his turpitude gave sufficiently clear warning to all who wished to be warned.

Hitler was going East ; every newspaper correspondent, every business house, every embassy and legation in Europe knew it and reported accordingly. " Czechoslovakia," wrote Coulondre to Bonnet in December, " which was established as a bulwark to stem the German drive, now serves the Reich as a battering-ram to demolish the gates to the East ".[3] Sir Nevile Henderson, moreover, writing later of this period, considered that though " Europe generally and the British public in particular were justifiably anxious and apprehensive " concerning the rumours current in December and January that Germany contemplated an invasion both of Holland and Switzerland and even a surprise bomb attack on London, " it was obvious that Hitler had other fish to fry before embarking on such adventures as these " and that there were, therefore " grounds for optimism ".[4]

It was these " other fish ", therefore, which supplied the source of British and French optimism. Mr. Chamberlain and M. Daladier and M. Bonnet hoped that, by conceding Central and Eastern Europe to Hitler as a field of economic exploitation, they would either choke him to death with cream or so glut his appetite

[1] Henderson, p. 176.   [2] *French Yellow Book*, p. 17.   [3] *Ibid.* p. 33.
[4] Henderson, p. 189.

that he would have no stomach for Western Europe. If this were not the case, and Hitler returned from his Eastern conquests still unsatiated, the rearmament of Britain and France would be completed and they would be in a position to meet him on a footing of equality or even of superiority. This, it would appear, was the cause of the blindness which afflicted the British and French leadership in the critical months which followed Munich, and there can be little doubt that had Hitler been content to obtain his aims and ambitions by " peaceful means ", that is to say by economic penetration and not by military occupation, he could have done so without a word of criticism or opposition from London or Paris. Central and Eastern Europe were his for the taking so long as the *convenances* were preserved, and, so far as France was concerned, every possible means of persuasion had been employed with her Eastern European allies to accept a " peaceful penetration " peacefully.

From all the evidence it was clear, after Funk's triumphal tour of Eastern Europe, that Rumania was the centre of Nazi penetration, yet, when King Carol visited Paris and London in November 1938, he was treated in the capital of his ally with a distinct *froideur* and found in London no glimmering of appreciation of Germany's economic intentions. On the contrary, the Prime Minister, supported by Sir Horace Wilson and with the approbation of some leading spirits of British industry, was wedded to the idea that diplomacy should be directed towards securing a comprehensive economic settlement with the Nazis. By the middle of February 1939 Sir Nevile Henderson was actually preparing the way for a visit to Berlin of the President of the Board of Trade, Mr. Oliver Stanley, and the Secretary of the Department of Overseas Trade, Mr. Robert Hudson,[1] a visit which was only cancelled by the events of mid-March. In every respect British policy, during these fateful five months, was to subordinate diplomatic advantage to economic convenience, to appease the Dictator in matters which vitally and directly concerned the interests of Britain. No better illustration is required than the timing of the decision to recognize the régime of General Franco in Spain (February 28), which occurred simultaneously with a declaration of Anglo-French solidarity and in the midst of the debate on the increase of armaments.

[1] Henderson, p. 191.

Britain and France had for all practical purposes retired behind the Rhine, leaving Central and Eastern Europe — a sphere from which, it was believed, they could withdraw without any great loss — as an area for German expansion. Their hope and expectation were that Germany would find it difficult to absorb territories ceded to her, and thanks to such difficulties, and to the opposition of Russia, the Reich would lose the capacity and the forcefulness to expand further. If, as a by-product of this policy, a war between Germany and Russia were to ensue, a conflict which could not fail to weaken both combatants, this also would prove advantageous to the Western Powers.

To this hope of German satiation Mr. Chamberlain clung, first with an almost child-like expectancy and later with purblind desperation. As the weeks passed and the evidence poured in of the manifest intention of Germany to make a further display of military might, it seemed incumbent upon the Prime Minister to assure and reassure the British public, both as to their own strength in armament and as to the improbability of their ever being called upon to demonstrate this strength in war.

Thus when Hitler, on January 30, 1939, assured the Reichstag that " in the future, we shall not tolerate the Western Powers attempting to interfere in certain matters which concern nobody but ourselves in order to hinder natural and reasonable solutions by their intervention ",[1] Mr. Chamberlain announced : " I very definitely got the impression that it was not the speech of a man who was preparing to throw Europe into another crisis. It seemed to me that there were many passages in the speech which indicated the necessity of peace for Germany as well as for other countries."[2]

An " inspired " campaign of optimism was launched in the press.[3] The " inspiration " was alleged to come from the Foreign Office and there was much talk among the less well-informed, though well-intentioned, critics of the Government of this broad-shouldered whipping-boy of Whitehall being continually " taken by surprise ". But the Foreign Office was not sleeping. From

[1] Baynes, vol. ii, p. 1572.

[2] *House of Commons Debates*, January 31, 1939, col. 81.

[3] Under a three-column headline, "This is why you can sleep soundly in 1939 ", the *Daily Express*, on January 2, 1939, published an article by Mr. George Malcolm Thomson which opened with these words : " There will be no great war in 1939. . . . Britain grows more formidable. Mr. Chamberlain tells us that. She is stronger in Europe. When the Singapore base is ready this year, she will be stronger in Asia." Later in the article the author stated that " Czechoslovakia is over and done with " and " Germany is boss east of the Rhine ".

each of its European outposts there came "ancestral voices prophesying war", and soon Lord Halifax was sharing the view held far earlier by a number of his officials that a new outbreak of the *furor teutonicus* was upon them.   The Foreign Office was not taken by surprise, but it did stand amazed and aghast at the audacity of those who, in the face of hard facts, continued to peddle official soporifics to an unsuspecting public.

The source of this "official inspiration" was indeed Downing Street, but it was not to be found in the Foreign Office ; it welled up from the Prime Minister's Department at No. 10, operating under the direction of Sir Horace Wilson.   Under this influence eighteen distinguished figures in British education, science, art, letters, medicine, and sport issued an appeal to "all men of good-will abroad" and "above all to the leaders and people of the great German Reich . . . to join with us in a supreme effort to lay the spectre of war and enmity between nations ".[1]   It was in obedience to this same source that the Prime Minister made his truly remarkable statement to the Lobby Correspondents on March 10 that "Europe was settling down to a period of tran-quillity, and that the Government was therefore contemplating the possibility of a general limitation of armament ".[2]

But nature is always more effective than art, and Sir Horace Wilson's efforts of inspiration were eclipsed by the free vent of expression of his patrons, of whom the most ineffable was the Home Secretary.   In the Munich debate, Sir Samuel Hoare had stated his belief that the new guarantee to Czechoslovakia would render her "as safe as Switzerland has been for many genera-tions ".   That balloon of fantasy had become rapidly deflated, but now, on March 10, 1939, when all indications pointed to a major crisis in Central Europe, Sir Samuel again ascended into "cloud cuckoo-land ", and, thus suspended, as it were, in a rosy nimbus, declaimed before his constituents of Chelsea an ecstatic vision of a proximate "Golden Age ", in which, "the long period of preparation [of armaments] having come to an end, a Five-

[1] For text of appeal see *The Times*, January 27, 1939.   The signatories included Mr. Montagu Norman, Lord Derby, Lord Willingdon, Lord Dawson of Penn, Mr. H. A. L. Fisher, Lord Eustace Percy, Sir Arthur Eddington, and the Poet Laureate.

[2] This statement of Mr. Chamberlain's called forth a prompt and forceful letter of protest from Lord Halifax, who pointed out the unfortunate effect which the encouragement of hopes of early progress in disarmament would have both in Berlin and in Paris.   The Foreign Secretary also drew attention to the difficulties arising from the failure to synchronize the press relations of No. 10 Downing Street with those of the Foreign Office (Feiling, pp. 396-7).

Year Plan would raise standards of living to heights we had never before been able to attempt ". The artificers of this elysium were to be " Five Men in Europe, the three Dictators and the Prime Ministers of England and France ", who " if they worked with a singleness of purpose and a unity of action to that end, might in an incredibly short time transform the whole history of the world. These five men working together might make themselves the eternal benefactors of the human race." [1]

[1] Speech at Chelsea, March 10, 1939 (*The Times*, March 11, 1939.)

CHAPTER TWO

"CZECHOSLOVAKIA HAS CEASED TO EXIST"

(i)

T H E disappointed man of Munich was Adolf Hitler. He had looked forward with relish to a local war in which the *Wehrmacht* could chastise the Czech Army ; he had not even shrunk from the possibility of a general European conflict, but the plain fact was that Mr. Chamberlain and M. Daladier had made so wholesale a surrender of Czechoslovakia that even Adolf Hitler could not find an excuse to go to war.[1]   Like the Amir of Afghanistan in Kipling's ballad :

> He has opened his mouth to the North and the South,
> They have stuffed his mouth with gold,

and, though he could not complain of the menu, the dish lacked just that relish which the blood of a conquered enemy could contribute.   The Czechs, he decided on reflection, had not really felt the weight of his displeasure.   To be sure, Beneš had been driven from Prague; the great line of Czech fortifications was in German hands ; and the Czechoslovak State was but a truncated torso, impotent both militarily and economically.   But German troops had only occupied the Sudetenland ; they had not penetrated into the fair provinces of Bohemia and Moravia proper ; they had not entered the capital.

" That fellow has spoiled my entry into Prague," Hitler said to Dr. Schacht on his return to Berlin,[2] with reference to Mr. Chamberlain, and forthwith he set about creating a situation within the remnant of Czechoslovakia which would make her continued existence impossible.

Nor was this state of mind occasioned entirely by a sense of frustration.   It will be remembered that, in the general plan of political strategy as originally conceived at the secret conference

---

[1] Cf. Lord Halifax's admission on January 20, 1940.   (See above, p. 194, footnote 2.)

[2] Statement made in evidence by Schacht before the International Military Tribunal at Nuremberg on May 2, 1946.   (See *Proceedings*, Part 13, p. 4).

in Berlin on November 5, 1937,[1] the acquisition of the Sudetenland and the subjugation of Czechoslovakia were not an end in
themselves. They were, together with the annexation of Austria,
but preliminary moves in the greater campaign for *Lebensraum*
in Eastern Europe at the expense of Poland and Russia. For
this purpose, therefore, Czechoslovakia must provide a bridge-
head for assault, not merely politically but physically. The result
of a German military victory over Czechoslovakia would have
meant both the cession of the Sudetenland to Germany on
terms similar to those imposed subsequent to the Munich Agreement by the International Commission in Berlin, and also the
military occupation of the remainder of the country. German
troops would have remained indefinitely in Czechoslovakia, con-
trolling completely the armaments industry of Pilsen and disposing
of the remnant of the Czech army.

It is evident, from the knowledge which we now possess, that
Hitler, from the moment the Pact of Munich was signed, began
to devise the means for undoing this agreement and completing
the work of annihilation to which he had, on his own admission,
set his hand on May 28, 1938.[2] He later confessed as much
at a staff conference on November 23, 1939, when he told his
Generals that he never had had any intention of abiding by the
Munich Agreement, that he had to have the whole of Czechoslovakia, and that this manœuvre was but the setting of the stage
for the attack on Poland, although there had at one time been
a moment of hesitation whether he should attack first in the
East or in the West.[3]

Within a week of the Munich Conference—while Mr. Chamberlain and M. Daladier were receiving their votes of confidence in
London and in Paris ; at a moment when the Prime Minister of
Britain was publicly proclaiming his belief in the integrity of the
Führer's word—Hitler was addressing to the High Command of
the *Wehrmacht* a questionnaire which is a sufficient indication of
his train of thought.[4] What reinforcements, he asked, were neces-

[1] See above, p. 11.
[2] See above, p. 100. Hitler reaffirmed his decision of May 28 in a speech delivered
in Munich on October 5, five days after the Munich Conference.
[3] Evidence produced by the prosecution before the International Military Tribunal
at Nuremberg. (See *Proceedings*, Part 2, p. 73.)
[4] The exact date of Hitler's questionnaire cannot be established, but the text of
Keitel's reply on October 11, 1938, which recapitulated the questions posed by the
Führer together with the answers, is given in *International Military Tribunal Document*,
No. 388–PS, item 48.

sary to break all Czech resistance in Bohemia and Moravia ? How much time would be required for regrouping or moving up such reinforcements ? How much time would it take to regroup or reinforce if the final operations were to be executed after the demobilization of the troops on the completion of " Operation Green " ?

What the reaction of Keitel was to the Führer's questions, which arrived at his headquarters before the final completion of the occupation of the Sudetenland, is unknown,[1] but in drawing up his reply he must doubtless have taken into consideration certain new factors which were every day being brought to his notice in reports from the Generals commanding the troops entering the Five Zones. As the progressive occupation took place it became increasingly apparent to the German commanders that, in strength and numbers, the Czech defences were far greater than had been suspected. Even the most weakly defended sector, the old Austrian border, where fortifications had only been begun in earnest in February 1938,[2] presented many surprises, and the neutral observers[3] who accompanied the German armies were amazed to see the unmistakable astonishment and awe on the faces of the German officers as they encountered defence after defence which did not appear on the carefully prepared maps provided by their Military Intelligence. When it came to the handing-over of the Czech " Maginot Line " the impression on the German Generals was even greater. Here indeed were formidable fortifications on which an assault might well have been held up for a considerable period. How right they had been, they thought to themselves, to urge restraint upon the Führer. These fortifications, now yielded up without a fight, would provide much valuable information for future reference in dealing with the French defences, should that eventuality arise. Bloodless victories had much to recommend them.[4]

[1] The completion of the occupation did not take place until October 12, and permission to demobilize was granted by the Führer on the following day at a staff conference at Essen. (See *International Military Tribunal Document*, No. 388–PS, item 47.)   [2] See above, p. 29.

[3] The British and Italian Military Attachés in Berlin accompanied the German occupying forces as neutral observers. The French Military Attaché begged leave to remain behind out of delicacy to a former ally.

[4] On August 11, 1939, Hitler remarked to Dr. Walther Burckhardt, then League of Nations High Commissioner in the Free City of Danzig : " When after Munich we were in a position to examine Czechoslovak military strength from within, what we saw of it greatly disturbed us : we had run a serious danger. The plan prepared by the Czech Generals was formidable." Keitel, for his part, admitted under cross-

In his reply to the Führer, telegraphed on October 11, Keitel was able to say that, though the operation concerned would have been no mean task before the Munich Agreement, it could now be undertaken with comparative ease.

It is possible that, in the first moments of his frustrated blood-lust, Hitler may have contemplated an immediate extension of military operations against Czechoslovakia. If so, other counsels prevailed ; he abandoned the idea, but not the policy. It was evident that much was to be gained by exploiting the present willingness of Britain and France to acquiesce in German economic expansion in the Balkans, and there were other plans which could be matured before the moment arrived for the final extinction of the Czechs. He therefore summoned Keitel to a conference (October 21) at which the future tasks of the *Wehrmacht* and the conduct of the war resulting from the tasks were discussed. The Führer reserved for himself complete freedom of decision as to when and where the *Wehrmacht* would next be employed, but he authorized the issue of a secret directive to the effect that, for the time being, the armed forces of the Reich " must be prepared at all times " for the " liquidation of the remainder of Czechoslovakia and the occupation of the Memel-land ".[1]

Thus the basic plan for German politico-military strategy as elaborated within two months of the Munich Conference was as follows : toward Britain a policy calculated to keep her alarmed and perplexed, yet not sufficiently so to overcome the natural hostility of Mr. Chamberlain to the idea of war ; toward France, a friendly attitude directed towards creating, if possible, a breach between herself and Britain ; toward Poland — the ultimate victim — a policy of the mailed fist in the velvet glove, attempting to bribe her to cede Danzig with promises of compensation elsewhere ; toward Czechoslovakia, a campaign of disintegration and destruction, which in the swiftest possible time would create a situation in which Germany could again intervene.

How far this plan had been successful in the cases of Britain and France we have already seen. With regard to Poland, her Ambassador in Berlin, M. Lipski, was invited to lunch at Berchtesgaden by Ribbentrop on October 24 for the express purpose of proposing a deal. In an attempt to capitalize on the inherent

examination at Nuremberg that the Munich Agreement had brought the greatest relief to the German High Command, who " did not believe themselves to be strong enough at that moment to break through the fortifications of the Czechoslovak frontier ".   [1] *International Military Tribunal Document*, C-136.

hostility of Poland for Russia, it was suggested that, in compensation for the return to Germany of Danzig and the granting of a corridor across the Polish Corridor by Poland, the Führer would extend the existing Polish-German non-aggression pact for a further twenty-five years and would guarantee the new frontier between the two States. Ribbentrop also dangled before the eyes of the Ambassador the alluring prospect of a wide sphere of co-operation between the two countries, and specified " a joint policy towards Russia on the basis of the Anti-Comintern Pact ".[1]

Caught, as so often before in her history, in the toils of her two powerful neighbours, Poland sought to appease both. She dared not break openly with Germany and yet was unwilling to accept guarantees from Russia. She temporized in her negotiations with Hitler and reaffirmed her friendship with Stalin.[2] The effect in Berlin was significant. On November 24 the *Wehrmacht* received a supplementary directive to that issued by Hitler and Keitel on October 21, adding " a surprise attack on the Free City of Danzig " to that category of eventualities for which the armed forces of the Reich " must be prepared at all times ".[3]

Hitler now directed his favours towards Hungary, whose geographical position made her of strategic importance in any policy regarding either Czechoslovakia or Russia. Hungarian territorial ambitions had been partially satisfied at the expense of Slovakia by the Vienna Award of November 2, and Hitler now dazzled M. de Kanya, the Foreign Minister, with visions of future annexations in Ruthenia. It was through the Ukrainians of Carpatho-Russia that Hitler now opened his political warfare offensive against Russia. On December 8 a so-called National Ukrainian Council met at Uzhorod and demanded the setting-up of a " Greater Ukraine " of 45,000,000 inhabitants.

This move had many facets, all advantageous to Germany. It created a diplomatic " incident " between Czechoslovakia and the U.S.S.R., who lodged a protest against this political interference with its Ukrainian citizens ; and it added generally to conditions of chaos and confusion which it was desired to create within the Czechoslovak State.

In their machinations against Czechoslovakia the Führer and

---

[1] *Polish White Book*, p. 47.
[2] A joint statement of Russo-Polish friendship was issued in Moscow and Warsaw on November 26, 1938 (*Polish White Book*, p. 181).
[3] *International Military Tribunal Document*, C-137.

his lieutenants moved with their accustomed deviousness. As in the case of Austria and the Sudetenland, they did not intend to rely on the *Wehrmacht* alone to accomplish their calculated objective. With the " reunion " of the Sudetenland to Germany, the cry " Home to the Reich " could no longer be used, but there remained within the remnant of the country a source of potential conflict between the main component elements of the Czechoslovak State, and to this end the full measure of their intrigue was directed toward fomenting this friction. As ready tools to their hand they found the venal elements of the Slovak Autonomist Party, who had been in Nazi pay long before Munich,[1] and also the quarter of a million Germans who had been left by the decision of the International Commission within the borders of the Czechoslovak State and who were now organized under the leadership of Henlein's old henchman, Karl Hermann Frank, into an active and efficient Fifth Column.

The object of the operation was to secure the disintegration of the Czechoslovak State in such a way that neither Britain nor France could find cause to oppose its dissolution. Such civil disturbance and instability must be created that no resistance could be offered to the invasion of German troops, who, to the outside world, would appear to be performing " an action of pacification and not a war-like undertaking ". Moreover, there would be the additional advantage that the operation could be carried out by the standing army and air force at their peace strength without giving, to Germany, the dislocation, and, to the world at large, the warning of preliminary mobilization.[2]

At no time does there seem to have entered into German calculations the possibility of Franco-British intervention in fulfilment of their guarantee of Czechoslovakia against unprovoked aggression. Hitler had taken the measure of Britain and France at Munich, and his intuition told him that, faced with a *fait accompli* and without time to prepare public opinion in their respective countries, Mr. Chamberlain and M. Daladier would do nothing. Another bloodless victory would result, but without the tiresome haverings of Munich. The Führer had been as inimical to the idea of Four-Power discussions as was Mr. Chamberlain to the idea of war.

---

[1] *International Military Tribunal Document*, 998–PS.

[2] See Supplementary Directive to the *Wehrmacht* issued on December 17, 1938 (*International Military Tribunal Document*, C–138).

(ii)

Meanwhile in Prague the First Republic was giving place to the Second and Czechoslovakia was being transformed into Czecho-Slovakia.[1] The process was rough and ready, but in two months the country had been transmogrified from a State with a centralized administration into a strange and ramshackle creation of Bohemia and Moravia and two autonomous provinces, Slovakia and Carpatho-Russia, each with its own Cabinet and Parliament, and maintaining but the most tenuous relation with the Central Government in Prague.

On November 30 General Syrový surrendered his office as President *ad interim* to Dr. Emil Hácha — elected by the National Assembly to succeed Dr. Beneš — and his position as Premier to Dr. Rudolph Beran,[2] the leader of the Agrarian Party. The new President, who had hitherto been Chief Justice of the Supreme Court, was a well-meaning but invertebrate figure of sixty-six, whose only distinction, outside his field of the law, had been his translation of Kipling's *Jungle Book* into the Czech language. Dr. Beran was a less attractive character. As an ardent opponent of the Russian affiliations of Czechoslovakia, he had coquetted with Henlein and the *Sudetendeutsche Partei*, and had come as near to treason as was possible without openly burning his fingers.

The new Foreign Minister was Dr. František Chvalkovsky, a professional diplomat, who had been Minister both in Berlin and in Rome and had imbibed both a knowledge of and respect for totalitarian policy.

When the new régime took office, the immediate external problems of the Czechoslovak State were supposed *in thesi* to be settled. The Agreement of November 20 had finally rounded off the new border of the Sudetenland ; Poland had demanded, and

---

[1] Under the First Republic it had been a punishable offence to write the name of Czechoslovakia with a hyphen. The change in spelling was first officially used on November 17, 1938, when, in the text of the Bill for the Autonomy of Slovakia presented to the National Assembly, the hyphen made its appearance in " Czecho-Slovakia ". Later, in the days immediately preceding and following the occupation of Prague, the term " Czechia " was current among the Germans, but this was soon abandoned.

[2] Dr. Beran was sentenced on April 21, 1947, on a charge of collaboration, to 20 years' imprisonment (ten with hard labour), loss of civil rights, and confiscation of property.

had inevitably been accorded (October 10), full satisfaction in regard to her claims to the Teschen District; while Hungary's claims had been dealt with by the Vienna Award.

The immediate Polish demands did not exceed the area round Teschen which had been in dispute between Poland and Czechoslovakia since 1918, and where the inhabitants were predominantly Polish ; *mais l'appétit vient en mangeant,* and no sooner had the original claims been satisfied than Colonel Beck, whose country, had he but known it, was the next destined victim for Nazi vivisection, proceeded to annex a number of districts farther to the westward which were indisputably Czech and to which Poland had never before laid claim. Latterly, in mid November, Poland also made substantial annexations in Teschen and in Slovakia, bringing her total acquisitions from Czechoslovakia up to a figure of 1000 square kilometres of territory, comprising 228,000 inhabitants of whom 133,000 were Czech. Moreover, in this transfer of territory more than 20,000 Germans exchanged Czech " tyranny " for Polish.

Against the depredations of the hated Hungarians the Prague Government had held out longer, and there had actually been armed clashes between Slovakian and Hungarian troops when the negotiations between the two countries failed and the Hungarians endeavoured to make good their claims by force (October 27). Then, however, the Dictators had stepped in, and, in open breach of the Munich Agreement, had authorized their deputies — Ribbentrop and Ciano — to arbitrate the issue at Vienna. The Award of November 2, while it disallowed Hungary's claim to Bratislava and Nitra in Slovakia, was in every other respect weighted in her favour, and resulted in her receiving some 12,000 square kilometres of territory, with a population of 850,000 souls (of which 500,000 were Magyars, 272,000 Slovaks and 38,000 Ruthenes).

For the Beran Government, with these agonies of amputation behind them, the principal tasks were to shore up the green and creaking structure of the new Federal State, and, at the same time, maintain good relations with Germany. Because of the nature of German intentions, the achievement of both these ends was manifestly impossible. The more the Prague Government endeavoured to pacify or discipline the provincial legislatures, the more the Germans sought to stir up trouble, and, as the attitude of the Government became progressively more severe with its contumacious subordinates, so the German wrath grew in fury and degree against Prague.

Meanwhile Nazi propagandists and Nazi research groups maintained close contact with the Slovakian Autonomist Movement, while from Austria the genius of Seyss-Inquart, Bürckel, and Baldur von Schirach combined in directing a campaign over the Vienna radio.[1] In Berlin, Göring and Ribbentrop received Slovak and Ruthenian autonomist leaders throughout the winter of 1938-9, and, as spring approached and the momentous month of March beckoned, the tempo of their negotiations and the definite nature of their promises increased accordingly.

By February things had reached so satisfactory a stage that Bela Tuka, the Vice-Premier of Slovakia, and Durčansky, the Foreign Minister, were received by Hitler in Berlin, where, in the course of the conversations, Tuka declared to the Führer : " I entrust the fate of my people to your care " (February 12, 1939).[2]

The attitude of the Government of the Reich towards Prague itself was unmistakably apparent in the interviews accorded by Hitler and Ribbentrop to Chvalkovsky on January 21, 1939, in which the terms of a German guarantee had been communicated to him.[3] From this it was evident that nothing short of grovelling lickspittle would satisfy Berlin, and this attitude not even the subservient Beran was prepared to adopt. With the return of Chvalkovsky to Prague began the final stage in the collapse of the Czechoslovak State, for it was painfully evident that, if the Prague Government did not comply in every detail with the demands made upon them, both they and Czechoslovakia would cease to exist. There was even speculation in Prague about the Ides of March, which, Europe had learned with dread, was the season at which an outbreak of the *furor teutonicus* might be expected.[4]

From the middle of January 1939 the premonitory symptoms of drastic action were open and significant. On January 21, the " moderate " Dr. Hjalmar Schacht was dismissed from the Presidency of the Reichsbank, to be succeeded by Walter Funk, an old Party member and one better attuned to the Führer's con-

[1] *French Yellow Book*, p. 99.
[2] *International Military Tribunal Document*, 2790-PS.
[3] See above, pp. 316-17.
[4] The declaration of rearmament had been in March 1935 ; the reoccupation o the Rhineland in March 1936 ; the annexation of Austria in March 1938.

ception of "emergency economy". As Minister of Economics Funk had toured the Balkans in October 1938 and had laid the foundations for the establishment of a German economic hegemony ; now his first act as President of the Reichsbank was to guarantee Germany's export trade, a measure which Schacht had refused to countenance.

Another casualty among the "moderates" was Fritz Wiedemann, the Führer's personal adjutant and sometime company commander, who was persistently importuning his former corporal to reach an understanding of friendship with the United States. Intolerant of criticism at all times, and particularly now when he had great things afoot, Hitler, with some sense of Greek justice, exiled Wiedemann to San Francisco, where, as Consul-General, he could practise his own theories of amicability with the Americans.

Even Göring, who had been faint-hearted at the time of Munich, was granted a "long leave of absence" and left for San Remo early in March. Hitler was taking no chances this time that his plans might be jeopardized by "moderate" influences.

In his speech to the Reichstag on January 20, the Führer warned the Western Powers that he would not tolerate their interference in "certain matters which concern nobody but ourselves", and a month later (February 28) the final German reply to the "needling" of Britain and France in the matter of the guarantee to Czechoslovakia made it clear beyond peradventure that any Anglo-French *démarche* was regarded as an inadmissible interference in a sphere of influence which Germany looked upon as being entirely her own.

The stage was set for the final act.

(iii)

By the beginning of March the Prague Government were in possession of evidence from Ruthenia and Slovakia which convinced them that the dissolution of the Czechoslovak State was imminent unless preventive action were immediately taken. They were, therefore, in a grave dilemma. If they did not take action the Republic would break up round them and Hitler would annex the rubble, but, if they took the only action possible to shore up the tottering edifice, there would almost certainly develop a condition of civil disturbance so acute that it would provide the Government of the Reich with an excuse to intervene. In this quandary they chose the latter course — with the results feared. The Führer's plans had, therefore, succeeded in every respect, and he was even relieved of the necessity and responsibility of " creating an incident ". The one brave act of the Hácha régime was its undoing.

On March 6 President Hácha dismissed the Ruthenian Government. Julien Revay, the Autonomist leader, fled to Berlin and besought Ribbentrop to authorize a declaration of independence. Three days later (March 9) the President dismissed the Slovak Government also, and on the following day arrested the Premier, Monsignor Tiso, together with Bela Tuka and Durčansky, and proclaimed martial law. Durčansky escaped from custody and fled to Vienna, where he, too, sought Nazi aid.

At once the well-oiled machinery for intervention was put into motion. The Vienna radio proclaimed that a " Marxist plot " was being hatched in Prague which would set all Central Europe aflame with Communism, and, in the midst of a meeting of the new Slovak Cabinet at Bratislava on the evening of March 11, Bürckel and Seyss-Inquart appeared with five German Generals and ordered the Government to proclaim the independence of Slovakia. The new Premier, M. Sidor, hesitated and sought to negotiate with Prague. Whereupon Tiso, who had also escaped by this time from the monastery in which he had been confined, found himself virtually kidnapped by Bürckel, and was flown immediately to Berlin, where the Führer awaited him.[1]

Hitler received Tiso in the new Reich Chancery at 7.15 on the evening of March 13. With him were Ribbentrop, State Secretary Meissner, Generals Keitel and von Brauchitsch, and also Durčansky, who had been flown up from Vienna. The Führer was indignant that his commands for the declaration of Slovakian independence had not been complied with immediately.

" At Munich [he said] I did not take Bohemia and Moravia into the German *Lebensraum*. I left the Czechs only another five months, but for the Slovaks I have some sympathy. I approved the Vienna Award in the conviction that the Slovaks would separate themselves from the Czechs and declare their inde-

[1] *International Military Tribunal Document*, D-571.

pendence, which would be under German protection. That is why I refused Hungarian demands in respect of Slovakia. As the Slovaks appear to be agreeing with the Czechs it looks as though they have not respected the spirit of the Vienna Award. This I cannot tolerate. To-morrow at midday I shall begin military action against the Czechs, which will be carried out by General von Brauchitsch there (pointing at the General). Germany does not intend to take Slovakia into her *Lebensraum* and that is why you must immediately proclaim the independence of Slovakia or I will disinterest myself in her fate. I will give you until to-morrow at midday to make your choice. Then the Czechs will be crushed by the German steam roller."

Confronted with this attitude, Tiso made haste to obey. He thanked the Führer for his words, saying that he had long wished to hear from the Führer himself how he stood in regard to Tiso's people and country. He assured the Führer that Slovakia could be counted on to do as Germany willed, then he flew back to Bratislava.[1] The independence of Slovakia was proclaimed next day (March 14), with Tiso as President and Bela Tuka as Premier.[2] Ruthenia followed suit on the same day.

The pace of events now quickened. From March 12 onwards the German press assumed an increasingly violent tone towards Czechoslovakia, a tone reminiscent of the days of August and September 1938, and each day the tale of threats and assaults by Czech nationals upon peaceful Germans in Bohemia mounted into fantasy. Keitel issued his final orders to the *Wehrmacht* on March 11, and, by the 14th, 14 divisions — some 200,000 men — were massed on the frontier of Bohemia and Moravia. Field-Marshal Göring, urgently recalled from his Italian retreat, concentrated the *Luftwaffe* on adjacent airfields. As designed in the secret directive of December 17, these troop movements took place in such secrecy that the normal life of the country was in no way disturbed. Few realized the magnitude of the operations in hand ; fewer still guessed the far-reaching repercussions which the operations would bring in their wake.

And then, when all things were prepared, the summons to the victims went forth. During the afternoon of March 14, the German

---

[1] *International Military Tribunal Documents*, D–57 and 2802–PS.

[2] These two persons were arrested by American military authorities on June 8, 1945, and subsequently handed over for trial to the Czechoslovak Government. Tuka was condemned to death on August 14, 1946, and hanged six days later. Tiso's trial began on December 2, 1946, and continued until April 15, 1947, when he was condemned to death. His execution took place three days later, on April 18.

Legation in Prague made it known to the Czechoslovak Foreign Ministry without further explanation that the presence of President Hácha and M. Chvalkovsky was desired in Berlin, and, having done so, the Minister and his entire staff became *incommunicado*, in accordance with the explicit instructions of Ribbentrop, to all attempts of the Government to elucidate the situation.[1]

To Hácha there seemed no choice but to obey. He was aged beyond his years and in ill-health, bowed and broken with the burden of an office he had never sought. His daughter travelled with him as nurse and companion. On their arrival at the Tempelhof airport on the evening of the 14th, the President was accorded, ironically enough, the honours due to the head of a State. There was a bouquet of flowers for his daughter too, and when they reached their apartments at the Hotel Adlon, she was presented with a box of chocolates as a gift from the Führer !

While the President rested after his journey, M. Chvalkovsky had a preliminary interview with Ribbentrop, from which he derived little consolation, and then at one o'clock in the morning of the 15th the ordeal of Hácha began ; an ordeal to which the agony which Schuschnigg had endured at Berchtesgaden was as nothing.

With that devotion to legalistic formulae so characteristic of the German mind, it had been decided that the death-warrant of Czechoslovakia must take the form of a treaty to which Hácha himself must put his name. Lest he should prove obdurate, all the factors of mental and spiritual torture were employed. The hour had been chosen as that at which the human resistance is at its lowest, and, in case the victim should seek refuge in physical collapse, doctors were held in attendance to revive him. Few mediaeval torturers could have devised so perfect a setting.

The Führer was attended by Göring, Ribbentrop, State Secretaries Weizsäcker and Meissner, and the inevitable Keitel. On the table in front of Hitler lay the documents for signature.

After a long harangue, in the course of which Hitler took occasion to recapitulate " the evil record " of Dr. Beneš, which had led to his own momentous decision of May 28 and to the Munich Agreement, he came to the point with frank brutality. " Czechia " had failed to profit by the opportunities offered to her during the past five months. She had been half-hearted in her co-operation with Germany and this he would not tolerate.

---

[1] *International Military Tribunal Document*, 2815-PS.

He now intended to declare the provinces of Bohemia and Moravia a protectorate of the Reich. To enforce this decision German troops would cross the frontier of " Czechia " at six o'clock [1] — that is to say, in five hours' time — and the *Luftwaffe* would occupy the Czech airfields. Prague would be occupied by nine o'clock. There existed, therefore, two alternatives. The Czechs could either resist the German *Einmarsch*, in which case they would be " trodden underfoot " with absolute ruthlessness, or they could accept their fate peacefully and render the German occupation " bearable ". In the latter case he would grant " Czechia " a generous life of her own — autonomy and a certain national liberty, which she could never have hoped for under the old Austria. He added that it was useless for Hácha to consider the possibility of any intervention by Britain or France in his defence, since neither of these countries was " in a position to stand up for Czechoslovakia ".

The Führer then signed the documents and left the room. It was about two o'clock on the morning of March 15.

There followed a scene of pitiable tragedy. Confronted with the death of their country, Hácha and Chvalkovsky protested with all the vehemence at their command.

" If I sign that document," said the President, " I shall be for ever cursed by my people," and he threw down the pen and walked away.

But Göring and Ribbentrop were pitiless.[2] They hunted the unfortunate Czechs around the table, thrusting pens into their hands and the documents in front of them : threatening, ever threatening, the dire perils to " Czechia " if they persisted in refusal.

" Sign, sign ! " they cried. " If you do not, half Prague will be lying in ruins within two hours," and Göring grimly affirmed that hundreds of bombers stood ready loaded, only awaiting the signal to take off — and the signal would be given at six o'clock.[3]

---

[1] In point of fact German troops had already crossed the frontier when Hitler spoke, and Göring admitted as much to Sir Nevile Henderson at Karinhall on May 27, 1939 (*British Blue Book*, p. 19). This fact was also confirmed by Göring in evidence at Nuremberg.

[2] Ribbentrop's later comment on the episode, when on trial at Nuremberg, is illustrative of his general attitude to public affairs : " Anyway, England encompassed the whole globe, and it would be justifiable to take a little place like Czechoslovakia."

[3] Göring sought subsequently to explain to Sir Nevile Henderson that, though he had indeed used this threat, he had only done so because President Hácha had said that he could not guarantee that not one Czech soldier would fire on the invading German troops (*British Blue Book*, pp. 18-19).

The hours passed. The fate of Prague loomed before the President in all its horror. Still he refused to sign. In his anguish he collapsed from exhaustion, only to be revived with cold efficiency by the physician in waiting.

Still the time flew by. It was 4.30 A.M. The threats, the cajoleries, the blackmail had never ceased. Hácha fainted a second time, was revived again and finally surrendered. Yet he temporized. He must, he said, have the consent of his Cabinet before taking so fearful a decision. With a sardonic smile Ribbentrop told him that a direct line had been established to the meeting of the Cabinet then in session at Prague. It had been laid down in Czech territory by members of the German minority without the knowledge of the authorities.

In a voice weak with emotion Hácha spoke to Beran and advised acceptance. Then in a state of collapse, kept going only by means of injections, he resigned himself, with death in his soul, to give his signature.[1] As they left the Chancellery it was still dark, and Chvalkovsky, looking up into the March night, murmured brokenly : " Our people will curse us, and yet we have saved their existence. We have preserved them from a horrible massacre." [2]

In the conduct of the occupation of Bohemia and Moravia Hitler displayed all his bent for petty and cruel revenge. The appointment of Baron von Neurath as Lord Protector of the two provinces, though clearly intended as a cloak of " decency " for the personality of his two chief lieutenants, was nevertheless in itself an insult, since it had been he who, with Göring, had given assurances of Germany's good intentions towards Czechoslovakia only a year before. But to make the notorious gangster, Karl Hermann Frank,[3] Secretary of State, and Konrad Henlein head of the civilian administration of Bohemia, was to offer the Czechs

---

[1] The above account of Hácha's ordeal is based on the official minutes of the meeting recorded by Legationsrat Hewel (*International Military Tribunal Document*, 2798–PS), supplemented by the accounts of M. Coulondre and Sir Nevile Henderson, which, though derived at second hand, are none the less vivid in detail. (See *French Yellow Book*, pp. 96-7 ; Henderson, pp. 216-18.)

[2] M. Chvalkovsky subsequently became the representative in Berlin of the Government of the Protectorate of Bohemia and Moravia. He was killed in the course of an Allied air raid on Berlin in 1944. Dr. Hácha, who had been an invalid for much of the latter portion of his life, was arrested on May 14, 1945, after the liberation of Prague, and died soon after.

[3] Frank subsequently became Vice-Protector of Bohemia and Moravia, and after the assassination of Heydrich ordered the massacre of Lidice on June 10, 1942. He was tried as a war criminal and publicly hanged near Prague on May 22, 1946.

a contemptuous affront, as pointed as it was gratuitous. And finally, Hitler went to Prague himself, arriving before Hácha had returned and being greeted somewhat too warmly by General Syrový.[1] At last the Führer sat in the Hradschin Castle, in the Palace of the Kings of Bohemia, where Beneš had governed his little democracy. Hitler's revenge was complete. At the table where the former President had so often sat listening to the flood of invective poured forth against his country by the German radio, the Führer wrote the words : " Czecho-Slovakia has ceased to exist." [2]

---

[1] General Syrový was arrested after the liberation of Czechoslovakia, and, after a trial, on a charge of collaboration, lasting from January 30 to April 2, 1947, was sentenced on April 21, 1947, to 20 years' imprisonment (ten with hard labour), loss of civil rights, and confiscation of property.

[2] Proclamation to the German people, March 15, 1939. (For text see Baynes, vol. ii, p. 1585.) The independence of Slovakia was also recognized by Hitler in an announcement from Prague, but the " Republic of Carpatho-Ukraine " (Ruthenia), proclaimed on March 14, survived only twenty-four hours. Hitler awarded this territory to Hungary as a reward for her compliancy and co-operation, and the incorporation of Ruthenia was announced by the Prime Minister in the Hungarian Parliament on March 16, 1939.

By a treaty signed on June 25, 1945, the province of Ruthenia was ceded by Czechoslovakia to the U.S.S.R.

PART IV

THE AWAKENING

(MARCH–AUGUST 1939)

Honour has come back as a king to earth,

.   .   .   .   .

Nobleness walks in our ways again.

RUPERT BROOKE, *The Dead*

CHAPTER ONE

THE FURY OF PATIENT MEN[1]

(i)

THE destruction of Czechoslovakia struck Britain with all the suddenness of a clap of thunder in a blue summer sky ; a Britain still basking in the reassuring rays of Sir Horace Wilson's inspired "sunshine talks" and Sir Samuel Hoare's ecstatic vision of a "Golden Age ".[2] To the critics of the Government's policy it came as a confirmation of their worst fears ; to those who genuinely believed in the durability of the structure of peace erected on the basis of the Munich Agreement and the Anglo-German Declaration, it came as a hideous disillusionment ; but to the vast majority of Englishmen it came as a final awakening from the thraldom of a magician's spell in which their limbs had been chained and their senses numbed by some insidious narcotic.

Throughout the Munich crisis Hitler had reiterated that the cession of the Sudetenland represented his last demand in Europe. He had repeated that he wanted none but Germans within his German Reich. He had agreed to guarantee the frontiers of Czechoslovakia. Now, at one stroke, he had disclosed himself publicly as a liar and a cheat. He had outraged the Englishman's code of the " things no fellow can do ". He had aroused the slow fury of patient men.

Now there could no longer be any uncertainty about the infamy of Nazi Germany nor of its ultimate ambition for world domination. Those who had been prepared to seek an agreement with Hitler joined hands — albeit a little gingerly, for the quarrels of the past months had gone very deep — with those who had cried " Hitler means war ", and the country was united in

---

[1] " Beware the Fury of a Patient Man " (John Dryden, *Absalom and Achitophel*).

[2] " The editor of *Punch* instructed Mr. Bernard Partridge to design a happy cartoon for his issue of Wednesday, March 15. This cartoon, which was entitled ' The Ides of March ', depicted John Bull waking up from an appalling nightmare. The nightmare was itself shown escaping through the window in the guise of a scaremonger. John Bull exclaimed ' Thank God ! That's over ! ' [*sic*] " (Nicolson, *Why Britain is at War*, pp. 101-2).

THE IDES OF MARCH

John Bull. " Thank goodness that's over ! "
(Pessimists predicted " another major crisis " in the middle of this month)

MARCH 15, 1939

Reprinted by the special permission of the Proprietors of " Punch "

the thought that " Hitler must be stopped ".[1] Those who had defended Munich in the past did not abandon their belief that it had " saved the peace of Europe " and " gained time " ; those who had attacked the policy of appeasement continued to believe that precious time had been lost and good allies abandoned ; but, disregarding these fissures in opinion, the country was at last awake and aware of the danger on its doorstep, and it became clamorous for action to meet the emergency.

That this quick change of opinion was unappreciated in leading Government circles was made immediately apparent when the Prime Minister met the House of Commons and was subjected to numerous requests, first for information, and then for explanation of the conduct of the Government.

Throughout the months which had elapsed between the signature of the Munich Agreement and the annexation of Bohemia and Moravia, the British and French Ambassadors in Berlin had persistently warned their Governments of the growing tension in Central and Eastern Europe and of the evident fact that Germany regarded the engagements entered into at Munich as null and void. The Military Attachés, moreover, had reported to their respective War Departments in Paris and London that the spirit of aggressive efficiency which now permeated the German armed forces could only result in continued military adventures which might or might not result in war, according to the attitude adopted by the Western Powers. Despite this evidence, the British and French Governments had endeavoured to persuade their countries that all was still for the best, and now the day of reckoning had arrived.

The first news of German troop movements reached London and Paris on March 11, and rumours of the events in Slovakia and Ruthenia were current during the week-end. Mr. Chamberlain told the House of Commons on Monday (March 13) that there had been " a Cabinet crisis " in Slovakia but that " the situation appears to be outwardly calm ". He had, he said, received no information that Monsignor Tiso was on his way to Germany. When asked whether, if this proved to be correct, His Majesty's Government would make representations in Berlin in view of the Anglo-French Guarantee, the Prime Minister made no

---

[1] As is not unusual with converts, many of the former supporters of appeasement now sought to excel in zealous protestation. A case in point is that of a man who in September 1938 was fiercely denouncing the Czechs as imperilling the peace of Europe and in March 1939 was refusing to drink German wines.

answer.[1] But on that very day M. Bonnet and the British Ambassador in Paris, Sir Eric Phipps, had conferred on this guarantee and had agreed that it did not apply.

By the following day (March 14) the world knew that Tiso had indeed gone to Berlin, and had also a very good idea of what had happened when he got there. The House of Commons, therefore, was manifestly dissatisfied with the Prime Minister's guarded statement that though he, too, knew of this fact he had " no information of the nature of the discussions ", and that, despite an unconfirmed report that Slovakia had proclaimed its independence, the situation in Bratislava " still remained outwardly calm ".[2]

It was on this day that there occurred an amazing passage between the Prime Minister and Mr. Attlee, which was reported to Berlin without comment by the German Embassy in London :

" Mr. Attlee : Is it not clear that influences are being brought to bear to separate Slovakia from the rest of Czechoslovakia, and are not the Government bound by their guarantee under the Munich Agreement to have a very close interest in anything which concerns the integrity of the Czechoslovak State ?

" The Prime Minister : Without full information I should not like to express an opinion upon the first point which was raised by the Rt. Hon. Gentleman. Assuming it to be true, that would not be a ground for bringing into force the guarantee.

" Mr. Attlee : Does the Prime Minister say that the Government are merely waiting for a *fait accompli*, and have they taken any steps to have any consultations with the representatives of the Czechoslovakian Government or with the French Government or any other guarantor, seeing that there are rumours and implications, which can hardly be disregarded altogether, of a possible break-up of Czechoslovakia which this country has guaranteed ?

" The Prime Minister : I am not sure what the Rt. Hon. Gentleman thinks we should do. I might remind him that the proposed guarantee is one against unprovoked aggression on Czechoslovakia. No such aggression has yet taken place." [3]

Here was the language of Munich, the dialect of appeasement, and it had become an alien tongue to the House of Commons.

The Prime Minister made one final effort to ride out the storm. On the afternoon of March 15, while German troops were pouring

---

[1] *House of Commons Debates*, March 13, 1939, coll. 23-4.
[2] *Ibid.* March 14, 1939, col. 222.
[3] *Ibid.* coll. 223-4 ; *Second German White Book*, p. 277.

into Bohemia and Moravia, while Hitler was making his triumphal entry into Prague, Mr. Chamberlain informed Parliament that Czechoslovakia had " become disintegrated " ; that " a State containing Czechs, Slovaks, as well as minorities of other nationalities " was liable to " possibilities of change " ; and that " I have so often heard charges of breach of faith bandied about which did not seem to me to be founded upon sufficient premises, that I do not wish to associate myself to-day with any charges of that character ". With regard to the guarantee — which involved the good faith of Britain, and from which he had previously expressed the hope and belief that " the new Czechoslovakia will find a greater security than she has ever enjoyed in the past " [1] — the Prime Minister was quite clear. " The situation has radically altered since the Slovak Diet declared the independence of Slovakia. The effect of this decision put an end by internal disruption to the State whose frontier we had proposed to guarantee. His Majesty's Government cannot accordingly hold themselves any longer bound by this obligation." [2]

Finally, on the following day (March 16), when questioned by Sir Archibald Sinclair, the Prime Minister stated that so far no protest had been lodged with the German Government, and he could give no assurance that any such protest would be made. He added, however, that the recall of Sir Nevile Henderson to London for purposes of consultation was " under consideration ".[3] He also announced that the British Minister to Prague, Sir Basil Newton, would be transferred to Iraq.[4]

But this equivocal expression of thought on a direct act of German aggression upon a non-German people was not to be Britain's final word on the subject. Mr. Chamberlain's inability to gauge the changed temper of the country precipitated the most

[1] *House of Commons Debates*, October 3, 1938, col. 45.

[2] *Ibid.* March 15, 1939, col. 437. It is of interest to compare Mr. Chamberlain's interpretation of the nature of the guarantee on this occasion with the statement which he made on November 1, 1938, when he definitely avoided any commitment to guarantee frontiers and admitted only a tentative " offer " to guarantee the sovereign integrity of Czechoslovakia. (See above, p. 315.)

[3] *Ibid.* March 16, 1939, col. 614. Sir Nevile Henderson had seen the State Secretary, Baron von Weizsäcker, on March 14, and, though making it clear that he wished neither to make a *démarche* nor to create the impression that his Government were interfering in the affair, nevertheless, " adjured him to see that nothing was done to violate the Munich Agreement or to upset the Stanley-Hudson visit " (Henderson, pp. 211-12 ; *Second German White Book*, p. 278).

[4] Mr. Basil Newton had been awarded a K.C.M.G. in 1939 in recognition of his services during the Munich crisis.

severe crisis within his own Party since the inception of the National Government in 1931. Throughout March 15 and 16 there was a growing volume of criticism among Conservative Members of Parliament and in the country at large.[1] It was evident that, if Mr. Chamberlain insisted upon a blind adherence to the shibboleths of Munich and did not make a stronger statement of Britain's future policy toward Germany, his personal position as Prime Minister and leader of the Conservative Party would be in danger.

It was now that Lord Halifax emerged as the man of the moment.

The Foreign Secretary, as he himself later admitted frankly in the House of Lords, had given " the fullest co-operation " to the Prime Minister in the policy of Munich.[2] He had, though in a lesser degree than Mr. Chamberlain, exaggerated the actual achievement of the Munich Settlement. But he had never displayed such fanatical devotion as had Simon, Hoare, and Inskip, and, with his greater knowledge of men and affairs, he had read the writing on the wall sooner, more clearly and more accurately than his leader and his colleagues. For the past weeks he had been leaning increasingly toward the views of those of his senior advisers in the Foreign Office, who had long foreseen that a belief in Hitler's good faith was destined to be disastrously belied by events.

Lord Halifax had distinguished between belief and hope. It was legitimate to hope, but when hopes failed the failure must be remedied. He had urged the Prime Minister, immediately after Munich, to strengthen his Cabinet by the inclusion of national leaders of all parties, but he had not been able to carry his point. He had advocated a modified scheme of conscription, but here again he had failed to overcome the hesitation of Mr. Chamberlain to commit himself. He had gone along as far as loyalty demanded — and some thought farther — in his approval of the Prime Minister's attitude, but he was not prepared to see the Conservative Party founder on the rock of personal

---

[1] On March 16 *The Times*, the *Daily Telegraph* and the *Daily Express* roundly denounced the occupation of Bohemia and Moravia. Only the *Daily Mail* followed the line of the Prime Minister : " The final disintegration of Czecho-Slovakia was almost inevitable. The shock lies in the swift and brutal manner of its end. Britain has now no cause to interfere. The final split-up of Czecho-Slovakia was due to an internal aggression. One thing, and one thing only will save Britain — her own armed might." [2] *House of Lords Debates*, March 20, 1939, col. 313.

obstinacy.   He had been ready to serve as chief mate in the barque of appeasement but he had never nailed his colours to the mast.

Above all Lord Halifax was both an experienced politician and an experienced Master of Foxhounds.   In his fifteen years as Member of Parliament he had learned to know the House of Commons like his own pack of hounds and he recognized the signs of disobedience to the whip.

Now in the moment of crisis (March 15–16) he came to Mr. Chamberlain and put the issue squarely before him.   The country, the Party, and the House of Commons demanded that Britain's attitude toward German aggression should be stated clearly and without equivocation.   The Prime Minister was due to make a much-heralded speech at Birmingham on the night of March 17 — the eve of his seventieth birthday — and this was his great opportunity.   He need not repudiate the past but he must leave no doubt about the future.   Otherwise he would almost certainly be faced with a revolt in the Party and the House. This time Mr. Chamberlain listened to the counsel of Lord Halifax and on the eve of his departure for Birmingham he amended the draft of his speech.[1]

The Prime Minister's change of mind, however, was apparently either not shared by, or not communicated to, Sir John Simon, who in the House of Commons on March 16 delivered a speech in the manner of Munich, which roused the House to a pitch of anger rarely seen.   It was not so much the repetition of the outmoded and threadbare watchwords of the Munich Debate which angered the House as the apparently cynical nature of his argument.   After referring to Hitler's proclamation that Czechoslovakia had ceased to exist, Sir John proceeded to demonstrate that one could not guarantee something which was non-existent.   " It is indeed impossible to suppose that in these circumstances the guarantee to maintain the State of Czechoslovakia can have any meaning."   " It is really essential ", he added, " that we should not enter into any extensive general and

---

[1] *Viscount Halifax*, by Allen Campbell Johnson (London, 1941), pp. 510-13 ; *Lord Halifax*, by Stuart Hodgson (London, 1941), pp. 181-5.   The crisis within the Government was reported by the German Embassy in the following terms : (On March 17) " The difference of opinion between Chamberlain and Halifax, which has already shown itself occasionally, is becoming more and more evident, the latter advocating a stronger attitude ".   (On March 18) " The more extreme group within the Cabinet, represented especially by Lord Halifax, who is entirely under the influence of the Foreign Office, gained the upper hand " (*Second German White Book*, pp. 281 and 282).

undefined commitment with the result that, to a large extent, our foreign policy would depend, not on this country, this Parliament and its electors, but on a lot of foreign governments." [1]

The effect of this statement was the most eloquent proof of the change in British public opinion. In October 1938 Sir John Simon's view would have been supported, though with varying degrees of approval and reluctance, by the majority of the House of Commons. In March 1939 it provoked savage criticism of the Government's policy, and although the leading critics, Mr. Attlee, Mr. Eden, Mr. Law, and Sir Archibald Sinclair, were still those who had attacked the Munich Agreement in the first place, there was a perceptible change in the temper of the House at large, a clear indication that the supporters of the Government were unhappy about the views and tactics of their leaders.

The influence of Lord Halifax and those who shared his views became at once discernible. It was imperative that Sir John Simon's remarks should not be interpreted as an expression of Government opinion. They were jettisoned that very night when a Minister, Lord De La Warr, declared publicly and with official blessing that " aggression stands forth naked and arrogant in its shame ".[2]

The following night, at Birmingham, the Prime Minister sounded the keynote of the new British diplomatic revolution. It was no speech to light a fiery cross. It disclosed no apology for the past, no recantation on appeasement. It attempted no explanation of the fact that His Majesty's Government had for months condoned by their silence the failure of Germany to accord a guarantee to Czechoslovakia, and though he expressed sympathy for the Czechs — a fact omitted in his statement of March 15, and tactfully included by Sir John Simon on the following day — Mr. Chamberlain chose this occasion to repeat publicly what he had telegraphed privately to President Beneš in September 1938,[3] namely that, had Britain fought and defeated Germany at that time, " never could we have reconstructed Czechoslovakia as she was framed by the Treaty of Versailles ". The Czechs still remained for him the stumbling-block which had nearly prevented his agreement with Hitler in the past and had somehow succeeded by their very helplessness in ruining that agreement now. It was evident that he still believed that Hitler had been

---

[1] *House of Commons Debates*, March 15, 1939, coll. 546, 554.
[2] Speech at Walthamstow (*The Times*, March 17, 1939).   [3] See above, p. 155.

justified in his pre-Munich policy, and that, had he agreed to stand by the Munich Agreement and the Anglo-German Declaration, he, Mr. Chamberlain, would have found no ground for criticism.

Indeed, there was a note of petulance and wounded vanity throughout the speech. The Führer had let him down, had wantonly shattered the edifice of appeasement in which Mr. Chamberlain had enshrined his hopes and the basis of his policy. He repeated the assurances which Hitler had given him — and which he had believed. " Surely as a joint signatory of the Munich Agreement I was entitled, if Herr Hitler thought it ought to be undone, to that consultation which is provided for in the Munich Declaration. Instead of that, he has taken the law into his own hands." [1]

But despite the sadness of his disillusionment, the Prime Minister came out forcefully with his condemnation of aggression, and that it was to be considered as a pronouncement of Government policy was shown by the fact that the speech was broadcast to Britain and America, and the text subsequently included in the British Blue Book on the outbreak of hostilities.[2] After saying that Britain, in taking stock of her new position resulting from the abandonment of appeasement, would " naturally turn first to our partners in the British Commonwealth of Nations — and to France — to whom we are so closely bound, and I have no doubt that others too, knowing that we are not disinterested in what goes on in South-Eastern Europe, will wish to have our counsel and advice ", the Prime Minister came to the gravamen of his speech :

" I do not believe there is anyone who will question my sincerity when I say that there is hardly anything I would not sacrifice for

[1] In view of this statement by the Prime Minister it is interesting to find that, on March 24, the ever-vigilant German Embassy reported to Berlin that, on March 23, in answer to a question from Mr. Arthur Henderson whether His Majesty's Government would make representation to the German Government in view of the fact that the Government of the Reich had failed to consult on " recent developments in relation to Czechoslovakia, as Herr Hitler had promised in the Anglo-German Declaration," the Under-Secretary for Foreign Affairs, Mr. R. A. Butler, had replied : " I am not aware that the Declaration in question contained such a statement. The second part of the question does not therefore arise." This reply does not tally with that recorded in *Hansard*, which merely referred the questioner to an earlier reply, in which again these words do not appear. Nevertheless, the reply, as phrased here, was reported with the comment that " it can only be interpreted as meaning that the British Government's standpoint is that German action in the Czechoslovak question does not constitute a breach of the agreement to consult contained in the German-British declaration of September 29, 1938 " (*Second German White Book*, p. 284).

[2] *British Blue Book*, p. 5.

peace. But there is one thing I must except, and that is the liberty we have enjoyed for hundreds of years and which we will never surrender. That I, of all men, should be called upon to make such a declaration — that is the measure of the extent to which these events have shattered the confidence which was just beginning to show its head, and which, if it had been allowed to grow, might have made this year memorable for the return of all Europe to sanity and stability.

It is only six weeks ago that . . . I pointed out that any attempt to dominate the world by force was one which the Democracies must resist, and I added that I could not believe that such a challenge was intended. . . . Indeed, with the lessons of history for all to read, it seems incredible that we should see such a challenge.

I feel bound to repeat that, while I am not prepared to engage this country by new unspecified commitments operating under conditions which cannot be foreseen, yet no greater mistake could be made than to suppose that, because it believes war to be a senseless and cruel thing, this nation has so lost its fibre that it will not take part to the uttermost of its power in resisting such a challenge if it were made."

It is possible to imagine a more inspiring declaration of policy and also one more calculated to promote confidence in other potential victims of aggression — for the references to others in South-Eastern Europe " who will wish to have our counsel and advice " were carefully offset by a refusal to engage the country in " new and unspecified commitments ". It was not a speech which, on the face of it, would strike terror into the heart of one contemplating aggression, and its value as a deterrent may be judged from the fact that within a month of its delivery Hitler had seized Memel (March 22) and Mussolini had annexed Albania (April 7). It did not prevent the application by His Majesty's Government to the German Government for the grant of *exequaturs* for British Consuls-General in Prague and Bratislava, thereby according at least *de facto* recognition of the German annexation,[1] nor the handing over to Germany of the Czechoslovak gold assets in the Bank of England at the behest of the Reich Government and the Bank of International Settlements.[2]

[1] The negotiations for the grant of these *exequaturs* took place in May and June 1939.

[2] Late in March 1939 there occurred an event which Mr. Churchill described as " a public disaster, namely, the transfer of £6,000,000 of Czech money into the hands of those who have overthrown and destroyed the Czech Republic ".

On March 18 the " National Bank of Bohemia and Moravia ", which had replaced the Czechoslovak National Bank under the Protectorate, requested the Bank of

The new British diplomatic revolution began " not with a bang but a whimper " ; however, it saved Mr. Chamberlain's position with the country, the Party, and the House of Commons, and, despite all appearances to the contrary, it did mark the transition of British foreign policy from one of outright isolationist appeasement to one of active participation in the affairs of Continental Europe For, from this prosaic, circumscribed, and most unrevolutionary pronouncement was to emerge, not without pain and labour and delay, that system of guarantees against aggression which preceded the entry of Britain into the Second World War, and it therefore ranks, as such, among the important State Papers of our country.

(ii)

The development of the British diplomatic revolution was destined to be a thing of fits and starts, of shy hesitations and panic rushes. It must be believed that Mr. Chamberlain's indignation, as expressed at Birmingham on March 17, was real and heartfelt. He had refused so long to listen to warnings or to recognize a danger signal when he saw one, that, when brought face to face with the car of Juggernaut, which he had so long

International Settlements at Basle to order the transfer to the Reichsbank of the Czech gold assets which had been deposited by the Bank of International Settlements with the Bank of England, a request to which the Bank of International Settlements, on whose board were two directors of the Reichsbank, assented with remarkable readiness. On March 24 the French Government asked the British Government whether certain steps could be taken to prevent this transfer, but received the reply that " the matter was one which fell to be decided by the Bank of International Settlements ", and that, as Sir John Simon subsequently told the House of Commons, " I do not see how we can fail to obey them (Bank of International Settlements) without breaking our treaty obligations ".

The Bank of England complied without the slightest demur and transferred £6 millions to the Reichsbank. It was subsequently stated that in so doing the Bank of England did not realize that the gold was the property of the National Bank of Czechoslovakia, as " the Bank of England has no knowledge whether gold so held is in fact the absolute property of the Bank of International Settlements or is held by the latter in whole or in part for the accounts of others ". This somewhat equivocal excuse must be considered in concert with the fact that two directors of the Bank of England were also directors of the Bank of International Settlements who issued the transfer instructions.

The unfortunate episode was the subject of fierce debates in the House of Commons in May and June 1939, which exposed, in the words of Professor Berriedale Keith, " the lack of patriotic zeal on the part of the directors and the grave weakness of Sir John Simon ".

(See *House of Commons Debates*, May 26 and June 5, 1939 ; also *The Causes of the War*, by Arthur Berriedale Keith (London, 1940), p. 382 ; and *The Czechoslovak Cause in International Law*, by Eduard Táborský (London, 1944), pp. 49-61.)

persisted in regarding as nothing more dangerous than a circus waggon, he was genuinely shocked and sincerely resentful.

What emerged from the Birmingham speech was that Britain would resist any further act of aggression by Germany, but that she was still very uncertain, not to say fearful, about the means by which such resistance should be effected. The position would probably have remained in this unclarified and nebulous condition had it not been for two factors : the energy of Lord Halifax and the pressure of events.

The Foreign Secretary had been active even before he had completed the conversion of the Prime Minister. A mild Note of disapprobation had been delivered by Sir Nevile Henderson in Berlin on the morning of Wednesday, March 15, but late that evening Lord Halifax summoned the German Ambassador, the suave von Dirksen, to the Foreign Office, and there spoke his mind with considerable candour. In the relations between Germany and Britain, he told the Ambassador, the hands of the clock had been set back considerably and it was now impossible to contemplate the proposed visit to Berlin of the President of the Board of Trade and Mr. Hudson. The Ambassador seemed surprised at this reaction and expressed an inability to comprehend what connection existed between the recent events in Czechoslovakia and German-British economic relations.[1] Lord Halifax explained the connection clearly and succinctly.

Nor was this the only expression which Lord Halifax gave to his opinions. Sir Nevile Henderson had telegraphed from Berlin on the 15th : " His Majesty's Government will doubtless consider what attitude to adopt towards a Government which has shown itself incapable of honouring an agreement not six months old ",[2] and had thereby precipitated a difference of opinion between the Prime Minister and the Foreign Secretary. Lord Halifax had originally wished to withdraw the British Ambassador from Berlin altogether as a mark of the deep disapproval felt by His Majesty's Government at this destruction of the structure of Munich and also as a clear indication that Britain was not disinterested in German plans for conquest in Eastern and South-Eastern Europe. Mr. Chamberlain, however, had not yet progressed sufficiently far along the road from appeasement to take so drastic a step.

---

[1] *Second German White Book*, pp. 280-81. Göring, on being informed that the Stanley-Hudson visit could not take place, professed " the utmost indignation that it should be cancelled for such a trifle " (Henderson, p. 222).   [2] Henderson, p. 223.

A compromise was found in the formula adopted by the United States Government on the occasion of the Jewish pogrom in November [1] and Sir Nevile Henderson was " recalled for consultation ".

While Mr. Chamberlain was in the train bound for Birmingham, Lord Halifax gave the gist of the Prime Minister's forthcoming speech to the American Ambassador, Mr. Joseph Kennedy, and instructed Sir Robert Vansittart to make contact with the Soviet Embassy.   Both applauded the change of front and regarded the new departure in British policy as vitally important.

From France, however, the signs were less encouraging. M. Bonnet had received the portents of March 11 with even greater *sang-froid* than Mr. Chamberlain.   As late as March 14, Thouvenin and Pierre-Étienne Flandin — the one in *L'Homme Libre*, Bonnet's mouthpiece, the other in the *New York Herald-Tribune* — were inveighing against the " *Fausses Alertes ! Fausses Nouvelles !* " of those who uttered warnings against the danger to Britain and France inherent in the absorption of Czechoslovakia by Germany.[2]

That same day M. Bonnet went before the Foreign Affairs Committee of the Chamber and explained that the Anglo-French guarantee to Czechoslovakia had never been put into effect.   He spoke very calmly and used the Nazi term " Czechia ", remaining quite unperturbed by the bitter criticism levelled against him by Henri de Kérillis and the Communist leader, Gabriel Péri.   In the evening the Foreign Minister received Count Welczeck, who brought with him the text of the Agreement signed in the early hours of the morning by Hitler and Hácha.[3]   Concerning M. Bonnet's comments both the *French Yellow Book* and the *German White Book* are silent, but when, a few days later (March 18), M. Coulondre saw Weizsäcker in Berlin, the State Secretary told him frankly that M. Bonnet had given " verbal assurances " to Ribbentrop in December that Czechoslovakia was in future not to be a subject of " an exchange of views ", and added that, had the German Government supposed that it might be otherwise, Ribbentrop would never have signed the Franco-German Declaration.[4]

It was not until March 15 that the French Government

---

[1] See above, p. 298.

[2] The first reaction of M. Bonnet's Press Chief, Bressy, to the news of the occupation of Prague was : " *Ça vous étonne ?*   It is after all only a consequence of the blunders made in 1919 " (Werth, p. 357).   It was in just these terms that von Dirksen and Count Welczeck excused the affair to Lord Halifax and M. Bonnet.

[3] *French Yellow Book*, p. 83.   [4] *Ibid.* p. 98.

evinced any alarm at all concerning the fate of Bohemia, Moravia, and Slovakia, and then the only reaction of M. Daladier was to demand *pleins pouvoirs* from the Chamber. He refused to give any explanation for his request or to give any guarantee that these powers, if granted, would not be used to curb liberties or jeopardize social reform. The Premier did not mention Czechoslovakia on the first day of the debate and only expressed his sympathy for the Czech people on the second, but M. Léon Blum was cheered when he exclaimed : " A people has been reduced to slavery by the atrocious abuse of force in that year that is the 150th anniversary of the French Revolution."

To Lord Halifax, in a new fervour of zeal, this delay seemed lamentable. He " needled " the French Ambassador in London, and M. Corbin, who himself needed no incentive to action, sought to spur on Bonnet. The result was a somewhat meagre contribution on March 16, which, though it stated the need for Britain and France to take concerted action in Berlin — on the ground that " Governments, who gave their assent to a compromise intended to assure the survival of Czechoslovakia, cannot to-day watch in silence the dismemberment of the Czech people and the annexation of their territory without being accused in retrospect of compliance and moral complicity " — made no suggestion for the future. Acting on this, both Henderson and Coulondre made their protests (March 17), which were firmly rejected by Weizsäcker even as the British protest regarding Austria had been rejected by Neurath a year before.[1]

All this activity, however, had taken place before Mr. Chamberlain's Birmingham speech of March 17, and it might reasonably have been supposed, in view of the critical international situation then obtaining, that every activity of preparation would be prosecuted to the utmost extent.

The spoils of Bohemia and Moravia had brought to Hitler more than the accretion of economic resources and reservoirs of potential slave labour. The gold reserves of the Reichsbank, greatly depleted by the wild and adventurous policies of Walter Funk, were now supplemented by the £10 million sterling assets found in the vaults of the Czech National Bank, — and to this was shortly to be added the further £6 millions which reposed, in supposed safety, on deposit with the Bank of England.[2] In addition to this loot, the German Army had acquired complete

---

[1] See above, p. 23 (footnote 2).   [2] See above, p. 358 (footnote 2).

control of the Skoda armament works at Pilsen and the Brno wireless, and had taken over from the Czech armed forces, in weapons and equipment, what the Führer later described to the Reichstag as " a vast store of munitions ".[1]

Moreover, the frontiers of the Reich were now advanced to a point from which the *Wehrmacht* could strike either due east into Poland or south-east into Rumania.   In place of the long winding frontier which had separated Germany from Czechoslovakia, there was now substituted the much shorter and much more easily defended line from Austria to Silesia.   Germany had thus saved several divisions which would have had to watch the Czech frontier in the event of war.   Furthermore, the table-lands of Bohemia and Moravia afforded an excellent base for military operations of all kinds, but particularly for aircraft, and the first act of the *Wehrmacht* had been to make Vienna the headquarters of a new air fleet (the Fourth, South-East) which increased the power of the *Luftwaffe* beyond all expectations.   Hungary, a gorged jackal, lay temporarily in the way of a common Russo-German frontier, but it would not be difficult to bribe her with promises of restored *irredenta* in Transylvania.   For all practical purposes she was within the political and military orbit of Germany.

For the moment, however, the Führer was confronted with an *embarras de choix*.   As an official of the Ministry of Propaganda remarked at this time : " We have before us so many open doors, so many possibilities, that we no longer know which way to turn or what direction to take." [2]   Hitler himself, well knowing that he could not finally accomplish his high destiny in Eastern Europe until France had been crushed and Britain rendered impotent on the Continent, was meditating the advisability of a descent on the West before proceeding against Poland and Russia.   While he hesitated — as it were communing with his own god-like personality — he maintained pressure upon Warsaw for the return of Danzig and for " the corridor across the Corridor ", and upon Bucharest for the closing down of all existing industries, reverting solely to agriculture, and the granting to Germany of a complete monopoly over all Rumanian exports, especially grain and oil.

[1] Speech to the Reichstag, April 28, 1939.   The text included in Baynes, vol. ii, pp. 1605-56, omits the details of the armament acquisitions.   These included over 1500 planes (500 front-line), 469 tanks, over 500 A.A. guns, more than 43,000 machine guns and over a million rifles.   In addition the *Wehrmacht* became possessed of over 1,000,000,000 rounds of rifle ammunition and more than 3,000,000 rounds of field-gun ammunition.   [2] *French Yellow Book*, p. 106.

It seemed now clear beyond peradventure in London and in Paris that the diminishing returns of the policy of placation, of fending off calamity by throwing another baby to the wolves, had reached the point of extinction. German aggression had passed from expansion into conquest, and conquest which would prove boundless unless checked. Britain and France were now directly threatened. They now saw no choice save either to bow in due time to Hitler's will or, by uniting their forces, to build up a military machine, and especially an air force, strong enough to impress and, if need be, to resist Germany.

This was the view of Lord Halifax and a number of the Ministers within the Government, and of Winston Churchill, Anthony Eden, Duff Cooper, Harold Macmillan, and Richard Law, the dissident Conservative leaders. These persons favoured a policy of swift and decisive action — the co-operation of Britain, France, and Russia for positive resistance to further acts of aggression by Germany, and the immediate introduction of conscription in Britain.

Over against them were the former paladins of appeasement, but recently and imperfectly converted to the necessity for action. In this group the leader was the Chancellor of the Exchequer, Sir John Simon. Sir John had been annoyed at not having been informed before the Birmingham speech of the Prime Minister's change of front, an omission which had caused him to make his statement on March 16 a probably more fervent defence of the Munich policy than would otherwise have been wise or politic. Now he captained the forces of " moderation " within the Government, advocating limited liabilities on the Continent and a cautious policy towards the introduction of compulsory military service at home.

Between these warring groups among his associates Mr. Chamberlain tended to lean more naturally towards the views of Sir John Simon than to those of Lord Halifax. It is true that the Prime Minister had in the past been critical of Sir John as a Foreign Secretary,[1] but nevertheless he was more in tune with Mr. Chamberlain's inherent horror of war and his dislike of foreign commitments than were the *bellicistes* of the Conservative

[1] " Simon's weakness has given rise to much criticism ", Mr. Chamberlain wrote in his diary in January 1934. " He can always make an admirable speech in the House, to a brief, but . . . the fact is that his manner inspires no confidence, and that he seems temperamentally unable to make up his mind to action when a difficult situation arises " (Feiling, p. 249).

Party with whom Lord Halifax was now associated. In the events which followed, therefore, it is believed that the influence of Sir John Simon played a conspicuously important part in the Prime Minister's decisions — or in the lack of them.

What had emerged from the situation created by the Birmingham speech of March 17 was that Britain had finished with appeasement, but this alone was definite. There appeared to be no clear decision on the degree of co-operation to be obtained with other Great Powers, the degree of support to be offered to other potential victims of aggression, or the degree of sacrifice to be demanded from the British people.

On the Continent the great enigma remained the future attitude of the U.S.S.R. Excluded by common consent from the Munich discussions, the Soviet Government had preserved in the interval between October 1938 and March 1939, toward both Germany and the Western Powers, an attitude of watchful waiting and of bitter criticism. The Russian press, in addition to its usual fulminations against the Reich, had consistently proclaimed the error of the Munich policy and its inevitably disastrous results. " The special peculiarity of the war now being waged against Britain, France, and Russia is that the democratic countries pretend not to notice it," Molotov had declared on November 6. " They wash their hands of it because the democratic governments are still more afraid of workers' movements than of Fascism." [1]

Though the Soviet Government's attention had been partially deflected from the West by a series of border conflicts with the Japanese in Manchuria, they took two positive steps to mark their displeasure with both groups of Powers in Europe. Diplomatic relations were broken off with Hungary on February 22 as a result of her adherence to the Anti-Comintern Pact, and a few weeks later (March 3) the Soviet representatives were withdrawn from the International Non-Intervention Committee in London on the ground that that body " had long ago ceased functioning and had lost the sense of its own existence ". Finally, at the opening of the 18th Congress of the All-Union Bolshevik Party on March 10, Stalin himself castigated the Western Powers in no uncertain terms. " Britain and France ", he said, " have repudiated the policy of collective security, of giving a collective rebuff to aggressors, and have, in fact, taken up the position of non-intervention — the policy of neutrality. . . . This

[1] *Izvestia*, November 7, 1938.

WHAT, NO CHAIR FOR ME ?

SEPTEMBER 13, 1938

By courtesy of Mr. David Low and the " Evening Standard "

policy leads to war, and behind it one perceives the desire not to hinder the aggressors in their black business. For instance, Japan starts a war in China, or better still, against the U.S.S.R., or Germany gets deeply involved in European affairs and in a war with the U.S.S.R. Let all those participating in the war get stuck in the mud of war ; encourage them secretly ; let them exhaust each other ; and when they are sufficiently exhausted then enter the stage with fresh forces — ' in the interests of peace ', of course — and dictate your own conditions." [1]

Though Stalin's trenchant denunciation may have come dangerously near the truth,[2] it did, nevertheless, contain the germ of hope that, under different circumstances, the Soviet Union would still be prepared to co-operate on a basis of collective security against a common aggressor. It was in this hope that Lord Halifax had authorized Sir Robert Vansittart to confer with M. Maisky on the potential threat to Poland, and the same hope prompted the British Government to enquire in Moscow as to the attitude which the Soviet Union proposed to adopt to the threat which Hitler was then developing in Eastern Europe (March 17).

The response of Moscow to these advances was to repeat the manœuvre of the previous year, after the *Anschluss*.[3] The Soviet Government proposed an immediate conference of Britain, France, the U.S.S.R., Poland, Rumania, and Turkey to devise means of resistance to aggression.

This proposal came before the British Cabinet, which had been called in emergency session, on March 18. The situation was tense ; the threat to Rumania seemed imminent. Hitler's demands regarding grain and oil had been received in Bucharest and the Rumanian Cabinet was wavering ; but King Carol had given the impression that he would fight rather than submit to any attack on Rumanian territory or independence, and he had outlined a plan whereby, if Britain, France and Russia would guarantee their support, he believed he could rally Bulgaria,

[1] *Izvestia*, March 11, 1939.
[2] The Polish Ambassador in London wrote to Colonel Beck on March 29, 1939, as follows : " It was foreseen that war between Russia and Germany would ensue, which would weaken both, not without affording indirect advantage to the Western Powers. The rapid succession of events by which Germany acquired valuable, bloodless booty showed the weakness of their arguments. . . . Serious misgivings arose when Germany, instead of losing face as a result of its action in the East, attained additional strength. From this conviction resulted an entirely new tone toward Germany " (*Third German White Book*, pp. 55-6.)
[3] See above, p. 32.

Poland, and the Balkan Entente (Rumania, Greece, Turkey, and Yugoslavia) in resistance to German aggression.

Lord Halifax is said to have favoured the plan and the Soviet proposals seemed to indicate the willingness of Russia to participate in drawing the line against further Nazi penetration in South-Eastern Europe. But there were other counsels. The " moderate school " opined that it was useless to try to stop Hitler short of the Near East and that resistance should be made on a line drawn from Turkey, through Syria and Palestine, to Egypt. Moreover, they feared that the consequence of a conference such as Russia had proposed would involve Britain in those "unspecified commitments operating under circumstances which cannot be foreseen" which the Prime Minister had deprecated at Birmingham on the previous night.

Faced with the necessity of making a clear-cut decision as between these conflicting views, Mr. Chamberlain hesitated — with the result that Rumania virtually capitulated and signed a new commercial agreement with Germany, and compromised — with the result that M. Maisky was informed that the Soviet proposal was considered " premature ".

Three days later (March 21) the President of the French Republic and Mme. Lebrun, attended by Georges Bonnet, arrived in London to return the state visit of the British Sovereigns to France in the previous July. Conferences ensued, and those who remembered that from the previous occasion had evolved the Runciman Mission to Prague regarded them with apprehension.

It was now that Mr. Chamberlain produced his alternative to the Russian proposals, a proposition drafted by himself,[1] whereby Britain, France, the U.S.S.R., and Poland should make a public declaration as to their common attitude towards aggression, and their intention, " if thought useful ", to consult together in the interests of mutual defence were any further acts of aggression believed to be imminent. With this suggestion, which completely failed to take cognizance of the tense situation then obtaining in Europe and the need for immediate positive action rather than procrastination, M. Bonnet agreed, but argued for the inclusion of Belgium, Holland, and Switzerland in the guarantee. The Soviet Government also agreed to the British proposal with some reluctance for its inadequacy, but suggested that, in order to give it as much weight and authority as possible, the Prime Ministers

[1] Feiling, p. 403.

of the States concerned should sign the Declaration in addition to the Foreign Secretaries.[1]

The whole plan was, however, made conditional on Poland's acceptance, and was rendered abortive by her attitude. Just as in October 1938 Colonel Beck refused to accept Ribbentrop's invitation to adhere to the Anti-Comintern Pact against Russia,[2] so now he refused to sign any document with the U.S.S.R. against Germany, even though, at that very moment, the pressure brought to bear in regard to the cession of Danzig and of territory in the Corridor was being perceptibly increased.[3]   Caught in the vortex of her own destiny, Poland was unable to choose between her traditional hatreds.

The new trend of British policy, of which such high hopes had been entertained on the morrow of Mr. Chamberlain's speech, appeared a week later to be doomed to extinction. On March 23 the Prime Minister cast further gloom on its prospects by announcing in the House of Commons that, while Britain would oppose, " by all means in her power ", a procedure under which independent States were subjected to such pressure under threat of force as to be obliged to yield up their independence, yet His Majesty's Government had " no desire to stand in the way of any reasonable efforts on the part of Germany to expand her export trade ", and was not " anxious to set up in Europe opposing blocs of countries with different ideas about the form of their internal administration ".[4]

What did this mean, men asked themselves ? Had the Prime Minister really meant what he said at Birmingham or not ? Was this reference to " blocs " a reversion to that similar phrase with which he had dismissed the Soviet proposals of the previous year ?[5] And, anyway, for what purpose could Germany now be preparing to expand her trade other than for that of war ?

While these questions perplexed the minds of many, Hitler was again in action. On March 22, under threat of immediate occupation by German troops, the territory of Memel was ceded by Lithuania to the Reich, and twenty-four hours later Germany assumed responsibility for " the protection of the political inde-

[1] For text of the proposed Four-Power Declaration, see *Polish White Book*, p. 69.
[2] See above, p. 335.
[3] *Polish White Book*, pp. 61-9 ; *Second German White Book*, p. 210.
[4] *House of Commons Debates*, March 23, 1939, col. 1462.
[5] See above, p. 39 (footnote).

pendence of the State of Slovakia ".[1] The *Wehrmacht* had now completed the tasks allotted under the Directive of October 21, 1938. There remained the supplementary Directive of November 26 — its objective, Danzig and the Corridor.

(iii)

March 21, 1939, was a fateful date in the history of Poland. On that day Ribbentrop summoned the Polish Ambassador in Berlin " in order to discuss Polish-German relations in their entirety ". The German Foreign Minister put forward demands for the cession of Danzig and the settlement of the Corridor question in far more forceful language than had so far been employed in their previous conversations. He repeated the offer of the German guarantee of Poland's frontiers, but added that any undertaking between Poland and Germany " would have to include explicit anti-Soviet tendencies ".[2]

On the same day the British Ambassador in Warsaw brought to the Ministry of Foreign Affairs the proposals for a Four-Power Declaration which would place Poland in definite alignment with the Soviet Union.

In facing this dilemma the counsels of Poland were divided. There were those who, in blind hatred of Russia, advocated an agreement with Germany. There were others who favoured the acceptance of Russian support in a qualified degree. Others again were as suspicious of the Western Powers as of either of Poland's great neighbours and feared that, under Soviet influence, Poland would be pushed by Anglo-French diplomacy into the position of playing cat's-paw for Moscow's chestnuts. Such a one was M. Arciszewski, the Under-Secretary of State, who roundly declared that " Poland would never fight merely for the interests of other Powers ".[3] And there were yet others who, though in theory favouring the acceptance of Anglo-French support, remained distrustful of the ability and the ultimate willingness of Britain and France, on their past record, to translate professions of zeal into terms of actual performance.

The views of this latter school were trenchantly expressed by

[1] For texts of the Agreements signed with Germany by Lithuania and Slovakia, see *Polish White Book*, pp. 59-61.

[2] *Polish White Book*, p. 61 ; *Second German White Book*, p. 210.

[3] *Second German White Book*, p. 213.

M. Lukasiewicz, the Ambassador in Paris, who wrote frankly to his Minister that " in view of the experience of the last twenty years, during which England and France not only never fulfilled any of their international obligations, but were never in a position conveniently to fulfil their own interests, it is impossible to believe that any State of Central or Eastern Europe, even those located on the other side of the Rome-Berlin Axis, can seriously consider the English proposals, unless England decides to commit acts which without doubt would confirm its decision to break off its relations with Germany ".[1]

Amid this tangled skein of conflicting advice Beck clung to the thread of his strange and paradoxical principle : " Not a millimetre nearer to Berlin than to Moscow ". In pursuit of this principle he had employed over the past six years every artifice of diplomatic navigation. With ingenious skill he had tacked and gone about, trimmed his sails, yawed and zigzagged, in a desperate effort to keep the Polish ship of state on a safe course between the Nazi Scylla and the Soviet Charybdis. In the course of his voyage he had violated most codes of conduct and might even be arraigned upon charges both of international piracy and barratry. In the end he was to encompass his own utter confusion,[2] but at the moment he still thought to weather the dangers of navigation by dint of superior steersmanship. Poland already possessed pacts of non-aggression with Germany and Russia and two treaties of alliance with France. It might therefore be possible to obtain the support of Britain as an accessory buttress to this already existing framework, thereby avoiding the necessity of declaring Poland's realignment with either side.

Such was the immediate reaction of the Polish Foreign Minister to the British proposals, but before he could put them into force there came the news of successive German *coups de main* in Memelland and Slovakia. Poland was already disgruntled that the occupation of Bohemia and Moravia should have been carried out without preliminary notification to Warsaw, and, moreover, Beck had hoped to draw Slovakia into the Polish orbit. With this end in view he had recognized Slovakia's independence on the very day on which it was proclaimed. Now that the acts of March 22 and 23 were also executed without previous warning,

---

[1] *Third German White Book*, p. 52.

[2] On September 17, 1939, after the military *débâcle* of Poland, Colonel Beck crossed the Polish frontier into Rumania. He died there in a sanatorium in 1944.

the Polish Government recognized definite danger signals, and, without delay, took steps for the greater protection and security of the country.

A partial mobilization was ordered, and to his Ambassador in London Colonel Beck sent urgent instructions to request the conclusion of a bilateral agreement in the spirit of the declaration which the British Government had themselves suggested [1] (March 23). The Foreign Minister also instructed M. Lipski, in view of the threatening German attitude, to make it clear to Ribbentrop that the negotiations which had been proceeding for some months in respect of the revision of the status of Danzig and the Corridor could only continue on the basis of free and equal discussion and not in an atmosphere of force and threats (March 25).

For a week there was no reaction from London to the Polish counter-proposal, and in the meantime M. Lipski had again seen Ribbentrop, who this time had given him " a very cold reception " Pretending to see in the Polish measures of mobilization a potential threat to Danzig, Ribbentrop said that he feared that the Führer would, on returning from Bavaria, come to the conclusion that an understanding with Poland was impossible of attainment. He declared, moreover, that " aggression against the Free City of Danzig would be regarded as an aggression against Germany itself ",[2] and caused this to be repeated in Warsaw. To this the Polish Government replied, with spirit, that for their part they would regard any attempt by the German Government or by the Senate of the Free City to change the *status quo* in Danzig as an act of aggression against Poland.[3]

The air was tense and electric in Berlin, in Danzig, and in Warsaw. The Führer was indeed furious on his return from Munich and uttered threats against Poland. Still there came no word from London until, on March 30, the British Ambassador in Warsaw, Sir Howard Kennard, called on Colonel Beck to give him the general views of the British Government on his proposal. What the Ambassador had to say was neither positive nor definite. In diplomatic parlance, his visit was of an " explorative nature ", not one calculated to bring great assurance to the harassed Colonel. And then, even as they talked, something happened. Sir Howard's First Secretary, Mr. Robin Hankey, interrupted the conversations to bring the Ambassador a fresh instruction from London to ask the Polish Government " whether they had any

---

[1] *Polish White Book*, p. 70.   [2] *Ibid.* p. 96.   [3] *Ibid.*

objection " to a British guarantee to meet any action which clearly threatened Polish independence and which Poland was accordingly prepared to resist by force. Colonel Beck saw no objection ; he gratefully accepted the British Government's proposal.[1]

In Britain the interval between the proposals of the Government for a joint declaration and the ultimate offer to Poland of a unilateral guarantee had not been without incident. The proposals had been delivered in Warsaw on March 21, and two days later Mr. Chamberlain had seen fit to make his particularly depressing statement in the House of Commons, a statement which had caused many to doubt the sincerity of his previous declaration of policy at Birmingham. However, events then began to happen with the rapidity of machine-gun fire.

The German annexation of Memelland and her declaration of protection over Slovakia were followed on March 24 by the arrival at the Foreign Office of Count Raczyński bearing Colonel Beck's request for an " immediate " bilateral non-aggression treaty with Britain. Simultaneously there began to flood from Paris, from Berlin, from Warsaw, and from Danzig, rumours and reports of Polish mobilization and German troop concentrations on the Pomeranian border. Finally it became known that Germany had presented Poland with a set of demands regarding the retrocession of Danzig and the right to construct an " extra-territorial " motor road and railway line across the Corridor, and that these had been rejected by the Polish Government.

The British Cabinet met daily at this moment of crisis. As Mr. Chamberlain later admitted : " We did not know that Poland might not be invaded within a term which could be measured by hours and not by days ".[2] There was the same reaction in Downing Street as there had been at the moment of the May crisis in 1938, and a corresponding demand for action. The Prime Minister swung diametrically away from the " moderates " in the Cabinet and far outstripped the fullest expectations of the " activists ".

The " activists " had advocated a stern declaration of general policy regarding future aggression ; Colonel Beck had asked for a bilateral agreement ; but Mr. Chamberlain in his new zeal,

---

[1] *Polish White Book*, pp. 71-2. No. 68.
[2] *House of Commons Debates*, October 3, 1939, coll. 1876-7.

born not of a sense of guilt but of indignation, went much further and offered far more — and, moreover, he carried the French with him, despite the objections of M. Bonnet. His reply to Colonel Beck's request constitutes one of the most remarkable public declarations in the history of British foreign policy, only comparable in originality to Mr. Churchill's proposal in June 1940 for the union of Britain and France.

By the declaration which the Prime Minister made to the House of Commons on March 31, His Majesty's Government placed in the hands of a foreign Power the ultimate decision as to whether or not Britain went to war. " In the event of any action which already threatened Polish independence, and which the Polish Government accordingly considered it vital to resist with national forces, His Majesty's Government would feel themselves bound at once to lend the Polish Government all support in their power. . . . I may add that the French Government have authorized me to make it plain that they stand in the same position as does His Majesty's Government." [1]

The immense importance of this declaration and the degree to which British policy had veered from its earlier bases may be judged from a comparison with those statements which Mr. Chamberlain had made in the House on March 24, 1938, and even at Birmingham. A year before, he had declared that " His Majesty's Government were not prepared to agree to any proposals which might result in Britain finding herself in a position where the decision to go to war should be automatically removed from the discretion of the Government " ; [2] at Birmingham he had explicitly omitted from British obligations any " new unspecified commitments operating under conditions which cannot be foreseen " ; [3] now, in one year, in two weeks, these reservations had been thrown to the winds and the decision to go to war had been placed unreservedly in the hands of a Power which had participated in the dismemberment of Czechoslovakia and whose record throughout the last twenty years had been, to say the least of it, equivocal. The circumstances of Mr. Chamberlain's conversion were as remarkable as had been the persistence of his previous intransigence.

But, as Mr. Duff Cooper had reminded the House during the Munich debate, it was not Belgium or Serbia for whom Britain

---

[1] *House of Commons Debates*, March 31, 1939, col. 2415.   [2] See above, p. 39.
[3] See above, p. 358.

fought in 1914, nor Czechoslovakia for whom she would have been fighting in 1938 ; nor did the guarantee which Mr. Chamberlain proclaimed merely represent a gesture of support to Poland. It was far more important than that. It was a declaration to the world that Britain, after grave travail, was captain of her soul again and that she stood once more four-square against the tempests of aggression.

Yet one cannot ignore the irony of the situation. It would have been so much easier to make out a *prima facie* case for appeasing Germany in the case of Poland than had been possible in the case of Czechoslovakia. The Sudetenland had never been part of the German Reich, whereas the Free City of Danzig was not only a German city but had only comparatively recently been separated from the Reich. It was true that the Polish claim to the control of Danzig was based on economic, strategic, and historical considerations, but Mr. Chamberlain and M. Daladier had calmly abandoned the economic and traditional life of Czechoslovakia to Germany, together with all that country's fortifications, regardless of the fact that they contained the secrets of the Maginot Line. Certainly the minorities structure within the Czechoslovak State had not been perfect, but Poland had consistently and notoriously refused to execute her obligations in respect of minorities, and, as long ago as 1934, had openly repudiated the provisions of the Minorities Treaties which she had signed in 1919–20.

Finally, having abandoned, in 1938, an industrious democracy, loyal to the principles of the League of Nations, and an untiring worker in the field of collective security, Britain and France in 1939 placed the decision as to their declaration of war in the hands of a State ruled by an incompetent and purblind oligarchy who preferred government by junta rather than by parliament, and who, in the years 1920–38, had embarked upon military or diplomatic forays against Germany, Russia, Lithuania, and Czechoslovakia which had resulted in no small accretion of territory.

That Mr. Chamberlain was ethically right in giving a guarantee to Poland there can be no more doubt than that he was ethically wrong in abandoning Czechoslovakia. But, on the face of things, taking into consideration his own record in the past and that of Poland, it was essentially difficult for Mr. Chamberlain to convince his potential enemies (Germany), his possible ally (Russia), his critical neighbour (America) — or even the Poles themselves

—that he had beaten his furled umbrella into a flaming sword, and that he himself had become a mighty warrior before the Lord. Yet Mr. Chamberlain had indeed performed this remarkable metamorphosis, and, when challenged on the meaning of his statement of March 31, he answered clearly and unequivocally.

" The Thunderer of Printing House Square " was still lowing in the accents of September 1938. In commenting, on the morrow, on Mr. Chamberlain's statement, it took occasion to emphasize that the Prime Minister's offer to Poland involved no blind acceptance of the *status quo* : " On the contrary, his repeated references to free negotiation imply that he thinks that there are problems in which adjustments are still necessary " ; the editorial added that Germany was " admittedly bound to be the most powerful Continental State ", and that the new obligation did not bind Great Britain " to defend every inch of the present frontiers of Poland. The key word in the declaration is not ' integrity ' but ' independence '. The independence of every negotiating State is what matters." [1]

There was a terrible similarity between these words and those of the famous *Times* editorial of September 7, 1938,[2] which had given so much encouragement to the Führer, and had publicly proclaimed the doom of Beneš. With Colonel Beck expected to arrive in London on April 3, it was imperative that this apparent incitement to Hitler to make Danzig a second Sudetenland should not go unchallenged.

Forthwith there came an inspired disclaimer from the Foreign Office in no uncertain terms. It expressed surprise that " attempts should have been made in London to minimize the Prime Minister's statement in the House of Commons. The statement is regarded as of outstanding importance, the meaning of which is perfectly clear and logical. No doubt is felt in official quarters that in present conditions the Polish Government will wish to keep His Majesty's Government fully informed, although the latter do not seek in any way to influence the Polish Government in the conduct of their relations with the German Government." [3] In other words, unless Warsaw saw fit to make a distinction between " independence " and " integrity " no pressure would be put upon her from London to do so.

The result of this frank warning, though it had little or no effect on Hitler, inspired reassurance and confidence in the mind

[1] *The Times*, April 1, 1939. [2] See above, p. 95. [3] *The Times*, April 3, 1939.

of Colonel Beck, who, in the course of his visit to London, agreed to transform the unilateral British guarantee into a reciprocal bilateral agreement (April 6).[1]

That the Axis leaders placed little reliance on either the sincerity or the efficacy of the transformation of British foreign policy was soon evident. That self-styled " Sword of Islam ", Benito Mussolini, promptly elected to deprive a small Moslem people of their independence. On April 7 Albania was occupied by Italian troops, who met little resistance, and a week later the crown of Albania was added to those of the Kingdom of Italy and the Empire of Ethiopia already worn somewhat precariously by Victor Emmanuel.

To this, perhaps the most contemptible example of pre-war Axis aggression, the response was a remarkable display of Anglo-French solidarity. Just as Lord Halifax's influence had asserted itself in the British Cabinet, so M. Daladier, who was enjoying one of his periods of forceful courage, had triumphed over the shiftiness of M. Bonnet. Now fully awakened to the imminence of danger, Britain and France were at this moment working in effective accord and, within a month of the annexation of Albania, the buckler of the Anglo-French unilateral guarantee had been extended first to Greece and Rumania (April 13), then to Denmark, Holland, and Switzerland (April 16).[2]

Yet in all this feverish activity and protestation there were lacking two factors which were essential if real conviction was to be established that a second last-minute capitulation by Britain and France was now impossible. Britain had not introduced compulsory military service and there was no indication of any real anxiety to obtain the co-operation of Russia.

Even among Britain's old allies and new protégés the absence of the first of these factors was a source of disquiet and suspicion. Without conscription, asked the French, how could Britain make

[1] " *Accord de garantie mutuelle anglo-polonaise. Bougre !* " was Anatole de Monzie's comment in his diary on April 6 (*Ci-devant*, p. 103).

[2] See the Prime Minister's statements to the House of Commons (*House of Commons Debates*, April 13, 1939, coll. 5-15 ; April 18, 1939, col. 165).

Both Switzerland and the Netherlands, fearing that the statement on the part of Britain and France would impair their traditional status of neutrality, refused to accept this offer of a guarantee.

That the French Cabinet were not unanimously behind M. Daladier in support of Britain's initiative is evident from Anatole de Monzie's diary entry for April 14, 1939 : " *A chaque annexation correspond un nouveau traité de garantie franco-anglais. Nous garantissons de proche en proche toutes les nations menacées. Annexation, garantie ! Jeu de raquette de la guerre* " (*Ci-devant*, p. 106).

good the promise given by her Secretary for War that, in the event of hostilities, a British Expeditionary Force in France would comprise 19 divisions? [1] And the same uncertainty was felt by many Poles. Britain's professed intentions might be sincere enough, but how to bridge the gap between profession and performance? [2]

In Berlin, on the other hand, it was the second factor, the absence of an accord with Russia, which gave the greatest cause for satisfaction. Perhaps the only sound advice that Ribbentrop had ever given his Führer had been that " you need never fear England until you find her talking about Russia as an ally. Then it means she is really going to war ", and there was no presently apparent reason to believe that the situation in London had undergone any material change from that which the German Chargé d'Affaires had reported on March 23, namely, that " in British Conservative circles, now as always, there exists an opposition — not to be underrated — to the admittance of Russia to the system planned ".[3]

Thus, when on April 1 the Führer spoke at Wilhelmshaven (from behind a bullet-proof glass shield, it was observed), he went no further than to warn the small States that " he who declares himself prepared to pull the chestnuts out of the fire on behalf of these Great Powers must expect to get his fingers burned ",[4] and this phrase was used by Ribbentrop as the text for a circular instruction to German diplomatic representatives as to how they should deal, in discussion, with the subject of the Anglo-French guarantees. They were not to raise the matter themselves, wrote the German Foreign Minister on April 12, but, should it arise in conversation, they were to reply : " We do not expect that any other States will allow themselves to be hoodwinked by Great Britain. If, nevertheless, some other Governments were to snap at the British bait, we should regret this in the interest of the States concerned." [5]

Though the new and more spirited note in British policy provided a useful springboard from which Joseph Goebbels could

---

[1] See above, p. 325.

[2] The Polish Ambassador in Paris had written to Colonel Beck on March 29 apropos of the original British proposals for a Four-Power Declaration : " If, a few days following the proposals of Warsaw, England had assembled her fleet, putting into effect obligatory military service . . . then even such an unacceptable English proposal as that which was made to us could have been considered a proof of good faith and loyal collaboration " (*Third German White Book*, p. 52).

[3] *Second German White Book*, p. 296.

[4] Baynes, vol. ii, p. 1596.   [5] *Second German White Book*, pp. 308-9.

launch an internal propaganda campaign on the dangers of
Einkreisung, it is to be believed that the Führer and his associates
were not at this juncture unduly perturbed by the unilateral
guarantees so lavishly offered by Britain and France. Certainly
Hitler did not permit them to alter his plans in regard to Poland.
For as early as April 3 (the day on which Beck arrived in London)
a directive was issued from Keitel to the *Wehrmacht* for " Operation
White " directed against Poland, wherein was developed a time
schedule which was to remain unaltered until the eve of the
outbreak of hostilities.[1]

(iv)

By the middle of April 1939 Britain found that, whereas a
month before she had stood pledged solely, in Europe, to the defence of France and Belgium, her obligations now stretched from
the North Sea to the Black Sea and the Aegean. Within this vast
expanse were half a dozen States, any one of whom, should they
be menaced by aggression and elect to resist, could automatically
plunge Britain and France into war. The " Peace Bloc against
Aggression " had developed piecemeal as the tempo of events
dictated rather than in accordance with any carefully prepared
and co-ordinated plan, and to meet her greatly increased commitments Britain was in no better position in regard to armaments
and allies than she had been when Germany had annexed Bohemia
and Moravia a month before.[2]

It was at last borne in upon Mr. Chamberlain that, in order
that these promises, which he had made in all sincerity on
Britain's behalf, might not be merely symbolic and illusory, two
conditions were essential : first, he must take the plunge in
introducing conscription, and, secondly, he must overcome the
inherent aversion of himself and his party for Russia and make
a further approach to Moscow for her co-operation.[3]

With regard to conscription, the Prime Minister had been
under constant sniping fire from the dissident Tories ever since

---

[1] *International Military Tribunal Document*, C-120.
[2] At this time the British Regular Army had a strength of 204,000 men, and the
Territorial Army, which had recently been doubled in strength, totalled 247,000.
(See statement by the Secretary of State for War, *House of Commons Debates*, April 27,
1939, col. 1447.)
[3] For the account of the approach to Russia and consequences, see the following
chapter.

the annexation of Bohemia and Moravia, but he had not allowed himself to be stampeded out of his usual cautious approach.[1] Indeed his caution in approaching the question of compulsory service is in curious contrast to his prodigality in the matter of offering guarantees. Caution was certainly justified, but not to the point of procrastination. It was inevitable that opposition would be aroused, but the sooner this was overcome the better.

The Prime Minister met his first opposition within his own Cabinet, where there was considerable doubt in the minds of some on whether so fundamental a measure should be introduced without first consulting the electorate, more particularly in view of the fact that the Prime Minister had recently reaffirmed Lord Baldwin's pledge that compulsion would not be introduced in peace-time. This argument was clearly academic, since if, as Mr. Chamberlain said later, the unilateral guarantee to Poland had been given in circumstances which had led the Government to think that an armed attack upon Poland was possibly only a matter of days, there was manifestly no time to be spared for the wearisome and distracting business of a General Election.

Under the compulsion of events the opposition among Mr. Chamberlain's colleagues was overcome, it being realized that a constructive gesture was demanded by the occasion. That this was undoubtedly true may be judged from the fact that

---

[1] Immediately after the occupation of Bohemia and Moravia a meeting of the dissident Tories, called to consider their course of action in the grave situation thus created, decided to put down a motion for the immediate introduction of conscription. Notice of this was placed on the Order Paper of the House of Commons in the names of Mr. Churchill, Mr. Eden, Mr. Duff Cooper, Mr. Harold Macmillan, Mr. Amery, Viscount Wolmer, and thirty others, on March 29, 1939, in the following terms : " In view of the grave dangers by which Great Britain and the Empire are now threatened following upon the successive acts of aggression in Europe and increasing pressure on smaller States, this House is of opinion that these menaces can only successfully be met by the vigorous prosecution of the foreign policy recently outlined by the Foreign Secretary ; it is further of opinion that for this task a National Government should be formed on the widest possible basis, and that such a Government should be entrusted with full powers over the nation's industry, wealth and man-power, to enable this country to put forward its maximum military effort in the shortest possible time ".

An amendment to the motion was at once tabled, at the suggestion of the Conservative Whips, in the names of 180 " back-bencher " supporters of the Government, as follows : " Leave out from ' this House ' to end, and add ' affirms its complete confidence in the Prime Minister and deprecates any attempt at the present critical time to undermine the confidence of the House and the country in the Prime Minister and the Government ' ".

Both the motion and the amendment remained on the Order Paper until after the Prime Minister had made his own motion for conscription a month later.

the American press was beginning to refer to the British lion as " the lion of least resistance ".

The last half of April, therefore, witnessed events and decisions of importance. On April 19 Lord Halifax, in the House of Lords, clearly reaffirmed the Government's policy in regard to resistance and aggression,[1] thereby replying to the suggestions for appeasement and negotiation put forward by *The Times*. A day later, in the Lower House, the Prime Minister announced the decision to set up a Ministry of Supply, a step which he had steadfastly refused to take during the last three years, though it had frequently been proposed during that period,[2] and, perhaps because it had been a favourite project of the Liberal Party, he made the not very happy choice of a Simonite Liberal, Mr. Leslie Burgin, as the first Minister.[3]

The principal event, however, did not take place until April 26, when the Prime Minister gave notice of the Government's intention to introduce a Bill for a limited measure of compulsory service, coupled with assurances that armaments profits would be limited, and that, in case of war, profiteering would be penalized.[4]

It had been decided by the Cabinet that Sir Nevile Henderson, who had been recalled for consultation after the occupation of Prague, should return to Berlin to notify the German Government of so revolutionary a departure in British policy as the imposition of conscription in peace-time, and he made his notification at midday on the 26th.[5] If it was hoped that this message and the information which it contained would have a sobering effect upon the Führer, those who entertained such hopes were doomed to disappointment. The sequel to Mr. Chamberlain's statement was one which could not fail to prove a source of mingled satisfaction and contempt to Hitler.

In the debate which followed the introduction of the Government's conscription measures the Labour and Liberal Parties gave

[1] *House of Lords Debates*, April 19, 1939, coll. 684-98.

[2] Between 1936 and 1939 the Liberal Party, under Sir Archibald Sinclair, broached the subject of a Ministry of Supply on eight occasions : these proposals were consistently opposed by both Mr. Baldwin and Mr. Chamberlain.

[3] The Ministry of Supply did not, in fact, begin to function before August 1, 1939 — one month before the outbreak of war.

[4] A White Paper (Cmd. 6046) giving particulars of the armaments profits tax was published on June 20, 1939, on which day a motion for its authorization was tabled in the Ways and Means Committee of the House of Commons.

[5] Henderson, pp. 230-31.

as notable an exhibition of blind prejudice as had ever been displayed by the most myopic supporters of appeasement in the post-Munich period. In the previous October the Opposition had criticized the Munich policy with fervour and indignation. In the recent weeks which had followed the occupation of Prague they had questioned and attacked the Government for lack of resolution and fortitude, and had expressed doubts about the sincerity of the reversal of British policy after the Birmingham speech of March 17. Now, when it was within their power to accord to friend and foe alike on the continent of Europe a demonstration of Britain united in resistance to aggression ; when proof could have been afforded that Britain was at one in her readiness to make definite sacrifices in the cause of peace, to take practical steps to make good her pledges and protests, the Labour and Liberal Parties adopted an attitude of doctrinal pacifism and party prejudice.

The Prime Minister had appealed to the Opposition to avoid a hasty decision, to refrain from an irrevocable determination to resist the Government's proposals and thereby spread doubt in the minds of potential enemies and potential allies as to the willingness of Labour to play a full part in carrying through a policy towards aggression which they themselves had always advocated.[1] It was all to no purpose. In response to the Government's proposals — which amounted to no more than a request for power to call up about 200,000 young men to train in preparation for war — Mr. Attlee responded with a negative amendment : " We are opposed to the introduction of conscription because we believe that, so far from strengthening this country, it will weaken it and divide it at a time when it should be strong and united. . . . In the background of conscription, as every trade unionist knows, there is the danger of industrial conscription. . . ."[2] This country provides the greatest fleet in the world," continued Mr. Attlee. " It has a rapidly growing Air Force. It has to provide munitions . . . for its Allies, and it cannot, in addition to that, provide a great Continental Army." [3]

Equally negative was the Liberal leader, Sir Archibald Sinclair, who deplored the Bill as a measure which would " split

---

[1] *House of Commons Debates*, April 26, 1939, coll. 1150-8.

[2] It is ironical to remember that when industrial conscription was eventually introduced in 1940 it was carried out with admirable and ruthless efficiency by a trade union leader — Mr. Ernest Bevin.

[3] *House of Commons Debates*, April 27, 1939, coll. 1353-9.

the country " and create a " deep, dangerous and unnecessary cleavage in public opinion ".[1] It was not surprising that so unhelpful a contribution should call down upon it the wrath of Mr. Churchill, who reminded the House that " no one has been a more strenuous advocate of the enlargement of our responsibilities and of the vigorous championship of our rights and interests than my right honourable friend [Sir Archibald Sinclair], and it is somewhat discouraging to find that, at the first really awkward fence . . . with which he has been confronted, he has found it necessary to take such a very strong attitude of opposition ".[2]

Mr. Arthur Greenwood, in winding up the debate for Labour, predicted public revolt against the measure and declared that to make a break in the system of voluntary service " at the cost of creating new divisions inside this country is not merely fantastic ; it is criminal ".[3]

At the First Reading of the Bill on April 27, 138 Socialists and 7 Liberals voted against it. The debate on the Second Reading did not open until May 1, but in the meantime Hitler had addressed the Reichstag (April 28).[4]

His speech took full account of any possible weakness in the British, French, and Polish will to resist. The Führer left no weak spot unprobed. He made his first public demand for the return of Danzig to the Reich and denounced the German-Polish Agreement of 1934, but he offered Poland in exchange a twenty-five-year non-aggression pact. He simultaneously and unilaterally denounced the Anglo-German Naval Agreement of 1935, but coupled this blow with sugary expressions of his respect for Britain and her contribution to culture. He reaffirmed to France his pledge that the return of Saar Territory had done away with all territorial problems between herself and Germany and hailed this as a gesture on his part towards the removal of any cause of tension. " If this tension has nevertheless arisen," he warned his hearers, " the responsibility does not lie with Germany, but with those international elements which systematically produce such tension in order to save their capitalistic interests." [5] Finally, at con-

---

[1] *House of Commons Debates*, April 27, 1939, coll. 1361-70.
[2] *Ibid.* col. 1370.   [3] *Ibid.* coll. 1437-45.
[4] Baynes, vol. ii, pp. 1605-56.
[5] " They are convinced at the Wilhelmstrasse that, in the mind of the Führer, Danzig is a means, but not an end ", wrote M. Coulondre to Georges Bonnet on June 1. " They stress the fact that, in his speech of April 28, Herr Hitler mentioned Alsace with a certain reticence " (*French Yellow Book*, p. 171).

siderable length, he poured ridicule and heavy irony on the proposal of President Roosevelt (April 14) for a ten years' truce and on the list of some thirty countries which the President had suggested should be guaranteed against aggression.

It was a subtle, brutal speech and not one which might have been calculated to inspire confidence in the Führer's pacific intentions. It should, indeed, have sounded a note of alarm throughout the world, seeing that it now contained fresh terri-torial demands in Europe, but when Parliament reassembled on May 1, to renew its discussion of the Military Service Bill, it was clear that the Labour Party remained unmoved by this additional storm-warning from Berlin; they were as adamant as before in their opposition.

In vain did Mr. Eden appeal for the passage of the measure without a division, in order to show to " nations living on the edge of danger and much more conscious of the immediate conflict that might arise at any moment even than we are in this country " [1] the determination of Britain to resist aggression. Nothing could deter the Labour Party from their fanatical resistance.

" We have lost, and Hitler has won," announced Mr. Aneurin Bevan. " He has deprived us of a very important English insti-tution—voluntary service. . . . What argument have they [the Government] to persuade the young men to fight except in another squalid attempt to defend themselves against a redistri-bution of international swag ? " [2] And Sir Stafford Cripps de-manded that, as a preliminary to legislation for conscription of man-power, there should be conscription of wealth, democratiza-tion of the forces, safeguards for trades union rights (including the right to strike) and nationalization of land.[3]

Other members of the Labour Party gave vent to even more extreme views. " You may take it from me that it will not come off," exclaimed Mr. David Kirkwood. " There will be no con-scription on the Clyde. . . . I will do all I can to get not only the engineers on the Clyde but the engineers throughout Britain to down tools against conscription " ; [4] and Mr. Neil Maclean proclaimed : " I shall advise mothers not to allow their boys to go and I shall advise the boys not to be conscripted." [5]

The final argument adduced by Mr. Attlee on behalf of his

[1] *House of Commons Debates*, May 4, 1939, col. 2143.
[2] *Ibid.* col. 2136.   [3] *Ibid.* May 8, 1939, coll. 110-16.
[4] *Ibid.* May 4, 1939, col. 2190.   [5] *Ibid.* May 8, 1939, col. 128.

party was that "it is very dangerous to give Generals all the men they want", and he added the suspicion that "the feeling behind this Bill is not the desire to meet the immediate needs of this country but the desire for conscription. That desire will grow. . . . In the name of liberty our liberties may be destroyed." [1]

On the Second Reading of the Bill (May 8) the Labour Party increased their vote against it from 138 to 145. The Liberals, on the other hand, were divided ; five voted with the Government and the rest abstained. In committee the Labour Party forced twenty-four separate divisions and a final division on the Third Reading, which was thus delayed until May 18.

In the meantime, while precious days were lost in fruitless debate, for the passage of the Conscription Act was in any case a foregone conclusion in view of the Conservative majority, Hitler had taken his decision for war. On May 10 orders were issued for the capture of economic installations in Danzig, and six days later the *Wehrmacht* was alerted for "Operation White" (the attack on Poland) at any moment before September 1.[2] But the decisive note of intention was not sounded until May 23.

On this day the Führer summoned the chiefs of his armed services to the Reichskanzlei and there addressed to them a speech which ranks second only in importance to his oration of November 5, 1937.[3]   There were present Göring and Raeder, Keitel and von Brauchitsch, Halder, Milch, and Bodenschatz and seven other senior military and naval officers,[4] besides the Führer's indefatigable adjutant, Colonel Schmundt, who had kept the records of "Operation Green".

To this audience Hitler pronounced a lengthy discourse in which he showed clearly that he was prepared for war.[5] He had abandoned the idea of using Poland as a cat's-paw against Russia and was determined now upon her immediate destruction. Poland was no "supplementary enemy" ; she would always be

[1] *House of Commons Debates*, May 8, 1939, col. 152.
[2] *International Military Tribunal Document*, C-126.   [3] See above, p. 11.
[4] Others present were Rear-Admiral Schniewindt, Colonel Jeschonnek, Colonel Warlimont, Captain Engel, Lieutenant-Commander Albrecht, and Captain von Below.
[5] See minutes of the meeting kept by Colonel Schmundt (*International Military Tribunal Document*, L-79).

on the side of Germany's adversaries. Danzig, therefore, was not
the object of the dispute at all. " It is a question of our *Lebensraum* in the East, of securing our food supplies and of the settlement
of the Baltic problem."

" There will be war," he told them. " We cannot expect a
repetition of the Czech affair. Our task is to isolate Poland.
The success of the isolation will be decisive, for the Polish problem
is inseparable from conflict with the West. There is no question
of sparing Poland." But the war with Poland could only be
successful if the Western Powers kept out of it. There must be
no simultaneous conflict with Britain and France.

The Führer went on to analyse the position of the other Powers.
He recognized France as being but the follower of Britain.
" England is the driving force against Germany. The British are
proud, courageous, tenacious, firm in resistance, and gifted as
organizers. They know how to exploit every new development.
They have the love of adventure and bravery of the Nordic race.
The war with England will be a life-and-death struggle. The
aim will always be to force England to her knees, but she will not
be forced to capitulate in one day. I doubt the possibility of a
peaceful settlement with England. We must prepare ourselves
for the conflict."

If England and France intended that the German attack on
Poland should lead to a general conflict, they would support
Belgium and Holland in their neutrality and would make
them build fortifications with the ultimate intention of bringing
them into the war as allies against the Reich. This eventuality
must be avoided. Dutch and Belgian declarations of neutrality must be ignored and their airfields occupied with lightning
speed.

And then Hitler turned to Russia, with whom, he said,
economic relations were only possible if political relations improved. " If there were an alliance of France, Britain and Russia
against Germany, Italy and Japan, I would be constrained to
attack England and France with a few annihilating blows.
But," he added significantly, " it is not impossible that Russia
will show herself disinterested in the destruction of Poland."

To the attainment of these aims Hitler directed the whole
energies of his planning staff. " Secrecy is the decisive requirement for success. Our object must be kept secret even from Italy
or Japan." He himself must reserve the right to give the final

order for attack. "We shall not be forced into a war, but we shall not be able to avoid one."

A more barefaced blue-print of aggression could scarcely be imagined, yet the Führer's speech was more vitally important than merely this. For it held the germ, not only of his long-term policy, but of his policy in the immediate future.

CHAPTER TWO

THE RUSSIAN SPHINX

(i)

WHAT had occurred to make the Führer so emphatically certain on May 23 that Germany could expect " no repetition of the Czech affair ", and that " there will be war " ? The answer lies in his final statement that " it is not impossible that Russia will show herself disinterested in the destruction of Poland " ; it lies in events which had taken place in London and in Moscow, and in Ribbentrop's oft-repeated advice : " You need never fear Britain until you hear her talking of Russia as an ally. Then it means she is really going to war."

The decision of Mr. Chamberlain, taken in mid-April, to resume negotiations with the U.S.S.R. initiated a period of fantastically complicated transactions between London, Paris, and Moscow on the one hand, and Berlin and Moscow on the other, which were to constitute a penultimate phase of the years between the wars, and were to conclude in the complete discomfiture of the Western Powers.

Fully to appreciate the intricacies and apparent inconsistencies of this phase, it is necessary to recapitulate the position of the protagonists *vis-à-vis* one another, and to realize that the transcending factor in this whole period was profound and ineradicable suspicion on all sides. From April to August 1939 these groups of negotiators were involved in bargaining for the issue of peace and war. Yet each transacting party was a prey within itself to a fierce conflict between the rival claims of prejudice and misgiving versus those of self-interest and security. Few negotiations in history have been conducted in such a spirit of mutual mistrust among all parties.

Within the Anglo-French *bloc* the suspicion and fear of Russia were inherent. Despite the halcyon periods of the Year of Recognition (1924) and Russia's " Return to Europe " ten years later, there had remained the dread of Bolshevist propaganda and the impact of the Comintern upon the bourgeois-capitalist

388

structure of Western Europe.   In Britain the antagonism toward
Russia was as deeply centred in the Left as in the Right, for
whereas the Conservatives were separated from Communism by
ideological beliefs and ways of life which were mutually exclusive,
the Labour Party, in their capacity as the foundation-stone of the
Second International, regarded Moscow with doctrinal hostility.
To those who believed in the pure doctrine of Marxian Socialism
the Bolshevist ideology was a thing of perversion and distortion,
and, moreover, the Labour Party were fully aware that their way
of life was as much a target for Communist attacks as was that
of the Tories.

Thus, though separated on divers issues, many Conservatives
and Socialists entertained a common mistrust of Russia, but for
different reasons.   As the party in power the Conservatives
naturally came under fire from the Labour Opposition for their
tardiness in opening negotiations with Russia, but it is interesting
to speculate on whether, had the roles been reversed, the Socialists
would have been any more eager in their approach to Moscow
or that their approach would have been crowned with any greater
success.

In France the position was different.   The Popular Front of
M. Blum had wedded Communism with Socialism in an uneasy
" marriage of inconvenience ".   Its result had been to accentuate
the differences between the two participants of the Left, and the
" New Deal " legislation which they enacted had terrified the
Right into pacifism and reaction.

In Conservative circles, both in Britain and in France, there
was a deep-seated conviction that Russia wished to precipitate a
European war, from which she would remain aloof, and which
would result in the destruction or collapse of the capitalist system.
On the rubble and ruins of the bourgeois-capitalism Moscow
would erect a Dictatorship of the Proletariat which, though
differing from that of National Socialism, would be no better
and might indeed prove worse.   In addition, there was a strong
belief that, even if she wished to do so, Russia could not make an
effective military contribution.[1]

---

[1] That this general feeling was shared by Mr. Chamberlain personally may be
seen from his diary entry for March 26, 1939 : " I must confess to the most profound
distrust of Russia.   I have no belief whatever in her ability to maintain an effective
offensive, even if she wanted to.   And I distrust her motives, which seem to me to have
little connection with our ideas of liberty, and to be concerned only with getting
everyone else by the ears " (Feiling, p. 403).

Herein lies the germ of the antagonism toward the Czechs which existed in British and French Government circles during the Munich crisis and which made for a greater sympathy with Germany than would otherwise have been possible. The Nazi propaganda line that Czechoslovakia was but a pawn of the Soviet Union fell upon fertile ground both in London and in Paris, and there were many who were convinced that Russia, despite many professions of good faith, would not — or could not — have sent adequate assistance to Czechoslovakia once she had incited her to armed resistance and thereby provoked a war. In France the *bellicisme* of Moscow was the more suspect since it was the Communist Party alone which voted against the Munich Agreement in the Chamber of Deputies.

As a corollary to this there emerged the hope that if only German expansion could be directed toward the East it would cease to threaten Western civilization and the Russian trick might be turned against themselves. The on-march of German penetration would sooner or later dissipate its force on the steppes of Russia in a struggle which would exhaust both combatants for many years to come. This thought had existed in Conservative circles until the annexation of Bohemia and Moravia, and it was naturally no easy task for them to acquire the disposition of mind prerequisite for the conclusion of agreement or alliance with the Soviet Union.

The attitude of Germany to the Soviet Union was that of a split personality. From the days of Frederick the Great and the Empress Elizabeth the history of Russo-German relations had been characterized by a series of alienations distinguished for their bitterness, and *rapprochements* remarkable for their warmth.[1] Bismarck, however, when he had unified Germany and made her independent of both France and Russia, did not cease to preach the doctrine of Russian friendship, partly in deference to the prevailing dread of a " two-front war ", but also in the sincere belief in the " manifest destiny " of Germany and Russia to divide world power between them, and confident, not without reason, that together the two Powers could accomplish anything they so desired.

With the departure of Bismarck there grew up in the German

[1] See " The Course of Russo-German Relations, 1919–1939 ", by J. W. Wheeler-Bennett, in *Foreign Affairs*, October 1946.

Foreign Ministry and in the General Staff two schools of thought, between which existed an unbridgeable gulf and a passionate jealousy, and there developed that battle for power between those of the Eastern school who would follow the old Prince's policy of collaboration with Russia, and those of the Pan-German school, who favoured the aggrandizement of Germany, if necessary at Russia's expense.

In the course of the battle it was the victory of the Pan-German school which materially contributed to the outbreak of the First World War and it was this same school which dictated the rapacious terms of Brest-Litovsk, whereby Russia was deprived of the Baltic Provinces, together with Finland, Georgia and the Ukraine. Had Germany been ultimately victorious against the West in 1918, there existed plans for the complete elimination of Russia as a Great Power by means of partition and further annexation.[1]

This contest of thought and policy regarding Russia, which was rekindled in the fierce conflicts of the Weimar period, persisted under the Third Reich ; although the anti-Russian forces were greatly augmented by the ideological hostility of National Socialism to Communism, and although Hitler himself espoused in all ardour the annexationist views of Ludendorff and the Pan-Germans, the advocates of an understanding with Russia were not completely silenced, albeit at some danger to themselves.

Nor was the Führer entirely insensible to their point of view. His hatred of Communism was genuine and fanatical, his intention to establish in the fullness of time a German *Lebensraum* amid the rich black soil of the Ukraine and the riches of the Urals was sincere and fundamental, but he, like Bismarck, was not anxious to contend with a " two-front " war either in foreign affairs or in military operations, and, like Wilhelm II, he dreaded a successful development of the *Einkreisung* of Germany.

Hitler had been alarmed at the united front between Britain, France, and Russia on the occasion of the crisis of May 1938. He had turned his energies to destroying it and had apparently accomplished this with the Munich Agreement, which had rebuffed Russia and isolated Poland, while driving the Western Powers into a fastness of complacency. The Führer accepted as a cardinal factor of his foreign policy that there should be no

[1] See *Brest-Litovsk ; the Forgotten Peace*, by J. W. Wheeler-Bennett. (London, 1938.)

rapprochement between the Western Powers and the Soviet Union, and, from his observation of men and affairs in London and in Paris, he had not believed that this was either probable or possible. The failure of the earlier tripartite discussions which had immediately followed his coup in Bohemia and Moravia had confirmed this view. But, should the danger arise, it must be met with every weapon within the Nazi armoury of deceit and duplicity.   At whatever cost, the destruction of the Polish State, which was now his immediate objective, must be effected without Soviet interference. Therefore he watched London and he watched Moscow.

Over against these two contestant groups stood Russia, a dark-veiled mystery, enigmatic and sphinx-like. Ever since the Revolution of November 1917, the Bolsheviks had stood in fear and suspicion of the Western World. Both Lenin and Stalin knew well enough that by their actions and their policies they had declared an ideological war upon the rest of the world ; a war which was deathless ; a war which, though there might be long periods of truce, could not be concluded until one side or the other had gone down to irrevocable defeat.

They believed that in the long run every man's hand in Europe and in the world was against the U.S.S.R. and the Comintern, and that, though for reasons of their own the Western Powers (including Germany) might from time to time court Russian assistance in the interests of their internecine quarrels, there was no basic sincerity in their approaches, and that, could these quarrels be composed, however temporarily, there was the ever-present danger of a combined attack upon Russia by the forces of Capitalism and Bourgeoisie.

In these circumstances, the watchwords of the Soviet Union had become " Suspicion " and " Security " — suspicion of all men and security for Russia — and this formula had guided every Soviet act throughout the Munich crisis and long before. The danger of the Nazi menace had been recognized and appreciated in Moscow far earlier than in London or in Paris, for the sufficient reason that Moscow realized that Russia must be the ultimate enemy of the Third Reich, and not only doctrinally but politically. The ideological chasm between National Socialism and Communism was in itself a sufficient cause, but far more important was it that only at the expense of Russia could Germany's ambitions for *Lebensraum* be realized in their ultimate entirety.

Austria, Czechoslovakia, Memel, and Poland were but stepping-stones to the Baltic lands, the Ukraine, and the Urals, and eventually to world domination, a fact of which Moscow was only too vividly aware.

To combat this menace Russia was as equally ready as Germany to employ every artifice of diplomatic circumvention. If the Western democracies were prepared to resist Nazi aggression, well and good, Russia would participate in such resistance ; but if Britain and France were ready to acquiesce in Nazi aggression and to regard the deflection of this menace to another quarter as a desirable policy, then Russia would be forced back upon her own resources and must employ such means as were presented to her hand.

It was in this spirit that the Soviet Union had made her Return to Europe in 1934 and it was in this spirit that she had persisted until the Munich Settlement. Her choice lay between war with Germany, in association with Britain and France, or isolation and dependence upon her resources in order to build up her defences and her military machine against the day when the Nazi attack should come. That these were her alternative policies she had made abundantly clear during the Czech crisis.[1] The Munich Agreement had seemed to convey the answer of the Western Powers.[2] The events of the succeeding months had confirmed Soviet suspicion that Britain and France " strove to keep Germany from the West only by turning her to the East ". Finally, the half-hearted tone of the abortive negotiations of March 1939 had strengthened her conviction that, even in their own disillusionment regarding Nazi intentions, the leaders of Britain and France were profoundly unhappy at the necessity of

---

[1] Mr. Harold Nicolson recorded in his diary on August 22, 1938, on which day he lunched with the Soviet Ambassador : " He [M. Maisky] says that . . . Russia is profoundly disillusioned with the Western democracies. If we and France went to war on behalf of the Czechs, then Russia would help. But if we abandon Czecho-slovakia then Russia will become isolationist."

[2] On October 4, 1938, the Soviet Government issued an official communiqué in which the following statement occurred : " In the course of the interviews of M. Bonnet with M. Souritz and of Lord Halifax with M. Maisky, which took place during the final period [of the Munich crisis], the two Ambassadors of the Soviet Union were given no information other than what had appeared in the press. There was no sort of a conference and still less an agreement between the Governments of the U.S.S.R., France and England with regard to the fate of the Czechoslovak Republic or to the question of concessions to the aggressor. Neither France nor England consulted the U.S.S.R., but confined themselves merely to informing the Soviet Government of what had already happened."

collaboration with Russia, and would approach it with distaste and reservation.

(ii)

Such was the background against which the closing scenes of the pre-war drama were played ; a drama in which Britain and France were to vie with Germany for the favour of Russia.[1] It began haltingly, but the tempo quickened to feverish speed, ending with a crescendo of tragedy.

By mid-April Mr. Chamberlain had brought himself again to the point of seeking Russian co-operation, without which it was evident that the guarantees which Britain and France had offered to various potential victims of aggression in Eastern Europe lacked any effective power of implementation. In reaching this decision Mr. Chamberlain was influenced both by this clear and indisputable fact and also by the growing demand within the country that the " Peace Bloc ", which the British Government had announced its intention of forming against Nazi aggression, should be further cemented by an agreement with Russia.[2]

This demand was reflected in the rising tide of criticism in the House of Commons. When, on April 13, the Prime Minister announced the extension of the Anglo-French guarantees to Rumania and Greece and was on the point of sitting down without having made any reference to the Soviet Union, he was greeted with cries of " What about Russia ? " from both sides of the House. Mr. Chamberlain replied evasively in his favourite formula of triple negatives. If he had not mentioned Russia, he assured them, it did not mean that the Government were not keeping in the closest touch with representatives of that country.[3]

This was indeed true. M. Maisky had seen Lord Halifax and Sir Robert Vansittart quite frequently during the last few

[1] In dealing with this period the historian is hampered by the absence of any official documentary material. Neither the British, nor the French, nor the Soviet Government have yet made public their diplomatic despatches of the time, and, so far, the captured German documents are not available. The account of the Anglo-Russian negotiations in the third volume of the *History of Diplomacy*, published in Moscow in 1946 by the State Publishing House for Political Literature (Gospolitcizdal), may be regarded as semi-official, but it contains no textual material and gives no details of the German-Soviet negotiations.

Of the studies of the period which have so far appeared, that included by Professor Namier in his *Diplomatic Prelude, 1938–1939*, is the most complete and the most reliable.

[2] A Gallup Poll in Britain during the month of April resulted in 92 per cent of those canvassed declaring in favour of an alliance with the U.S.S.R. (*New York Herald-Tribune*, May 4, 1939.)   [3] *House of Commons Debates*, April 13, 1939, col. 15.

weeks, but nothing concrete had come of these conversations. Now, however, on April 14, the Soviet Ambassador was received again, and to him was put the request that Russia should make a unilateral declaration guaranteeing Poland and Rumania. This proposal was repeated on the following day by the British Ambassador in Moscow.

The Soviet reply was made on April 17, and went far beyond the scope of the British request. Deeply distrustful of London, Paris, and Berlin alike, and firmly convinced that she herself was the ultimate aim of Nazi aggression, the Soviet Union sought to provide for her own protection, while at the same time erecting an edifice of general security. In reply to the restricted request of Britain for a unilateral guarantee to two Powers, Moscow proposed a triple pact of mutual assistance between France, Great Britain, and Russia, a military convention reinforcing such a pact, and a triple guarantee of all the border States from the Baltic to the Black Sea.

The Russian reply was starkly realistic. It faced Britain and France with the quandary of whether, in their opposition to German aggression, they were prepared to become full partners in an alliance with the Soviet Union — and all that that implied. Moreover, in demanding a guarantee for all the border States, the Soviet Government had touched on a point of political and strategic importance. The Baltic lands represented to Germany a Naboth's vineyard and to Russia a *terra irredenta*. Ceded by Russia and annexed by Germany after the Peace of Brest-Litovsk, they had later achieved and preserved an uneasy independence. But neither the German nor the Russian General Staffs had forgotten Marshal von Hindenburg's famous reply to Baron von Kühlmann when, on the eve of his departure for the Brest-Litovsk Conference in December 1917, the German Foreign Minister had asked why the Field-Marshal so particularly wanted the eastern border States for Germany — " I need them," Hindenburg had replied in his deep growling voice, " I need them for the manœuvring of my left wing in the next war." [1]

In the Soviet concept of Russian security Germany must be kept out of the Baltic States at all costs, for, with the Germans in Kovno and Riga and Tallinn, the fate of Leningrad might well be sealed. The Russian desire was to develop for herself an over-all military alliance with the Western Powers and a defence in depth

[1] Wheeler-Bennett, *Brest-Litovsk*, p. 109.

on her own Western border. For this purpose it was necessary to bring not only Poland and Rumania but also the Baltic States and Finland into one gigantic framework of strategy, and, since Russia would be the dominant military influence within this combination, she would inevitably exercise a certain political control also.

Confronted with the Soviet counter-proposals and all that they implied, the British and French Governments hesitated in consternation, for they saw therein merely an attempt to expand Russian influence in Eastern Europe. Many believed that, even if Moscow's conditions were granted and the Triple Alliance should be called into operation, Russia would simply march her troops into the border States and remain there, without fighting. Britain and France would thereby be placed in the position of condoning aggression by an ally on an even grander scale than that proclaimed by Germany.

Moreover, the reaction of Europe as a whole was largely unfavourable. Poland and Rumania, fearing that Stalin's motto was dangerously akin to the inimitable Mr. Jorrocks's " Where I dines, I sleeps ", let it be known that they were profoundly reluctant to permit Red Army troops and aircraft to cross their borders (April 20). Estonia and Latvia sent identical Notes to Moscow and to London, emphasizing that they were in no danger of war and therefore in no need of military assistance, and shortly thereafter (May 7) both States announced their readiness to follow Lithuania's lead and sign non-aggression pacts with Germany.[1] Portugal threatened to oppose Britain in the event of an Anglo-Soviet military alliance and Spain openly joined the Anti-Comintern Pact.

To the French Government also the Soviet proposals were distasteful and unwelcome. Bonnet knew well that, once a formal alliance had been concluded with Moscow, it would be impossible, or at least very much more difficult, for him to continue to coquette with Berlin and with Rome. This he still hoped to be able to do, particularly in the case of the Italian Government. Bonnet had not forgotten the technique of Munich, and he still regarded Mussolini as the Groom of the Backstairs to the Führer.

[1] Lithuania had signed a non-aggression pact with Germany on March 23, 1939, immediately after the Memel coup. Latvia and Estonia followed suit on June 7, 1939. Finland declined a similar agreement. The U.S.S.R. had concluded non-aggression pacts with Lithuania in 1926 and with Finland, Latvia, and Estonia in 1932.

In this connection he welcomed a move by the Pope — in agreement, it was said, with the Duce — to mediate between Germany and Poland.[1] Such a proceeding would be impossible if France were allied to Russia.

This M. Bonnet represented to the Cabinet on May 6 when he reported on the Russian negotiations and on the Papal proposals. At the conclusion of the Cabinet meeting it was officially announced that " the French Government is lukewarm to the Russian idea of a sweeping guarantee to the small States ".

Criticized at home for inaction, and abroad for the reaction which action had provoked, Mr. Chamberlain waited until May 1 to reach a decision. At that time, after Hitler had denounced the German-Polish Non-Aggression Pact and the Anglo-German Naval Agreement (April 28), the British Government agreed to decline the Russian proposals, presumably on the ground put forward by *The Times*, that " a hard-and-fast alliance with Russia might hamper other negotiations and approaches ".[2] Mr. Chamberlain had not abandoned all hopes of a peaceful settlement and he believed that to enter into binding agreements with Russia would render this impossible and war inevitable.

Shortly thereafter (May 9) the British Government repeated their proposals of April 15 for a unilateral guarantee by Russia of Poland and Rumania, but this time it was suggested that the guarantee should only become operative on the decision of the British Government. No mention was made of any reciprocal assistance to be accorded to Russia by Britain and France. The Soviet Union replied on May 14, themselves ignoring in their turn the British proposal and repeating their own requirements.

Thus by the middle of May, after a month of desultory activity, the negotiations between the Western Powers and Russia were at a deadlock. They had had, however, one result of very considerable importance. On May 3, the day following the rejection by Britain of the Soviet proposals, Maxim Litvinov, the advocate of collective security and of collaboration with Britain and France, had been removed as Peoples' Commissar for Foreign Affairs and had been succeeded by Viacheslav Molotov, who was widely believed to favour an " Agreement of Accommodation " with Germany.[3]

---

[1] *Osservatore Romano*, May 3, 1939.   [2] *The Times*, May 3, 1939.

[3] M. Litvinov disappeared into obscurity. He held the office of Head of the Foreign Affairs Bureau of the Party and retained a room in the Narkomindel, but he never again appeared publicly until after the German invasion of the Soviet Union.

(iii)

On the evidence available to-day, it is not possible to give the exact date on which Adolf Hitler took his great decision to perform a political *volte-face* in regard to Russia, but " premonitory symptoms " of such a move became apparent almost simultaneously with the receipt of the intelligence of the Soviet proposals for a formal Anglo-French-Russian alliance (April 17). Previously to this the Führer had been of the opinion that he could employ Poland as a cat's-paw against Russia, thus encompassing the destruction of both of them, and had made three proposals to this effect between October 1938 and March 1939.[1]

The conclusion of an agreement with Russia had not, however, lacked advocates both in the Army and in the Foreign Ministry. Among the General Staff there was a fundamental tradition against a " two-front war ", and, to a lesser degree, a school of thought — the Seeckt school — which favoured active collaboration with Russia. In the course of the purge of the *Reichswehr* in February 1938, which resulted in the elimination of both von Blomberg and von Fritsch, the Führer, then in his most Russophobe mood, had taken occasion to send into temporary retirement the remnants of the followers of General von Seeckt. But the tradition persisted ; von Brauchitsch had been nurtured in it, and even Keitel, lackey though he was, could not ignore the salient principles of strategy. During the Munich crisis they had believed that Russia would fight in support of Britain and France, and it had caused them wakeful nights.[2] In

In September 1941, during the visit of Lord Beaverbrook and Mr. Averell Harriman to Moscow, Litvinov was invited to a reception at the Kremlin and thus began his return to public life. In October he was appointed Ambassador to Washington, where he arrived on December 7 a few hours before the Japanese attack on Pearl Harbour. There he remained until August 1943, when he was recalled to Moscow as Deputy Commissar for Foreign Affairs. From this position Litvinov was summarily dismissed on August 24, 1946 ; once again, at the whim of Stalin, he disappeared into obscurity.

M. Maisky was also recalled to Moscow in August 1943 in order to become a Deputy Commissar for Foreign Affairs, in which capacity he attended the Allied Conferences of Yalta and Potsdam, and the Moscow Conference on Reparation Payments in the autumn of 1945. In 1946 he was " relieved of his duties " at the Narkomindel and was placed in charge of the Party Bureau of History. He was elected to the Soviet Academy of Sciences in August of that year.

[1] *French Yellow Book*, p. 135 ; *Polish White Book*, pp. 47, 53 and 61.
[2] Under cross-examination at Nuremberg, Keitel admitted frankly that, " had there been, in place of the Munich Conference, a collaboration between Great Britain, France and the U.S.S.R., it would have been impossible for us to strike ".

the ensuing period they had not ceased to urge that in the event of war with Poland, which might mean war with Britain and France, some arrangement for the neutrality of Russia and the safeguarding of the German rear should be obtained.

In the Foreign Ministry Joachim von Ribbentrop was equally enthusiastic. Dreading a combination of Britain, France, and Russia, he was confident that, if a German-Russian *rapprochement* could be achieved, the two Western Powers would be too shattered by the event to continue their support of Poland. Faced with Soviet defection, they would either force the Poles to accept a second Munich or would abandon them to their fate, or, at worst, go through the motion of declaring war in their defence and accept a negotiated peace after the inevitable *débâcle* of the Polish Army.

Ribbentrop had, therefore, joined the ranks of those who advocated an agreement with Russia, and in Moscow he found an able supporter in the German Ambassador, Count Werner von der Schulenburg. But there was a difference in Schulenburg's attitude from that of the other advocates of the pro-Russian policy. Almost alone among them he was genuinely pro-Russian, and whereas they sought to buy time and security to overcome their other victims in Eastern and Western Europe, and then finally to turn upon Russia, Schulenburg remained true to the tenets of his diplomatic upbringing.

A disciple of Baron von Maltzan and Count von Brockdorff-Rantzau, who, with von Seeckt, had forged the Rapallo policy of the 'twenties, Schulenburg remained almost the last veteran of the Eastern school in the German Foreign Ministry. Trained in the principles of Bismarck, he regarded an approach to Russia as a return to sanity on the part of German foreign policy. His advocacy was based upon the hope of a permanent agreement and not upon the intention of a pact of perfidy.[1]

Such were the various forces which combined in the spring of 1939 to influence the Führer towards an apparent reversal of the principles of National Socialism and of the Anti-Comintern Pact, a diplomatic revolution as great as that which had occurred in British foreign policy.

---

[1] There is good reason to believe that von der Schulenburg was genuinely and deeply shocked by the surprise attack on Russia on June 22, 1941. As a result he joined the conspiracy of the Generals against Hitler which culminated in the abortive *Putsch* of July 20, 1944. In the purge which followed, von der Schulenburg was arrested and executed, together with the remaining members of the Eastern school in the German General Staff.

Hitler was not an easy convert, but he saw the value of using the idea of a Russo-German agreement as a weapon of political warfare against the British and the French. He also realized the value of preventing an agreement between the Western Powers and Russia, and he listened, at any rate, to his Generals, even if he did not pay much attention to what he heard. Both Keitel and von Brauchitsch were asked their views no whether an armed conflict would, in existing circumstances, turn in favour of Germany. Both replied that much depended on whether Russia remained neutral or not.

" If she does remain neutral ? " asked the Führer.

" Yes," answered Keitel, the sycophant.

" Probably," replied the more cautious von Brauchitsch.

Both Generals agreed that, if Germany had to fight against Russia in addition to the Western Powers she would have little chance of winning.[1]

When, therefore, the news arrived of the Russian proposals to London and to Paris for a triple alliance, the Führer authorized a qualified approach to Moscow. Forthwith the Soviet Ambassador was summoned to the German Foreign Ministry and the Soviet Military Attaché to the offices of the General Staff. Both then left immediately for Moscow.[2]

It is probable that at this moment Hitler had no greater objective than that of using the idea of Russo-German *rapprochement* as a negative element to frustrate the negotiations then in process between London, Paris and Moscow. The idea of a pact between Germany and Russia was almost ostentatiously aired by the Nazi leaders for the benefit of the British and French Ambassadors, in order both to terrify them with a bogy and increase the suspicions which their Governments already entertained towards Russia.[3]

No definite move, however, was made until some indication could be gained as to the success or failure of the Russian proposals to Britain and France.[4] This was provided by *The Times*

---

[1] *French Yellow Book*, p. 171.   [2] *Ibid.* p. 148.

[3] On May 6 a member of the French Embassy Staff was informed by " one of the Führer's associates " that Ribbentrop had recently remarked : " It may well be that we shall witness a Fourth Partition of Poland ; in any case, we shall soon see that something is brewing in the East " (*French Yellow Book*, pp. 145-6).

[4] Ambassador Joseph E. Davies informed the United States Department of State, from Brussels on May 17, that he had received a report from Captain von Rintelen to the effect that General Jan Syrový, former head of the Czechoslovak State, had been sent twice to Moscow as Hitler's secret emissary to contact army officers and friends in Russia (*Mission to Moscow*, by Joseph E. Davies (New York, 1941), p. 443).

editorial of May 3, and confirmed in no uncertain manner by the announcement on the same day of the accession of Molotov to the Commissariat of Foreign Affairs.

It was now considered in Berlin that events were running sufficiently in Germany's favour to warrant a more exact approach, and, according to American sources,[1] Schulenburg received instructions to propose to Molotov a *détente* in German-Russian relations and the development of closer trade and economic connections. Somewhat to the Ambassador's surprise, Molotov's response to this covert approach was to say frankly that closer trade relations were all very well but what Stalin most desired was closer political relations.[2]

This frankness was received with a certain suspicion in Berlin and the Ambassador was instructed to pursue, for the moment, negotiations for a commercial agreement only. Conversations, however, proceeded between Ribbentrop and Ciano on the question of placing their relations with the Soviet Union on a normal footing and so neutralizing Russia as to " prevent her from participating in the encirclement of Germany by the Great Powers ".[3]

All in all, the Führer felt sufficiently confident on May 23, the morrow of his signature of a military alliance with Italy,[4] to

[1] *American White Paper*, by Joseph Alsop and Robert Kintner (New York, 1940), p. 53. Since much of the information in this publication was derived from conversations between the authors and the Hon. Adolph Berle, at that time Assistant Secretary of State, it may be regarded as a quasi-official document.

[2] In his address to the staff conference at the Obersalzberg on August 22, 1939, Hitler stated categorically that the first proposition for a pact came from Russia. (See below, p. 415.)

[3] See Count Ciano's speech before the Fascist Chamber, December 16, 1939 (*Giornale d' Italia*, December 17, 1939).

[4] Ribbentrop had originally put forward proposals at the close of 1938 for the transformation of the Anti-Comintern Pact into a military alliance between Germany, Italy, and Japan. Negotiations had proceeded along these lines until April 1939, when the new situation created by the approaches of Britain and France to Russia had raised difficulties. Japan favoured an uncompromising front against the U.S.S.R. Ribbentrop was unwilling to accept this in view of the desirability of reaching an understanding with Moscow. Ciano supported him, though without being fully aware of all the implications. The Japanese, however, remained obdurate, and, at the meeting between Ribbentrop and Ciano at Milan, on May 6–7, it was agreed to proceed with the conclusion of a bilateral treaty of military alliance to which Japan could later adhere if she became so minded. This agreement was signed in Berlin by the two Foreign Ministers on May 22. (*Ciano Diaries*, pp. 3, 39, 72, 78 and 82.) It was evidently on account of their respective attitudes towards Russia — the one of peace, the other of war — that Hitler warned his hearers on May 23 that Germany's plans and objectives must be kept absolutely secret, " even from Italy and Japan ". (See above, p. 386.)

state categorically to his military leaders : " There will be war ".
He did not take them into his full confidence regarding Russia, but
it is doubtful whether he would have been so positive if he were
not already moderately well assured of Soviet neutrality, for after
all, war could only be of his own making.

(iv)

" I cannot help feeling," said Mr. Chamberlain wearily in the
House of Commons on the afternoon of May 19, after a burst of
criticism from the Labour Opposition and the dissident Tories on
the dilatory policy of the Government in regard to a Russian
alliance, " I cannot help feeling that there is a sort of veil, a sort
of wall, between the two Governments, which it is extremely
difficult to penetrate." [1]

A week of deadlock had ensued since the receipt of the last
Soviet Note, and, though in the interim M. Maisky had kept in
touch with Lord Halifax, there was no definite result from their
conversations.   Meanwhile Britain had offered her unilateral
guarantee to Turkey; Count von der Schulenburg had been
received in Moscow; and Germany and Italy had signed a pact
of military alliance " without mental or other reservations ".   It
was also becoming increasingly evident that a crisis — of what
proportion none could tell, for it was like lighting matches in a
powder magazine — was developing round the militarization of
the Free City of Danzig.

Still Britain and France hesitated to abandon all hope of peace
by negotiation with Germany, but at length, in deference to a
barrage of criticism from Labour, Liberals, and Conservatives
alike, Mr. Chamberlain bowed to the storm.   On May 27 he
instructed the British Ambassador in Moscow, Sir William Seeds,
to agree to the discussion of a Pact of Mutual Assistance and a
Military Convention.   In regard to the question of the guarantee,
Britain and France — for the French Ambassador, M. Naggiar,
presented similar proposals — sought to safeguard themselves
against possible Soviet territorial ambitions by restricting it to
Poland and Rumania.[2]

Before replying to this new *démarche*, M. Molotov made his first

---

[1] *House of Commons Debates*, May 19, 1939, col. 1839.
[2] *Pravda*, May 30, 1939.

public pronouncement as Commissar for Foreign Affairs in a speech before the Supreme Council of the U.S.S.R. on May 31. He took occasion to castigate the British and French Governments for the paucity and half-heartedness of their proposals, and to demonstrate the logical superiority of those of the Soviet Union. He also welcomed the resumption of commercial conversations with the Axis Powers, saying that, while conducting negotiations with Britain and France, " we by no means consider it necessary to renounce business relations with Germany and Italy ".[1]

Having delivered this body blow, Molotov followed it up two days later (June 2) with fresh counter-proposals. It was suggested that, in addition to the conclusion of a triple alliance, there should be an agreement for the U.S.S.R. to give assistance to five out of the seven States which had been guaranteed by Britain and France (Belgium, Greece, Rumania, Poland, and Turkey) ; a further pact whereby the Three Powers should assist the Baltic States should their neutrality be violated ; and a concrete agreement about the methods, form, and extent of the help to be given.[2] For good measure, M. Molotov also proposed that Lord Halifax should come himself to Moscow.

This invitation Lord Halifax declined. He agreed, however, that the seat of the negotiations should be moved to Moscow and he deputed Mr. William Strang, head of the Central Department of the Foreign Office, to assist the British Ambassador in conducting them.

Should Lord Halifax have gone to Moscow ?

Certainly he was criticized for not going. It was pointed out by the critics of the Government that Lord Halifax had paid a visit — albeit an " unofficial " visit — to Hitler at Berchtesgaden, and that he had accompanied Mr. Chamberlain on his visits to M. Daladier and to the Duce. Surely, it was asked, if the British Government were in earnest in their efforts to reach an accord with Russia, Lord Halifax should at least pay the same courtesy to Moscow as he had to Paris and Rome ; and there were many who shared the opinion of Sir Charles Stewart on the occasion of Lord Castlereagh's failure to accompany the Emperor Alexander I into Paris in 1814 : " It is deeply to be regretted that His Majesty's Secretary of State for Foreign Affairs, by accidental occurrences, has been thrown out of the way of affording

[1] *Izvestia*, June 1, 1939.   [2] *Pravda*, June 7, 1939.

that incalculable benefit which his presence could not fail of producing here at this moment ".[1]

Why did Lord Halifax not go ?

It may well be that he felt that the risk of failure was too great ; that if the British Foreign Secretary went to Moscow and failed to reach agreement it would prove too great a source of satisfaction to Hitler. It was better, therefore, that a lesser light should undertake the negotiations, whose failure — if fail he must — would be less conspicuous. It is probable, moreover, that Lord Halifax would have proved unacceptable as a negotiator in Moscow after the speech which he delivered in the House of Lords on June 8, when he once more expressed his distaste for " division into politically hostile groups ", offered to Germany the idea of a conference for the " adjustment of rival claims ", and spoke of the consideration of *Lebensraum.*[2]

To the Russians this speech spelled an unmistakable retrogression towards appeasement and it provided an inauspicious beginning for the negotiations which opened with the British and French representatives on June 15 in Moscow.

These conversations, which dragged out their wearisome and abortive course for eight long weeks, produced a series of *impasses* centring upon the Soviet demands to station troops in the Baltic States in case of emergency and the reluctance of the British and French to agree to this step, which they regarded in the light of a veiled annexation and a negation of the whole principle on which the negotiations were supposed to be based.

At the end of June the irritation of the Soviet Government was ventilated in an article in *Pravda* contributed by Zhdanov, a member of the Politbureau and President of the Foreign Affairs Committee of the Soviet Union. Writing " as a private individual and not committing his Government ", M. Zhdanov said frankly :

" It seems to me that the British and French Governments are not out for a real agreement acceptable to the U.S.S.R., but only for talks about an agreement in order to demonstrate before the public opinion of their own countries the alleged unyielding attitude of the U.S.S.R. and thus facilitate the conclusion of an agreement with the aggressors. The next few days will show whether this is so or not." [3]

[1] Letter from Sir Charles Stewart to Lord Liverpool, April 4, 1814, quoted by Harold Nicolson in *The Congress of Vienna* (London, 1946), p. 86.

[2] *House of Lords Debates*, June 8, 1939, col. 361.

[3] *Pravda*, June 29, 1939. Point was given to M. Zhdanov's remarks by the fact

There followed the July crisis over the militarization of the Free City of Danzig. This measure, which the Germans and the Senators of the Free City protested was purely defensive in nature and in anticipation of a Polish attack, was proceeding apace. The fact that the so-called " safety measures " were equally adaptable for offensive purposes naturally alarmed the Poles, who were also aware that arms were being openly smuggled into the city. For their own protection the Polish Government reinforced their customs inspectors with a considerable number of frontier guards, and, by way of reprisal, they also took certain economic measures of a nature prejudicial to the trade of the Free City.[1]

These retaliatory measures by the Poles convinced Hitler, that Poland was not to be intimidated by threats nor further wooed by illusory promises of aggrandizement at the expense of Russia. He thereupon determined to crush her by war, and, to ensure that Britain and France should not this time talk him out of his " local conflict ", he decided upon a stratagem which should at once isolate Poland and terrorize the Western Powers into acquiescence in her fate.

Ribbentrop had consistently maintained that, if an agreement were reached between Germany and Russia, Britain and France would never dare to go to war on account of Poland. The Führer was now disposed to agree. He had shifted a little from the position he had outlined on May 23, but still held to the basic principle that the war with Poland must be conducted without the intervention of Britain and France. By purchasing Russian neutrality Hitler thought to complete the isolation of Poland and ensure the success of his " little war ". Russian neutrality must therefore be bought, at however high a price. Poland must then be destroyed, and, if necessary, partitioned with Russia. In due course, thereafter, Germany would turn upon the Western Powers and defeat them either by diplomatic terrorization or military might, and then, the West having been subjugated, she would crush Russia, taking back all that had been conceded and more besides.

In the annex entitled " Political Hypotheses and Aims " attached to the general directive for " Operation White ", which had been issued by Hitler and Keitel to the *Wehrmacht* on April 11,

that, on the same day that the article appeared (June 29), General von Brauchitsch arrived in Helsinki to return the visit which the Finnish Commander-in-Chief had recently paid to Berlin.   [1] Henderson, pp. 251-2.

it had been specifically stated that, as a preliminary to war, " quarrels with Poland should be avoided ", and, in accordance with this precept, there now settled upon German-Polish relations an ominous calm which was gladly welcomed by the optimistic as a *détente*.   At the same time, fresh instructions were sent to von der Schulenburg to enquire the Soviet terms for a pact of non-aggression and neutrality.

It was now the middle of July.   Stalin had become convinced that the British and French negotiators were not serious in their efforts and that Britain would do a deal with Germany at the expense of Russia if the occasion presented itself.   This latter view gained confirmation when, on July 18, Dr. Wohltat, a leading German economic expert and chief assistant on Göring's planning staff, arrived in London and was received by Mr. Robert Hudson, Parliamentary Secretary of the Overseas Trade Department, and by officials of the Treasury.   As a result of these conferences, the press of the world rang with talk of economic appeasement and of a possible loan to Germany of £500 millions, and, though Mr. Chamberlain denied that Dr. Wohltat's mission had extended beyond questions arising out of the Whaling Conference and in connection with the refugees problem,[1] his denials did not seem to carry great conviction and certainly had very little result.

In Moscow the effect was disastrous, more especially as it was soon to be followed by a widely circulated rumour that " an economic mission " was to proceed to Danzig in order to effect a compromise between Germany and Poland, similar to that which Lord Runciman had sought to achieve in Czechoslovakia.

It seemed that nothing more could be achieved, but on July 25 the British and French Governments agreed to a Soviet proposal that staff talks should begin at once for the conclusion of a military convention.   This decision had been accelerated by the fact that General Sir Edmund Ironside, Chief of the Imperial General Staff, had returned to London from Warsaw on July 21, bearing with him the news that in Polish General Staff circles it was believed that Germany would attack Poland towards the end of August.

The agreement for staff talks was reached on July 25 ; it was announced by Mr. Chamberlain in the House of Commons on July 31.   The Joint Staff Mission did not leave London until August 5, and, travelling not by plane or fast cruiser, but by slow

---

[1] *House of Commons Debates*, July 24, 1939, coll. 1025-28.

boat, arrived in Moscow on August 11.[1] By that time they might as well have stayed at home, for within a few days of their arrival a momentous thing happened. On August 15 Count von der Schulenburg informed M. Molotov that Germany was prepared to negotiate a pact of non-aggression with Russia.[2]

(v)

There is no reason to believe that Stalin received the approaches of Adolf Hitler with either greater or lesser suspicion than he had those of Mr. Chamberlain. He knew well that both were driven to their present pass from sheerest necessity and that neither would ever willingly have found himself in such a situation. He knew that Mr. Chamberlain, and that part of the Conservative Party which followed him, distrusted and feared the Soviet régime almost as much as did Hitler and the Nazi Party. Could either of them have got along without Russia they would certainly have done so. Stalin, believing that a war in which Russia would be sooner or later involved against Germany was now inevitable, and considering that, in this case, the interests of Russian security were paramount, pitched his terms to the maximum point at which these interests could be best safeguarded.

In so doing, Stalin was reverting to the age-old Russian policy of the *peredyshka* (the breathing space) which had been employed by Alexander I in dealing with Napoleon at Tilsit in 1807 and by Lenin in negotiating the Treaty of Brest-Litovsk one hundred and ten years later. Russia was not, in 1939, sufficiently prepared

---

[1] The composition of the British Staff Mission gave rise to some comment both in London and in Moscow. The distinguished careers of the persons selected were undoubtedly impressive, but they were despatched to Russia with no greater preparation than a hasty briefing. Those who considered that Lord Halifax should have conducted the political conversations in person, now felt that, if the negotiations with Russia were seriously intended, the Staff Mission should have been headed by the Chief of the Imperial General Staff — who had only recently visited Poland — supported by a Naval officer of corresponding rank and importance. In practice, however, the appointment of Sir Edmund Ironside to this assignment might have met with opposition from Moscow, where his occupation of Archangel in 1918–19 had not endeared him to the Bolsheviks.

[2] Hitler's final decision to sign the pact with Moscow was taken during the night of August 4–5 and was communicated to Berlin from the Berghof by telephone. Speaking at Kilmaronaig on the day before (August 3), Sir Thomas Inskip told his audience that war was unlikely, and the Government had very good reasons for saying that.

"IF THE BRITISH DON'T, MAYBE WE WILL"

JUNE 29, 1939

By courtesy of Mr. David Low and the "Evening Standard"

to withstand the military might of Germany. She needed time to make up the leeway in her armaments programme ; above all, she needed additional territory in the West to provide for her defence in depth. She was prepared to follow the same course which Britain and France had pursued at Munich — to buy peace and time for preparation at the expense of small nations, and to turn away from herself for a time the menace of Nazi aggression. She was prepared, if necessary, to hoist the Western Powers with their own petard, and to make a considerably more profitable thing out of appeasement than they had been able to do.

To Germany Russia stated the same terms that she had put to Britain and France, but in different language. Molotov did not talk to von der Schulenburg in terms of guarantees against aggression and pacts of mutual assistance. He spoke in the more brutal tones of *Realpolitik* and said bluntly that Russia's price for neutrality was a free hand in the Baltic States and in Finland, a share in the partition of Poland up to the line of Brest-Litovsk, and the cession by Rumania of the province of Bessarabia, which had been awarded her by the Paris Conference in 1920 without the consent of Russia, of whose territory it had since formed a part.

Such were the terms which von der Schulenburg reported back to Berlin, and for the space of three weeks there ensued in Moscow the fantastic tragi-comedy of two sets of parallel negotiations in process between rival contestants for an alliance with Russia.

For, though Berlin pressed for an immediate decision, Moscow refused to be pushed into precipitate action. Hitler, once his decision had been taken, would have signed at once ; diplomatic formulae and niceties of drafting were as nothing to him. He intended to abandon the pact at the first possible occasion, but for the moment he must have it quickly.

This urgency was reflected in Ribbentrop's telegrams and in von der Schulenberg's approaches. Molotov, however, was adamant in his insistence that all should be done " decently and in order ". The Nazis were forced to make their choice as between the three models of non-aggression treaties then in force in Soviet practice, and to agree that the signature of the commercial treaty should precede that of the political agreement. Finally, in response to an almost hysterical appeal from Hitler and Ribbentrop, Stalin and Molotov agreed that the German Foreign Minister should arrive in Moscow on August 23.

Not only were the British and French unaware that negotiations were taking place with the Germans, but, since the Anglo-French-Soviet conversations had been transformed into staff talks — Mr. Strang had wearily taken his departure on August 11 — they were now conducted on behalf of the Russians by Marshal Voroshilov, the Commissar for War, and it is not entirely impossible that he was also in the dark as to what his colleague at the Narkomindel was saying to von der Schulenburg.

Whether the Marshal's ignorance was genuine or not, it is certain that M. Molotov knew what he himself was about and also the necessity of keeping that knowledge from coming into general circulation. Thus, when, as a result of rumours in London, Paris, and Washington, the British, French and American Ambassadors enquired whether there was any truth in the reports that Russia was negotiating with Germany, they were met with a bland denial from Molotov and loud protests from Voroshilov.[1]

The Marshal went so far as to assure Sir William Seeds and M. Naggiar and their colleagues of the Joint Staff Mission on August 12 that, if Poland and Rumania would only admit the Red Armies within their frontiers, the Soviet Union would join without more ado in their guarantee, a proposal which, when relayed to Warsaw, resulted in the most emphatic rejection from the horrified Government concerned.

But soon the portents of approaching climax became unmistakable. A new incident in connection with the Customs authorities at Danzig on August 5 evoked a spirited exchange of Notes between Berlin and Warsaw. Again the Poles refused to be intimidated, but this time Hitler was more certain of his ground.

---

[1] Mr. Leonard Steinhart, the American Ambassador in Moscow, had since July kept up a constant stream of warnings to Washington of an impending German-Russian Agreement. As a result of these President Roosevelt had charged Oumansky, the Soviet Ambassador to Washington, on his departure for Moscow, to warn Stalin that, if Russia joined with Germany, " it was as certain as that the night followed the day that as soon as Hitler had conquered France, he would turn on Russia ". On July 18 the President asked Mr. Joseph Davies, the United States Ambassador to Belgium, to send this same word to Stalin by any channel on which he could rely (*Mission to Moscow*, p. 450).

Steinhart's warnings to the President and the State Department were relayed to the Embassies in Washington of those Governments whom the President considered vitally concerned, and, as a result, Marshal Chiang Kai-shek sent an emissary by special plane from Chungking to Paris to seek confirmation from Ambassador William C. Bullitt. The information which he cabled back to Chungking caused the Generalissimo to refuse to conclude a treaty then being offered to China by Russia, which he had been urgently pressed to sign by several influential members of the Executive Yuan (*American White Paper*, pp. 53-4).

At once the Goebbels orchestration of press and radio began its fierce premonitory cacophonies of aggression.   By August 8 the propaganda attack was in full blast with its lurid accounts of Polish maltreatment of the German minority, and a week later a full-size mobilization was in process.[1]

It was on this same day (August 15) that Baron von Weizsäcker could contain himself no longer.   At the conclusion of a conversation with Sir Nevile Henderson, the State Secretary, who had been arrogant and confident throughout the interview, permitted himself to say that not only would Russian assistance to the Poles be entirely negligible, " but that the U.S.S.R. would even in the end join in sharing in the Polish spoils ".[2]   Four days later (August 19) the negotiations for a commercial agreement between Germany and Russia, which had been the screen for Schulenburg's other conversations, were brought to a successful conclusion, and the official communiqué announcing the agreement closed with an unmistakably significant sentence : " This may constitute an important step in the task of further improving not only the economic but the political relations between the U.S.S.R. and Germany ".[3]

Amid these burgeoning storm signals the British and French Staff Missions continued to pursue their course with unabated, if frustrated, zeal.   There were even one or two official dinner-parties with Marshal Voroshilov and the Red General Staff, at which, so observers present reported, the atmosphere was one of extreme cordiality and toasts and compliments were exchanged.[4]

But when the end came to this tragic farce it came with theatrical suddenness.   On August 23 Joachim von Ribbentrop arrived by plane from Berlin, and, during the night, he signed with Molotov a Pact of Neutrality and Non-Aggression,[5] together with

---

[1] *French Yellow Book*, p. 269.   [2] *British Blue Book*, p. 91.
[3] *Pravda*, August 19, 1939.
[4] According to M. Daladier's statement before the Constituent Assembly on July 18, 1946, he sent a telegram to General Doumenc, head of the French Military Mission, authorizing him to sign the military convention.   The General received these instructions at ten o'clock in the evening of the 21st, and early next morning he asked Marshal Voroshilov for a meeting of the delegations that afternoon.   The Marshal asked him to come and see him alone at 6.30 P.M., when he gave further reasons for delaying the conclusion of the convention.   As General Doumenc left the Marshal's office he was informed that the Deutsches Nachrichtenbüro in Berlin had announced that day that Ribbentrop would arrive in Moscow on the morrow (August 23) to sign a pact of non-aggression with Russia (*Journal Officiel*, *op. cit.* p. 2681).
[5] For text, see Appendix M.

a Secret Agreement in which was embodied the price exacted by
Russia and paid by Germany for the former document.[1]

It was not until August 25 that Voroshilov summoned the
stunned and bewildered members of the Allied Staff Missions to
inform them that " in view of the Soviet-German Agreement the
Soviet Government feels that to continue the conference would
be fruitless ".

(vi)

The world shuddered at the announcement of the Soviet-
German pact ; shuddered and then groaned in anguished apprehension. None doubted that this amazing event could betoken
anything other than war, but what, men asked themselves, was at
the root of this circumstance which had suddenly rendered the
impossible possible, the inconceivable an accomplished fact ?

Had Hitler forgotten what he himself had written, that " a
Russo-German coalition waging war against Western Europe, and
probably against the whole world on that account, would be
catastrophic ", and, again, that " the fact of forming an alliance
with Russia would be the signal for a new war, and the result of
that would be the end of Germany " ? [2]

Had Stalin forgotten his reference to " Fascist beasts " and
his denunciation of Nazi aggression as " mean and despicable " ?

What of those thousands in Germany who had been im-
prisoned, and many executed, on a charge of " Communism ",
and that even greater number who had met their deaths in Russia
on account of their " Fascist " sympathies ?

Had Nazi Germany abandoned the basic doctrines of *Mein
Kampf*, the dreams of exploitation of the Ukraine and the Baltic
lands, the proud boastings of the Anti-Comintern Pact and the
Rome-Berlin Axis ? Were these to find with Soviet protestations
of collective security, the " Peoples' Front ", and the anti-Fascist

[1] The texts of the secret Soviet-German protocols have not yet been published
officially, either in Britain or America. An English translation, however, appeared
in the *Manchester Guardian* of May 30, 1946, and later in the *St. Louis Post-Despatch*
of November 20, 1946.

In deference to Soviet susceptibilities the protocols were not introduced as evidence
before the International Military Tribunal at Nuremberg, but Baron von Weizsäcker,
the former State Secretary of the German Foreign Ministry, was permitted to refer
to their contents under cross-examination on May 21, 1946.

The English version, as it appeared in the *Manchester Guardian*, is printed in
Appendix N.

[2] *Mein Kampf* (English translation, London, 1939), pp. 537, 539.

line of the Comintern, a common grave over which was to be piled the Pelion of perjury upon the Ossa of betrayal ? [1]

These and many other wild conjectures perplexed men's minds on that August day as they read the news from Moscow and tried, with fear and bewilderment, to fathom the incomprehensible.

Yet the answers were not so difficult to supply. No two men had ever entered into an agreement in cooler sanity nor with greater cynicism than Hitler and Stalin as they accepted their " pact of mutual suspicion ". Neither had abandoned one iota of his fundamental doctrinal beliefs; Stalin had not become a Fascist, Hitler had not become a Bolshevik, but for the nonce they had both elected to employ that great facility for mental and political acrobatics which is only given to authoritarian rulers.

For the moment both had gained their immediate objectives. Germany had obtained Russian neutrality in her attack upon Poland and had secured her rear in the event of war with Britain and France. Russia, on the other hand, had gained her *peredyshka* and could concentrate on preparing for that inevitable day when Germany should turn upon her. When that moment came, with the surprise attack of June 22, 1941, the fact that the Soviet armies were able to extricate themselves from the disastrous results of the initial German onslaught and to organize an effective defence of Moscow and Leningrad is evidence of the good use to which Stalin put the " breathing-space " that he had bought from Hitler.[2]

[1] That these same questions continued to perplex Mussolini as late as January 2, 1940, is evident from a letter which he wrote on that day to the Führer, pointing out that Ribbentrop's hopes of British and French non-intervention as a result of the Nazi-Soviet Pact had not materialized and that Russia remained the greatest beneficiary from the war and without firing a shot. The Duce then proceeded to give advice — as one " who was born a revolutionary and has not modified his position " — that Hitler must not sacrifice the fundamental principles of his revolution to the tactical exigencies of a phase of given policy, and expressed concern lest the new German-Russian alignment should have a catastrophic effect on German-Italian relations (*Les Lettres secrètes échangées par Hitler et Mussolini* (Paris, 1946), p. 55).

[2] In his broadcast to the Russian people on July 3, 1941, Stalin said : " What did we gain by concluding a non-aggression pact with Germany ? We secured peace for our country for one and a half years, as well as an opportunity of preparing her forces for defence, if Fascist Germany risked attacking our country in defiance of the pact. This was a definite gain for our country and a loss for Fascist Germany." Yet though he was so far-sighted in his suspicions of Hitler's intentions, Stalin was almost equally distrustful of the Western Powers, whom he suspected of consistent efforts to inveigle Russia into the war against Germany. It was this belief which prompted him to reject all warnings which reached him from British and American sources regarding the forthcoming German attack. These he dismissed as unsolicited meddling and transparently self-interested interference.

(vii)

There was no more satisfied man in Europe on the evening of August 22, 1939, than Adolf Hitler in his mountain eyrie of the Berghof, gazing across the chill beauty of the Bavarian Alps ; meditating on the success of his manœuvres, the infallibility of his intuition, and the glories that he was about to confer upon the German Reich.

The course of events had been extraordinarily favourable. Russia had accepted the bait and had sold her neutrality for a fairly substantial mess of pottage. It was true that in this transaction the Führer had had to abandon the Baltic lands, but he would withdraw his good *Volksdeutsche*, and repay them with better and broader lands when they returned again to the Baltic shores. Poland was now isolated. When confronted with that German-Soviet Pact which Ribbentrop would sign on the morrow, Britain and France, despite the clear warnings which their Ambassadors had so recently given,[1] would either be too terrified by the German-Soviet Pact to defy Germany in a " one front war ", or too sensible to embark on a war for Poland in which the object of their protection would be crushed and destroyed before their assistance could come to hand. The Poles themselves were utterly *verrückt*, and he believed that " their attitude would be such as to free Britain and France from any obligation to follow blindly every eccentric step on the part of a lunatic ".[2]

And now he would get his " little war " at last ; that " little war " of the satisfaction of which Chamberlain and Daladier had robbed him a year before by their too generous capitulation at Munich. Poland should suffer more than Czechoslovakia ; Warsaw should endure the fate he had intended for Prague.

It had been a wonderful day. In the morning he had bidden farewell to Ribbentrop on his departure for Moscow and then, later, at the Obersalzberg, he had addressed to a staff conference of his senior Army and Navy commanders a speech of some importance reflecting his mood of the moment, which was sig-

---

[1] Both Sir Nevile Henderson and M. Coulondre had had long interviews with Baron von Weizsäcker, the State Secretary, on August 15, in the course of which they had emphatically stated that Britain and France would go to war with Germany in the event of an attack on Poland (*British Blue Book*, p. 88 ; *French Yellow Book*, p. 264 ; *Second German White Book*, pp. 455, 457).

[2] This remark was actually made by Baron von Weizsäcker to Sir Nevile Henderson on August 15, " and he gave me to understand ", commented the Ambassador, " that the phrase was not his own " (*British Blue Book*, No. 48, p. 90).

nificantly more optimistic than on May 23. The Führer did not let slip the chance of reading his soldiers a lesson. He reminded them that in September 1938 there had been many who had said : " England will intervene in favour of Czechoslovakia, even with her armed forces ". When this did not come off, these doubters had admitted their error. " We admit we were wrong, and the Führer was right," they said. " He won because he had better nerves to stick it out." But this had created the impression abroad that he had been bluffing, and that, if only Britain and France had accepted his challenge of a threat of war, he would have given in. This impression was now detrimental to Germany's policies, for it was essential that the attack on Poland should be unencumbered by a war in the West, and, because of the idea that he was again bluffing, there had been an added determination in the British and French attitudes which had been lacking a year before.

Now, however, the danger of an attack from the West would be largely obviated when the news of the Moscow Pact became known. " The likelihood of an intervention by the Western Powers in a conflict is, in my opinion, not great," Hitler told his Generals. " It seems impossible to me that any responsible British statesman would take the risk of a war for England in this situation." And as for France, she could not afford a long and bloody war ; she had been dragged along, against her will, by England.

" I have struck this instrument [the assistance of Russia] from the hands of the Western Powers," declaimed the Führer. " Now we can strike at the heart of Poland. To the best of our knowledge the military road is free."

" I shall give a good propaganda excuse for starting the war," Hitler told them. " Never mind whether it is plausible or not.[1] In the starting and making of war it is not Truth that matters but Victory. We must steel our heart and make it hard, for Providence has made us the leaders of one of the greatest races on earth and has given us the task of securing the necessary *Lebensraum* for this German people, who are compressed, 140 persons to the square

[1] That Hitler had already begun his preparations for " a good propaganda excuse " is shown by the fact that, as early as the middle of August, he had instructed Admiral Canaris, head of German Intelligence, to furnish Heydrich, then head of the Gestapo under Himmler, with Polish uniforms. (See record of a conversation between Canaris and Keitel, August 17, 1939, *International Military Tribunal Document*, 795–PS.)

kilometre. The greatest harshness can mean the greatest mercy in the accomplishment of such a task." [1]

And then, at the close of the conference, the Führer had given the order to put " Operation White " into effect. X-Day was to be August 26 ; Y-time, 0430 hours ; [2] the object of the Operation, " The elimination of living forces in Poland ".

In three days' time the field-grey armies would cross the Polish borders at dawn, and the great air fleets of Germany would begin their work of destruction. The campaign would not be a long one ; it would be over in two months, and then he would hurl 160 divisions against the Western Powers, if they should prove so unwise as to oppose his plans. Britain and France, however, would surely not be so foolhardy.

But the Führer was destined to have a surprise on the morrow. The premonitory symptoms of a Russo-German Agreement had not been neglected by the British Government. The reaction was one of anxiety mingled with relief. The gravity of Russia's defection could not be ignored, but her decision had freed Britain from a disconcerting incubus. It would now no longer be necessary to consider as an ally a Power who was deeply suspected of harbouring as ruthless annexationist ambitions as the Nazis themselves, and there was the comforting thought that Colonel Lindbergh had always said that the Russians would be very poor allies from the military point of view. Some satisfaction was also derived from the fact that the action of Stalin in shaking hands with Hitler would put an effectual quietus to the many critics of the Government in the House of Commons who had evinced such a glowing admiration for Moscow.

What Hitler had ignored in his calculations was the indomitable obstinacy and courage of the British people when in a " tight spot ", and it was a miscalculation which he was to make again and again. On this occasion the British public, though staggered and perturbed by the amazing contradictions of the Nazi-Soviet Pact, were not one whit deterred from their conviction that " Hitler must be stopped now ", and they went about

---

[1] See official minutes of the staff conference (*International Military Tribunal Document*, 1014–PS), and also the notes of the Führer's speech set down by General-Admiral Hermann Boehmer on the same evening on his return to the " Vier Jahreszeiten Hotel " at Munich after the conference (*Defence Document Book*, No. 2, in the case of Grand-Admiral Erich Raeder, No. 27, p. 144).

[2] Cf. Jodl's diary entry for August 23, 1939 (*International Military Tribunal Document*, 1780–PS).

their summer holidays shouldering their gas-masks as coolly as if these had been golf clubs or tennis racquets. There was absolute support for the Government in whatever measures they might take, and a fatalistic acceptance of the fact that these measures might — and in all probability would — betoken war.

By a curious combination of circumstances, therefore, the German-Soviet Pact, far from having a deterrent effect on the British Government, impelled them to reiterate their intention to stand by their obligations to Poland, and this fact was made public in a communiqué issued at the close of the Cabinet meeting on August 22,[1] at which it had been decided to summon Parliament on Thursday, August 24, in order to receive the Emergency Powers Bill, to call up the Army, Navy, and Royal Air Force Reserves, and to alert the A.R.P. and Defence Organizations. Mr. Chamberlain also decided to put the matter directly to the Führer in a personal letter, and it was with this letter that Sir Nevile Henderson was flying from Berlin to Berchtesgaden on the morning of August 23.

Mr. Chamberlain wrote with simple sincerity. He told the Führer that the defence measures which the British Government had decided to put into effect had been occasioned by the military movements in Germany and by the fact that apparently the announcement of a German-Soviet Agreement was taken in some quarters in Berlin to indicate that intervention by Great Britain on behalf of Poland was no longer a contingency that need be reckoned with. To disabuse the Führer's mind of this impression the Prime Minister then stated categorically that " whatever may be the nature of the German-Soviet Agreement, it cannot alter Great Britain's obligation to Poland, which His Majesty's Government have stated in public repeatedly and plainly and which they are determined to fulfil ".

Two other points followed : first, the readiness of Britain, if a peaceful atmosphere could be created, to discuss all problems and issues between herself and Germany ; and, secondly, Britain's anxiety to see immediate and direct discussion initiated between Germany and Poland in regard to the reciprocal treatment of minorities.

[1] " The Cabinet also took note of the report that a non-aggression pact between the German and Soviet Governments was about to be concluded. They had no hesitation in deciding that such an event would in no way affect their obligation to Poland, which they had repeatedly stated in public and which they are determined to fulfil " (*The Times,* August 23, 1939).

" In view of the grave consequences to humanity, which may follow from the action of their rulers," Mr. Chamberlain concluded, from the depths of his soul, " I trust that Your Excellency will weigh with the utmost deliberation the considerations which I have put before you." [1]

The gist of this letter had been telephoned to the Berghof from Berlin on the morning of the 23rd, and had effectually shattered the complacent calm which had been the Führer's mood on the previous evening. The prophecies which he had made then to his Generals and Admirals at the Obersalzberg were not to be fulfilled. Incredibly the British were persistent in their attitude of idiotic quixotism toward Poland — or was it hatred of Germany rather than quixotism ? At any rate, Ribbentrop's trick had not worked, and when the Führer received the British Ambassador in the early afternoon, he was in a rage. In language " violent, recriminatory and exaggerated ", he abused Britain and Poland impartially. The Poles had maltreated their German minority and the British had encouraged them to do so. If Britain wanted war she should have it. Germany had nothing to lose thereby and Britain much. He did not desire a general war but he would not shrink from it if it was necessary. His patience was at an end.[2]

But the Führer consented to send a reply to the Prime Minister's letter, and the Ambassador withdrew to wait while it was written. He received it late that afternoon, and it was as uncompromising a document as might have been expected. As undeterred by Mr. Chamberlain's threats as Mr. Chamberlain had been by the Soviet-Nazi Pact, the Führer refused to modify his policy to Poland ; he was prepared, he wrote, to accept even a long war rather than sacrifice German national interests and honour, and, if Britain persisted in her military preparations, he would at once order mobilization of the whole of the German forces.[3]

At his second interview with Sir Nevile Henderson, however, the Führer was quite calm. His rage of a few hours before had spent itself, but he was no less obdurate. He spoke of England more in pain than in anger ; of his admiration for her, of his efforts to reach an agreement, of his past regard for Mr. Chamberlain. Now everything was England's fault. He could no longer trust Mr. Chamberlain, who had given a blank cheque to Poland.

[1] *British Blue Book*, p. 96.   [2] *Ibid.* p. 98 ; *Second German White Book*, p. 462.
[3] *British Blue Book*, p. 102.

If he must have war, he preferred to have it when he was fifty than when he was fifty-five or sixty, and he stated categorically that he would attack the Poles " if another German were ill-treated in Poland ".[1] With this he dismissed the Ambassador and resumed his solitary meditations.

And now there appears to have occurred another of those striking changes which were so formidable a part of Hitler's temperament. A year before, on September 27, 1938, he had raged and stormed at Sir Horace Wilson when he also had brought to him a letter from Mr. Chamberlain. He had threatened war and declared utter lack of concern as to whether Britain came into it or not. Yet a few hours later he had sat down and written a letter to Mr. Chamberlain so restrained in character that it had a marked effect on the Prime Minister's subsequent conduct of affairs.[2]

Then also the Führer had talked of his regard for England and his general desire to reach agreement with her. So now he underwent another of his schizophrenic impulses toward Britain. Just as he had threatened her with war in the presence of her Ambassador, so now he became amenable to the love side of his " love-hate " complex. He would make one more gesture to Britain in an endeavour to keep her out of war, not solely from consideration for Britain, but because her abstention was essential to his success.

Throughout August 24 Hitler was expecting almost hourly to hear of the fall of the Chamberlain and Daladier Governments under the pressure of popular opposition to war in Britain and France. Until late in the evening, when he returned to Berlin, he continued to ask for press and radio reports on " the governmental crises in London and Paris ", and the non-appearance of such tidings threw him into a fury.

On his return to Berlin on the night of August 24 the Führer was informed that the Japanese Government had formally protested against the conclusion of the German-Soviet Pact as a breach of faith and of the Anti-Comintern Pact,[3] but this dis-

---

[1] *British Blue Book*, p. 100 ; Henderson, pp. 269-70.   [2] See above, pp. 160-63.

[3] The Russo-German Pact struck Japan like a bombshell, where it was at once interpreted as a betrayal of every agreement that had previously been entered into between Germany and Japan. The Cabinet was forced to resign, and the Japanese Ambassador in Berlin refused to be mollified either by Ribbentrop's apologies for keeping him in the dark or his assurances that, though concluded for a period of ten years, the pact with Russia would in reality only remain in force " until after the Polish and Danzig problems has been settled " (*Ciano Diaries*, p. 126).

turbed him less than the apparent obstinacy of Britain and France in their support of Poland. He first summoned Sir Nevile Henderson to the Chancellery in the early afternoon (1.30) of the 25th and made him a verbal communication in which he urged the immediate necessity of a settlement of the dispute between Germany and Poland, and offered a treaty of alliance to Britain on condition that his colonial claims were met in due course and that his obligations to Italy remained unaltered. He also emphasized " the irrevocable determination of Germany never again to enter into conflict with Russia ".

In regard to the British Empire, Hitler declared that he would not only guarantee its existence but, if necessary, he would give an assurance of German assistance regardless of where such assistance should be necessary. He was, he repeated, " a man of *ad infinitum* decisions " by which he himself was bound, and this was his last offer.[1]

Having dealt with Britain, Hitler turned to France. He received M. Coulondre later the same afternoon (about 5.30) and despatched by his hand to M. Daladier a message of which the general purport was that France, with whom Germany had no quarrel, should refrain from giving further support to the Poles.[2]

Shortly after the French Ambassador had left the Chancellery there arrived an item of news which had a profound effect upon the Führer's future actions. It became known that, that very afternoon, the British Government had announced the transformation of their existing agreement with Poland into a formal treaty of alliance, whereby the contracting parties reaffirmed their previous undertakings to one another and agreed further that, should they become involved in war, they would not conclude an armistice or a treaty of peace without mutual consent.[3]

From this latter provision it was clear that every contingency had been considered, and that, though as a result of hostilities Poland might be overrun by the German armies before British and French assistance could reach her, the war would not end there, and Britain would prosecute it to a victorious finish provided that Poland remained an ally.[4]

---

[1] *British Blue Book*, p. 120.   [2] *French Yellow Book*, p. 302.

[3] The Anglo-Polish Treaty was signed at the Foreign Office by Lord Halifax and the Polish Ambassador, Count Edward Raczyński, at 5.40 P.M. on August 25. The news would, therefore, have reached Berlin shortly after six o'clock.

[4] For text see Appendix O. It is of interest to note that, though Britain and Poland had entered into a compact before the outbreak of war not to conclude a

The British Government had taken this step in the hope that Hitler might still be reluctant to incur a general European war and that a formal treaty might impress him more than the informal assurance of Mr. Chamberlain. In this latter surmise they were correct. The announcement of the Anglo-Polish Alliance caused considerable concern in Berlin.

Ribbentrop was particularly disconcerted, for this apparent intransigence on the part of Britain was a denial of all that he had so long poured into the Führer's ear and a negation of the arguments which he had used in advocating the conclusion of the agreement with Russia. " We want war," he had told Count Ciano at Fuschl on August 11, and had gone on to make a bet with him of an Italian painting against a suit of old armour that Britain and France would not come to the assistance of Poland.[1] In wagering this — though he did not say so to Ciano — Ribbentrop had banked heavily on the effect of the agreement which he was intending to sign in Moscow. Now he had returned with the agreement in his pocket and one of the principal objects for which it had been made — to keep Britain and France out of the war — was escaping him. Not only was he in danger of losing his bet, but the Führer was not the man to be merciful in regard to the miscalculation on the part of his Foreign Minister.[2]

The effect of the news of the Anglo-Polish Alliance upon Hitler was immediate and vital. All now depended on the reply of Britain to his offer. Meanwhile they must mark time. He conferred with Ribbentrop and Keitel and at once cancelled the orders for " Operation White " to go into effect on August 26 ; he then telephoned to Göring to tell him that he had done so.

" Is this just temporary or for good ? " asked the Field-Marshal.

" No," was the Führer's reply. " But I must see whether we

separate armistice or treaty of peace, it was not until March 28, 1940, when the war had been in progress for six months, that France would agree to a similar obligation — and within two and a half months she had broken it, while Poland remained faithful to her word.

[1] *Ciano Diaries*, p. 582. Count Ciano recorded it as his private opinion : " I am certain that, even if the Germans were given more than they ask for, they would attack just the same, because they are possessed by the demon of destruction " (*Diaries*, p. 119).

[2] Hitler had recently remarked to the wife of the Italian Ambassador, Signor Attolico : " Whatever has been said about him [Ribbentrop] it must be admitted that this man has a swelled head " (*Ciano Diaries*, p. 86).

can eliminate British intervention," [1] and he urged Henderson to take his offer by fast plane to London.[2]

In the meantime appeals for peace were flooding into Berlin and Warsaw from all quarters. They came on August 23 from King Leopold II, in the name of Belgium, Denmark, Luxemburg, the Netherlands, Norway, Sweden and Finland ; on August 24 from Pope Pius XII and President Roosevelt ; and on August 26 from Mr. Mackenzie King, Prime Minister of Canada. But appeals from these august persons weighed little with the Führer. He was anxiously awaiting the return of the two doves which he had sent out to London and to Paris.

The reply of M. Daladier arrived first (August 26) and consisted in a dignified reaffirmation of the obligations of France to Poland. " I owe it to you, I owe it to our two peoples," wrote the French Premier, " to say that the fate of peace still rests solely in your hands ", and he urged that there was not one of the grievances invoked by Germany against Poland in connection with the Danzig Question that might not be submitted to decision by methods of free conciliation with a view to a friendly and equitable settlement.[3]   To this the Führer at once returned a long and abusive reply, of which the key sentence remained : " Danzig and the Corridor must return to Germany ".[4]

The British reply was handed to the Führer at 10.30 on the evening of the 28th.   Its preparation had received almost continuous consideration by the Cabinet for two days, during which time Lord Halifax had been in communication with Warsaw. He had sought and obtained agreement from Colonel Beck that negotiations would be begun between Germany and Poland and that, in order to facilitate their success, Poland would accept the principle of exchange of populations, and would also agree to a corps of neutral observers in the disputed territory.

The British Government informed Hitler of these developments, and urged that direct negotiations should be opened at

---

[1] See Göring's testimony taken at Nuremberg, August 29, 1945 (*International Military Tribunal Document*, TC.—90, pp. 7-8).   Göring was at this moment actively engaged in his own efforts to keep Britain from going to war through the agency of Hr. Dahlerus of Stockholm.   For an account of this gentleman's mission see both his own and Göring's evidence before the International Military Tribunal at Nuremberg on March 19 and 21, 1946.   (*Proceedings*, Part 9, pp. 210-32, 232-37, and 299-303; also *Sista Försöket, London-Berlin, Sommaren, 1939* (*The Last Attempt, London-Berlin, Summer, 1939*), by Birger Dahlerus (Stockholm, 1945).)

[2] Sir Nevile Henderson flew to London on the morning of August 26 (Henderson, p. 272).   [3] *French Yellow Book*, p. 311.   [4] *Ibid.* p. 321.

once " on a basis which would include . . . the safeguarding of Poland's essential interests and the securing of the settlement by an international guarantee." The British obligations to Poland were reaffirmed and it was added guardedly that " if, as His Majesty's Government hope, such discussion led to agreement, the way would be open to the negotiation of that wider and more complete understanding between Great Britain and Germany which both countries desire ".[1]

When the British Ambassador notified the Reichskanzlei of his return and of his readiness to communicate the British reply, no effect was omitted by the German officials which might emphasize the importance of the occasion. Sir Nevile Henderson was received with a guard of honour in the forecourt of the gigantic New Chancellery ; a roll of drums announced his arrival and he was greeted on the steps by Meissner, the Minister of State, and by Bruckner, the Führer's A.D.C. and body-guard.[2] It was evident that every attention was to be paid to Britain's envoy in the hope that the reply of the British Government would announce their willingness to abandon Poland to her fate.

Hitler's reception of this document, on his first perusal of it on the night of August 28, was " calm and even conciliatory ". He kept the Ambassador with him till midnight and listened in an apparently reasonable frame of mind to Sir Nevile Henderson's reiteration of the British point of view. He must study the reply in detail, the Führer said, and would give an answer on the following evening.[3]

The Ambassador retired to bed in a relatively optimistic spirit, but with the day came further portents of evil. The German press of August 29 carried a glaring story of the murder of six German nationals in Poland, and Sir Nevile Henderson recalled what the Führer had said he would do " if one more German were maltreated in Poland ".

The 29th was a vitally important day. The morning was spent by Hitler and his advisers in drafting proposals to be put before the Poles in such a manner that Beck would either have to accept or reject them immediately. If Poland signed on the dotted line, a diplomatic victory was assured for Germany ; if not, the Führer still persisted in the belief that he would have his " little war ". As the afternoon wore on, however, Hitler's

---

[1] *British Blue Book*, p. 126.   [2] Henderson, p. 276.
[3] *British Blue Book*, p. 128 ; Henderson, p. 277.

confidence in this respect appears to have waned, and he began
to realize that the British and French really meant what they said.
They were again about to cheat him of his " little war ", and
this time it was not to be by way of appeasement. Forthwith he
flew into a paroxysm of rage and paced his study snarling like an
animal. " I have never heard sounds like that coming from a
human mouth," said one present.

Ribbentrop, who had now recovered some of his evil self-
assurance, fanned the flames of his master's anger, advocating
war in the hope that, confronted with a *fait accompli* in the shape
of a complete *débâcle* in Poland, Britain and France, even if they
had gone through the motions of declaring war on Germany,
would soon become amenable to a negotiated peace. Moreover,
the General Staff, who had been somewhat bewildered by the
sudden order of the 25th to postpone " Operation White ",
were now urging immediate action on the ground that they
could not afford to lose further time if the lightning attack, on
which the Operation was based, was to be fully accomplished
before the autumn rains turned the plains of Poland into a
quagmire in which mechanized divisions could not operate.

The choice lay with Hitler. He knew now that an attack
on Poland would mean war with the Western Powers, whereas
the British reply gave him an opportunity of a settlement by
peaceful means. He knew, for his Generals had told him, that
if the British and French attacked immediately and in force,
they could penetrate the Siegfried Line and break into the lower
plain of Germany. In face of all these factors he could not bring
himself to forgo the blood-lust of war and the satisfaction of
crushing Poland as he had wished to crush Czechoslovakia. He
chose war, a choice which was to lead him to the highest pinnacle
of military conquest — but, finally, to suicide and a nameless
grave in the gardens of the Reichskanzlei. After holding *Weltmacht*
within his grasp for one illusive moment, he found that it was,
after all, only *Niedergang* that he had encompassed as the destiny
of Germany.

But now, as ever, he was anxious to appear the injured party,
and it was therefore imperative that the demands upon Poland
should be made in such a manner that they were impossible of
fulfilment. Thus, when Sir Nevile Henderson arrived on the
evening of the 29th, he found a very different atmosphere from that
which he had left the night before. Hitler was now cold and

uncompromising. He would accept the principle of negotiation with Poland but a Polish representative with full plenary powers must arrive in Berlin by next day (Wednesday, August 30).[1] The Ambassador protested that this was tantamount to an ultimatum, to which both Hitler and Ribbentrop virtuously protested, as they had at Godesberg a year before,[2] that it was not a " *Diktat* but a reply to the British Memorandum ". " But," added the Führer significantly, " my soldiers are asking me, ' Yes ' or ' No '." [3]

There followed frenzied telephone calls between Berlin and London, London and Warsaw. But Colonel Beck was not to be stampeded either by his friends or his enemies. He was ready to enter into negotiations with Germany on a basis of decency and equality, but he was not going to Berlin to be bullied like Schuschnigg or chased round a table like Hácha, and he clearly said so. He would instruct his Ambassador to receive German proposals but not a German ultimatum. He proposed that the negotiations should be carried on in a neutral capital and suggested Rome.[4]

By 4 A.M. on August 30, the British Ambassador had told Ribbentrop that it would be impossible and indeed unreasonable to expect that the British Government could produce a qualified Polish representative in Berlin in twenty-four hours.[5] Later in the day it was suggested that the German proposals should be communicated through the Polish Ambassador.

At midnight Ribbentrop again received Sir Nevile Henderson. With studied discourtesy he read, very rapidly and in German, a list of Germany's demands on Poland, and refused to furnish a written copy. In vain the Ambassador protested ; it was not till 9.15 on the evening of the 31st that he received the terms in writing, and by that time they were useless.[6]

Early on the morning of August 31 the order so long expected, so long desired, was finally issued to the *Wehrmacht*. " Operation White " would begin at 0445 on September 1. Its object — " to destroy Polish military strength and to create, in the East, a situation which satisfies the requirements of defence ".[7]

The sequel to Munich was over. The Prologue had ended. The curtain had risen on the Tragedy.

[1] *British Blue Book*, p. 135.   [2] See above, p. 136.   [3] Henderson, p. 280.
[4] *British Blue Book*, p. 148; *Polish White Book*, p. 118.
[5] Henderson, p. 282.   [6] *British Blue Book*, p. 145.
[7] The change in the hour from that in the original order of August 22 is accounted for by the fact that dawn on September 1 would be fifteen minutes later than on August 26.

AT WESTMINSTER

(August 1942)

It is perhaps curious that the war was all but three years old before the British Government formally announced that it did not regard itself as being bound by the Agreement of Munich.

Czechoslovak troops had fought with hopeless gallantry in the Battle of France ; Czechoslovak airmen had fought with conspicuous courage and success throughout the Battle of Britain ; in Czechoslovakia itself the smooth and oily rule of Neurath had given place to the bloody repression of Heydrich, which had brought its own Nemesis in the assassin's bullet and its own sequel in the hideous massacre of Lidice. All these things had taken place before the British Government saw fit to make formal redress of that great wrong to Czechoslovakia which it had condoned.

To be sure Mr. Winston Churchill had stated on September 30, 1940, that the Munich Agreement had been destroyed by the Germans and the Czechoslovak Provisional Government had been officially recognized by Britain and France in July 1941, but in the late summer of 1942 His Majesty's Government had not formally denounced the Munich Agreement.

The reasons for the delay were many and various. The mentality of appeasement had died hard. The councils of Britain had remained divided on the matter of Czechoslovakia, and there had existed for some time that school of thought which found expression in Mr. Chamberlain's telegram to President Beneš of September 28, 1938, that even in the event of a successful war with Germany Czechoslovakia could not be reconstituted within her existing frontiers. In 1940 and 1941 there were still those who thought that the Sudetenland, and even Austria, should form a part of post-war Germany. All these obstacles had to be cleared away before the decision to make formal denunciation of the Munich Agreement could be taken, and it took the best part of three years to remove them.

The event, when it came at last, on August 5, 1942, was free from all dramatics and received but little publicity. It was

accomplished in the most unemotional, almost prosaic, tradition
of British parliamentary procedure.

The scene was the House of Commons but the setting was a
different one from that of September 1938. The Palace of West-
minster was now battle-scarred. The Chamber in which Mr.
Chamberlain had been so hysterically acclaimed on his departure
for Munich, and so glowingly eulogized on his return, was now an
empty shell, open to the sky, mute witness to the bombing of May
10–11, 1941 ; the Commons now sat upon the scarlet benches of
the House of Lords. Here too were changes. Mr. Chamberlain
had been dead for nearly two years and Mr. Churchill had
reigned in his stead for a still longer period. The Prime Minister,
however, was not in his place to-day. He was in Cairo on his
return from Moscow, whence came dour news of the German
advance into the Caucasus. Lord Halifax no longer sat in the
Peers' Gallery but in the British Embassy in Washington, and
Mr. Anthony Eden had returned to the Foreign Office. Of that
team which had so ably and readily supported Mr. Chamberlain
in the Munich debates not one remained in the House. Lord
Simon now sat upon the Woolsack as Lord High Chancellor of
England ; Sir Thomas Inskip (now Viscount Caldecote) had
become Lord Chief Justice, and Sir Samuel Hoare (soon to become
Viscount Templewood) was writing decorous despatches from
Madrid.

Of those who had sat tight-packed among the diplomats on
September 28, 1938, only two were there to-day. Dirksen had
returned to Germany; Corbin was in voluntary exile; Maisky,
though still in the Soviet Embassy in London, was not present
on this occasion, having accompanied Mr. Churchill to Moscow.
Only the Polish Ambassador, Count Edward Raczyński, and Jan
Masaryk remained. M. Masaryk was now Foreign Minister of
his country and it was the first time that he had entered the
House of Commons since that day four years before when, with
death in his heart, he had watched the hysterical pandemonium
break out in the Chamber below him.

With Sir Robert Bruce Lockhart, who had been British Representative with the Czechoslovak Provisional Government from
1939 to 1941 and had played a leading role in the struggle to
obtain its recognition by the British Government, I had been
invited to be present in the House on this occasion, and we sat
together in the Officials' Gallery.

It was just three o'clock on the afternoon of August 5, 1942, when Sir Derrick Gunston, one of those dissident Tories who had harried Mr. Chamberlain during the " Golden Age " of Appeasement, rose to ask the Foreign Secretary a question — it had, of course, been all arranged beforehand, and the affair partook of well-rehearsed theatrecraft : " Having regard to the recognition of the Czechoslovak Government in July 1941 and to the resistance being offered to German aggression by the Czechoslovak people," queried Sir Derrick, " do His Majesty's Government still consider themselves bound in any way by the terms of the Munich Agreement ? "

When Mr. Eden rose to reply he was smiling. It was a happy moment for him, a bright ray striking through the darkness of the reverses which at that moment encompassed the fortunes of Allied arms, a fitting sequel to that golden encomium which he had offered to the Czechs during the Munich debate and which had so touched the heart of President Beneš that he carried the text about with him in his pocket-book.

" I am glad [said the Foreign Secretary] to have this opportunity to inform the House that I have to-day exchanged Notes with the Czechoslovak Minister of Foreign Affairs in which I stated that the policy of His Majesty's Government in the United Kingdom in regard to Czechoslovakia was guided by the formal act of recognition of the Czechoslovak Government by His Majesty's Government in July 1941 and by the Prime Minister's Statement of September 30, 1940, that the Munich Agreement had been destroyed by the Germans. I added that, as Germany had deliberately destroyed the arrangements concerning Czechoslovakia reached in September 1938, His Majesty's Government regard themselves as free from any engagements in this respect, and that at the final settlement of the Czechoslovak frontiers to be reached at the end of the war, His Majesty's Government would not be influenced by any changes effected in and since 1938.

In reply, M. Masaryk informed me that the Czechoslovak Government accepted my Note as a practical solution of the questions and difficulties of vital importance for Czechoslovakia which emerged between our two countries as the consequence of the Munich Agreement, while maintaining their political and juridical position with regard to that Agreement and to the events which followed it.

The text of this Exchange of Notes is being laid as a White Paper.[1]

I should not like to let this occasion pass without paying tribute

[1] *British White Paper*, Cmd. 6379.

on behalf of His Majesty's Government to the tenacious and courageous stand which the Czechoslovak people are making against their ruthless German oppressors. Acts such as the destruction of Lidice have stirred the conscience of the civilized world and will not be forgotten when the time comes to settle accounts with their perpetrators." [1]

The House cheered this statement in sincere congratulation, and it would perhaps have been better if the matter had ended there. But Sir Derrick Gunston was a purist and a good friend of Czechoslovakia ; he was anxious to have full satisfaction. Now he was on his feet again to congratulate the Government on their denunciation of Munich, but also to ask whether the Foreign Secretary's statement in any way affected the frontiers between Czechoslovakia and Poland.

An awkward situation this ; the question of Teschen, seized by Poland from Czechoslovakia in October 1938, had remained a bone of contention between the two Governments-in-exile. But to-day they were allies in a common fight against a common oppressor and the Polish Ambassador was sitting next to Jan Masaryk in the Diplomatic Gallery.

Mr. Eden, however, is well skilled in handling awkward situations and he was more than equal to this one. With his most disarming smile he replied to his honourable and gallant but over-zealous friend that the statement which he had made dealt only with the Munich Agreement, and the point which Sir Derrick Gunston had made, " if I understand him aright, concerns the frontiers between two Allied countries and I have every confidence that it will be dealt with on the basis of the close and friendly relations which now exist between them ".

At the conclusion of this felicitous exchange Mr. Eden, M. Masaryk, Count Raczyński, Sir Robert Bruce Lockhart, Mr. Gerald Palmer, and I gathered to toast the event in House of Commons sherry. But here occurred an anti-climax. The Polish Ambassador had heard Sir Derrick Gunston's supplementary question imperfectly and asked for it to be repeated to him. This was done with some embarrassment, but he and M. Masaryk laughed pleasantly over it and the gathering broke up with mutual assurances of agreement.[2]

---

[1] *House of Commons Debates*, August 5, 1942, coll. 1004-5.
[2] It is worth recording that the Teschen area remained a matter for dispute between the reconstituted Governments of Czechoslovakia and Poland until March 11, 1947,

Thus was the Ghost of Munich laid to rest, and an inglorious chapter in British history was closed with honour.[1]

Such is the story of Munich — a story which, as the great Bishop Stubbs once wrote of the study of history, " though it may make you wise, . . . cannot fail to make you sad ". It is a story in which the human frailties and virtues are inextricably commingled. Vacillation and tenacity ; faith and suspicion ; trust and betrayal ; over-confidence and under-estimation ; conduct courageous and conduct ignoble — they are all there. It is a gloomy story.

Let us say of the Munich Agreement that it was inescapable ; that, faced with the lack of preparedness in Britain's armaments and defences, with the lack of unity at home and in the Commonwealth, with the collapse of French morale, and with the uncertainty of Russia's capacity to fight, Mr. Chamberlain had no alternative to do other than he did ; let us pay tribute to his persistence in carrying out a policy which he honestly believed to be right. Let us accept and admit all these things, but in so doing let us not omit the shame and humiliation which were ours ; let us not forget that, in order to save our own skins — that because we were too weak to protect ourselves — we were forced to sacrifice a small Power to slavery. It is of no avail to say that we saved Czechoslovakia from that fate which was later suffered by our ally Poland, that, but for Munich, Bohemia and Moravia would have been devastated as were the provinces of Cracow and Lodz and Warsaw. In reality it was the Czechs who saved us, for, had President Beneš elected to fight with Russian support and thus precipitate an Eastern European war, it is impossible to believe that Britain and France could have kept aloof, however reluctantly they might have been dragged into participation.

In fairness to Mr. Chamberlain it must be said that he was the victim of circumstances which he had previously foreseen and had striven to prevent. The blame for the delay in British re-

when a protocol to the twenty years' Treaty of Friendship and Mutual Assistance signed on that day by Czechoslovakia and Poland stated that " all territorial questions between them at present unsettled " were by mutual agreement to be settled not later than two years after the date of signature.

[1] It was not until August 22, 1944, that by common declaration the French Provisional Government and the Czechoslovak Government confirmed the final repudiation by France of the Munich Agreement and the re-establishment of the mutual relations which had existed prior to September 1938.

armament lies not so much at Mr. Chamberlain's door as at those
of Mr. Baldwin and Mr. MacDonald, and the credit for the fact
that Britain began to rearm even in 1936 is due in great measure
to their Chancellor of the Exchequer. But, because of these sins
of omission between 1933 and 1937, Britain was forced to other
sins of commission in 1938; because she was too weak to do
otherwise, she was compelled to condone chicanery, aggression
and injustice and to become an accessory to these outrages.
There is nothing for pride or congratulation in the story of this
whole period; British statesmanship has never been so humbled
by a foreign Power since the Dutch burned the British Fleet in
the Medway. In that time Britain attempted to play the part of
a Great Power " on the cheap ". She assumed obligations which
she had not the will to carry out. From the original violations of
the Treaty of Locarno in 1936, when Britain was forced to admit
that she had put her name to a treaty which she could no longer
maintain, to the Munich Agreement, when Germany achieved
the full measure of her demands, there was a fundamental failure
of leadership which resulted in the complete lack on the part of
the British public, at any time between the wars, to realize how
far their vital interests lay in Europe. It is true that Mr. Baldwin
had declared in 1934 that " our frontier is on the Rhine ", but
he had never followed up this statement.

The apologists for Munich cannot have it both ways. Either
Britain was so ill-armed and undefended that she was, with great
reluctance, forced to a certain course of action in order to ensure
peace, or else she *was* in a position to fight, and, of her own free
will, chose not to do so. In neither case is there cause for self-
approbation, but there is less ground for contrition in the first
than the second. It may be true that we could not " stand up
to Hitler and damn the consequences ", but if so we should not
be proud of it.

Moreover, it must not be forgotten that the whole basis of the
defence of Munich shifted midway between October 1938 and
March 1939. The original argument of Mr. Chamberlain, Sir
John Simon, Sir Samuel Hoare, and Sir Thomas Inskip was
that the Prime Minister had saved the world from war and
had brought back " Peace for Our Time ". Later, however,
when the international situation began to deteriorate, the
Munich Agreement began to be hailed by its supporters not so
much as a great act of statesmanship which had preserved

anew the palladium of peace, as an astute act of diplomacy by which Britain had " bought time " in order to complete her rearmament and build up her defences. Of this last argument there was no sign in October 1938, and, in any case, whichever claim is made for Munich, it was a failure. It brought neither peace with honour nor for our time, and not until it had been destroyed by the march into Prague did His Majesty's Government take the crucial decision to introduce conscription.

Should we have fought in October 1938 ? On this point the military authorities on the highest level are divided. There are those who believe that, considering our lack of preparation, that Germany was from two to three years ahead of us in armaments, that France was in little better state than ourselves and Russia an unknown quantity, we were not only more than justified in not fighting in 1938, but were guilty, in Lord Trenchard's phrase, of " sheer audacity in going to war in 1939 ". Others maintain that, although our essential weakness must be admitted, it would have been better to have fought in 1938, since war with Germany was inevitable, with the military forces of Czechoslovakia and Russia on our side than later when Germany had been able to destroy the one and neutralize the other. They point out, in addition, that the German defences in the West were not completed in 1938 and that, in obtaining at Munich the necessary time for this, Germany profited more from the breathing-space than did Britain and France, since for her it represented a year's work at full speed, and to them only seven months' work at a varying tempo.

It is true that the interval between September 1938 and September 1939 enabled Mr. Chamberlain to meet the Polish crisis with the support of a united Britain and a united Commonwealth, and that the British Government no longer felt that it was useless to go to war if the immediate object of their assistance was to be at once overwhelmed by Germany. This had been the argument employed with Czechoslovakia in 1938, but by 1939 it had been realized that Hitler must be fought and beaten even with the certainty of initial reverses.

Yet it is equally true that if, in 1939, it was the hope of British statesmanship to avoid war, the chances of so doing had been materially diminished by the events of 1938, since Hitler can hardly be blamed for thinking that those Powers who had abandoned an unassailably strong moral and political position in respect of Czechoslovakia, would not proceed to extremes in the

case of Poland. Just as Mr. Chamberlain had failed to comprehend the depths of German infamy, so, in his turn, Hitler under-
estimated the capacity of the British for illogical virtue.

In the United States of America great harm was done to
British prestige by the policy of Munich, harm of which the full
degree was not to be realized until after the outbreak of the
Second World War. France and Britain lost more friends in
America, and the forces of Isolationism gained more recruits, by
reason of the Munich Agreement than by almost any other event
in the years between the wars. Though there was no great body
of American opinion which would have favoured intervention on
the side of Britain had she gone to war in 1938, the fact remains
that the hands of those who bitterly opposed the granting of
American aid in 1939–41 were substantially strengthened by the
suspicion and mistrust of British policy which was engendered by
her surrender at Munich, and the protagonists of the " all-aid-
short-of-war " movement before Pearl Harbour numbered among
them many former friends of Britain, who openly proclaimed
that their motives were opposition to Hitler and not friendship for
Britain. Those supporters of outright intervention, such as Miss
Dorothy Thompson, found difficulty in undoing in 1939 and 1940
the harm which their own vituperation against Britain had
effected in 1938, and the American public, ever prone to adopt
an anti-British attitude, were more deeply moved by the writings
of Professor Frederick Schuman and Mr. Louis Bromfield after
Munich than by the eloquent appeals of Mr. Herbert Agar
after Dunkirk.[1] The ill-effects of the Munich policy were only
partially obliterated by the appearance of Mr. Churchill as
Prime Minister of Britain, and it cannot yet be said that the
seeds of suspicion then implanted have been completely eradicated.

[1] Professor Frederick Schuman was a particularly severe and more than unusually
inaccurate critic of British policy. In his book, *Europe on the Eve*, he fostered, if he did
not create, the fantastic theory of the " Pre-Munich Plot ", a secret agreement between
Mr. Chamberlain and Hitler conceived and concluded long before the Munich
Conference, which was alleged to have been merely a well-rehearsed *coup de théâtre*.
It is difficult to recognize Mr. Chamberlain in a role which would demand a combination of the genius of Machiavelli, Talleyrand, and Metternich !

Mr. Louis Bromfield, in a singularly socially conscious pamphlet, *England a
Dying Oligarchy*, which achieved a wide circulation, did not scruple to abuse the
hospitality of those whose society he had never refused to frequent.

Mr. Herbert Agar, editor of the *Louisville Courier*, was the leader of a far-seeing,
hard-hitting group of American interventionists known as the " Fight for Freedom
Committee ", who, in the days before Pearl Harbour, called for even more drastic
action on the part of the United States than " all aid short of war ".

There remains the enigma of Russia, ever a sphinx, ever a mystery. Had Britain and France made in 1938 the advances to Moscow which they made a year later, would the result have been different? That Russia was prepared to fight at the time of Munich is more than a strong probability ; it is only the effectiveness and capacity of her intervention which are in doubt. If Mr. Chamberlain had not deemed " premature " the Soviet proposals for consultation put forward after the annexation of Austria and the occupation of Prague, would Russia to-day be the object of the world's suspicion and concern ? These questions can only be pondered. Their answer is unknown. The fact, however, remains that, with the Munich Agreement, Soviet policy was radically reorientated, and that to-day we are confronted with a parallel in history of which the possibilities are terrible in the extreme.

But, above all, the salient point of the story of Munich is not so much its immediate importance as its significance as an analysis of a case-history in the disease of political myopia which afflicted the leaders and the peoples of the world in the years between the wars. For the problem posed then is the same which confronts us now — and remains unsolved. It is not, fundamentally, a political or a technical problem ; it is psychological and spiritual. Can we, with the experience of two world wars behind us, admit, both consciously and subconsciously, the essential truth that peace is one and indivisible ; that, in our efforts " to seek peace and ensue it ", we must realize that a threat to the peace of any country is a threat to ourselves — and must be recognized as such ?

This is the challenge with which we are confronted to-day, and on our capacity to accept that challenge hangs the future of our civilization and our way of life.

APPENDICES

BIBLIOGRAPHY

INDEX

APPENDIX A

FRANCO–CZECHOSLOVAK TREATY OF MUTUAL ASSISTANCE

(October 16, 1925) [1]

[Translation]

The President of the French Republic and the President of the Czechoslovak Republic ;

Equally desirous to see Europe spared from war by a sincere observance of the undertakings arrived at this day with a view to the maintenance of general peace :

Have resolved to guarantee their benefits to each other reciprocally by a treaty concluded within the framework of the Covenant of the League of Nations and of the treaties existing between them ;

And have to this effect, nominated for their plenipotentiaries :

Who, after having exchanged their full powers, found in good and due form, have agreed on the following provisions :—

Article 1

In the event of Czechoslovakia or France suffering from a failure to observe the undertakings arrived at this day between them and Germany with a view to the maintenance of general peace, France, and reciprocally, Czechoslovakia, acting in application of article 16 of the Covenant of the League of Nations, undertake to lend each other immediately aid and assistance, if such a failure is accompanied by an unprovoked recourse to arms.

In the event of the Council of the League of Nations, when dealing with a question brought before it in accordance with the said undertakings, being unable to succeed in making its reports accepted by all its members other than the representatives of the parties to the dispute, and in the event of Czechoslovakia or France being attacked without provocation, France, or reciprocally Czechoslovakia, acting in application of article 15, paragraph 7, of the Covenant of the League of Nations, will immediately lend aid and assistance.

Article 2

Nothing in the present treaty shall affect the rights and obligations of the high contracting parties as members of the League of Nations,

[1] *British White Paper*, Cmd. 2525, No. 3.

or shall be interpreted as restricting the duty of the League to take whatever action may be deemed wise and effectual to safeguard the peace of the world.

Article 3

The present treaty shall be registered with the League of Nations, in accordance with the Covenant.

Article 4

The present treaty shall be ratified. The ratifications will be deposited at Geneva with the League of Nations at the same time as the ratification of the treaty concluded this day between Germany, Belgium, France, Great Britain and Italy, and the ratification of the treaty concluded at the same time between Germany and Czechoslovakia.

It will enter into force and remain in force under the same conditions as the said treaties.

The present treaty done in a single copy will be deposited in the archives of the League of Nations, and the Secretary-General of the League will be requested to transmit certified copies to each of the high contracting parties.

Done at Locarno the 16th October 1925.

APPENDIX B

FRANCO-SOVIET TREATY OF MUTUAL ASSISTANCE

(MAY 2, 1935) [1]

Le comité central exécutif de l'Union des Républiques soviétiques socialistes, et le président de la République française,

Animés du désir d'affermir la paix en Europe et d'en garantir les bienfaits à leurs pays respectifs en assurant plus complètement l'exacte application des dispositions du pacte de la Société des nations visant à maintenir la sécurité nationale, l'intégrité territoriale et l'indépendance politique des États,

Décidés à consacrer leurs efforts à la préparation et à la conclusion d'un accord européen ayant cet object et, en attendant, à contribuer, autant qu'il dépend d'eux, à l'application efficace des dispositions du pacte de la Société des nations,

Ont résolu de conclure un traité à cet effet et ont désigné pour leurs plénipotentiaires, savoir :

---

[1] *L'Europe Nouvelle* (Documents Supplement, No. 16), June 8, 1935.

Le comité central exécutif de l'Union des Républiques soviétiques socialistes :

M. Vladimir Potemkine, membre du comité central exécutif, ambassadeur extraordinaire et plénipotentiaire de l'Union des Républiques soviétiques socialistes près le président de la République française.

Le président de la République française :

M. Pierre Laval, sénateur, ministre des Affaires étrangères,

Lesquels, après avoir échangé leurs pleins pouvoirs reconnus en bonne et due forme, sont convenus des dispositions suivantes

Article Premier

Au cas où la France ou l'U.R.S.S. serait l'objet d'une menace ou d'un danger d'agression de la part d'un État européen, l'U.R.S.S. et réciproquement la France s'engagent à procéder mutuellement à une consultation immédiate en vue des mesures à prendre pour l'observation des dispositions de l'article 10 du pacte de la Société des nations.

Article 2

Au cas où, dans les conditions prévues à l'article 15, paragraphe 7, du pacte de la Société des nations, la France ou l'U.R.S.S. serait, malgré les intentions sincèrement pacifiques des deux pays, l'objet d'une agression non provoquée de la part d'un État européen, l'U.R.S.S. et réciproquement la France se prêteront immédiatement aide et assistance.

Article 3

Prenant en considération que, d'après l'article 16 du pacte de la Société des nations, tout membre de la Société qui recourt à la guerre contrairement aux engagements pris aux articles 12, 13 ou 15 du pacte est *ipso facto* considéré comme ayant commis un acte de guerre contre tous les autres membres de la Société, la France et réciproquement l'U.R.S.S. s'engagent, au cas où l'une d'elles serait, dans ces conditions et malgré les intentions sincèrement pacifiques des deux pays, l'objet d'une agression non provoquée de la part d'un État européen, à se prêter immédiatement aide et assistance en agissant par application de l'article 16 du pacte.

La même obligation est assumée pour le cas où la France ou l'U.R.S.S. serait l'objet d'une agression de la part d'un État européen dans les conditions prévues à l'article 17, paragraphes 1 et 3, du pacte de la Société des nations.

Article 4

Les engagements ci-dessus stipulés étant conformes aux obligations des Hautes Parties Contractantes en tant que membres de la Société des nations, rien dans le présent traité ne sera interprété comme restreignant la mission de celle-ci de prendre les mesures propres à sauvegarder efficacement la paix du monde ou comme restreignant les obligations découlant pour les Hautes Parties Contractantes du pacte de la Société des nations.

Article 5

Le présent traité, dont les textes français et russe feront également foi, sera ratifié et les instruments de ratification seront échangés à Moscou aussitôt que faire se pourra. Il sera enregistré au Secrétariat de la Société des nations.

Il prendra effet dès l'échange des ratifications et restera en vigueur pendant cinq ans. S'il n'est pas dénoncé par une des Hautes Parties Contractantes avec un préavis d'un an au moins avant l'expiration de cette période, il restera en vigueur sans limitation de durée, chacune des Hautes Parties Contractantes pouvant alors y mettre fin par une déclaration à cet effet avec préavis d'un an.

Fait à Paris en double expédition, le 2 mai 1935.

(L.S.) PIERRE LAVAL   (L.S.) POTEMKINE

PROTOCOLE DE SIGNATURE

Au moment de procéder à la signature du traité d'assistance mutuelle franco-soviétique en date de ce jour, les plénipotentiaires ont signé le protocole suivant qui sera compris dans l'échange des ratifications du traité :

I

Il est entendu que l'effet de l'article 3 est d'obliger chaque Partie Contractante à prêter immédiatement assistance à l'autre en se conformant immédiatement aux recommandations du Conseil de la Société des nations, aussitôt qu'elles auront été énoncées en vertu de l'article 16 du pacte. Il est également entendu que les deux Parties Contractantes agiront de concert pour obtenir que le Conseil énonce ses recommandations avec toute la rapidité qu'exigeront les circonstances et que, si néanmoins le Conseil, pour une raison quelconque, n'énonce aucune recommandation ou s'il n'arrive pas à un vote unanime, l'obligation d'assistance n'en recevra pas moins application.

Il est également entendu que les engagements d'assistance prévus dans le présent traité ne visent que le cas d'une agression effectuée contre le territoire propre de l'une ou de l'autre Partie Contractante.

II

L'intention commune des deux gouvernements étant de ne contre-dire en rien, par le présent traité, les engagements précedemment assumés envers des États tiers par la France et par l'U.R.S.S. en vertu de traités publiés, il est entendu que les dispositions dudit traité ne pourront pas recevoir une application qui, étant incompatible avec des obligations conventionnelles assumées par une Partie Contractante, exposerait celle-ci à des sanctions de caractère international.

III

Les deux gouvernements, estimant désirable la conclusion d'un accord régional qui tendrait à organiser la sécurité entre États con-tractants et qui pourrait comporter ou que pourraient accompagner d'autre part des engagements d'assistance mutuelle, se reconnaissent la faculté de participer, de leur consentement mutuel, le cas échéant, à de semblables accords dans telle forme, directe ou indirecte, qui paraîtrait appropriée, les engagements de ces divers accords devant se substituer à ceux résultant du présent traité.

IV

Les deux gouvernements constatent que les négociations qui vien-nent d'avoir pour résultat la signature du présent traité ont été engagées, à l'origine, en vue de compléter un accord de sécurité englo-bant les pays du Nord-Est de l'Europe, à savoir, l'U.R.S.S., l'Alle-magne, la Tchécoslovaquie, la Pologne et les États Baltes voisins de l'U.R.S.S. ; à côté de cet accord devait être conclu un traité d'assis-tance entre l'U.R.S.S., la France et l'Allemagne, chacun de ces trois États devant s'engager à prêter assistance à celui d'entre eux qui serait l'objet d'une agression de la part de l'un de ces trois États.

Bien que les circonstances n'aient pas jusqu'ici permis la conclusion de ces accords, que les deux parties continuent à considérer comme désirables, il n'en reste pas moins que les engagements énoncés dans le traité d'assistance franco-soviétique doivent être entendus comme ne devant jouer que dans les limites envisagées dans l'accord tripartite antérieurement projeté. Indépendamment des obligations découlant du présent traité, il est rappelé en même temps que, conformément au pacte franco-soviétique de non-agression signé le 29 novembre 1932, et sans porter par ailleurs atteinte à l'universalité des engage-ments de ce pacte, au cas où l'une des deux parties deviendrait l'objet d'une agression de la part d'une ou de plusieurs tierces puissances européennes non visées dans l'accord tripartite ci-dessus mentionné, l'autre Partie Contractante devra s'abstenir, pendant la durée du conflit, de toute aide ou assistance directe ou indirecte à l'agresseur ou aux agresseurs, chaque partie déclarant d'ailleurs n'être liée par aucun accord d'assistance qui se trouverait en contradiction avec cet engagement.

Fait à Paris, le 2 mai 1935.

(L.S.) PIERRE LAVAL
(L.S.) POTEMKINE

APPENDIX C

SOVIET-CZECHOSLOVAK TREATY OF MUTUAL ASSISTANCE

(MAY 16, 1935)[1]

THIS treaty was signed at Prague on May 16, 1935, by Dr. Beneš and the Soviet Minister in Prague, and ratifications were exchanged during the visit of Dr. Beneš to Moscow on June 8. It is identical with the Franco-Soviet Pact except for the Protocol of Signature, the text of which reads as follows :

PROTOCOLE DE SIGNATURE

Au moment de procéder à la signature du traité d'assistance mutuelle entre la République tchécoslovaque et l'Union des Républiques soviétiques socialistes, en date de ce jour, les Plénipotentiaires ont signé le protocole suivant qui sera compris dans l'échange des ratifications du traité.

I

Il est entendu que l'effet de l'article 3 est d'obliger chaque Partie Contractante à prêter immédiatement assistance à l'autre en se conformant immédiatement aux recommandations du Conseil de la Société des nations, aussitôt qu'elles auront été énoncées en vertu de l'article 16 du pacte. Il est également entendu que les deux Parties Contractantes agiront de concert pour obtenir que le Conseil énonce ces recommandations avec toute la rapidité qu'exigeront les circonstances et que, si néanmoins le Conseil, pour une raison quelconque, n'énonce aucune recommandation ou s'il n'arrive pas à un vote unanime, l'obligation d'assistance n'en recevra pas moins application. Il est également entendu que les engagements d'assistance prévue dans le présent traité ne visent que le cas d'une agression effectuée contre le territoire propre de l'une ou de l'autre Partie Contractante.

---

[1] *Documents on International Affairs* (R.I.I.A.), 1935, Vol. 1, pp. 138-9.

II

Les deux gouvernements constatent que les engagements stipulés dans les articles 1, 2 et 3 du présent traité, conclu en vue de contribuer à l'établissement dans l'Europe Orientale d'un système régional de sécurité, qui a été inauguré par le traité franco-soviétique du 2 mai 1935, se borneront aux mêmes limites que celles fixées au paragraphe 4 du protocole de signature dudit traité. En même temps, les deux gouvernements reconnaissent que les engagements d'assistance mutuelle joueront entre eux seulement en tant que se trouveraient réunies les conditions prévues dans le présent traité et que serait prêté de la part de la France assistance à la partie victime de l'agression.

III

Les deux gouvernements, estimant désirable la conclusion d'un accord régional qui tendrait à organiser la sécurité entre États contractants et qui pourrait comporter ou que pourraient accompagner d'autre part des engagements d'assistance mutuelle, se reconnaissent la faculté de participer, de leur consentement mutuel, le cas échéant, à de semblables accords dans telle forme, directe ou indirecte, qui paraîtrait appropriée, les engagements de ces divers accords devant se substituer à ceux résultant du présent traité.

Fait à Praha, le 16 mai 1935.

(L.S.) Édouard Benes   (L.S.) S. Alexandrovski

APPENDIX D

RUNCIMAN REPORT

(September 21, 1938)

Lord Runciman to the Prime Minister [1]

Westminster S.W.1,
September 21, 1938.

My dear Prime Minister,

When I undertook the task of mediation in the controversy between the Czechoslovak Government and the Sudeten German party, I was, of course, left perfectly free to obtain my own information and to draw my own conclusions. I was under no obligation to issue any kind of report. In present circumstances, however, it may be of assistance to you to have the final views which I have formed as a

---

[1] *British White Paper*, Cmd. 5847, No. 1. A similar letter was addressed by Lord Runciman to President Beneš on September 21, 1938.

result of my Mission, and certain suggestions which I believe should be taken into consideration, if anything like a permanent solution is to be found.

The problem of political, social and economic relations between the Teuton and Slav races in the area which is now called Czechoslovakia is one which has existed for many centuries with periods of acute struggle and periods of comparative peace. It is no new problem, and in its present stage there are at the same time new factors and also old factors which would have to be considered in any detailed review.

When I arrived in Prague at the beginning of August, the questions which immediately confronted me were (1) constitutional, (2) political and (3) economic. The constitutional question was that with which I was immediately and directly concerned. At that time it implied the provision of some degree of home rule for the Sudeten Germans within the Czechoslovak Republic ; the question of self-determination had not yet arisen in an acute form. My task was to make myself acquainted with the history of the question, with the principal persons concerned, and with the suggestions for a solution proposed by the two sides, viz. by the Sudeten German party in the " Sketch " submitted to the Czechoslovak Government on the 7th June (which was by way of embodying the 8 points of Herr Henlein's speech at Karlsbad), and by the Czechoslovak Government in their draft Nationality Statute, Language Bill, and Administrative Reform Bill.

It became clear that neither of these sets of proposals was sufficiently acceptable to the other side to permit further negotiations on this basis, and the negotiations were suspended on the 17th August. After a series of private discussions between the Sudeten leaders and the Czech authorities, a new basis for negotiations was adopted by the Czechoslovak Government and was communicated to me on the 5th September, and to the Sudeten leaders on the 6th September. This was the so-called 4th Plan. In my opinion — and, I believe, in the opinion of the more responsible Sudeten leaders — this plan embodied almost all the requirements of the Karlsbad 8 points, and with a little clarification and extension could have been made to cover them in their entirety. Negotiations should have at once been resumed on this favourable and hopeful basis ; but little doubt remains in my mind that the very fact that they were so favourable operated against their chances with the more extreme members of the Sudeten German party. It is my belief that the incident arising out of the visit of certain Sudeten German Deputies to investigate into the case of persons arrested for arms smuggling at Mährisch-Ostrau was used in order to provide an excuse for the suspension, if not for the breaking off, of negotiations. The Czech Government, however, at once gave way to the demands of the Sudeten German party in this matter, and preliminary discussions of the 4th Plan were resumed on the 10th September. Again, I am convinced that this did not suit the policy of the Sudeten extremists, and that incidents were provoked and instigated on the 11th September and, with greater effect after Herr Hitler's speech, on the 12th September. As a result of the bloodshed and disturbance thus caused, the Sudeten delegation refused to meet the Czech authorities as had been arranged on the 13th September. Herr Henlein and Herr Frank presented a new series of demands — withdrawal of State police, limitation of troops to their military duties, etc., which the Czechoslovak Government were again prepared to accept on the sole condition that a representative of the party came to Prague to discuss how order should be maintained. On the night of the 13th September this condition was refused by Herr Henlein, and all negotiations were completely broken off.

It is quite clear that we cannot now go back to the point where we stood two weeks ago ; and we have to consider the situation as it now faces us.

With the rejection of the Czechoslovak Government's offer on the 13th September and with the breaking off of the negotiations by Herr Henlein, my functions as a mediator were, in fact, at an end. Directly and indirectly, the connection between the chief Sudeten leaders and the Government of the Reich had become the dominant factor in the situation ; the dispute was no longer an internal one. It was not part of my function to attempt mediation between Czechoslovakia and Germany.

Responsibility for the final break must, in my opinion, rest upon Herr Henlein and Herr Frank and upon those of their supporters inside and outside the country who were urging them to extreme and unconstitutional action.

I have much sympathy, however, with the Sudeten case. It is a hard thing to be ruled by an alien race ; and I have been left with the impression that Czechoslovak rule in the Sudeten areas for the last twenty years, though not actually oppressive and certainly not " terroristic ", has been marked by tactlessness, lack of understanding, petty intolerance and discrimination, to a point where the resentment of the German population was inevitably moving in the direction of revolt. The Sudeten Germans felt, too, that in the past they had been given many promises by the Czechoslovak Government, but that little or no action had followed these promises. This experience had induced an attitude of unveiled mistrust of the leading Czech statesmen. I cannot say how far this mistrust is merited or unmerited ; but it

certainly exists, with the result that, however conciliatory their statements, they inspire no confidence in the minds of the Sudeten population. Moreover, in the last elections of 1935 the Sudeten German
party polled more votes than any other single party ; and they actually
formed the second largest party in the State Parliament. They then
commanded some 44 votes in a total Parliament of 300. With subsequent accessions, they are now the largest party. But they can
always be outvoted ; and consequently some of them feel that
constitutional action is useless for them.

Local irritations were added to these major grievances. Czech
officials and Czech police, speaking little or no German, were appointed
in large numbers to purely German districts ; Czech agricultural
colonists were encouraged to settle on land transferred under the
Land Reform in the middle of German populations ; for the children
of these Czech invaders Czech schools were built on a large scale ;
there is a very general belief that Czech firms were favoured as
against German firms in the allocation of State contracts and that
the State provided work and relief for Czechs more readily than for
Germans. I believe these complaints to be in the main justified.
Even as late as the time of my Mission, I could find no readiness on
the part of the Czechoslovak Government to remedy them on anything
like an adequate scale.

All these, and other, grievances were intensified by the reactions
of the economic crisis on the Sudeten industries, which form so
important a part of the life of the people. Not unnaturally, the
Government were blamed for the resulting impoverishment.

For many reasons, therefore, including the above, the feeling
among the Sudeten Germans until about three or four years ago was
one of hopelessness. But the rise of Nazi Germany gave them new
hope. I regard their turning for help towards their kinsmen and
their eventual desire. to join the Reich as a natural development in
the circumstances.

At the time of my arrival, the more moderate Sudeten leaders still
desired a settlement within the frontiers of the Czechoslovak State.
They realised what war would mean in the Sudeten area, which
would itself be the main battlefield. Both nationally and inter-
nationally such a settlement would have been an easier solution than
territorial transfer. I did my best to promote it, and up to a point
with some success, but even so not without misgiving as to whether,
when agreement was reached, it could ever be carried out without
giving rise to a new crop of suspicions, controversies, accusations and
counter-accusations. I felt that any such arrangement would have
been temporary, not lasting.

This solution, in the form of what is known as the " Fourth Plan ", broke down in the circumstances narrated above ; the whole situation, internal and external, had changed ; and I felt that with this change my mission had come to an end.

When I left Prague on the 16th September, the riots and disturbances in the Sudeten areas, which had never been more than sporadic, had died down. A considerable number of districts had been placed under a régime called Standrecht, amounting to martial law. The Sudeten leaders, at any rate the more extreme among them, had fled to Germany and were issuing proclamations defying the Czechoslovak Government. I have been credibly informed that, at the time of my leaving, the number of killed on both sides was not more than 70.

Unless, therefore, Herr Henlein's Freikorps are deliberately encouraged to cross the frontier, I have no reason to expect any notable renewal of incidents and disturbances. In these circumstances the necessity for the presence of State Police in these districts should no longer exist. As the State Police are extremely unpopular among the German inhabitants, and have constituted one of their chief grievances for the last three years, I consider that they should be withdrawn as soon as possible. I believe that their withdrawal would reduce the causes of wrangles and riots.

Further, it has become self-evident to me that those frontier districts between Czechoslovakia and Germany where the Sudeten population is in an important majority should be given full right of self-determination at once. If some cession is inevitable, as I believe it to be, it is as well that it should be done promptly and without procrastination. There is real danger, even a danger of civil war, in the continuance of a state of uncertainty. Consequently there are very real reasons for a policy of immediate and drastic action. Any kind of plebiscite or referendum would, I believe, be a sheer formality in respect of these predominantly German areas. A very large majority of their inhabitants desire amalgamation with Germany. The inevitable delay involved in taking a plebiscite vote would only serve to excite popular feelings, with perhaps most dangerous results. I consider, therefore, that these frontier districts should at once be transferred from Czechoslovakia to Germany, and, further, that measures for their peaceful transfer, including the provision of safeguards for the population during the transfer period, should be arranged forthwith by agreement between the two Governments.

The transfer of these frontier districts does not, however, dispose finally of the question how Germans and Czechs are to live together peacefully in future. Even if all the areas where the Germans have a majority were transferred to Germany there would still remain in Czechoslovakia a large number of Germans, and in the areas transferred to Germany there would still be a certain number of Czechs. Economic connexions are so close that an absolute separation is not only undesirable but inconceivable ; and I repeat my conviction that history has proved that in times of peace the two peoples can live together on friendly terms. I believe that it is in the interests of all Czechs and of all Germans alike that these friendly relations should be encouraged to re-establish themselves ; and I am convinced that this is the real desire of the average Czech and German. They are alike in being honest, peaceable, hard-working and frugal folk. When political friction has been removed on both sides, I believe that they can settle down quietly.

For those portions of the territory, therefore, where the German majority is not so important, I recommend that an effort be made to find a basis for local autonomy within the frontiers of the Czechoslovak Republic on the lines of the " Fourth Plan ", modified so as to meet the new circumstances created by the transfer of the preponderantly German areas. As I have already said, there is always a danger that agreement reached in principle may lead to further divergencies in practice. But I think that in a more peaceful future this risk can be minimised.

This brings me to the political side of the problem, which is concerned with the question of the integrity and security of the Czechoslovak Republic, especially in relation to her immediate neighbours. I believe that here the problem is one of removing a centre of intense political friction from the middle of Europe. For this purpose it is necessary permanently to provide that the Czechoslovak State should live at peace with all her neighbours and that her policy, internal and external, should be directed to that end. Just as it is essential for the international position of Switzerland that her policy should be entirely neutral, so an analogous policy is necessary for Czechoslovakia — not only for her own future existence but for the peace of Europe.

In order to achieve this, I recommend :—

(1) That those parties and persons in Czechoslovakia who have been deliberately encouraging a policy antagonistic to Czechoslovakia's neighbours should be forbidden by the Czechoslovak Government to continue their agitations ; and that, if necessary, legal measures should be taken to bring such agitation to an end.

(2) That the Czechoslovak Government should so remodel her foreign relations as to give assurances to her neighbours that

she will in no circumstances attack them or enter into any aggressive action against them arising from obligations to other States.

(3) That the principal Powers, acting in the interests of the peace of Europe, should give to Czechoslovakia guarantees of assistance in case of unprovoked aggression against her.

(4) That a commercial treaty on preferential terms should be negotiated between Germany and Czechoslovakia if this seems advantageous to the economic interests of the two countries.

This leads me on to the third question which lay within the scope of my enquiry, viz. the economic problem. This problem centres on the distress and unemployment in the Sudeten German areas, a distress which has persisted since 1930, and is due to various causes. It constitutes a suitable background for political discontent. It is a problem which exists ; but to say that the Sudeten German question is entirely or even in the main an economic one is misleading. If a transfer of territory takes place, it is a problem which will for the most part fall to the German Government to solve.

If the policy which I have outlined above recommends itself to those immediately concerned in the present situation, I would further suggest : (a) That a representative of the Sudeten German people should have a permanent seat in the Czechoslovak Cabinet. (b) That a Commission under a neutral chairman should be appointed to deal with the question of the delimitation of the area to be transferred to Germany and also with controversial points immediately arising from the carrying out of any agreement which may be reached. (c) That an international force be organised to keep order in the districts which are to be transferred pending actual transfer, so that Czechoslovak State police, as I have said above, and also Czechoslovak troops, may be withdrawn from this area.

I wish to close this letter by recording my appreciation of the personal courtesy, hospitality and assistance which I and my staff received from the Government authorities, especially Dr. Beneš and Dr. Hodza, from the representatives of the Sudeten German party with whom we came in contact, and from a very large number of other people in all ranks of life whom we met during our stay in Czechoslovakia.

Yours very sincerely,

RUNCIMAN OF DOXFORD

APPENDIX E

ANGLO–FRENCH PROPOSALS TO THE CZECHOSLOVAK GOVERNMENT

(September 19, 1938) [1]

The representatives of the French and British Governments have been in consultation to-day on the general situation, and have considered the British Prime Minister's report of his conversation with Herr Hitler. British Ministers also placed before their French colleagues their conclusions derived from the account furnished to them of the work of his Mission by Lord Runciman. We are both convinced that, after recent events, the point has now been reached where the further maintenance within the boundaries of the Czechoslovak State of the districts mainly inhabited by Sudeten Deutsch cannot, in fact, continue any longer without imperilling the interests of Czechoslovakia herself and of European peace. In the light of these considerations, both Governments have been compelled to the conclusion that the maintenance of peace and the safety of Czechoslovakia's vital interests cannot effectively be assured unless these areas are now transferred to the Reich.

2. This could be done either by direct transfer or as the result of a plebiscite. We realise the difficulties involved in a plebiscite, and we are aware of your objections already expressed to this course, particularly the possibility of far-reaching repercussions if the matter were treated on the basis of so wide a principle. For this reason we anticipate, in the absence of indication to the contrary, that you may prefer to deal with the Sudeten Deutsch problem by the method of direct transfer, and as a case by itself.

3. The area for transfer would probably have to include areas with over 50 per cent of German inhabitants, but we should hope to arrange by negotiations provisions for adjustment of frontiers, where circumstances render it necessary, by some international body, including a Czech representative. We are satisfied that the transfer of smaller areas based on a higher percentage would not meet the case.

4. The international body referred to might also be charged with questions of possible exchange of population on the basis of right to opt within some specified time-limit.

5. We recognise that, if the Czechoslovak Government is prepared

[1] *British White Paper*, Cmd. 5847, No. 2.

452

to concur in the measures proposed, involving material changes in the conditions of the State, they are entitled to ask for some assurance of their future security.

6. Accordingly, His Majesty's Government in the United Kingdom would be prepared, as a contribution to the pacification of Europe, to join in an international guarantee of the new boundaries of the Czechoslovak State against unprovoked aggression. One of the principal conditions of such a guarantee would be the safeguarding of the independence of Czechoslovakia by the substitution of a general guarantee against unprovoked aggression in place of existing treaties which involve reciprocal obligations of a military character.

7. Both the French and British Governments recognise how great is the sacrifice thus required of the Czechoslovak Government in the cause of peace. But because that cause is common both to Europe in general and in particular to Czechoslovakia herself they have felt it their duty jointly to set forth frankly the conditions essential to secure it.

8. The Prime Minister must resume conversations with Herr Hitler not later than Wednesday, and earlier if possible. We therefore feel we must ask for your reply at the earliest possible moment.

APPENDIX F

CZECHOSLOVAK REPLY

(September 20, 1938) [1]

THE Czechoslovak Government thank the British and French Governments for the report transmitted, in which they express their opinion on a solution of the present international difficulties concerning Czechoslovakia. Conscious of the responsibility they bear in the interests of Czechoslovakia, her friends and allies, and in the interest of general peace, they express their conviction that the proposals contained in the report are incapable of attaining the aims which the British and French Governments expect from them in their great effort to preserve peace.

These proposals were made without consultation with the representatives of Czechoslovakia. They were negotiated against Czechoslovakia, without hearing her case, though the Czechoslovak Government have pointed out that they cannot take responsibility for a declaration made without their consent. It is hence understandable that the proposals mentioned could not be such as to be acceptable to Czechoslovakia.

[1] *Documents on International Affairs* (R.I.I.A.), 1938, Vol. 2, pp. 214-16.

The Czechoslovak Government cannot for constitutional reasons take a decision which would affect their frontiers. Such a decision would not be possible without violating the democratic régime and juridical order of the Czechoslovak State. In any case it would be necessary to consult Parliament.

In the view of the Government, the acceptance of such a proposal would amount to a voluntary and complete mutilation of the State in every respect. Czechoslovakia would be completely paralysed in regard to economics and communications and, from a strategic point of view, her position would become extremely difficult. Sooner or later she would fall under the complete domination of Germany.

Even if Czechoslovakia should make the sacrifices proposed, the question of peace would by no means be solved.

(a) Many Sudeten Germans would, for well-known reasons, prefer to leave the Reich and would settle in the democratic atmosphere of the Czechoslovak State. New difficulties and new nationality conflicts would be the result.

(b) The mutilation of Czechoslovakia would lead to a profound political change in the whole of Central and South-Eastern Europe. The balance of forces in Central Europe and in Europe as a whole would be completely destroyed : it would have the most far-reaching consequences for all other States and especially for France.

(c) The Czechoslovak Government are sincerely grateful to the Great Powers for their intention of guaranteeing the integrity of Czechoslovakia ; they appreciate it and value it highly. Such a guarantee would certainly open the way to an agreement between all interested Powers, if the present nationality conflicts were settled amicably and in such a manner as not to impose unacceptable sacrifices on Czechoslovakia.

Czechoslovakia has during recent years given many proofs of her unshakable devotion to peace. At the instance of her friends, the Czechoslovak Government have gone so far in the negotiations about the Sudeten German question that it has been acknowledged with gratitude by the whole world — also a British Government pronouncement stressed that it is necessary not to exceed the bounds of the Czechoslovak Constitution — and even the Sudeten German Party did not reject the last proposals of the Government but publicly expressed its conviction that the intentions of the Government were serious and sincere. In spite of the fact that a revolt has just broken out among a part of the Sudeten population which has been instigated from abroad, the Government have again declared solemnly that they still adhere to the proposals which had met the wishes of the Sudeten German minority. Even to-day they consider this solution as realizable as far as the nationality questions of the republic are concerned.

Czechoslovakia has always remained faithful to her treaties and fulfilled her obligations resulting from them, whether in the interests of her friends or the League of Nations and its members or the other nations. She was resolved and is still resolved to fulfil them under any circumstances. If she now resists the possibility of the application of force, she does so on the basis of recent obligations and declarations of her neighbour and also on the basis of the arbitration treaty of October 16, 1925, which the present German Government have recognized as valid in several pronouncements. The Czechoslovak Government emphasize that this treaty can be applied and ask that this should be done. As they respect their signature, they are prepared to accept any sentence of arbitration which might be pronounced. This would limit any conflict. It would make possible a quick, honourable solution which would be worthy of all interested States.

Czechoslovakia has been always bound to France by respect and most devoted friendship and an alliance which no Czechoslovak Government and no Czechoslovak will ever violate. She has lived and still lives in the belief in the great French nation, whose Government have so frequently assured her of the firmness of their friendship. She is bound to Great Britain by traditional friendship and respect with which Czechoslovakia will always be inspired, by the indissoluble co-operation between the two countries and thus also by the common effort for peace, whatever conditions in Europe prevail.

The Czechoslovak Government appreciate that the effort of the British and French Governments have their source in real sympathy. They thank them for it sincerely. Nevertheless, for reasons already stated, they appeal again and for the last time and ask them to reconsider their opinion. They do so in the conviction that they are defending, not only their own interests, but also the interest of their friends, the cause of peace and the cause of healthy development in Europe. At this decisive moment, it is not only a question of the fate of Czechoslovakia, but also the fate of other countries, and especially of France.

Sketch Map based on the Map annexed to the Memorandum handed to the Prime Minister by the Reichschancellor on September 23, 1938.

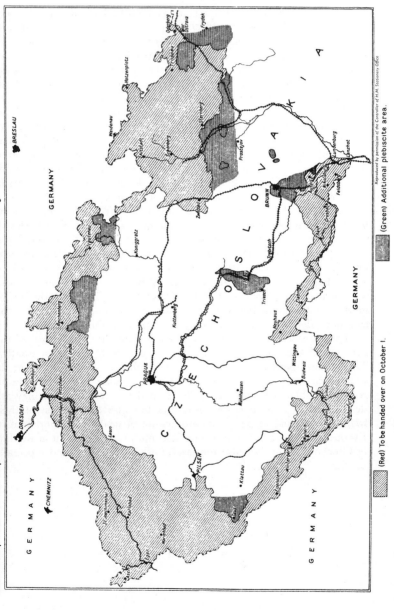

(Red) To be handed over on October 1.

(Green) Additional plebiscite area.

APPENDIX G

GODESBERG MEMORANDUM

(September 23, 1938) [1]

[Translation]

REPORTS which are increasing in number from hour to hour regarding incidents in the Sudetenland show that the situation has become completely intolerable for the Sudeten German people and, in consequence, a danger to the peace of Europe. It is therefore essential that the separation of the Sudetenland agreed to by Czechoslovakia should be effected without further delay. On the attached map [2] the Sudeten German area which is to be ceded is shaded red. The areas in which, over and above the areas which are to be occupied, a plebiscite is also to be held are drawn in and shaded green.

The final delimitation of the frontier must correspond to the wishes of those concerned. In order to determine these wishes, a certain period is necessary for the preparation of the voting, during which disturbances must in all circumstances be prevented. A situation of parity must be created. The area designated on the attached map as a German area will be occupied by German troops without taking account as to whether in the plebiscite there may prove to be in this or that part of the area a Czech majority. On the other hand, the Czech territory is occupied by Czech troops without regard to the question whether, within this area, there lie large German language islands, the majority of which will without doubt avow their German nationality in the plebiscite.

With a view to bringing about an immediate and final solution of the Sudeten German problem the following proposals are now made by the German Government : —

1. Withdrawal of the whole Czech armed forces, the police, the gendarmerie, the customs officials and the frontier guards from the area to be evacuated as designated on the attached map, this area to be handed over to Germany on the 1st October.

2. The evacuated territory is to be handed over in its present condition (see further details in appendix). The German Government agree that a plenipotentiary representative of the Czech Government or of the Czech Army should be attached to the headquarters of the German military forces to settle the details of the modalities of the evacuation.

[1] *British White Paper*, Cmd. 5847, No. 6. [2] See map facing this page.

3. The Czech Government discharges at once to their homes all Sudeten Germans serving in the military forces or the police anywhere in Czech State territory.

4. The Czech Government liberates all political prisoners of German race.

5. The German Government agrees to permit a plebiscite to take place in those areas, which will be more definitely defined, before at latest the 25th November. Alterations to the new frontier arising out of the plebiscite will be settled by a German-Czech or an international commission. The plebiscite itself will be carried out under the control of an international commission. All persons who were residing in the areas in question on the 28th October, 1918, or were born there prior to this date will be eligible to vote. A simple majority of all eligible male and female voters will determine the desire of the population to belong to either the German Reich or to the Czech State. During the plebiscite both parties will withdraw their military forces out of areas which will be defined more precisely. The date and duration will be settled by the German and Czech Governments together.

6. The German Government proposes that an authoritative German-Czech commission should be set up to settle all further details.

Godesberg, September 23, 1938.

Appendix

The evacuated Sudeten German area is to be handed over without destroying or rendering unusable in any way military, commercial or traffic establishments (plants). These include the ground organization of the air service and all wireless stations.

All commercial and traffic materials, especially the rolling-stock of the railway system, in the designated areas, are to be handed over undamaged. The same applies to all utility services (gas-works, power stations, etc.).

Finally, no food-stuffs, goods, cattle, raw materials, etc., are to be removed.

APPENDIX H

CZECHOSLOVAK REPLY

(SEPTEMBER 25, 1938) [1]

September 25, 1938

SIR,

My Government has instructed me just now, in view of the fact that the French statesmen are not arriving in London to-day, to bring to His Majesty's Government's notice the following message without any delay : —

The Czechoslovak people have shown a unique discipline and self-restraint in the last few weeks regardless of the unbelievably coarse and vulgar campaign of the controlled German press and radio against Czechoslovakia and its leaders, especially M. Beneš.

His Majesty's and the French Governments are very well aware that we agreed under the most severe pressure to the so-called Anglo-French plan for ceding parts of Czechoslovakia. We accepted this plan under extreme duress. We had not even time to make any representations about its many unworkable features. Nevertheless, we accepted it because we understood that it was the end of the demands to be made upon us, and because it followed from the Anglo-French pressure that these two Powers would accept responsibility for our reduced frontiers and would guarantee us their support in the event of our being feloniously attacked.

The vulgar German campaign continued.

While Mr. Chamberlain was at Godesberg the following message was received by my Government from His Majesty's and the French representatives at Prague : —

" We have agreed with the French Government that the Czechoslovak Government be informed that the French and British Governments cannot continue to take the responsibility of advising them not to mobilize."

My new Government, headed by General Syrový, declared that they accept full responsibility for their predecessor's decision to accept the stern terms of the so-called Anglo-French plan.

Yesterday, after the return of Mr. Chamberlain from Godesberg, a new proposition was handed by His Majesty's Minister in Prague

[1] *British White Paper,* Cmd. 5847, No. 7.

to my Government with the additional information that His Majesty's Government is acting solely as an intermediary and is neither advising nor pressing my Government in any way. M. Krofta, in receiving the plan from the hands of His Majesty's Minister in Prague, assured him that the Czechoslovak Government will study it in the same spirit in which they have co-operated with Great Britain and France hitherto.

My Government has now studied the document and the map. It is a *de facto* ultimatum of the sort usually presented to a vanquished nation and not a proposition to a sovereign State which has shown the greatest possible readiness to make sacrifices for the appeasement of Europe. Not the smallest trace of such readiness for sacrifices has as yet been manifested by Herr Hitler's Government. My Government is amazed at the contents of the memorandum. The proposals go far beyond what we agreed to in the so-called Anglo-French plan. They deprive us of every safeguard for our national existence. We are to yield up large proportions of our carefully prepared defences, and admit the German armies deep into our country before we have been able to organize it on the new basis or make any preparations for its defence. Our national and economic independence would automatically disappear with the acceptance of Herr Hitler's plan. The whole process of moving the population is to be reduced to panic flight on the part of those who will not accept the German Nazi régime. They have to leave their homes without even the right to take their personal belongings or, even in the case of peasants, their cow.

My Government wish me to declare in all solemnity that Herr Hitler's demands in their present form are absolutely and unconditionally unacceptable to my Government. Against these new and cruel demands my Government feel bound to make their utmost resistance, and we shall do so, God helping. The nation of St. Wenceslas, John Hus and Thomas Masaryk will not be a nation of slaves.

We rely upon the two great Western democracies, whose wishes we have followed much against our own judgment, to stand by us in our hour of trial.

I have, etc.

JAN MASARYK

APPENDIX I

MUNICH AGREEMENT

(SEPTEMBER 29, 1938) [1]

I

GERMANY, the United Kingdom, France and Italy, taking into consideration the agreement, which has been already reached in principle for the cession to Germany of the Sudeten German territory, have agreed on the following terms and conditions governing the said cession and the measures consequent thereon, and by this agreement they each hold themselves responsible for the steps necessary to secure its fulfilment : —

1. The evacuation will begin on the 1st October.

2. The United Kingdom, France and Italy agree that the evacuation of the territory shall be completed by the 10th October, without any existing installations having been destroyed and that the Czechoslovak Government will be held responsible for carrying out the evacuation without damage to the said installations.

3. The conditions governing the evacuation will be laid down in detail by an international commission composed of representatives of Germany, the United Kingdom, France, Italy and Czechoslovakia.

4. The occupation by stages of the predominantly German territory by German troops will begin on the 1st October. The four territories marked on the attached map [2] will be occupied by German troops in the following order : the territory marked No. I on the 1st and 2nd of October, the territory marked No. II on the 2nd and 3rd of October, the territory marked No. III on the 3rd, 4th and 5th of October, the territory marked No. IV on the 6th and 7th of October. The remaining territory of preponderantly German character will be ascertained by the aforesaid international commission forthwith and be occupied by German troops by the 10th of October.

5. The international commission referred to in paragraph 3 will determine the territories in which a plebiscite is to be held. These territories will be occupied by international bodies until the plebiscite has been completed. The same commission will fix the conditions in which the plebiscite is to be held, taking as a basis the conditions of the Saar plebiscite. The commission will also fix a date, not later than the end of November, on which the plebiscite will be held.

[1] *British White Paper*, Cmd. 5848. No. 4.
[2] See sketch map based on the original, p. 464.

6. The final determination of the frontiers will be carried out by the international commission. This commission will also be entitled to recommend to the four Powers, Germany, the United Kingdom, France and Italy, in certain exceptional cases minor modifications in the strictly ethnographical determination of the zones which are to be transferred without plebiscite.

7. There will be a right of option into and out of the transferred territories, the option to be exercised within six months from the date of this agreement. A German-Czechoslovak commission shall determine the details of the option, consider ways of facilitating the transfer of population and settle questions of principle arising out of the said transfer.

8. The Czechoslovak Government will within a period of four weeks from the date of this agreement release from their military and police forces any Sudeten Germans who may wish to be released, and the Czechoslovak Government will within the same period release Sudeten German prisoners who are serving terms of imprisonment for political offences.

ADOLF HITLER
NEVILLE CHAMBERLAIN
ÉDOUARD DALADIER
BENITO MUSSOLINI

Munich,
September 29, 1938

Annex to the Agreement

His Majesty's Government in the United Kingdom and the French Government have entered into the above agreement on the basis that they stand by the offer, contained in paragraph 6 of the Anglo-French proposals of the 19th September,[1] relating to an international guarantee of the new boundaries of the Czechoslovak State against unprovoked aggression.

When the question of the Polish and Hungarian minorities in Czechoslovakia has been settled, Germany and Italy for their part will give a guarantee to Czechoslovakia.

ADOLF HITLER
NEVILLE CHAMBERLAIN
ÉDOUARD DALADIER
BENITO MUSSOLINI

Munich,
September 29, 1938

[1] See Appendix E.

Declaration

The Heads of the Governments of the four Powers declare that the problems of the Polish and Hungarian minorities in Czechoslovakia, if not settled within three months by agreement between the respective Governments, shall form the subject of another meeting of the Heads of the Governments of the four Powers here present.

ADOLF HITLER
NEVILLE CHAMBERLAIN
ÉDOUARD DALADIER
BENITO MUSSOLINI

Munich,
September 29, 1938

Supplementary Declaration

All questions which may arise out of the transfer of the territory shall be considered as coming within the terms of reference to the international commission.

ADOLF HITLER
NEVILLE CHAMBERLAIN
ÉDOUARD DALADIER
BENITO MUSSOLINI

Munich,
September 29, 1938

Composition of the International Commission

The four Heads of Government here present agree that the international commission provided for in the agreement signed by them to-day shall consist of the Secretary of State in the German Foreign Office, the British, French and Italian Ambassadors accredited in Berlin, and a representative to be nominated by the Government of Czechoslovakia.

ADOLF HITLER
NEVILLE CHAMBERLAIN
ÉDOUARD DALADIER
BENITO MUSSOLINI

Munich,
September 29, 1938

Sketch Map based on the Map annexed to the Agreement signed at Munich on September 29, 1938.

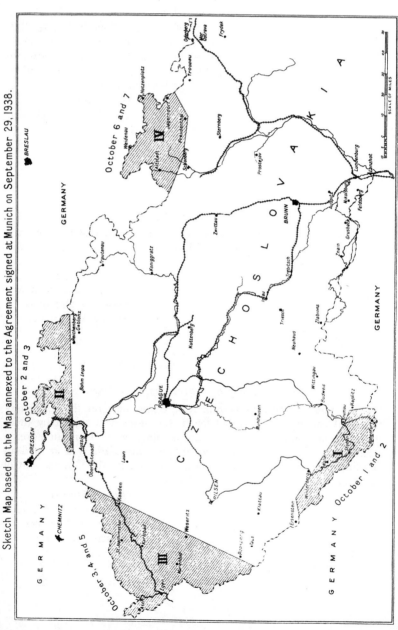

APPENDIX J

COMPARISON OF THE TERMS OF THE ANGLO–FRENCH
PROPOSALS, THE GODESBERG MEMORANDUM, THE
CZECHOSLOVAK COMMENTS, AND THE MUNICH
AGREEMENT

I.—ANGLO-FRENCH PROPOSALS, SEPTEMBER 19, 1938 [1]

II.—GERMAN (GODESBERG) MEMO-RANDUM, SEPTEMBER 23, 1938 [1]

1. Cession and Evacuation.

" We are both convinced that, after recent events, the point has now been reached where the further maintenance within the boundaries of the Czechoslovak State of the districts mainly in-habited by Sudeten Deutsch cannot, in fact, continue any longer without imperilling the interests of Czechoslovakia herself and of European peace. In the light of these considerations, both Governments have been com-pelled to the conclusion that the maintenance of peace and the safety of Czechoslovakia's vital interests cannot effectively be assured unless these areas are now transferred to the Reich."

" The area for transfer would probably have to include areas with over 50 per cent of German inhabitants. . . . We are satisfied that the transfer of smaller areas based on a higher percentage would not meet the case."

1. Cession and Evacuation.

" Withdrawal of the whole Czech armed forces, the police, the gendarmerie, the customs officials and the frontier guards from the area to be evacuated as designated on the attached map, this area to be handed over to Germany on October 1."

" The area designated on the attached map as a German area will be occupied by German troops without taking account as to whether in the plebiscite there may prove to be in this or that part of the area a Czech majority."

" The evacuated territory is to be handed over in its present con-dition " (*i.e.* according to an Ap-pendix), " without destroying or rendering unusable in any way military, commercial or traffic establishments (plants). These include the ground organization of the air service and all wireless stations.

" All commercial and traffic ma-terials, especially the rolling-stock of the railway system, in the desig-nated areas, are to be handed over undamaged. The same applies to all utility services (gas-works, power stations, etc.).

" Finally, no food-stuffs, goods, cattle, raw materials, etc., are to be removed."

[1] Texts in *British White Paper*, Cmd. 5847.

III.—Comments of the Czecho-slovak Government on the Godesberg Memorandum, September, 25, 1938

1. Cession and Evacuation.

(*Extracts from Note of the Czecho-slovak Government, September 25, 1938*) [1].

" His Majesty's and the French Governments are very well aware that we agreed under the most severe pressure to the so-called Anglo-French plan for ceding parts of Czechoslovakia. We accepted this plan under extreme duress. . . . Nevertheless we accepted it because we understood that it was the end of the demands to be made upon us. . . .

" My Government has now studied the document " (the German Memorandum) " and the map. It is a *de facto* ultimatum of the sort usually presented to a vanquished nation. . . . The proposals go far beyond what we agreed to in the so-called Anglo-French plan. They deprive us of every safeguard for our national existence. We are to yield up large proportions of our carefully prepared defences, and admit the German armies deep into our country before we have been able to organize it on the new basis or make any preparations for its defence. Our national and economic independence would automatically disappear with the acceptance of Herr Hitler's plan. The whole process of moving the population is to be reduced to

IV.—Munich Agreement, September 30, 1938 [2]

1. Cession and Evacuation.

" Evacuation will begin on October 1." (§ 1)

It " shall be completed by October 10, without any existing installations having been de-stroyed. . . . The Czecho-slovak Government will be held responsible for carrying out the evacuation without damage to the said installations." (§ 2)

" The conditions of the evacua-tion will be laid down in detail by an International Commission composed of representatives of Germany, the United Kingdom, France, Italy, and Czechoslo-vakia " (§ 3)

" The occupation by stages of the predominantly German terri-tory by German troops will begin on October 1 . . . " (the four zones to be occupied successively between October 1 and October 7 were specified). " The remaining territory of preponderantly Ger-man character will be ascertained by the aforesaid International Commission forthwith and be occupied by German troops by October 10." (§ 4)

---

[1] Text in *British White Paper*, Cmd. 5847.   [2] *Ibid.* Cmd. 5848.

I.—(*contd.*)   II.—(*contd.*)

2. Plebiscite.

" We realize the difficulties involved in a plebiscite and we are
aware of your objections already
expressed to this course.   .   .   .
We anticipate . . . that you may
prefer to deal with the Sudeten
Deutsch problem by the method
of direct transfer, and as a case
by itself."

2. Plebiscite.

" The areas in which, over and
above the areas which are to be
occupied, a plebiscite is also to be
held are drawn in " (on the map).
. . . " The German Government
agrees to permit a plebiscite to
take place in those areas, which
will be more definitely defined,
before, at latest, November 25."

" During the plebiscite both
parties will withdraw their military forces out of areas which will
be defined more precisely."

" The plebiscite itself will be
carried out under the control of
an international commission. All
persons who were residing in the
areas in question on October 28,
1918, or were born there prior to
this date will be eligible to vote.
A simple majority of all eligible
male and female voters will deter-

III.—(*contd.*)

panic flight on the part of those who will not accept the German Nazi régime. They have to leave their homes without even the right to take their personal belongings or, even in the case of peasants, their cow. . . . Herr Hitler's demands in their present form are absolutely and unconditionally unacceptable. . . ."

(*Other comments issued by Czechoslovak Legation in London.*)[1]

" The territory included in the Anglo-French plan contains 382,000 Czechs, whereas the territory to be surrendered by October 1 contains 836,000 Czechs."

2. Plebiscite.

" As a settlement of the further appurtenance of the plebiscite territory depends, for all practical purposes, only on Germany, Germany can decide that to the large territorial areas inhabited by a German population in a large majority are to be added a series of adjacent Czech districts, with the result that the plebiscite area thus formed will contain a German majority and Germany will appropriate by this operation further Czech territory in addition to that which, according to the map, is already to be surrendered to Germany." " It does not grant the right of voting to persons now settled there, if they do not fulfil the condition of the de-

IV.—(*contd.*)

2. Plebiscite.

"The International Commission . . . will determine the territories in which a plebiscite is to be held. These territories will be occupied by international bodies until the plebiscite has been completed. The same Commission will fix the conditions in which the plebiscite is to be held, taking as a basis the conditions in the Saar plebiscite. The Commission will also fix a date, not later than the end of November, on which the plebiscite will be held." (§ 5)

[1] Text in *Bulletin of International News* (Royal Institute of International Affairs), October 8, 1938.

I.—(*contd.*)

II.—(*contd.*)

mine the desire of the population. . . . "

3. *Supervision.*

" We should hope to arrange by negotiations provisions for adjustment of frontiers, where circumstances render it necessary, by some international body, including a Czech representative."

3. *Supervision.*

" Alterations to the new frontier arising out of the plebiscite will be settled by a German-Czech or an international commission."

4. *Other Provisions.*

4. *Other Provisions.*

" An authoritative, German-Czech commission should be set up to settle all further details."

" The international body referred to might also be charged with questions of possible exchange of population on the basis of right to opt within some specified time-limit."

" The Czech Government discharges at once to their homes all Sudeten Germans serving in the military forces or the police anywhere in Czech State territory."

" The Czech Government liberates all political prisoners of German race."

III.—*(contd.)*

mand." The Plebiscite areas contain " 1,116,000 Czechs and only
144,000 Germans ".

IV.—*(contd.)*

3. Supervision.

" The final determination of the
frontiers will be carried out by
the International Commission.
This Commission will also be
entitled to recommend to the
four Powers . . . in certain
exceptional cases minor modifications in the strictly ethnographical
determination of the zones which
are to be transferred without
plebiscite." (§ 6)

4. Other Provisions.

" All further details not mentioned in the plan are to be dealt
with by a German-Czechoslovak
Commission . . . *i.e.* with the
exclusion of the Western Powers.
This means that all financial,
currency, economic, transport,
judicial and other problems connected with the surrender of the
territory are left to Germany to
be dealt with in any arbitrary
fashion she may think fit." This
applies particularly to (*a*) the portion of the Czechoslovak State
debt to be allotted to the territory
surrendered ; (*b*) the separation
of the currency and securing of
Czechoslovak banknotes in circulation ; (*c*) complicated economic
questions ; (*d*) transport problems, *i.e.* intersection by German
territory of main railway lines
Prague — Brno — Bratislava, and
Prague — Vitkovice — M. Ostrava

4. Other Provisions.

" All questions which may arise
out of the transfer of the territory
shall be considered as coming
within the terms of reference to
the International Commission."
(*Supplementary Declaration*)

" There will be a right of option
into and out of the transferred
territories, the option to be exercised within six months from the
date of this agreement. A German-
Czechoslovak Commission shall
determine the details of the option,
consider ways of facilitating the
transfer of population, and settle
questions of principle arising out
of the said transfer." (§ 7)

" The Czechoslovak Government will, within a period of four
weeks from the date of this agreement, release from their military
and political forces any Sudeten-
Germans who may wish to be
released, and the Czechoslovak

I.—(*contd.*)   II.—(*contd.*)

5. *Guarantees.*   5. *Guarantees.*

" H.M. Government in the   None.
United Kingdom would be pre-
pared, as a contribution to the
pacification of Europe, to join in
an international guarantee of the
new boundaries of the Czechoslovak State against unprovoked
aggression. One of the principal
conditions of such a guarantee
would be the safeguarding of the
independence of Czechoslovakia
by the substitution of a general
guarantee against unprovoked
aggression in place of existing
treaties which involve reciprocal
obligations of a military character."

III.—(*contd.*)

(by way both of Silesia and of Olomouc).

5. Guarantees.

" For the territory left to Czechoslovakia there is no guarantee of security. It will be controlled by Germany from the mountainous territory surrendered, it will lose all the fortresses . . . [and] the great majority of its industries producing war material, it will be torn into two parts joined only, north of Brno, by a narrow corridor only about 20 miles across which contains no railway route and only some secondary roads leading from west to east."

" There is no reference to Hitler's attitude regarding Polish and Magyar demands. . . . There is absolute silence concerning a guarantee on the part of Germany towards what is left of Czechoslovak territory after the amputation, and, finally, no account is taken of that condition in the Anglo-French plan which grants Czechoslovakia a general guarantee of her territory by way of compensation."

IV.—(*contd.*)

Government will, within the same period, release Sudeten-German prisoners who are serving terms of imprisonment for political offences." (§ 8)

5. Guarantees.

" His Majesty's Government in the United Kingdom and the French Government have entered into the above agreement on the basis that they stand by the offer, contained in paragraph six of the Anglo-French proposals of September 19, relating to an international guarantee of the new boundaries of the Czechoslovak State against unprovoked aggression.

"When the question of the Polish and Hungarian minorities in Czechoslovakia has been settled, Germany and Italy, for their part, will give a guarantee to Czechoslovakia." (*Annex*)

"The Heads of the Governments of the four Powers declare that the problems of the Polish and Hungarian minorities in Czechoslovakia, if not settled within three months by agreement between the respective Governments, shall form the subject of another meeting of the Heads of the Governments of the four Powers." (*Declaration*)

APPENDIX K

ANGLO-GERMAN JOINT DECLARATION
(September 30, 1938) [1]

WE, the German Führer and Chancellor and the British Prime Minister, have had a further meeting to-day and are agreed in recognizing that the question of Anglo-German relations is of the first importance for the two countries and for Europe.

We regard the agreement signed last night and the Anglo-German Naval Agreement as symbolic of the desire of our two peoples never to go to war with one another again.

We are resolved that the method of consultation shall be the method adopted to deal with any other questions that may concern our two countries, and we are determined to continue our efforts to remove possible sources of difference and thus to contribute to assure the peace of Europe.

[1] *Documents on International Affairs* (R.I.I.A.), 1938, Vol. 2, p. 291.

APPENDIX L

FRANCO-GERMAN JOINT DECLARATION
(December 6, 1938) [1]

M. GEORGES BONNET, ministre des affaires étrangères de la République française,

Et M. Joachim von Ribbentrop, ministre des affaires étrangères du Reich allemand,

Agissant au nom et d'ordre de leurs gouvernements sont convenus de ce qui suit, lors de leur rencontre à Paris le 6 décembre 1938 :

I — Le gouvernement français et le gouvernement allemand partagent pleinement la conviction que des relations pacifiques et de bon voisinage entre la France et l'Allemagne constituent l'un des éléments essentiels de la consolidation de la situation en Europe et du maintien de la paix générale. Les deux gouvernements s'emploieront en conséquence de toutes leurs forces pour assurer le développement dans ce sens des relations entre leurs pays.

II — Les deux gouvernements constatent qu'entre leurs pays aucune question d'ordre territorial ne reste en suspens et ils recon-

[1] *Le Temps*, December 7, 1938.

naissent solennellement comme définitive la frontière entre leurs pays telle qu'elle est actuellement tracée.

III — Les deux gouvernements sont résolus, sous réserve de leurs relations particulières avec des puissances tierces, à demeurer en contact sur toutes les questions intéressant leurs deux pays et à se consulter mutuellement au cas où l'évolution ultérieure de ces questions risquerait de conduire à des difficultés internationales.

En foi de quoi, les représentants des deux gouvernements ont signé la présente déclaration, qui entre immédiatement en vigueur.

Fait en double exemplaire, en langues française et allemande.

A Paris, le 6 décembre 1938.

GEORGES BONNET
JOACHIM VON RIBBENTROP

APPENDIX M

NON-AGGRESSION PACT BETWEEN GERMANY AND THE UNION OF SOVIET SOCIALIST REPUBLICS

(AUGUST 23, 1939) [1]

THE Government of the German Reich and the Government of the Union of Soviet Socialist Republics, guided by the desire to strengthen the cause of peace between Germany and the Union of Soviet Socialist Republics, and taking as a basis the fundamental regulations of the Neutrality Agreement concluded in April 1926 between Germany and the Union of Soviet Socialist Republics, have reached the following agreement :—

Article 1.—The two Contracting Parties bind themselves to refrain from any act of force, any aggressive action and any attack on one another, both singly and also jointly with other Powers.

Article 2.—In the event of one of the Contracting Parties becoming the object of warlike action on the part of a third Power, the other Contracting Party shall in no manner support this third Power.

Article 3.—The Governments of the two Contracting Parties shall in future remain continuously in touch with one another, by way of consultation, in order to inform one another on questions touching their joint interests.

Article 4.—Neither of the two Contracting Parties shall participate in any grouping of Powers which is directed directly or indirectly against the other Party.

---

[1] *British Blue Book*, Cmd. 6106, No. 61.

Article 5.—In the event of disputes or disagreements arising between the Contracting Parties on questions of this or that kind, both Parties would clarify these disputes or disagreements exclusively by means of friendly exchange of opinion or, if necessary, by arbitration committees.

Article 6.—The present Agreement shall be concluded for a period of ten years on the understanding that, in so far as one of the Contracting Parties does not give notice of termination one year before the end of this period, the period of validity of this Agreement shall automatically be regarded as prolonged for a further period of five years.

Article 7.—The present Agreement shall be ratified within the shortest possible time. The instruments of ratification shall be exchanged in Berlin. The Agreement takes effect immediately after it has been signed.

For the German Reich Government :

RIBBENTROP

For the Government of the Union of Soviet Socialist Republics :

MOLOTOV

Moscow, *August* 23, 1939.

APPENDIX N

(i)

FIRST SECRET ADDITIONAL PROTOCOL TO SOVIET-GERMAN PACT OF NON-AGGRESSION

(AUGUST 23, 1939) [1]

ON the occasion of the signature of a pact of non-aggression between the German Reich and the U.S.S.R., the undersigned plenipotentiaries of both parties raised in a strictly confidential exchange of views the question of the mutual delimitation of the spheres of interest of both parties. This exchange led to the following results :

1. In the event of a territorial and political transformation of the areas belonging to the Baltic States, Finland, Estonia, Latvia, Lithuania, the northern frontier of Lithuania automatically constitutes the frontier between the German and Russian spheres of interest, while both parties recognise Lithuania's claim to the territory of Wilno.

---

[1] *Manchester Guardian*, May 30, 1946.

2. In the event of a territorial and political transformation of the territories belonging to the Polish State, the spheres of interest of Germany and the U.S.S.R. will be delimited approximately on the Narev – Vistula – San line. The question whether in the interest of both parties the maintenance of an independent Polish State will be considered desirable will be definitely decided only in the course of the further development of political events. In any case, both Governments will solve this question in friendly understanding.

3. Where South-eastern Europe is concerned, on the Russian side, interest in Bessarabia is emphasised. On the German side, complete disinterestedness is proclaimed in regard to that territory.

4. This protocol will be treated by both parties as strictly secret.

(ii)
SECOND SECRET ADDITIONAL PROTOCOL
(SEPTEMBER 28, 1939) [1]

The secret additional protocol signed on August 23, 1939, is changed in its first point in such a way that the area of the Lithuanian State comes into the sphere of influence of the Soviet Union, while, on the other hand, Lublin Province and part of Warsaw Province come into the sphere of influence of the German Reich. Compare the map attached to the Frontier and Friendship Agreement signed to-day.

From the moment the Soviet Government takes special steps on Lithuanian territory for the purpose of realising its interests, the present German-Lithuanian frontier will be rectified in such a way that the Lithuanian territory which lies to the south and south-west of the line indicated on the attached map will fall to the Germans.

[1] *Ibid.*

APPENDIX O

AGREEMENT OF MUTUAL ASSISTANCE BETWEEN THE UNITED KINGDOM AND POLAND [WITH PROTOCOL]

(AUGUST 25, 1939)[1]

THE Government of the United Kingdom of Great Britain and Northern Ireland and the Polish Government :

Desiring to place on a permanent basis the collaboration between their respective countries resulting from the assurances of mutual assistance of a defensive character which they have already exchanged ;

Have resolved to conclude an Agreement for that purpose and have appointed as their Plenipotentiaries :

The Government of the United Kingdom of Great Britain and Northern Ireland :

The Rt. Hon. Viscount Halifax, K.G., G.C.S.I., G.C.I.E., Principal Secretary of State for Foreign Affairs ;

The Polish Government :

His Excellency Count Edward Raczyński, Ambassador Extraordinary and Plenipotentiary of the Polish Republic in London ;

Who, having exchanged their Full Powers, found in good and due form, have agreed on the following provisions :—

Article 1

Should one of the Contracting Parties become engaged in hostilities with a European Power in consequence of aggression by the latter against that Contracting Party, the other Contracting Party will at once give the Contracting Party engaged in hostilities all support and assistance in its power.

Article 2

(1) The provisions of Article 1 will also apply in the event of any action by a European Power which clearly threatened, directly or indirectly, the independence of one of the Contracting Parties, and was of such a nature that the Party in question considered it vital to resist it with its armed forces.

(2) Should one of the Contracting Parties become engaged in hostilities with a European Power in consequence of action by that

---

[1] *British White Paper*, Cmd. 6616 (1945). The Agreement only was first issued in 1939 (Cmd. 6144).

Power which threatened the independence or neutrality of another European State in such a way as to constitute a clear menace to the security of that Contracting Party, the provisions of Article 1 will apply, without prejudice, however, to the rights of the other European State concerned.

Article 3

Should a European Power attempt to undermine the independence of one of the Contracting Parties by processes of economic penetration or in any other way, the Contracting Parties will support each other in resistance to such attempts. Should the European Power concerned thereupon embark on hostilities against one of the Contracting Parties, the provisions of Article 1 will apply.

Article 4

The methods of applying the undertakings of mutual assistance provided for by the present Agreement are established between the competent naval, military and air authorities of the Contracting Parties.

Article 5

Without prejudice to the foregoing undertakings of the Contracting Parties to give each other mutual support and assistance immediately on the outbreak of hostilities, they will exchange complete and speedy information concerning any development which might threaten their independence and, in particular, concerning any development which threatened to call the said undertakings into operation.

Article 6

(1) The Contracting Parties will communicate to each other the terms of any undertakings of assistance against aggression which they have already given or may in future give to other States.

(2) Should either of the Contracting Parties intend to give such an undertaking after the coming into force of the present Agreement, the other Contracting Party shall, in order to ensure the proper functioning of the Agreement, be informed thereof.

(3) Any new undertaking which the Contracting Parties may enter into in future shall neither limit their obligations under the present Agreement nor indirectly create new obligations between the Contracting Party not participating in these undertakings and the third State concerned.

Article 7

Should the Contracting Parties be engaged in hostilities in consequence of the application of the present Agreement, they will not conclude an armistice or treaty of peace except by mutual agreement.

Article 8

(1) The present Agreement shall remain in force for a period of five years.

(2) Unless denounced six months before the expiry of this period it shall continue in force, each Contracting Party having thereafter the right to denounce it at any time by giving six months' notice to that effect.

(3) The present Agreement shall come into force on signature.

In faith whereof the above-named Plenipotentiaries have signed the present Agreement and have affixed thereto their seals.

Done in English in duplicate, at London, the 25th August 1939. A Polish text shall subsequently be agreed upon between the Contracting Parties and both texts will then be authentic.

(L.S.) HALIFAX

(L.S.) EDWARD RACZYŃSKI

PROTOCOL

THE Polish Government and the Government of the United Kingdom of Great Britain and Northern Ireland are agreed upon the following interpretation of the Agreement of Mutual Assistance signed this day as alone authentic and binding :

1.—(*a*) By the expression " a European Power " employed in the Agreement is to be understood Germany.

(*b*) In the event of action within the meaning of Articles 1 or 2 of the Agreement by a European Power other than Germany, the Contracting Parties will consult together on the measures to be taken in common.

2.—(*a*) The two Governments will from time to time determine by mutual agreement the hypothetical cases of action by Germany coming within the ambit of Article 2 of the Agreement.

(*b*) Until such time as the two Governments have agreed to modify the following provisions of this paragraph, they will consider : that the case contemplated by paragraph (1) of Article 2 of the Agreement is that of the Free City of Danzig ; and that the cases contemplated by paragraph (2) of Article 2 are Belgium, Holland, Lithuania.

(*c*) Latvia and Estonia shall be regarded by the two Governments as included in the list of countries contemplated by paragraph (2) of Article 2 from the moment that an undertaking of mutual assistance between the United Kingdom and a third State covering those two countries enters into force.

(*d*) As regards Roumania, the Government of the United Kingdom refers to the guarantee which it has given to that country; and the Polish Government refers to the reciprocal undertakings of the Roumano-Polish alliance which Poland has never regarded as incompatible with her traditional friendship for Hungary.

3. The Undertakings mentioned in Article 6 of the Agreement, should they be entered into by one of the Contracting Parties with a third State, would of necessity be so framed that their execution should at no time prejudice either the sovereignty or territorial inviolability of the other Contracting Party.

4. The present protocol constitutes an integral part of the Agreement signed this day, the scope of which it does not exceed.

In faith whereof the undersigned, being duly authorised, have signed the present Protocol.

Done in English in duplicate, at London, the 25th August, 1939. A Polish text will subsequently be agreed upon between the Contracting Parties and both texts will then be authentic.

> (signed)   HALIFAX
> (signed)   EDWARD RACZYŃSKI

BIBLIOGRAPHY

I. OFFICIAL DOCUMENTS

Proceedings of the International Military Tribunal sitting at Nuremberg. November 1945–October 1946. (London, 1946–47).

Documents presented in evidence by the Prosecution and the Defence before the International Military Tribunal at Nuremberg.

Czechoslovak State Archives.

German White Books. No. 1. Verhandlungen zur Lösung der sudetendeutschen Frage. (Berlin, 1938.)

No. 2. Dokumente zur Vorgeschichte des Krieges. (Berlin, 1939.) Documents on the Events preceding the Outbreak of the War. (Berlin, 1939 ; New York, 1940.)

No. 3. Polnische Dokumente zur Vorgeschichte des Krieges. (Berlin, 1940.) The German White Paper of Polish Documents. (New York, 1940.)

British Blue Books. Documents concerning German-Polish Relations and the Outbreak of Hostilities between Great Britain and Germany on September 3, 1939. Cmd. 6106. Miscellaneous No. 9. (1939.)

Protocols determining the frontiers between Germany and Czechoslovakia. Berlin. November 20-21, 1938. Cmd. 5908. Miscellaneous No. 11. (1938.)

French Yellow Book. Documents diplomatiques 1938–1939. (Paris, 1939.) The French Yellow Book. (New York, 1940.)

Polish White Book. Les Relations polono-allemandes et polono-soviétiques au cours de la période 1933–1939. (Paris, 1940.) The Polish White Book ; Official Documents concerning Polish-German and Polish-Soviet Relations (1933–1939). (London, 1940.)

British White Papers. Correspondence respecting Czechoslovakia September, 1938. Cmd. 5847. Miscellaneous No. 8. (1938.)

Further Documents respecting Czechoslovakia, including the Agreement concluded at Munich on September 29, 1938. Cmd. 5848. Miscellaneous No. 8. (1938.)

Agreement between the Government of the United Kingdom and the Polish Government regarding Mutual Assistance [with Protocol]. London, August 25, 1939. Cmd. 6616. Poland No. 1. (1945.)

Parliamentary Debates (House of Commons).

Parliamentary Debates (House of Lords).

Journal Officiel de la République Française.

London Gazette.

League of Nations Official Journal.

U.S. Department of State Press Releases.

II. UNOFFICIAL COLLECTIONS OF DOCUMENTS, SPEECHES, ETC.

Documents on International Affairs. Published annually by the Oxford University Press for the Royal Institute of International Affairs.

My New Order. (Hitler's Speeches, 1922–1941.) Edited by Count Raoul de Roussy de Sales. (New York, 1941.)

Hitler's Speeches, 1922–1939. Edited by Norman H. Baynes. 2 vols. (Oxford, 1942.)

Arms and the Covenant. (Speeches of the Rt. Hon. Winston S. Churchill. 1928–1938.) Compiled by Randolph S. Churchill. (London, 1939.)

Into Battle: Speeches of the Rt. Hon. Winston S. Churchill, 1938–1940. Compiled by Randolph S. Churchill. (London, 1941.)

The Struggle for Peace: Speeches by the Rt. Hon Neville Chamberlain, 1937–1939. (London, 1939.)

Speeches on Foreign Policy by the Rt. Hon. Viscount Halifax, 1934–1940. (Oxford, 1940.)

Against Aggression: Speeches of Maxim Litvinov. (New York, 1939.)

The Ciano Diaries: Personal Diaries of Count Galeazzo Ciano, 1939–1943. (New York, 1946.)

Les Lettres secrètes échangées par Hitler et Mussolini. (Paris, 1946.)

III. BOOKS

ALSOP, JOSEPH, and KINTNER, ROBERT. American White Paper. (New York, 1940.)

ANGELL, NORMAN. Peace with the Dictators. (London, 1938.)

ARMSTRONG, HAMILTON FISH. When there is no Peace. (New York, 1938.)

AURIOL, VINCENT. Hier-Demain. (Paris, 1945.)

BOIS, ÉLIE J. The Truth on the Tragedy of France. (London, 1941.)

BONNET, GEORGES. Défense de la Paix. Vol. I: De Washington au Quai d'Orsay. (Geneva, 1946.)

BROGAN, D. W. The Development of Modern France. 1870–1939. (London, 1940.)

BROMFIELD, LOUIS. England, a dying oligarchy. (New York, 1939.)

BUK, PAUL. La Tragédie Tchécoslovaque. (Paris, 1939.)

CAILLAUX, JOSEPH. Mes mémoires. (Paris, 1943.)

CAMERON, ELIZABETH A. Prologue to Appeasement, a Study in French Foreign Policy. (Washington, 1942.)

" CATO." Guilty Men. (London, 1940.)

CHARLTON, AIR COMMODORE LIONEL. War Over England. (London, 1936.)

CHAUVINEAU, GENERAL. Une Invasion, est-elle encore possible? (Paris 1939.)

COOPER, RT. HON. ALFRED DUFF. The Second World War. (London, 1939.)

COQUET, JAMES I.E. Le Procès de Riom. (Paris, 1945.)

COT, PIERRE. Le Procès de la République. (New York, 1944.)

CRUTTWELL, C. R. M. F. A History of Peaceful Change in the Modern World. (Oxford, 1937.)

DAHLERUS, BIRGER. Sista Försöket. London-Berlin. Sommaren, 1939. (The Last Attempt. London-Berlin. Summer 1939.) (Stockholm, 1945.)

DALLIN, DAVID. Soviet Russia's Foreign Policy, 1939–1942. (New Haven, 1942.)

DAVIES, JOSEPH E. Mission to Moscow. (New York, 1941.)

DEAN, VERA MICHELES. Europe in Retreat. (New York, 1939.)

DOMINIQUE, PIERRE. Après Munich : veux-tu vivre ou mourir ? (Paris, 1938.)

DOUHET, GENERAL GIULIO. The Command of the Air. (London, 1927.)

DUHAMEL, GEORGES. The White War of 1938. (London, 1939.)

EINZIG, PAUL. Appeasement before, during and after the War. (London, 1942.)

FABRE-LUCE, ALFRED. Histoire secrète de la négotiation de Munich. (Paris, 1938.)

FEILING, KEITH. The Life of Neville Chamberlain. (London, 1946.)

FRANÇOIS-PONCET, ANDRÉ. Souvenirs d'une ambassade à Berlin. (Paris, 1946.)

GAFENCU, GRÉGOIRE. Prelude to the Russian Campaign. (London, 1945.) Derniers Jours de l'Europe. (Paris, 1946.)

GAMELIN, GENERAL M.-G. Servir. (Paris, 1946.)
Vol. I : Les Armées françaises en 1940.
Vol. II : Le Prologue du Drame, 1930–39.

GAULLE, CHARLES DE. Vers l'armée de métier. (Paris, 1934.)

GEDYE, G. E. R. Betrayal in Central Europe. (New York, 1939.)

GEORGE, G. J. They Betrayed Czechoslovakia. (London, 1938.)

GISEVIUS, G. B. Bis zum bitteren Ende. (Zurich, 1946.)

GLASGOW, GEORGE. Peace with the Gangsters. (London, 1939.)

GRANT-DUFF, SHEILA. Europe and the Czechs. (London, 1938.)

GUÉHENNO, JEAN. Journal d'une " révolution " 1937–1938. (Paris, 1939.)

HADLEY, W. W. Munich : Before and After. (London, etc., 1944.)

HALÉVY, DANIEL. 1938, une année d'histoire. (Paris, 1938.)

HENDERSON, ALEXANDER. Eye-Witness in Czechoslovakia. (London, 1939.)

HENDERSON, SIR NEVILE. Failure of a Mission. (New York, 1940.) Water under the Bridge. (London, 1945.)

HENRIOT, PHILIPPE. Comment mourut la Paix. (Paris, 1942.)

HITLER, ADOLF. Mein Kampf. (Munich, 1926.)

HODGSON, STUART. Lord Halifax. (London, 1941.)

HUTTON, GRAHAM. Survey after Munich. (Boston, 1939.)

JOHNSON, ALLEN CAMPBELL. Viscount Halifax. (London, 1941.)

KEITH, ARTHUR BERRIEDALE. The Causes of the War. (London, 1940.)

KENNEDY, JOHN. Why England Slept. (New York, 1940.)

KÉRILLIS, HENRI DE. The Causes of the War. (London, 1939.)

KILLANIN, MICHAEL. Four Days. (London, 1938.)

LAZAREFF, PIERRE. De Munich à Vichy. (New York, 1944.)

LEBRUN, ALBERT. Témoignage. (Paris, 1946.)

LENNHOFF, EUGENE. In Defence of Dr. Beneš and Czechoslovakia. (London, 1938.)

LÉVY, LOUIS. The Truth about France. (London, 1941.)

LOCKHART, SIR R. H. BRUCE. Guns or Butter. (London, 1939.) Comes the Reckoning. (London, 1947.)

LOMBARD, PAUL. Le Chemin de Munich. (Paris, 1938.)

Le Quai d'Orsay. (Paris, 1939.)

LONDONDERRY, MARQUESS OF. Ourselves and Germany. (London, 1938.)

MANN, GOLO. The Secretary of Europe. (New Haven, 1946.)

MANN, THOMAS. This Peace. (New York, 1938.)

MAUGHAM, VISCOUNT. The Truth about the Munich Crisis. (London, 1944.)

MAUROIS, ANDRÉ. Tragedy in France. (New York, 1940.)

MICAUD, CHARLES A. The French Right and Nazi Germany. 1933–1939. (Durham, N.C., 1943.)

MONTHERLANT, HENRI DE. L'Équinoxe de Septembre. (Paris, 1938.)

MONZIE, ANATOLE DE. Ci-devant. (Paris, 1941.)

NAMIER, L. B. Diplomatic Prelude. 1938–1939. (London, 1948.)

NICOLSON, HAROLD. Why Britain is at War. (London, 1939.)

The Congress of Vienna. (London, 1946.)

NIETZSCHE, FRIEDRICH. Complete Works. (Edinburgh and London, 1910.)

NIZAN, PIERRE. Chronique de septembre. (Paris, 1939.)

NOËL, LÉON. L'Agression allemande contre la Pologne. (Paris, 1946.)

ORMESSON, VLADIMIR D'. France. (London, 1939.)

PAUL-BONCOUR, J. Entre deux guerres. (Paris, 1946.)

" PERTINAX." The Gravediggers of France. (New York, 1944.)

POL, HEINZ. Suicide of a Democracy. (New York, 1940.)

PRITT, D. N., K.C. Light on Moscow. (London, 1939.)

RAUSCHNING, HERMANN. Germany's Revolution of Destruction. (London, 1939.)

REIBEL, CHARLES. Pourquoi nous avons été à deux doigts de la guerre. (Paris, 1938.)

REYNAUD, PAUL. La France militaire. (Paris, 1937.)

La France a sauvé l'Europe (Paris, 1947).

RIBET, MAURICE. Le Procès de Riom. (Paris, 1945.)

RIPKA, HUBERT. Munich : Before and After. (London, 1939.)

ROTHERMERE, VISCOUNT. Warnings and Predictions. (London, 1939.)

SAMUEL, VISCOUNT. Memoirs. (London, 1945.)

SCHUMAN, FREDERICK L. Europe on the Eve. (New York, 1939.)

SETON-WATSON, R. W. Munich and the Dictators. (London, 1939.)

SHIRER, WILLIAM. Berlin Diary. (New York, 1941.)

SIMON, YVES R. The Road to Vichy. 1918–1938. (New York, 1942.)

SIMONE, ANDRÉ. J'Accuse ! The Men who betrayed France. (London, 1941.)

TÁBORSKÝ, EDUARD. The Czechoslovak Cause in International Law. (London, 1944.)

TABOUIS, GENEVIÈVE. Blackmail or War ? (London, 1939.)

Ils l'ont appelée Cassandra. (New York, 1942.)

TARDIEU, ANDRÉ. L'Année de Munich. (Paris, 1939.)

TAYLOR, EDMOND. The Strategy of Terror. (Boston, 1940.)

THOMAS, LOUIS. Histoire d'un jour. Munich, 29 septembre, 1938. (Paris, 1939.)

TISSIER, LIEUT.-COLONEL PIERRE. The Riom Trial. (London, 1942.)

TORRES, HENRY. Campaign of Treachery. (New York, 1942.)

WALTER-SMITH, DEREK. Neville Chamberlain. (London, 1940.)

WELLES, SUMNER. The Time for Decision. (New York, 1944.)

WERTH, ALEXANDER. The Twilight of France, 1933–40. (London, 1942.)

WHEELER-BENNETT, J. W. The Wreck of Reparations. (London, 1932.)

Disarmament and Security since Locarno. (London, 1932.)

Disarmament Deadlock. (London, 1934.)

Hindenburg, the Wooden Titan. (London, 1936.)

Brest-Litovsk. The Forgotten Peace. (London, 1938.)

WINTER, GUSTAV. This is not the end of France. (London, 1942.)

WISKEMANN, ELIZABETH. Czechs and Germans. (Oxford, 1938.)

WOLFERS, ARNOLD. Britain and France between Two Wars. (New Haven, 1940.)

YOUNG, EDGAR P. Czechoslovakia. (London, 1938.)

ZAY, JEAN. Carnets secrets de Jean Zay. (Paris, 1942.)

Souvenirs et Solitude. (Paris, 1945.)

IV. NEWSPAPERS AND PERIODICALS

Great Britain

The Times
Daily Telegraph
Daily Mail
Daily Express
Daily Herald
Daily Worker
Evening Standard
Star
Forward
The Observer
The Sunday Times

U.S.A.

New York Times
New York Herald-Tribune
Chicago Daily News
Chicago Tribune
Foreign Affairs

France

Le Temps

Le Soir
Le Petit Parisien
Le Figaro
L'Europe Nouvelle
La République
Gringoire
L'Œuvre
L'Écho de Paris
L'Humanité

Italy

Giornale d' Italia
Osservatore Romano

Germany

Leipziger Zeitung
Deutsche Diplomatische-politische Korrespondenz
Völkischer Beobachter

U.S.S.R.

Izvestia
Pravda

INDEX